ELIEZER BEN HYRCANUS

THE TRADITION AND THE MAN

PART TWO

STUDIES IN JUDAISM IN LATE ANTIQUITY

FROM THE FIRST TO THE SEVENTH CENTURY

EDITED BY

JACOB NEUSNER

VOLUME FOUR

ELIEZER BEN HYRCANUS

THE TRADITION AND THE MAN

PART TWO

LEIDEN
E. J. BRILL
1973

ELIEZER BEN HYRCANUS

THE TRADITION AND THE MAN

BY

JACOB NEUSNER

Professor of Religious Studies
Brown University

PART TWO

ANALYSIS OF THE TRADITION

THE MAN

LEIDEN
E. J. BRILL
1973

ISBN 90 04 03754 3

PRINTED IN THE NETHERLANDS

TABLE OF CONTENTS

PART TWO

List of Abbreviations XI
Transliterations XII

ANALYSIS OF THE TRADITION

V. The Tradition as a Whole 1

VI. Forms 18
i. The Forms of Eliezer's Tradition 18
ii. Forms and Particular Masters 31
iii. History of Forms 32
iv. Form (C) 39
v. The Houses and Yoḥanan ben Zakkai and "The Mishnah" before 70 44
vi. Eliezer b. Hyrcanus and "The Mishnah" before 70 . 49
vii. Collections of Traditions 53
viii. Conclusion 60

VII. Attestations 63
i. Survey of Attested Pericopae 63
ii. Chains of Traditions 73
iii. Suppressed Traditions 82
iv. Other References to the Formation and Transmission of Eliezer's Traditions 85
v. Conclusion 87

VIII. The Best Traditions 92
i. Yavnean Attestations 92
ii. The Laws 95
iii. Eliezer's Attestations of Houses' Disputes 115
iv. Eliezer and the Traditions about pre-70 Masters . . 118
v. Eliezer and the Traditions about Yoḥanan b. Zakkai 119
vi. Yavnean Chains of Traditions 120
vii. Judah b. Ilai's Traditions 124
viii. The Earliest Eliezer 129

IX. The Better Traditions 143
i. The ʿAqiban Eliezer 143
ii. The Laws 144
iii. The Chains 158
iv. The Ushan Eliezer and Yoḥanan b. Zakkai. The Houses 160
v. The Better Traditions 167

X. The Fair Traditions 170
i. Attestations of the Circle of Judah the Patriarch . . 170
ii. Pericopae First Attested by Appearance in Mishnah-Tosefta 172
iii. The Authenticity of Pericopae First Appearing in Mishnah-Tosefta 200

XI. Suppressed Traditions 205
i. Definition 205
ii. The Laws 206
iii. Sayings about the Value of Eliezer's Traditions . . 219
iv. Conclusion 223

XII. The Poor Traditions. 225
i. Definition and Criteria. 225
ii. Traditions First Appearing in Tannaitic Exegetical Compilations 226
iii. The Tannaitic Stratum of the *Gemarot* 233
iv. Amoraic and Later Contributions to the Traditions about Eliezer 236
v. Conclusion 243

THE MAN

XIII. Earlier Views of Eliezer ben Hyrcanus 249
i. Introduction 249
ii. Compilations of Stories and Sayings 250
iii. Special Studies 255
iv. Ben Zion Bokser and Louis Finkelstein. 259
v. Alexander Guttmann 263
vi. Yitzhak D. Gilat 265
vii. The Eliezer of History and the Eliezer of Biography 277

XIV. The Eliezer of History 287
i. Introduction 287
ii. Origins, Early Life, Education 294
iii. Eliezer's Active Career 296
iv. Eliezer's Historical Situation, Pharisaism and Rabbinism. 298
v. Eliezer and the Houses 307
vi. Eliezer and the Old Law 310
vii. Eliezer's Own Contribution 316
viii. The Application of Eliezer's Law 322
ix. Eliezer's Program for Yavneh 325
x. Eliezer and the Christians 330

XV. The Eliezer of Tradition 335
i. Introduction 335
ii. Origins, Early Life, Education 343
iii. Eliezer's Active Career 346
iv. Eliezer's Historical Situation. Pharisaism and Rabbinism. 347
v. Eliezer and the Houses 351
vi. Eliezer and the Old Law 352
vii. Eliezer's Own Contribution 356
viii. The Application of Eliezer's Law 361
ix. Eliezer's Program for Yavneh 365
x. Eliezer and the Christians 365
xi. Forms and the Formation of Traditions about Eliezer 367
xii. The Formation of the *Eliezer* + *Sages*-Type of Tradition 368
xiii. The Formation of the *Eliezer* + *Named Master*-Type of Tradition 371
xiv. The Distribution of Traditions from Identifiable Sources 377
xv. Eliezer and the Tannaim (1): Yavneh 384
xvi. Eliezer and the Tannaim (2): Usha 385
xvii. Conclusion 386

XVI. Eliezer's Exegeses 387
i. Introduction 387
ii. Legal Exegeses. 387

iii. Plain *vs.* Fanciful Interpretations 392
iv. Techniques of Exegeses 394
v. Redactional Devices 396
vi. Conclusion 397

XVII. The Eliezer of Legend 399
i. Introduction. Eliezer and the Amoraim 399
ii. Origins, Early Life, Education 403
iii. Eliezer's Active Career. Eliezer and Hillel. 407
iv. Eliezer's Historical Situation 416

Appendix I: G. S. Aleksandrov. *The Role of ʿAqiba in the Bar Kokhba Rebellion.* Translated by Sam Driver 422

Appendix II: *Development of a Legend. Studies on the Traditions Concerning Yoḥanan ben Zakkai*: Corrections, Revisions, and Reconsiderations 437

Indices 459

I. Bible 459
II. Mishnah 464
III. Tosefta 475
IV. Sifra. 480
V. Sifré. 481
VI. Mekhilta DeR. Ishmael 481
VII. Mekhilta DeR. Simeon. 482
VIII. Other Midrashic Compilations 482
IX. Palestinian Talmud 484
X. Babylonian Talmud 488
XI. General Index 495

PART ONE

THE TRADITION

Preface. xiii
Foreword xv
List of Abbreviations xix
Transliterations xx

I. Introduction 1
i. Locating the Traditions about Eliezer b. Hyrcanus 1
ii. Texts Consulted. 14
iii. Purpose of the Comments 16

II. The Legal Traditions 18
i. Berakhot 18
ii. Pe'ah 34
iii. Demai 36
iv. Kila'im 38
v. Shevi'it 39
vi. Terumot 45
vii. Ma'aserot 70
viii. Ma'aser Sheni 72
ix. Ḥallah 76
x. 'Orlah 82
xi. Bikkurim 84
xii. Shabbat 85
xiii. 'Eruvin 100
xiv. Pesaḥim 117
xv. Sheqalim 135
xvi. Yoma, Sukkah, Beṣah 138
xvii. Rosh HaShanah, Ta'anit, Megillah, Mo'ed Qaṭan, Ḥagigah . . 154
xviii. Yevamot 163
xix. Ketuvot 181
xx. Nedarim, Nazir, Soṭah 185
xxi. Giṭṭin, Qiddushin 204
xxii. Bava Qamma, Bava Meṣi'a', Bava Batra 211
xxiii. Sanhedrin, Makkot, Shavu'ot, 'Avodah Zarah, Horayot . . . 217
xxiv. Zevaḥim, Menaḥot 222
xxv. Ḥullin, Bekhorot, 'Arakhin 246
xxvi. Temurah, Keritot, Me'ilah, Tamid 252
xxvii. Kelim 276
xxviii. Ohalot, Nega'im 287
xxix. Parah 302
xxx. Ṭoharot, Miqva'ot 315
xxxi. Niddah 323
xxxii. Makhshirin, Zabim, Yadaim, 'Uqṣin 330
xxxiii. 'Eduyyot 337

Appendix to Chapter Two: Legal Pericopae Not Demonstrably Part of the Traditions about Eliezer ben Hyrcanus 346

III. Historical and Biographical Traditions. Wisdom Sayings 394

IV. Exegetical and Theological Traditions 453

LIST OF ABBREVIATIONS

Ah. = Ahilot
Ant. = Josephus, *Antiquities*
Ar. = ʿArakhin
ARN = Avot deRabbi Natan
A.Z. = ʿAvodah Zarah
b. = Bavli, Babylonian Talmud
b. = ben
B.B. = Bava Batra
B.M. = Bava Meṣiʿaʾ
B.Q. = Bava Qamma
Ber. = Berakhot
Beṣ. = Beṣah
Bik. = Bikkurim
Dem. = Demaʾi
Development = *Development of a Legend. Studies on the Traditions Concerning Yoḥanan ben Zakkai* (Leiden, 1970)
Ed. = ʿEduyyot
Eruv. = ʿEruvin
Git. = Giṭṭin
Hag. = Ḥagigah
Hal. = Ḥallah
Halivni, *Meqorot* = David Weiss Halivni, *Meqorot uMesorot* (Tel Aviv, 1968)
Hor. = Horayot
Hul. = Ḥullin
Kel. = Kelim
Ker. = Keritot
Kil. = Kilaʾim
M. = Mishnah
M.Q. = Moʿed Qaṭan
M.S. = Maʿaser Sheni
M.T. = Midrash Tannaʾim
Ma. = Maʿaserot
Mak. = Makkot
Maksh = Makshirin
Me. = Meʿilah
Meg. = Megillah
Mekh. = Mekhilta
Men. = Menaḥot
Mid. = Middot
Miq. = Miqvaʾot
Naz. = Nazir
Ned. = Nedarim
Neg. = Negaʿim
Nez. = Nezirot
Nid. = Niddah
Nusaḥ = J. N. Epstein, *Introduction to the Text of the Mishnah* (*Mavo leNusaḥ HaMishnah* [Jerusalem, 1964²])
Oh. = Ohalot
Orl. = ʿOrlah
Par. = Parah
Pes. = Pesaḥim
Phar. = *The Rabbinic Traditions about the Pharisees before 70* (Leiden, 1971), *I. The Masters. II. The Houses. III. Conclusions*
Qid. = Qiddushin
R. = Rabbi
Rabbi = Rabbi Judah the Patriarch
R.H. = Rosh Hashanah
Sanh. = Sanhedrin
Shab. = Shabbat
Shav. = Shavuʿot
Sheq. = Sheqalim
Shev. = Sheviʿit
Sot. = Soṭah
Suk. = Sukkah
Ta. = Taʿanit
Tan. = J. N. Epstein, *Introductions to Tannaitic Literature* (*Mevoʾot leSifrut HaTannaʾim* [Jerusalem, 1957])
Tem. = Temurah
Ter. = Terumot
Toh. = Ṭohorot
Tos. = Tosefta
T.Y. = Ṭevul Yom
Uqs. = ʿUqṣin
y. = Yerushalmi, Palestinian Talmud
Y.T. = Yom Ṭov
Yad. = Yadaim
Yev. = Yevamot
Zab. = Zabim
Zer. = Zeraʿim
Zev. = Zevaḥim

TRANSLITERATIONS

א	= ʼ	מ ם	= M
ב	= B	נ ן	= N
ג	= G	ס	= Ś
ד	= D	ע	= ʻ
ה	= H	פ	= P
ו	= W	צ ץ	= Ṣ
ז	= Z	ק	= Q
ח	= Ḥ	ר	= R
ט	= Ṭ	שׁ	= Š
י	= Y	שׂ	= S
כ ך	= K	ת	= T
ל	= L		

ANALYSIS OF THE TRADITIONS

CHAPTER FIVE

THE TRADITION AS A WHOLE

Our analysis of the traditions about Eliezer ben Hyrcanus begins with a summary which shows that legal materials strikingly predominate in the first stage in the tradition's formation. By the completion of Mishnah-Tosefta, nearly all legal themes, sayings, and stories had registered in some form or other. The topics of Eliezer's laws had been laid out, though their further articulation continued in the Tannaitic Midrashim, the *baraita*-stratum of the *Gemarot*, and beyond. By contrast, important exegetical and biographical themes do not surface until later compilations; much of the exegetical tradition was unknown until the late Amoraic collections, e.g., Gen. R. and Lev. R., and even into post-Talmudic times.

Of approximately 228 separate items of legal interest, only the following were unknown in the primary stratum, Mishnah-Tosefta: Nos. 3, 6 (but these are closely linked to nos. 1 and 2, and 5, respectively, and cannot be regarded as thematically distinct), 4, 8, 9, 32, 41, 61, 63, 68, 71, 72, 73, 82, 88, 89, 90, 91, 101, 102, 144 (an issue faced by earlier authorities)—that is, a maximum of 19 items, or approximately 8 %. Of the above excluded items, moreover, the following occur in the Tannaitic midrashim: Nos. 4, 6, 32, 71, 72, 73, 82, 90,—7 out of 19. Among the remaining items, the *baraita*-stratum accounts for Nos. 3, 8 (Who is *ʿam haʾareṣ*), 9 (wipe with left hand), 41 (vermin on Sabbath), 61 (repeat lesson four times), 63 (making *maṣṣah*), 68 (study on the festival), 91 (mourners *re* festival), 101 (*re* uncircumcized eating Heave-offerings), 102 (proselyte does not have to immerse), and 144 (date of Pentecost). That leaves a negligible number of legal traditions first known in the Amoraic stratum, three in all, 1.3 %. (Of the items first occurring in the *baraita*-stratum, Nos. 8, 9, 61, and 67 pertain to the rituals of 'being a rabbi.') We may therefore conclude with certainty that problems of law constituted the predominant interest in the primary formation of the traditions about Eliezer.

Biographical and exegetical materials are apt to make an appearance only later on. Of approximately 29 items of biographical and historical interest, 7 first occur in Mishnah-Tosefta, an additional 3 in the

Tannaitic midrashim, and 5 more in the *baraita*-stratum. Fifteen begin in the Amoraic or later collections. Thus while approximately 92 % of all legal materials begin in the Tannaitic stratum, only 24 % of biographical and historical materials first occur there, 34 % if one adds the Tannaitic-Midrashim, and approximately 49 % if one further includes the *baraita*-stratum of the *Gemarot.* So, by any count, approximately 51 % of the biographical-historical traditions begin in the Amoraic stratum, against perhaps 1 % of the legal ones.

The presence of some biographical-historical materials in Mishnah-Tosefta and other Tannaitic and related collections indicates that such materials *could* have been shaped in the earliest process of formation and transmission but evidently were not produced in any abundance. One therefore cannot claim that it is merely the normal characteristic of Mishnah-Tosefta to give emphasis to legal, as against other kinds of traditions, which explains the differences we have observed. The differential is disproportionate to the difference in emphasis, especially so when one includes both the other compilations commonly regarded as Tannaitic and the Talmuds' *baraita*-stratum.

When, furthermore, we review the attestations, we shall see that, while dozens of legal traditions yield Yavnean and Ushan attestations, scarcely a single biographical historical, theological or exegetical tradition seems to have elicited attention—at least so as to produce a clear attestation—before the compilation of the document in which it first occurs, Mishnah-Tosefta, Mekhilta, Sifré, and so forth. This seems to me decisive evidence that legal materials constitute the primary stratum of the traditions about Eliezer.

Nor should we ignore the extraordinary disproportion represented by the absolute number of legal traditions measured against the absolute number of the non-legal traditions. Of approximately 321 items in all, no fewer than 228, or approximately 71 %, concern legal matters. These figures would be still more disproportionate if we deducted the biographical traditions in which Eliezer plays no important role, e.g., how he and others met Abba Yudan, or how he helped Yoḥanan b. Zakkai to escape from Jerusalem. These, strictly speaking, are not items of much significance in the tradition about Eliezer b. Hyrcanus; his place in the formulary structure of a pericope, unless he stands at the head, likewise cannot be regarded as significant. He is just a name on a list.

The exegetical traditions, numbering 61, or approximately 18 % of the whole, appear only episodically in Mishnah-Tosefta—4 items, 3 in a single pericope (and these are essentially the same ruling about several different matters); in addition 23 items occur first in the compilations of Tannaitic Midrashim, with another 11 in the *baraita*-stratum of the *Gemarot*, 34 in all, or approximately 55 % —not much different from the historical and biographical traditions.

The following chart, indicating the first occurrence of each item in the tradition, therefore will show that the legal part of the Eliezer-tradition not only predominates in quantity, but also in substance probably originates earlier than the non-legal part; and that the biographical and exegetical parts of the tradition in quantity and point of origin do not materially differ from one another.

Item	I Mishnah-Tosefta	II Tannaitic Midrashim	III *Baraita*-Stratum	IV Amoraic Materials	V Later Compilations
1. Read *Shema*ʿ in evening	M. Ber. 1 : 1			b. Ber. 26	
2. Read *Shema*ʿ in morning	M. Ber. 1 : 2				
3. Night has three watches			b. Ber. 3a		
4. *Shema*ʿ requires intention		Mid. Tan. Deut. 6 : 6	b. Ber. 13a		
5. No fixed text for Prayer	M. Ber. 4 : 5				
6. Short Prayer		Mekh. I, p. 216; II, p. 9-72; Mekh. R. Sim. p. 57, p. 103, Sifré Num. 105	b. Ber. 29b b. Ber. 34a		
7. Say *Havdalah* in Thanksgiving	M. Ber. 5 : 2				
7A. Say Sanctification of the Day in Thanksgiving	Tos. Ber. 3 : 10, 3 : 11				
8. Who is *ʿam haʾareṣ?*			b. Ber. 47b		
9. Why wipe with left hand?			b. Ber. 62a		
10. Ground liable for *Peʾah*	M. Peʾah 3 : 6				
11. Vineyard entirely composed of defective clusters	M. Peʾah 7 : 7	Mid. Tan. Deut. 24 : 2; Sifra Qed. 3 : 1; Sifré Deut. 285			
12. First-fruits in valley *re demai*	Tos. Dem. 1 : 3		y. Dem. 1 : 1		
13. Thorns in vineyard	M. Kil. 5 : 8	Sifré Deut. 230	y. Kil. 1 : 1, 5 : 7		
14. Handkerchiefs etc., *re Kilaʾim*	M. Kil. 9 : 3 Tos. Kil. 5 : 18				
15. Arum after Seventh Year	M. Shev. 5 : 3 Tos. Shev. 4 : 3		y. Shev. 5 : 2		

	I	II	III	IV	V
16. Hide anointed with Seventh Year oil	M. Shev. 8 : 9-10			y. Shev. 8 : 8	
17. Three vegetables in jar	M. Shev. 9 : 5	Sifra Behar 3 : 4	y. Shev. 9 : 4		
18. Seventh-Year fruits as gift	M. Shev. 9 : 9				
19. Heave-offering from clean for unclean	M. Ter. 2 : 1; Tos. Ter. 3 : 18			y. Ter. 2 : 1	
20. Increase Heave-offering	M. Ter. 4 : 5				
21. Neutralize Heave-offering in 101	M. Ter. 4 : 7				
22. Neutralize Heave-offering + other rules and cases	M. Ter. 4 : 8, 9, 10, 11 Tos. Ter. 5 : 10, 11 M. Ter. 5 : 2, 4, 5, 6 Tos. Ter. 6 : 4			y. Ter. 4 : 6, 8	
23. Restore misappropriated Heave-offering	M. Ter. 6 : 6 Tos. Ter. 7 : 9, 10	Sifra Emor 6 : 6			
24. Liability for act begun legitimately but proved illicit	M. Ter. 8 : 1, 2, 3				
25. Disposition of possibly unclean Heave-offering and protection of Heave-offering	M. Ter. 8 : 8, 9, 10, 11			b. Bekh. 34a	
26. Non-priest consumes date-honey, etc.	M. Ter. 11 : 2 Tos. Ter. 9 : 8, 9				
27. Olives from press *re* Tithes	M. Ma. 4 : 3			y. Ma. 4 : 2	
28. Tithing dill	M. Ma. 4 : 5				
29. Tithing caperbush	M. Ma. 4 : 6				
30. Tithing mustard	Tos. Ma. 3 : 7				
31. Purchasing saffron with Tithe-money	Tos. M.S. 1 : 14				
32. Reliability for Second, First Tithe	Tos. M.S. 3 : 16				
33. Not buy coffin with tithes		Sifré Deut. 303			
34. Gave Principle, not Fifth	Tos. M.S. 4 : 5-6				
35. Produce from Palestine abroad—*re Ḥallah*	M. Hal. 2 : 1	Sifré Num. 110			
36. Dough in *qavs re Ḥallah*	M. Hal. 2 : 4				
37. Dough-offering clean for unclean (= No. 19)	M. Hal. 2 : 8				
38. Israelite farmers in Syria *re* Tithes and Seventh Year	M. Hal. 4 : 7				
39. Cakes of Thank-offering of Nazir	Tos. Hal. 1 : 6 [= M. Hal. 1 : 6; Anonymous]				
40. Curdle milk with sap of *ʿorlah*	M. Orl. 1 : 7				
41. *Etrog* like tree	M. Bik. 2 : 6				
42. Not kill vermin on Sabbath			b. Shab. 12a, 107b		

	I	II	III	IV
43. Baking before Sabbath	M. Shab. 1 : 10			
44. Wick for Sabbath lamp	M. Shab. 2 : 3			
45. Weapons on Sabbath	M. Shab. 6 : 4			
46. Tiara on Sabbath	Tos. Shab. 4 : 6			
47. Spice-box on Sabbath	Tos. Shab. 4 : 11			
48. Scratch on flesh on Sabbath	M. Shab. 12 : 4 Tos. Shab. 11 : 15		y. Shab. 12 : 4 b. Shab. 104b	
49. Weave threads on Sabbath	M. Shab. 13 : 1 Tos. Shab. 12 : 1			
50-50A. Window-shutter [Add to building] + spread out filter	M. Shab. 17 : 7, 20 : 1 Tos. Shab. 12 : 14		y. Shab. 20 : 1	
51. Circumcision on Sabbath	M. Shab. 19 : 1 Tos. Shab. 15 : 16		y. Shab. 19 : 1 b. Shab. 131a-b	
52. Erred by circumcising wrong child on Sabbath	M. Shab. 19 : 4 Tos. Shab. 15 : 10		b. Shab. 137b	
53. Rendering alleyway valid	M. Eruv. 1 : 2 Tos. Eruv. 1 : 2			y. Eruv. 1 : 2 b. Eruv. 11b-12a
54-55-56. Carry in garden; hart's tongue; not prepare *ʿeruv*	M. Eruv. 2 : 6 Tos. Eruv. 2 : 7-8			
57. Two *ʿeruvs* for Sabbath + festival	M. Eruv. 3 : 6 Tos. Eruv. 4 : 1-2			
58. *ʿEruv* with any food	M. Eruv. 7 : 10			
59. Buy *ʿeruv* with coins	M. Eruv. 7 : 11			
60. Breach between courtyard and public domain	M. Eruv. 9 : 2			
61. Repeat lesson four times			b. Eruv. 54b	
62. Burn unclean *ḥameṣ* separately from clean	M. Pes. 1 : 7			
63. Make *maṣṣah* with fruit juice			b. Pes. 36a, y. Pes. 2 : 7	
64. Do not designate Dough-offering on 15 Nisan until dough is baked	M. Pes. 3 : 3 Tos. Pis. 3 : 7			
65. Measure of dough	Tos. Pis. 3 : 8			
66-67. Passover overrides Sabbath in all respects	M. Pes. 3 : 8 Tos. Pis.	Sifré Zuṭṭa 9 : 2		
68. Study on festival			b. Pes. 68b	
69. Offerings eligible as Passover slaughtered under other designation	M. Pes. 6 : 5 Tos. Pis. 5 : 4			
70. Anyone not in Temple keeps second Passover	M. Pes. 9 : 2 Tos. Pis. 8 : 2	Sifré Num. 69		
71. Passover not from tithes		Mekh. deR. Simeon, p. 39, ls. 7-14	b. Yev. 46a b. Men. 82a-b	
72. Barbecue Passover [May not be our Eliezer]		Mekh. Ishmael, Lauterbach, I, p. 50		

	I	II	III	IV	V
73. Sacrifice Passover in evening		Sifré Deut. 133	b. Ber. 9a		
74. Sanctified property including cattle—disposition	M. Sheq. 4 : 7 Tos. Sheq. 2 : 10				
75. Burn unclean sanctities inside/outside	M. Sheq. 8 : 7 Tos. Sheq. 3 : 16				
76. Prefect + high priest choose lots	Tos. Kip. 2 : 10				
77. High priest counts sprinklings	Tos. Kip. 2 : 16				
78. High priest sprinkled in place	M. Yoma 5 : 5				
79. If goat fell ill	Tos. Kip. 3 : 14		b. Yoma 66b		
80. Lambs offered in morning	M. Yoma 7 : 3 Tos. Kip. 3 : 19				
81. *Sukkah* like cone-shaped hut	M. Suk. 1 : 11 Tos. Suk. 1 : 10				
82. Spreading cloth over *Sukkah*	Tos. Suk. 1 : 9				
83. Bake for Sabbath + festival		Mekh. Ishmael, Lauterbach, II, p. 118			
84. Sweeping chips etc. on festival	M. Bes. 4 : 6-7 Tos. Y.T. 3 : 18				
85. Animal and offspring in pit	Tos. Y.T. 3 : 2				
86. When to say rain prayer	M. Ta. 1 : 1				
87. Rained before fast was done	M. Ta. 3 : 9				
88. *ʿAṣṣeret* like Sabbath	M. M.Q. 3 : 6				
89. Mourners + *tefillin*				y. M.Q. 3 : 5	
89A. Mourners overturn beds				y. M.Q. 3 : 5 b. M.Q. 21a	
90. Leper + *tefillin*		Sifra Tazriʿa 12 : 6			
91. Mourners *re* festival			b. M.Q. 20a		
92. Eunuch *re ḥaliṣah*	M. Yev. 8 : 4				
93. *Ḥaliṣah* at night	M. Yev. 12 : 2				
94. Said words but did not spit at *ḥaliṣah*	M. Yev. 12 : 3 Tos. Yev. 12 : 11	Sifré Deut. 291			
95. Deed of female minor is nothing	M. Yev. 13 : 2 Tos. Yev. 13 : 3-5, 12 : 12			Story: y. Yev. 13 : 2	
96. Divorce wife + remarry her—she cannot marry Levir	M. Yev. 13 : 6				
97. Minor told to exercise rite of refusal	M. Yev. 13 : 7				
98. Permitted to deceased Levirs = permitted to all	M. Yev. 16 : 2 Tos. Yev. 14 : 3				
99. Widow may not remarry on evidence of one witness	M. Yev. 16 : 7				

	I	II	III	IV	V
100. One offering for each act of sin (see No. 158)	Tos. Yev. 11 : 4				
101. Uncircumcized priest may not eat Heave-offering			b. Yev. 70a		
102. Proselyte does not have to immerse			b. Yev. 46a		
103-106. Claims of virginity, etc.—rules of evidence	M. Ket. 1 : 6-9 Tos. Ket. 1 : 6				
107. Orphan has right to usufruct	Tos. Ket. 11 : 4				
108. Nurse for 24 months	Tos. Nid. 2 : 3		b. Yev. 34b, 60b y. Ket. 5 : 6 y. Nid. 1 : 4		
109-110. Releasing vows	M. Ned. 9 : 1-2				
111. Husband annuls vows of *bogeret*	M. Ned. 10 : 5				
112. Levir annuls vows	M. Ned. 10 : 6				
113. Annul vow in advance	M. Ned. 10 : 7 M. Ned. 6 : 5				
114-116. Unclean Nazir loses 7/30 days	M. Naz. 3 : 3-5 Tos. Naz. 2 : 2-13 4 : 8				
117. Nazir unclean during sacrifices loses all	M. Naz. 6 : 11 Tos. Naz. 4 : 9-10				
118. High priest and Nazir *re* neglected corpse	M. Naz. 7 : 1				
119. Warn wife before two	M. Sot. 1 : 1				
120. Do not teach daughter Torah	M. Sot. 3 : 4				(Num. R. 9 : 48)
121. Evidence against wife	M. Sot. 6 : 1				
122-124. Neglected corpse	M. Sot. 9 : 2-4				
125. Testify *re Geṭ*	M. Git. 1 : 1				
126. Exception in divorce	M. Git. 9 : 1 Tos. Git. 9 : 1-5				
127. New-produce-taboo applies abroad	M. Qid. 1 : 9				
128. Purify *mamzer*	M. Qid. 3 : 13				
129. Guilt-offering subject to rule of Sin-offering	M. Zev. 1 : 1 M. Yad. 4 : 2				
130. Other animal sacrificed on 14th of Nisan offered for Passover	Tos. Pis. 4 : 5-6				
131. Slaughter with wrong intention	M. Zev. 3 : 3 Tos. Zev. 2 : 16				
132. If no blood, no flesh; but if no flesh, there is blood	Tos. Zev. 4 : 1-2				
133. Whole-offering of bird offered below line subject to laws of sacrilege	M. Zev. 7 : 4 Tos. Zev. 7 : 16-20		b. Zev. 67a (Joshua wins)		
134. Limbs of Sin-offering mixed with those of Whole-offering	M. Zev. 8 : 4 Tos. Zev. 8 : 15				

	I	II	III	IV
135-140. Mixture of limbs, bloods, etc.	M. Zev. 8 : 5, 7, 8, 9, 10, 11, 12 Tos. Zev. 8 : 19, 20, 21, 23, 24			
141. Meal-offering with wrong intention	M. Men. 3 : 1 Tos. Men. 2 : 16			
142. Residue of Meal-offering contracted uncleanness —sacrifice is valid	M. Men. 3 : 4 Tos. Men. 4 : 2, 5, 6			
143. Bread is sanctified even if Thank-offering is blemished	M. Men. 7 : 3 Tos. Men. 8 : 19			
144. Date of Pentecost			b. Men. 65b	
145. Slaughter dying animal	M. Hul. 2 : 6 Tos. Hul. 2 : 11			
146. Cock-partridge	M. Hul. 12 : 2			
147. Redeem firstling with hybrid	M. Bekh. 1 : 5			
148. Liability for redemption-money set aside for firstling	M. Bekh. 1 : 6 M. Ed. 7 : 1			
149. Slit ear of firstling	M. Bekh. 5 : 3			
150. Dedicated goods—*re* divorce	M. Ar. 6 : 1			
151. No pledge of utensils of one's livelihood	M. Ar. 6 : 3 Tos. Ar. 4 : 6			
152. Cannot dedicate to Temple all of one's goods	M. Ar. 8 : 4 Tos. Ar. 4 : 24			
153. Progeny of Peace-offerings may not be offered as Peace-offerings	M. Tem. 3 : 1			
154. Progeny of Guilt-offering	M. Tem. 3 : 3 C-E			
155. Guilt-offering whose owner has died	M. Tem. 3 : 3 F-H			
156. Progeny of *ṭerefah*	M. Tem. 6 : 3			
157. Sin-offerings for many instances of single sin	M. Tem. 6 : 3 M. Ker. 3 : 10	Sifra Vayiqra 1 : 13		
158. Sin-offering when not sure of which sin has been committed	M. Ker. 4 : 2-3 Tos. Ker. 2 : 12-15			
159. Suspensive Guilt-offering offered any time	M. Ker. 6 : 1, 3 Tos. Ker. 4 : 4			
160-162. Flesh of Most Holy Things which went out before sprinkling of blood are subject to law of sacrilege, etc.	M. Me. 1 : 2-3 Tos. Me. 1 : 4, 6 Tos. Men. 4 : 10, 4 : 14-15 Tos. Zev. 4 : 5, 8			
163. Fire in own property	M. B.Q. 6 : 4 Tos. B.Q. 6 : 22			
164. Acquire property by walking [?]	Tos. B.B. 2 : 11			

	I	II	III	IV	V
165. Verbal division of property	M. B.B. 9 : 7 Tos. B.B. 10 : 12				
166. No trial for wild animals	M. Sanh. 1 : 4 Tos. Sanh. 3 : 1				
167. Hang those stoned to death	M. Sanh. 6 : 4 Tos. Sanh. 9 : 6	Sifré Deut. 221			
168. Liability for unawareness of creeping thing + Temple	M. Shav. 2 : 5 Tos. Shav. 1 : 6				
169. Comb of watercooler unclean	M. Kel. 2 : 8 Tos. Kel. B.Q. 2 : 8 Tos. Ed. 2 : 1				
170. Size of hole to render lamp insusceptible to uncleanness—*peruṭah*	M. Kel. 3 : 2				
171. Oven of ʿAkhnai	M. Kel. 5 : 10 Tos. Ed. 2 : 1 M. Ed. 7 : 7		b. B.M. 59b		
172. Insect in divided oven does not render food unclean	M. Kel. 8 : 1 Tos. Kel. B.M. 6 : 4				
172A. Metal vessel = no. 170	M. Kel. 14 : 1 Tos. Kel. B.M. 4 : 2				
173. Clean broken metal vessel	M. Kel. 14 : 7 Tos. Kel. B.M. 4 : 14				
174. Baker's shelf attached to wall is clean	M. Kel. 15 : 2 M. Ed. 7 : 7 Tos. Ed. 2 : 1, 3 : 1, M. Ed. 7 : 7				
175. Wooden vessel = no. 170	M. Kel. 17 : 1				
176. Money pouch is unclean	M. Kel. 26 : 2 Tos. Kel. B.B. 4 : 3				
177. Shoe on last is clean	M. Kel. 26 : 4 Tos. Kel. B.B. 4 : 7 Tos. Ed. 2 : 1				
178. Throwing away piece of new cloth does not make it clean	M. Kel. 27 : 2				
179. Small cloth used as rag is clean	M. Kel. 28 : 2				
180. Worm from corpse is unclean	M. Oh. 2 : 2F				
181. Ashes of cremated corpse	M. Oh. 2 : 2I				
182. Grave-stone renders unclean by carrying	M. Oh. 2 : 4 Tos. Ah. 3 : 7				

	I	II	III	IV	V
183. Vessels under bier are clean	M. Oh. 6 : 1 Tos. Ah. 7 : 1				
184. Uncleanness of tomb	M. Oh. 9 : 15				
185. Projecting window-sill does not bring in uncleanness	M. Oh. 12 : 3 Tos. Ah. 13 : 3				
186. Olive's bulk of corpse on threshold makes house unclean	M. Oh. 12 : 8 Tos. Oh. 13 : 10				
187-188. Wall projection house unclean (= Nos. 185-6)	M. Oh. 14 : 4-5 Tos. Ah. 13 : 12				
189. Grave-area makes grave-area	M. Oh. 17 : 2				
190-191. One who intentionally removed signs of uncleanness—signs of purification	M. Neg. 7 : 4-5				
192. Shut up him who has bright spot on palm of hand	M. Neg. 9 : 3				
193. Leprosy sign on checkered garment	M. Neg. 11 : 7				
194-197. Rules of selecting Red Heifer	M. Par. 1 : 1, 2 : 1, 2 : 3, 2 : 5 Tos. Par. 2 : 1-2				
198-199. Heifer-sacrifice is not subject to usual Temple rules	M. Par. 4 : 1, 4 : 3				
200. Reed-pipe for heifer	M. Par. 5 : 4 Tos. Par. 5 : 6				
201. Depositing heifer-water with bailiff	M. Par. 7 : 1 Tos. Par. 7 : 7				
202. Heifer-water mixed with other water may be used	Tos. Par. 9 : 3, 9 : 5				
203. Mouse makes heifer-water invalid	M. Par. 9 : 3				
204. False intention regarding heifer-water renders it invalid	M. Par. 9 : 4 Tos. Par. 9 : 6				
205. Mixture of heifer-ashes and other ashes is valid	M. Par. 9 : 7				
206. Uncleanness due to corpse is not unclean with *maddaf*-uncleanness	M. Par. 10 : 1 Tos. Par. 10 : 4				
207. Jar of heifer-ashes on top of creeping thing	M. Par. 10 : 3 Tos. Par. 10 : 5 (Tos. Ah. 7 : 11) M. Ed. 7 : 5				
208. Loosely fastened boards are unclean in what concerns Sin-offering water	M. Par. 11 : 2				
209. Berries *re* hyssop	M. Par. 11 : 7				

	I	II	III	IV	V
210. First-grade uncleanness produces first-grade uncleanness	M. Toh. 2 : 2 Tos. Toh. 2 : 1				
211. Uncertainty about corpse-uncleanness treated leniently	M. Toh. 6 : 5				
212. Outer parts of vessels made unclean by liquids do not make food unclean	M. Toh. 8 : 7 Tos. T.Y. 1 : 8				
213. Sap exuded by crushed olives is clean	M. Toh. 9 : 3				
214. Quarter-*log* of drawn water at the outset invalidates ritual pool	M. Miq. 2 : 4 Tos. Miq. 3 : 1				
215. Using water collected in pot in ritual pool	M. Miq. 2 : 8				
216. May not immerse in ritual pool	M. Miq. 2 : 10				
217. Four types of women rely on normal period in determining cleanness	M. Nid. 1 : 3				
218. Also a woman past menopause	M. Nid. 1 : 5				
219. Hard labor three days out of eleven + 24 hrs. of relief = she is one who gives birth while in flux	M. Nid. 4 : 4				
220. Hard labor during eighty days of female-purification produces unclean blood	M. Nid. 4 : 6				
221. *Zab* who examined first and seventh day is presumed to have been clean throughout intervening days	M. Nid. 10 : 3 Tos. Nid. 9 : 13				
222. *Zab's* semen does not render susceptible to uncleanness	M. Maksh. 6 : 6				
223. He who carries carrion is unclean	M. Zab. 5 : 3				
224. He who carries flux of *Zab*, etc., is unclean	M. Zab. 5 : 7 Tos. Zab. 5 : 2				
225. Beehive is like real estate	M. Shev. 10 : 7 = M. Uqs. 3 : 10 Tos. Uqs. 3 : 15				
226. Woman may wear tiara on Sabbath	M. Ed. 2 : 7 (M. Shab. 6 : 1) Tos. Ed. 1 : 10				
227. Pigeon-racers are ineligible to give testimony	M. Ed. 2 : 7 (M. Sanh. 3 : 3—anonymous) Tos. Ed. 1 : 10				

	I	II	III	IV	V
228. Limb from a living being even less than olive's bulk is unclean	M. Ed. 6 : 2-3				
229. Destruction of Temple marked decline of sages (Tos.: When *Eliezer* died)	M. Sot. 9 : 15 Tos. Sot. 15 : 3				
230. Three sayings	M. Avot 2 : 10			b. Shab. 153a	ARN Chap. 15, etc.
231. Built Temple walls outside curtains	M. Ed. 8 : 6				
232. Gathering cucumbers by sorcery	Tos. Sanh. 11 : 5 (ʿAqiba)		y. Sanh. 7 : 13 (Joshua)		
233. Eliezer arrested for *minut*	Tos. Hul. 2 : 24		b. A.Z. 16b-17a		
234. Ammon and Moab pay poorman's tithe	M. Yad. 4 : 3 Tos. Yad. 2 : 16		(b. Yev. 16a = Dosa)		
235. Eliezer sick + Ṭarfon, Joshua, Eleazar b. ʿAzariah, ʿAqiba visit him		Mekh. Baḥodesh 10 : 58-86			
236. Eliezer at wedding of Gamaliel's son		Sifré Deut. 38			
237. Eliezer's court is a good one		Sifré Deut. 144	b. Sanh. 32a		
238. Death-scenes (various types)			y. Shab. 2 : 7 b. Sanh. 68a, etc.	y. Sot. 9 : 16 y. A.Z. 3 : 1	
239. Whoever has a scrap of bread and fears for the morrow has no faith			b. Sot. 48b		
240. Oven of ʿAkhnai			b. B.M. 59b		
241. Eye of Leviathan			b. B.B. 74b		
242. On 15th of Av wood no longer cut			b. B.B. 121b		
243. *Tefillin* at all times				y. Ber. 2 : 3	
244. Onqelos's Targum on the authority of Eliezer + Joshua				y. Meg. 1 : 9	
245. Eliezer + Joshua at home of Abbuya *re* circumcision of Elisha				y. Hag. 2 : 1	
246. ʿAqiba studied with Eliezer + Joshua				y. Naz. 7 : 1 b. Ned. 50a	
247. Yoḥanan b. Zakkai ordained Eliezer + Joshua				y. Sanh. 1 : 2	
248. Collected funds with Joshua + ʿAqiba				y. Hor. 3 : 4	
249. Eliezer and Joshua helped Yoḥanan escape from Jerusalem				b. Git. 56a	ARN Chap. 4

	I	II	III	IV	V
250. Honor father before mother				b. Qid. 31a	(Num. R. 1 : 15)
251. To have sons, give to the poor, etc.				b. B.B. 10a	Kallah R. 52b
252. Had intercourse at midnight				b. Ned. 20b	
253. Children born with defects because women refuse intercourse					Kallah R. 1 : 1, 51b
254. *Mamzer* is boldfaced					Kallah R. 2 : 1, 52a
255. Eliezer knew seventy languages				b. Sanh. 17b	
256. The origins of Eliezer					ARN Chap. 6, Gen. R. 42 : 1, Tanhuma, Buber I, 34b-35a, PRE Chaps. 1-2
257. Comforted Yoḥanan b. Zakkai when his son died					ARN Chap. 14
258-259. Eliezer, Joshua, and proselytes					Gen. R. 70 : 5, Num. R. 8 : 9, Qoh. R. 7 : 8 : 1; Qoh. R. 1 : 8 : 4

	I	II	III	IV	V
260-262. Generation of wilderness have share in world to come; Qoraḥ will be forgiven; Ten Tribes will return, etc.	M. Sanh. 10 : 3 Tos. Sanh. 13 : 10		b. Sanh. 110b		
263. Gentiles have no share in world to come	Tos. Sanh. 13 : 2		b. Sanh. 105a		Mid. Ps. 9 : 5
264. Men of Sodom have *no* portion in world to come					ARN Chap. 3 : 6
265. Ex. 12 : 1		Mekh. Pisḥa 1 : 114			
266. *Sukkoth* was place where they built booths		Mekh. Pisḥa 14 : 11-22 Sifra Emor 17 : 11			
267. Idol crossed sea with Israelites		Mekh. Pisḥa 14 : 95 Sifré Num. 84			
268. Redemption will come in Tishri, not Nisan		Mekh. Pisḥa 14 : 113; Mekh. deR. Simeon to Ex. 12 : 42			
(268A. World created in Tishri)			b. R.H. 10b-12a		
269. Ex. 13 : 18		Mekh. Beshallaḥ 1 : 57-69			

	I	II	III	IV	V
270. Ex. 14 : 2: What were *Ḥirot?*		Mekh. Beshallaḥ 2 : 8-15			
271. 200 plagues at sea		Mekh. Beshallaḥ 7 : 109-121			
272. Taste of Manna		Mekh. Vayassa 6 : 27-9			
273. Ex. 15 : 2		Mekh. Vayasa 1 : 1-12			
274. Ex. 17 : 16		Mekh. Amalek 2 : 186-192			
275. Ex. 17 : 13		Mekh. Amalek 1 : 173-175			Mid. Ps. 9 : 10
276. Blot out memory of Amalek					Lam. R. 3 : 66
277. Rephidim and Shiṭṭim			b. Bekh. 5b; b. Sanh. 106a		
278. How God saved Moses at Pharaoh's court		Mekh. Amalek 3 : 127-140			
279. Ex. 19 : 5—What is covenant?		Mekh. Baḥodesh 2 : 43-5; Mekh. deR. Simeon to Ex. 13 : 10, 19 : 5			Pes. R. 23 Aggad. Ber. 17 : 2
280. Ex. 19 : 19		Mekh. Baḥodesh 4 : 36-44			
281. God revealed self in bush to show redemption follows degradation		Mekh. deR. Simeon, p. 1, ls. 12-18			
282. Milk + honey		Mekh. deR. Simeon to Ex. 13 : 5			
283. Aaron's sons died outside tent		Sifra Mekh. deMil. 2 : 35			
284. God warns before punishing people		Sifra Beḥ. 5 : 1			
285. Deut. 3 : 26		Sifré Deut. 29 Mid. Tan. to Deut. 3 : 26			
286. With all your soul *vs.* might		Sifré Deut. 32			
287. Moses saw whole land		Sifré Num. 136; Sifré Deut. 338			
288. Serving Temple brings man to study Torah		Mid. Tan. to Deut. 14 : 22			
289. Man's agent is like himself		Sifré Zuṭṭa 13 : 34			
290. Is. 1 : 18			y. Shab. 9:3		
291. Redemption depends on repentence			y. Ta. 1:1, b. Sanh. 97a-98a		
292. Deut. 28 : 10 refers to *tefillin*			b. Ber. 6a		

	I	II	III	IV	V
293. Gen. 49 : 4 *re* Reuben			b. Shab. 55b		
294. Qoh. R. 11 : 2 refers to creation, circumcision				b. Eruv. 40b	Pes. R. Kah. p. 419, ls. 10-13
295. Psalms refer to David himself			b. Pes. 117a		
296. World draws water from ocean			b. Ta. 9b		Gen. R. 13 : 9-10
297. Ezekiel's dead sang I Sam. 2 : 6			b. Sanh. 92b		
298. World is like *exedra*			b. B.B. 25a-b		
299. World created from center			b. Yoma 54b		
300. Earth created from earth, heaven from heaven			b. Yoma 54b		Gen. R. 12 : 11
301. Job sought to turn the dish upside down			b. B.B. 16a		
302. Patriarchs could not stand before divine reproof			b. Ar. 17a		
303. Reprove until beaten			b. Ar. 16b		
304. Gen. 40 : 10 refers to patriarchs			b. Hul. 92a		
305. Prov. 14 : 34				b. B.B. 10b	Pes. deR. Kah. p. 20, ls. 6 - 11 etc.
306. Divine names in reference to Naboth are sacred				b. Shav. 35b	
307. Solomon built gates for bridegrooms and mourners					Soferim 42b
308. Sea absorbed waters—Ps. 93 : 3					Gen. R. 5 : 3
309. Planets functioned during flood					Gen. R. 25 : 2
310. Sow early and late					Gen. R. 61 : 3
311. Gen. 49 : 3					Gen. R. 98 : 4
312. Wickedness at court—Qoh. 3 : 16					Lev. R. 4 : 1
313. Job. 38 : 8 + Lev. 12 : 2					Lev. R. 14 : 4
314. Song 5 : 11					Lev. R. 19 : 1
315. Reuben—Gen. 37 : 29					Pes. deR. Kah., p. 356, ls. 6-11
316. Ps. 139 : 16					Pes. Rab. 23 : 1 Tanḥ. Ber. 28
317. Recompense for woman falsely accused (Num. 5 : 28)					Num. R. 9 : 25
318. Angel spoke through Balaam					Num. R. 20 : 18
319. Ruth 4 : 1					Ruth R. 7 : 7
320. Song 6 : 10					Mid. Ps. 22 : 12
321. Ps. 90 : 15					Ps. 90 : 4

Viewed as a whole the bulk of the traditions about Eliezer b. Hyrcanus appear to lay a strong *prima facie* claim on credibility. Many were produced through a process of formulation and transmission beginning in the time in which Eliezer lived and among men whom he had known and taught. They concerned living issues of his, and immediately subsequent, times. The vitality of those issues surely produced distortion of the detailed opinions transmitted in Eliezer's name, but that vitality also suggests the thematic agenda was pretty much what it had been in his own day and school. Controls over the formation of traditions in Eliezer's name ought to have been relatively strong, for, both in the face of continuing opposition to Eliezer and in the presence of a group of men who had been his students or the students of his students, it was difficult to introduce materials utterly extraneous to Eliezer's teachings. Obviously, the opposition might exchange Eliezer's opinion for that of his opponent so as to misrepresent him. But the misrepresentation would then stand in the apodosis, never in the protasis. We may thus confidently claim to know much of what Eliezer talked about, if not exactly what he said, the precise words he used, or the fixed formulae assigned by Eliezer himself to convey his opinions.

Eliezer's legal materials, some exegetical ones, and perhaps a few biographical items may therefore be said to constitute a *tradition.* That is, they were formed and handed on in a continuous chain from Eliezer and the circle of his disciples to those who ultimately reduced them either to writing or to the fixed formulations found in Mishnah-Tosefta. By contrast, a considerable part of the exegetical corpus, and even more of the biographical materials would seem to form the Eliezer-*legend.* They were stories told about, or sayings attributed to, Eliezer, without much direct, or even indirect contact with the corpus of living traditions, certainly without roots in the historically sound materials beginning in the circle around Eliezer in his own day.

That fact does not mean exegetical and biographical materials are to be dismissed. Our task as historians would be all too convenient were we to assign to Mishnah-Tosefta the sole value as the corpus of authentic, living traditions, and to the Amoraic strata of the *Gemarot* and the Amoraic compilations of Midrashim no historical value at all. But materials first occurring in later compilations or strata obviously will have considerably diminished interest, especially if either we see no links to the antecedent tradition—as is often the case in the exegetical corpus—or we equally readily discern the ways in which antecedent traditions have been taken up, expanded, and embellished.

In the analysis of the traditions, our task is to trace the stages in their formation, according to the method of attestations described in *Phar.* III, pp. 180-238. We shall first isolate the forms in which the tradition was handed on, following the procedures of *Phar.* II, pp. 1-5, and III, pp. 1-100. Only then shall we be able, with some confidence, to consider both the history and the substance of the traditions about Eliezer, and so posit some hypotheses about the man (Part III).

In some measure the analyses in parts II and III produce repetition. We shall first analyze the tradition according to the stages in which it took shape, then go back over the same tradition for the purpose of offering hypotheses about Eliezer as a historical figure. In part III, Chapters XIV, section i, XV, section i, and XVII, section i, I have briefly recapitulated the substance of traditions dealt with in Chapters VIII, section ii, IX, section ii, and X, section ii. In Part III my intent is to offer a mosaic of traditions and this has produced the necessity to repeat in a new context and for a new purpose what in part II has already been discussed.

CHAPTER SIX

FORMS

i. The Forms of Eliezer's Tradition

Eliezer's traditions appear in six well-defined variations of one form.

A.

Statement of a Legal Problem + X says... Y says...

1. He who passes through dangerous place + prayers
   b. Ber. 29b
2. Vineyard entirely defective clusters—Eliezer, ʿAqiba
   M. Peʾah 7 : 7
   + Exegetical exchange
3. Preserving thorns in vineyard—Eliezer and sages
   M. Kil. 5 : 8
4. Arum after Seventh Year—Eliezer and Joshua
   M. Shev. 5 : 3
5. Hide anointed with Seventh-Year oil—Eliezer and sages
   M. Shev. 8 : 9
6. He who pickles three kinds of vegetables in one jar—Eliezer, Joshua and Gamaliel
   M. Shev. 9 : 5
7. Seventh-Year fruits as gifts—Eliezer and sages
   M. Shev. 9 : 9
8. Give more Heave-offering—Eliezer, Ishmael, Ṭarfon, ʿAqiba
   M. Ter. 4 : 5
9. Dried figs in mouth of jar—Eliezer, Joshua
   M. Ter. 4 : 10
10. Heave-offering in mouth of a store-jar
   M. Ter. 4 : 11

11-12-13-14. *Seʾah* of unclean Heave-offering in a hundred *seʾahs* of clean unconsecrated food, etc.
M. Ter. 5 : 2, 5 : 4, 5 : 5, 5 : 6

15-16-17. Woman eating Heave-offering, etc.—Eliezer, Joshua
M. Ter. 8 : 1, 2, 3

18-19-20-21. Jar of Heave-offering—Eliezer, Joshua + Gamaliel [8 : 8 only]
M. Ter. 8 : 8, 8 : 9, 8 : 10, 8 : 11C-E

22. Non-priest drank date-honey—Eliezer, Joshua
   M. Ter. 11 : 2
23. Gave principle but not fifth
   Tos. M.S. 4 : 5-6

24. Produce from Palestine abroad *re Ḥallah*—Eliezer, ʿAqiba
M. Hal. 2 : 1

25. Israelites sharecropping in Syria *re* Tithes, etc.—Eliezer, Gamaliel
M. Hal. 4 : 7

26. Catch flea on Sabbath—Eliezer and Joshua
b. Shab. 107b

[N.B. Eliezer: He who kills vermin—b. Shab. 12a]

27. Wick twisted, not singed—Eliezer and ʿAqiba
M. Shab. 2 : 3

28. He who scratches on flesh—Eliezer and Joshua
M. Shab. 12 : 4

29. Window shutter—Eliezer and sages
M. Shab. 17 : 7, Tos. Shab. 12 : 4

30. Two babies to circumcize—Eliezer and Joshua
M. Shab. 19 : 4

31. On that day—Eliezer and Joshua
Tos. Shab. 1 : 17

32. Rendering alley-way valid—Houses and Eliezer
M. Eruv. 1 : 2

33. Breach between courtyard and public domain--Eliezer and sages
M. Eruv. 9 : 2

34. Offerings appropriate for Passover slaughtered for other purpose—Eliezer *vs.* Joshua + debate
M. Pes. 6 : 5

35. Sanctified property, including cattle valid for altar—Eliezer *vs.* Joshua and ʿAqiba
M. Sheq. 4 : 7

36. High priest counted sprinklings—Judah → Eliezer
Tos. Kip. 2 : 16

37. How high priest sprinkled
M. Yoma 5 : 5

38. Sukkah like cone-shaped hut—Eliezer *vs.* sages
M. Suk. 1 : 11

[39. Egg born on festival—Eliezer *only* + Houses
Tos. Y.T. 1 : 1]

40. Animal and offspring fell into pit—Eliezer and Joshua
Tos. Y.T. 3 : 2

41. Read *ḥaliṣah*-words but did not spit—Eliezer *vs.* ʿAqiba
M. Yev. 12 : 3

42. If husband of adult woman died—Eliezer *vs.* Gamaliel and Joshua
M. Yev. 13 : 7

43. Remarried etc.—one sacrifice for all *vs.* for each
Tos. Yev. 11 : 4

44. Proselyte circumcized but not immersed—Eliezer *vs.* Joshua
b. Yev. 46a

45-46-47. Various claims *re* virginity—Eliezer and Gamaliel *vs.* Joshua
M. Ket. 1 : 6-9

48-49-50. Levirs and releasing vows—Eliezer, Joshua, ʿAqiba, sages
M. Ned. 10 : 5-7

51. Nazir unclean while sacrifices were underway—Eliezer *vs.* sages
M. Naz. 6 : 11, Tos. Nez. 4 : 9-10

52. High priest and Nazir—Eliezer *vs.* sages
M. Naz. 7 : 1

53. Warn wife—Eliezer *vs.* Joshua
M. Sot. 1 : 1

54. Evidence against wife—Eliezer *vs.* Joshua
M. Sot. 6 : 1

55-56. Neglected corpse—various forms—Eliezer *vs.* ʿAqiba
M. Sot. 9 : 2-4

57. Make woman drink against her wishes—Eliezer *vs.* ʿAqiba
Sifré Zuṭṭa 24

58. Divorce for all but one man—Eliezer *vs.* sages
M. Git. 9 : 1

59. Law of sacrilege *re* Whole-offering of bird offered below line—Eliezer *vs.* Joshua
M. Zev. 7 : 4

60. Limbs of sin-offering mixed with those of Whole-offering—Eliezer *vs.* sages
M. Zev. 8 : 4

61. Limbs of Whole-offering mixed with those of blemished animals—Eliezer *vs.* sages
M. Zev. 8 : 5

62-66. Mixtures of blood—Eliezer *vs.* sages
M. Zev. 8 : 8, 9, 10, 11, 12

67. Residue of meal-offering contracted uncleanness—Eliezer *vs.* Joshua
M. Men. 3 : 4

68. Bread sanctified if Thank-offering is blemished
M. Men. 7 : 3

69. Slaughter dying animal—Gamaliel *vs.* Eliezer, Simeon
M. Hul. 2 : 6

70. Liability for redemption money for firstling
M. Bekh. 1 : 6

71. Slit ear of firstling
M. Bekh. 5 : 3

72. Dedicated goods—*re* divorce—Eliezer *vs.* Joshua
M. Ar. 6 : 1

73. Progeny of Peace-offerings may not be offered as Peace-offerings
M. Tem. 3 : 1

74. Substitute of Guilt-offering, etc.—Eliezer *vs.* Eleazar
M. Tem. 3 : 3

75. Progeny of *ṭerefah*—Eliezer *vs.* sages
M. Tem. 6 : 5

76. Sin-offering when not sure what sin has been committed
M. Ker. 4 : 2-3

77. Suspensive Guilt-offering any time
M. Ker. 6 : 1, 3

78. Flesh of Most Holy Things which went out before the sprinkling of the blood—Eliezer *vs.* ʿAqiba
M. Me. 1 : 2

79. Flesh of Less Holy Things which went out before sprinkling of blood—Eliezer *vs.* ʿAqiba
M. Me. 1 : 3

80. Verbal division of property
M. B.B. 9 : 7

81. Comb of water-cooler—Eliezer *vs.* sages
M. Kel. 2 : 8

82. Oven of ʿAkhnai—Eliezer *vs.* sages
M. Kel. 5 : 10

83. Baker's shelf fixed to wall—Eliezer *vs.* sages
M. Kel. 15 : 2

84. Money pouch—Eliezer *vs.* sages
M. Kel. 26 : 2

85. Shoe on last—Eliezer *vs.* sages
M. Kel 26 : 4

86. Worm from corpse—Eliezer *vs.* sages
M. Oh. 2 : 2

87. Ashes of cremated corpse—Eliezer *vs.* sages
M. Oh. 2 : 2

88. Tomb equal top and bottom—Eliezer *vs.* Joshua
M. Oh. 9 : 15

89. Projecting windowsill—Eliezer *vs.* Joshua
M. Oh. 12 : 3

90. Olive's bulk of corpse on threshhold—Eliezer *vs.* Joshua
M. Oh. 12 : 8 (2 laws)

91-92. Wall projection—Eliezer *vs.* Joshua
M. Oh. 14 : 4-5

93. If one intentionally cut off bright spot—Eliezer *vs.* sages
M. Neg. 7 : 5

94. Heifer born of Caesarean section—Eliezer *vs.* sages
M. Par. 2 : 3

95. Black hair on Red Heifer—ʿAqiba, Eliezer, Joshua b. Batyra
M. Par. 2 : 5

96. Reed pipe for Sin-offering—Eliezer *vs.* Joshua
M. Par. 5 : 4

97. Heifer-water mixed with other water—Eliezer *vs.* sages
M. Par. 9 : 1

98. False intention *re* heifer-water
M. Par. 9 : 4

99. *Maddaf*-uncleanness—Eliezer *vs.* sages
M. Par. 10 : 1

100. Jar of sin-offering water above creeping thing—Eliezer *vs.* sages
M. Par. 10 : 3 = M. Ed. 7 : 5

101. Uncertainty about corpse-uncleanness
M. Toh. 6 : 5
102. Outer parts of vessels made unclean make liquids unclean—Eliezer *vs.* Joshua *vs.* Simeon brother of ʿAzariah
M. Toh. 8 : 7
103. Sap exudes from pressed olives—Eliezer *vs.* sages
M. Toh. 9 : 3
104. Use of water collected in pot left in ritual pool—Eliezer *vs.* Joshua
M. Miq. 2 : 8
105. Water and mud in ritual pool—Eliezer *vs.* Joshua
M. Miq. 2 : 10
106. Hard labor three days out of eleven—Eliezer *vs.* Joshua
M. Nid. 4 : 4
107. *Zab* who examined self on first and seventh day is presumed clean throughout—Eliezer *vs.* Joshua *vs.* ʿAqiba
M. Nid. 10 : 3
108. Bee-hive—Eliezer *vs.* sages
M. Shev. 10 : 7 = M. Uqs. 3 : 10
109. Psalms—Eliezer, Joshua, sages
b. Pes. 117a
110. Names mentioned in connection with Naboth, Gibeah of Benjamin (I Kings 21 : 10, Judges 20 : 18-28)—Eliezer *vs.* Joshua
b. Shav. 35b

B.

Closely related to the foregoing, indeed merely the same form used for different materials, is the following: *Citation of Scripture + X says... Y says...* or, alternatively, *Citation of Scripture + Comment + the words of X. And Y says...*

1. Reciting *Shemaʿ*— b. Ber. 13a
2. Ex. 14 : 15, Mekh. I, p. 216
3. Deut. 26 : 14, *re* confession—Sifré Deut. 303
4. Mekh. Lauterbach, I, p. 50—Barbecue Passover, ʿAqiba *vs.* Eliezer
5. Sifré Deut. 133, Sacrifice Passover in evening—Eliezer *vs.* ʿAqiba (b. Ber. 9a: *vs.* Joshua)
6. Mekh. Lauterbach, II, p. 118—Eliezer on baking for Sabbath and festival (b. Bes. 15b + Joshua)
7. Sifra Tazriʿa 12 : 6—Lev. 13 : 43 + Eliezer and ʿAqiba
8. Sifré Deut. 212—Deut. 21 : 12 + Eliezer, ʿAqiba
9. Sifré Deut. 213—Deut. 21 : 12 + Eliezer, ʿAqiba
10. Sifré Num. 24—Num. 6 : 4—Eliezer
11. b. Qid. 18b, Ex. 21 : 8—ʿAqiba *vs.* Eliezer
12. b. Men. 68b, Lev. 2 : 14, *ʿomer* of barley—Eliezer *vs.* ʿAqiba on how to prove it. Compare Sifra Vayiqra 13 : 4.
13. M. Sanh. 10 : 3, Num. 14 : 35 *re* generation of wilderness—ʿAqiba *vs.* Eliezer (3 cases)

14. ARN Chap. 36, Gen. 13 : 13, Men of Sodom have no portion in world to come—Eliezer *vs.* Joshua
15. Mekh. Pisḥa Lauterbach, 1 : 114, Ex. 12 : 1—Ishmael *vs.* Eliezer
16. Mekh. Pisḥa Lauterbach, 14 : 11, Ex. 12 : 37—Eliezer, sages, ʿAqiba
17. Mekh. Pisḥa 14 : 113, Ex. 12 : 42—Eliezer *vs.* Joshua
18. Mekh. Beshallaḥ 1 : 57, Ex. 13 : 18—Eliezer *vs.* Joshua
19. Mekh. Beshallaḥ 2 : 8, Ex. 14 : 2—Eliezer *vs.* Joshua
20. Mekh. Beshallaḥ 7 : 109, Ex. 14 : 31—Simeon b. Yoḥai, Eliezer, ʿAqiba
21. Mekh. Vayassa 6 : 47, Ex. 16 : 3—Joshua *vs.* Eliezer
22. Mekh. Vayassa 1 : 1-12, Ex. 15 : 22—Joshua *vs.* Eliezer
23. Mekh. Amalek 2 : 186, Ex. 17 : 6—Joshua, Eleazar of Modiʿim, Eliezer
24. Mekh. Amalek 1 : 173, Ex. 17 : 13—Joshua *vs.* Eliezer
25. Mekh. Amalek 1 : 131, Ex. 17 : 11—Eliezer [alone]
26. b. Sanh. 106a, Num. 25 : 1—Eliezer *vs.* Joshua
27. Mekh. Amalek 3 : 127, Ex. 18 : 4—Joshua *vs.* Eliezer
28. Mekh. Baḥodesh 2 : 43, Ex. 19 : 5—Eliezer *vs.* ʿAqiba
29. Mekh. Baḥodesh 4 : 36, Ex. 19 : 19—Eliezer *vs.* ʿAqiba
30. Mekh. deR. Simeon to Ex. 13 : 5—Eliezer *vs.* ʿAqiba
31. Sifra Mekh. deMil. 2 : 35, Lev. 16 : 1—Eliezer *vs.* ʿAqiba
32. Sifra Beḥuq. 5 : 1, Lev. 26 : 18—Eliezer *vs.* Joshua
33. Sifré Deut. 29, Deut. 3 : 26—Eliezer *vs.* Joshua
34. Sifré Num. 136, Deut. 34 : 1—ʿAqiba *vs.* Eliezer
35. Sifré Deut. 338, Deut. 32 : 49—Eliezer *vs.* Joshua [Same as No. 34 in content.]
36. Mid. Tan. to Deut. 14 : 22—Eliezer and Ishmael [No difference in substance.]
37. b. Shab. 55b, Gen. 49 : 4—Eliezer, Joshua, Gamaliel
38. b. Eruv. 40b, Qoh. 11 : 2—Eliezer *vs.* Joshua
39. b. B.B. 16a, Job. 9 : 24—Eliezer *vs.* Joshua

C.

Anonymous Law + X Says = Gloss or Differing Opinion (*Sometimes*: + *Others*). This form also characterizes most pericopae in the Appendix to Chapter Two, so it may be considerably under-represented in the following catalogue

1. Say *Havdalah* in 4th blessing + ʿAqiba, Eliezer
   M. Ber. 5 : 2
2. Liability of first fruits + Ilai—Eliezer
   Tos. Dem. 1 : 3
3. Handkerchiefs etc. *re* diverse seeds
   M. Kil. 9 : 3
4. Give Heave-offering from what is clean for what is unclean
   M. Ter. 2 : 1
5. Take olives from press—*re* liability for tithes
   M. Ma. 4 : 3

6. Tithe dill
M. Ma. 4 : 5
7. Prepare dough in *qavs* and they contact one another
M. Hal. 2 : 4
8. Clean *Ḥallah* for unclean
M. Hal. 2 : 8 (Compare Tos. Hal. 1 : 10)
9. Do not put bread into oven at dusk + Eliezer
M. Shab. 1 : 10
10. Wear weapons on Sabbath + Eliezer + sages
M. Shab. 6 : 4
11. Woman not wear key on Sabbath + Eliezer allows spice-box + sages allow perfume flask
Tos. Shab. 4 : 11
12. Passover overrides Sabbath + debate
M. Pes. 6 : 1, 2
13. Prefect chooses lots, etc.
Tos. Kip. 2 : 10
14. Fasted and it rained
M. Ta. 3 : 9
15. Levirate law + Eliezer—Houses
M. Yev. 13 : 1-2
16. *Ḥaliṣah* at night, etc.
M. Yev. 12 : 2
17. He who divorces wife and remarries her—she is permitted to Levir *vs.* Eliezer
M. Yev. 13 : 6
18. Levirs died, etc. + Eliezer
M. Yev. 16 : 2 (Tos. Yev. 14 : 3)
19. Woman may remarry on evidence of one witness *vs.* Eliezer + Joshua: May not
M. Yev. 16 : 7
20-21-22. Nazir unclean—anonymous rule + Eliezer's gloss
M. Naz. 3 : 3-5
23. Agent testifies *re Geṭ*—glossed by Gamaliel, Eliezer
M. Git. 1 : 1
24. Commandments dependent on land—glossed by Eliezer
M. Qid. 1 : 9
25. Guilt-offering is subject to rule of Sin-offering
M. Zev. 1 : 1
[Tos. Zev. 1 : 1, Joshua *vs.* Eliezer without statement of problem.]
26. Slaughter with wrong intention
M. Zev. 3 : 3
27. Blood of fit sacrifices mixed with unfit—Eliezer *vs.* sages
M. Zev. 8 : 7
28. Meal-offering with wrong intention renders invalid (as No. 26)
M. Men. 3 : 1
29. Cock-partridge—Eliezer *vs.* sages, *re* Deut. 22 : 6-7
M. Hul. 12 : 2

30. Redeem firstling with hybrid
M. Bekh. 1 : 5

31. Farmer allowed to keep yoke if he dedicated self—no pledge of livelihood—utensils are taken
M. Ar. 6 : 3

[Minor gloss.]

32. Wild animals judged by court *vs.* Eliezer + ʿAqiba
M. Sanh. 1 : 4

33. Measure of break in lamp—*peruṭah*
M. Kel. 3 : 2

32. Insect in subdivided oven + debate
M. Kel. 8 : 1

35. Measure of break in metal vessel to render clean + Eliezer and ʿAqiba
M. Kel. 14 : 1

36. Measure of break in wooden vessel to render clean
M. Kel. 17 : 1

37. Throwing away rag *re* cleanness of cloth
M. Kel. 27 : 12

38. Grave-stone renders unclean by carrying + Eliezer and Joshua + ʿAqiba + debate
M. Oh. 2 : 4

39. Vessels under bier
M. Oh. 6 : 1

40-41. Red Heifer slaughtered not under own name; by priest with washed hands; or subject to wrong intention
M. Par. 4 : 1, 3

42. Depositing heifer-water
M. Par. 7 : 10

43. If mouse drinks heifer-water, it has made the water invalid
M. Par. 9 : 3

44. Ashes valid mixed with stove-ashes
M. Par. 9 : 7

45. Loosely fastened boards are unclean in what concerns heifer-water
M. Par. 11 : 2

46. Berries *re* hyssop for heifer-rite
M. Par. 11 : 7

47. Deem woman clean after their period—four types—Eliezer and Joshua gloss rule of House of Shammai
M. Nid. 1 : 3

48. Woman who misses period—enough for her is her time
M. Nid. 1 : 5

49. Hard labor during eighty days of purifying etc.
M. Nid. 4 : 6

50. Liquids render unclean—Eliezer excludes item on list
M. Maksh. 6 : 6

51-52. He that carries carrion is unclean. (Addition to list.)
M. Zab. 5 : 3, 7

[53-54. M. Ed. 6 : 2-3; Eliezer, Joshua, Neḥunya discuss the substance of the law in M. Oh. 1 : 7: *should* produce gloss of that law.]

D.

Question + (Differing) Answers

1. From what time do they read *Shemaʿ* + *Maʿaśeh* M. Ber. 1 : 1, M. Ber. 1 : 2
2. Who is *ʿam haʾareṣ* b. Ber. 47b
3. Why wipe with left hand b. Ber. 62a
4. How separate Dough-offering in uncleanness on 15 Nisan—Eliezer *vs.* Judah b. Bathyra M. Pes. 3 : 3
5. What is a distant journey—Eliezer *vs.* ʿAqiba M. Pes. 9 : 2
6. When do they say rain prayer M. Ta. 1 : 1
7. When do mourners turn over beds y. M.Q. 3 : 5
8. Who is a minor who exercises right of refusal + Eliezer: Minor cannot do so M. Yev. 13 : 2
   [Compare Tos. 13 : 3-5: Eliezer's saying stands independently.]
9. How do we know *vs.* ʿAqiba: It is unnecessary b. Yev. 70a
10. How much time for intercourse—Eliezer, Joshua, + others Tos. Sot. 1 : 2
11. Fire in own property M. B.Q. 6 : 4
12. When does he [who removed signs of uncleanness] become clean? Eliezer *vs.* sages M. Neg. 7 : 4
    [See A. 93]
13. They asked Eliezer: What is law *re* bright spot in palm of hand? M. Neg. 9 : 3
14. Leprosy sign on checkered garment—They asked Eliezer—lo, it is on one check only M. Neg. 11 : 7
15. What to do to have male children—Eliezer and Joshua b. B.B. 10b

E.

Simple Saying without protasis: *X says* + *lemma* in direct (sometimes in indirect) discourse

1. Eliezer says b. Ber. 3a

2. Eliezer used to say
M. Shev. 8 : 10
3. Simeon in name of Liezer—*re* saffron as to Tithe-money
Tos. M.S. 1 : 14
4. Leazar b. R. Yosah etc. in name of Liezer—*re* ʿ*orlah* abroad
Tos. Orl. 1 : 8
5. Eliezer: He who kills vermin
b. Shab. 12a
6. Liezer: Woman wears tiara on Sabbath
Tos. Shab. 4 : 6 [M. Ed. 2 : 7]

[7. R. Eliezer and R. Joshua agree they burn this by itself, etc.
M. Pes. 1 : 7 = M. Ter. 8 : 8 is summarized]

8. Nathan in name of Liezer *re* measure of dough
Tos. Pis. 3 : 8
9. Eliezer: ʿ*Aṣṣeret* like Sabbath
M. M.Q. 3 : 6
[+ Gamaliel, not on same subject.]
10. Eliezer: Minor can do nothing
Tos. Yev. 13 : 3-5
[Compare M. Yev. 13 : 2]
11. Liezer: Orphan has right to usufruct
Tos. Ket. 11 : 4
12. Eliezer: Teach daughter
M. Sot. 3 : 4
13. Cannot dedicate all of one's goods—the words of R. Eliezer
M. Ar. 8 : 4
14. Eliezer: Raising dogs is like raising pigs
Tos. B.Q. 8 : 17

[15. M. Ed. 2 : 7 *should* produce: R. Eliezer says, "A woman may go out . . ." and "Pigeon-flyers are. . ."]

16. M. Sot. 9 : 15, Eliezer says, From the day on which the Temple was destroyed. . .
17. M. Avot 2 : 10—Three sayings [Repent-saying developed into chria: b. Shab. 153a]
18. Tos. Sanh. 11 : 5: ʿAqiba, "Three hundred laws *re* sorceress [Ex. 22 : 17] did Eliezer expound, etc." produces M. Sanh. 7 : 11. y. Sanh. 7 : 13: Joshua
19. b. Sot. 48b—Eliezer, "Whoever has a scrap of bread. . ."
20. b. B.B. 121b—Eliezer, 15th Av *re* wood-offering
21. Mekh. Pisḥa 14 : 95—Eliezer, "Idol passed through Red Sea with Israelites." [y Suk. 4 : 3: + ʿAqiba]
22. b. Ber. 6a—Eliezer, Deut. 28 : 10 refers to *tefillin*
23. b. Arakh. 17a—Eliezer, "Even Patriarchs could not stand before divine reproof."

F.

Closely related to the foregoing are juxtaposed, differing opinions, given without a protasis. These sometimes rely on the first opinion for a definition of the context, issue, or meaning, but often each saying stands independent of the other. Thus simply: *X says... Y says...*

1. Prayer—Gamaliel, Joshua, ʿAqiba, Eliezer
M. Ber. 4 : 3-4
2. Eliezer, Joshua, Ṭarfon, Judah b. Bathyra, ʿAqiba—*re* liability for *Pe'ah*
M. Pe'ah 3 : 6
3. Eliezer, Joshua
M. Ter. 4 : 7
4. Joshua, Eliezer, ʿAqiba
M. Ter. 4 : 8 [+9]
5. Eliezer, ʿAqiba
M. Ter. 6 : 6 [statement of problem = 6 : 1]
6. Gamaliel, Eliezer, ʿAqiba—*re* tithes
M. Ma. 4 : 6
7. Liezer, sages—Believed for Second Tithe, also First Tithe
Tos. M.S. 3 : 16
8. Eliezer *vs.* Joshua *re* curdling milk with sap of *ʿorlah*
M. Orl. 1 : 7
9. *Etrog*—Gamaliel *vs.* Eliezer
M. Bik. 2 : 6
10. Eliezer *vs.* sages *re* weaving
M. Shab. 13 : 1
11. Eliezer: May bring knife for circumcision on Sabbath, etc., *vs.* ʿAqiba: Every kind of work which can be done before the Sabbath...
12. Eliezer *vs.* sages *re* stretching out filter on festival
M. Shab. 20 : 1
13. Two *ʿeruvs* for festival and Sabbath—Eliezer *vs.* sages
M. Eruv. 3 : 6
14. Make an *ʿeruv* with all food *vs.* only whole loaf—Eliezer *vs.* Joshua
M. Eruv. 7 : 10
15. Baker buys *ʿeruv* for money—Eliezer *vs.* sages
M. Eruv. 7 : 11
16. Repeat lesson four times *vs.* no limit—Eliezer, ʿAqiba
b. Eruv. 54b
17. Passover not from tithes—Eliezer *vs.* ʿAqiba
Mekh. Simeon, p. 39, ls. 7-14
18. Burning unclean sanctities—Eliezer *vs.* ʿAqiba *re* Houses
M. Sheq. 8 : 7
19. Unblemished lambs offered with evening *vs.* morning sacrifice —Eliezer *vs.* ʿAqiba
M. Yoma 7 : 3
20. Sweeping chips on festival, etc.
M. Bes. 4 : 6-7

21. Lev. 23 : 24—Eliezer *vs.* ʿAqiba
Tos. R. H. 2 : 10

23. Mourners and *tefillin*—Eliezer *vs.* Joshua
y. M.Q. 3 : 5

24. Mourners and couch *re* festival—Eliezer *vs.* Joshua
b. M.Q. 20a

25. Nurse: two *vs.* four/five years—Eliezer *vs.* Joshua
y. Ket. 5 : 6 = b. Ket. 60a

26-27. Eliezer release from vow *vs.* sages prohibit
M. Ned. 9 : 1-2

28. Releasing vows—Scriptural support—Eliezer *vs.* Joshua
b. Hag. 12a

29. *Mamzers* can be purified—Ṭarfon *vs.* Eliezer
M. Qid. 3 : 13

30. Blood, flesh—Eliezer *vs.* Joshua
Tos. Zev. 4 : 1-2

31. Date of Pentecost—Eliezer *vs.* Joshua, Ishmael, etc.
b. Men. 65b

32. Acquire property by walking—Eliezer *vs.* sages
Tos. B.B. 2 : 11

33. Eliezer *vs.* sages *re* hanging those who have been stoned
M. Sanh. 6 : 4

34. Eliezer *vs.* ʿAqiba *vs.* Ishmael *re* liability for unawareness of creeping thing + Temple
M. Shav. 2 : 5

35. Eliezer *vs.* Joshua *re* cleaning broken metal vessel
M. Kel. 14 : 7

36. Eliezer *vs.* Joshua *vs.* ʿAqiba *re* cleanness of small rag
M. Kel. 28 : 2

37. Eliezer *vs.* Joshua *re* grave-area makes grave-area
M. Oh. 17 : 2

38. Eliezer *vs.* sages *re* unclean dirt
M. Oh. 17 : 5

39-40. Eliezer *vs.* sages *re* Parah
M. Par. 1 : 1, 2 : 1

41. Eliezer *vs.* Joshua *re* grades of uncleanness
M. Toh. 2 : 2

42. Eliezer *vs.* sages *re* rendering ritual pool unfit
M. Miq. 2 : 4

43. Eliezer *vs.* Joshua *re* world made in Tishri
b. R.H. 10b-12a

44. Eliezer *vs.* Joshua *re* revelation from bush
Mekh. deR. Simeon, p. 1, ls. 12-18

45. Eliezer *vs.* ʿAqiba *re* Deut. 4 : 6
Sifré Deut. 32

46. ʿAqiba, Joshua, Eliezer—how do we know a man's agent is like himself?
Sifré Zuṭṭa

47. Eliezer *vs.* Joshua *re* Is. 1 : 18
y. Shab. 9 : 3
48. Eliezer *vs.* Joshua—Redemption depends on repentence
y. Ta. 1 : 1
49. Eliezer *vs.* Joshua—Whole world draws water from ocean
b. Ta. 9b
[Gen. R. 13 : 9 supplies narrative framework]
50. Eliezer + Joshua—Dead whom Ezekiel raised sang song
b. Sanh. 92b
51. Eliezer *vs.* Joshua—World is like an *exedra* *vs.* tent
b. B.B. 25a
52. Eliezer *vs.* Joshua—Gen. 40 : 10 refers to Patriarchs *vs.* Moses
b. Hul. 92a
53. Eliezer *vs.* Joshua—World created from center *vs.* sides; earth came from earth, heaven from heaven
b. Yoma 54b

G.

A variation on F is the first-person report of an opinion, *X says [said], I asked... I heard...*

1. Ilai: I asked Joshua, then Eliezer
Tos. Hal. 1 : 6 (M. Hal. 1 : 6 has Eliezer's opinion, anonymously)
2. Ilai: I heard from Eliezer
M. Eruv. 2 : 6 (+ three unrelated laws)
3. Joshua: I heard + ʿAqiba + Eliezer
M. Yev. 8 : 4
4. ʿAqiba: I reasoned before Eliezer
M. Naz. 7 : 4
5. ʿAqiba: I asked Eliezer
M. Ker. 3 : 10
6. Eliezer: I have heard a tradition *re* building Temple + Joshua, I have heard *re* sacrifices without Temple
M. Ed. 8 : 6

H.

Not constituting well-defined forms are stories, brief and long respectively.

1. *Brief stories*

1. Eliezer's disciple at prayer
Mekh. II, p. 91-92
2. ʿAqiba: I was staying with Eliezer and Joshua—*re maṣṣah*
b. Per. 36a, y. Pes. 2 : 7
3. Eyes of Leviathan
b. B.B. 74b
4. *Tefillin* of Eliezer used at all times
y. Ber. 2 : 3

5. Honor father before mother
b. Qid. 31a

2. *Long stories*

1. They asked Eliezer *re* goat fell ill, *mamzer*, etc.
Tos. Kip. 3 : 14, Tos. Yev. 3
2. Yoḥanan b. Ilai + Eliezer *re* spreading cloth over *Sukkah*
Tos. Suk. 1 : 9
3. Eliezer arrested for *minut*
Tos. Hul. 2 : 24
4. Ammon and Moab in Seventh Year
M. Yad. 4 : 3
5. Eliezer sick: Ṭarfon, Joshua, Eleazar b. ʿAzariah, ʿAqiba
Mekh. Baḥodesh 10 : 58-86
6. Eliezer at wedding of Gamaliel's son
Sifré Deut. 38
7. Death-scenes
b. Sanh. 68a, y. Shab. 2 : 7, etc.
8. Oven of ʿAkhnai
b. B.M. 59b
9. Origins of Eliezer
ARN Chap. 6, etc.

ii. Forms and Particular Masters

While almost all Houses' materials are in dispute-form, no form is disproportionately associated with Eliezer, by himself or with a particular contemporary. We therefore cannot hypothesize that the tradents responsible for the formation, preservation, and transmission of materials about, e.g., Eliezer and ʿAqiba, or Eliezer and Joshua, made use of one form in preference to some other:

Form (A):

Eliezer *vs.* ʿAqiba:	10
Eliezer *vs.* sages:	32
Eliezer *vs.* Joshua:	32

Form (B):

Eliezer *vs.* ʿAqiba:	17
Eliezer *vs.* sages:	1
Eliezer *vs.* Joshua:	16

Form (F):

Eliezer *vs.* ʿAqiba:	11
Eliezer *vs.* sages:	11
Eliezer *vs.* Joshua:	22

These approximate figures show that pericopae containing disputes between Eliezer and a named sage or "the sages", were not set into one form in preference to another.

The low incidence of the use of form (B) for Eliezer + sages-materials apparently reflects nothing more than the general preference of the framers of *aggadic* exegetical pericopae for assigning materials to named authorities, rather than to a named sage *vs.* "the sages".

All together (A) + (B) are as follows: E/A—27; E/S—33; E/J—48. We then notice that form (F) exhibits pretty much the same proportions: E/A—11; E/S—11 E/J—22. All one may conclude is that more pericopae are assigned to E/J than to either E/A or E/S. But as to the use of the several well-defined forms for materials of one set over another, no significant differences occur. As stated, I take this to mean that the imposition of forms had nothing to do with the redactional preferences of a given circle of tradents, for instance, the circle of Eliezer's disciples in association with that of Joshua's. No form can be thought to originate among the disciples of Eliezer, either by themselves or in association with those responsible for the redaction of teachings of any other master of his generation. Since, moreover, the same, or closely-related, teachings may come in different forms in Mishnah and Tosefta, the question of the formation of such forms as are not either original to, or unique in, a given master's materials has to be dealt with in the larger context of the formation of Mishnah-Tosefta.

iii. History of Forms

It follows that the history of no form may be considered primarily in the context of Eliezer's traditions, except for (C), as we shall presently note. Let us review the history of the other forms.

Forms (A), (B), and (F) are essentially variations on the dispute-form, already well-known to us from the rabbinic traditions about the Pharisees, and abundantly attested, within those traditions, in the Yavnean stratum. Since the attestations of the form occur in the names of Eliezer, Joshua, ʿAqiba, and most other early Yavneans, we may take it for granted that the *terminus ante quem* for the form must be the earliest years of the Yavnean period, and that it was used in the first instance for the redaction of Houses' materials (*Phar.* II, pp. 1-5, and III, pp. 199-209.)

The Yavnean attestations of the dispute-form used for Houses' pericopae are as follows:

Eliezer: M. Ter. 5 : 4/Tos. Ter. 6 : 4; Tos. Ter. 3 : 16; b. Yoma 80a; M. Ket. 5:6; b. Yev. 89b; M. Nid. 5 : 9; Tos. Nid. 5 : 5-7/M. Nid. 4 : 3;
Joshua b. Ḥananiah: b. Eruv. 6a; M. Yev. 1 : 4/Tos. Yev. 1 : 7-14; Tos Ah. 3 : 4/M. Ed. 1 : 7; Tos. Ah. 5 : 11. M. Oh. 5 : 4/M. Ed. 1 : 14; M. Nid. 2 : 4; M. Maksh. 1 : 2-4;
Eliezer + Joshua: Tos. Ar. 4 : 5;
Eliezer + ʿAqiba: Sifra Ṣav 8 : 6, M. M.S. 3 : 9/M. Sheq. 8 : 6; M. Eruv. 1 : 2;
Abba Saul [Late Yavneh or early Usha]: M. Bes. 2 : 4, Tos. Hag. 2 : 10/M. Hag. 2 : 2; M. Yev. 3 : 1/Tos. Yev. 5 : 1;
Gamaliel II: b. Ber. 43b; M. Bes. 1 : 8; M. Kel. 28 : 4; M. Toh. 9 : 1, 5, 7;
Eleazar b. R. Ṣaddoq: Tos. Pisḥa 7 : 14; Tos. Kel. B.M. 4 : 16;
Eleazar b. ʿAzariah: M. Yev. 3 : 1/Tos. Yev. 5 : 1; M. Yev. 1 : 4/Tos. Yev. 1 : 7-14;
Eleazar b. ʿAzariah + Joshua: M. Pe'ah 6 : 2;
Eleazar b. ʿAzariah + Ishmael: M. Ber. 1 : 3;
Ṭarfon: y. Shev. 4 : 2/M. Shev. 4 : 4; M. Ber. 1 : 3B; M. M.S. 2 : 9; Tos. Yev. 1 : 7-13/M. Yev. 1 : 4; M. Naz. 5 : 1, 2, 3, 5;
Ṭarfon + ʿAqiba: M. Pes. 10 : 6/Tos. Pisḥa 10 : 9;
ʿAqiba: M. M.S. 2 : 4; M. M.S. 2 : 9; Sifra Vayiqra 13 : 13/M. B.M. 3 : 12; Sifré Deut. 269/M. Git. 9 : 10; b. Ber. 23a; M. R.H. 1 : 1/Tos. Shev. 4 : 2; M. M.S. 2 : 7; M. M.S. 3 : 7 [Yosi: "This is the Mishnah of R. ʿAqiba"]; Tos. Pisḥa 1 : 6; M. Yev. 4 : 3/M. Ket. 8 : 6/M. B.B. 9 : 8-9; M. Bekh. 5 : 2/Tos. Bekh. 3 : 15-16; M. Kel. 20 : 2; M. Oh. 5 : 1-4/M. Kel. 9 : 2; M. Zab. 1 : 2/Tos. Zab. 1 : 4; M. Uqs. 3 : 8.

To ʿAqiba's list one must add ʿAqiban exegeses in support of the opinion of the House of Hillel for six Houses-disputes (*Phar.* III, p. 207). We have further, later Yavnean attestations of the dispute-form used for Houses' materials in the names of Yoḥanan b. Nuri, Ilai, and others (*Phar.* III, pp. 208-9). We may be absolutely certain, therefore, that the dispute-form was known to the early Yavneans; indeed, pericopae set into the dispute-form constitute the vast majority of Houses' materials first attested in one way or another by the Yavneans.

The Houses' materials normally were set into the following form:

Statement of Problem:
House of Shammai say...
House of Hillel say...

The apodosis of the Houses' sayings almost always consisted of mnemonically carefully constructed elements (*Phar.* III, pp. 119-143).

The dispute-form without an antecedent statement of the subject of the dispute occurs in reference to the following:

1. Shemaʿiah *vs.* Abṭalion—Mekh. Beshallaḥ 4 : 58-60 M. Nid. 1 : 1
2. Hillel *vs.* Shammai—M. Ed. 1 : 1, 2, 3/Tos. Ed. 1 : 3
3. Houses—M. Ed. 1 : 7
4. Houses—b. Bes. 16a

[5. Ishmael, Ḥanina Prefect of the Priests—M. Men. 10 : 1]
[6. Hanina Prefect of the Priests, Dosa b. Harkinas, ʿAqavyah b. Mehallel + ʿAqiba—M. Neg. 1 : 4]

7. Houses—M. Ber. 1 : 3A
8. Houses—M. Pe'ah 6 : 1
9. Houses—M. Dem. 6 : 6
10. Houses—M. Shev. 5 : 8
11. Houses—M. M.S. 2 : 7, etc.

But in most of the Houses' exempla, the lemma of the House of Shammai contains the definition of the dispute, and when this is restored as a superscription, the Houses' sayings are balanced (listed in *Phar.* III, pp. 132-134).

By contrast, the dispute-form as applied to Eliezer-materials will occur either with or without an introductory statement of the legal problem or issue. When the Houses' materials lacked such a statement, as noted, it often would be included in the saying of the House of Shammai. When Eliezer's materials have no statement of the problem, however, it is supplied not by the construction of the saying either of Eliezer or of his opponent, but, at best, by the context, or even by the substance of the two opposed sayings (F).

A second, even more striking contrast is that when the dispute-form is used for Eliezer's sayings, we rarely, if ever, are able to locate an interest in mnemonic considerations. Sayings seldom are carefully balanced, stated in the same words, built upon some clearcut pattern, or otherwise so phrased as to facilitate memorization. So while the dispute-form occurs in its three closely related versions—(A), with statement of the legal issue, (F), without such a statement, and (B), in exegeses of Scriptures—it is materially changed from the simple version used for the Houses' disputes. With the Houses' materials the form is apt not to vary and exhibits concern for mnemonic patterns of a highly disciplined sort.

What do these changes in the dispute-form mean? As to the second: mnemonic considerations obviously were irrelevant to the parties responsible for the formation of Eliezer's traditions. Perhaps they did not intend the materials to be memorized and so did not pay attention to the mnemonic requirements. But in the Houses' materials it was only the apodosis, never the protasis, that was mnemonically structured. So questions of memorization cannot have predominated. Then why should the Houses' materials have exhibited such sustained concern for a balanced and orderly statement of the Houses' opinions (*Phar.* III, pp. 126-136)? Perhaps the problem was not literary and mnemonic but political. If elements of the original Houses were responsible for the compromise that permitted the traditions of the two groups to be redacted in a single, set pattern, then the parity in the apodoses preserved throughout may reflect a part of that compromise. In the formation of a given tradition, neither party will have a great deal more to say than the other. The opinions in effect will be a simple affirmative or negative, with little added by way of explanation or elaboration.

If so, ought not Eliezer's materials (among those of other masters), when redacted along with those of other masters, e.g., ʿAqiba or Joshua, also have such abbreviated apodoses? But what if neither Eliezer nor his immediate disciples, e.g. Ilai, supervised the redaction of his materials when set into juxtaposition with those of Joshua or ʿAqiba? The biographical traditions are clear that both Joshua and ʿAqiba outlived Eliezer. It is quite certain that some of Eliezer's materials were reworked by unsympathetic authorities. Joshua and ʿAqiba, however, do not seem to have been among those unsympathetic to Eliezer—no tradition suggests otherwise—and the disciples of both, if in charge of the matter, would have had no strong motive drastically to revise in favor of their own masters and against Eliezer the materials they had received and clearly intended to preserve in Eliezer's name. And it is a well-established fact that Joshua and ʿAqiba or circles of their disciples *did* preserve Eliezer's materials—or otherwise we should have very little in his name. It would seem, therefore, that the masters in charge of setting Eliezer's materials together with those of ʿAqiba, Joshua, and "the sages" did not work under the burden of intense partisanship necessitating closely meted out phrases. No one seemed to care that one party had a longer saying than another, or expressed his opinion in language quite different from, indeed unrelated to, that of the other. It would thus seem plausible that the difference in the development of the dispute-apodoses in Eliezer materials reflects a different redactional situation. While with the Houses it was important to preserve a meticulous balance—because of evident hostilities between them—with Eliezer's dispute-materials it was not necessary to do so, because of a quite different relationship between Eliezer and the Joshua-ʿAqiba-"sages"-circles.

The dispute-form in Eliezer-materials produces interesting variations. Of these, (B) is the least important. What has changed is simply the use of the same dispute-form for a different *sort* of tradition, one involving not law but the explanation of Scripture. When, in the Houses-materials, we observed occasional use of the form for the same purpose, however, it was seldom *well* used. The disciplined structure was almost invariably broken; all one was left with was "The House of Shammai say... The House of Hillel say..." The amount of non-legal pericopae was slight. As with Eliezer, none of the Houses' non-legal dispute-pericopae was attested before occurrence in the document in which it was contained. Houses' non-legal pericopae in the dispute-form are as follows:

1. b. Eruv. 13b: The Houses dispute the law—in general—but no specific opinions are spelled out. Then the echo says both are the words of the living God, but the law follows the House of Hillel.
   —This does not conform to the dispute-form at all.
2. b. Hag. 12a, y. Hag. 2 : 1: The House of Shammai say, "Heaven was created first, then earth."
   The House of Hillel say, "Earth was created first, then heaven."
   —The dispute-form here has been followed in every regard.
3. b. Ket. 17a: How does one dance before the bride? The House of Shammai say, "The bride as she is." The House of Hillel say, "Beautiful and graceful bride."
   —The dispute-form is followed in general, but the apodosis is not balanced.
4. Tos. Sanh. 13 : 3: House of Shammai say, Three groups—one for eternal life, one for eternal shame, and one in the middle. House of Hillel say, "He that abounds in grace..."
   —The dispute-form is followed in general, but the sayings of the Houses are formally unrelated to one another.
5. b. Eruv. 13b: For two and a half years the Houses disputed whether it would have been better for man not to have been created... They voted...
   —The dispute-form here is wholly ignored.

These are, to my knowledge, all the instances in which the Houses are represented as disputing about non-legal issues. Only No. 2 conforms to the pattern well established in the legal materials. What changes with Eliezer's materials, therefore, is that a considerably larger portion of non-legal materials is assigned to him than was assigned to the Houses. His non-legal materials generally follow the dispute-form as set forth in other Houses-pericopae. So (B) does not mark an important variation in the dispute-form. What has changed is the nature of the traditions, not the form in which they are preserved.

(F) seems more important, and at least some of its materials are attested before their appearance the third-century compilations. (F) permits the statement of a dispute *without* the provision of a protasis, thus consisting simply of juxtaposed, differing opinions. Now the Houses-materials are apt not to occur without some sort of introductory clause, if only *Concerning the Meal* (M. Ber. 8 : 1, *Phar.* II, pp. 43-48, 324-326). Presenting a dispute without an introduction of any sort—whether articulated as a separate introductory clause or inserted into the saying of the House of Shammai—must be regarded as a loosening up of the disciplined dispute-form known to us in Houses-materials. I should further guess that this "looser" form comes later than the "tighter" one. It allows for greater variation in the construction of a dispute. The sayings of the juxtaposed masters will not be balanced in word choice, diction, or meter, or be tied together by a common introductory clause. So the substance of the dispute, as worded by the individual masters, must carry the whole weight. The tightly worked-out form is now less important. All that is left of what seems to be the "original" form is the juxtaposition of two masters' sayings on a closely related, or common, problem. The result will be highly supple, for instance:

> R. Eliezer says, "If they had not brought the implement on the eve of the Sabbath, it may be brought openly on the Sabbath."

or

> R. Eliezer said, "They may cut wood to make charcoal in order to forge an iron implement."

vs.

> R. ʿAqiba said a general rule, "Any act of work that can be done..."

Eliezer has a very specific rule; ʿAqiba has the opposite. Yet without a protasis of any kind, the nature of the dispute is entirely clear, and the principles under debate are well spelled-out.

Such freer use of the dispute-form ought to represent a development over its more disciplined and rigid implementation. This conclusion seems certain because almost all the materials attributed to the Houses are carefully structured around an introductory statement; and because it is primarily with Eliezer and ʿAqiba/Joshua that we find variation (F). Perhaps the evident absence of partisan considerations in the formation of Eliezer's materials by his disciples in relationship to Joshua and ʿAqiba and their disciples also permitted greater flexibility in the use of the dispute-form.

Form (D) seems close to form (A). Instead of a statement of a problem followed by two opposed sayings completing the opening statement or ruling on it, (D) states the problem as a question, and then, as before, the apodosis will contain the answers to the question, which are formally not much different from completions of an opening statement. Thus (D) may be regarded as a further, though minor, variation of the dispute-form. Indeed, not a few Houses' disputes are introduced by questions, e.g., M. Shev. 1 : 1.

Form (E) is not entirely new, for we observed (*Phar.* III, pp. 5ff.) that a few masters who lived about the time of the destruction of the Temple had simple sayings, as follows:

1. b. Qid. 43a: Shammai the Elder said in the name of Haggai...
2. Sifra Ṣav. 1 : 9: Ḥananiah Prefect of the Priests says, Father would reject...
3. M. Pes. 1 : 6: Ḥananiah the Prefect of the Priests says...
4. M. Zev. 12 : 4: R. Ḥananiah Prefect of the Priests said, Never have I seen... R. ʿAqiba said, We learn from his words...
5. b. Yoma 39a/b. Sot. 42a: R. Ḥananiah Prefect of the Priests said, For what is the prefect of the priests appointed? (*Or*) Why does the prefect of the priests stand at the right?

We have a couple of *X says...*—sayings, without contrasting opinions, in the name of Naḥum the Mede as well. So the form cannot be thought to begin with Eliezer. But it was uncommon before his time. (In so stating, we of course ignore M. Avot 1 : 1-18; but none of those sayings is attested in Yavnean times, while, as is evident from No. 4 above, ʿAqiba supplies an important attestation for a Ḥananiah-saying, and others, not indicated, also are attested by Yavneans.) Since Ḥananiah himself is partially a Yavnean figure (*Phar.* I, pp. 400-413), we must conclude that with Yavneh one finds the beginning of the redaction of a saying, without protasis and without an opposed saying, in the name of a single master, in the form *X says....*But Eliezer's simple sayings, not set in dispute with someone else's opinion and not given an introductory statement or other sort of protasis, are considerably more numerous. Since he comes at the beginning of the Yavnean tradition, we may suppose a form employed slightly before 70 for a few, relatively unimportant names now was taken up and used far more extensively, beginning with Eliezer.

Alternatively, more sayings attributed to Eliezer than to earlier masters survived in this form. It is hard to say whether it is a matter of accident, or whether a greater stress on formulating materials simply as *X says* characterized the early Yavnean tradents.

(G) is similar in form to (F). It has no protasis and normally will not permit inclusion of a dispute. But the form cannot be said to characterize *Eliezer's* materials in particular. He has only one "I" saying; it hardly is a form important in the formulation of his materials.

(H) is not to be regarded as a form at all, as noted (*Phar.* III, pp. 43-55).

iv. Form (C)

The anonymous statement of a law followed by a gloss in the name of a particular master does not constitute a new form. Such a construction is used, if less commonly, in reference to traditions attributed to, or told about, Yoḥanan ben Zakkai and the Houses of Shammai and Hillel, though it never occurs with reference to named masters of the period before 70. It would seem to have been worked out toward the end of the Jerusalem period or in the earliest years of Yavneh.

What is of interest is the *form,* not the fact that an antecedent rule may in some way be discussed, explained, or elaborated. Few if any legal sayings attributed to pre-70 Pharisees or early Yavneans supply the definition of a wholly new law. Most take for granted the general principles of the law and deal with minor details. Whether the laws discussed by Pharisaic masters were originally Pharisaic, or derived from Scriptures, or came from some other sect, or were part of the common law, or were produced by the government of Jewish Palestine, is not our problem. What is important is to seek evidence of a law-*code* antecedent to the discussants and available to them in its *present* form. If it can be shown that a pericope attested in early Yavnean times has been added to an antecedent rule and has been shaped with the language, not merely the substance, of the antecedent rule in mind, then we may plausibly propose that that antecedent rule derives from the period before the early Yavnean pericope was formulated. This must mean that pre-70 Pharisaism did have some sort of law-*code* and that elements of that law-*code* have survived in Mishnah-Tosefta. Since Eliezer is the beginning of the Yavnean tradition, his traditions provide the first important opportunity for exploring this problem. And the fact that a large number of his traditions occur in form (C)—larger, by twice, as we shall see, than those of the Houses of Shammai and Hillel—is of considerable interest.

The form of a gloss by itself, however, does not guarantee that the antecedent rule comes before the time of the Houses. In a number of instances, e.g., No. 12, the Houses' gloss seems to date after the anonymous law, but in fact is the work of Ushans. Later generations were quite capable of formulating glosses in the names of the Houses—and therefore also of post-70 generations—which seemed to clarify a law already set down before their time, but in fact were formulated later on and attached as a gloss to a unanimously accepted, anonymous rule.

The following are the pericopae in form (C) attributed to masters before Eliezer. I have omitted the numerous pericopae in which a general law is given, followed by a Houses' dispute in which one or another party takes the position already formulated as a general law, e.g. M. Yev. 3 : 1 (*Phar.* II, p. 194):

1. M. M.S. 3 : 12B-13:

   A. If wine was designated Heave-offering before the jars were sealed [and they were confused with others], they are neutralized in a hundred and one. But if they were later sealed up, they render holy [others with which they are confused] in any quantity.

   B. Until he has sealed them up, he may give Heave-offering from one for all; afterward, he must give Heave-offering from each by itself.

   C. The House of Shammai say, "He opens and empties them into the winepress."

   And the House of Hillel say, "He opens them but need not empty them."

   —The Houses' dispute takes for granted the antecedent rule (B) and relies upon its language for the definition of the subject matter of the dispute. Without B, C is incomprehensible.

2. M. Orl. 2 : 4:

   Whatsoever is leavened, flavored, or mingled with Heave-offering, *ʿorlah*-fruit, or Diverse Kinds of the Vineyard is forbidden.

   The House of Shammai say, "It can also convey uncleanness."

   The House of Hillel say, "It can never convey uncleanness..."

   —The Houses' dispute concerns an emendation of the antecedent rule, on which they are agreed.

3. M. Pes. 1 : 1:

   A. On the night of the fourteenth [of Nisan] the *ḥameṣ* must be searched for by the light of a lamp. Any place into which *ḥameṣ* is never brought needs no searching.

B. Then why have they said, "Two rows in a wine-vault?"

They are a place into which *ḥames* might be brought.

C. The House of Shammai say, "The two rows on the whole surface of the wine-vault."

And the House of Hillel say, "Only the two outermost rows that are uppermost."

—The Houses clearly gloss the foregoing rule (B). For the meaning of the passage, see *Phar.* II, pp. 140-1.

4. M. Pes. 4 : 5

—Similar in form to the foregoing. See *Phar.* II, p. 141.

5. M. Bes. 2 : 1-2:

If a festival-day fell on the eve of the Sabbath, one may not cook on the festival-day food for the Sabbath, but he may cook food for the festival-day, and if any is left over, it is left over for the Sabbath; or he may prepare a dish on the eve of the festival-day and depend on it for the Sabbath.

The House of Shammai say, "Two dishes."

And the House of Hillel say, "One dish."

—The form is clearly that of a gloss. But the meaning is unclear, see *Phar.* II, pp. 166-170.

6. M. Hag. 1 : 1 says all but children are liable to appear before the Lord. Then the Houses define who is deemed a child, thus exempt from the afore-stated liability.

7. M. Ned. 3 : 4:

They vow to murderers, robbers, etc.

The House of Shammai say, "They vow in all forms except an oath."

The House of Hillel say, "Even in the form of an oath," etc.

—The Houses' dispute (and the list that follows, *Phar.* II, pp. 212-214) supplies details that depend upon the antecedent rule.

8. M. Qid. 1 : 1:

By three means is the woman acquired... by money.

By money—the House of Shammai say, "By a *denar...*"

And the House of Hillel say, "By a *peruṭah...*"

—The Houses' dispute defines the foregoing rule and relies upon its language.

9. M. Hul. 1 : 2:

If one slaughtered with a hand-sickle... what he slaughters is valid. They slaughter with any implement excepting a reaping-sickle since it chokes... If a man slaughtered with a reaping-sickle, drawing the blade backwards—

The House of Shammai declare it invalid.

And the House of Hillel declare it valid.

—The Houses gloss the foregoing general rule. The Shammaites say one may not draw the blade backward, lest he draw it in the other direction. The Hillelites do not prohibit one movement on account of the other. The Houses therefore take for granted the rule that one should not do so.

10. M. Kel. 14 : 2:

A staff with a club-headed nail is susceptible to uncleanness. But when nails are put in only for adornment, it is insusceptible...

When does it become insusceptible?

The House of Shammai say, "So soon as it has suffered damage."

The House of Hillel say, "So soon as it is fastened on."

—The Houses define the *time* of the application of the antecedent, anonymous rule (for details, see *Phar.* II, pp. 255-256). Further examples of the same phenomenon are cited without quotation.

11. M. Kel. 20 : 6

—See No. 10

12. Tos. Kel. B.M. 4 : 5

—See No. 10. But here the Houses' opinions are attributed to Meir and Judah.

13. M. Oh. 2 : 3:

These convey uncleanness... a backbone in which aught is lacking...

How much must be lacking in the backbone?

The House of Shammai say, "Two links."

And the House of Hillel say, "Even one link."

—The Houses again define a detail of an antecedent, anonymous rule.

14. M. Oh. 7 : 3:

If a corpse lay in a house to which were many entrances, all is unclean. If one entrance was opened, it alone is unclean. If there was the intention to take the corpse out through one of them or through a window... it affords protection to all the others.

The House of Shammai say, "The intention must have been formed before the man was dead."

And the House of Hillel say, "Even afterward."

—This is in essence no different from No. 10. But it is both attested by, and evidently the creation of, Judah.

15. M. Toh. 9 : 1

—See No. 10. But the pericope is Ushan, see *Phar.* II, p. 289.

16. M. Miq. 1 : 5

—See No. 10.

17. M. Miq. 5 : 6A gives a list of places where one may immerse. Then the Houses debate whether one may immerse vessels in a rain-stream.

—The authority is Yosi, M. Ed. 5 : 2.

18. M. Nid 2 : 1: The daughters of Israel use two test rags when they have sexual relations.
M. Nid. 2 : 4:
The House of Shammai say, "She needs two test rags for every act of intercourse. . ."
And the House of Hillel say, "Two test-rags suffice for the whole night."
—The Houses gloss the rule of M. Nid. 2 : 1.
19. M. Nid. 2 : 6:
Five kinds of bloods are unclean. . .
The House of Shammai say, "Also a color like water. . ."
And the House of Hillel declare clean.
—The Houses dispute the antecedent rule, debating whether it is to be emended.
20. M. Maksh. 5 : 9:
Any unbroken stream of liquid remains clean, except a stream of thick honey or batter.
The House of Shammai say, "Also one of porridge. . ."
—Here the Shammaites alone supply a gloss.
21. M. Ket. 13 : 1-2: Yoḥanan b. Zakkai comments on the antecedent rule of Ḥanan: "Ḥanan spoke well. Let her swear only at the end."
And: "Ḥanan spoke well. The man laid his money on the horn of the gazelle."
—We have no attestations for these sayings, but, in their present form, they clearly take for granted not only the rule of Ḥanan, but also the language of that rule. See *Development*, pp. 47-8, and below, p. 48.
22. M. Kel. 17 : 16: A beam of a balance, etc.—these are susceptible to uncleanness.
And of all these Rabban Yoḥanan ben Zakkai said, "Woe is me if I speak of them, and woe is me if I do not speak of them."
—To Yoḥanan is attributed a comment on the foregoing, anonymous rule.
23. M. Ber. 6 : 5:
If one said a Benediction over the savory, he is not exempt from saying it over the bread.
The House of Shammai say, "Or over aught that was cooked in the pot."
—This Shammaite gloss does not supply a commentary on an undisputed, antecedent law, for the House of Hillel take a contrary position (*Phar.* II, pp. 42-3). But the Houses together take for granted the foregoing rule. Therefore we may regard the rule of A as antecedent to the Houses. But we have no attestation.
24. M. Shev. 8 : 3:
Seventh Year produce may not be sold by bulk, weight or number.
The House of Shammai say, "Nor in bundles."

And the House of Hillel say, "What is usually tied up in bundles..."

—The Houses take for granted the antecedent rule and debate a further detail. But we have no attestation.

To this list, Y. N. Epstein [*Mevo'ot leSifrut HaTanna'im* (Jerusalem, 1957), pp. 23-24] adds the following:

25. M. Oh. 11 : 1

—See No. 10; *Phar.* II, pp. 271ff.

26. M. Kel. 15 : 1: A chest that holds not less than forty *se'ahs* of liquid is not susceptible to uncleanness.

M. Kel. 18 : 1:

A chest—

The House of Shammai say, "Is measured on the inside."

The House of Hillel say, "Is measured on the outside."

—See No. 10; *Phar.* II, pp. 255-256.

27. M. Miq. 4 : 1:

If a man put vessels under the waterspot... they render the immersion-pool invalid.

The House of Shammai say, "It is all the same whether they were set there or left in forgetfulness."

And the House of Hillel declare clean if they were left in forgetfulness.

—The Houses' debate takes for granted the foregoing rule.

28. M. Pes. 10 : 6

—See *Phar.* II, p. 142. I do not think this is a valid example.

Epstein says there are "many such as those he cites" (in addition to Nos. 23-26, he also lists M. Oh. 2 : 3, M. Qid. 1 : 1, M. Pes. 1 : 1, etc.), but he has not listed "all of them." Without saying why, he explicitly rejects "many" of the similar items in the list compiled by Y. I. Halevy, *Dorot HaRishonim*, Vol. I c, pp. 206-311. In Eliezer-materials, by contrast, we were able to locate (above, pp. 23-26) a minimum of 54 pericopae, reliably attributed to Eliezer, which are constructed in the form of a comment on an antecedent law, or a difference from such a law. We shall review these pericopae below (section vi).

v. The Houses and Yoḥanan ben Zakkai and "The Mishnah" before 70

In some respects form (C) in fact is not much different from (A), (B), and (F). The statement of a legal problem characteristic of (A) and the statement of a law characteristic of (C) are much the same. A protasis consisting of [If] *a se'ah of unclean Heave-offering fell into a hundred of clean*, such as we would find in (A), is completed by the apodosis, *The House of Shammai prohibit/The House of Hillel permit.* Now one might easily formulate the law according to one or the other House: *A se'ah of unclean Heave-offering* [*which*] *fell into a hundred of clean* [*renders the whole*] *prohibited/permitted.* If we had the law as formulated by one of the respective Houses *without* the opinion of the contrary House, the statement of the problem (protasis) together with the solution to the problem (apodosis) would together have constituted nothing more than the equivalent of form (C)'s opening element. The addition, then, of an additional comment in the name of a particular master or House turns form (C) into the functional equivalent of the dispute-form. Only now, instead of having two parties dispute about a common antecedent statement of a problem, the anonymous party makes a statement, which is in some way or other revised or glossed by the named opposition. On this basis one cannot readily distinguish the dispute-form from the gloss- or commentary-form before us.

That will be the case where two *distinct* legal opinions, the one anonymous and phrased as a complete, one-sentence statement of law, the other named, and phrased as a different legal opinion, are before us. But what if the *opinion* attributed to a named master or the *issue* attributed to both disputants takes for granted the substance and wording of what has gone before and *then* glosses it? Here we no longer deal with a dispute at all. All parties are in agreement. The purpose of the second opinion now is to clarify or modify the antecedent law—"antecedent" in a quite historical sense: the named authority actually knows, and therefore for our purposes attests the prior existence of, the anonymous rule or opinion.

This distinction among the varied exempla of form (C) requires two theories as to the history of the form. The first deals with form (C) when it is functionally not much different from a dispute-form. Here we cannot propose other than the theory already given for the dispute-form: the juxtaposition of the opposed opinions of two named masters would seem to develop at the beginnings of the Yavnean academy, if not toward the end of the Jerusalem-period. Likewise, the phrasing of a law as a simple anonymous rule, followed by a contrary opinion in the name of a particular master need not have developed otherwise.

But the use of form (C) for the purposes of commentary is another matter entirely. When a given master comments on an antecedent law he evidently knew and the authority of which he takes for granted, then I think we may reasonably claim the law commented upon comes before the named master. Consequently, the existence of that law, in something much like its present form, should likewise be attested by the named master's presence in the completed pericope. Form (C) in this second sense may be called the *commentary-form.* The function of the form is to preserve an antecedent law, together with a gloss of a master subsequent to the formulation of that law. Since commentary-form is not attested before Yavnean traditions, it must be thought to start in Eliezer's generation. And that would necessarily mean that some sort of pre-70 Pharisaic law, formulated in something like its present language, ought to have come down to Yavneans, beginning with Eliezer, from pre-70 times, and to have required his (and others') exegetical attention. On the face of it, the commentary-form, coming shortly after 70, begins in the need of the early Yavneans to take up the study of pre-existing, already formulated legal materials.

Let us now test this hypothesis against pericopae in commentary—or gloss-form attributed to the Houses and Yoḥanan ben Zakkai. Because of the demonstrated tendency of the later masters, particularly Ushans, to create their own forms for either traditions they had received in earlier masters' names or traditions they themselves invented and attributed to earlier masters, we shall have to eliminate pericopae not attested by the end of Yavnean times. Post-Yavnean pericopae, we may assume, could have been formulated by Ushans in commentary-form and therefore cannot testify to the state of pre-70 legal materials. But if, by early in the Yavnean period, a pericope evidently had reached its present state, it seems less likely that it would have been fabricated out of whole cloth so as to make an early comment appear to gloss a still earlier legal formulation. While some evidence indicates that Yavneans did phrase a few disputes of Eliezer and Joshua—and some others—in the names of the Houses and in dispute-form, this evidence applies to a small part of the whole Yavnean corpus. It would seem reasonable that for the main part later Yavneans reliably formulated or transmitted materials of earlier Yavneans pretty much as they had been received. If, for instance, Ilai knows about a comment attributed to Eliezer which clearly is a gloss on a law evidently not formulated by, and therefore probably antecedent to, Eliezer, I take it that attestation will provide important and reliable evidence on the state of affairs by ca. 90-100 A.D.

Let us now isolate the usable exempla of form (C) and isolate those possibly useful in ascertaining the existence and state of a pre-70 "Mishnah." After ascertaining the pericopae deriving from Yavneh, we shall note those exhibiting true *commentary*-form.

1. M. M.S. 3 : 12B-13
   —Simeon b. Leazar, Tos. M.S. 2 : 18, supplies a late attestation.
2. M. Orl. 2 : 4
   —Dositheus of Kefar Yatmah cannot be thought to attest the dispute.
3. M. Pes. 1 : 1
   —No attestation.
4. M. Pes. 4 : 5
   —Simeon b. Gamaliel appears in the pericope, but does not attest the Houses' dispute.
5. M. Bes. 2 : 1-2
   —Simeon b. Eleazar attests the dispute and explains it.
6. M. Hag. 1 : 1
   —No attestation.
7. M. Ned. 3 : 4
   —No attestation.
8. M. Qid. 1 : 1
   —No attestation.
9. M. Hul. 1 : 2
   —No attestation.
10. M. Kel. 14 : 2
    —No attestation.
11. M. Kel. 20 : 6
    —ʿAqiba participates in the pericope. Epstein says the present form is Yosi's, hence an Ushan attestation. I do not see how ʿAqiba's *participation* permits us to assign the pericope to Yavneh.
12. Tos. Kel. B.M. 4 : 5
    —Certainly Ushan.
13. M. Oh. 2 : 3
    —No firm attestation. See *Phar.* II, pp. 277-280. Joshua does not attest this pericope.
14. M. Oh. 7 : 3
    —Judah b. Ilai provides an Ushan attestation.
15. M. Toh. 9 : 1
    —Ushan. Gamaliel's participation does not permit assigning the pericope to Yavneh.
16. M. Miq. 1 : 5
    —Certainly Ushan.
17. M. Miq. 5 : 6A
    —The authority is Yosi, see *Phar.* II, p. 296.

18. M. Nid. 2 : 1/M. Nid. 2 : 4
—Joshua supplies a firm attestation, see b. Nid. 16b, *Phar.* II, p. 299
19. M. Nid. 2 : 6
—No attestation.
20. M. Maksh. 5 : 9
—No attestation.
21. M. Ket. 13 : 1-2
—b. Ned. 33b: Dosa b. Harkinus attests; see *Development*, p. 100.
22. M. Kel. 17 : 16
—No attestation.
23. M. Ber. 6 : 5
—No attestation.
24. M. Shev. 8 : 3
—No attestation.
25. M. Oh. 11 : 1
—Ushan.
26. M. Kel. 15 : 1/18 : 1
—Ushan.
27. M. Miq. 4 : 1
—Ushan.
28. M. Pes. 10 : 6
Ṭarfon and ʿAqiba supply a firm attestation to the Houses' dispute, see *Phar.* II, p. 142.

Of the twenty-eight exempla of the commentary-form in the names of the Houses and Yoḥanan, only Nos. 18, 21, and 28 may reliably be regarded as Yavnean.

The form of No. 18 is not ideal, for M. Nid. 2 : 1 is not followed by the Houses' debate. But if we restore the pericope to what ought to have been its original form, it appears to be as follows:

The daughters of Israel use two test rags when they have sexual relations.
The House of Shammai say, "Two for every act of intercourse."
The House of Hillel say, "Two for the whole night."

We cannot regard No. 18 as a dispute in gloss-form; the Houses' sayings in every respect depend upon the antecedent rule, the validity of which both acknowledge, and on the language of which both depend. So here we have a well-attested, very early exemplum of the commentary-form.

No. 21, M. Ket. 13 : 1-2, is attested by a *baraita*-saying of Dosa

b. Harkinus, an early Yavnean. But Dosa appears in the body of the pericope. Still, the saying of Yoḥanan would seem to come early and to supply a commentary on a pre-existing pericope of a law-code—but we do not know that it was a code produced by Pharisees in particular.

No. 28 contains a Houses' dispute on how much of the *Hallel* one is supposed to say, with Ṭarfon's and ʿAqiba's dispute then depending on the Houses'. But the Houses' pericope is *not* in the form of a gloss on an antecedent law, e.g., "One recites the Hallel. How far does one recite it? The House of Shammai say..." Therefore, as observed, Epstein errs in assigning M. Pes. 10 : 6 to the list of Houses' glosses of antecedent laws.

We may now state with some, if limited, certainty that form (C) as a gloss on a pre-existing law by early Yavnean times was applied to one Houses' pericope and one pericope of Yoḥanan ben Zakkai. The latter is an excellent example of form (C), and we may conclude that the Ḥanan (and other) materials in M. Ket. 13 : 1-2 probably existed as a little list of rulings on the Jerusalem Temple courts, glossed by Yoḥanan ben Zakkai. The Mishnah therefore contains at least one pericope which, in its present form, is apt to come from Temple times or from the very earliest years of the Yavnean period. It is striking that that pericope is unique; I can think of no other equivalent to M. Ket. 13 : 1-2—that is, another list containing rulings made by authorities who are named and who evidently were not Pharisees, taken over and glossed by Pharisees.

As to the Houses' pericope, here things seem to me less certain. It is difficult to maintain that the whole of the pre-70 Pharisaic law-*code* consisted of M. Nid. 2 : 1 + M. Nid. 2 : 4. But on this basis we may reasonably suppose that some such a law-code may have existed, and that at least one pericope within it has survived in its pre-70 form from, at the very latest, early Yavnean times.

vi. Eliezer b. Hyrcanus and "The Mishnah" before 70

We shall now review the Eliezer-pericopae in form (C), eliminating those pericopae which are essentially disputes, and then seeking Yavnean attestations for those which seem to supply a commentary for an already-formulated law. But our purpose, it must be stressed, is to find the actual literary remnants of a pre-70 law-*code,* not to speculate on the *substance* of pre-70 law. The larger problem of Eliezer's relationship to pre-70 Pharisaic and other law will be raised below, pp. 310ff.

1. M. Ber. 5 : 2
   —ʿAqiba and Eliezer differ about a detail of a law otherwise unanimously accepted. No attestation, but Eliezer and ʿAqiba *should* supply an attestation for the foregoing law.
2. Tos. Dem. 1 : 3
   —Ilai supplies a firm attestation for Eliezer's opinion. But Eliezer seems simply to dispute with the foregoing opinion, not to gloss it.
3. M. Kil. 9 : 3
   —Dispute.
4. M. Ter. 2 : 1
   —Dispute. But see above, Vol. I, pp. 45ff.
5. M. Ma. 4 : 3
   —Dispute.
6. M. Ma. 4 : 5
   —Dispute.
7. M. Hal. 2 : 4
   —Dispute.
8. M. Hal. 2 : 8
   —Dispute.
9. M. Shab. 1 : 10
   —Dispute.
10. M. Shab. 6 : 4
    —Dispute.
11. Tos. Shab. 4 : 11
    —Gloss, but Ushan attestation.
12. M. Pes. 6 : 1, 2
    —Dispute.
13. Tos. Kip. 2 : 10, M. Yoma 5 : 5
    —Dispute.
14. M. Ta. 3 : 9
    —Dispute.
15. M. Yev. 3 : 1
    —Dispute.
16. M. Yev. 12 : 2
    —Dispute.
17. M. Yev. 13 : 6
    —Dispute.
18. M. Yev. 16 : 2
    —Dispute.
19. M. Yev. 16 : 7
    —Dispute.

20-21-22. M. Naz. 3 : 3-5
    —Disputes.

23. M. Git. 1 : 1
 —Dispute.
24. M. Qid. 1 : 9
 —Gloss; but no attestation. Yoḥanan b. Nuri does not know Eliezer's opinion in M. Qid. 1 : 9.
25. M. Zev. 1 : 1
 —This is a true gloss. But Tos. shows the argument is with *Joshua*, and Eliezer's gloss in M. Zev. 1 : 1 therefore comes out as a dispute with Joshua.
26. M. Zev. 3 : 3
 —Dispute.
27. M. Zev. 8 : 7
 —Dispute.
28. M. Men. 3 : 1
 —Dispute.
29. M. Hul. 12 : 2
 —Dispute.
30. M. Bekh. 1 : 5
 —Dispute.
31. M. Ar. 6 : 3
 —Good gloss; but no attestation.
32. M. Sanh. 1 : 4
 —Dispute. Anonymous rule is ʿAqiba's.
33. M. Kel. 3 : 2
 —Dispute.
34. M. Kel. 8 : 1
 —Dispute.
35. M. Kel. 14 : 1
 —Dispute.
36. M. Kel. 17 : 1
 —Dispute.
37. M. Kel. 27 : 12
 —Good gloss; but no attestation.
38. M. Oh. 2 : 4
 —The dispute of Eliezer and Joshua glosses the opening rule, but we have no firm attestation.
39. M. Oh. 6 : 1
 —Dispute.

40-41. M. Par. 4 : 1, 3
 —Disputes.

42. M. Par. 7 : 10
 —Dispute.
43. M. Par. 9 : 3
 —Gloss, along with Gamaliel, of foregoing rule. But we have no attestation. M. Par. 11 : 1 knows nothing of Eliezer's rule.
44. M. Par. 9 : 7
 —Dispute.

45. M. Par. 11 : 2

—Eliezer glosses the foregoing rule, but we have no attestation.

46. M. Par. 11 : 7

—Eliezer adds to the foregoing rule, but his saying is not attested.

47. M. Nid. 1 : 5

—Eliezer and Joshua clearly gloss the rule of the House of Shammai, that a woman may rely on her usual time; or they give a separate rule in ignorance of that of the House of Shammai. We have no firm attestation.

48. M. Nid. 4 : 6

—Dispute.

49. M. Maksh. 6 : 6

—Dispute.

50-51. M. Zab. 5 : 3, 7

—Eliezer glosses the foregoing rules in both cases. We have no attestation.

52-53. M. Ed. 6 : 2-3

—Joshua, Neḥunya, and Eliezer are in the position of explaining an antecedent rule, but they debate its substance without clear reference to a fixed, prior text.

One may further note:

54. M. Neg. 7 : 4-5

—Eliezer and the sages take for granted the foregoing law and dispute a further problem issuing from it. Furthermore ʿAqiba, Gamaliel, and Joshua provide a valuable terminus for the whole problem.

55. M. Neg. 11 : 7

—Eliezer is in a similar position, explaining a problem emerging from the acceptance of an antecedent rule.

In both of these cases, however, the *form* is not that of a gloss or commentary on the antecedent law. All we may say, therefore, is that the substance of the law had evidently been known to the early Yavneans, but we cannot be sure that the form in which we now have it is the form which lay before them.

Our results therefore turn out to be entirely negative. We do not have any significant evidence that a corpus of Mishnah—whether in writing or orally formulated and then orally transmitted in exactly the language of the original formulation—lay before Eliezer. Among the many instances of what seems to be a gloss of a foregoing rule, most turn out, on closer inspection, to be nothing more than a variation or development of form (A), a dispute. What has changed is simply that instead of an introductory clause stating a problem, we have a complete sentence stating a law. Then the opinion of the second party, normally Eliezer, comes as a separate statement of law, in contradiction to the first. While this looks like a gloss or a comment on an already formulated law, in fact it is nothing more than a different opinion on the same problem of law, thus, as noted, form (A) all over again. The few exceptions of course are interesting, but they lack the attestations necessary to render them important evidence about a pre-70 code of some sort. So in the end we cannot propose a history for form (C) much different from that already adduced for forms (A), (B), and (F). No form used for the traditions attributed to Eliezer begins in his school or circle of disciples or in a school or circle of disciples devoted chiefly to work on his and some contemporary's teachings. Forms, however, already in existence by his time or shaped during his time—particularly the dispute-form well attested, including by Eliezer himself, for Houses-materials—clearly have been subjected to some variation and development.

vii. Collections of Traditions

The collection is made up of intermediate units, themselves composed of individual pericopae, which are formed by small units of tradition, such as a statement of the problem or the opinion on the stated problem in the name of Eliezer (see *Phar.* III, pp. 5ff.). A *collection*, or compilation, of traditions is formed by combining two or more separate legal opinions, given in two or more completed pericopae, into a single, normally contiguous unit. A *composite* will consist of two or more separate legal opinions, with a single superscription, given in a single, but complex or developed, pericope. Thus if we have one superscription followed by several opinions, revealing a single principle, spelled out in several closely related issues of law, we generally have a composite. But if there are two or more superscriptions, or two or more discrete expressions of opinion as, "Rabbi Eliezer says..." or "the words of Rabbi Eliezer," then we have a collection.

The difference between a composite and a collection is important with respect to the origin of the complex pericope, but not with respect to its function in the larger setting of a chapter of Mishnah-Tosefta. I assume a composite has been worked out by a single hand or at a single time, while a collection follows upon the completion of its individual components, which have then been put together. A composite therefore will have a history somewhat similar to that of a simple pericope, while a collection will probably be the work of more than a single redactional stage, hand, or stratum. In our analysis, we shall treat the two complexes of materials as one. Both constitute larger units of tradition, rather than a single, simple legal pericope.

The collections and composites of Houses' pericopae are as follows:

1. Sifré Deut. 143, *Phar.* II, p. 35f. = M. Hag. 1 : 1-3, *Phar.* II, pp. 183f.: 1. Who is a child? 2. Limit for *re'iyyah/ḥagigah.* The collection combines laws on the festal pilgrimage. The unifying principle is Deut. 16 : 16f.
2. M. Ber. 8 : 1-8, *Phar.* II, pp. 43ff.: Differences between the Houses with respect to the meal. The composite is unified, both in theme and in a tight mnemonic patterns, with the opinions of the Houses differentiated merely by reversal of the order of the substantives—day/wine *vs.* wine/day. Tos. preserves the composite, but elaborates it with explanations for the opinions given in abbreviated form in Mishnah.
3. Tos. Ber. 3 : 13, *Phar.* II, p. 49: 1. New Year coincides with Sabbath. 2. Festival coincides with Sabbath. Two units in a single collection on a common problem.
4. M. Pe'ah 6 : 1, 2, 3, 5, *Phar.* II, pp. 55ff.: Rules of forgotten sheaf, corner of the field. Simple collection.
5. M. Pe'ah 7 : 6, *Phar.* II, pp. 59ff.: Grapes of the Fourth-Year Vineyard—several rules. But these could have been stated in a simple pericope, with a long saying for the House of Shammai, followed by a brief saying, that the House of Hillel hold the laws of Second Tithe apply in all respects. The development into a collection therefore results from mnemonic considerations.
6. M. Kil. 4 : 1, *Phar.* II, pp. 67f.: Vineyard patch—two rules.
7. M. Shev. 4 : 2, 4, *Phar.* II, pp. 72ff.: Four rules of Seventh Year: preparing the field and eating its produce.
8. M. M.S. 2 : 3, 4, 7, 8, 9, *Phar.* II, pp. 95ff.: Heave-offering of fenugreek; changing Second Tithe coins, four rules. These are discrete pericopae, not a composite. 2 : 7-9 are linked together only by the common theme.
9. M. M.S. 3 : 6, 7, 9, *Phar.* II, pp. 99ff.: Produce fully harvested and passed through Jerusalem; not yet fully harvested; tree stands within the wall with its boughs outside; entrances to olive presses in the wall and their contained space outside; Second Tithe brought to Jerusalem and contracts uncleanness, etc. The single principle of the affect of Jerusalem on the Seventh-Year produce is spelled out in a number of quite distinct cases. This is a collection of separate pericopae which in fact could have been spun out from a single general principle.
10. M. Shab. 1 : 4-9, *Phar.* II, pp. 120ff.: Completing on the Sabbath

work begun before sundown. The single principle under dispute is spelled out in a number of cases, but the cases are worded according to a single pattern. This is a good example of a composite.

11. M. Shab. 3 : 1, *Phar.* II, pp. 125f.: Put hot water but not cooked food on stove heated with peat; remove but not put back. Two rulings about the same situation.
12. M. Sheq. 2 : 3, *Phar.* II, pp. 147f.: If a man said, Lo, These are for my *sheqel*... I shall bring from them for my *sheqel.* Two rulings spell out the same principle.
13. M. Bes. 1 : 1, 2, 3, 5, 6, 7, 8, 9, *Phar.* II, pp. 159ff.: Twelve rulings, chiefly on preparation of food on festivals, mostly in the form, *The House of Shammai say, They do not... and the House of Hillel permit.* This is a composite, for the antecedent pericopae have been reworked so as to follow a single form. Only M. Bes. 1 : 1B is out of place, an evident interpolation.
14. M. Bes. 2 : 1-7, *Phar.* II, pp. 166ff.: Four rulings on preparation of food and on sacrifices for the festivals. This is a collection, not a composite. The several elements are in various forms.
15. M. Hag. 2 : 3-4, *Phar.* II, pp. 185f.: Peace-offerings on festival, Pentecost on Friday *re* slaughtering—two related rulings, on the same principle, but in respect to different matters, and in different forms.
16. M. Yev. 1 : 4, *Phar.* II, pp. 190-192: Levirate marriage between co-wives and surviving brothers—the simple rule at the outset is spun out with reference to a number of cases, thus a composite.
17. M. Yev. 13 : 1, *Phar.* II, pp. 198-200: Exercising the rite of Refusal—five rules, composite in a simple form, "Only they..." *vs.* "Both they and they...."
18. M. Ned. 3 : 2-4, *Phar.* II, pp. 212ff.: Three rules of vowing, all on the same principle, and all in the form, "They do not..." + "They even do..."—a composite.
19. M. Naz. 1 : 1-2, *Phar.* II, p. 215: Two cases on the same principle, each introduced by a separate superscription.
20. M. Naz. 5 : 1, 2, 3, 5, *Phar.* II, pp. 218ff.: Principle regarding a thing dedicated in error, followed by a series of cases. A composite in form, for the cases lack individual superscriptions. Compare Tos. Nez. 3 : 19, *Phar.* II, pp. 224ff.
21. M. Git. 8 : 8-9, *Phar.* II, pp. 230-2: Two possible impairments of a writ of divorce, each with a separate superscription—a collection.
22. M. B.M. 3 : 12, *Phar.* II, pp. 235f.: Two laws about misuse of property, first, using for private gain what has been left as a bailment; second, expressing an intention to do so. A collection of closely related, but separate problems.
23. M. B.B. 9 : 8-9, *Phar.* II, pp. 237f.: How to divide estate when it is not clear who has died first. Two cases, same principle.
24. Tos. Zev. 4 : 9, *Phar.* II, pp. 241-2: Two sprinklings make fit and render *piggul* + *how so* + four examples. Collection of examples of a single principle.

25. Tos. Bekh. 3 : 15-16, *Phar.* II, p. 246: Two rulings on firstlings.
26. M. Kel. 22 : 4, *Phar.* II, pp. 257-258: Two rulings on the cleanness of stools.
27. M. Kel. 29 : 8, *Phar.* II, p. 259: Two rulings on trowels.
28. Tos. Kel. B.B. 5 : 7-8, *Phar.* II, pp. 265-266: Two rulings on girdles.
29. M. Oh. 2 : 3, *Phar.* II, p. 266-7: Two rulings on Tents and corpses.
30. M. Oh. 5 : 1-4, *Phar.* II, pp. 267-269: Baking oven with the house *re* Tent. A sequence of rulings on the same problem, according to the same principles, applied to differing situations.
31. M. Oh. 7 : 3, *Phar.* II, pp. 269-270: As in No. 30.
32. M. Oh. 11 : 1, 3, 4, 5, 6, 8, *Phar.* II, pp. 271-273: As in No. 30.
33. M. Oh. 13 : 1, 4: Two rulings on a covered light-hole, as in No. 30.
34. M. Oh. 18 : 1, 4, 8: Related rulings on examining a grave-area.
35. M. Toh. 8 : 1, 5, 7, *Phar.* II, p. 289: Olives receive uncleanness, three rulings.
36. M. Nid. 4 : 3, *Phar.* II, pp. 299-300: Uncleanness of blood of gentile woman, woman after childbirth. Collection.
37. M. Nid. 10 : 1, *Phar.* II, pp. 301-3: Girl who had not yet suffered a flow and was married. Three rulings.
38. M. Maksh. 1 : 2-4, *Phar.* II, pp. 310-312: Three rulings on *If water be put*, with the same principle applied to several situations.
39. M. Maksh. 4 : 4-5, *Phar.* II, p. 313: Three rulings, as above, No. 38.
40. M. Zab. 1 : 1-2, *Phar.* II, pp. 316-318: Four rulings on *Zab,* several situations worked out in terms of consistent principles.
41. M. T.Y. 1 : 1, *Phar.* II, pp. 322-3: Two rulings on unrelated cases. A collection.

Note also: M. Ed. 1 : 7-14, 4 : 1-12, 5 : 1-5, *Phar.* II, pp. 327-343: Collections of separate pericopae, strung together as lists of the lenient rulings of the House of Shammai and the strict rulings of the House of Hillel.

The Houses-collections are of four sorts.

First, we find a compilation of separate, but closely-related pericopae in which the Houses differ on the same principle. These are arranged because of the common principle and the internally consistent rulings of the respective Houses.

Second, we notice a highly developed composite, in which a single superscription will serve a whole range of disagreements, carefully constructed according to a single mnemonic principle.

Third, we see the development of a simple pericope into a collection on account of mnemonic or other editorial considerations.

Finally, we observe the simple compilation of several Houses' rulings on the same theme, in which a number of principles are at issue.

These four sorts of collections comprise the following examples:

1. 9, 11, 12, 15, 19, 23, 37, 38, 39;
2. 2, 10, 13, 16, 17, 18;
3. 5, 20, 24, 30, 31, 32, 33, 40;
4. 1, 3, 4, 6, 7, 8, 14, 21, 22, 25, 26, 27, 28, 29, 34, 35, 36, 41.

The several sorts of collections all are relatively sophisticated. They exhibit the marks of careful construction, and, as noted, in general are tightly organized according to both cogent principles under discussion and mnemonic traits. Only a modest part of the collections is based merely upon a common theme, without centering on a single principle and a careful articulation of that principle through a set of examples or different applications.

Collections of Yoḥanan b. Zakkai-pericopae are as follows:

1. M. Suk. 3 : 12, *Development*, p. 43: Two post-70 decrees are linked together in a single list, though they do not relate to one another.
2. M. R.H. 4 : 1-4, *Development*, pp. 43-6: Four decrees issued after 70. No. 1 and No. 2 exhibit the same form: *Before time they used to do such-and-such. When the Temple was destroyed, Yoḥanan ordained....*
3. M. Ket. 13 : 1, 2, *Development*, pp. 47-8: Yoḥanan's opinions on the two decrees are given in the same language but with different glosses.
4. M. Sot. 5 : 2, 5: The two pericopae are not joined in context, but follow the same pattern: *That same day X expounded...* Then: *R. Joshua said, "Who will take away the dust..."* Yoḥanan's "collections" thus tend to be built on the repetition of the same formulae.
5. Tos. B.Q. 7 : 3-7, *Development*, pp. 71-73: Five exegeses *kemin ḥomer*, each introduced by a question or a citation of Scripture, then followed by a comment of Yoḥanan.

Yoḥanan b. Zakkai-collections are of another order than the Houses'. They are built in general upon the repetition of a single formula or of a single construction, e.g., formula: No. 3; pattern: Nos. 1, 2, 4, 5. Yoḥanan's collections are marked by a pronounced historical interest; only No. 5 is not constructed explicitly in terms of a single historical-legal problem. Otherwise Yoḥanan's collections tend to be put together for historical reasons, to list either Yoḥanan's opinions of what had been done by others, or Yoḥanan's expectations of what would be said by others, or Yoḥanan's changes in the law on account of a historical turning point. The several collections thus are not composed chiefly for legal purposes.

Collections of Eliezer b. Hyrcanus-pericopae are as follows:

1. M. Ter. 4 : 7, 8, 9, 10, 11: Eliezer and Joshua differ about a single principle, spelled out in several specific cases.
2. M. Ter. 5 : 4, 5, 6: Eliezer and the sages differ on a single principle, articulated in a number of cases: the problem of misplaced Heave-offering.
3. M. Ter. 8 : 1, 2, 3: Eliezer and Joshua differ about the principle of an act begun licitly and completed illicitly, spelled out in several examples.
4. M. Ter. 8 : 8, 9, 10, 11: Eliezer and Joshua differ on pretty much the same principle as in No. 3, with more examples.
5. M. Ter. 11 : 2: Eliezer and Joshua differ on a specific case, then on the general principle underlying the case.
6. Tos. M.S. 4 : 5-6: Two rules on a related problem.
7. M. Hal. 4 : 7: Status of Jewish farmers in Syria, two closely related rulings based on a single principle.
8. M. Eruv. 2 : 6: Ilai has a list of three rulings of Eliezer, on unrelated topics: "I heard from. . ."
9. M. Eruv. 7 : 10-11: Two rules on making, taking part in, *ʿeruv.*
10. M. Suk. 1 : 11: Two unrelated rules on the *Sukkah.*
11. M. Bes. 4 : 6-7: Two unrelated rules on festival/Sabbath law.
12. b. Ta. 25b: Two stories about fasting.
13. M. Yev. 12 : 3-4: Two closely related rules on performing the rite of *ḥaliṣah.*
14. M. Ket. 1 : 6, 7, 8, 9: Principle of evidence is illustrated in four separate, but closely-related cases.
15. M. Ned. 9 : 1-2: Two rules on the release of vows, closely related in principle, but presented as separate pericopae: *R. Eliezer says. . . And further did R. Eliezer say. . .*
16. M. Ned. 10 : 5, 6, 7: The release of vows of various women in ambiguous legal status—two cases; releasing vows in advance of their being made—one case plus debate. This group is not a collection of pericopae, but merely thematically related, separate items. 10 : 5, 6 would seem to be a collection.
17. M. Naz. 3 : 3, 4, 5: Three cases of a Nazir who became unclean at the end of his period of Naziriteship—based on the same principle.
18. M. Sot. 9 : 2, 3, 4: Three rulings on the rite for a neglected corpse. These are logically arranged: 1. What if he is exactly between two cities? Then 2. Bring head to body, *vs.* ʿAqiba: body to the head; 3. From where do they measure—refers back to No. 1. This is the closest one comes to a composite.
19. M. Sanh. 6 : 4: Those who are stoned are hung, a man is hung facing the people—two closely related rules, in Eliezer's name (*vs.* contrary view of sages).
20. M. Zev. 8 : 7, 8, 9, 10, 11, 12: Mixtures of various sacred matter—blood, limbs—and how they are disposed of. A single principle unites the several discrete rulings. That principle is exactly the same as enunciated in M. Ter. 5 : 2.

21. M. Bekh. 1 : 5-6: Rules of redemption of firstlings, separate but thematically related.
22. M. Tem. 3 : 3: Several rules on disposal of substitutes, based on the same principle: A Guilt-offering substitute is treated like a Sin-offering substitute.
[23. M. Ker. 4 : 2 Several cases with a single ruling at the end. But this is not a collection or a composite.]
24. M. Oh. 2 : 2: Quantities of corpse-residue subject to the law of Tents. Two rulings; no principle in common.
25. M. Oh. 12 : 8: Two rulings on Tents, following a single principle.
26. M. Oh. 14 : 4-5: Two rulings on Tents, following a single principle.
27. M. Neg. 7 : 4-5: Two rulings on intentionally removing signs of leprosy, following a single principle.
28. M. Par. 9 : 1: Two rulings on Sin-offering water, following a single principle.
29. M. Nid. 4 : 4, 6: Two disputes, Eliezer *vs.* Joshua, *re* blood appearing in hard labor; the disputes follow a single principle.
30. M. Sanh. 10 : 1: Three disputes of Eliezer *vs.* ʿAqiba, following a single principle.

Note also Tos. Ed. 2 : 1

Eliezer's collections tend to be put together as illustrations of a single principle of law, applied to a number of discrete, but closely related cases. M. Ker. 4 : 2, which is not a collection, is the form a collection should have had before it was fully worked out; that is, it contains several cases, to which a single opinion was attached. Later on, the several cases would each be given its own ruling in Eliezer's name and so produce a collection. Collections of cases illustrating a single principle include the following: 1, 2, 3, 4, 5, 7, 13, 14, 15, 17, 18 (like a Houses' composite), 19, 20, 25, 26, 27, 28, 29, 30. Less tightly organized collections, put together on the basis of a common legal theme or problem, but not joined by a common principle, are as follows: 6, 9, 10, 11, 12, 16, 21, 22, 24.

Ilai's collection, No. 8, stands quite by itself. It is the first instance of a collection formed by a single master for a purpose other than spelling out legal materials of a simple, principled sort. Ilai's list is of three discrete rulings. One may suppose behind ʿAqiba's suppressed Eliezer-rulings in M. Shev. 8 : 9-10 might be a similar list of two items. So what is striking is that for Eliezer, unlike the antecedent authorities and circles, a little list of *unrelated* legal traditions was put together. (This recalls Yosi b. Yoʿezer's purity-rulings in M. Ed. 8 : 4, but Yosi's are all on a single theme, pretty much like the Houses' materials.) Listing teachings of a master on various topics is not unknown; we found M. Ed. to be a collection of complex pericopae, put together primarily on the basis of a given master's list of several sorts of individual pericopae of a given sort, e.g., the lenient rulings of the House of Shammai. While M. Ed. is an Ushan document, collected by ʿAqiba's disciples, its dominant trait seems to be prefigured by the little lists of Ilai and ʿAqiba; Ilai's and ʿAqiba's were lists of teachings of Eliezer's traditions which no one else seemed to know, while the collected pericopae of M. Ed., with regard to the Houses, were known elsewhere. And Eliezer's materials in M. Ed. (above, Vol. I, pp. 329-338) are not little lists at all.

As with other forms already considered, we notice that, while Eliezer's traditions follow patterns familiar from the Houses' and Yoḥanan b. Zakkai's traditions, they also produce developments of, or variations on, these forms. In the case of Eliezer, the little list of Ilai is the sole example of something apparently new in the formation of traditions, namely, the use of an organizing principle consisting of nothing more than the master's own name and authority. In the traditions of Yoḥanan and of the Houses, something beyond the name of Yoḥanan of the Houses would invariably be present to turn a list into a more coherent unit of tradition.

viii. Conclusion

Our analysis of the forms of Eliezer's tradition has produced six facts.

First, the huge corpus of his legal traditions was reduced to a remarkably small number of forms. Indeed, since forms (A), (B), (D) and (F), all are variations on the dispute-form, and since the majority of instances of (C) likewise turn out to be nothing more than disputes, we may say that almost the whole of the preserved tradition was redacted in variations on that single form. (G) turned out not to apply to materials attributed to Eliezer at all, and (H) is not a form. Only (E), the simple saying, was not much in evidence before Eliezer. Yet the dispute is built of sets of simple sayings. So in all, the form characteristic of the Houses' materials, the dispute, appears to be the primary, and strikingly predominant, form for Eliezer's as well. We observe, however, an important difference: the Houses-materials exhibit virtually no variation on the simple dispute: *Statement of law, X says... Y says...*, with the apodosis mnemonically arranged. But Eliezer's materials show a marked tendency to vary, and probably even to develop, the simple dispute. To be sure, developments are matters of degree. One can find in Houses-materials occasional adumbrations of these (probably later) variations. But in one important aspect Eliezer's materials do differ, for most Houses' pericopae normally exhibit careful mnemonic balance, and practically none of Eliezer's does.

Second, form (C) produces the phenomenon of a gloss or commentary on a law already formulated before the comment of Eliezer is added. This does seem to be a new development of an older tendency. The Houses supply a fair amount of commentary to pre-existing law. But Eliezer's materials yield a great many more instances of commentary-*form.* Again, therefore, we observe a tendency to take up and exploit what may be an older pattern for the redaction of legal materials.

Third, we found no significant evidence that the Houses', Yoḥanan ben Zakkai's, and Eliezer's glosses or comments on already formulated laws demonstrate the existence, before their time, of a law-code (written or orally formulated) in exactly the language of the pericopae in our hands. Since the Ushans were quite capable of constructing a pericope in the form of an anonymous law followed by a comment, gloss, or disagreement attributed to an early, named master, we asked for Yavnean attestations as the first step toward verifying the existence of an early code now embedded in our Mishnah. We discovered insufficient evidence for the Houses, inconsequential evidence for Yoḥanan, and no evidence at all for Eliezer. That the themes and even the details of pre-70 Pharisaic law now are in our hands seems to me beyond question; that is shown by the early attestation of the substance of laws. But we could not attest the wording of the law, thus the availability of a *code*, at a point early enough to make it likely that present formulations derive from a period before Eliezer and the Yavnean redactors of the Houses' materials.

Fourth, we noted that while the principles for the collection of Houses' materials into composites and collections were operative in the formation of Eliezer's materials into collections, we could find—if only in one, or possibly two instances—the application of a quite new principle as well, a collection of pericopae on diverse subjects linked only by attribution to a single authority. This too suggests that the formation of Eliezer's traditions in a few, disciplined forms involved not only the use of already available literary conventions, but also the development of those conventions in new ways.

Fifth, we have found out nothing about the life-situation reflected by, or underlying, the several forms. We have taken for granted that all the forms derive from a single circumstance, and that is the master-disciple circle, whether at Yavneh, or Lud, or some other locale. As to which school or circle of disciples produced which form we can say nothing. We observed at the outset that no form seems disproportionately associated with a given master or set of redactors. We therefore cannot attribute to the redactors of Eliezer-ʿAqiba disputes a preference, e.g., for form (A) over form (B). As to form (C), it seems possible that it was used chiefly by redactors of materials in which Eliezer appears by himself or in disagreement with "them"—the anonymous sages, whether named as such or simply given the opening saying in a two-element pericope. But who those sages were cannot definitely be stated (but see below, pp. 367-377). We cannot take for granted they were never ʿAqiba, or Joshua, or Gamaliel. In some instances, they probably were. So we are left with a life-situation too vague to be meaningful: circles of disciples. And this we had supposed at the outset.

Sixth, the analysis of the forms and the form-history of Eliezer's traditions produces no important guide to the historical usefulness of the contents of the tradition. It contributes, if modestly, only toward the history of the Mishnaic forms themselves. Perhaps the variations, by Eliezer's tradents, of forms evidently known in earliest Yavnean times may show that the materials were worked out relatively soon after these earliest, rigid forms had been fixed. This might mean that for Eliezer's materials looser forms were used, developed in his own time and very shortly thereafter. But those same forms were systematically used long afterward as well. So the mere employment of a form that seems to come from the early stages of the development of Yavnean materials cannot signify that the materials set into that form likewise emerge in early Yavnean times. Form-history, while interesting, cannot be decisive in settling questions about the substance of traditions about Eliezer.

CHAPTER SEVEN

ATTESTATIONS

i. Survey of Attested Pericopae

We are able to isolate five stages in the formation of the tradition. The first three are marked by allusions of masters of Yavneh, Usha, and the circle around Judah the Patriarch. The fourth is occurrence in Mishnah-Tosefta. Finally, the Tannaitic Midrashim and designation as a Tannaitic tradition in the two *Gemarot* form a stratum in the formation of the tradition. I have not listed items first attested by appearance in the Amoraic stratum of the *Gemarot* or in the early or late compilations of Midrashim. As noted, only legal materials produce attestations before the final formulation of Mishnah-Tosefta and the Tannaitic collections, not to mention the Tannaitic strata in the *Gemarot*. Non-legal materials are rarely attested at all.

1. *Yavneh*

1. Tos. Ter. 3 : 18/M. Ter. 2 : 1—Clean Heave-offering given for unclean (Ilai).
2. Tos. Hal. 1 : 10/M. Hal. 2 : 8—Clean Dough-offering given for unclean (Ishmael).
3. Tos. Hal. 1 : 6/M. Hal. 1 : 6—Ilai *re* cakes of Thank-offering of Nazirite.
4. Tos. Orl. 1 : 8—Yoḥanan b. Nuri *re* *ʿOrlah* outside of Palestine.
5. Tos. Shev. 4 : 21/M. Bik. 2 : 6—ʿAqiba—*Etrog* like tree.
6. M. Eruv. 2 : 5—Ilai: (1) carry in garden (2) not prepare *ʿeruv* (3) ʿQRBNYM.
7. M. Pes. 3 : 3—Eliezer: Do not designate Dough-offering on 15 Nisan until it is baked *vs.* Judah b. Bathyra. Joshua comments on Eliezer's and Judah's opinions, but stands outside the legal framework of the pericope. But Tos. Pis. 3 : 7 frames the dispute to include Joshua. Compare M. Ter. 8 : 11.
8. M. Sheq. 4 : 7—Property sanctified includes cattle fit for altar—Eliezer *vs.* Joshua. ʿAqiba: I prefer Eliezer's opinion. (N.B. Tos. Sheq. 2 : 10: Yosah + Simeon)
9. M. Sheq. 8 : 7/Tos. Sheq. 3 : 16—Eliezer + ʿAqiba *re* Houses on burning unclean sanctities inside/outside.
10. Tos. Yev. 13 : 3-5/M. Yev. 13 : 2—Ishmael *re* Eliezer, Deed of female-minor is of no effect. [Also serves Tos. Yev. 12 : 12/M. Yev. 12 : 4; and story: y. Yev. 13 : 2, b. Yev. 89b, etc.]

11. M. Yev. 13 : 7—Levir is refused by minor—Eliezer *vs.* Gamaliel. Joshua comments on case and opinions, but is external to original dispute.
12-13. M. Ned. 9 : 1-2—Releasing vows. Ṣaddoq comments on completed pericope involving Eliezer and sages.
14. Tos. Git. 9 : 1-5/M. Git. 9 : 1—Divorce with limitation. Attested by story *re* Ṭarfon, ʿAqiba, Yosi, Joshua.
15. b. Qid. 39a/M. Qid. 1 : 9—Yoḥanan b. Nuri—Eliezer: No *ʿorlah*-taboo abroad. = No. 4.
16. M. Bekh. 1 : 6D—Joshua + Ṣaddoq have a precedent for Eliezer's opposition in 1 : 6B-C.
17. M. Ar. 8 : 4B—Eleazar b. ʿAzariah comments on Eliezer in A, *re* not dedicating all of one's property.
18. Tos. Kel. B.M. 6 : 4/M. Kel. 8 : 1—Yoḥanan b. Nuri *re* Eliezer in M. Kel. 8 : 1 on insect in subdivided oven, "I said to R. Eliezer..." Yosi b. Ḥalafta further attests Yoḥanan b. Nuri.
19. b. Sanh. 68a/M. Kel. 26 : 4, Tos. Kel. B.B. 4 : 7—Shoe on last is clean—referred to by Eleazar b. ʿAzariah in Eliezer's deathscene; also Tos. Kel. B.B. 4 : 7—Simeon Shezuri; b. Shab. 141b—Judah [b. Ilai] in name of Eliezer.
20. M. Ed. 2 : 7/Tos. Ed. 1 : 10—Testimony before ʿAqiba *re* opinions of Eliezer (1. Woman wears tiara on Sabbath, 2. Pigeon-racers are ineligible to testify) should mean a Yavnean, or early Ushan, attestation.
21. ARN Chap. 15/M. Avot 2 : 10 = b. Shab. 153a—Repent-saying is given a chain of tradents beginning with Ilai. But ARN is not a likely source for attestations, and produces no others. To this list are to be added Eliezer's attestations of Houses' pericopae, p. 33.

2. *Usha*

1. Tos. Peʾah 3 : 2—Houses *re* forgotten sheaf.
[2. Tos. Dem. 1 : 3—Ilai + Eliezer: First fruits always liable *re demai.* Yavnean chain.]
3. Tos. Kil. 5 : 18/M. Kil. 9 : 3—Handkerchiefs, etc., *re kilaʾim*: Meir *vs.* Judah.
4. Tos. Ter. 5 : 10-11/M. Ter. 4 : 8-9-10-11—Meir + Judah *re* neutralizing Heave-offering.
5. Tos. Ter. 7 : 10/M. Ter. 8 : 3—Nathan *re* deed begun licitly and discovered to be illicit. [*May* attest principle of M. Ter. 8 : 1, 2 as well.] *See No. 12.*
6. Tos. Ter. 9 : 8-9/M. Ter. 11 : 2—Nathan, Judah (+ Jacob, Judah the Patriarch) *re* date-honey, cider, etc.—liability for tithes, capacity to render unclean as liquid.
7. Tos. Shab. 15 : 10/M. Shab. 19 : 4—Joshua + Eliezer: Erred by circumcizing wrong baby on Sabbath. Simeon [b. Yoḥai] + b. Shab. 137a = Simeon b. Eleazar.

[8. M. Eruv. 3 : 6/Tos. Eruv. 4 : 1-2—Judah rules consistently with Eliezer—a slight warrant both for assigning law to Eliezer b. Hyrcanus and for attestation.]

9. M. Eruv. 7 : 11—Judah glosses dispute of Eliezer and sages (= M. Eruv. 3 : 1).

[10. M. Eruv. 9 : 2—Judah cites Eliezer in b. B.B. 100a in an opinion consistent with this one.]

11. b. Eruv. 54b—Judah comments on story illustrating Eliezer's view that one repeats lesson four times.

12. M. Pes. 1 : 7/Tos. Pis. 1 : 5—Meir, Yosi, Simeon *re* Eliezer + Joshua on burning clean and unclean Heave-offering *ḥameṣ* together. Also attests M. Ter. 8 : 3.

13. Tos. Pis. 3 : 8—Measure of dough—Nathan in name of Liezer.

14. M. Pes. 6 : 5/Tos. Pis. 5 : 4—Meir, Simeon *re* Eliezer, Joshua on slaughter of animal appropriate for Passover for some other purpose.

15. Tos. Sheq. 2 : 10/M. Sheq. 4 : 7—Yosah + Simeon. *See Yavneh No. 8.*

16. Tos. Kip. 2 : 10—Judah + Eliezer: High priest and prefect choose lots.

17. Tos. Kip. 3 : 1/M. Yoma 5 : 5—Judah + Eliezer: High priest sprinkled standing in place.

18. Tos. Kip. 3 : 19/M. Yoma 7 : 3—Judah + Eliezer: When unblemished lambs offered?

19. b. Suk. 19b—Nathan *re* Eliezer, M. Suk. 1 : 1, Tos. Suk. 1 : 10, on cone-shaped *sukkah*.

20. Tos. Y.T. 1 : 3/M. Bes. 1 : 1—Judah + Eliezer *re* Houses on egg born on festival.

21. Tos. Y.T. 3 : 18/M. Bes. 4 : 6-7—Simeon *re* sweeping courtyard on festival.

22. Tos. R.H. 2 : 10—Lev. 23 : 24—Judah + Eliezer.

23. b. Ta. 2b/M. Ta. 1 : 1—Judah b. Ilai refers to Eliezer's opinion *re* fasting for rain.

24. b. M.Q. 19a—Judah cites Eliezer. M. M.Q. 3 : 4 has Judah *without* Eliezer's authority.

25. b. M.Q. 10a—Judah + Eliezer *re* setting up mill on festival.

26. Tos. Yev. 12 : 11/M. Yev. 12 : 2—*Ḥaliṣah* with wooden sandal: Judah says Eliezer would have approved. But Eliezer is not cited as authority of that element of M. 12 : 2.

27. Tos. Ket. 11 : 4/M. Ket. 11 : 6—Judah + Eliezer *re* orphan/ *usufruct.*

28. b. Ket. 52a—He who forbids wife by vow from benefit has to redeem her. Nathan asks Symacchus *re* Joshua's contrary opinion.

29-31. Tos. Nez. 2 : 12-13/M. Naz. 3 : 3, 4, 5—Judah *re* Eliezer on how many days Nazir loses if he becomes unclean at end of his period. 2 : 13: Judah + Eliezer: General rule.

32. M. Git. 1 : 2/M. Git. 1 : 1—Judah knows M. Git. 1 : 1, *re* testifying on origin of *Geṭ*.

33. Tos. Zev. 4 : 1-2/b. Pes. 77a—Yosi *re* Eliezer *vs.* Joshua: If no flesh

there is blood. N.B.: Serves to attest M. Me. 1 : 2-3, Tos. Me. 1 : 6, Tos. Men. 4 : 10, 4 : 14-15, Tos. Zev. 4 : 5, 8.

34. Tos. Zev. 8 : 15/M. Zev. 8 : 4—Judah defines dispute *re* limbs of Sin-offering mixed with those of Whole-offering.

35. Tos. Zev. 8 : 20/M. Zev. 8 : 5, 7, 8, 9, 10, 11, 12—Judah again attests the *issues* of M. Zev. 8 : 5-12, namely, mixtures of various sacrificial objects of differing status. Specific attestation for M. Zev. 8 : 8.

[36. Tos. Men. 2 : 16/M. Men. 8 : 1—Meal-offering with wrong intention: Judah follows Eliezer. *See Bet Shearim No. 6.*]

37. Tos. Men. 4 : 5/M. Men. 3 : 4 (Tos. Men. 4 : 2, 6)—Yosi *re* debate. *See above, No. 33*—same issue, same attestation.

38. Tos. Men. 8 : 19/M. Men. 7 : 3—Meir *vs.* Judah *re* sanctification of Bread-offering where Thank-offering is blemished. See M. Zev. 9 : 3. N.B.: Judah interprets dispute *re* bread as matter of intention, not blemished animal, as in No. 36 above.

[38A. M. Ar. Ar. 6 : 1D—Simeon b. Gamaliel is consistent with Eliezer in M. Ar. 6 : 1 A-C, 6 : 1 A-C, divorce in case of dedication of goods to Temple.]

39. M. Tem. 3 : 1E–F: Simeon [b. Yoḥai] *re* Eliezer *vs.* sages in 3 : 1A–D: Progeny of Peace-offerings may not be offered as Peace-offerings.

40. M. Ker. 4 : 23—Sin-offering when not sure exactly what sin has been done: Yosi + Judah *re* Eliezer *vs.* Joshua. Also: Tos. Ker. 2 : 12-15, 3 : 5-8.

41. b. B.B. 157a—Meir + Judah *re* Eliezer *vs.* Joshua on verbal will—M. B.B. 9 : 7, Tos. B.B. 10 : 12.

42. Tos. Sanh. 9 : 6/M. Sanh. 6 : 4—Judah *re* Eliezer on hanging criminal who has been stoned to death.

43. Tos. Kel. B.M. 6 : 4/M. Kel. 8 : 1—Yosi attests Yoḥanan b. Nuri. *See Yavneh No. 18.*

44. Tos. Kel. B.M. 4 : 14/M. Kel. 14 : 7—Nathan attests Eliezer + Joshua *re* cleaning metal vessel.

45. Tos. Kel. B.B. 4 : 3/M. Kel. 26 : 2—Nathan *re* Eliezer *vs.* sages on uncleanness of money-pouch.

46. *See Mishnah-Tosefta, No. 92.*

47. Tos. Ah. 7 : 3/M. Oh. 6 : 1-2—Judah cites Eliezer.

48. Tos. Ah. 9 : 7/M. Oh. 8 : 6—Judah has a dispute of Eliezer and Joshua, but they do not occur in M. Oh. 8 : 6. Issue: Jars each with half-olive's bulk of corpse. Eliezer is authority behind M. Oh. 8 : 6, so Goldberg, *Massekhet Ohalot*, p. 66.

49. Tos. Ah. 13 : 10/M. Oh. 12 : 8—Simeon [b. Yoḥai] *vs.* Jacob *re* Eliezer and Joshua on olive's bulk of corpse on treshhold.

50. Tos. Ah. 17 : 6/M. Oh. 17 : 5—Judah *re* dirt of grave area combines with dirt from abroad.

51. Tos. Neg. 3 : 5/M. Neg. 7 : 4-5—Judah *re* Eliezer *vs.* sages on purification after intentionally removing signs of uncleanness.

52. Tos. Par. 7 : 7/M. Par. 7 : 10—Judah *re* Eliezer on depositing Heifer-water.

53-56. M. Par. 9 : 4—Yosi comments on dispute of Eliezer and Joshua *re* false intention in Heifer-water. Also Tos. Par. 9 : 6 serves for whole set of pericopae, M. Par. 9 : 1, 3, 4, 7.

57. M. Eruv. 9 : 4/M. Toh. 6 : 5, Tos. Toh. 7 : 7, 9—Judah in M. Eruv. 9 : 4 is consistent with Eliezer in Tos. Toh. 7 : 9, on which basis the pericopae are assigned to Eliezer, and consequently Judah supplies an attestation (no more positive than his warrant, to be sure!).

58. M. Toh. 9 : 3F/M. Toh. 9 : 3C–E—Simeon [b. Yoḥai] attests dispute of Eliezer and sages *re* moisture exuded by crushed olives.

59. Tos. Nid. 9 : 13/M. Nid. 10 : 3—Yosi and Simeon attest dispute of Eliezer, Joshua, ʿAqiba *re Zab.*

60. Tos. Uqs. 3 : 15/M. Uqs. 3 : 10 = M. Shev. 3 : 10—Judah *re* Eliezer and sages on beehive.

61. Tos. Ah. 2 : 7/M. Ed. 6 : 2-3, Tos. Ed. 2 : 10—Simeon *re* Eliezer on uncleanness of limb from living being.

62. b. Sanh. 110b—Joshua b. Qorḥai *re* generation of wilderness in world to come, *seems* to attest M. Sanh. 10 : 3/Tos. Sanh. 13 : 2.

3. *Bet Shearim*

1. *See Usha No. 6.*
2. *See Usha No. 7* [Simeon b. Eleazar].
3. Mourners' couch *re* festival—b. M.Q. 20A—Eliezer and sages = the Houses, according to Simeon b. Eleazar.
4. Deed of female minor—Judah the Patriarch approves Eliezer's opinion—b. Yev. 108a, for M. Yev. 13 : 2. *See Yavneh No. 10.*
5. Yosi b. R. Judah—Tos. Sot. 1 : 1/M. Sot. 1 : 1 quotes Eliezer *re* warning wife before two witnesses. [N.B.: y. Sot. 1 : 1: Leazar b. Yosi.]
6. Tos. Zev. 2 : 16/M. Zev. 3 : 3—Rabbi says Joshua differs from Eliezer *re* slaughter with improper intention. [N.B.: Sifra Ṣav 8 : 1: Eliezer *vs.* ʿAqiba.]
7. Tos. Kel. B.M. 8 : 8/M. Kel. 18 : 9—Rabbi *vs.* Simeon *re* purifying bed (connector).
8. b. Nid. 9b/M. Nid. 1 : 3, 5/Tos. Nid. 1 : 5—Rabbi ruled in accord with Eliezer *re* women who may rely on their period in determining uncleanness.

4. *Mishnah-Tosefta*

The use of brackets ([ ]) indicates a case illustrating an established law.

1. M. Ber. 1 : 1—*Shemaʿ* in evening.
2. M. Ber. 1 : 2—*Shemaʿ* in morning.
3. M. Ber. 4 : 3-4—Fixed text for Prayer.
4. M. Ber. 5 : 2—Where insert *Havdalah*?
5. M. Peʾah 3 : 6—Liability for *peʾah.*
6. M. Peʾah 7 : 7—Vineyard wholly composed of defective clusters.
7. M. Kil. 5 : 8—Thorns in vineyard.
8. M. Shev. 5 : 3—Arum after Seventh Year.

[9. M. Shev. 8 : 9-10—Hide anointed with Seventh-Year-oil.]
10. M. Shev. 9 : 5—Three kinds of vegetables pickled in one jar.
11. M. Shev. 9 : 9—Seventh-Year-produce as gift.
12. M. Ter. 4 : 5—Increase Heave-offering.
13. M. Ter. 5 : 2, 4, 5, 6—Unclean Heave-offering in clean, unconsecrated food.
14. M. Ter. 6 : 6—Ate Heave-offering in error.
[15. M. Ter. 8 : 8, 9, 10, 11—Protecting Heave-offering from uncleanness.]
16. M. Ma. 4 : 3—Olives from press *re* tithes.
17. M. Ma. 4 : 5—Tithing dill.
18. M. Ma. 4 : 6—Tithing caperbush.
19. Tos. Ma. 3 : 7—Tithing mustard.
[20. Tos. M.S. 1 : 14—Saffron not purchased with Tithe-money (cited by Simeon).]
21. Tos. M.S. 3 : 16—Reliability for Second, First Tithes.
22. Tos. M.S. 4 : 5-6—Gave principle, not fifth *re* eating.
23. M. Hal. 2 : 1—Produce from Palestine abroad *re Ḥallah.*
24. M. Hal. 2 : 4—Dough in *qavs re Ḥallah.*
25. M. Hal. 4 : 7—Israelite farmers in Syria *re* Tithes and Seventh Year.
26. M. Orl. 1 : 7—Curdle milk with sap of *ʿorlah.*
27. M. Shab. 1 : 10—Baking before Sabbath.
28. M. Shab. 6 : 4—Weapons of war on Sabbath.
29. M. Shab. 2 : 3—Wick for Sabbath-lamp.
30. Tos. Shab. 4 : 6—Wear tiara on Sabbath.
31. M. Shab. 12 : 4—Scratch self on Sabbath.
32. M. Shab. 13 : 1—Weave on Sabbath.
33. M. Shab. 17 : 7—Window-shutter.
[34. M. Shab. 19 : 1—Circumcision on Sabbath.]
35. M. Shab. 20 : 1—Stretch out filter.
36. Tos. Shab. 1 : 17—*Re on that day* (M. Shab. 1 : 4).
37. M. Eruv. 1 : 2—Rendering alley-way valid—Eliezer and Houses. [Eliezer ignored in other comments on law.]
38. M. Pes. 6 : 1-2, Tos. Pis. 5 : 1—Passover overrides Sabbath in all respects (*vs.* Joshua, ʿAqiba). [This ought to have been known in Usha.] (*See No. 34.*)
39. M. Pes. 9 : 2, Tos. Pis. 8 : 2—Distant journey.
40. Tos. Kip. 3 : 14—If goat fell ill, etc.
41. Tos. Suk. 1 : 9—Spreading cloth over *Sukkah.*
42. Tos. Y.T. 3 : 2—Animal and offspring in pit.
43. M. Ta. 1 : 1—When say rain-prayer?
44. M. Yev. 8 : 4—Eunuch *re ḥaliṣah.*
45. M. Yev. 12 : 2—*Ḥaliṣah* at night, with left foot.
46. M. Yev. 12 : 3—Read but not spit.
47. M. Yev. 13 : 6—Divorce, remarry orphan-minor: she is prohibited to Levir.
48. M. Yev. 16 : 2—Once woman is permitted to Levir, if he dies, she may marry anyone.

49. M. Yev. 16 : 7—Woman may not remarry on evidence of single witness.
[50. Tos. Yev. 11 : 4—Sacrifice for each and every sin.]
51-54. M. Ket. 1 : 6-9—Virginity-claims, etc.
55-56. M. Ned. 10 : 5-6—Releasing vows of *bogeret* and woman awaiting Levirate marriage.
57. M. Ned. 10 : 7—Annul vows in advance.
58. M. Naz. 6 : 11—Uncleanness hits Nazir during final sacrifices.
59. M. Naz. 7 : 1—High priest, Nazir, and neglected corpse.
60. M. Naz. 7 : 4—ʿAqiba before Eliezer *re* quantity of uncleanness and Nazir.
61. M. Sot. 3 : 4D—Not teach daughter Torah.
62. M. Sot. 6 : 1—Testimony against wife.
63-65. M. Sot. 9 : 2-4—Neglected corpse-laws.
66. M. Qid. 3 : 13—Purify *mamzer* through marriage.
67. M. Zev. 1 : 1, Tos. Zev. 1 : 1, Tos. Pis. 4 : 8 etc.—Sin-offering and Guilt-offering.
68. M. Zev. 7 : 4—Bird-whole offering below line subject to sacrilege.
69. M. Hul. 2 : 6—Slaughter dying animal.
70. M. Hul. 12 : 2—Cock-partridge.
71. M. Bekh. 1 : 5—Redeem firstling with hybrid.
[72. M. Bekh. 1 : 6F-G—Firstling of ass died.]
73. M. Bekh. 5 : 3—Slit ear of firstling.
74. M. Ar. 6 : 3—Not take oxen as pledge to Temple.
75. M. Tem. 3 : 3—Substitute of Guilt-offering, etc.
76. M. Tem. 6 : 5—Progeny of *ṭerefah.*
[77. M. Ker. 3 : 10—How many Sin-offerings for one type of sin repeated many times. *But see Usha, No. 40.*]
78. M. Ker. 6 : 1, 3—Suspensive-guilt-offering when man has not sinned.
79. M. B.Q. 6 : 4—Fire in own property.
80. Tos. B.B. 2 : 11—Acquire property by walking.
81. M. Sanh. 1 : 4, Tos. Sanh. 3 : 1—No trial for wild animals.
[82. M. Shav. 2 : 5, Tos. Shav. 1 : 6—Unawareness of creeping thing and Temple: How many liabilities?]
83. M. Kel. 2 : 8, Tos. Kel. B.Q. 2 : 8—Comb of water-cooler.
84. M. Kel. 3 : 2—Hole to render lamp clean—*perutah.*
85. M. Kel. 5 : 10—Oven of ʿAkhnai.
86. M. Kel. 14 : 1—Hole to render metal vessel clean—*perutah.*
87. M. Kel. 15 : 2, M. Ed. 7 : 7—Baker's shelf attached to wall is clean.
88. M. Kel. 17 : 1—Hole to render wooden vessel clean.
89. M. Kel. 27 : 12—New cloth not purified when thrown out.
90. M. Kel. 28 : 2—Small rag always unclean.
91. M. Oh. 2 : 2—Worm from corpse, ashes of cremated corpse.
92. M. Oh. 2 : 4, Tos. Ah. 3 : 7—Grave-stone renders unclean by carrying. [N.B.: Tos. Ah. 3 : 8—Simeon (b. Yoḥai) carried forward debate.]
93. M. Oh. 9 : 15 + Tos. Ah. 10 : 8—Uncleanness of tomb.

94. M. Oh. 12 : 3, Tos. Ah. 13 : 3—Projecting windowsill.
95-96. M. Oh. 14 : 4-5, Tos. Ah. 13 : 12—Wall projection.
97. M. Oh. 17 : 2—Grave-area makes grave-area.
98. M. Neg. 9 : 3—Bright spot on palm of hand.
99. M. Neg. 11 : 7—Leprosy sign on checkered garment.
100-102. M. Par. 1 : 1, 2 : 1, 3, 5—Rules of selection of Red Heifer.
103-104. M. Par. 4 : 1, 3—Heifer-sacrifice is not subject to ordinary Temple rules.
105. M. Par. 5 : 4, Tos. Par. 5 : 6—Reed-pipe for heifer ceremony + rules of cleanness.
106. M. Par. 10 : 1—*Maddaf*-uncleanness *re* corpse-uncleanness.
107. M. Par. 10 : 3—Jar of heifer-ashes on top of creeping thing.
108. Tos. Par. 10 : 4—One clean for Sin-offering rite who moved creeping thing is clean.
109. M. Par. 11 : 2—Loosely-fastened boards are unclean in what concerns Sin-offering water.
110. M. Par. 11 : 7—Berries *re* hyssop.
111. M. Toh. 2 : 2—First-grade uncleanness.
112. M. Miq. 2 : 4—Quarter-*log* of drawn water at outset invalidates ritual pool.
113. M. Miq. 2 : 7—Water caught in jars *re* ritual pool.
114. M. Miq. 2 : 8—Water collected in pot in ritual pool.
115. M. Miq. 2 : 10—Mud in ritual pool.
116. M. Nid. 4 : 4—Hard labor three days out of eleven.
117. M. Nid. 4 : 6—Hard labor during eighty days of purification.
118. M. Maksh. 6 : 6—*Zab's* semen.
119-120. M. Zab. 5 : 3, 7—Carrying carrion, flux of *Zab.*
121. M. Sot. 9 : 15—Temple's destruction marked decline in sages.
122. M. Avot 2 : 10—Three sayings.
123. M. Ed. 8 : 6—Built Temple walls outside of curtains.
124. Tos. Sanh. 11 : 5, y. Sanh. 7 : 13 [M. Sanh. 7 : 11]—Gathering cucumbers by sorcery prohibited.
125. Tos. Hal. 2 : 24—Eliezer arrested for *minut.*
126. M. Yad. 4 : 3/Tos. Yad. 2 : 16—Ammon and Moab give Poorman's Tithe in Seventh Year.
[127. M. Sanh. 10 : 3/Tos. Sanh. 13 : 10—Generation of wilderness, etc. have portion in world to come. *But see Usha, No. 62.*]
128. Tos. Sanh. 13 : 2—Gentiles have no portion in world to come.

5. *Tannaitic Stratum of Gemarot and Tannaitic Midrashim*

1. b. Ber. 3a—Night has three watches [*vs.* Judah the Patriarch].
2. b. Ber. 13a, Mid. Tan. Deut. 6 : 6—Intention in saying *Shemaʿ.*
3. b. Ber. 29b—Short Prayer.
4. Mekh. Ishmael, Besh. Lauterbach, I, p. 216, etc.—Pray according to appropriate length—briefly or lengthily.
5. b. Ber. 47b—Who is an *ʿam ha'areṣ?*
6. b. Ber. 62a—Wipe with left hand.

7. Sifré Deut. 303—Not buy shrouds or coffin with tithes.
8. b. Shab. 12a, 107b—Kill fleas, vermin on Sabbath.
9. b. Pes. 36a, y. Pes. 2 : 7—Make *maṣṣah* with fruit juice. ʿAqiba *re* Eliezer and Joshua.
10. Mekh. Simeon, p. 39, ls. 7-14—Passover not from tithes.
11. Mekh. Ishmael Pisḥa 6 : 88-91—Barbecue Passover.
12. Sifré Deut. 133 (b. Ber. 9a)—Sacrifice Passover in evening.
13. Mekh. Ishmael Vayassa 5 : 41-50—Bake for Sabbath and festival.
14. Sifra Tazriʿa 12 : 6—Leper and *tefillin.*
15. b. Yev. 70a—Uncircumcized priest may not eat Heave-offering *re* Ex. 12 : 45.
16. b. Yev. 46a—Proselyte need not immerse.
17. Sifré Deut. 212, 213—*Re* Deut. 21 : 12.
18. b. Yev. 34b, y. Ket. 5 : 6—Nurse 24 months.
19. b. Hag. 10a—Grounds for releasing vows.
20. Mekh. Nez. 9 : 29-30, b. Git. 42b, etc.—Deed of emancipation of slave injured by master.
21. b. Qid. 18b—*Re* Ex. 21 : 8.
22. Sifra Vayiqra 13 : 4—*Re* Lev. 2 : 14: *ʿOmer* from barley.
23. Mekh. Baḥodesh 10 : 58-86—Eliezer is sick; suffering is good.
24. Sifré Deut. 38—Gamaliel's son's wedding; Gamaliel should serve as good host.
25. Sifré Deut. 144—Eliezer's court is a good one.
26. b. Sanh. 68a, y. Shab. 2 : 7, etc.—Death-scene(s).
27. b. Sot. 48b—Have faith.
28. b. B.M. 59b—Oven of ʿAkhnai debate.
29. b. B.B. 74b—Eye of Leviathan.
30. b. B.B. 121b—15th of Av.
31. ARN Chap. 36—Men of Sodom.
32. Mekh. Pisḥa 1 : 114-118—Ex. 12 : 1.
33. Mekh. Pisḥa 14 : 11-22—Ex. 12 : 37 (*Succoth*). [Also: Sifra Emor 17 : 11.]
34. Mekh. Pisḥa 14 : 95-97—Idol crossed sea with Israelites.
35. Mekh. Pisḥa 14 : 113-117, Ex. 12 : 42—Israel will be redeemed in Nisan, not Tishri.
36. Mekh. Beshallaḥ 1 : 57-69, Ex. 13 : 18—God tried to tire Israelites by detour.
37. Mekh. Beshallaḥ 2 : 8-15, Ex. 14 : 2—What were *Ḥirot*?
38. Mekh. Beshallaḥ 7 : 109-121, Ex. 14 : 31—Egyptians smitten at sea by 200 plagues.
39. Mekh. Vayassa 6 : 47-9, Ex. 16 : 3—Taste of manna.
40. Mekh. Vayassa 1 : 1-12, Ex. 15 : 22—All journeys in wilderness made at command of God.
41. Mekh. Amalek 2 : 186-192—Ex. 17 : 16.
42. Mekh. Amalek 1 : 173-5—Ex. 17 : 13.
43. b. Bekh. 5b—*Rephidim* and *Shiṭṭim* were place-names.
44. Mekh. Amalek 3 : 127-140—How God saved Moses at court of Pharaoh.

45. Mekh. Baḥodesh 2 : 43-5, Ex. 19 : 5—Covenant is Sabbath or circumcision.
46. Mekh. Baḥodesh 4 : 36-44—Ex. 19 : 19.
47. Mekh. deR. Simeon, p. 1, ls. 12-18—Why revelation in bush? Redemption comes when people are at lowest point.
48. Mekh. deR. Simeon, p. 38, ls. 22-25—Ex. 13 : 5.
49. Sifra Mekh. deMil. 2 : 35—Aaron's sons died outside tent.
50. Sifra Beḥuq. 5 : 1—Lev. 26 : 18: God warns before punishing people.
51. Sifré Deut. 29—*Re* Deut. 3 : 26.
52. Sifré Deut. 32—Deut. 4 : 6: Some love life more than money, or *vice versa.*
53. Sifré Num. 136, Deut. 338—Deut. 34 : 1, 32 : 49: Moses saw all of land.
54. Mid. Tan. to Deut. 14 : 22—When man comes to Temple, he is moved to study Torah.
55. Sifré Zuṭṭa 13 : 34—Man's agent like himself.
56. y. Shab. 9 : 3—Is. 1 : 18.
57. y. Ta. 1 : 1—If Israel do not repent, they will not be redeemed.
58. b. Ber. 6a—Deut. 28 : 10 refers to *tefillin.*
59. b. Shab. 55b—Gen. 49 : 4 *re* Reuben.
60. b. Pes. 117a—David said Psalms with reference to himself.
61. b. Ta. 9b—World draws water-supply from ocean.
62. b. Sanh. 92b—Ezekiel's dead sang I Sam. 2 : 6.
63. b. B.B. 25a-b—World is like *exedra.*
64. b. Yoma 54b—World created from center.
65. b. Yoma 54b—Heaven made from heaven, earth from earth.
66. b. B.B. 16a—Job 9 : 24.
67. b. Ar. 17a—Patriarchs could not stand before divine reproof.
68. b. Hul. 92a—Gen. 40 : 10 refers to patriarchs.
69. Midrash Tannaim to Deut. 6 : 6—*Kavvanah* in *Shemaʿ.*
70. Sifra Shemini 2 : 32-3—Nadav and Abihu died for teaching law before Moses.
71. Sifré Deut. 140—A person must have his own *Sukkah.*
72. Sifré Zuṭṭa 24—A woman may be forced to drink as a Soṭah.
73. Sifré Num. 153—A man's agent is like himself.
74. Sifré Deut. 61—One must uproot an *asherah.*
75. Sifra Shemini 10 : 5-6—An oven is completely finished without being heated up.
76. Mekhilta deR. Simeon b. Yoḥai, p. 106, ls. 23-26—A man should have enough faith not to worry about his food for the morrow.
77. Mekhilta Vayassa 7 : 68-74—People in the wilderness obeyed God only because he would fulfill their needs.
78. Mekhilta deR. Simeon b. Yoḥai, p. 143, ls. 3-8—The people at the sea had faith.
79. Mekhilta Neziqin 18 : 9-16—The stranger has a strong inclination to do evil.
80. b. A.Z. 7b—Ask first for own needs, then Prayer.

81. b. Eruv. 54b—Teaching traditions.
82. b. Ta. 25b—Eliezer fails to produce rain.
83. y. Ber. 2 : 8—Eliezer regards slave as mere property.
84. y. B.Q. 4 : 5, b. B.Q. 41b-42a—Proof for opinion in M. B.Q. 4 : 5.

ii. Chains of Traditions

Eliezer b. Hyrcanus is the first Tannaitic master for some of whose sayings we have chains of tradition, that is, authorities who say, "I heard from..." or, more commonly, *Rabbi X says/said that Rabbi Y says that R. Eliezer b. Hyrcanus says/said.* In addition, some of the Toseftan traditions about Eliezer, like many of those about disputes of the Houses, contain redefinitions of the substance of a dispute, or of the protasis of the pericope, preserving the apodosis just as it appears in the Mishnah. These constitute important evidence about the formation of Eliezer's sayings; they tell us that a given authority knew and did not accept the specification of an opinion of Eliezer or of a matter about which he and others disputed, as given anonymously, but preferred a different formulation of the matter. Finally, we have, primarily from Judah b. Ilai, a number of opinions for Eliezer which are either consistent with (or contradict) anonymous Mishnaic laws, but which do not appear in the Mishnah in Eliezer's name.

Chains of tradition are different from attestations. The latter supply a general notion as to the time at which a given tradition attributed to Eliezer may have been known. The former give more precise information about the authorities responsible for the preservation and transmission of teachings attributed to Eliezer. We shall now review the names of authorities behind Eliezer's tradition through the Tannaitic stratum of the *Gemarot.* All such chains of tradition pertain to legal materials, except for the one, which may or may not be authentic, for M. Avot 2 : 10, in ARN. After listing the traditions ascribed to several masters, we shall review all the materials for which no chain at all is available. This will indicate for how small a proportion of Eliezer's materials we have any chain of tradition at all. Square brackets ([ ]) indicate an item listed only for the sake of completeness, which does not, however, contain a chain of tradition.

1. *ʿAqiba*

1. M. Shev. 8 : 9-10—ʿAqiba declines to reveal Eliezer's rule *re* hide anointed with oil of Seventh Year, bread of Samaritans. [Attested by Yosi, y. Shev. 8 : 8.]

[2. M. Ed. 2 : 7/Tos. Shab. 4 : 6 + M. Sanh. + Tos. Shab. 4 : 11—

Stated before ʿAqiba in name of Eliezer *re* woman wearing tiara, pigeon-racers' testimony.]

3. M. Sheq. 4 : 7—ʿAqiba: I prefer Eliezer's opinion to Joshua's *re* sanctification of cattle to Temple.
4. M. Ker. 3 : 10—ʿAqiba: I asked Eliezer.

2. *Ishmael*

[1. M. Hal. 2 : 8/Tos. Hal. 1 : 10—Even *he* has grounds for his opinion, *re* giving Dough-offering for unclean from clean dough.]

3. *Ilai*

1. Tos. Dem. 1 : 3, y. Dem. 1 : 1—First fruits are always liable for they are guarded [no Mishnaic equivalent].
2. M. Ter. 2 : 1/Tos. Ter. 3 : 18—They give Heave-offering for what is unclean from what is clean.
3. Tos. Hal. 1 : 6—Cakes of Thank-offering are free of liability unless sold. M. Hal. 1 : 6 omits Eliezer.
4. M. Eruv. 2 : 5—I heard from Eliezer *re* two rules on *ʿEruvin*, one on Passover.

[5. Tos. Suk. 2 : 1—*Story* about Ilai and Eliezer *re* studying on festival.]

6. ARN Chap. 15/M. Avot 2 : 10—Yosi b. R. Judah + Judah b. Ilai + Ilai—Eliezer the Great *re* repent, etc.

4. *Judah b. Ilai*

1. Tos. Ter. 9 : 9C/M. Ter. 11 : 2—Clean olives and clean grapes may be made into liquids.
2. Sifré Num. 110/M. Hal. 2 : 1—Fruit from abroad is free of liability for tithes.

[3. M. Eruv. 1 : 2—Epstein, *Tan.*, p. 119, says Judah is the authority.]

4. M. Eruv. 7 : 11—Judah comments on Eliezer + sages *re* acquiring an *ʿeruv* with coins.
5. Tos. Kip. 2 : 10—Eliezer cited *re* lots.
6. Tos. Kip. 2 : 16—Eliezer cited *re* counting.
7. Tos. Kip. 3 : 1/M. Yoma 5 : 5—Eliezer cited *re* sprinkling.
8. Tos. Kip. 3 : 19/M. Yoma 7 : 3—Eliezer cited *re* continual offering, etc.
9. Tos. Y.T. 1 : 3, 1 : 1 [M. Bes. 1 : 1]—Judah cites Eliezer *re* Houses' dispute on egg.
10. Tos. R.H. 2 : 10—Eliezer cited *re* meaning of solemn rest.
11. b. M.Q. 19a/M. M.Q. 3 : 4—Eliezer cited *re* spinning blue thread for fringe. Not in Mishnah.
12. b. M.Q. 10a/M. M.Q. 1 : 9—Eliezer *re* setting up millstones in festival week. Not in Mishnah.
13. Tos. Ket. 11 : 4/M. Ket. 11 : 6—Eliezer *re* right of orphan to *melog.* Not in Mishnah.

14-16. Tos. Nez. 2 : 12-13/M. Naz. 3 : 3, 4, 5,—Judah in Liezer's name *re* losing days of Naziriteship.

17. b. B.B. 157a/M. B.B. 9 : 7—M. B.B. 9 : 7 follows Judah's version, against Meir.
18. Tos. Sanh. 9 : 6/M. Sanh. 6 : 4—Eliezer *re* hanging woman.
[19. Tos. Zev. 2 : 16/M. Zev. 3 : 3—Judah is consistent with Eliezer, and Judah the Patriarch comments on that fact; but Judah does not cite Eliezer.]
[20. Tos. Zev. 8 : 15/M. Zev. 8 : 4—Judah comments on the dispute but is *not* the authority behind M. Zev. 8 : 4.]
[21. Tos. Zev. 8 : 20/M. Zev. 8 : 8A—as above.]
[22. Tos. Men. 2 : 16/M. Men. 3 : 1—as above.]
23. Tos. Ah. 7 : 3/M. Oh. 6 : 2—Judah cites Eliezer, but Eliezer's opinion is omitted from M. Oh. 6 : 2. It is, however, consistent with M. 6 : 1.
24. Tos. Ah. 9 : 7/M. Oh. 8 : 6—Judah has an opinion of Eliezer and Joshua; Eliezer is left out of M. Oh. 8 : 6, but the opinion is consistent with Toh. Ah. 9 : 7.
25. Tos. Ah. 17 : 6/M. Oh. 17 : 5—Judah redefines dispute of M. Oh. 17 : 5 *re* dirt from abroad.
26. Tos. Neg. 3 : 5/M. Neg. 7 : 4-5—Judah redefines dispute *re* cutting off signs of leprosy.
27. Tos. Par. 5 : 9/M. Par. 5 : 7—Judah supplies opinion for Eliezer, which M. Par. 5 : 7 drops.
28. M. Par. 7 : 10/Tos. Par. 7 : 7—Judah is authority for Eliezer's saying *re* guarding water.
29. Tos. Uqs. 3 : 15/M. Uqs. 3 : 10 = M. Shev. 3 : 10—Judah redefines dispute about beehive.

5. *Meir + Judah*

1. M. Kil. 9 : 3/Tos. Kil. 5 : 18—Handkerchiefs etc. *re* mixed seeds. M. Kil. follows Meir's view of Eliezer's opinion, *vs.* Judah.

2-6. M. Ter. 4 : 7, 8, 9, 10, 11/Tos. Ter. 5 : 10-11—Mixture of black white figs neutralizes *re* Heave-offering—when known it will (+/— not) neutralize.

7. Tos. Men. 8 : 19/M. Men. 7 : 3—Judah *vs.* Meir *re* blemished animal and incense. M. Men. 7 : 3 follows Meir's version.

6. *Simeon*

1. Tos. M.S. 1 : 14—Saffron is not purchased from money of tithe.
2. Tos. Shab. 15 : 10/M. Shab. 19 : 1, 4—Circumcision on Sabbath [b. Shab. 137a: + Meir].
3. Tos. Pis. 1 : 5/M. Pes. 1 : 7—Burning doubtfully unclean with unclean Heave-offering.
4. Tos. Pis. 5 : 4/M. Pes. 6 : 5—Sacrificed what is valid for Passover-offering for the sake of Passover.
5. Tos. Sheq. 2 : 10—Simeon + Yosah deny a dispute exists between Eliezer + Joshua in M. Sheq. 4 : 8.

[6. Epstein, *Tan.*, p. 359, attributes M. Bes. 4 : 6-7 to Simeon.]

7. Tos. Hul. 2 : 11/M. Hul. 2 : 6D-F—Simeon cites Eliezer.
8. Tos. Kel. B.M. 8 : 8/M. Kel. 18 : 9—Simeon *vs.* Judah the Patriarch *re* purifying bed.
9. Tos. Ah. 13 : 10/M. Oh. 12 : 8—Simeon and Jacob redefine dispute of M. Oh. 12 : 8.
10. M. Toh. 9 : 3—Simeon redefines Eliezer's and Joshua's dispute about liquids.

7. *Nathan*

1. Tos. Ter. 7 : 10C/M. Ter. 8 : 3—Eating grapecluster before Sabbath.
2. Tos. Ter. 9 : 8/M. Ter. 11 : 2—Honey is free of liability for tithes [9 : 9 + Judah].
3. M. Suk. 1 : 11, Tos. Suk. 1 : 10/b. Suk. 19b—Nathan is represented as citing Eliezer *re* Sukkah without roof.
4. Tos. Kel. B.M. 4 : 14/M. Kel. 14 : 7C-D—Nathan cites the dispute of Eliezer and Joshua *re* purifying a metal vessel.
5. M. Kel. 26 : 2/Tos. Kel. B.B. 4 : 3—Nathan redefines dispute *re* money pouch.

8. *Yoḥanan b. Nuri*

1. Tos. Orl. 1 : 8—Leazar b. R. Yosah + Yosah b. Durmasqit + Yosah the Galilean + Yoḥanan b. Nuri + Liezer the Great: *ʿOrlah*-laws inapplicable abroad. Compare M. Qid. 1 : 9, b. Qid. 39a. Epstein, *Tan.*, p. 178: The authority is Eliezer b. R. Yosi.

[2. Tos. Kel. B.M. 6 : 4/M. Kel. 8 : 1—Yoḥanan b. Nuri, "I said to Eliezer. . ."—Not as authority for the saying.]

9. *Simeon Shezuri*

1. M. Kel. 26 : 4/Tos. Kel. B.B. 4 : 7—Simeon redefines dispute *re* shoe on the last.

10. *Yosi b. R. Judah*

1. Tos. Sot. 1 : 1 (M. Sot. 1 : 1)—*Re* warning wife before witnesses
2. b. Git. 82a-b (M. Git. 9 : 1)—Divorce with limitations. [Note also Story *re* Ṭarfon, ʿAqiba, Yosi, Eleazar b. ʿAzariah.]

11. *Yosi, Simeon Shezuri, Judah*

1. M. Ker. 4 : 2-3 + Tos. Ker. 2 : 12-15 + Sifra Vayiqra 7 : 26-31—*Re* Eliezer *vs.* Joshua on Sin-offering where one is not sure of liability.

12. *Traditions without Chains or Named Tannaitic Authorities*

1. M. Ber. 1 : 1
2. b. Ber. 3a
3. Mekh. Pisḥa 6 : 40-43
4. Mid. Tan. to Deut. 6 : 6
5. M. Ber. 4 : 3-4
6. Tos. Ber. 3 : 7

7. Mekh. Beshallaḥ 4 : 1-9
8. M. Ber. 5 : 2
9. b. Ber. 47b
10. b. Ber. 62a
11. M. Pe'ah 3 : 6
12. M. Pe'ah 7 : 7
13. M. Kil. 5 : 8
14. M. Shev. 5 : 3 [But Judah follows Eliezer.]
15. M. Shev. 9 : 5
16. M. Ter. 4 : 5
17. M. Ter. 5 : 2
18. M. Ter. 5 : 4
19. M. Ter. 5 : 5
20. M. Ter. 5 : 6
21. M. Ter. 6 : 6
22. M. Ter. 8 : 1
23. M. Ter. 8 : 2
24. M. Ter. 8 : 8
25. M. Ter. 8 : 9
26. M. Ter. 8 : 10
27. M. Ter. 8 : 11
28. M. Ma. 4 : 3
29. M. Ma. 4 : 5
30. M. Ma. 4 : 6
31. Tos. M.S. 3 : 16
32. Sifré Deut. 303
33. Tos. M.S. 5 : 15-16
34. M. Hal. 2 : 4
35. M. Hal. 4 : 7
36. M. Orl. 1 : 7
37. M. Orl. 2 : 11
38. M. Orl. 2 : 13
39. M. Bik. 2 : 6
40. b. Shab. 12a, 107b
41. M. Shab. 1 : 10
42. M. Shab. 2 : 3
43. M. Shab. 6 : 4
44. M. Shab. 12 : 4
45. M. Shab. 13 : 1
46. M. Shab. 17 : 7
47. M. Shab. 20 : 1
48. Tos. Shab. 1 : 17
49. M. Eruv. 3 : 6
50. M. Eruv. 7 : 10
51. M. Eruv. 9 : 2 [b. B.B. 100a: Judah b. Ilai is consistent with Eliezer, but does not cite this ruling. Note also Tos B.B. 2 : 1.]
52. b. Eruv. 54b [Judah b. Ilai comments on story, but does not tell it.]
53. Sifra Shemini 2 : 32-3

54. M. Pes. 3 : 3
55. M. Pes. 6 : 1-2
56. M. Pes. 9 : 2
56A. Mekh. deR. Simeon, p. 39, ls. 7-14
57. Sifré Deut. 133
58. Tos. Kip. 3 : 14
59. Tos. Kip. 4 : 3
60. Tos. Suk. 1 : 9
61. b. Suk. 27a-b = Sifré Deut. 140
62. Mekhilta Vayassa 5 : 41-50
63. M. Bes. 4 : 6
64. M. Bes. 4 : 7
65. Tos. Y.T. 3 : 2
66. M. Ta. 1 : 1
67. M. M.Q. 3 : 6
68. y. Ber. 3 : 1 = b. M.Q. 27a
69. y. M.Q. 3 : 5
70. y. Ber. 2 : 8 = b. Ber. 16b
71. Sifra Tazriʿa 12 : 6
72. M. Yev. 8 : 4
73. M. Yev. 12 : 2
74. M. Yev. 13 : 2 [Ishmael attests, but is not the authority for, Eliezer's saying, Tos. Yev. 13 : 3-5.]
75. Tos. Yev. 12 : 12
76. y. Yev. 13 : 2
77. M. Yev. 13 : 6
78. M. Yev. 13 : 7
79. M. Yev. 16 : 2
80. M. Yev. 16 : 7
81. Tos. Yev. 3
82. Tos. Yev. 11 : 4
83. b. Yev. 70a
84. b. Yev. 46a
85. Sifré Deut. 212
86-89. M. Ket. 1 : 6-9
90. b. Ket. 52a
91. b. Yev. 34b, y. Ket. 5, 6
92. M. Ned. 9 : 1
93. M. Ned. 9 : 2
94. b. Hag. 10a [M. Hag. 1 : 1]
95. M. Ned. 10 : 5
96. M. Ned. 10 : 6
97. M. Ned. 10 : 7
98. M. Naz. 6 : 11
99. M. Naz. 7 : 1
100. M. Naz. 7 : 4
101. Tos. Sot. 1 : 2
102. M. Sot. 3 : 4

103. M. Sot. 6 : 1
104. M. Sot. 9 : 2
105. M. Sot. 9 : 3
106. M. Sot. 9 : 4
107. Sifré Zuṭṭa 24
108. y. Sot. 1 : 1
109. M. Git. 1 : 1
110. Mekh. Nez. 9 : 29-30
111. b. Qid. 18b
112. M. Qid. 3 : 13
113. Tos. Qid. 1 : 4
114. b. Sanh. 76a
115. b. Yev. 61b
116. M. B.Q. 6 : 4
117. y. B.Q. 4 : 5 [Not in M. B.Q. 4 : 5]
118. M. Sanh. 1 : 4
119. M. Shav. 2 : 5
120. b. Shav. 113b
121. Sifré Num. 153
122. Sifré Deut. 61
123. M. Zev. 1 : 1
124. M. Zev. 3 : 3 [Judah is consistent with Eliezer, Tos. Zev. 2 : 16.]
125. Sifra Ṣav 8 : 1
126. M. Zev. 7 : 4
127. M. Zev. 8 : 4
128-133. M. Zev. 8 : 5, 7, 8, 9, 10, 11
134. M. Men. 3 : 1 [Judah is consistent, Tos. Men. 2 : 16.]
135. M. Men. 3 : 4
136. b. Men. 65b
137. b. Men. 68b
138. M. Hul. 2 : 6A-C
139. M. Hul. 12 : 2
140. M. Bekh. 1 : 5
141. M. Bekh. 1 : 6/M. Ed. 7 : 1
142. M. Bekh. 5 : 3
143. M. Ar. 6 : 1
144. M. Ar. 6 : 3
145. M. Ar. 8 : 4
146. M. Tem. 3 : 1 = M. Ed. 7 : 6
147. M. Tem. 3 : 3
148. M. Tem. 6 : 5
149. M. Ker. 6 : 1A
150. M. Ker. 6 : 3
151. M. Me. 1 : 2
152. M. Me. 1 : 3 + Tos. Me. 1 : 4, 6, Tos. Men. 4 : 10, 4 : 14-15, Tos. Zev. 4 : 5, 4 : 8
153. Tos. Zev. 4 : 1-2
154. M. Kel. 2 : 8

155. M. Kel. 3 : 2
156. M. Kel. 5 : 10
157. M. Kel. 14 : 1
158. M. Kel. 15 : 2/M. Ed. 7 : 7
159. M. Kel. 17 : 1
160. M. Kel. 27 : 12
161. M. Kel. 28 : 2
162. M. Oh. 2 : 2
163. M. Oh. 2 : 4
164. M. Oh. 6 : 1
165. M. Oh. 9 : 15
166. M. Oh. 12 : 3
167. M. Oh. 14 : 4
168. M. Oh. 14 : 5
169. M. Oh. 17 : 2
170. M. Neg. 9 : 3
171. M. Neg. 11 : 7
172. M. Par. 1 : 1
173. M. Par. 2 : 1
174. M. Par. 2 : 3
175. M. Par. 2 : 5
176. M. Par. 4 : 1
177. M. Par. 4 : 3
178. M. Par. 5 : 4
179. M. Par. 9 : 1
180. M. Par. 9 : 3
181. M. Par. 9 : 4 [*vs.* Yosi: Tos. Par. 9 : 6]
182. M. Par. 9 : 7
183. M. Par. 10 : 1
184. M. Par. 10 : 3/M. Ed. 7 : 5
185. Tos. Par. 10 : 4
186. Tos. Ah. 7 : 11
187. M. Par. 11 : 2
188. M. Par. 11 : 7
189. M. Toh. 2 : 2
190. M. Toh. 6 : 5
191. M. Toh. 8 : 7
192. M. Miq. 2 : 4
193. M. Miq. 2 : 7
194. M. Miq. 2 : 8
195. M. Miq. 2 : 10
196. M. Nid. 1 : 3
197. M. Nid. 1 : 5
198. Tos. Nid. 2 : 3
199. Tos. Nid. 5 : 6
200. Tos. Nid. 6 : 8
201. M. Nid. 4 : 4
202. M. Nid. 4 : 6

203. M. Nid. 5 : 9
204. M. Nid. 10 : 3
205. M. Maksh. 6 : 6
206. Tos. Maksh. 1 : 4
207. M. Zab. 5 : 3
208. M. Zab. 5 : 7
209. M. Yad. 4 : 2
210. M. Yad. 4 : 3
211. Tos. Ed. 1 : 4
212. M. Ed. 2 : 7 (M. Shab. 6 : 1, Sanh. 3 : 5)
213. Tos. Ed. 2 : 1, 2 : 8
214. M. Ed. 6 : 2
215. M. Ed. 6 : 3
216. M. Sot. 9 : 15
217. M. Ed. 8 : 6
218. Tos. Sanh. 11 : 5
219. Tos. Hul. 2 : 24
220. Mekh. Baḥodesh 10 : 56-86
221. b. Sanh. 10a-b
222. Sifré Deut. 38
223. Sifré Deut. 144
224. Sifré Deut. 188
225. y. Shab. 2 : 7
226. b. Ber. 28b, y. Sot. 9 : 16
227. y. A.Z. 3 : 1 (Jacob b. R. Idi + Joshua b. Levi)
228. y. Meg. 1 : 9
229. b. Sot. 48b
230. Mekh. deR. Simeon, p. 143, ls. 3-8
231. Mekh. Vayassa 7 : 68-74
232. b. B.M. 59a-b, y. M.Q. 3 : 1
233. b. B.B. 74b
234. b. B.B. 121b
235. y. Ber. 2 : 3
236. y. Meg. 1 : 9 (Jeremiah + Ḥiyya b. Ba)
237. y. Hag. 2 : 1
238. y. Naz. 7 : 1
239. y. Sanh. 1 : 2 (R. Ba)
240. y. Hor. 3 : 4
241. b. Ned. 50a
242. b. Git. 56a
243. b. Qid. 31a
244. b. B.B. 10b
245. b. Ned. 20b
246. ARN Chap. 6
247. ARN Chap. 14
248. M. Sanh. 10 : 3, Tos. Sanh. 13 : 2, 10
249. Mekh. Pisḥa 1 : 114-119
250. Mekh. Pisḥa 14 : 11-22

251. Mekh. Pisḥa 14 : 95-7
252. Mekh. Pisḥa 14 : 113-117
253. b. R.H. 10b-12a
254. Mekh. Beshallaḥ 1 : 57-69
255. Mekh. Beshallaḥ 2 : 8-15
256. Mekh. Beshallaḥ 7 : 109-121
257. b. Sanh. 95b
258. Mekh. Vayassa 6 : 47-9
259. Mekh. Vayassa 1 : 1-12
260. Mekh. Amalek 2 : 186-192
261. Mekh. Amalek 1 : 173-175
262. Mekh. Amalek 1 : 131-137
263. b. Bekh. 65b
264. Mekh. Amalek 3 : 127-140
265. Mekh. Baḥodesh 2 : 43-5
266. Mekh. Baḥodesh 4 : 36-44
267. Mekh. deR. Simeon, p. 1, ls. 12-18
268. Mekh. deR. Simeon, p. 38, ls. 22-25
269. Sifra Mekhilta de Miluʾim 2 : 35
270. Sifra Beḥuqotai 5 : 1
271. Sifré Deut. 29
272. Sifré Deut. 32
273. Sifré Num. 136, Deut. 338
274. Mid. Tan., pp. 77-8
275. Sifré Zuṭṭa 13 : 34
276. y. Shab. 9 : 3
277. y. Ta. 1 : 1
278. b. Ber. 6a
279. b. Shab. 55b
280. b. Eruv. 70b
281. b. Pes. 117a
282. b. Ta. 9b
283. b. Sanh. 92b
284. b. B.B. 25a-b
285. b. Yoma 54b
286. b. B.B. 16a
287. b. Ar. 17a
288. b. Ar. 16b
289. b. Hul. 92a
290. b. B.B. 10b
291. b. Shav. 35b

iii. Suppressed Traditions

Mishnah-Tosefta contain considerable evidence, both explicit and implicit, that Eliezer-traditions were suppressed or ignored; that traditions of his were given anonymously in the Mishnah; that attribution of a tradition to him meant it would not be regarded as normative; and other indications that the transmission of traditions attributed to Eliezer was significantly impaired. Here we shall list the cases in which Eliezer should have been included in a Mishnaic pericope, either as the authority of a law now given anonymously or as the holder of an *omitted* opinion contrary to that given in the Mishnah. In addition, one must take note of the variant traditions (above, pp. 73-76), in which later Tannaim comment upon, and alter, opinions of Eliezer or disputes in which Eliezer appears with Joshua. But these variant traditions or efforts to redefine disputes do not signify a deliberate effort to falsify or to suppress Eliezer's opinions. It was perfectly routine for later masters to define disputes of earlier teachers around ever finer points of law; this was commonplace in the Houses-materials, among others.

1. M. Shev. 7 : 6/b. Nid. 8a—Rose etc. subject to law of Seventh Year. Eliezer is omitted in M. Shev., but Pedat in b. Nid. 8a says this is his teaching.
2. M. Maksh. 6 : 4—According to Tos. Ter. 9 : 8D, Eliezer would differ, but the difference is omitted.
3. M. M.S. 5 : 12/Sifré Deut. 303—Not use Second Tithe for corpse-shrouds.
4. M. M.S. 5 : 2/Tos. M.S. 5 : 15, 16—Story about Eliezer not reflected in M. M.S. 5 : 2.
5. M. Hal. 1 : 6/Tos. Hal. 1 : 6—Cakes of Thank-offering, etc., exempt from Dough-offering.
6. M. Orl. 2 : 4 omits the differing opinion of Eliezer, M. Orl. 2 : 11. The "sages" of 2 : 11 are the anonymous authority for 2 : 4, 8-9.
7. M. Shab. 6 : 1/Tos. Shab. 4 : 6—Eliezer's lenient ruling is omitted by M. Shab. 6 : 1. But compare M. Ed. 2 : 7. Then M. Shab. 6 : 5 gives Eliezer's opinion *without* attributing it to him.
8. M. Bes. 5 : 2/Tos. Y.T. 4 : 4—Eliezer's distinction between Sabbath and festival is alluded to in M. Bes. 5 : 2, but it is repeated and Eliezer is not mentioned.
9. M. Eruv. 3 : 1/M. Eruv. 7 : 10A—Eliezer's opinion in the latter is given anonymously in the former.
10. Tos. Pis. 1 : 5—Simeon has a dispute of Eliezer and Joshua which is unknown to M. Pes. 1 : 7, but is congruent to M. Ter. 8 : 8.
11. Tos. Kip. 2 : 10/M. Yoma 4 : 1—Judah's tradition *re* Eliezer is omitted in M. Yoma 4 : 1.
13. Tos. Kip. 3 : 14—Eliezer's opinion is not cited in M. Yoma 6 : 3ff.
14. M. Yoma 7 : 3/Tos. Kip. 3 : 19—M. Yoma 7 : 3 contains only part of Eliezer's opinion.
15. Tos. Y.T. 1 : 1/M. Bes. 1 : 1—Eliezer's explanation of the Shammaite position is omitted in M. Bes. 1 : 11.
16. M. Bes. 2 : 1 is in accord with Eliezer, Mekh. Bayassa 5 : 41-50, but Eliezer does not appear in M. Bes. 2 : 1.

17. Tos. Y.T. 3 : 2/M. Bes. 3 : 4—M. Bes. 3 : 4 omits reference to the issue defined by Eliezer and Joshua in Tos. Y.T. 3 : 2.
18. M. Ta. 2 : 10 omits the contrary opinions of Eliezer and Joshua in Tos. Ta. 2 : 5.
19. M. M.Q. 3 : 4 omits reference to Judah's opinion in Eliezer's name in b. M.Q. 19a.
20. M. Ber. 3 : 1 omits reference to the pertinent opinions of Eliezer and Joshua in y. M.Q. 3 : 5.
21. M. M.Q. 1 : 9 omits Eliezer's condition about not completing work, b. M.Q. 10a.
22. Tos. Yev. 12 : 11/M. Yev. 12 : 2—Judah alludes to an opinion of Eliezer, about which M. Yev. 12 : 2 knows nothing.
23. Tos. Yev. 12 : 12/M. Yev. 12 : 4—M. Yev. 12 : 4 has Eliezer's opinion in his exact words, but does not cite him. Compare M. Yeb. 13 : 2B.
24. M. Yev. 16 : 7—Eliezer's and Joshua's opinion, contrary to Gamaliel's, is not formulated as a generalized law, but left as a story.
25. Tos. Yev. 11 : 4/M. Yev. 10 : 2—M. Yev. 10 : 2 omits Eliezer's opinion on how many offerings are required.
26. M. Ket. 16 : 6 omits Judah's tradition of Eliezer's contrary opinion in Tos. Ket. 1 : 4.
27. Sifré Deut. 206 has an opinion opposed to that of Eliezer in M. Sot. 9 : 2, which there stands without contradiction.
[28. M. Qid. 1 : 9 and Tos. Orl. 1 : 8 do not correlate with one another.]
29. M. B.Q. 4 : 5 is Eliezer's opinion, so b. B.Q. 41b-42a=y. B.Q. 4 : 5. But Eliezer is not credited with M. B.Q. 4 : 5.
30. Tos. Ar. 4 : 5/M. Ar. 6 : 1—M. Ar. 6 : 1 omits Eliezer's opinion on whether the couple may remarry.
31. M. Zev. 2 : 4 is in accord with Joshua in Tos. Zev. 4 : 1-2. Eliezer's name and opinion are omitted altogether.
32. M. Kel. 23 : 1 omits reference to Eliezer's contrary opinion given in b. Sanh. 68b.
33. M. Oh. 6 : 2 omits Eliezer's opinion given by Judah, in Tos. Ah. 7 : 3.
34. M. Oh. 8 : 6 omits Eliezer's and Joshua's dispute in Tos. Ah. 9 : 7, and M. Oh. 8 : 6 follows Eliezer.
35. M. Oh. 12 : 8D knows nothing of Eliezer's opinion in Tos. Ah. 13 : 10.
36. M. Par. 5 : 7 omits reference to Judah's tradition of Eliezer's opinion, contrary to M. Par.; see Tos. Par. 5 : 9.
37. M. Par. 11 : 1 omits the position of Eliezer, M. Par. 9 : 3.
38. Tos. Toh. 7 : 9—Eliezer qualifies M. Toh. 6 : 6 but is not mentioned there.
39. M. Sanh. 3 : 3/M. Ed. 2 : 7—M. Sanh. 3 : 3 has Eliezer's opinion in his words but omits his name.
40. M. R.H. 1 : 8 is Eliezer's opinion but omits his name, supplied in y. R.H. 1 : 7.

41. M. Toh. 4 : 2 is consistent with Eliezer in Tos. Ed. 1 : 10H-K.
42. Tos. Ah. 2 : 7 supplements M. Oh. 2 : 6, where Eliezer does not occur.
43. M. Sanh. 7 : 11 certainly is Eliezer's teaching, so ʿAqiba in Tos. Sanh. 11 : 5. But M. Sanh. is given in Joshua's name.

In addition, Y. N. Epstein, *Mevo'ot leSifrut HaTanna'im* (Jerusalem-Tel Aviv, 1957), pp. 65-70, points out that Eliezer's (alleged) association with the House of Shammai impaired the value of his traditions in the eyes of later tradents. That he was excommunicated likewise limited his influence and led to the disappearance of his teachings. Epstein notes instances in which *beraitot* give versions of Eliezer's opinions either different from those in the Mishnah or entirely excluded from the Mishnah. He would further add to the foregoing list the following items:

44. M. Eruv. 3 : 3—Eliezer's opinion is switched with that of the sages.
45. M. Yoma 7 : 3
46. M. Oh. 18 : 7
47. M. Neg. 13 : 1

iv. Other References to the Formation and Transmission of Eliezer's Traditions

In addition to the internal evidence, surveyed above, we have a number of sayings that indicate impairment of the formation and transmission of teachings attributed to Eliezer. Some of these are explicit, as in the case of ʿAqiba and Ilai (Nos. 1, 3). Others (e.g., No. 2), are indirect testimonies that it was not wise to cite Eliezer directly. Still others either imply or state that Tannas switched Eliezer's opinions with those of other masters, to make his view acceptable by supplying it with a better authority.

But, on the contrary, many other sayings and stories exhibit respect for Eliezer and his traditions. He is the model of the student who accurately preserves his own master's sayings and doings. He was among the most learned men of his day. He would have received the holy spirit, like Hillel, had the generation been worthy of it. The heavenly echo even confirmed the accuracy of his tradition.

Beyond these explicit references to the excellence of Eliezer's tradition lies the whole corpus of his sayings, which, with the exceptions noted below, implicitly shows respect to Eliezer and his teachings and takes for granted that these are important traditions and supply useful precedents. So the sayings and stories that either cast doubt upon the value of Eliezer's traditions, or claim that those traditions were not accurately formulated and transmitted, or suggest that it was necessary to hide his opinions under the names of others, or allege that no one would verify his opinions—those sayings and stories are strikingly few and exceptional when measured against the whole corpus.

The following are the more important sayings about the value of Eliezer's teachings and the accuracy of their transmission:

1. M. Shev. 8 : 9-10—ʿAqiba says he will not report the real opinion of Eliezer, which is probably the lenient one, that a) a hide anointed by Seventh-Year-oil is not to be burned, and b) it is permitted to eat Samaritan cooking. y. Shev. 8 : 8 confirms (a) and provides an alternative to (b).
2. Tos. Hal. 1 : 10/M. Hal. 2 : 8—Ishmael's students suppress Eliezer's name behind M. Hal. 2 : 8. He approves the rule, then they reveal the authority, and Ishmael admits Eliezer has grounds for his opinion. Compare Tos. Yev. 13 : 3-5.
3. M. Eruv. 2 : 6—Ilai has traditions of Eliezer and cannot find anyone else who knows them. But M. Eruv. 2 : 5 has a completely different rule for Eliezer/Eleazar, and the other rulings are ignored.

[4. Sifra Shemini Mekhilta deMiluʾim 2 : 32-3—Eliezer says one will die who teaches law in the presence of his master.]

5. M. Sheq. 4 : 7—R. Pappyas: "I have heard traditions according to both Eliezer and Joshua."
6. b. Suk. 28a: Eliezer: "I never said anything I did not hear from my masters."
7. Tos. Yev. 13 : 3-5—Ishmael says only Eliezer is fully consistent *re* minor females and says he approves his opinion.
8. M. Neg. 9 : 3, 11 : 7—Judah b. Batyra supports Eliezer's tradition.
9. M. Par. 1 : 1/Midrash Tanḥuma Ḥuqat 24—God, to Moses, praises Eliezer's traditions.
10. M. Toh. 8 : 7—Simeon brother of ʿAzariah rejects Eliezer's and Joshua's traditions as inaccurate.
11. Tos. Nid. 1 : 9, b. Nid. 7b/M. Nid. 1 : 3, 5—When Eliezer was alive, people followed his ruling.
12. b. Nid. 9b—Rabbi ruled in accordance with Eliezer, and, when he realized it, he said it is all right to do so in an emergency.
13. M. Yad. 4 : 3/b. Yev. 16a—Eliezer has a tradition from Yoḥanan b. Zakkai, back to Sinai.
14. Tos. Ed. 1 : 4—Eliezer is mentioned as an individual to indicate the law is contrary to his view. M. Ed. 1 : 6: Judah does not mention Eliezer explicitly.
15. Tos. Sot. 15 : 3—When Eliezer died, Torah was annulled.
16. Tos. Hul. 2 : 24—Eliezer learned something from Jesus.

17. Sifré Deut. 188—Tannas would confuse Eliezer's and Joshua's opinions, contrary to Deut. 19 : 14.
18. y. M.Q. 3 : 1—The Tannas mix up Eliezer's opinions with those of others, so states Judah the Patriarch, who says otherwise he should teach the law in accord with Eliezer's view.
19. b. Sanh. 68a-b—Eliezer: No one asked me questions, so much learning dies with me.
20. y. A.Z. 3 : 1—Jacob b. R. Idi + Joshua b. Levi: Eliezer would have received the holy spirit, but the generation is unworthy.
21. b. B.M. 59b—Heaven itself endorsed Eliezer's opinion.
22. y. Sanh. 1 : 2—Ba: Yoḥanan b. Zakkai ordained Eliezer.

v. Conclusion

The data we have surveyed make possible the development of sound criteria for the evaluation of the relative usefulness of various traditions about Eliezer b. Hyrcanus. We must regard as the best traditions, and probably reliable reports, materials for which we have chains of tradition and Yavnean attestations. The reason is that, concerning such materials, we know how a tradition was framed and handed on. We therefore can assess the possible presence of special interests or tendencies which may have affected its formation and transmission. We have reason to claim the responsible authority knew, or should have known, what he was talking about. And we stand very close to the person of Eliezer himself. A tradition already attested at Yavneh on the face of it should be dependable, for Eliezer himself is supposed to have lived through much of the Yavnean period—to about 90 at the least—and therefore should have exerted some control over the formulation and transmission of sayings he originally produced. The larger numbers of such sayings, moreover, come down in the names of, or are attested by, masters alleged to have been Eliezer's own students and colleagues. We therefore are on firm ground in postulating that the master has been accurately represented by authorities who knew what they were talking about on the basis of direct, first-hand experience. The traditions attested at Yavneh and with Yavnean chains of traditions therefore constitute the most reliable corpus of materials, against which all others are to be tested.

Traditions attested by, or in the name of, Judah b. Ilai, moreover, ought to be no less dependable, for Judah's father, Ilai, is repeatedly described as Eliezer's disciple, so Judah should have known from his father, if not directly from Eliezer, what the master had taught.

Even the best traditions, however, cannot be regarded as

stenographic reports of what Eliezer actually said. Indeed, it is difficult to imagine that a report consisting of

> One does not give Heave-offering for the unclean from the clean. R. Eliezer says, "One gives Heave-offering from the clean for the unclean. . ."

begins in a little dialogue, in which one master, or an anonymous chorus of masters, states the first line, and Eliezer, in the solo part, pronounces the second. Whatever Eliezer originally taught has been reworked for inclusion in an objective and neutral framework of laws, organized along logical and orderly lines, independent of Eliezer's own agendum, viewpoint, and circle of disciples. At some point before the Bar Kokhba War, however, something very like the opinion of Eliezer must have been stated in his name, for later masters in the middle or late period of Yavneh's history evidently knew both the anonymous opinion and Eliezer's. We cannot be sure that they knew these opinions in the exact form and wording now before us. But for our purposes, it is sufficient to be able to show that Eliezer held such an opinion. It is important to know whether he said it in the words before us only if we propose a close exegesis *not* of the legal theme, but of the language of the opinion in the very formulation now at hand; and this, while desirable, is not necessary for our limited historical-biographical purposes. In claiming that Yavnean traditions attested at Yavneh, with or without sound chains of transmission, are relatively reliable testimonies, I thus suggest that what is reliable is the substance of the opinion attributed to Eliezer. As to both the form in which it occurs and the exact wording, we as yet are able to say nothing.

This, however, means that even the best traditions about Eliezer —and these certainly are better than the preserved traditions about pre-70 masters, the Houses, or Yoḥanan b. Zakkai—are not so good as we might hope. They are not traditions to which Eliezer has given final form; they are not autobiographical; they are not in exactly Eliezer's language; and they were not finally redacted under the ultimate control of Eliezer himself. Others in his own time and for a long while thereafter had a share in the redaction of even these traditions (below, pp. 365-383). But from the viewpoint of the history of the rabbinic tradition, these are the first comparatively useful historical materials about an individual master.

One cannot compare their historical usefulness, however, to that of the sorts of traditions a man might produce for and about himself. For all his limitations, Josephus, for example, has given us the record of his own view of things in pretty much his own language. That record seems not to have undergone a process of transmission, and therefore revision and 'improvement,' for hundreds of years before it reached the form now before us. Nor did the opinion of Josephus carry preponderant weight, so as to form the basis for appeal to 'ancient authorities.' This fact generally preserved Josephus from the fabrications of the pious of later times, since, apart from the alleged Christian interpolations, no one had any practical interest in counterfeiting in his name stories made up only later on. But since, like all the other Tannaitic masters, Eliezer's opinion was authoritative long after he died—if only to assure acceptance of the opposite view—it was in some measure normal for a later master, or tradent, or even a scribe, to add a negative, or to switch Eliezer's opinion with that of the majority, or to give in Eliezer's name the opinion of his opponent—and in later Tannaitic and early Amoraic times, these things certainly were done. We know of a few instances. We do not know in how many more Eliezer's words have been subjected to the improvement of people with a vested interest in having him say something other than what he or his disciples had originally handed on.

The best traditions, therefore, are excellent primarily by comparison with traditions first attested later on, at Usha, and those lacking a chain of tradition. These we may regard as better traditions. They are better than materials attested later on or not at all because they find attestation in comments of masters who were taught by Yavneans. In Eliezer's case, moreover, the Ushan masters ought to have had accurate information, for they had studied with ʿAqiba—so we are told—and therefore had direct access, if primarily through him, to Joshua's and Eliezer's teachings. If Eliezer's materials transmitted through the circles around ʿAqiba are less credible than materials deriving from Eliezer directly or from Ilai and Judah b. Ilai, they are considerably more credible than materials the derivation of which we do not know at all. When we considered Ushan attestations of Houses' pericopae, we noticed that the Ushans generally revised the earlier definitions both of their protases and of their apodoses. We could take seriously the thematic agenda of Houses' laws attested by the Ushans, but we found it difficult to accept the exact definitions of those disputes and decided laws. If the Ushans tended to refine the legal disputes of the Houses, it probably was because they had before them a statement of those disputes in a grosser form, concerning a more fundamental question, than later seemed appropriate for debate. But with Eliezer the Ushans ought to have done less by way of revision of the received materials, because of the presence of Judah b. Ilai, on the one side, and because of the information coming from ʿAqiba himself, on the other. These attestations ought, therefore, to be more reliable than the Ushan ones for the Houses' pericopae.

The fair traditions are those attested at Bet Shearim, in the circle of masters around Judah the Patriarch. That they might uncover reliable Eliezer-traditions unknown for a century seems unlikely, but not impossible; we cannot claim that the formulation and redaction of the traditions from Yavneh, and even Usha, proceeded in so thorough, systematic, and orderly a way as to leave out nothing and to include everything authentic.

What first surfaces in Mishnah-Tosefta cannot be dismissed, but, so far as possible, must be measured against the contents of materials already well-attested before then. Before a more detailed picture of the formation of Mishnah-Tosefta and of the ways in which earlier materials were preserved until inserted in that compilation is available, however, we can offer no very firm opinion on the usefulness of such material as first occurs there. That few chains of tradition extend from Yavneh through the Mishnah seems to me an important limitation on the credibility of materials first known in Mishnah-Tosefta.

The suppressed traditions form an important problem. Together with the various sayings and stories about the impairment of the transmission of Eliezer's traditions, they raise the question of how complete, accurate and reliable a picture we have of the whole lot. In studying the suppressed traditions, we must wonder whether considerations of original content have proved decisive, or whether the politics surrounding the final formation of Judah the Patriarch's Mishnah somehow produced a prejudice against Eliezer's name and authority. We shall ask whether what seems to be Eliezer's tradition, according to Tosefta or the allegation of a *baraita*, or because of consistency with what Eliezer says in some other place, or because of something contained in a later story, in fact is Eliezer's and has been suppressed. Or is it someone else's idea which is merely congruent to Eliezer's known views but not originally and uniquely his—therefore not a sign of deliberate revision or suppression?

The predominant question in our analysis of the traditions is, What attitude toward Eliezer appears in the several discrete pericopae? Particularly among the best and the better traditions, are we able to discern specific tendencies, not articulated, concerning Eliezer's authority and the accuracy of his legal traditions? And if we do see such tendencies, where do they occur and how consistently? We have not raised these larger questions in the analysis of the discrete pericopae, for until the survey of attestations was completed, we had no reason to think a given pericope might reflect the conditions of one circle or school in preference to some other. I erred in *Development of a Legend* in taking for granted that ʿAqiban agenda lay hidden behind every pericope in an ʿAqiban compilation, Ishmaelean agenda behind each in an Ishmaelean one. This produced a monomanic interpretation concerning war and peace, as though the discrete pericopae had all been redacted at a time at which that one issue predominated. The interpretation of tendencies of the discrete pericopae has to follow, not precede, the establishment, where possible, of the historical circumstances pertinent to that interpretation.

CHAPTER EIGHT

THE BEST TRADITIONS

i. Yavnean Attestations

We assume that if a later Yavnean master gives evidence of having known a teaching in the name of Eliezer, then that teaching in Eliezer's name may be presumed to have been in existence, in substance if not in the exact form and language now before us, before the time of said master. But in so assuming, do we not take for granted in the case of the later Yavnean what we deny to Eliezer, namely, that the saying attributed to the master in question has actually been said by him? Having denied a mere allegation that Eliezer made a statement is to be taken for granted, we thus seem to accept at face value the allegation that someone *after* Eliezer has made a statement with respect to Eliezer and his opinions. Furthermore, in regard to the Houses' traditions, we likewise assumed that if a statement is attributed to Eliezer about a dispute between the Houses of Shammai and Hillel, the dispute between the Houses comes before Eliezer's time. He knew the dispute, it has been claimed, in pretty much its present formulation, and commented on it. So as we proceed from the earliest strata to the later ones, we seem to postpone the inevitable problem of the veracity of both attributions and what is attributed, taking for granted when studying the former generations the validity of sayings attributed to their successors, then bringing into doubt those very sayings as we proceed to examine the traditions attributed to the successors themselves. Why take at face value what is attributed to Eliezer in reference to the Houses but raise questions about sayings attributed to Eliezer in reference to issues evidently current in his own time or subjects untreated by antecedent authorities?

The answer lies in the original definition of attestations (*Phar.* III, pp. 180-184): By attestation is meant the effort to find a *terminus ante quem* for a pericope in some evidence outside the structure of the pericope itself. If a saying is attributed to a later master concerning a pericope, but the master evidently stands outside of the pericope, we suppose that the issue or opinion given in the pericope was known to him. That assumption is based upon the principle that, if a saying is attributed to a master, he supplies a firm *terminus a quo* for the saying.

Within the rabbinic circles no one earlier was likely to have said it, if the substance of the saying begins with him, for such a claim of priority simply is not made in respect to that saying by the rabbinic tradents later on. Obviously, it was common enough pseudepigraphically and anachronistically to attribute to an early authority an opinion formulated only after on, so as to gain greater credence for the opinion. But we need not claim more than did the pseudepigraphs themselves. If they were willing to go to an early Yavnean authority but not to Simeon the Just or Hillel, then we hardly are justified in reading the saying in anything like its present form back into Simeon's or Hillel's time. The pseudepigraphs thus supply a limit to the possible anachronisms to be taken into account.

When, moreover, we suppose Eliezer supplies an attestation for a dispute between the Houses, we claim only that that dispute was known *in Yavnean times.* In *Phar.* III, pp. 199-209, 223-231, we treated Yavnean attestations as a group, for our claim was only that what evidently was known to Yavneans may *as a whole* be taken to represent the state of the Houses' tradition by the end of the Yavnean period. Our stress was on the themes of the allegedly attested pericopae, not on their specific wording or rulings. We did not take for granted more than that a saying attributed to Eliezer glossing a Houses' dispute did not come before the time of Eliezer. Unless shown otherwise, we further supposed the Houses' dispute was not formulated all at once so as to include Eliezer's gloss. It was, after all, commonplace to include Yavneans (e.g., ʿAqiba) within the structure of Houses' dispute and therefore unnecessary to construct pericopae in such a way as to leave the Yavneans solely in the position of mere commentators or glossators—unless that is exactly what they were.

For detailed information we never relied on a single pericope with its attestation or on the attestations of a single master. What we found were remarkable thematic consistencies *among* the attestations of the several Yavnean masters. Taken together, they seemed to show that the Yavneans had in hand Houses' materials in a narrowly-circumscribed range of subjects: agricultural tithes, offerings and taboos; uncleanness laws; and Sabbath and festival laws (*Phar.* III, p. 227). Because the sayings attributed to a large number of individual Yavnean masters seemed to reflect knowledge of much the same agendum, it seemed likely that the Yavneans as a group knew about Houses' materials appropriate to that agendum. That was our sole claim about the substance of the Houses' pericopae in Yavnean times. It also seemed likely that the Houses' form was known to Yavneans, for practically everyone at Yavneh knew pericopae in that form. So what we have taken at face value is only attributions of sayings about given subjects to particular Yavnean masters, not the veracity in detail of all that is attributed. Our view therefore is that if to the more important Yavneans is attributed knowledge of the Houses' dispute-form, that form probably comes no later than those Yavneans. If, likewise, many Yavneans are supposed to have known about Houses' rulings on a certain, limited legal agendum, then those rulings are apt to come no later than the group of Yavneans to which the sayings are attributed. We are very far indeed from taking at face value pretty much everything attributed to the early Yavneans about the Houses' disputes.

All we have really postulated is that the several masters' materials were not pseudepigraphically produced all at once, in a single circle, by the same hand, when Mishnah-Tosefta was compiled, that is, long after the period in question. We have supposed that those materials were produced in various places, times, and circles, by differing authorities, some of them nearer, others farther, from the period of the masters themselves. When, therefore, we notice important points in common among discrete sources, we legitimately suppose that those points in common are to be taken—in a general way—as testimony about the state of affairs prevailing at the very latest by the middle or latter part of the Yavnean period.

Yavnean attestations of Eliezer's traditions likewise cannot be taken to mean that the traditions were, individually and in detail, in their present form by the end of the Yavnean period and generally known to Yavnean masters. We therefore do not take at face value what Yavneans other than, and after, Eliezer were supposed to have said, while calling into question what Eliezer himself is alleged to have taught. We seek a picture of what several individuals or circles of disciples in different places and at different times in the Yavnean period seem to have known in regard to Eliezer. We do take for granted that those several individuals were not in collusion but approached the Eliezer-materials from varying perspectives; further, that the traditions of the several individuals were handed on in different ways to different circles. Hence points of agreement among the various authorities ought to suggest a few reliable generalities about the state of opinion about Eliezer before ca. 120 A.D. We shall first review the pericopae with Yavnean attestations, and then suggest what may be said on the basis of the best traditions.

ii. The Laws

1-2. *Clean Heave-offering for Unclean*

Tos. Ter. 3 : 18/M. Ter. 2 : 1 and Tos. Hal. 1 : 10/M. Hal. 2 : 8 concern a fundamental principle in the giving of Heave-offering. The anonymous rule states that one does not give Heave-offering from what is clean for what is unclean, but if one has done so, the Heave-offering is acceptable. Eliezer holds a still more lenient view, that one may do so in the first place. Likewise, Eliezer says one may take clean Dough-offering for the unclean. Eliezer obviously will accept the principle that one may not give from worse for better produce, hence unclean for clean; otherwise people would routinely give the poorer for the better. But the whole complex of rules about not giving Heave-offering from one variety of produce for some other variety of produce here finds its first major exception. Eliezer's ruling, if brought to its logical conclusion, ought to have loosened up other rules as well and in later stages of development to have allowed the giving of Heave-offering from grapes for wine, or from raisins for grapes. In M. Ter. 1 :4 we have a Houses' dispute about giving Heave-offering from olives for oil or grapes for wine. One does not do so. If one has done so, the House of Shammai say, "It may still be deemed Heave-offering for the olives or grapes themselves"—but not for the wine. Eliezer does not rule on that question, but in allowing an exception in the rigid rules, he might, as observed, have come to such a conclusion. At any rate he is in a lenient position *vis à vis* the anonymous rule, as is the House of Shammai *vis à vis* the House of Hillel.

Tos. Ter. 3 : 18 provides a chain of tradition for M. Ter. 2 : 1. Ilai here quotes Eliezer in exactly the language given in M. Ter. in Eliezer's name without Ilai's attestation. He further explains that in Eliezer's opinion dry (therefore, clean) produce may be given as Heave-offering even if it is not nearby.

Tos. Ter. 3 : 16 has Eliezer supply a Houses' dispute on a related issue. If a man give Heave-offering of grapes intended for eating but then made the grapes into raisins, it is Heave-offering—even though this produce whose preparation has been eventually completed serves as Heave-offering for produce whose preparation has not been completed, for one does not have to give Heave-offering a second time. Eliezer says the House of Shammai say one does not have to give Heave-offering a second time—the anonymous ruling—and the

House of Hillel say one does have to give Heave-offering a second time.

I can imagine no reason for Ilai to have invented in Eliezer's name so novel a position. It is possible, to be sure, that Ilai had to attribute to his master a position he himself originated, so as to secure acceptance of his own opinion. But in Tos. Ter. 3 : 16 Eliezer himself is alleged to have given as a dispute between the Houses, with the House of Shammai in a position congruent to his own, what was also known as an undisputed law. M. Ter. 1 : 4 has the dispute in Eliezer's version—that is, as an argument between the Houses—but Eliezer is not cited as formulator of the dispute.

Accordingly, three versions of the matter existed: (1) An anonymous, unanimous statement of the law in accord with the opinion attributed by Eliezer to the House of Shammai; (2) Eliezer's statement that the matter is disputed by the Houses; (3) the representation of the matter as disputed by the Houses without Eliezer's allegation to that effect. Now one fact seems sure: after ca. 100-120 A.D. a master who wanted his ideas to be accepted would attribute them to the House of Hillel or to a unanimous rabbinical consensus. By the Bar Kokhba War the tendency of rabbinic circles, particularly under ʿAqiba's leadership, was to favor the opinion of the House of Hillel. With the reconstitution of the rabbinical authority at Usha it was perfectly clear that the law would follow the opinion of the House of Hillel. So we have no reason whatever to suppose a post-120 master would attribute to the House of Shammai an opinion he wished to have accepted. Yet Eliezer is supposed—by Ilai's testimony—to have taken a position roughly congruent to that of the Shammaites, and he is supposed—by Tos. Ter. 3 : 16A—to have claimed that what someone knew as a unanimous opinion was in fact only that of the House of Shammai. I see two possible explanations. Either he agreed with the opinion and attributed the dispute to the Houses and his own view to the House of Shammai, because the pericope was early and a Shammaite attribution would strengthen the possibility of acceptance of his view. Or a later master wished to set aside the testimony of an anonymous, unanimous law, with which he in fact differed, and therefore put into Eliezer's mouth the allegation that the law was the opinion of the House of Shammai and disputed by the House of Hillel. Doing so at once set aside the authority of the anonymous version and called into question the acceptability of its (=the House of Shammai's) opinion. Since Eliezer was (later on) taken to be a Shammaite, he would be expected to know the facts of the matter. In that case the Tos. Ter. 3 : 16B-evidence would derive from a period long after Yavneh. Between these two possibilities, the evidence of Ilai seems to me to favor the former. It was Eliezer's real opinion. Ilai knew it with respect to the problem of Heave-offering and attributed it to Eliezer because he had learned it from Eliezer.

3. *Cakes of Thank-offering of Nazirites*

Tos. Hal. 1 : 6/M. Hal. 1 : 6 deals with the liability for giving the Dough-offering of cakes from the Thank-offering made by the Nazirite. Ilai reports he asked Joshua, who said they were free of liability. He asked Eliezer, who said that, if made for the Nazir's own use, they are free of liability; but, if for sale, they are liable. Eleazar b. ʿAzariah then states his approval of Eliezer's opinion, saying that it comes from Mount Horeb. But M. Hal. 1 : 6 gives Eliezer's opinion in exactly his words without citing his name. Then b. Pes. 38b has the same structure, built upon a question of Ilai. But this time Ilai asks Eliezer about fulfilling with the cakes of the Thank-offering of the Nazirite one's obligation on Passover to eat *maṣṣah.* Eliezer says he does not know. He then asks Joshua, who gives the rule in M. Hal. 1 : 6, but now, with reference to Passover *maṣṣah.* Then Ilai tells Eliezer, who affirms Joshua's teaching comes from Sinai (not Horeb).

It is difficult to assess this pericope. If we take for granted Ilai really stated what he is alleged to have said, then it follows that M. Hal. 1 : 6 indeed is Eliezer's formulation. Eleazar b. ʿAzariah really said Eliezer's traditions are as good as if revealed at Sinai. And Joshua did not know the law. But we do not know how such a story, told in the first-person, was made up and transmitted. It is patently self-serving for the cause of Eliezer; it represents him as the most reliable authority of his own time. While we may regard that inference as clear and present, we do not know for sure it comes from Ilai. And we are not certain it would not have surprised Eleazar b. ʿAzariah.

I am inclined to ignore the version of b. Pes. 38b, which follows the form but bypasses the substance of Tos.

As to M. Hal. 1 : 6—and other Mishnaic pericopae in which a teaching attributed to Eliezer is given either anonymously or in someone else's name—it is difficult to say whether Eliezer has deliberately been dropped or was left out for some other reason. One such reason would be that a number of authorities held the same opinion, which was neither originated by, nor unique to, Eliezer himself. Perhaps the authority behind M. Hal. 1 : 6 did not know the allegation that Eliezer had in the first place laid down that particular law; or, if he knew it, perhaps he simply did not accept the attribution as valid. So we cannot be sure that the omission of Eliezer's name here was because of a desire to suppress his teachings. Nor do we know that it was because of a hope to secure greater acceptance of the law by giving it anonymously rather than in Eliezer's own name (if it was Eliezer's to begin with). Nor may we be sure that Tos. Hal. 1 : 6 has not been invented by someone who does not agree with M. Hal. 1 : 6 and therefore wishes to attribute the already-redacted tradition to Eliezer so as to secure its rejection—though the nature of the story in Tos. Hal. 1 : 6 seems to me too friendly to Eliezer to support this last alternative.

4. [= *No. 15*] *ʿOrlah-Laws Abroad*

Tos. Orl. 1 : 8 deals with the application of the *ʿorlah*-taboo outside of Palestine. A chain extending from Yavneh to the circle of Rabbi—Leazar b. R. Yosah + Yosah b. Durmasqit + Yosah the Galilean + Yoḥanan b. Nuri + Liezer the Great—says the taboo does not apply outside of the land. The foregoing, anonymous rule states that when in doubt, the *ʿorlah*-taboo does not apply in Syria and abroad; Judah says the case in doubt in Syria is treated as in Palestine, that is, *ʿorlah*-fruit is prohibited.

M. Qid. 1 : 9, without a chain of tradition, has Eliezer add the law of new produce to a list specifying that *ʿorlah* and mixed seeds *are* observed abroad.

Eliezer's saying in Tos. Orl. has nothing to do with the status of Syria. But Judah's certainly does, and in later strata Eliezer is represented as claiming Syria for the Jews, just as does Judah.

5. *The Status of the Etrog*

Tos. Shev. 4 : 21/M. Bik. 2 : 6 deal with the status of an *etrog.* Gamaliel says it is like a tree in three ways, and like a vegetable in one; Eliezer says it is like a tree in all respects. Tos. Shev. has a story that ʿAqiba picked an *etrog* on the first of Shevaṭ and did with it according to the opinions of both Houses (*Phar.* II, pp. 80-81), who had disputed the date of the New Year of the trees. Then Yosah b. R. Judah says ʿAqiba also followed the opinions of both Gamaliel and Eliezer. Yosah thus glosses the story to introduce the issue debated by Eliezer and

Gamaliel—which does not occur in the *maʿaśeh*. The original story therefore cannot attest to Yavnean knowledge of the dispute in M. Bik.

But Yosah—grandson of Ilai—does supply an additional clause to associate ʿAqiba with Eliezer as much as with Gamaliel. Incidentally, he also has Eliezer as the second party, parallel to the form of M. Bik., and parallel also to the normal position of the House of Hillel. Eliezer says with respect to tithes one follows the formation of the fruits. Since the *etrog* formed its fruits in the second year, it is liable to Second Tithe—in conformity with the Hillelite opinion, but not for the same reason. So Eliezer, according to the tradition of Ilai's grandson, stands more or less with the House of Hillel.

6. *Ilai's List*

M. Eruv. 2 : 5-6 has Ilai's list of three things heard from Eliezer: 1. "And even if it is about a *kor's* space;" 2. Forgetting to prepare an *ʿeruv*; 3. Hart's tongue as a bitter herb. Ilai's saying (1) is formulated so as to take for granted the language of M. Eruv. 2 : 5, the debate between Judah b. Bava, Judah [b. Ilai], ʿAqiba, Eliezer/Eleazar, and Yosi—a strange mixture. "And even if it is about a *kor's* space" cannot be understood outside of the context of M. Eruv. 2 : 5 and refers explicitly to the saying of Judah b. Bava, "The garden and the outer area which are not more than seventy cubits and two-thirds by seventy cubits and two-thirds." Eliezer is supposed, therefore, to have said a *kor's* space, and not the small space defined by Judah b. Bava + ʿAqiba. So we have a development of a debate between ʿAqiba and Eliezer, with Ilai attesting the existence of Eliezer's opinion. But this is curious, for Judah b. Bava does not allude to ʿAqiba as the authority for clause (1) of his opinion. Then the next two items on the list are formulated as complete statements of laws, without contrary opinions. And finally we have the formula, "I besought... and found no colleague [who knew these same opinions]." Judah b. Bava's version thus has the antecedent dispute about the size of a field surrounded by a wall; ʿAqiba says what is decisive is the size; Eliezer says the presence of a wall makes all the difference. It seems Ilai's saying should constitute adequate attestation of some such dispute between ʿAqiba and Eliezer.

As to (2) we notice Eliezer is in a lenient position *vis à vis* M. Eruv. 6 : 3, which prohibits all from using the courtyard; Eliezer says the one who forgot to make an *ʿeruv* is prohibited, but the others are permitted to use it.

Likewise in (3) Eliezer says one may fulfill his obligation with colopendrium. The opposite opinion can only be, One does *not* fulfill his obligation. b. Pes. 39a has Ilai find a *ḥaver* in the person of Eliezer b. Jacob.

Ilai thus represents Eliezer as a more lenient authority than others. His list has survived, but only outside the framework of the pericopae in which the individual items of the list should have been included. The exclusion of Eliezer's lenient rulings, *but* their preservation in Ilai's list, is striking.

ʿAqiba also asserted in M. Shev. 8 : 9-10, that he knew traditions about Eliezer which are suppressed or not available to the disciples. The law here, however, comes in two versions. M. Shev. 8 : 9B-D has a simple dispute between Eliezer and the sages about hide anointed with oil of the Seventh Year. Eliezer says it is to be burned. The sages say otherwise. Then in E-F, we have a colloquy between ʿAqiba and "them." "They" cite Eliezer, as in C, and ʿAqiba says he will not tell Eliezer's real opinion. The same pattern, but now without the antecedent, generalized formulation of the law, occurs in M. Shev. 8 : 10. "They" tell ʿAqiba that Eliezer says one cannot eat the bread of Samaritans. ʿAqiba responds that he will not tell Eliezer's real opinion. In the former instance there can be no doubt Eliezer's opinion was that one may indeed make use of the hide anointed with Seventh-Year oil. In the second it seems plausible that Eliezer took up a lenient position with respect to the Samaritan bread. In M. Shev. ʿAqiba does not present a "list," but once he is made to give one suppressed ruling, he gives the second as well. Since it is not related to the subject of the first, ʿAqiba ought to have had a little list of Eliezer's lenient rulings, just as did Ilai. These would seem similar to the lists of the lenient rulings of the House of Shammai in M. Ed. (*Phar.* II, pp. 324-343).

Do these assertions, attributed to Ilai and ʿAqiba, constitute probative evidence of the existence, by the end of Yavnean times, of such lists of rulings of Eliezer. Admittedly, we cannot take at face value an allegation that ʿAqiba or Ilai has said something about Eliezer, if we are not prepared to grant credence to what is alleged in regard to Eliezer himself or in regard to other sayings of Ilai and ʿAqiba. So we cannot regard the two pericopae as probative attestations concerning Eliezer's opinions. We have no Tannaitic attestions for either pericope. Both occur for the first time in the Mishnah-Toseftan stratum.

But the differences between the two lists seem important. First, they are attributed to different authorities—Ilai, ʿAqiba. Second, they are in different form. Ilai has a little list, depending on M. Eruv. ʿAqiba's pericope is in the form of two separate stories, constructed according to a single pattern. Third, they are about different subjects—Ilai's on the *ʿeruv* and on Passover, ʿAqiba's on Seventh Year laws and on the Samaritans. It seems to me difficult to suppose the lists derive from a single circle.

Nor is it reasonable that the lists come only from a very late authority, who has a special interest in fabricating and assigning these opinions to Eliezer so that they either will be accepted or rejected by his contemporaries. As to acceptance, later on that is excluded—by definition. As to rejection, in both sets of rulings Eliezer is an individual, as against "the sages" or "them," so there is no reason to fabricate a pericope to do what the accepted or normative tradition has already done. In ʿAqiba's list, the opinion that 'it is to be burned' is Eliezer's, as against the sages. The second is problematical. In Ilai's list, Eliezer's first opinion is opposed by ʿAqiba; his second stands against a majority opinion, given anonymously, in 6 : 3. The third has no equivalent. It would hardly seem likely, therefore, that the Ilai- and ʿAqiba-lists have been made up at the end of Tannaitic times—or indeed, at any time much after the beginning of Usha—for the purpose of securing rejection of what was formerly the accepted law.

Accordingly, the lists of both masters come from their respective circles and were not formulated by a single hand to make a single point or worked out only later in Tannaitic times. If so, we may take very seriously indeed what the two lists have in common: first, that Eliezer took a very lenient position on several matters of law; second, that his lenient views have been suppressed in the formulation of the normative tradition; third, that his disciples, Ilai and ʿAqiba, kept alive the memory of those original rulings. So someone has chosen to represent Eliezer in more strict positions than he held, so as to secure the acceptance of the lenient opinion (or of an opinion congruent to Eliezer's lenient viewpoint) originated by Eliezer in the first place. Who can that have been? It ought not to have been Ilai. He does not seem to have been important in the formulation of normative materials. But it could well have been ʿAqiba, who publicly taught one thing and privately another; the formulation of the law as both a story and as a generalized dispute in M. Shev. claims exactly that. If it was ʿAqiba, then he must have had a reason for revising what he had learned from Eliezer and accepted from him. That reason can be only some important event in the relationship between Eliezer and the larger body of the sages, an event which rendered Eliezer's traditions no longer acceptable within the consensus developing in Yavnean times or at Yavneh itself. At that point it became necessary for ʿAqiba to gain entry for Eliezer's opinions—which, after all, were regarded by him as valid and right—by claiming in Eliezer's name the opposite of what he originally had said. Ilai did otherwise; he simply preserved the traditions as best he could, and sought others who might testify both that Eliezer had said them and that they represented normative tradition. But, as noted, Ilai seems to have had a much smaller role in the formation of the preserved Yavnean materials than did ʿAqiba.

What was so controversial about these particular rulings? As to Ilai's: A wall around an area of any size would be sufficient to obviate the need for further provision of an *ʿeruv*. The contrary view imposes the requirement for an *ʿeruv* even where, at first glance, one ought not to be required. So the importance of the *ʿeruv* was to be enhanced. Likewise if one party to a joint *ʿeruv* forgot it, according to Eliezer that party alone was penalized. According to the opposite view, *everyone* was penalized. So social pressure on non-conformists in respect to the *ʿeruv* was greatly increased by the decided law. Since the validity of the *ʿeruv* was one of the points at issue between Pharisees and others, these two rulings of Eliezer put him outside of the circle of partisans of the strict enforcement of pre-70 Pharisaic rules.

As to Harts-tongue on Passover, I can say nothing other than that the ruling on the face of it is lenient.

With respect to ʿAqiba's: Eliezer clearly takes the view that the enforcement of the laws of Seventh-Year produce will be lenient. The agricultural taboos too were a central part of pre-70 Pharisaic rules. If a person disobeyed them, according to the opposition, he would be penalized by losing valuable property. Eliezer held contrariwise. So Eliezer was in the position of imposing no penalty at all in the enforcement of one Seventh-Year rule, again contrary to what surely was the emphasis of the circle holding to the pre-70 Pharisaic position.

As to the Samaritans, if Eliezer said one might eat Samaritan bread, that meant he supposed the Samaritans should be regarded in respect to cooking as no different from Israelites. We do not know the attitude of pre-70 Pharisaism toward the Samaritans. But the Gospel stories, reaching final form at this same time, introduce the same issue. Mt. 10 : 5 has Jesus tell the disciples to keep out of Samaria. Lk. 10 : 51

has the Samaritans refuse to receive Jesus. But as to the Pharisees, the good Samaritan is preceded by a Priest and a Levite, but not a Pharisee (Lk. 10 : 29-37). While we do not know Eliezer's position *vis à vis* that of pre-70 Pharisaism in general, we may say that the issue of the Samaritans was important after 70, and on it Eliezer took the view that they were to be treated, so far as pertinent, like Israelites.

ʿAqiba or some of those responsible for the redaction of his materials took a highly favorable view of the opinions of Eliezer and made efforts to secure the acceptance of those opinions, even at the expense of assigning them to someone other than Eliezer himself. Both ʿAqiba and Ilai had difficulty in advancing Eliezer's views. And if our suggestion about the substance of the laws is correct, it must further mean that Eliezer took a substantially more liberal view of the law than others in his time. Specifically, he was prepared to limit the enforcement of two important laws of pre-70 Pharisaism, the *ʿeruv*, about which Pharisees and Sadducees are supposed to have disputed (and here the evidence is very strong indeed), and the rigid enforcement of rules on the use of Seventh Year produce. Whether or not Eliezer was himself a Pharisee in pre-70 times or at least represented at Yavneh a viewpoint within pre-70 Pharisaism is a question we cannot yet raise. Nor are we presently able to speculate on the relationship between Eliezer and the pre-70 Houses. But we may propose that in post-70 times, Eliezer was among those who would have defined the law in such a way as to make relatively easy the acceptance of the Pharisaic discipline by non-Pharisees, both by placing limits on social pressures exerted on them, and by liberal interpretation of a law on agricultural produce of the Seventh Year. This second point is congruent to what we have already proposed with respect to the rules on giving Heave-offering; Eliezer proposed to suspend some of the rigid distinctions imposed upon different categories of produce deriving from the same species, beginning with clean and unclean produce—a fundamental matter.

7. *Dough-Offering on the Fifteenth of Nisan*

In M. Pes. 3 : 3, Joshua seems to stand outside the framework of the already-completed pericope involving a dispute between Eliezer and Judah b. Batyra. The issue is how to separate Dough-offering in uncleanness on the fifteenth of Nisan. Eliezer says the woman should not designate it as such until the dough is baked. Judah says she should put the dough in cold water. Then Joshua rejects the problem entirely. The woman should simply do things in the normal way (not on the 15th of Nisan at all!). He says that the prohibition of leaven on Passover is not the woman's problem, parallel to his view in M. Ter. 8 : 11. Eliezer's opinion likewise is consistent with his rulings in M. Ter. 8 : 8-11: One has to avoid violating the law by taking affirmative action. Joshua there says one need do nothing at all, and if the law is broken, it is broken.

The same principle is debated, moreover, in the collection of M. Zev. 8 : 5-12. The issue there is what to do with blood to be sprinkled once which was mixed with blood to be sprinkled four times. Eliezer says the whole mixture should be sprinkled four times, Joshua, once. Eliezer's principle is that if one does not sprinkle the whole four times, he violates the law not to diminish observance of the commandments. Joshua says if one does so, he violates the law against adding to the commandments. Then Joshua says, "When you sprinkled, you transgressed *You shall not add* and transgress with your own hand, but when you do not sprinkle, you transgress *You shall not diminish*, but you do *not* do a sin with your own hand." In 8 : 11, Eliezer does not participate in solving a parallel problem, but he opposes ʿAqiba, who takes a position inconsistent with his own in 8 : 10. The whole complex in M. Zev. has several Ushan attestations, most notably in Tos. Zev. 8 : 20: Judah b. Ilai, who turns out to be the authority responsible for the bulk of M. Zev. 8 : 8 as we now have it.

Three quite unrelated cases revolve around the same legal principle and involve several Yavnean circles: Eliezer + Judah b. Batyra, Eliezer + ʿAqiba, and Eliezer + Joshua. The issue in all three cases is whether a man must exert himself to prevent an illegal situation, or whether he may simply stand by while such a situation takes shape on its own. Eliezer's view is clear and consistent, and Judah b. Batyra agrees with him. But Joshua and ʿAqiba do not. Their disagreement occurs in quite unrelated pericopae, which do not seem to have been spun out by a single hand. What is decisive in assigning the disputes to the best traditions is Judah's attestation, along with the evident attributions to a number of Yavnean authorities of disputes on the same principle, but wholly discrete details. No case of the Houses focuses on this principle; its attribution to dominant circles of early Yavneans strongly suggests the issue itself was first faced in Yavnean times.

Eliezer himself thus held the view that when one has the choice of action or inaction in the possible violation of the law, one should take action and possibly transgress, rather than do nothing and certainly allow a transgression to happen on its own.

8. *Sanctifying Cattle Fit for the Altar*

M. Sheq. 4 : 7 presents a dispute between Eliezer and Joshua on the disposition of cattle found in property sanctified to the Temple. Eliezer says the males are to be sold to people who require Whole-offerings, the females, to those who need Peace-offerings, and the proceeds of the sale are to be used for Temple funds. Joshua says the males themselves are sacrificed.

The issue is the intent of the man who made the gift. Did he intend that whatever was fit for the altar should be sacrificed on it? Or that the whole thing should be sold for the treasury unless otherwise specified? Eliezer says that, without an explicit statement of the man's intention, the whole thing is deemed intended for the Temple fund. Joshua says one may interpret the man's intention that the animals fit for sacrifice are to be offered, even though the man has said nothing.

The Yavnean attestations are impressive. First, we have ʿAqiba's comment, entirely outside the framework of the legal dispute. ʿAqiba commends Eliezer for his consistency. Then Pappyas says he has traditions which accord with each master's opinion; but in fact his traditions provide an explanation for the dispute. One tradition is that if a man is explicit in his donation, one follows his directions; then if he says nothing about the cattle, we assume he wants done what Eliezer has instructed. But if he says nothing at all, then one follows Joshua's opinion. But this is pretty much what Joshua has maintained at the outset. So the "tradition" is convenient from Joshua's viewpoint.

ʿAqiba's commendation of Eliezer's consistency accords with Ishmael's expression of the same opinion. Eliezer consistently holds that the deeds of a female minor are of no legal effect. Tos. Yev. 13 : 3-5 has the following for Ishmael: "I have reviewed all the logic of the sages and have found no one whose logic is consistent in respect to minor girls, except for Liezer." Then ʿAqiba's saying here is repeated—perhaps interpolated?—"For R. Liezer is consistent, and R. Joshua is inconsistent." Since other traditions in Ishmael's name are hostile to Eliezer, this is impressive testimony. It becomes apparent that Eliezer's ruling consistently according to a single principle about a number of different cases was commended by middle Yavneans —ʿAqiba, Ishmael—and later on as well.

The problem of intention is much debated in Houses' pericopae. In general, the House of Shammai hold intention is not taken into account in assessing an action. Thus, in M. Naz. 5 : 1-5, if a man says, "I am a Nazir," he is a Nazir, no matter how he then completes his sentence. The Hillelites hold a dedication made in error is not binding, therefore one takes account of a person's intention. This issue is attested as early as Ṭarfon. Here we have Eliezer in a position more or less parallel with that of the House of Shammai; unless one is *explicitly* informed of the man's intention, he ignores all but what in fact has been done, therefore treats the whole gift as for the Temple fund. Joshua is consistent with the House of Hillel in his willingness to interpret what the man has done without explicit knowledge of his plans. But the masters' opinions here could not by themselves have produced the Houses' dispute of M. Naz.

9. *Burning Unclean Sanctities*

M. Sheq. 8 : 6 deals with the flesh of Most Holy Things which contracted uncleanness, "whether from primary or secondary sources of uncleanness, whether inside or outside the court." The House of Shammai say everything is to be burned inside the court, except what has been made unclean by a primary source of uncleanness, which is to be burned outside. The House of Hillel take the opposite position: all is burned outside, save what is unclean from a derived uncleanness, which is burned inside.

M. Sheq. 8 : 7 then has Eliezer and ʿAqiba debate the same issue. What has contracted uncleanness from a primary source of uncleanness should be burned outside, from a derived source, inside—so Eliezer. ʿAqiba then says the location is decisive, not the source of uncleanness, therefore where uncleanness is contracted, there the holy things should be burned. Tos. Sheq. 3 : 16 supplies an Ushan attestation: Judah says Eliezer is consistent with the House of Shammai, ʿAqiba with the House of Hillel. But M. Sheq. 8 : 7 contains no allusion to the Houses and their dispute. And the dispute of M. Sheq. 8 : 6 seems to ignore the opinions of both Eliezer and ʿAqiba, for the House of Shammai say that what is decisive is uncleanness contracted from a primary source, which is to be burned outside, and the House of Hillel say what is decisive is uncleanness contracted from a secondary source, which is burned inside—both according to the principle of Eliezer (!).

Here we must consider M. M.S. 3 : 13: If Second Tithe was brought to Jerusalem and contracted uncleanness, whether from a primary or a secondary source of uncleanness, whether inside or outside the wall of Jerusalem, rather than the Temple court as above, the House of Shammai say all is to be redeemed and consumed within [the walls] except what is made unclean by a primary source of uncleanness, which is taken care of outside the walls. The House of Hillel say all is redeemed outside, except what was made unclean by a secondary source of uncleanness, which is redeemed inside the walls. Clearly, the two disputes between the Houses are about an identical problem, namely, where the holy produce or holy offerings are to be disposed of. The operative words are *inside/outside.* Both disputes are formulated according to Eliezer's view of what is decisive; the source of uncleanness, not the place in which the uncleanness was contracted, will be at issue. The superscriptions of both pericopae then ignore the substance of the Houses' opinions, by explicitly alluding to *whether within or without* the wall of Jerusalem—a consideration important only from ʿAqiba's perspective and then ignored by the body of the pericopae. But the superscriptions also say, *Whether from a primary or a secondary source of uncleanness*—thus rejecting the distinction important to ʿAqiba. So the superscriptions represent a compromise; the opinions of both masters are explicitly alluded to (and rejected!). But, as stated, the pericopae themselves then follow Eliezer's viewpoint in M. Sheq. 8 : 7.

Tos. M.S. 2 : 16 makes it clear that M. M.S. 3 : 13 is Judah b. Ilai's formulation of the dispute. Here is a case in which Judah's tradition clearly comes from his father, thence from Eliezer. But Meir also formulates matters so that the issue of the source of uncleanness is predominant. Then Leazar—obviously it should be Liezer—gives the opinion of Eliezer in M. Sheq. 8 : 7, and ʿAqiba's opinion in M. Sheq. is repeated. Tos. M.S. 2 : 16 further has Leazar/Liezer and ʿAqiba ignore the Houses' form entirely, just as they do in M. Sheq. 8 : 7 (!).

The opinion of ʿAqiba and Ḥanina Prefect of the Priests in M. Pes. 1 : 6 comes first of all. Ḥanina says, "The priests never refrained from burning flesh that had become unclean from a primary uncleanness, although they thereby added uncleanness to its uncleanness." Before one may debate on *where* such a burning may take place, he must acknowledge *that* it may take place at all. ʿAqiba in M. Pes. 1 : 6 states, "The priests never refrained from burning in a lamp rendered unclean by one that had contracted corpse-uncleanness [= a primary source of uncleanness.] [Heave-offering-]oil that was rendered unfit by one that had immersed himself the selfsame day [= a secondary source of uncleanness], although they thereby added uncleanness to its uncleanness." ʿAqiba's and Ḥanina's opinions are identical, but Ḥanina spoke in general terms, rather than specifying the primary and secondary sources, and he referred to meat, while ʿAqiba spoke in specific terms about the sources of uncleanness and alluded to oil. Accordingly, the sayings of ʿAqiba and Ḥanina stand at the beginning of the matter. Then follows the dispute of Eliezer and ʿAqiba.

It is striking that Ḥanina and ʿAqiba take for granted what is decisive is the *source* of uncleanness, rather than the location. And Eliezer makes this explicit. But in M. Sheq. ʿAqiba then introduces the further problem of where the uncleanness has been contracted. That issue does not contradict his former opinion; it simply produces the complication which then yields the dispute between the Houses(!)—a dispute which, according to Eliezer, ought not to take place at all, at least, not in terms of *inside/outside.*

Judah b. Ilai's and Meir's attestations of the dispute and Judah's conformity to Eliezer's opinion in formulating it seem important evidence of Eliezer's original opinion. And that opinion is consistent with the view of Ḥanina and ʿAqiba that the burning of the variously unclean holy things may take place all at once; but Eliezer opts for a simpler definition of the matter. None of these formulations of the problem(s) can have had practical consequences in early Yavnean times. The situation in the Temple obviously is not going to be illuminated by the Yavneans' disputes, especially so when at issue clearly is theory, not practice.

Judah b. Ilai thus has assured that Eliezer's opinion not only would register in its own terms but also would predominate in the definition of the Houses' dispute. Judah's observation about the consistency of Eliezer and ʿAqiba with the Shammaites and the Hillelites, respectively, may reflect the later imposition of the Houses' names on materials originally given in the names of the early Yavneans. For M. Sheq. 8 : 7 indicates that at the outset Eliezer and ʿAqiba knew nothing about the Houses' involvement in the *same* issue and so would have been surprised by the allegation that they represented one or the other of the Houses. Now, since Judah alludes to the Houses' disputing the matter, sometime toward the end of Yavnean times the issue ought to have been formulated in the names of the Houses of Shammai and Hillel, instead of Eliezer and ʿAqiba. This theory depends upon the supposition that M. Sheq. 8 : 7 was early but preserved after the formulation of the dispute in the Houses' names had been put forward. Then Judah, who had learned the Eliezer/ʿAqiba-version, commented on the fact that the Houses-formulation was parallel. But he evidently knew both.

10. *Deed of a Female Minor*

M. Yev. 13 : 2 contains Eliezer's general ruling, "The deed of a female child is nothing." This is then applied to the problem of a minor's exercising the right of refusal: "She is like one who has been seduced." The right of refusal therefore lies quite outside Eliezer's legal framework. His position is at variance with the Houses' view (M. Yev. 13 : 1), which accepts the validity and necessity of the right of refusal. Tos. Yev. 13 : 3-5 then defines the issue of the *Ketuvah* of a girl who has exercised the right of refusal. But Liezer says the action is null in law, therefore there is no issue. The attestation comes in Ishmael's praise of Liezer's consistency, in two lemmas, "I have reviewed all the logic..." and "I prefer..." Of the two, the first seems primary, the second an interpolated cliché.

Ishmael's attestation of Eliezer's consistency in applying his principles seems to me strong, because of ʿAqiba's parallel assertion. As to the specific issues before us, I see no reason to reject Ishmael's saying, for I can imagine no reason for someone's making it up later on and attributing it to him.

11. *Levir Refused by Minor*

M. Yev. 13 : 7 has a dispute between Eliezer and Gamaliel concerning the case of two sisters, one an adult, the other a minor, who were deaf-mutes. If the husband of the adult died, the minor is instructed to exercise the right of refusal, according to Eliezer. Gamaliel holds that, ideally, the minor should wait until she is of age, and at that point the widow is exempt from Levirate marriage as the "sister of his wife." On this dispute Joshua comments, "Woe to him..." Joshua's comment takes for granted the antecedent opinions, so should attest them. But Joshua's saying in fact contains a still stricter rule than that of either Eliezer or Gamaliel. So Joshua takes a position on the disputed issue, rather than commenting on it, and cannot attest the dispute. Further, Eliezer's opinion is inconsistent with his view that the deed of a minor female is of no legal consequence. So M. Yev. 13 : 7 cannot be said to have a Yavnean attestation, and the ruling attributed to Eliezer ought not to be his at all.

12-13. *Releasing Vows*

M. Ned. 9 : 1-2 presents two rulings in Eliezer's name, which, if adopted, would have ended the complications presented by the making of vows. Eliezer holds that one may release a man from his vow by reference to "the honor" of his father and mother. The sages prohibit doing so. Then Ṣaddoq says that, if so, one may release vows with reference to the honor of God, and consequently vows would no longer be effective. Then other "sages" modify the position attributed to the former sages. In relationship to a man's own dealings with his parents, vows may be released, but not on account of the "honor" of parents in general. Ṣaddoq cannot be thought identical to the first "sages," for he comments upon, and agrees with, their position. But he also is not identical with the second, for obvious reasons. The second "sages" seem to take account of Ṣaddoq's criticism. In all, then, Ṣaddoq evidently stands outside the pericope involving Eliezer and the (first) sages. If so, he supplies a very early Yavnean attestation for Eliezer's opinion.

Eliezer's view in M. Ned. 9 : 2 is consistent with the foregoing. One may release a man from a vow by reason of what happens unexpectedly. The sages differ. Eliezer's opinion is then applied to specific cases. Since 9 : 1 is to be assigned to Eliezer, 9 : 2, which reflects the same viewpoint, ought also to be both early and his. Eliezer's first ruling, carried to its logical conclusion in the second, would nullify the effects of vowing.

14. *Conditional Divorce*

In M. Git. 9 : 1 Eliezer rules that a conditional writ of divorce is valid. The ruling is attested by Yosi b. R. Judah, so b. Git. 82a-b. Tos. Git. 9 : 1-5 has a story about how, after Eliezer had died, Ṭarfon, Yosi, Eleazar b. ʿAzariah, and ʿAqiba met to refute the position of Eliezer. The y. and b. versions add that Joshua reproved them. The story itself draws together four proofs for the view contrary to Eliezer's. But the proofs are not equally valid and also tend to repeat one another. Yosi is repeated by Eleazar, Ṭarfon and ʿAqiba have essentially the same argument. So merely in order to state—in dramatic form—four separate objections to Eliezer's view it was unnecessary to invent such a story. It turns out in later rabbinic opinion that Eleazar b. ʿAzariah's is best. ʿAqiba's circle therefore is not the likely source of the story.

How valid an attestation do we have in this story? The story itself is not attested before the third century. It follows standard rabbinic form: four opinions expressed in a dramatic setting, thus a well-developed chria. The story-line of the tale consists of the introductory clause, that Eliezer had died, and the sages got together to refute his opinion—not an uncommon motif in Yavnean materials. But the sages, all middle- and later-Yavneans, are taken to be specific, differentiated individuals—a sign of authenticity. At the very least the story should indicate that the circles of disciples around four masters registered an opinion different from Eliezer's. But it also strongly suggests that the masters or their circles independently knew and rejected Eliezer's position. The assemblage of the four ought further to reflect a fairly wide-spread opposition to Eliezer. Other stories of Eliezer's death and legal issues introduced in that connection know nothing of the conditional divorce. Some of the same masters are involved in these stories—Eleazar b. ʿAzariah and ʿAqiba in particular, Joshua as well. From the tendency to link the death of Eliezer to legal issues I learn that a tendency of story-tellers—whether Yavnean or otherwise we cannot say—was to ask whether controversial opinions of Eliezer had ultimately been retracted by him, and whether his associates and their associates had refuted them.

Clearly, Eliezer's approval of a conditional writ of divorce represents a most controversial opinion. It is lenient in the extreme to allow a divorce to take effect if a woman is allowed by the husband to marry almost anyone else; the exclusion in no way is supposed to impair the force of the document. Divorce is all the easier; the husband may have revenge on a wife he conceives, without firm evidence, to have been unfaithful, even though he has no better recourse. Eliezer surely is consistent with the very lenient attitude of the House of Hillel (*Phar.* II, pp. 37-39) and with the position attributed to ʿAqiba in the same pericope. Eliezer's opinion here is consistent also with his strict position in M. Sot. 1 : 1: a husband, having warned his wife before two witnesses, may make her undergo the rite of the suspected adulteress merely on the basis of his own evidence. And his opinion in M. Sot. 6 : 1 is equally relevant; virtually any sort of evidence at all is acceptable. All this accords with his view, M. Sot. 3 : 4, that a man should not allow his daughter to study the Torah. While not conclusive, it is highly suggestive that a number of opinions of Eliezer on quite separate issues reveals an entirely consistent position, in favor of a man's rights over a woman's. Perhaps Eliezer's consistency in the matter led him to the extreme view attributed to him in M. Git. 9 : 1.

16. *Liability for Lost Redemption-lamb*

M. Bekh. 1 : 6 contains a dispute between Eliezer and sages on the responsibility for a redemption lamb, set aside for the firstling of an ass, which has died. Eliezer says the owner is liable and has to make it up. The sages differ. Then Joshua and Ṣaddoq testify about the issue, holding that the priest has no claim, thus consistent with the sages. But they are not represented as the sages; they stand outside the formulation of the argument. Their "testimony" is stated as though no contrary view existed, then attached to the pericope. Their saying supplies independent corroboration that the issue addressed by Eliezer was raised in his time, and that it was resolved in a way contrary to his opinion. Were Joshua's opinion included in Eliezer's pericope, it would provide no useful attestation. But standing outside, it indicates that a circle outside of Eliezer's faced the problem and resolved it in both form and substance in a way different from Eliezer.

17. *Dedicating Property*

In M. Ar. 8 : 4, Eliezer says a person may dedicate part of his flock but not all of it. Then Eleazar b. ʿAzariah has a saying taking for granted the foregoing and deriving a lesson from it, that people must not squander their property. As presently formulated, Eleazar's saying certainly attests knowledge of Eliezer's.

18. *Partitions in a 'Tent'*

In M. Kel. 8 : 1 Eliezer rules that food in a bee-hive hung in the air-space of an oven will not be made unclean on account of the presence of an insect in the oven. He then provides an argument in favor of his viewpoint, against the contrary opinion and argument of the sages. Yoḥanan b. Nuri in Tos. Kel. B.M. 6 : 4 comments on the debate: "I said to R. Eliezer." Then Yosi: "I said to Yoḥanan b. Nuri." Finally, *Rabbi said*, "The answer of R. Yosi is the same as the answer of R. Yoḥanan b. Nuri." It would seem, therefore, that Tos. supplies attestations from late Yavneh, Usha, and the time of Rabbi. M. characteristically omits all but the original dispute and debate. But both should have been in their present form by Yoḥanan b. Nuri's time, for he clearly stands outside their framework and comments on the substance of the debate. Whether he actually said *to* Eliezer, or merely with reference to Eliezer's opinion, what is attributed to him, we cannot say. Yosi's saying then takes for granted what has preceded, and Judah the Patriarch's likewise. I cannot see how the later masters may be held responsible for the formulation of the original dispute and debate. If they had, they should have stated matters in such a way as to convey their own opinions, not merely giving reasons for those of others and supplementing their formulation of a dispute of others with those opinions. So these would seem very strong attestations indeed.

At issue, then, is a matter of logic: Will the bee-hive not save from uncleanness what is in an earthenware vessel, seeing that it has the capacity to preserve the contents from the more severe corpse-uncleanness. The sages' reply is that partitions afford protection in a 'Tent,' but partitions do not afford protection in earthenware vessels. This in substance is a repetition of their original ruling, but now as a statement of argument, rather than as a legal opinion. So Eliezer's argument represents an effort to move beyond the decided law—which ought to accord with the sages' opinion—on the basis of a logical extension of *other* decided law. The sages' reply is simply to stand pat and to regard the decided law as imposing not merely the rule but also its own logic. Yoḥanan b. Nuri says to Eliezer merely what the sages have already said. Yosi then repeats, in other language, the same "argument." And Rabbi comments on that fact.

19. *A Shoe on the Last*

M. Kel. 26 : 4 has Eliezer's ruling that a shoe still on the last is insusceptible to uncleanness. Simeon b. Shezuri supplies a firm Ushan attestation by redefining the dispute in more complicated terms, so Tos. Kel. B.B. 4 : 7. We have what seems to be a further attestation in the death-stories of Eliezer, b. Sanh. 68a. Eleazar b. ʿAzariah there makes explicit reference to this pericope and affirms that to the end Eliezer remained certain the shoe was clean. Further, Judah b. Ilai provides an Ushan attestation for the problem, but not the issue of cleanness. Judah in the name of Eliezer says if the shoe on the last is loose, it is permitted to remove it on the Sabbath. Judah's issue is whether the shoe is regarded as finished if it is removed and returned to the last. The sages hold the work is not yet finished. The pericope recurs in Tos. Ed. 2 : 1, but without a usable attestation.

That the pericope is well attested by Judah b. Ilai and Simeon Shezuri seems beyond question. But what sort of attestation derives from the stories, themselves unattested, about Eliezer's death? Here matters seem less clear than with reference to the story accompanying M. Git. 9 : 1, for the story here simply alludes to Eliezer's opinion, rather than spelling out, in detail, opinions of several contemporary masters about that opinion. I am inclined, therefore, to dismiss b. Sanh. 68b as a strong, Yavnean attestation. The story could well come long after the pericope—it itself is unattested in Tannaitic strata—and simply allude to a random, earlier tradition. But that does not mean the story contains no valid information about Eliezer's legal rulings; as noted, it certainly has independent evidence about opinions nowhere else cited in reference to Eliezer, and this evidence seems to me not readily ignored.

20. *Reports to ʿAqiba*

M. Ed. 2 : 7/Tos. Ed. 1 : 10 contains two rulings introduced by a redactional formula alleging that they were said before ʿAqiba in the name of Eliezer: a woman may go out on the Sabbath wearing a golden city, and pigeon-racers are not eligible to give testimony. M. Shab. 6 : 1 and M. Sanh. 3 : 3 know nothing about Eliezer's holding such an opinion. M. Shab. 6 : 1 decides contrariwise, and M. Sanh. 3 : 3 rules as does Eliezer. Tos. Ed. adds that ʿAqiba did not rule on the questions one way or the other.

The allegation that these opinions were stated before ʿAqiba seems to me worth taking seriously. ʿEduyyot consists chiefly of traditions in the name of ʿAqiba's Ushan continuators, which on the face of it should be strong. The reports here clearly are independent of those behind M. Shab. and M. Sanh. One cannot suppose Eliezer's opinions have been deliberately suppressed, as was evidently the case with Ilai's, and probably ʿAqiba's, list, on account of the unacceptability of Eliezer's opinions or a desire to secure acceptance for those opinions by giving him the opposite view from what he really held. As to the pigeon-racers, M. Sanh. *accepts* Eliezer's view; on the question ʿAqiba had none. So why should the Ushan or later masters behind M. Sanh. have had reason either to include or to exclude Eliezer's name? M. Shab. gives a more strict ruling than Eliezer's, but the matter does not seem to have been of fundamental importance. So the redactional formula seems worthwhile evidence that the opinions attributed to Eliezer do come from Yavnean times, probably from Eliezer himself.

21. *Repent before Death*

ARN presents a chain, beginning with Ilai, for Eliezer's ruling about repentance before death. It is possible that the tradition persisted for a while before surfacing in ARN; in that case Eliezer taught what is attributed to him. If so, this would be the sole excellent tradition on other than a legal problem. We have no reason whatever to reject the whole corpus of non-legal materials and to posit that all Eliezer ever taught had to do with law.

iii. Eliezer's Attestations of Houses' Disputes

Most attestations in the name of Eliezer for rabbinic traditions about pre-70 times (*Phar.* III, pp. 199-202) pertain to the Houses:

1. M. Ter. 5 : 4/Tos. Ter. 6 : 4 (*Phar.* II, pp. 83-86): Eliezer corresponds to the position of the House of Shammai, the sages to the House of Hillel. But Eliezer does not stand outside of, and comment on, the pericope. His disagreement with the sages is attached with the phrase, *After they had agreed*, so the redactor evidently had two versions of an apodosis for a single protasis. y. Pes. 3 : 6 has Judah refer to the Houses, but not to Eliezer; presumably he knew nothing about Eliezer's participation.

2. Tos. Ter. 3 : 16 (*Phar.* II, pp. 88-89): The pericope opens with an anonymous rule that one who gives Heave-offering of grapes but eventually makes them into raisins need not repeat the offering. Then Eliezer says the House of Shammai is responsible for that rule, the House of Hillel taking a contrary position, and then the Houses have a debate, with the House of Shammai at the end, saying the last word. As noted above (p. 95), Eliezer himself rules in a way more or less consistent with the House of Shammai in M. Ter. 1 : 4, 9-10. We may have no doubt this too is our Eliezer. Representing Eliezer as an authority for a Houses' dispute seems to me not motivated by a hostile view, at least in early Yavnean times when the Houses' representatives could not have been of grossly unequal strength.

But why should Eliezer have taken an anonymous law and assigned it to the Shammaites? Perhaps the saying of Eliezer should have begun with a statement of the problem, without the anonymous rule. Then Eliezer supplied the Houses' dispute. But another version, giving as a unanimous opinion the view of the House of Shammai, also circulated. Then the two were put together in a simple, efficient way, by dropping the duplicated protasis. So Eliezer would not have changed an anonymous and unanimously accepted rule into a matter debated by the Houses. He would simply stand behind one version of the matter. Then another version—surely emanating from Shammaite circles—would have existed alongside his. Eliezer here does not appear as a Shammaite, but as a person involved in the formulation of pre-70 disputes. But if our surmise is correct in regard to M. Ter. 1 : 4, 9-10, then Eliezer also agreed in this instance with the Shammaite position. If so, however, he has not shown a bias toward the Shammaites, such as would be indicated by his turning a Shammaite opinion into a unanimous law, but has honestly preserved what he evidently had received, at the same time making up his mind on the issues.

3. b. Yoma 80a (*Phar.* II, pp. 149-150): The Houses dispute how much one must have drunk to be culpable for drinking on the Day of Atonement. The House of Shammai say a fourth, the House of Hillel, a mouthful. Then Judah in Eliezer's name says, "As much as a mouthful"—close to the view of the House of Hillel, the difference being whether it is an exact or an approximate measure. Judah is good authority for Eliezer's view. Here he assigns Eliezer to the Hillelites. But Eliezer does not attest the existence of the Houses' dispute.

4. Tos. M.Q. 2 : 9, b. M.Q. 20a (*Phar.* II, pp. 182-3): Eliezer b. Jacob differs from an antecedent, anonymous rule about overturning the couch as a sign of mourning three days before the festival. Then Leazar b. R. Simeon has the Houses differ on the same question, with the Hillelites using the same mnemonic as Liezer b. Jacob. b. M.Q. 20a presents Eliezer as the authority for the anonymous rule; the sages take the place of Liezer b. Jacob; and Simeon b. Eleazar gives the Houses, but with different opinions. In no way can Eliezer be thought to attest the existence of the pericope; it would seem that b. has a garbled version, and we cannot be sure that b.'s *Eliezer* is ours. He probably is not.

5. M. Ket. 5 : 6 (*Phar.* II, pp. 207-208): Eliezer's saying is attached to a Houses' dispute, but does not allude to, and cannot attest it. Further, we are not sure this is our Eliezer.

6. b. Yev. 89b, M. Ket. 8 : 6, M. Yev. 4 : 3 (*Phar.* II, pp. 209-211): In b. Yev. 89b the Houses dispute the question, At what time is a husband entitled to inherit his wife if she dies as a minor? The Shammaites say, "When she attains adulthood." The Hillelites say, "When she enters the bridal chamber." Eliezer says, "When sexual relations have taken place"—that is, pretty much the same view as the Hillelites. Eliezer b. Hyrcanus, praised for his consistency in ruling that the minor-female can effect no legal act, should rule as do the Shammaites. This Eliezer ought not to be ours. In any case, since Eliezer stands within the structure of argument, he cannot supply an attestation for it.

7. M. Nid. 5 : 9 (*Phar.* II, pp. 300-301): Eliezer here clearly attests the Houses' dispute on the signs of adulthood, but his saying does not stand at the end of the formulation of the dispute. Nor are we sure this is our Eliezer.

8. Tos. Nid. 5 : 5-7/M. Nid. 4 : 3 (*Phar.* II, pp. 308-309): Eliezer does not attest the Houses' dispute. Simeon b. Judah in Simeon [b. Yoḥai]'s name gives as a Houses' dispute what in M. Nid. 4 : 4 is debated by Eliezer and Joshua. Thus the Eliezer-Joshua dispute evidently was not before the Ushans, but was available to the editor(s) of the Mishnah. For our present purposes it is sufficient to note we have here no firm attestation by an Eliezer, let alone our Eliezer, of this Houses' dispute.

9. M. Ed. 5 : 5 *re* M. Nid. 4 : 3, M. Yev. 3 : 1 (= Tos. Nid. 5 : 5) (*Phar.* II, pp. 336-337): This is almost certainly not our Eliezer, but most likely the Ushan Eliezer, for in M. Yev. Simeon [b. Yoḥai] is involved. MS evidence varies, but Tos. is firm on Eleazar.

10. M. M.S. 3 : 9, M. Sheq. 8 : 6: See above, p. 106.

11. M. Eruv. 1 : 2 (*Phar.* II, pp. 135-136): Eliezer participates, along with the Houses and differing from both, in a discussion of rendering an alley-entry valid by means of an *ʿeruv.* The whole pericope is attested by Ishmael's disciple + ʿAqiba. But Eliezer does not attest it, and the middle-Yavnean attestation does not allude to Eliezer's opinion, only to the Houses'.

12. Tos. Ar. 4 : 5 (*Phar.* II, pp. 248-250): Joshua and Eliezer stand for the House of Hillel and the House of Shammai, respectively. b. Ar. 23a has a clearer version of the same, and Eleazar b. Simeon states what is given in Tos. as an anonymous observation. The whole corresponds to M. Ar. 6 : 1 (above, Vol. I, p. 250). Two versions thus seem to have come down to Usha, one in the name of Eliezer/Joshua, the other, House of Shammai/House of Hillel. Eliezer/Joshua cannot be said to supply an attestation for the existence of the Houses' dispute before their time. It would seem that the Ushans received versions of the same disputes in the names of both the early Yavnean masters and the Houses, although, because of the unclarity of Tos.'s text, one could not prove that fact on the basis of this pericope alone.

In sum, Eliezer's attestations for Houses' disputes do not add up to much. For the purposes of *Phar.* they seemed to me adequate to supply some evidence about the nature of the legal themes debated by the Houses according to Yavnean authorities. For that limited purpose the attestations suffice, for what is not our Eliezer's may belong to

Eleazar b. ʿAzariah; or, at the latest, we have evidence from early Usha—and ʿAqiba's disciples—if not from Yavneh.

But one cannot derive much information about the state of Eliezer b. Hyrcanus's own tradition *vis à vis* the Houses. No. 1 is highly suggestive; along with Nos. 2 and 12, it seems to indicate that versions of a single dispute reached the Ushans, in the name, on the one hand, of Eliezer/sages, on the other, of the Houses. This would suggest that later Yavneans and Ushans, probably the former, revised early Yavnean materials and replaced Eliezer's name with that of the House of Shammai, or *vice versa.* But while No. 1 then represents Eliezer as a Shammaite, No. 2 does not. No. 3 sees him as a Hillelite—and this is the testimony of Judah b. Ilai (!). Nos. 4, 5, 6, 7, 8, 9 are not useful. No. 10 is another matter, as already shown. No. 11 has Eliezer disputing with both Houses, but we have no attestation for his opinion. In No. 12 we have the same situation as in Nos. 1-2. We find no consistent viewpoint on Eliezer's own relationship to the Houses. He seems to emerge as either a Shammaite or a Hillelite or neither.

iv. Eliezer and the Traditions about pre-70 Masters

In *Phar.* III, pp. 199-202, I alleged that Eliezer attests the following stories about pre-70 masters:

1. Sifré Deut. 221/M. Sanh. 6 : 4 (*Phar.* I, pp. 90-91, 92-3): Eliezer cites the hangings of Simeon in Ashqelon. Judah's participation means that we need not doubt this is our Eliezer, and the attestation is a good one.
2. M. Ker. 6 : 3 (*Phar.* I, p. 389): Eliezer's opinion that one may always offer a Suspensive Guilt-offering except the day after the Day of Atonement is illustrated by the story about Baba b. Buṭa. But Eliezer is not cited as the authority for the story, nor does his saying suggest he knew it.
3. Sifra Shemini 8 : 5/M. Ed. (*Phar.* I, pp. 61-2): In a dispute between Eliezer and ʿAqiba, Eliezer says, "Uncleanness in no way pertains to liquids. You may know that this is so, because Yosi b. Ṣeredah gave testimony. . ." ʿAqiba replies to the issue, but not to the precedent. The MSS evidence and other versions of the same matter also have Eleazar, instead of Eliezer, but the presence of ʿAqiba provides some warrant for choosing our Eliezer. What is less clear is whether Eliezer's saying originally alluded to Yosi, or whether that passage has been interpolated later on. As presently formulated, Eliezer states that uncleanness does not pertain to liquids at all—his sole proof then is the precedent of Yosi. ʿAqiba's reply is the argument that an insect renders liquids unclean and the liquids render vessels unclean, and the vessels render food unclean—so the three are

made unclean by the insect. Since Eliezer has nothing more than Yosi's precedent behind his opinion, it would seem that precedent is integral, not tacked on as an additional proof. ʿAqiba's position is consistent with Joshua's in M. Toh. 8 : 7 (Vol. I, p. 318): the outer parts of vessels make liquids unclean, and liquids render the food invalid. Eliezer says the outer parts make the liquids unclean, but they do *not* then make the food unclean. That still is not wholly consistent with Eliezer's position *vis à vis* ʿAqiba.

This evidence seems somewhat better than that in section iii. No. 3 has Eliezer and ʿAqiba debating a problem raised, in other ways, in Eliezer-Joshua materials; the reference to Yosi appears to be intrinsic to Eliezer's saying. Since two circles of (presumably) Yavnean tradents, Joshua's and ʿAqiba's, both represent Eliezer as concerned with the problem of the uncleanness of liquids, perhaps that is an accurate representation. The details, to be sure, are different. But Eliezer's reference to Yosi seems to provide a valid attestation both for Yosi's pericope and for Eliezer's interest in the matter. No. 2 is not so firm an attestation. Eliezer's view is consistent with the story about Baba, but Eliezer does not attest the story, and the literary framework does not allege otherwise. No. 1, a singleton, is a less useful attestation than No. 3

v. Eliezer and the Traditions about Yoḥanan b. Zakkai

Eliezer does not supply a single useful attestation for a tradition attributed to, or story told about, Yoḥanan b. Zakkai. Some of his traditions standing by themselves are related, or parallel to, Yoḥanan's, as follows:

1. Sifré Num. 123 (*Development*, pp. 19-20): Eliezer says white garments are required by Num. 19 : 1. A story about Yoḥanan contains the same view. The story is then glossed by a reference to Hillel, but that reference has nothing to do with Eliezer's law. The equivalent story in Tos. Ah. 16 : 8 knows nothing about Eliezer's law; Tos. Par. 4 : 7 has the law, but not Eliezer.
2. Sifré Deut. 144 (*Development*, pp. 30-21): Yoḥanan's and Eliezer's are good courts.
3. M. Yad. 4 : 3 (*Development*, pp. 58-60; above, Vol. I, pp. 332ff.): "I have received a tradition from Rabban Yoḥanan b. Zakkai..." The saying is in the context of a story. The pericope cannot be adduced as evidence that Eliezer attests knowledge of Yoḥanan's law—that is the point of the story itself. And Dosa b. Harkinus knows nothing either about Eliezer or about Yoḥanan in respect to the identical law, as noted above, Vol. I, p. 335.

4. b. Ber. 28b (*Development*, pp. 87-8): Yoḥanan's and Eliezer's death-scenes are linked together. y. Sot. 9 : 16 (*Development*, p. 137) has a similar relationship, but different death-scenes.
5. b. Suk. 28a adds to an encomium about Yoḥanan, "And so did his disciple R. Eliezer behave after him."
6. b. R.H. 31b, b. Bes. 5a, and Tos. M.S. 5 : 15 do not present Eliezer as attesting Yoḥanan's rule; they allege that he did not know it.

The association of Eliezer and Yoḥanan clearly is taken for granted by the redactors responsible for Nos. 1, 2, and 4; the glossator of No. 5 has the same idea in mind. No. 3 assumes Eliezer learned Yoḥanan's traditions; that idea is intrinsic to the narrative. But Eliezer cannot be said to attest the tradition. No. 6 is the opposite of an attestation.

While we have a few instances, therefore, in which it may be shown that Eliezer provides independent attestations of stories about pre-70 masters and debates between the Houses, not a single saying attributed to Eliezer with reference to Yoḥanan ben Zakkai is of the same order. Later masters tell stories taking for granted the association of the two, but no one has given us a saying in Eliezer's name which both stands outside, and indicates knowledge, of a story or teaching attributed to Yoḥanan. This seems strong *prima facie* evidence that the connection to Yoḥanan has not played a role in the formation of the earliest stratum of Eliezer's materials. The first solid attestations of Yoḥanan's traditions occur with Judah b. Ilai in Usha, though one might argue that some later Yavnean materials may be interpreted as indicating knowledge of Yoḥanan's sayings and doings. The unavailability of such evidence in respect to Eliezer therefore cannot be regarded as inconsequential. But admittedly, the whole Yoḥanan-corpus is slight.

vi. Yavnean Chains of Traditions

Chains of tradition in the names of Yavneans derive from ʿAqiba and Ilai. Ishmael occurs in a single passage, which does not contain a chain at all. The evidence made available by the chains therefore points to Ilai and ʿAqiba as the students of Eliezer chiefly responsible for handing on his materials and including them in the normative tradition. Though he seems to have survived Eliezer, Joshua hands on nothing in his name. Eleazar b. ʿAzariah, Gamaliel, Yosi the Galilean, Ṭarfon, and others of the succeeding Yavnean generation (as in Tos. Git., above, p. 110), never quote Eliezer or allude to his opinions except within the structure of the pericope in which those opinions occur. Eliezer, like Ishmael later on, appears as an isolated figure, whose traditions were preserved—along with the claim that they were worthwhile because they contained nothing of his own, only what his master had said—but who exerted little influence outside of his immediate circle of disciples and close associates. That impression, however, will become more reliable when we have similar accounts of other important Yavneans and how their materials are attested; then it will be clear to what extent important figures were quoted in chains of tradition and how commonly their opinions were alluded to or attested in their own and the immediately succeeding generation.

We shall now review those attested pericopae which seemed (pp. 73-76) to present a chain of tradition.

1. *ʿAqiba*

We have already discussed M. Shev. 8 : 9-10, M. Ed. 2 : 7, and M. Sheq. 4 : 7.

The fourth alleged chain is M. Ker. 3 : 10, ʿAqiba says, "I asked R. Eliezer..." The problem is theoretical. If one does many individual acts of work of a single category in a single period of unawareness, does he bring one Sin-offering for all, or one for each act? Eliezer replies that an offering for each act is required. ʿAqiba then reports that he replied to Eliezer's reasoning, and at the end of the exchange of views, it turns out that ʿAqiba has relied on a set of facts different from Eliezer's. M. Ker. 3 : 7ff. exhibits identical form. ʿAqiba reports he asked Gamaliel and Joshua about the same principle. But the reply of Gamaliel and Joshua is different from Eliezer's. He has given a ruling based on logic. They say, "We have heard no tradition about this, but we heard a tradition about a similar matter." Their received tradition accords with Eliezer's logic.

M. Shav. 2 : 5 has a not dissimilar issue. If a man contracted uncleanness in the Temple court, and the uncleanness was forgotten, though he was aware he was in the Temple; or if he forgot he was in the Temple but was aware of his uncleanness; or if he forgot both but stayed too long—he is liable to a Rising and Falling Offering. Eliezer then provides an exegesis to prove that the man is liable for the unawareness of the creeping thing, but not for the Temple. ʿAqiba agrees. Ishmael holds him liable for both. Tos. Shav. 1 : 6 has *R. Eliezer and R. ʿAqiba say*—a simpler version. M. seems an expansion, in the form of a colloquy. Or Tos. is a summary. Clearly, the theory of penalties for closely related transgressions was at issue in early

Yavnean times; major authorities were involved in discussing it.

The form of M. Ker. 3 : 7-10 is not precisely that of a chain of tradition, for we do not have, *R. ʿAqiba said that R. Eliezer said.* But the form is close to a chain. It gives in the first person what, in the third person, would be nothing other than the expected chain. The first-person form for ʿAqiba's saying seems to me noteworthy. Other forms were used for the redaction of his sayings. Employment of this one in particular therefore seems to indicate that the substance of the saying had come to the redactors in the first-person, and that the redactors preserved what they received, rather than restating the whole in the (far more common) third-person.

2. *Ishmael*

M. Hal. 2 : 8/Tos. Hal. 1 : 10 contains the opinion of Eliezer that one may take Dough-offering from clean for unclean dough. Tos. Hal. 1 : 10 has a little story about how "they" said before Ishmael that *so-and-so* in the south teaches Dough-offering is taken from the clean for the unclean dough. Ishmael approves the teaching "by the priestly garment which father wore." Then "they" tell him it is Eliezer's teaching. Ishmael says that even (ʾP) *he* has support for his opinion.

This strange colloquy seems to provide sound evidence that Ishmael was regarded as hostile to Eliezer's teachings, probably to Eliezer himself. That supposition is supported by the very rare occurrences of Ishmael in the corpus of Eliezer's legal traditions. This means that the redaction of Eliezer's materials proceeded quite apart from the circles of Ishmael's followers. The story does not constitute a "chain" of tradition. But it does supply additional attestation for the presence of Eliezer's opinion on the subject in the earliest stratum of Yavnean tradition.

3. *Ilai*

Tos. Dem. 1 : 3 (y. Dem. 1 : 1) has a chain: *Leʿii in the name of Liezer*, saying that the first fruits in the garden are always liable, for they are guarded. The landowner does take account of them, so they are obligated for Heave-offering and tithes. The anonymous rule is that first fruits are free of liability.

The issue of whether produce is guarded, therefore of value to the owner and to be tithed, is further raised by the Houses, Sifra Behar 1 : 5/M. Shev. 4 : 28 (*Phar.* II, pp. 26-30). The problem is whether one may eat the produce of the Seventh Year. The House of Shammai say one does not eat the produce of the Seventh Year if it is by favor. The House of Hillel say one does. Judah then reverses matters. According to Judah the Shammaites do not prohibit the use of produce which is guarded and therefore do not forbid a person to take it under conditions which require him to be obligated to anyone. Here Eliezer is of the view that first fruits which are guarded are liable—thus consistent with the House of Hillel's view in the version of Judah b. Ilai. The opinion reported by Ilai and that reported by Judah are on different subjects, but the principle is the same and is, according to Judah, the Hillelite view. As to Eliezer, Judah ought to have known what he was talking about—but Eliezer does not occur in M. Shev. 4 : 2B. I do not know why Judah should be a reliable witness to the view of the House of Hillel. Nor do I know that Ilai's tradition in Tos. Dem. 1 : 3 would have been thought by Judah to be relevant to the Houses' dispute in M. Shev. 4 : 2.

As noted, Ilai says in the name of Eliezer, "They give Heave-offering from what is clean for what is unclean" (Tos. Ter. 3 : 18). This seems to me among the most reliable traditions about Eliezer.

Ilai also gives a first-person saying, Tos. Hal. 1 : 6, about Eliezer's opinion on the cakes of the Thank-offering of the Nazirite with respect to liability for Dough-offering. Another first-person saying occurs in M. Eruv. 2 : 5 (above, pp. 99-103). ARN Chap. 15 contains an extended chain for M. Avot 2 : 10 (above, p. 115). Tos. Suk. 2 : 1 has a story about Ilai and Eliezer, but it is not told in the first-person and does not contain, or constitute, a chain of tradition about Eliezer's opinion on studying on the festival.

In all, therefore, the Yavnean chains are as follows:

ʿAqiba:	M. Shev. 8 : 9-10: I shall not tell you
	M. Ed. 2 : 7: They said before ʿAqiba
	M. Sheq. 4 : 7: I prefer Eliezer's opinion
	M. Ker. 3 : 10: I asked Eliezer
[Ishmael:	Tos. Hal. 1 : 10: Attestation, not a chain.]
Ilai:	Tos. Dem. 1 : 3: Leʿii in the name of Eliezer
	Tos. Ter. 3 : 18: Ilai in the name of Eliezer
	Tos. Hal. 1 : 6: I asked Liezer
	M. Eruv. 2 : 5: I heard from Eliezer
	[Tos. Suk. 2 : 1: Story]
	ARN Chap. 15: Yosi b. R. Judah + Judah b. Ilai + Ilai + Eliezer the Great

What we have called a chain appears solely in the preserved traditions in the name of Ilai. ʿAqiba's "chains" are nothing more than first-person accounts; but as observed, in the third-person they would as well have been phrased, *R. ʿAqiba in the name of R. Eliezer.* Ilai has two chains in regard to laws on agricultural matters, two first-person sayings, and ARN. So where specific chains exist in the Yavnean stratum, they are Ilai's.

It seems legitimate to attribute to Ilai (or to his circle of disciples) the development of the chain as a form. Judah his son has a great many sayings in the form of a chain. We therefore may not suppose the use of a chain was provoked by either the state of the material transmitted or the particularly contested nature of specific laws. Nor may we say it was a generally available form, routinely employed for Eliezer's sayings.

We have already observed that Ilai seems responsible for the organization of a collection as a list of a master's teachings on diverse subjects, rather than as a list of materials on a single theme or problem. Eliezer himself attests Yosi b. Yoʿezer's sayings in M. Ed. 8 : 4/Sifra Shemini 8 : 5 (p. 118). Perhaps, therefore, it was from Eliezer that Ilai got the idea of forming collections of different teachings around the name of a specific authority; perhaps also for adding to the collected materials the name of the master responsible for making the collection—but for this we have no evidence at all. Still, the same organizing principle is used in ʿEduyyot, which is constructed of lists of teachings on different subjects in the name of a single authority. The logical next step is to add on the name of the tradent responsible for making up and transmitting the list, as is the case with ʿEduyyot, e.g., Judah's list of three lenient rulings, on diverse topics, of the House of Shammai.

4. *Yoḥanan b. Nuri*

Yoḥanan b. Nuri's sole chain is in Tos. Orl. 1 : 8, above, p. 98.

vii. Judah b. Ilai's Traditions

1. *Chains and Other Direct Attributions*

The following, numbered according to the list on p. 74, are instances in which Judah directly cites Eliezer or otherwise indicates he gives Eliezer's exact words. Pericopae in which Judah simply rephrases a whole dispute—*they differed not about this but about that, and R. Eliezer says... R. Joshua says...*—are considered among attestations, p. 127.

2. Sifré Num. 110/M. Hal. 2 : 1: Judah says, "Even fruit from abroad which entered the land, R. Eliezer declares free of liability." As a chain, the saying would read, *Judah says Eliezer says.* As it stands, *Even fruit...* is out of place.
5. Tos. Kip. 2 : 10: Judah in the name of Eliezer *re* drawing lots.
6. Tos. Kip. 2 : 16: Judah in the name of Liezer *re* how the high priest would count.
7. Tos. Kip. 3 : 1/M. Yoma 5 : 5: Judah in the name of Liezer [M. omits Judah] *re* where the high priest would stand.
8. Tos. Kip. 3 : 19/M. Yoma 7 : 3: Judah in the name of Liezer on the whole-offerings.
9. Tos. Y.T. 1 : 3: Judah in the name of Liezer—The dispute is still in its place, *re* eating an egg born on the festival. b. Bes. 4a then spells out the Houses' dispute. Judah has Eliezer in the position of the House of Hillel.
10. Tos. R.H. 2 : 10: Judah in the name of Liezer *re* Lev. 23 : 24. Then: *ʿAqiba said to him*, meaning Eliezer.
11. b. M.Q. 19a: Judah in his [Eliezer] name *re* spinning the blue-wool for the fringe. M. M.Q. 3 : 4 has Judah without the citation of Eliezer.
12. b. M.Q. 10a/M. M.Q. 1 : 9: Judah in his name—They set up the new millstone in the festival week. This is different from Judah's opinion in M. M.Q. 1 : 9. Where Judah has his own opinion but gives another in the name of Eliezer, we may be reasonably sure the representation of Eliezer is accurate.
13. Tos. Ket. 11 : 4/M. Ket. 11 : 6: Judah in the name of Liezer—The orphan has the right to usufruct [of *melog*-property.] Liezer by himself rules on the orphan's right to worn-out articles. M. Ket. 11 : 6 has the contrary rule: A minor who has exercised the right of refusal is not entitled to the right to usufruct or to worn-out articles. Since Eliezer holds the right of refusal exercised by a minor is of no effect, he is consistent in his rulings here—in all, a very well-attested tradition.

14-16. Tos. Nez. 2 : 12-13/M. Naz. 3 : 3-5: Two sayings of Judah in the name of Liezer *re* the Nazir's losing thirty, or seven, days in the event of his contracting uncleanness at the last minute. Then: *This is the general rule that R. Judah said in the name of R. Liezer.*

17. b. B.B. 157a/M. B.B. 9 : 7: TNYʾ: Meir says, *Eliezer said... Joshua said... Judah says, Eliezer said... Joshua said.* These cannot be regarded as chains of tradition. But the form is strikingly close to a chain. Had Meir been omitted, or had Joshua's disagreement not been recorded, then we should have regarded the pericope as a chain.
18. Tos. Sanh. 9 : 6/M. Sanh. 6 : 4: "At a distance of four cubits they would cover a woman front and behind [before hanging]"—the words of Judah in the name of Eliezer *vs.* the sages. M. Sanh. 6 : 4 does not have the words attributed to Judah-Eliezer here, but the substance of the opinion is the same.

23. Tos. Ah. 7 : 3/M. Oh. 6 : 2: Judah in the name of Eliezer, "Even though the door is open, the house is clean, because the lock is unclean." The saying is pertinent to Mishnah 6 : 2, but is omitted there.
27. Tos. Par. 5 : 9/M. Par. 5 : 7: Judah in the name of Eliezer, "If he made for it a crown of mud..." M. Par. 5 : 7 omits reference to Eliezer's view and gives the opposite opinion.
28. Tos. Par. 7 : 7/M. Par. 7 : 10: Tos. has *Eliezer says*: He who hands over his water to one who is unclean... Then: R. Judah says in his name, "If the unclean person did work, the water is valid. If the owner did work..." The first is Eliezer's ruling in M. Par. 7 : 10. Judah's rule is consistent and follows from the foregoing. This may mean Judah by his own logic has concluded what Eliezer's opinion ought to have been and has then attributed it to Eliezer.

While ʿAqiba has only four chains—all of them in other than standard form—and Ilai has two, or possibly three, Judah has no fewer than eighteen. Clearly, it was commonplace to use the form *Judah says/said + Eliezer says.* Judah also has a substantial number of attestations, so we cannot suppose that the chain was used as the conventional way of having Judah comment upon Eliezer's traditions. This is virtually certain, for some of Judah's traditions differ from those given by Judah in Eliezer's name on the same problem. Certainly, the chain was used because of Judah's allegation that what he taught was *verbatim* what he had heard from Eliezer.

But Judah never studied with Eliezer. His father did. And Judah does not say *My father Ilai says/said + Eliezer says.* His chains are only in his own name plus Eliezer's. What this means is difficult to ascertain. The obvious implication is that Judah alleges he has exact verbal records of Eliezer's laws; perhaps it was taken for granted that these came through his father, but we do not find evidence that anyone supposed so before the end of Ushan times. Later on, to be sure, this conclusion was reached.

Strikingly, while Judah supplies chains or attestations for a wide range of laws, few, if any, of his laws represent a continuation or a development of materials already attested at Yavneh. Some of them, to be sure, deal with the same principles, for instance, the rule about the minor-female's claims after she has exercised the right of refusal. The rulings on the right of the orphan who has exercised the right of refusal are probably Eliezer's, for they are consistent with quite well-attested sayings about Eliezer's opinion on the subject. But most of the others are unrelated to earlier themes. We hear nothing about some of the most important Yavnean principles, e.g. Heave-offering from clean for unclean produce, conditional divorce, or the problem of intention. The chains pertain chiefly to laws of Moᶜed—Nos. 5, 6, 7, 8, 9, 10, 11, 12. The rest are scattered: Zeraᶜim: No. 2; Nashim: Nos. 13, 14, 15, 16; Neziqin: Nos. 17, 18; Qodashim: None; Ṭoharot: Nos. 23, 27, and 28. These certainly do not conform to the proportions of Eliezer's laws devoted to the respective orders, for the larger parts are in Zeraᶜim, Ṭoharot, and Qodashim; Moᶜed does not predominate in his traditions.

The single chain in respect to agricultural laws deals with fruit from abroad, a topic also pertinent to No. 25, below. Four chains following a single pattern have to do with the rites in the Temple on the Day of Atonement. They account for half of the chains in Moᶜed and therefore for the imbalance. Perhaps Judah formulated a set of traditions in Eliezer's name on the rite of Atonement; but none of these made its way into the Mishnah. One chain deals with a Houses' dispute, another has Judah + Eliezer debate with ᶜAqiba. But we do not know, since Judah hands on Eliezer's, who formulated ᶜAqiba's saying. Perhaps it is a theoretical argument, spun out in response to Judah's tradition in Eliezer's name. No. 12 is a very reliable tradition, as noted. But M. M.Q. 1 : 9 gives Judah's opinion and omits Eliezer's.

The chains about the Nazir who has contracted uncleanness at the end of his period of Naziriteship are spun out of the general rule at the end. Or they have led to the formulation of a general rule out of the several specific cases. I tend to think the former, for Eliezer seems to have laid down a number of general principles which then were aplied to specific cases, as in legal incapacity of the minor female.

The two rulings on the Sin-offering water are not closely related to one another. We have a cluster of rulings in Eliezer's name in M. Par.

2. *Attestations*

Judah, along with other Ushans, also attests to pericopae involving Eliezer, usually along with other masters in a dispute. The attestations, numbered according to the list on p. 74, are as follows:

1. Tos. Ter. 9 : 9C/M. Ter. 11 : 2: Judah, Jacob, and Rabbi differ on the topic of a dispute between Joshua and Eliezer about making olives and grapes into oil and wine, respectively. The Mishnah accords with Judah's view of Joshua's opinion. The issue of M. Ter. 11 : 2 is whether liquids other than the seven that render unclean are regarded as liquids capable of becoming unclean. Eliezer says they are; Joshua, they are not.

3. M. Eruv. 1 : 2: Not pertinent.
4. M. Eruv. 7 : 11: Judah defines a dispute between Eliezer and sages regarding acquisition of a share in an *'eruv.*
19. Tos. Zev. 2 : 16: Not pertinent.
20. Tos. Zev. 8 : 15/M. Zev. 8 : 4: Judah redefines a dispute between Eliezer and sages, holding the dispute is on a more subtle issue than is debated in the version of M. Zev. 8 : 15.
21. Tos. Zev. 8 : 20/M. Zev. 8 : 8a: Judah attests the dispute about the disposition of the blood of unblemished offerings which has been confused with that of blemished offerings. Note that for M. Ter. 5 : 2/M. Zev. 8 : 5 we here have a further attestation.
22. Tos. Men. 2 : 16/M. Men. 3 : 1: Judah and Eleazar debate on an issue between Eliezer and Joshua. Judah is consistent with Eliezer. Judah certainly attests Eliezer's opinion.
24. Tos. Ah. 9 : 7/M. Oh. 8 : 6: Judah defines a dispute between Eliezer and Joshua; M. Oh. 8 : 6 knows nothing of the dispute.
25. Tos. Ah. 17 : 6/M. Oh. 17 : 5: Judah: Eliezer and the sages did not differ concerning dirt that comes from the grave area, etc.
26. Tos. Neg. 3 : 5/M. Neg. 7 : 4-5: Judah: Eliezer and the sages did not differ concerning him who cut if off along with living flesh, that he cannot be purified, but concerning him who cut off the leprosy-sign as dead flesh. M. Neg. 7 : 5 does not have this dispute.
29. Tos. Uqs. 3 : 15/M. Uqs. 3 : 10 = M. Shev. 3 : 10: Judah: Eliezer and sages did not differ concerning honey-combs, that they do not receive uncleanness, but concerning the Sabbath and Seventh Year. Thus Judah redefines the dispute about the beehive to exclude one of the four elements under discussion.

In addition, Judah along with Meir attests the following:

1. M. Kil. 9 : 2/Tos. Kil. 5 : 18: Meir and Judah differ on the opinions of Eliezer and the sages with respect to the application of the law of diverse kinds to handkerchiefs. Meir has Liezer *prohibit*, Judah has Liezer *permit*. M. Kil. 9 : 3 follows Meir.

2-6. M. Ter. 4 : 7-11/Tos. Ter. 5 : 10-11: Meir and Judah differ on Eliezer's and Joshua's opinions in M. Ter. 4 : 8. M. Ter. 4 : 8 follows Judah's definition of the matter.

7. Tos. Men. 8 : 19/M. Men. 7 : 3: Meir and Judah differ on the definition of the dispute between Eliezer and Joshua. Judah then invents a debate along the lines of his dispute. Judah's tradition is materially different from Meir's. M. Men. follows Meir.

Judah's attestations, like his chains, deal with subjects formerly not dealt with at all. The most important are in Zevaḥim and Menaḥot; of these, the principle applied to the mixture of blood of unblemished and blemished offerings is identical to that applied in M. Ter. 5 : 2. Eliezer consistently rules that what has fallen into a mixture is what is then removed—theoretically, the prohibited substance remains separate from the permitted—and therefore we have a series of lenient rulings on different matters.

Judah's differences with Meir seem to me far less valuable attestations of Eliezer's opinions, though they do indicate themes likely to have been the subject of his opinions. If Meir says Eliezer prohibits and Judah has him permit a mixture of diverse kinds in handkerchiefs, then clearly no firm tradition existed even in Ushan times. The same applies to Nos. 2-6 and 7.

viii. The Earliest Eliezer

Eliezer's rulings sometimes contain general principles; either he states such a principle, along with diverse applications, or he rules in such a way as to produce out of specific cases a general law. This seems to be an innovation, for to the earlier masters, the Houses, and Yoḥanan b. Zakkai are attributed few, if any, generalizations; rules assigned to the former generations apply to discrete cases. Perhaps Eliezer attempted to legislate according to a coherent philosophy, but we have only a little evidence to suggest so.

While we have some evidence of hostility toward Eliezer, few of the best traditions—such as Ilai's and ʿAqiba's lists—give us information on the grounds for such hostility or contain expressions of a negative view of Eliezer's teachings, as in Ishmael's story. Eliezer's opinions were carefully preserved; no one seems to have formulated a legal pericope indicating that Eliezer's laws were not to be taken seriously. We found no evidence, except for Ilai's and ʿAqiba's lists, of deliberate falsification of Eliezer's opinion to secure acceptance of either what he said or the opposite of what he said. The existence of chains does not lead to the inference that it was necessary to protect particularly controversial opinions by testifying as to their transmission.

We shall now review the best traditions and systematically inquire as to the attitude toward Eliezer expressed in those traditions. The pericopae are numbered according to the foregoing sections in which they are considered.

ii-1-2. One may give Heave offering from what is clean for what is unclean. Eliezer stands within the Shammaite opinion, but rules in a still more lenient way than do the Shammaites. Not hostile.

ii-3. Cakes of Thank-offering of Nazirites are free of liability to the Dough-offering if made for the Nazir's own use, but liable if made for sale. Eleazar b. ʿAzariah stated that Eliezer's opinion was given at Sinai. Eliezer's origination of the law—if he indeed made it up—is not alluded to in M. Hal. 1 : 6. We do not know why. Eleazar: friendly. Pericope: not hostile.

ii-4-15. *ʿOrlah*-taboos do not apply outside of Palestine. M. Qid. 1 : 9 has an opinion for Eliezer that *ʿorlah* and mixed-seeds-taboos are observed abroad. Here we have a serious confusion. Tos. Orl. is well attested; M. Qid. 1 : 9 is not. I should tend, therefore, to regard the former as authoritative; either the latter is not our Eliezer, or it is our Eliezer and therefore is false. Not hostile.

ii-5. The *etrog* is like a tree in all respects, against Gamaliel's view that it is in some ways like a vegetable. ʿAqiba followed the opinions of both Gamaliel and Eliezer, both the Houses of Shammai and Hillel as well. Eliezer stands close to the Hillelite opinion. Not hostile.

ii-6. Ilai's list indicates Eliezer ruled leniently with respect to making an *ʿeruv* for a field, however large, surrounded by a wall; likewise he held if one party to a collective *ʿeruv* in a courtyard has failed to take part, the others may still make use of the courtyard on the Sabbath—also a lenient ruling. ʿAqiba shows Eliezer held that the Seventh-Year produce might be used under specified conditions, and that Israelites might consume Samaritan bread. These rulings do seem highly controversial; both sets were preserved only privately, and neither master could find much support for them. ʿAqiba indeed taught his laws only privately. But the lists *were* preserved in the Mishnah, so at some point they became public and were accepted as important records, albeit of private opinions. Reflects hostility, but does not contain a negative view.

ii-7. One should take affirmative action to prevent the violation of the law. Not hostile.

ii-8. If intention is not spelled out, it is of no account. Therefore one does not interpret a man's intention on the basis of his action. ʿAqiba observes that Eliezer is to be praised for his consistency. Eliezer is more or less in accord with the view of the House of Shammai. ʿAqiba: friendly. Pericope: not hostile.

ii-9. Eliezer and ʿAqiba debate the principle of whether the source of uncleanness or the location in which the uncleanness is contracted is decisive in deciding where to burn unclean holy things. Judah says Eliezer is consistent with the House of Shammai. This is one of the few explicit allegations that Eliezer and the House of Shammai exhibit an affinity. But Eliezer's view predominates in the formulation of the Houses' dispute. Not hostile.

ii-10. Eliezer holds that a female minor can effect no legal action. Ishmael praises Eliezer for his consistency in rulings on that subject. Ishmael: friendly. Pericope: not hostile.

ii-11. The dispute among Eliezer, Gamaliel, and Joshua on the Levirate marriage of sisters that were deaf-mutes cannot be considered among the best traditions. Not hostile.

ii-12, 13. Eliezer holds vows may be released on account of the 'honor' of parents and even on account of what happens unexpectedly after the vow has been made. Consequently, Eliezer would make it easy to release people from their vows, so easy, in fact, that vows are no longer of any account. Not hostile.

ii-14. Eliezer holds a conditional writ of divorce is valid. This view in general is consistent with the lenient tendency of the House of Hillel with respect to grounds for divorce. Pericope: not hostile. The story is respectful of Eliezer's opinion but also shows one must and can refute it.

ii-16. Eliezer holds the owner is liable to make up a lost redemption-lamb set aside for the firstling of an ass. Not hostile.

ii-17. Eliezer says that a person may not dedicate the whole of his flock to the Temple, but only part of it. Not hostile. Eleazar: friendly.

ii-18. Eliezer holds that a bee-hive hung in the air space of an oven will save from uncleanness what is contained within an earthenware vessel, because it has the capacity to preserve its contents from the more severe effect of corpse-uncleanness. Therefore he holds one may allow logic to guide the ruling. The sages say that one thing does not affect the other. Not hostile.

ii-19. Eliezer says a shoe on the last is incomplete, therefore is insusceptible to uncleanness. Not hostile. Story: friendly.

ii-20. Two reports, given before ʿAqiba, say Eliezer ruled a woman goes out on the Sabbath wearing a tiara, and pigeon racers may not testify in a court of law. The first opinion is not accepted, the second is, in the Mishnah; Eliezer is not credited with either. The exclusion of Eliezer's name is not explained. Not hostile.

ii-21. One should repent before he dies. Not hostile.

iii-1. Eliezer rules in a way consistent with the view of the House of Shammai that if a *se'ah* of unclean Heave-offering fell into a hundred of clean, it should be taken up and burned but is not lost through its scantiness. The House of Shammai *forbid* the mixture, the House of Hillel *permit* it. Eliezer's view is not exactly the same as the House of Shammai's, for he does not *forbid* the mixture, but allows for the extraction of the prohibited produce. Not hostile. The redactor relates Eliezer to the House of Shammai and sets them parallel to one another; but had the pericope been divided, we should not have supposed Eliezer's opinion to exhibit an affinity with that of the Shammaites; it seems closer to the Hillelites'.

iii-2. Eliezer rules consistently with the House of Shammai that one who gives Heave-offering for grapes but eventually makes the grapes into raisins need not repeat the offering. Not hostile.

iii-3. Eliezer rules consistently with the House of Hillel that one who drinks about a mouthful of liquid on the Day of Atonement is culpable. Not hostile.

iii-4. Not usable.

iii-5. Not usable.

iii-6. Eliezer rules consistently with the House of Hillel that a husband inherits his minor-wife only after sexual relations have taken place. Not hostile.

iii-7. Not usable.

iii-8. Not usable.
iii-9. Not usable.
iii-10. = ii-9.
iii-11. Not usable.
iii-12. Joshua and Eliezer stand for the Houses of Hillel and Shammai respectively. Not hostile.
iv-1. Eliezer holds that a woman is either not hanged at all, or not hanged in the nude. He knows that Simeon b. Sheṭaḥ hung women in Ashqelon. Not hostile.
iv-2. Not usable.
iv-3. Eliezer holds that uncleanness does not pertain to liquids and cites the testimony of Yosi b. Yoʿezer. Not hostile.
v-1, 2, 3, 4, 5, 6. Not usable.
vi-1. Eliezer holds that if a person does many individual sins of a single category in a single period of unawareness, he has to bring a Sin-offering for each one. ʿAqiba differs. Not hostile.
vi-2. The same rule as ii-1, 2. The story claims Ishmael was hostile to Eliezer. Pericope: not hostile. Ishmael: explicitly hostile.
vi-3. Eliezer says the first fruits in the garden are obligated to the agricultural offerings because they are guarded. This is consistent with Judah b. Ilai's view of the opinion of the House of *Hillel.* Not hostile.
vii-2. Fruit from abroad is not liable to agricultural offerings. Not hostile.
vii-5, 6, 7, 8. Eliezer has several rules on the rite of Atonement. None hostile.
vii-9. Eliezer is consistent with the House of Hillel in respect to eating an egg born on the festival. Not hostile.
vii-10. Eliezer supplies an exegesis for Lev. 23 : 24 with respect to the liturgy of the New Year. Not hostile.
vii-11. Eliezer rules on spinning the blue wool for the fringe. M. M.Q. 3 : 4 omits Eliezer's name. Not hostile.
vii-12. Eliezer says they set up a new millstone in the festival week. Not hostile.
vii-13. The orphan who has exercised the right of refusal has the right of usufruct of *melog*-property, consistent with ii-10. Not hostile.
vii-14, 15, 16. Eliezer says if a Nazir contracts uncleanness at the very end of his period, he loses a small number of days, rather than the whole period. A general rule is given. Not hostile.
vii-17. Not usable.
vii-18. = iv-1.
vii-23. Eliezer rules on the laws of 'Tents.' Not hostile.
vii-27, 28. Eliezer rules on the laws of preparing the Sin-offering water. Not hostile.
vii-1. Not usable.
vii-4. Eliezer holds one may acquire a share in an *ʿeruv* by means of a payment of money. Not hostile.
vii-19. Not usable.
vii-20. If members of a Sin-offering were confused with the members of

a Whole-offering, they all may be put on the altar-fire, so Eliezer. The mixture is valid. Not hostile.

vii-21. Blood of unblemished offerings which has been confused with the blood of blemished offerings may be offered—essentially the same principle as in vii-20. Not hostile.

vii-22. If someone took Meal-offering with the wrong intention, the handful is invalid. Not hostile.

vii-24. Eliezer rules on a matter of 'Tents.' Not hostile.

vii-25. Eliezer rules more strictly than the opposed sages on the uncleanness of dirt from a foreign country. Not hostile.

vii-26. Eliezer rules on how one who has deliberately cut off leprosy-signs becomes clean. Not hostile.

vii-29. Eliezer rules on status of honey-combs *vis à vis* Sabbath and Seventh-year law. Not hostile.

Meir's and Judah's differences on Eliezer's opinions are not among the best traditions.

Not a single legal tradition is phrased in such a way as to reflect hostility toward Eliezer b. Hyrcanus. Apart from the saying of Ishmael—contradicted by another—and the lists of Ilai and ʿAqiba, we have no evidence that the formulation and transmission of Eliezer's teachings were subject to extraordinary or negative circumstances. Eleazar b. 'Azariah, Joshua, Gamaliel, and especially ʿAqiba regularly occur with Eliezer. Whatever the history of those pericopae, it does not include an effort to denigrate Eliezer, whose opinions register at parity with his opposition, whose reasoning is clearly spelled out, and who is treated with unfailing respect. We cannot claim that these are signs of a favorable opinion of Eliezer. But they certainly yield no hint of hostility toward him or his traditions. Overall, the traditions about Eliezer derive from friendly or neutral sources, ʿAqiban and otherwise. So far as evidence permits, we may suppose those sources include Eliezer's own disciples. Of Ilai there can be no doubt. ʿAqiba occurs chiefly as an equal; we see no hint that he was Eliezer's disciple. The numerous instances in which ʿAqiba presents an opinion contrary to Eliezer's do not suggest he was a disciple. But this fact makes all the more striking the considerable involvement of ʿAqiba in Eliezer's materials.

The earliest Eliezer exhibits no affinity to, or relationship with, Yoḥanan b. Zakkai, whose name is entirely absent, and whose legal rulings—such as they may have been at the end of Yavnean times—are strikingly ignored. Eliezer never appears as a co-disciple with Joshua. If both masters studied with the same authority, we have no evidence of that fact.

Eliezer is not consistently associated with the House of Shammai. In some instances, such as ii-1, 2; ii-8, ii-9; iii-1 (?), iii-2, iii-12, he rules in a way not inconsistent with the House of Shammai. In others, such as ii-5, ii-14, [iii-1 (!)], iii-3, iii-6, iii-9, he seems closer to the Hillelites. In still other pericopae involving the Houses, Eliezer stands apart from the opinions of both. He would seem closer to the Shammaites in six (or five) pericopae, to the Hillelites in five (or six). What is most important is that in none of these cases is association with the House of Shammai regarded as a reason to reject Eliezer's opinion, nor do we see an effort to tie Eliezer to the House of Shammai in order to exclude his opinions from consideration. The picture is confused; I discern no effort at systematization.

The subject-matter of Eliezer's rulings attested at Yavneh covers much the same ground as the Houses' rulings (*Phar.* III, pp. 223-230), but introduces new issues as well. The two bodies of material compare as follows (" " = Eliezer rules on or in the same pericope):

Houses	*Eliezer*
	A. *Temple Law, Jerusalem, Pilgrimage, and Priestly Dues*
1. Burning unclean with clean meat	1. " "
2. Laying on of hands	2. —
3. Bitter-water ritual	3. —(But Eliezer rules on other aspects of the ritual, M. Sot. 1 : 1)
4. Israelites eat first-born with priests	4. —
5. Children make pilgrimage	5. —
6. —	6. Cattle given to the Temple are not sacrificed but sold.
7. —	7. Liability for lost redemption-lamb set aside for firstling of an ass.
8. —	8. One may not dedicate all one's property to Temple.
9-10. —	9-10. Preparing Sin-offering water—two rulings.
11. —	11. Whole-offering parts confused with Sin-offering parts are burned together.
12. —	12. Blood from blemished offerings mixed with blood from unblemished offerings is sprinkled.
13. —	13. Wrong intention renders Meal-offering invalid.

B. *Agricultural Tithes, Offerings, and Taboos*

1. Unclean Heave-offering mixed with clean (Eliezer b. Hyrcanus)	1. —
2. Giving Heave-offering of grapes and the remainder is eventually made into raisins (Eliezer b. Hyrcanus)	2. —
3. Removing old produce at Nisan (Joshua b. Ḥananiah)	3. —
4. *Pe'ah* from olives, carobs—how given (Gamaliel II)	4. —
5. Forgotten-sheaf-rules (Eliezer b. ʿAzariah, Joshua b. Ḥananiah)	5. —
6. Seventh-year-produce rules (Ṭarfon)	6. —
7. Second-tithe money in Jerusalem (Ṭarfon, Ben Zoma, Ben ʿAzzai, ʿAqiba)	7. —
8. Heave-offering vetches (ʿAqiba)	8. —
9. Fleece-offering (ʿAqiba)	9. —
10. Date of New Year for trees (ʿAqiba)	10. —
11. Olive-presses in walls of Jerusalem (ʿAqiba)	11. —
12. Fourth-year-fruit rules (ʿAqiba)	12. —
13. Mixed seeds in vineyard (ʿAqiba)	13. —
14. Heave-offering from black and white figs (Ilai)	14. " "
15. —	15. Clean-Heave-offering for unclean. [= No. 2]
16. —	16. Cakes of Thank-offering of Nazirite exempt from Dough-offering
17. —	17. *ʿOrlah*-laws abroad
18. — [But compare No. 10.]	18. Status of *etrog*
19. —	19. Seventh-Year oil may be used for anointing hide.
20. —	20. Dough-offering on 15 Nisan.
21. — [But compare M. Shev. 4 : 2B.]	21. First-fruits in garden are guarded, therefore liable.
22. —	22. Fruit from abroad is free of liability.
23. —	23. Making olives and grapes into oil and wine.

C. *Sabbath-Law*

1. *ʿEruv* in public domain (Ḥananiah, nephew of Joshua)	1. —
2. *ʿEruv* for separate kinds of food (Ḥananiah, nephew of Joshua)	2. —

3. *ʿEruv* for alley (Eliezer b. Hyrcanus + ʿAqiba + disciple of Ishmael)	3. " "
4. Gentile/Sadducee in alley *re ʿeruv* (Gamaliel II = Meir + Judah)	4. — [But see No. 7.]
5. Work started before Sabbath (ʿAqiba)	5. —
6. —	6. No *ʿeruv* if field has wall.
7. — [But see No. 4.]	7. Failure of partner to participate in *ʿeruv* does not restrict others.
8. —	8. Woman may wear tiara on Sabbath.
9. —	9. Acquiring a share in the *ʿeruv*.

D. *Festival Law*

1. How much does one drink to be liable on the Day of Atonement (Eliezer b. Hyrcanus)	1. " "
2. Large cakes *re* Passover Gamaliel II)	2. —
3. Pick pulse on festival (Gamaliel II)	3. —
4. Other festival rules (Gamaliel II)	4. —
5. Size of *Sukkah* (Eleazar b. R. Ṣaddoq)	5. —
6. —	6. Hart's-tongue on Passover.
7.-10.	7-10. Rulings on rite of Atonement.
11.— [Eliezer attests Houses' dispute, M. Bes. 1 : 1.]	11. Egg born on festival.
12. —	12. New millstone on festival week.

E. *Liturgy*

1. Order of blessing: Oil *vs.* myrtle (Gamaliel II)	1. —
2. Proper position of saying *Shemaʿ* (Eleazar b. ʿAzariah, Ishmael, Ṭarfon)	2. —
3. How far recite *Hallel* at *Seder* (Ṭarfon, ʿAqiba)	3. —
4. *Tefillin* in privy (ʿAqiba)	4. —
5. Where shake *Lulav* (ʿAqiba, *re* Gamaliel, Joshua)	5. —
6. Limit *re ṣiṣit* (Jonathan b. Batyra)	6. —
7. Circumcision of child born circumcized (Eleazar b. R. Ṣaddoq)	7. —
8. —	8. New Year liturgy (Lev. 23 : 24).

F. *Uncleanness Laws*

1. Quarter-*qab* of bones in 'Tent' (Joshua b. Ḥananiah)	1. —

2. Woman kneading in 'Tent' (ʿAqiba, Joshua b. Ḥananiah)	2. —
3. If man shook tree—preparation for uncleanness by reason of water (Joshua b. Ḥananiah)	3. —
4. Uncleanness of liquids—Yosi b. Yoʿezer (Eliezer b. Hyrcanus + ʿAqiba)	4. " "
5. Uncleanness of scroll-wrappers (Gamaliel II)	5. —
6. When do olives receive uncleanness in harvest (Gamaliel II)	6. —
7. Mustard-strainer (Eleazar b. R. Ṣaddoq)	7. —
8. Itch inside itch (cleanness rite) (ʿAqiba)	8. —
9. Insusceptibility of sheet (ʿAqiba)	9. —
10. Searching grave-area (ʿAqiba)	10. —
11. Issue of semen in third day (ʿAqiba)	11. —
12. Uncleanness of fish (ʿAqiba)	12. —
13. —	13. Partitions in 'Tent.'
14. —	14. Shoe on the last is incomplete, therefore clean.
15. —	15. Even though door is open, house is clean—*re* 'Tents.'
16. —	16. Jars tightly covered with bit of corpse inside.
17.	17. Dirt from grave-area.
18. —	18. Leprosy sign deliberately removed.
19. —	19. Ritual status of honey-comb.

G. *Civil Law, Torts, and Damages. Criminal Law.*

1. Damaged bailment (ʿAqiba)	1. —
2. —	2. Woman hanged +/— naked.

H. *Family Law and Inheritances*

1. Vow not to have intercourse (Eliezer).	1. [May not be our Eliezer]
2. Husband's inheritance when wife dies as a minor (Eliezer b. Hyrcanus)	2. " "
3. Signs of adulthood (Eliezer b. Hyrcanus)	3. " "
4. Levirate rules *re* brothers married to sisters (Eliezer b. Hyrcanus, Eleazar b. ʿAzariah, Abba Saul)	4. " "
5. Levirate rules *re* co-wives (Ṭarfon,	5. —

Eleazar b. ʿAzariah, ʿAqiba, Joshua b. Ḥananiah)	
6. Test rags for each act of intercourse (Joshua b. Ḥananiah).	6. —
7. Sanctifies property and intends to divorce wife (Joshua b. Ḥananiah + Eliezer b. Hyrcanus)	7. " "
8. Wife remarries on testimony of one witness (ʿAqiba, Gamaliel II).	8. —
9. Grounds for divorce (ʿAqiba)	9. —
10. Dividing estate where order of deaths is unclear (ʿAqiba)	10. —
11. Blood of woman who has given birth and not immersed (Eliezer).	11. " "
12. — [But see No. 2.]	12. Deed of a female-minor is null.
13. —	13. Levir refused by minor.
14. — [But see No. 9.]	14. Conditional divorce valid.
15. —	15. Minor who has exercised right of refusal still controls usufruct of *melog.* [= 12]

I. *Miscellany*

1. Taboo against drinking gentile wine (Gamaliel II)	1. —
2. Eliezer b. Hyrcanus *re* overturning couch before festival, b. M.Q. 20a, is given by Eleazar b. R. Simeon as Houses-dispute, Tos, M.Q. 2 : 9.	2. " "

Eliezer Alone

1. Releasing vows made easy.
2. Gambler may not testify.
3. Samaritan bread permitted to Israelites.
4. Repent before death.
5. Many sinful acts of a single type are punished by an equivalent number of Sin-offerings.
6. Spinning blue-wool for fringe.

7-9. Nazir who contracts uncleanness on last day of his period—various rulings.

The themes of Eliezer's rulings are much the same as those of the Houses, and the proportions seem about right, with one exception. In this stratum Eliezer is strikingly silent on liturgical matters. This would accord with the (presently unattested) ruling that a fixed liturgy is not to be followed; if so, Eliezer would not issue many rulings on the subject.

But the substance in detail of Eliezer's rulings strikingly differs from that of the Houses. Eliezer paid attention to dedications to the Temple; the pericopae of the Houses attested at Yavneh ignore the subject. He has important rulings on the preparation of Sin-offering water—and others, not attested at Yavneh, are likely to be valid traditions. The Houses do not rule on the subject. He solves through logic various problems of mixtures of diverse holy materials and how they are to be disposed of. The Houses do not enter that problem at all. He deals—at length, as we shall see later on—with the problem of intention in the cult. The Houses do not. His rulings on the Temple thus concern strikingly fundamental matters. The tendency of those rulings is to figure out the logic and consistent order to be imposed on the Temple cult. What actually was done never enters his framework of discussion. He seems to have attempted to develop a coherent and internally logical set of rules on the Temple cult and its conduct.

While some of the rules on agricultural taboos concern both the Houses and Eliezer, others involve Eliezer alone. These tend to represent striking innovations in antecedent laws. Two themes seem important, first, the status of the produce of foreign countries; second, and of fundamental importance, the easing of the distinctions in produce subject to Heave-offering.

As to Sabbath law, for both the Houses and Eliezer the *ʿeruv* appears as a predominate concern. In respect to festival law, Eliezer has important new rulings on the rite of the Day of Atonement—appropriate for his agendum for the Temple, which concentrates on the conduct of the cult.

The subject-matter of the uncleanness rules is pretty much the same, but the specific rulings of Eliezer are original. Again, we observe a tendency to solve a problem through abstract reasoning, rather than through a simple edict or citation of established practice. This would account for the difference between the discrete rules attributed to the Houses on when and whether various objects are susceptible to uncleanness, in contrast to Eliezer's effort on the same themes to give reasons for rulings, applying to more than the single case at hand.

Civil and criminal law is virtually ignored by both the Houses and Eliezer.

The interest in family law and inheritances is much the same; vows, inheritances, Levirate rules, and divorces concern both parties. But Eliezer's generalization about the nullity of the deed of a female minor and the rule, susceptible to generalization and expansion, about the conditional divorce, are unknown to the Houses and constitute far-reaching theoretical innovations.

Entirely new legal themes involve releasing vows, rules of testimony, the law of the Nazirite who has become unclean, and the general principle about liability for various similar sinful acts. These do not yield completely new agenda of legislative legal interest. But they are, individually, quite novel topics, on which the Yavnean pericopae of the Houses are silent.

Why do we have a corpus of materials, with and without Yavnean attestations, so much larger on Eliezer than on Yoḥanan b. Zakkai? Perhaps ʿAqiba is the key, for he is credited with the major role in the formation and transmission of the Yavnean tradition. Since he evidently had much to do with, and may have been the disciple of, Eliezer, and had little, if anything, to do with Yoḥanan, he and his disciples preserved a very substantial record of Eliezer, and little of Yoḥanan. But ʿAqiba is alleged also to have been associated with Joshua. Between Eliezer and Joshua he ought to have known a good deal about Yoḥanan. The most likely answer is that in Yavnean times Yoḥanan's position as master of Eliezer and Joshua was not known. The reason is either that he was not their master at all or that it was advantageous to both disciples to suppress what they had received from Yoḥanan and to give in their own names what were actually his traditions. I tend to think the former is more likely.

Clearly Eliezer was a post-70 continuator of pre-70 Pharisaism. But what evidence do we have that Yoḥanan was a Pharisee in pre-70 times? If we examine his legal rulings, we find strikingly few pertinent to the predominant agenda of pre-70 Pharisaism:

1. Sifré Num. 123: Heifer sacrifice carried out in white garments. Story.
2. Sifra Shemini 7 : 12: "Third" loaf is unclean by the second.
3. Sifra Emor 16 : 9: *Lulav* taken as a memorial to the Temple.
4. Sifra Emor 16 : 9: New produce is prohibited on the entire Day of Waving.
5. M. Shab. 16 : 17: One may cover a scorpion on the Sabbath.
6. M. Shab. 22 : 3: One may open a jar to eat dried figs, but not pierce the plug of a jar on the Sabbath.
7. M. Sheq. 1 : 4: Priests have to pay the *sheqel.*
8. M. Suk. 2 : 5: Food must be eaten in the *Sukkah* even for a random meal.
9. M. R.H. 1 : 1: The *shofar* may be sounded on the Sabbath.

10. M. R.H. 4 : 4: Witnesses may testify about the New Moon throughout the day.
11. M. Ket. 13 : 1: A woman swears at the end with respect to maintenance.
12. M. Ket. 13 : 2: A person who maintains another man's wife has no claim to recompense.
13. M. Sanh. 5 : 2: Evidence should be carefully tested.
14. M. Ed. 8 : 3, 7: Courts can not tell the priests whom to marry.
15. M. Kel. 2 : 2: Broken sides of large jugs are not susceptible to uncleanness.
16. M. Kel. 17 : 16: A beam of a balance (etc.) is susceptible to uncleanness. (Not attributed to Yoḥanan.)
17. M. Yad. 4 : 3: Ammon and Moab give Poorman's Tithe in the Seventh Year.
18. M. Yad. 4 : 6: Scriptures render the hands unclean. (Not attributed to Yoḥanan.)

The Mishnaic evidence deals, therefore, with the following:

Temple and Priesthood: Nos. 1, 7, 14
Agricultural Rules: Nos. 4, 17
Festival Law: Nos. 5, 6
Liturgy: Nos. 3, 8, 9, 10
Uncleanness Laws: Nos. 2, 15, 18
Civil Law, Torts, Damages, Criminal Law: Nos. 11, 12, 13
Family Law and Inheritances:—

Pre-70 Pharisees and Eliezer tend to rule primarily on agricultural law, Sabbath and festival rules, and uncleanness. Yoḥanan's traditions are scattered; most of those on the festival have to do with the problems posed by the Destruction. The law in Nos. 11, 12, 17, and 18 is not accredited to Yoḥanan; he simply approves what others have done. In all, Yoḥanan's legal agenda hardly correspond to those of the pre-70 Houses—about which he knows nothing—and seem on the whole to focus upon the Temple, the priests, and the liturgical consequence of the Destruction, rather than upon any other matter. The greater number of his other rulings has to do with Sabbath and festival laws. To be sure, the whole thing adds up to very little. But while, on the basis of the extant laws, one may reasonably claim Eliezer was a Pharisee, on the same basis one cannot claim the same for Yoḥanan. At best one may say he *might* have been a Pharisee. The external evidence does not help; Luke-Acts knows Gamaliel; Josephus knows Simeon b. Gamaliel; but no external source knows about Yoḥanan, despite the decisive role in events of the day claimed for him by the later story-tellers.

The earliest Eliezer therefore stands within the framework of pre-70 Pharisaism. We need not doubt he was one of the major continuators of the sect. Assuming he came to Yavneh as an adult, he probably had sound information on the sect's beliefs and practices before 70. This makes all the more interesting the striking innovations he evidently introduced. The chief one would seem to be the tendency to work out the logic behind discrete rulings or to apply logic to superficially unrelated problems. A second would be the extension of the legal agenda to include the exact conduct of the Temple cult. Whether or not others were preserving a record of what had been done in Jerusalem, Eliezer certainly attempted to produce an orderly account of what should be done in the future. But his rulings pertain to exceptional and theoretical circumstances—mixtures of holy materials which should not normally be mixed up—and this must mean that the basic procedures of the Temple were well-established and acceptable to him. A third innovation is the effort to simplify what may formerly have been complicated and perhaps internally contradictory rules, for example, on the status of the female-minor, the releasing of vows, the giving of Heave-offering from related, but slightly different substances, and the like. In all these matters Eliezer seems to have sought to impose a single, comprehensive, and, on the whole, lenient rule, one which in general would uncomplicate the status of individuals and straighten out the complex application of taboos. In all, therefore, the earliest Eliezer emerges as an important, original lawyer. His legal rulings were carefully worked out and transmitted in the circle of the leading authority of the following generation, ʿAqiba, and involved the major figures of his own day, particularly ʿAqiba, Joshua, Gamaliel, and Eleazar b. ʿAzariah.

CHAPTER NINE

THE BETTER TRADITIONS

i. The ʿAqiban Eliezer

It is generally taken for granted that the founders of the Ushan academy consisted of the disciples of ʿAqiba, so that Ushan traditions are based primarily upon, or evolve from, the ʿAqiban part of the Yavnean corpus. Whether this supposition is correct or not I cannot say. But it is certainly a fact that the largest number of pericopae attested at Yavneh for which we are at all able to propose a redactional authority are to be attributed to Ilai. In the assumption that a pericope involving Eliezer and another master derives not from Eliezer himself, but from him and the other master, or, more likely, from his disciples and those of said master, we may assign the Yavnean pericopae as follows (the items are enumerated according to appearance in Chapter Eight, Section ii):

ii-1, 2. Ilai
ii-3. Ilai
ii-4 [15]. Yoḥanan b. Nuri
ii-5. Ilai
ii-6. Ilai
ii-7. Joshua + ʿAqiba
ii-8. — (ʿAqiba approves)
ii-9. Judah b. Ilai
ii-10. —
ii.-11. —
ii-12. —
ii-13. —
ii-14. —
ii-16. —
ii-17. Eleazar b. ʿAzariah(?)
ii-18. —
ii-19. —
ii-20. —(Reports *to* ʿAqiba)
ii-21. Ilai

Where we have any evidence at all on the basis of which to assign responsibility for a pericope to a particular authority or circle, we seem to come back to Ilai, for six of the twenty-one pericopae, with Judah his son behind a seventh. Strikingly, we have no basis on which to assign the formation of even a single pericope to ʿAqiba himself, though ii-20 might belong to his circle (assuming it is Yavnean). When, furthermore, we add to the list the still larger number of pericopae attested by a chain involving Judah b. Ilai, we see that a considerable proportion of the best traditions seems to go back to Ilai and his son (and grandson). They would form an independent stem of Eliezer's tradition, separate from that shaped by the Ushan ʿAqibans, an earlier tradition in attestation, and considerably more reliable, on the face of it, deriving, as it does, from Eliezer's own student.

The better traditions thus represent a distinct strand in the whole corpus of Eliezer's materials. They bear not only a later attestation, but also a quite different probable point of origin, with ʿAqiba's disciples at Usha. If ʿAqiba studied with Eliezer, they should be not much less reliable than the best traditions, except that they stand one step removed from Eliezer, with the disciple's disciples, rather than the disciple himself, taking the chief part in their formulation and redaction. This trait becomes evident in the Ushans' difficulty in agreeing upon the definition of the protases of Eliezer's pericopae. They had in common a thematic agenda, but not much else.

ii. The Laws

We enumerate according to the list of attestations by Ushans, above, p. 75. Judah b. Ilai's chains and related pericopae have already been considered (pp. 124-129).

1. *Forgotten Sheaves*

Tos. Peʾah 3 : 2 (*Phar.* II, pp. 60-63) has a first-person saying of Ilai, "I asked Joshua... And when I came and asked Leazar..." The Leazar almost certainly should be Eliezer, since the conclusion is, as above, "And when I came and laid the matters out before Leazar b. ʿAzariah." The issue is the definition of a Houses' dispute in M. Peʾah 6 : 2 about whether the law of the forgotten sheaf applies to a sheaf left near a wall or some other identifiable object. M. follows Joshua's definition, as against Leazar's, but, as above, Eleazar b. ʿAzariah endorses the latter's view. If the text had read Liezer, the pericope would belong among the best traditions. It certainly has been formulated so as to affirm the accuracy of Eliezer's traditions on the Houses. The pericope is classified as friendly to Eliezer.

2. *Tos. Dem. 1 : 3*

See above, p. 122.

3. *Handkerchiefs and 'Diverse Kinds'*

Judah and Meir dispute the opinions of Eliezer and the sages on whether handkerchiefs, wrappers for Torah-scrolls, and bath towels come under the law of 'diverse kinds.' Eliezer "prohibits" in M. Kil.

9 : 3—the view of Meir. Judah says he permits and the sages prohibit, so Tos. Kil. 5 : 18. Judah's tradition places Eliezer in the lenient position. This accords with his father's tendency, but also ʿAqiba's, as exemplified in their respective lists (above, p. 99). But since ʿAqiba's tendency was along the same lenient lines, we cannot suppose Meir here exemplifies an ʿAqiban effort to represent Eliezer as more strict than he really was. The pericope is not hostile.

4. *Neutralizing Heave-Offering*

Tos. Ter. 5 : 10-11/M. Ter. 4 : 8-11 deal with neutralizing Heave-offering which has fallen into a large quantity of secular produce. Eliezer holds a hundred and one parts are required to neutralize; Joshua, a hundred and a bit more—a negligible difference.

Joshua then holds (M. Ter. 4 : 8) that black figs neutralize white, and *vice versa*; Eliezer denies it. ʿAqiba says if one knows what has fallen into the mixture, the black cannot neutralize the white, but if not, they can—essentially Eliezer's opinion.

In Tos. Ter. 5 : 10, Meir and Judah differ on the opinions of Eliezer and Joshua. Meir holds Eliezer's opinion is that when what has fallen in is known, it will not neutralize, but when not, it will; Joshua says whether known or unknown, it will not neutralize. So Meir's Eliezer is the same as the Mishnah's, but his Joshua is in a position still more strict than the Mishnah's Eliezer.

Judah then says Eliezer says, Whether known or not known, it will not neutralize; and Joshua says, Whether known or not known, it will neutralize; Judah introduces ʿAqiba's compromise. Thus Meir's Eliezer is Judah's ʿAqiba; Meir's Joshua is Judah's Eliezer! Meir clearly has placed Eliezer in the position of his teacher, ʿAqiba—about whose involvement in the pericope Meir knows nothing. Similarly in Tos. Ter. 5 : 11 Judah has Eliezer in the strict position, but then defines for Joshua a still more strict opinion.

What is attested by the Ushans, therefore, is that the early Yavneans disputed about the principles of the neutralization of Heave-offering. But exactly what position was held by which master cannot be said to have been clearly known at Usha, if, as is obvious, a wide range of positions leaves room for several, incompatible opinions to be assigned to each master. While from the best traditions we derive knowledge of the exact opinions held by Eliezer, from the better ones we seem reliably to locate the themes or legal agenda on which he evidently laid down laws, but not the exact opinions he actually held.

Nor can we extrapolate from the best to the better traditions an opinion which Eliezer ought, on the basis of the former, to have held in connection with the latter. We have no clear idea of Eliezer's tendency in the materials before us. To be sure, he ruled in a lenient way about giving Heave-offering from clean to unclean produce. But that does not justify supposing that here, too, he would rule, in a lenient spirit, that the Heave-offering may be easily neutralized, for the legal principles are not the same and are not even related.

The pericope is not hostile.

5. *A Deed Begun Licitly and Completed Illicitly*

Nathan's saying in Tos. Ter. 7 : 10C attests to M. Ter. 8 : 3: If a person was eating a grapecluster and went from the garden to the courtyard on the eve of the Sabbath, and it got dark, Eliezer says the man may finish the grapes, and Joshua says he may not. Eliezer therefore holds what is begun licitly may be concluded, even though in the meantime it is no longer licit. Nathan says Eliezer says he may finish eating only when the Sabbath is over—so he makes Eliezer's opinion into Joshua's, and both are strict. The contrary tradition of Eliezer's opinion, represented in the Mishnah, is consistent for all cases; Nathan's applies only for this one. Eliezer's position in general accords with that of the House of Hillel in M. Shab. 1 : 4-8. Accordingly, Nathan's saying should attest to the dispute between Eliezer, Joshua, and Gamaliel in M. Ter. 8 : 8.

While Nathan may be said to attest to the principle under dispute, he does not seem to supply important evidence about Eliezer's position in the matter. On the contrary, since he so defines Eliezer's view as to make it equivalent to Joshua's, it would seem Eliezer's view in the opinion of others is that what has begun licitly may be completed, even though in the meantime it has become illicit.

6. *The Definition of Liquids*

M. Ter. 11 : 2 has Joshua and Eliezer debate the definition of liquids. Eliezer holds that date-honey, cider, vinegar from winter grapes, or other juices (except wine and oil) are regarded as liquids and are capable of becoming unclean and rendering produce susceptible to uncleanness. Joshua says there are seven kinds of liquid which render unclean, and all other liquids do not. In Tos. Ter. 9 : 8 we find Nathan's definition of the issue. He says Eliezer agrees date-honey is not liable to tithes and does not render unclean as a liquid; if water is put into it, then (naturally) it is liable and does render unclean. Nathan again remakes Eliezer's opinion into the equivalent of Joshua's.

Tos. Ter. 9 : 9 has further attestations of the dispute, in the names of Meir, Jacob, Judah, and, finally, Rabbi. Here the issue is turning into oil Heave-offering-olives which are clean, and the same of grapes into wine. Jacob in Meir's name has a dispute between Liezer and Joshua on unclean olives. Eliezer says they may not be made into oil. Joshua says they may. Judah says they agree on olives and grapes, that, when clean, they be made into oil and wine; but they differ on the unclean, with Liezer in the negative position. Rabbi says they differ neither on the clean olives, which may be made into liquid, nor on the unclean grapes, which may not be made into wine, but only concerning unclean olives and clean grapes. Thus all possible positions have been stated. M. Ter. 11 : 3 knows no distinction between olives and grapes, clean or unclean, indeed nothing of Tos.'s disputes. Thus subject-matter of the dispute is well-attested; but the exact opinion of Eliezer (and of Joshua) therefore again eludes us.

The pericope is not hostile.

7. *Circumcision and the Sabbath*

Tos. Shab. 15 : 10/M. Shab. 19 : 4 deals with circumcision on the Sabbath. The attested issue concerns a child supposed to be circumcized after the Sabbath, who is actually circumcized on the Sabbath. Eliezer and Joshua, according to Simeon b. Yoḥai, agree that the man is liable. But if the child is to be circumcized on Friday, and the operation is done on the Sabbath, Eliezer declares the man liable for Sin-offering. Then a debate is supplied.

M. Shab. 19 : 4 has a confusion of *two* babies, but the problem is the same: circumcizing on the Sabbath when it is not the eighth day after birth. Then, in b. Shab. 137a, Simeon b. Eleazar has them disagree on a confusion of two infants; Meir attests a dispute on the same case, but on different days. Simeon b. Eleazar deals with Friday and Saturday; Meir, Saturday and Sunday. These constitute strong attestations not only for the theme of the dispute, but also of Eliezer's opinion in principle. Eliezer certainly holds that one who circumcizes on the Sabbath when that is not the eighth day after birth will be liable to a Sin-offering. According to M. Shab. 19 : 4, the obligation to circumcize is such that if the eighth day does not coincide with the

Sabbath, the obligation is sufficiently diminished so that one should not do so on the Sabbath.

M. Shab. 19 : 1 has Eliezer take a lenient position with respect to ʿAqiba's. One may do anything at all in respect to a circumcision on the Sabbath. ʿAqiba holds one may do on the Sabbath only what cannot be done beforehand, that is, the actual operation. Judah the Patriarch attests to this dispute, but the construction of Tos. Shab. 15 : 16, involving Yosi b. Ḥalafta, then Eliezer and ʿAqiba, is such that 19 : 1 ought to be accorded an Ushan attestation as well.

If so, we have two opinions for Eliezer, one quite lenient, allowing anything at all to be done in connection with a circumcision on the Sabbath, the other quite strict, holding that an error in circumcizing on the Sabbath a child that needs to be circumcized on some other day produces the liability to a Sin-offering. These principles are not in contradiction. The leniency of the first imposes the strictness of the second: one may do what needs to be done on the Sabbath, but one must be sure that the operation actually has to be performed on the Sabbath. The pericope is not hostile.

8. *Making Two ʿEruvs*

Judah b. Ilai rules consistently with Eliezer's opinion, in Tos. Eruv. 4 : 1-2, M. Eruv. 3 : 6-7. This constitutes warrant for assigning the pericope to our Eliezer, but, since the consistency is not made explicit, it is hardly sufficient evidence for a strong Ushan attestation.

9. *Acquiring an ʿEruv*

M. Eruv. 7 : 11D contains Judah b. Ilai's gloss of a dispute between Eliezer and sages on purchasing a share in an *ʿeruv* with coins. Judah explains the principle at hand. One may gain an advantage for a person without his knowledge but may not obligate him without his knowledge. Therefore in respect to the *ʿeruv* of courtyard, one may do so without the man's knowledge. But since placing the *ʿeruv* for the Sabbath obligates a man to rely upon that, and not some other, *ʿeruv*, one may not do so.

The pericope is not hostile.

10. *M. Eruv. 9 : 2/b. B.B. 100a*

Judah's consistency with Eliezer's opinion does not constitute an explicit, Ushan attestation, but merely a warrant for supposing the opinion belongs to our Eliezer.

11. *Repeating a Lesson*

The story about how Moses taught the Mishnah to Aaron, b. Eruv. 54b, contains a gloss of Judah b. Ilai: Aaron sat on the right of Moses. Judah provides a firm *terminus ante quem* for the story, which illustrates Eliezer's view that one must teach his disciple a given tradition four times, against ʿAqiba's view that the tradition is to be repeated until the disciple has learned it, however many times. Since the story accords with the opinion attributed to Eliezer, and since Judah b. Ilai clearly knows the story, it stands to reason that the story and appended dispute accurately reflect Eliezer's opinion on the procedures of oral transmission of traditions.

The pericope is not hostile.

12. *Burning Together Clean and Unclean Heave-offering-Ḥameṣ*

M. Pes. 1 : 7/Tos. Pis. 1 : 5 contain a dispute between Eliezer and Joshua about burning Heave-offering of *ḥameṣ* that is unclean together with what is clean. Eliezer says each is burned by itself, apart from the other. Joshua says they may be burned together. Then Yosi [b. Ḥalafta] claims the dispute concerned burning together what is doubtfully unclean with what is certainly unclean, with the same opinions following. Now this Ushan dispute is appended to the earlier one, M. Pes. 1 : 6, which has both ʿAqiba and Ḥanina hold one *may* burn flesh made unclean from a derived uncleanness together with that made unclean from a primary source of uncleanness. So Eliezer and Joshua are represented in the Ushan stratum in a position considerably more strict than that assigned to ʿAqiba and Ḥanina—and well attested by the participation of Eliezer in the definition of the Houses' dispute on the same subject, above, p. 106(!).

But Eliezer may well have distinguished between the sacrificial refuse, which is to be burned, and the Heave-offering, for he has held—in a well-attested Yavnean pericope—that one must under no circumstances permit Heave-offering to be made unclean if one can do anything to stop it. So the Ushan stratum follows and depends upon M. Ter. 8 : 8-11, and might be logically inferred from it.

The pericope is not hostile.

13. *The Measure of the Dough*

Tos. Pis. 3 : 8 supplements M. Pes. 3 : 3. Nathan has an opinion for Eliezer that one may knead a certain amount of dough and keep it from fermenting on Passover. The issue of M. Pes. 3 : 3 is adequately attested in the Yavnean stratum, and the opinion of Eliezer seems to be accurately represented there.

The pericope is not hostile.

14. *The Passover Slaughtered for Some Other Purpose*

M. Pes. 6 : 5/Tos. Pis. 5 : 4 (+M. Zev. 1 : 1, Tos. Zev. 1 : 1, Tos. Pis. 4 : 5-6) deal with the sacrifice of a Passover for some purpose other than the Passover-offering. Eliezer holds that if one sacrifices on the Sabbath-Passover an animal eligible for the Passover sacrifice for a purpose other than the Passover, he is liable for a Sin-offering. Joshua says he is not liable. Eliezer's argument is that while it is permitted to sacrifice the Passover on the Sabbath for the sake of the Passover, if one does so on the Sabbath for some other purpose, the man is liable. Other sacrifices, *not* to be done on the Sabbath, should then produce the same liability. The man must not only do the right thing, but also do so with the correct intention. Joshua says doing the right thing is sufficient—even with the wrong intention.

In Tos. Simeon redefines the argument. Liezer and Joshua differ not about things *not* valid for the Passover, but about things *valid* to come as a Passover, which have been slaughtered for the sake of the Passover—that is, what M. takes for granted as acceptable. Liezer is in the same position, but on the much more refined issue. If a man has sacrificed animals on the Sabbath which were appropriate for the Passover and has done so for the sake of the Passover, he still is supposed to be held liable by Eliezer. Simeon seems to me not only to attest to the dispute, but also to show the version of M. Pes. to be the earlier formulation of the dispute.

Eliezer moreover is consistent with his view that the matter of intention must be fully spelled out in the proper way. We therefore may definitely assign that position to him and observe that Ushans are consistent with the Yavneans about Eliezer's opinion on the subject.

The pericope is not hostile.

M. Pes. 6 : 5 does not help us to find an attestation for M. Pes. 6 : 1-3.

15. *Sanctifying Cattle Fit for the Altar*

In Tos. Sheq. 2 : 10 Yosah and Simeon attest to the dispute of M. Sheq. 4 : 7, above, p. 105.

16-18. *Traditions on the Atonement Rite*

See above, p. 125.

19. *A Cone-shaped Sukkah*

b. Suk. 19b/M. Suk. 1 : 11/Tos. Suk. 1 : 10 deal with a cone-shaped *Sukkah.* Eliezer says it is unfit because it has no roof, so M. Suk. Tos. Suk. is consistent: Liezer says if there is any sort of roof at all, it is acceptable. b. Suk. has Nathan's tradition of Eliezer's view: It is invalid because it has no roof—an Ushan attestation for Eliezer's opinion. The pericope is not hostile.

20. *Egg Born on the Festival*

See above, Vol. I, p. 150.

21. *Sweeping the Courtyard on the Festival*

Tos. Y.T. 3 : 18/M. Bes. 4 : 6-7 present Eliezer's ruling that on a festival one may make use of a splinter with which to pick his teeth, even though the wood has not been set aside for that purpose on the preceding day. He is consistent with the general tendency of the House of Hillel. Tos.'s gloss, in the name of Simeon, may supply an Ushan attestation. But Tos. as it stands has Liezer argue with Simeon—scarcely a sign that this is our Eliezer at all. Simeon attests the Houses' dispute on the same principle so he has made an Eliezer (if not ours) into a Hillelite.

22. *Tos. R.H. 2 : 10*

See above, Vol. I, p. 154, and above, p. 125.

23. *The Powers of Rain*

In M. Ta. 1 : 1 Eliezer says one says 'the powers of rain' from the first day of Sukkot, Joshua, from the last. b. Ta. 2b has Judah [b. Ilai] refer to Eliezer's opinion. If so, it is an Ushan attestation. The pericope is not hostile.

24. *b. M.Q. 19a*

See above, p. 125.

25. *b. M.Q. 10a*

See above, p. 125.

26. *Ḥaliṣah with a Wooden Sandal*

Judah evidently had a tradition in Eliezer's name about not using a wooden sandal for *ḥaliṣah.* He says in Tos. Yev. 12 : 11 that if Eliezer knew the wooden sandal of the present time, he would have accepted it for the *ḥaliṣah*-rite. Eliezer does not occur in M. Yev. 12 : 2. The saying is not hostile.

27. *Tos. Ket. 11 : 4/M. Ket. 11 : 6*

See above, p. 125.

28. *Ransoming a Wife*

Eliezer and Joshua dispute what is to be done when a man has forbidden his wife by vow from enjoying benefit from him, and she is taken captive. Eliezer says he is to redeem her and give her the *Ketuvah.* Joshua says he is not to redeem her. Nathan alludes to the discussion, so signifies a valid *terminus.* The pericope is not hostile.

29-31. *The Unclean Nazir*

See above, p. 125.

32. *Testifying about the Writ of Divorce*

M. Git. 1 : 1 includes a gloss of Gamaliel and Eliezer on the testimony required for a *Geṭ* from foreign parts. Eliezer says a *Geṭ* brought from Kefar Ludim to Lud must be verified by the agent that in his presence it was written and sealed. Gamaliel and Eliezer do not greatly differ, but both do differ from the sages. In M. Git. 1 : 2 Judah refers to Gamaliel's opinion, but not to Eliezer's. He would seem to know the pericope, so to supply a usable attestation. The tradition is not hostile.

33. [= 37]. *Impairment in the Sacrificial Process*

Tos. Zev. 4 : 1-2/b. Pes. 77a/M. Me. 1 : 2-3/Tos. Me. 1 : 6/Tos. Men. 4 : 10, 4 : 14-15/Tos. Zev. 4 : 5-8 all deal with the disposition of the appurtenances of a sacrifice when the meat of the sacrifice is unfit. Eliezer consistently holds that "the blood without the meat" is ineffectual; ʿAqiba says that "the blood without the meat" is effectual. The sprinkling of the blood is at issue. In Tos. Zev. Eliezer holds if there is no sprinkling of blood, the meat is unfit.

We have a number of Ushan attestations. b. Me. 7a has a saying of Simeon b. Yoḥai, that an old man asked him whether ʿAqiba really holds the sprinkling is of effect where the offering has been taken out from its proper location. b. Pes. 77a has Yosi agree with the position of Eliezer in respect to meal-offerings and animal sacrifices, and with Joshua in respect to animal sacrifices and meal-offerings.

The pericopae reveal no hostility to Eliezer.

4. *Limbs of Sin-offering Mixed with Whole-offering*

See above, p. 104.

35. *Mixtures of Cultic Materials*

See above, p. 104.

36. *Meal-offering with Wrong Intention*

See below, p. 170.

38. *Dedicating Property and Paying the Ketuvah*

In M. Ar. 6 : 1, Eliezer holds that a man who dedicated his property to the Temple and is liable for his wife's *Ketuvah* will have to make the wife vow to yield no benefit to him when he divorces her. Joshua says it is unnecessary to make such a vow. Simeon rules consistently with Eliezer, so would supply an Ushan attestation of the *issue*, if not of Eliezer's opinion on it.

39. *The Progeny of Peace-offerings*

Eliezer says the progeny of Peace-offerings may not be brought as Peace-offerings, so M. Tem. 3 : 1. The sages say it may. Simeon b. Yoḥai then claims the difference concerns not the progeny of the progeny of Peace-offerings, but the progeny itself. Joshua and Pappyas then testify that the progeny of Peace-offerings *may* be brought as Peace-offerings. Simeon provides an attestation, though a strange one, since, as noted, he says the dispute is on exactly the stated problem. Joshua and Pappyas agree with Eliezer's opposition. But the pericope is not hostile.

40. *A Sin-offering When in Doubt*

In M. Ker. 4 : 2-3/Tos. Ker. 2 : 12-15, 3 : 5-8, Eliezer and Joshua dispute about a series of cases, all of which pertain to the same problem: Does a man give a Sin-offering when he is not certain exactly what sin he has done, when or whether he has sinned at all?

The first definition of the dispute is on the problem, What if the man sinned but does not know exactly how or when he has sinned? Yosi then redefines the details of the dispute, but not the opinion of the masters. Then Judah comments on the same problem. Finally, Simeon Shezuri and Simeon b. Yoḥai have them dispute concerning a transgression falling within two classes.

Clearly, leading Ushans were certain of the existence of a dispute between Eliezer and Joshua; they knew too that Eliezer would consistently declare the man liable for a Sin-offering, and Joshua would consistently exempt him. But the exact terms of argument seem to have been greatly refined in the course of time, so that the original dispute, if any, ought to have been on the question of whether the man knew he had sinned at all.

In this regard, one recalls Eliezer's opinion that one might bring a Suspensive Sin-offering every day except the Day after the Day of Atonement. These pericopae should provide Ushan attestations for M. Ker. 6 : 1 and 6 : 3, both of which have as Eliezer's opinion that one may as well bring a Suspensive Guilt-offering, for if it is not on account of one sin, it inevitably will cover some other.

No hostile view of Eliezer or of his traditions is implied in any of these versions.

41. *A Verbal Will*

See above, p. 125.

42. *Hanging Women*

See above, p. 118.

43. *Tos. Kel. B.M. 6 : 4/M. Kel. 8 : 1*

See above, p. 112.

44. *Cleaning a Metal Vessel*

Tos. Kel. B.M. 4 : 14/M. Kel. 14 : 7 present the dispute of Eliezer and Joshua on metal vessels. Eliezer holds they may contract uncleanness and be rendered clean when broken. Joshua says it can only be when they are whole. In Tos. Nathan says attests to Eliezer's part of the dispute.

The pericope is not hostile.

45. *Money Pouch*

In Tos. Kel. B.B. 4 : 3/M. Kel. 26 : 2, Nathan attests a dispute between Eliezer and the sages on a money-bag. The version of M. is that they dispute whether it is unclean or not. In Tos. Nathan says they agreed it is clean—the sages' opinion—but differed on a bag for pearls, with the same apodosis as earlier.

No hostile opinion about Eliezer is to be inferred.

46. *See Mishnah-Tosefta No. 92.*

47. *Tos. Ah. 7 : 3/M. Oh. 6 : 2*

See above, p. 126.

48. *Jars Containing Remnant of a Corpse*

Tos. Ah. 9 : 7 has a saying of Judah that Eliezer and Joshua ruled on the case, in M. Oh. 8 : 6, of two jars, each containing a half-olive's bulk of a corpse. They remain clean, but the house is unclean if they are stopped up. If one is open, it and the house are unclean, but the other is clean. Judah then says that Eliezer and Joshua agree concerning two jars which open into a house, that the house is unclean. They differ about two *rooms* in the house. Then the sages say they differed about two jars. In both cases the Mishnah explicitly says the House is unclean, so follows Eliezer.

The pericope is not hostile.

49. *Olive's-bulk of Corpse on Threshhold*

Tos. Ah. 13 : 10/M. Oh. 12 : 8 presents a dispute between Eliezer and Joshua about an olive's cleaving to the outer side of the door-jamb of the threshhold. Eliezer says the house is unclean, Joshua, that it is clean. Tos. Ah. has Simeon b. Yoḥai: They did not differ about a case in which the corpse-matter was *under* the threshhold. The house then is clean. The difference comes when the corpse-matter is *on* the threshold. Eliezer then says it is unclean, Joshua, clean. Simeon thus provides a good *terminus* for the dispute as defined by M. Oh. 12 : 8.

The pericope is not hostile.

50. *Tos. Ah. 17 : 6/M. Oh. 17 : 5*

See above, p. 128.

51. *Removing Leprosy-Signs*

See above, p. 128.

52. *Tos. Par. 7 : 7/M. Par. 7 : 10*

See above, p. 126.

53-56. *Intention in Respect to Sin-offering Water*

M. Par. 9 : 4/Tos. Par. 9 : 6/M. Par. 9 : 1, 3, 7 deal with the wrong intention in respect to Sin-offering-water. If one intends to drink it, without actually doing so, Eliezer says he has nonetheless rendered the water unfit. Joshua says not intention, but actually turning the flask up to drink from it, is what renders it unfit.

Yosi then says that rule pertains to water that has not been sanctified. But if the water has been sanctified, then it is when one turns up the flask, according to Eliezer, and when he actually drinks, according to Joshua, that it is unfit—so M. Par. 9 : 4. Rabbi further attests M. Par. 9 : 1. Yosi in Tos. Par. 9 : 6 further says that Eliezer's tendency in respect to the Red-Heifer rite is to rule leniently, alluding to the opinion given in 9 : 4.

The pericope is not hostile.

57. *M. Eruv. 9 : 4, M. Toh. 6 : 5.*

See above, Vol. I, p. 317.

58. *Moisture Exuded by Crushed Olives*

M. Toh. 9 : 3F/M. Toh. 9 : 3C-3 present Simeon b. Yoḥai's attestation of a dispute between Eliezer and the sages on whether the sap of crushed olives is capable of receiving uncleanness. Eliezer says they are clean, the sages say they are unclean. Then Simeon says the dispute concerns not the sap of olives but what exudes from the oil vat.

The pericope is not hostile.

59. *The Zab*

Tos. Nid. 9 : 13/M. Nid. 10 : 3 has a dispute among Eliezer, Joshua, and ʿAqiba about a *Zab* or a *Zabah* who examined themselves on the first and seventh day of their periods and found themselves clean, but did not examine themselves on the intervening days. Eliezer says they are clean; Joshua rules they are clean only for the days on which they examined themselves. ʿAqiba says only the seventh day is regarded as clean. Yosi and Simeon allude to the dispute, saying they think Eliezer gives a better ruling than Joshua, but ʿAqiba's ruling is best of all. But the law, they say, follows Eliezer—the first such saying we have seen. The pericope certainly is not hostile.

60. *The Beehive.*

See above, p. 128.

61. *An Olive's Bulk of Flesh from the Limb of a Living Person*

The dispute in M. Ed. 6 : 2-3 is attested by Simon's remark in Tos. Ah. 2 : 7, "I should be astonished if Eliezer declared it unclean under all circumstances." Simeon then says Eliezer held it was unclean only when there is sufficient flesh on the limb so that it might render unclean in contact, carrying, and in a 'Tent.' The pericope is not hostile.

62. *The Generation of the Wilderness in the World to Come*

Joshua b. Qorḥa's remark in b. Sanh. 110b attests M. Sanh. 10 : 3/Tos. Sanh. 13 : 2. Joshua alludes to Eliezer's exegesis of Ps. 50 : 5 and says it refers *not* to the generation of the wilderness but to Ḥananiah, Mishael, and ʿAzariah, on the one side, and to ʿAqiba and his companions, who were martyred, on the other. If the saying is genuine, then Joshua certainly knew what Eliezer said in respect to the application of the Scripture to the generation of the wilderness. The pericope is not hostile, but Joshua supports Eliezer against ʿAqiba—the only instance in which an Ushan sides against Eliezer and in favor of the alleged father of the Ushans' traditions.

None of the pericopae reflects the slightest hostility toward Eliezer. No Ushan alleges, as do Ilai and ʿAqiba, that Eliezer's traditions have been, or must be, suppressed. Eliezer's teachings are carefully analyzed and taken to be important legal materials. Just as the Houses' materials in the Ushan stratum concentrate on issues of law and ignore historical and political questions—alleging that the Houses had really loved one another anyhow—so tradents of Eliezer's pericopae likewise seem oblivious to whatever controversy centered upon his name in Yavnean times. The Ushan attestations include leading figures, not only Judah, though he stands at the head of the list, but also Meir, Simeon, Nathan, Simeon Shezuri, and others. This seems to me important evidence that for Ushans Eliezer was a name of importance, not a source of partisan dispute.

iii. The Chains

We earlier (pp. 74-76) alleged that Ushan materials yield chains in the names of Simeon, Nathan, Simeon Shezuri, Yosi b. R. Judah [b. Ilai], and one complex, Yosi + Simeon + Simeon Shezuri + Judah. We shall now consider the Ushan chains of traditions.

1. *Simeon*

1. Tos. M.S., Vol. I, p. 72: Simeon said in the name of Liezer, Saffron is not purchased with the money of Tithe. Simeon's tradition is allegedly in Eliezer's own words. It is followed by a separate teaching, in the name of Judah b. Gaddish *before* Liezer. But Liezer does not answer. Present text reads, *They* said.

2. Tos. Shab. 15 : 10/M. Shab. 19 : 1, 4, Vol. I, p. 96: Simeon said, Liezer and Joshua did not argue about... Concerning what did they differ... —An attestation, not a chain.

3. Tos. Pis. 1 : 5/M. Pes. 1 : 7, Vol. I, p. 117.—An attestation, not a chain.

4. Tos. Pis. 5 : 4/M. Pes. 6 : 5, Vol. I, p. 130.—An attestation, not a chain.

5. Tos. Sheq. 2 : 10/M. Sheq. 4 : 8, Vol. I, p. 136.—An attestation, not a chain.

6. Not pertinent.

7. Tos. Hul. 2 : 11/M. Hul. 2 : 6D-F, Vol. I, p. 246: Tos. Hul. 2 : 11 has *R. Simeon says in the name of R. Eliezer*, "He who slaughters at night and in the morning finds the walls of the neck filled with blood—it is valid..." M. Hul. 2 : 6 has Simeon's ruling, without attribution to Eliezer, and then: "This is according to the ruling of Eliezer." Simeon's chain is in proper form but may represent an alternative version of M., which has Simeon in accord with, but separate from, Eliezer. In any event this seems a good attestation, if not a chain. Still, Judah's chains in Tos. will frequently enough appear in M. either as Judah's own ruling or as Eliezer's ruling without Judah's name attached.

8. Tos. Kel. B.M. 8 : 8/M. Kel. 18 : 9, Vol. I, p. 283: M. Kel. concerns the effect of a connector for uncleanness in the event that only one piece of the bed has become unclean, and in respect to a connector if the owner dipped both parts of the bed into a ritual pool. In Tos. Simeon explains the ruling, as against Judah the Patriarch's view of Eliezer's opinion—an attestation, not a chain.

9. Tos. Ah. 13 : 10/M. Oh. 12 : 8, Vol. I, p. 294; An attestation, not a chain. Simeon redefines the argument of Eliezer and Joshua.

10. M. Toh. 9 : 3, Vol. I, p. 320: Simeon redefines the argument and attests the *theme* of the pericope.

2. *Nathan*

1. Tos. Ter. 7 : 10C/M. Ter. 8 : 3, Vol. I, p. 61: Nathan said, Liezer *would* say, Let him wait, etc. An attestation, not a chain. But the form is close to a chain.

2. Tos. Ter. 9 : 8/M. Ter. 11 : 2, Vol. I, p. 66: Nathan said, Liezer agrees—an attestation, not a chain.

3. M. Suk. 1 : 11/Tos. Suk. 1 : 10/b. Suk. 19b, Vol. I, p. 145: Nathan says Eliezer invalidates the cone-shaped *Sukkah* because it has no roof—not a chain, but a good attestation.

4. Tos. Kel. B.M. 4 : 14/M. Kel. 14 : 7C–D, Vol. I, p. 281: Nathan says Eliezer says, A metal vessel which was unclean and broken and repaired, etc. This would be a chain, were it not for the provision of an equivalent saying for Joshua—thus nothing more than an attestation.

5. M. Kel. 26 : 2/Tos. Kel. B.B. 4 : 3, Vol. I, p. 284: Nathan attests the *theme* by redefining the dispute: not a money-pouch but a bag for pearls.

3. *Simeon Shezuri*

1. M. Kel. 26 : 4/Tos. Kel. B.B. 4 : 7, Vol. I, p. 285: Not a chain, but an attestation.

4. *Yosi b. R. Judah*

As the son of Judah b. Ilai, Yosi's materials may fall into the category of the best traditions:

1. Tos. Sot. 1 : 1/M. Sot. 1 : 1: "R. Yosi b. R. Judah says in the name of R. Eliezer, He who warns his wife does so on the evidence of *one* witness or on his own evidence and causes her to drink on the evidence of *two*." Yosi has a good chain, but it is the opposite of M. Sot. 1 : 1, which says Eliezer says, He warns before *two* and makes her drink before *one* or on his own testimony.

2. b. Git. 82a-b/M. Git. 9 : 1: Yosi b. R. Judah said, Eliezer and the sages did not differ concerning...—An attestation for an already-attested pericope.

Note also M. Ker. 4 : 2-3Tos. Ker. 2 : 12-15/Sifra Vayiqra 7 : 26-31, Vol. I, p. 259: Not a chain but a very good Ushan attestation.

5. *The Ushan Chains*

By contrast to Judah b. Ilai, no other Ushan has an impressive number of chains of tradition for Eliezer. Simeon b. Yoḥai has two, one on the use of Tithe-money for the purchase of saffron, the other about slaughtering at night and awaking to find the walls of the neck filled with blood. Other items turn out to be nothing more than attestations, and what is attested is the theme of Eliezer's legislation, not his exact opinion. Nathan and Simeon Shezuri attest other materials. Yosi b. R. Judah has a chain alleging Eliezer says the opposite of what is attributed to him in M. Sot. 1 : 1—strikingly parallel to the situation with Simeon's chain of Tos. Hul., which in M. Hul. becomes Simeon's own opinion. In general, therefore, the chains are preserved chiefly in Tos., and M. ignores either the chain or the attribution to Eliezer, and then leaves the tradition in the name of the person to whom the chain is attributed.

We cannot locate in the laws validated by chains anything that would have required the affirmative evidence supplied by a later authority in the form, *X says Y says...* Why chains were needed for rulings on saffron, ritual slaughter, and warning a woman suspected of adultery—not a practical matter for a century, if it ever was—I cannot say.

iv. The Ushan Eliezer and Yoḥanan b. Zakkai. The Houses

In the better traditions, as in the best ones, Eliezer bears no relationship whatever to Yoḥanan b. Zakkai. He does not allude to Yoḥanan's teachings; no one refers to his having studied with Yoḥanan; he does not even legislate on the issues important to Yoḥanan b. Zakkai, either in Yoḥanan's corpus as a whole or in the Judah b. Ilai-pericopae of Yoḥanan

Pericopae attested at Usha involving Eliezer and the Houses are as follows (enumerated according to the list in section ii):

ii-1. Eliezer and Joshua define a Houses' dispute. Neither party participates in the issue.

ii-12. The Houses are not referred to, though the dispute is parallel to theirs on the same subject.

ii-21. Eliezer's ruling is consistent with the tendency of the House of Hillel, and the form of the pericope is the same as that of the Houses' version. But no one seems to have linked Eliezer to the House of Hillel.

The better traditions know nothing about Eliezer as a Shammaite. The only pertinent pericope has him as a Hillelite. The issue of Eliezer's relations to the Houses is scarcely raised.

The comparison of Eliezer's Ushan attestations and those of the Houses is clear in the following (*Phar.* III, pp. 231-233):

Houses	*Eliezer*
	A. *History*
1. Echo to Simeon the Just and Yoḥanan the High Priest (Judah b. Baba)	1. —
2. Echo to Hillel, Samuel the Small, etc. (Judah b. Baba)	2. — [Eliezer added much later]
3. Hillel came up at 40 (Post-ʿAqibans?)	3. —
4. Rise of Hillel (Tos. Pisḥa 4 : 13)	4. —
5. Hillel expounded language of common folk (Meir + Judah?)	5. —
6. Disputes come from poor (Yosi)	6. —
7. End of Grapeclusters (Judah b. Baba)	7. —
8. Trough of Jehu (Judah b. Ilai)	8. —
9. Hillel: Scatter/gather (Simeon b. Yoḥai)	9. —
10. Who prepared heifer-sacrifices (Meir)	10. —
11. Lay/not lay (Meir + Judah)	11. —
12. Temple of Onias (Meir + Judah)	12. —
13. Simeon b. Sheṭaḥ *vs.* Judah b. Ṭabbai as *Nasi* (Meir + Judah)	13. —
14. Letter of Gamaliel to Diaspora (Judah)	14. —
15. Yoḥanan b. Gudgada's sons (Judah)	15. —
B. *Temple Law, Jerusalem, Pilgrimage, and Priestly Dues*	
1. Two sprinklings of sacrificial blood (Eliezer b. Jacob)	1. —
2. Coins for *sheqel* (Simeon b. Yoḥai)	2. —
3. Burn flesh inside/outside (Meir + Judah)	3. —
4. —	4. The Passover slaughtered for some other purpose (M. Pes. 6 : 5/Tos. Pis. 5 : 4 + M. Zev. 1 : 1 etc.) (Simeon b. Yoḥai)

5. —	5. Impairment in sacrificial process (Tos. Zev. 4 : 1, M. Me. 1 : 2-3, etc.) (Simeon, Yosi)
6. —	6. Progeny of Peace-offerings (M. Tem. 3 : 1) (Simeon)
7. —	7. Sin-offering when in doubt (M. Ker. 4 : 2-3/Tos. Ker. 2 : 12-15, etc.) (Yosi, Simeon Shezuri, Simeon b. Yoḥai)

C. *Agricultural Tithes, Offerings, and Taboos*

1. Watering plants until New Year of Seventh Year (Yosi b. Kifar, or Eleazar b. R. Ṣaddoq)	1. —
2. Israelite woman eats *Terumah* (Yosi)	2. —
3. Dough for *Ḥallah* (Yosi)	3. —
4. Heave-offering of oil for crushed olives (Yosi)	4. —
5. Produce not fully harvested passed through Jerusalem (Yosi)	5. —
6. Olive-presses in walls of Jerusalem (Yosi)	6. —
7. *Demai re ʿomer* (Simeon b. Yoḥai)	7. —
8. *Demai re Ḥallah* (Simeon b. Yoḥai)	8. —
9. Change silver and produce (Meir)	9. —
10. Heave-offering of fenugreek (Meir + Judah)	10. —
11. Fruit of prepared field in Seventh Year (Judah)	11. —
12. Vineyard patch (Judah)	12. —
13. Burn doubtful Heave-offering (Judah)	13. —
14. Young shoot over stone (Simeon b. Gamaliel, Yosi + Meir)	14. —
15. Assigning produce to past/coming year *re pod* (Simeon b. Gamaliel)	15. —
16. Fruit of fourth year vineyard *re* Fifth, Removal (Simeon b. Gamaliel)	16. —
17. *Demai re* sweet oil (Nathan)	17. —
18. —	18. Forgotten sheaves (Houses) (Tos. Pe'ah 3 : 2)
19. —	19. Handkerchiefs and 'Diverse kinds' (Tos. Kil. 5 : 18) (Meir + Judah)

20. —	20. Neutralizing Heave-offering (Tos. Ter. 5 : 10-11) (Meir + Judah)
21. —	21. Definition of liquids (M. Ter. 11 : 2, Tos. Ter. 9 : 9) (Nathan, Meir, Jacob, Judah, Rabbi)
22. —	22. Burning clean and unclean Heave-offering—*Ḥameṣ* together (M. Pes. 1 : 7, Tos. Pis. 1 : 5) (Yosi)
23. —	23. Saffron not purchased with Tithe-money (Tos. M.S. 1 : 14) (Simeon)

D. *Sabbath Law*

1. Clearing table on Sabbath (Yosi)	1. —
2. Work started before Sabbath, completed on Sabbath (Yosi)	2. —
3. *ʿEruv* with Sadducee (Meir + Judah)	3. —
4. Put back on stove (Meir + Judah)	4. —
5. Food for Sabbath (Judah)	5. —
6. Work to gentile launderer before Sabbath (Simeon b. Gamaliel)	6. —
7. Charity on Sabbath (Simeon b. Gamaliel)	7. —
8. *ʿEruv* for cistern (Simeon b. Gamaliel)	8. —
9. —	9. Completing the eating of a grapecluster (Tos. Ter. 7 : 10C) (Nathan) N.B. Compare the Houses in Nos. 2 and 5 above.
10. —	10. Circumcision and Sabbath (Tos. Shab. 15 : 10/M. Shab. 19 : 4) (Yosi, Simeon b. Eleazar, Simeon b. Yoḥai)
[11. —	11. Making two *ʿeruvs* (Tos. Eruv. 4 : 1-2) (Judah b. Ilai)]
12. —	12. Acquiring an *ʿeruv* (M. Eruv. 7 : 11) (Judah b. Ilai)

E. *Festival Law*

1. Proselyte on day before Passover (Yosi)	1. —
2. Gifts on festival (Yosi + Judah)	2. —
3. Return *pesaḥ* whole (Simeon b. Yoḥai)	3. —
4. Tying pigeon (Simeon b. Yoḥai)	4. Below, No. 12.
5. Egg laid on festival (Meir)	5. As above.

6. Prepare spices, salt on festival (Meir)	6. —
7. Timber-roofing of *Sukkah* (Meir + Judah)	7. —
8. Pick pulse on festival (Judah)	8. —
9. More vessels on account of need (Simeon b. Gamaliel)	9. —
10. —	10. Measure of dough for Passover (Tos. Pis. 3 : 8) (Nathan)
11. —	11. Cone-shaped *Sukkah* (b. Suk. 19b/M. Suk. 1 : 11) (Nathan)
12. Above, No. 4.	12. May use splinter (Tos. Y.T. 3 : 18/M. Bes. 4 : 6-7) (Simeon b. Yoḥai)

F. *Liturgy*

1. Order of *Havdalah* (Meir + Judah)	1. —
2. —	2. Powers of rain (M. Ta. 1 : 1) (Judah)

G. *Uncleanness Laws*

1. Vessels before *ʿam haʾareṣ* (Dosetai b. R. Yannai)	1. —
2. Uncleanness of weasel (Yosi)	2. —
3. Burn clean and unclean meat together (Yosi)	3. —
4. Measure chest (Yosi)	4. —
5. Split in roof (Yosi)	5. —
6. Gather grapes in grave-area (Yosi)	6. —
7. Lid-chain connector (Yosi)	7. —
8. Place water (M. Maksh. 1 : 4) (Yosi + Judah)	8. —
9. Vessel under waterspout (Yosi + Meir)	9. —
10. Water from roof leaked into jar (Yosi + Meir)	10. —
11. Uncleanness of *Qohelet* (Yosi + Simeon)	11. —
12. Uncleanness of girdle (Simeon b. Yoḥai)	12. —
13. Removing pot for Heave-offering (Simeon b. Yoḥai)	13. —
14. Uncleanness of her who has difficulty giving birth (Simeon b. Yoḥai)	14. —

15. Sin-offering water that has fulfilled its purpose (Simeon b. Yoḥai)	15. —
16. How much lacking in skull (Tent) (Meir)	16. —
17. When is tube clean (Meir + Judah)	17. —
18. When is sheet clean (Meir + Judah)	18. —
19. Stool on baking-trough (Meir + Judah)	19. —
20. Menstrual blood of gentile woman (Meir + Judah)	20. —
21. Quarter-*qab* of bones in tent (Judah)	21. —
22. When to make the vat unclean (Judah)	22. —
23. Open hole to let out uncleanness (Judah)	23. —
24. Anoint self with clean oil (Judah)	24. —
25. Blood of carcass (Judah)	25. —
26. Water-skin (Judah)	26. —
27. Sell food to *ḥaver* (Simeon b. Gamaliel)	27. —
28. When is ritual pool deemed clean (Simeon b. Gamaliel)	28. —
29. —	29. Cleaning a metal vessel (Tos. Kel. B.M. 4 : 14/M. Kel. 14 : 7) (Nathan)
30. —	30. Money-pouch (M. Kel. 26 : 2/Tos. Kel. B.B. 4 : 3) (Nathan)
31. —	31. Jars containing remnant of corpse (Tos. Ah. 9 : 7) (Judah)
32. —	32. Corpse-piece on treshhold (Tos. Ah. 13 : 10/M. Oh. 17 : 8) (Simeon b. Yoḥai)
33. —	33. Intention in Sin-offering water (M. Par. 9 : 4/Tos. Par. 9 : 6) (Yosi)
34. —	34. Moisture of crushed olives (M. Toh. 9 : 3) (Simeon b. Yoḥai)
35. —	35. *Zab* (Tos. Nid. 9 : 13/M. Nid. 10 : 3) (Yosi, Simeon)
36. —	36. Olive's bulk of flesh from living person unclean (M. Ed. 6 : 2-3/Tos. Ah. 2 : 7) (Simeon)
37. —	37. Connector in bed (Tos. Kel. B.M. 8 : 8/M. Kel. 18 : 9) (Simeon b. Yoḥai)

H. *Civil Law, Torts, and Damages*

1. Hillel and futures (usury) (Meir, Judah, Simeon)	1. —
2. Restore beam or value (Simeon b. Gamaliel)	2. —

I. *Family Law and Inheritances*

1. Lewdness with minor son (Yosi)	1. —
2. Cohabitation with mother-in-law (Yosi + Judah)	2. —
3. Girl married before flow (Meir, Simeon b. Gamaliel, Judah)	3. —
4. Nursing mother remarries (Meir + Judah)	4. —
5. Betrothed woman disposes of goods (Judah)	5. —
6. How many children before desisting from marital life (Nathan)	6. —
7. Annuling daughter's vows (Nathan)	7. —
8. Three betrothe woman—witness/agent (Nathan)	8. —
9. —	9. *Ḥaliṣah* with wooden sandal (Tos. Yev. 12 : 11)(Judah)
10. —	10. Ransoming a wife (Nathan)
11. —	11. Attesting a writ of divorce (M. Giṭ. 1 : 1-2) (Judah)
12. —	12. Dedicating property and paying the *Ketuvah* (M. Ar. 6 : 1) (Simeon b. Gamaliel)
13. —	13. Warning wife before witnesses (M. Soṭ. 1 : 1/Tos. Soṭ. 1 : 1) (Yosi b. R. Judah)

J. *Miscellany*

1. *Targum* of Job (Yosi)	1. —
2. Nazir: Erroneous vow (Yosi; Judah)	2. —
3. Chicken and cheese (Yosi)	3. —
4. Nazirite vow for longer period (Judah)	4. —
5. —	5. Repeating a lesson (b. *Eruv.* 54b) (Judah b. Ilai)
6. —	6. Generation of wilderness in world to come (Tos. Sanh. 13 : 2) (Joshua b. Qorḥa)
7. —	7. Slaughter (Tos. Hul. 2 : 11) (Simeon b. Yoḥai)

The Ushan attestations of Eliezer's traditions differ from those of the Houses' materials in two important respects. First, the Ushans have no traditions in Eliezer's name on any historical question pertaining to either pre- or post-70 times. Second, Eliezer's Temple laws attested by Ushans greatly exceed in numbers and importance the Houses' equivalent materials—a pattern already observed in the best traditions. I see no Ushan expansion in the range of interests attributed to Eliezer. In general, as in the Yavnean materials, so in the Ushan ones, with the noted exception, Eliezer rules on pretty much the same legal agenda as were faced by the Houses and in roughly the same proportions.

But the subject-matter of Eliezer's rulings bears slight relationship to that of those of the Houses attested at Usha. We find no points of contact. Apart from the considerable, but familiar, innovation in his theorizing on the cult, we find a wide range of unrelated rulings, none with a parallel among the Houses'. The only set bearing a general resemblance to Houses' rulings pertains to issues of ritual uncleanness.

v. The Better Traditions

The better traditions exhibit no important differences from the best ones. The Ushan Eliezer stands within the framework both of pre-70 Pharisaism and of the Yavnean Eliezer. The Ushans seem to have innovated little, if at all, in the themes of laws attributed to Eliezer. The Ushan attestations serve to establish the agenda on which Eliezer legislated, but provide little evidence of the exact opinions which he held or were attributed to him.

Let us review the main results of our survey of the better traditions. Eliezer ruled on whether the taboo against 'Diverse Kinds' applies to handkerchiefs, scroll-wrappers, and bath towels. He legislated on mixtures of one hundred-and-one parts of secular produce and one part of Heave-offering, in general taking a more lenient position than Joshua. He said, again in the lenient position, that a deed begun licitly might be completed, even illicitly. He and Joshua debated the definition of liquids capable of rendering produce susceptible to uncleanness. In respect to circumcision on the Sabbath, he held that performing such an act when it is not actually required—that is, not on the eighth day—will produce liability to a Sin-offering. He ruled one may acquire an *ʿeruv* with coins. He taught a law with respect to memorizing traditions: the master must teach a tradition four times. He said one might not burn unclean Heave-offering-*ḥameṣ* with clean.

He stated that a Passover offered for some other purpose than the Passover-sacrifice will impose liability for a Sin-offering—this on the basis of logic. A cone-shaped *Sukkah* is not acceptable; the *Sukkah* must have a roof. Like the House of Hillel, he taught that one might use on the festival what was not set aside on the preceding day. *The Powers of Rain*-prayer is to be said from the first, not the last, day of *Sukkot.* One who has forbidden his wife from benefiting from him must nonetheless redeem her if she is taken captive, as explicitly required by the *Ketuvah.* He glossed a rule about bringing a writ of divorce from foreign parts, applying the rule even to neighboring villages. He held that sprinkling the blood when the meat-offering is impaired is of no effect; conversely, if the sprinkling of the blood has not properly taken place, the meat-offering is likewise unacceptable. The progeny of Peace-offerings may not be brought as Peace-offerings. An important general rule is that when one is not certain exactly what sin he has done or even whether he has sinned at all, he must still bring a Sin-offering. A metal-vessel in parts may contract uncleanness and be cleansed. A money-bag or a pearl-pouch is capable of receiving uncleanness. He gave several rules in respect to 'Tents.' Sin-offering-water may be rendered unfit by the wrong intention, even though one has not actually done anything to carry out his intention. He ruled on the moisture exuded by crushed olives or by the olive vat. He decreed in a lenient way concerning the ritual cleanness of a *Zab* who examined himself only on the first and seventh day of his period of uncleanness. He held that an olive's bulk of flesh from the limb of a living person is capable of conveying uncleanness. And he held that the generation of the Wilderness would acquire a portion in the world to come.

As stated, the themes are already familiar from the best traditions: agricultural laws, a few Sabbath and festival rules, some teachings on the matter of marriage and divorce, and ritual uncleanness. The cult, in theory if not in practice, continued to take an important place in his traditions, and the method of producing laws on the cult—logic rather than tradition—continued as before. No area of law dealt with in the best traditions is neglected in the better ones; no legal theme is introduced to the already established agendum. The specific opinions, to be sure, are on different subjects. But we are unable to find contradictions between principles used in deciding cases in the best traditions and those employed in the better ones. We observe an essential consistency between Yavnean and Ushan materials, both in an affirmative sense, in the selection of legal problems, and in a negative sense, in the absence of contradictions of established principles. This seems to me a considerable argument in favor of the authenticity of the laws attributed to Eliezer.

In all of these traditions we discern not the slightest hint of hostility toward Eliezer. Detailed rules of course occur here which have not been seen before. But if the Ushan Eliezer is the ʿAqiban Eliezer, then we may say that no important trait of Ilai's Eliezer is absent in ʿAqiba's; both schools or circles seem to have a fairly consistent and harmonious picture of the man. The two sets of traditions differ only in the degree of accuracy imputed to the one over the other. Among the best traditions we seem to find reliable evidence about specific opinions; among the better ones, usable data are chiefly about probable themes, but not commonly about the exact legal opinion to be attributed to Eliezer. Where we have some evidence on the formation of Eliezer's traditions and how the responsible tradent knew what he attributed to Eliezer, we thus find a single picture of the man. And that picture emerges from a wide range of authorities, who cannot be thought to have conspired with one another to make up a false view or to have laid down laws in Eliezer's name on the basis of a plan to misrepresent him.

CHAPTER TEN

THE FAIR TRADITIONS

i. Attestations of the Circle of Judah the Patriarch

1. Judah the Patriarch attests the dispute on whether date-honey and cider are liable for tithes and have the capacity to render unclean as a liquid, Tos. Ter. 9 : 8-9/M. Ter. 11 : 2; above, Usha, No. 6, p. 146.

2. Simeon b. Eleazar attests Tos. Shab. 15 : 10; above, Usha, No. 7, p. 147.

3. Simeon b. Eleazar provides the opposite of an attestation for the dispute about overturning the couch in mourning in respect to the festival, b. M.Q. 20a. Eliezer says if one overtures the couch three days before the festival, he does not do so afterward; the sages say that is the rule even if one has done so only a day or an hour before. Then Simeon b. Eleazar assigns the dispute to the Houses. So Simeon knows nothing of the attribution of the dispute to Eliezer. y. Meg. 3 : 1 has Eliezer b. R. Ṣaddoq. This seems to mean the pericope should be excluded from our Eliezer's tradition.

4. Judah the Patriarch approves Eliezer's opinion, b. Yev. 108a/M. Yev. 13 : 2, that the deed of a female minor is null and void; above, Yavneh, No. 10, p. 109.

5. Yosi b. R. Judah, Tos. Soṭ. 1 : 1/M. Soṭ. 1 : 1 attests Eliezer's opinion about warning a wife before two witnesses; above, Ushan chains, p. 159.

6. Tos. Zev. 2 : 16/M. Zev. 3 : 3: Rabbi attests the issue of M. Zev.: the wrong intention in a sacrifice renders the act invalid. If a man intended to eat what is not usually eaten or to burn what is not usually burned, the slaughter is retroactively invalid. The issue is phrased in Tos. Zev. 2 : 16 in terms of the sages, who say it is valid, and Judah, who says it is not. Rabbi introduces the names of Eliezer and Joshua in place of the sages and Judah.

The pericope continues with a story that Rabbi taught the tradition to Issi, who told Rabbi that Judah b. Ilai said it was invalid. Rabbi then says, "Judah is the disciple of Ilai, and Ilai is the disciple of Eliezer. Therefore he teaches the Mishnah of Eliezer." In this instance, therefore, we may reliably assign the pericope of M. Zev. to Rabbi and explain the assignment just as is done in Tos.: Rabbi has through his own reasoning introduced Eliezer's name instead of Judah b. Ilai's. But this is the only instance of the sort. Sifra Ṣav 8 : 1 has Eliezer *vs.* ʿAqiba on the same principle. Eliezer proves that intention may retroactively invalidate a sacrifice. M. Me. 1 : 2, attested above, p. 152, deals with a parallel issue of the affect of intention on the cult. It may be that Rabbi has extended Eliezer's position from the one case to the other, and that Judah b. Ilai has done the same. The attestations then serve for the exact opinion, not only the principle.

7. Tos. Kel. B.M. 8 : 8/M. Kel. 18 : 9, Rabbi *vs.* Simeon b. Yoḥai; above, Simeon, chains, No. 8.

8. b. Nid. 9b/M. Nid. 1 : 3, 5/Tos. Nid. 1 : 5: M. Nid. 1 : 1 has a dispute of Shammai and Hillel. Shammai says, "For all women it is enough for them to be deemed unclean only from their time of suffering a flow." Hillel says "A woman is deemed unclean from examination to examination." Eliezer says, "Four types of women may rely on the normal occurrence of their period, the virgin, the pregnant woman, the nursing mother, and the old woman." Joshua says this rule applies only to the virgin. Yosi then says the rule applies to a pregnant woman and a nursing mother for whom three periods have passed without menstruation, but he does not allude to Eliezer + Joshua. Eliezer's rule is contrary to those of both Shammai and Hillel. He knows nothing about the Shammaite rule. b. Nid. 9b has a story and a saying attributed to Rabbi. He ruled in agreement with Eliezer. And he said, "Eliezer is reliable for emergencies." This seems meant to account for the Mishnah's statement that the law follows Eliezer; but it also supplies an attestation in the name of Judah the Patriarch.

The dispute between Shammai and Hillel is not attested before its appearance in M. + Tos. Ed. 1 : 1. Apart from Tos. Nid. 9 : 13/M. Nid. 10 : 3. This is the only pericope on the menstrual woman for which we have an attestation before the stratum of Mishnah-Tosefta. M. Nid. 10 : 3 is about the *Zab.*

We see, therefore, that the attestations of Rabbi's circle closely resemble those of the Ushans and the Yavneans, in that order; Nos. 1, 2, 4, 5, and 7 are well-attested before Rabbi's time; No. 3 is anomalous. That leaves No. 6, about a principle closely related to debates attested earlier. Only No. 8 introduces into the agendum of Eliezer's legal rulings a quite new theme. Overall, therefore, the attestations seem limited to remarkably narrow agenda, and from one stratum to the next the range of agenda does not appreciably expand.

ii. Pericopae First Attested by Appearance in Mishnah-Tosefta

1-2. *The Shema*ʿ

M. Ber. 1 : 1 and 1 : 2 have rulings of Eliezer, sages, and Gamaliel about saying the *Shema*ʿ in the evening; 1 : 2 has Eliezer and Joshua on the time to say the *Shema*ʿ in the morning. Defining laws about saying the *Shema*ʿ is well attested for Yavneh, with the Houses' pericopae attested by Ishmael, Ṭarfon and Eleazar b. ʿAzariah. So it would seem reasonable that Eliezer ruled on such a subject. The opinions of the several masters do not reveal important differences in principle or even in detail.

3-4. *The Prayer*

In M. Ber. 4 : 4 Eliezer says one should not make his prayer routine but should ask for something new and pray in a different way from one day to the next. The tendency of the Yavneans clearly was to lay out the main requirements of the daily liturgy. But Eliezer stands in opposition to this part of the project, though he obviously agrees that a time is to be fixed for saying the *Shema*ʿ.

In M. Ber. 5 : 2 the issue is where one inserts the *Havdalah*-prayer. Eliezer says it is in the Thanksgiving prayer. ʿAqiba says it is said by itself as a fourth blessing. If Eliezer holds that the substance of the prayer is not to be set down, then he would have no choice but to include it in the fixed, concluding blessings. y. Ber. 5 : 2 has Isaac Rabbah in the name of Rabbi: The law follows Eliezer. This should be a valuable attestation.

If the Yavneans were laying down details for a formerly undefined matter of personal piety (*Phar.* III, pp. 234ff.), then Eliezer would seem to oppose the whole operation and to prefer to keep the situation as before. Ordinary folk would be expected to say their prayers, but the details of the matter would be left open.

5-6. *Liability for Pe*ʾ*ah, Defective Clusters*

In M. Peʾah 3 : 6 Eliezer, Joshua, Ṭarfon, Judah b. Batyra, and ʿAqiba define the amount of land liable for *peʾah*—a strikingly fundamental issue. M. Peʾah 7 : 7 has Eliezer and ʿAqiba discuss the liability to the law of defective clusters of a vineyard made up wholly of imperfect grape-clusters. The two have exegeses in support of their respective positions. M. Peʾah 7 : 4 has a ruling of Judah b. Ilai in harmony with Eliezer's. In 7 : 6 the Houses rule on even more basic problems. It would seem that these pericopae are authentic records of themes of Eliezer's ruling.

7. *Thorns in the Vineyard*

M. Kil. 5 : 8 gives Eliezer's rule about forfeiting vines adjacent to thorns kept in a vineyard. Sages say the opposite, since people do not usually preserve thorns. The issue is the application of the taboo against 'mixed seeds' to thorns. The problem of intention lies in the background. Eliezer is not willing to supply a theory of the man's intention; he interprets in an obvious way what is actually done. If the man has kept the thorns, that is evidence that he *intended* to keep them, and the taboo applies. M. Kil. 3 : 6 distinguishes between a case in which intention is articulated, and one in which one does not know what the man really intends. Eliezer seems to accord with the position of the House of Shammai.

8. *Arum after the Seventh Year*

M. Shev. 5 : 3 has Eliezer's and Joshua's dispute about arum which has remained after the Seventh Year. Eliezer says if the poor have not gathered the leaves, then they have a share in the crop. Joshua says they have no claim on the arum. Eliezer's view is that the poor may eat after the Removal at the beginning of the Seventh Year. In M. Shev. 9 : 8 Judah rules in accord with Eliezer's position, Yosi follows Joshua. While these are not attestations, they do provide strong warrant for assigning the opinion to our Eliezer.

9. *Hide Anointed with Seventh Year Oil*

See above, p. 100.

10. *Three Kinds of Vegetables Pickled in One Jar*

M. Shev. 9 : 5 deals with the problem of when, on the eve of the Seventh Year, one must stop eating several kinds of vegetables pickled in a single jar. The problem is that one may eat what is in the house only so long as like produce is still found free in the field. Eliezer holds when the first species is gone, the others are prohibited; Joshua takes the opposite position, and Gamaliel has a compromise—but the compromise is along the lines of Joshua's opinion. I can think of no similar ruling in Eliezer's name, but the topic—Seventh Year laws—is very well attested for early Yavneh.

11. *Seventh Year Produce as a Gift*

When one is given Seventh Year produce as a gift, Eliezer's problem is that, if the fruit is sold, the money will be prohibited because of the Seventh Year. The sages hold that is no problem—the proceeds are to be given out as freely as Seventh Year produce. Eliezer is consistent with the House of Shammai's view that one may eat produce of the Seventh Year both by favor and not by favor.

12. *Giving Heave-offering*

In M. Ter. 4 : 5 we find a set of rules on how much one may increase his gift of Heave-offering beyond the specified minimum. The problem follows upon the Houses' definitions of the proper measure, so the rules would seem to stand in logical sequence. Eliezer says one may give as much as a tenth more, Ishmael says one may give as much as a half; Ṭarfon and ʿAqiba rule that one may give virtually his whole crop. I see no reason to reject the ruling; the subject matter is attested at Yavneh for the Houses and Yavneh, and the logical sequence—Houses, then Eliezer and the other Yavneans—does not appear to be invented.

13. *Unclean Heave-offering Mixed with Clean Unconsecrated Food*

A *seʾah* of unclean Heave-offering which fell into a hundred of clean unconsecrated food is to be raised up and burned but does not render the whole forbidden, so Eliezer in M. Ter. 5 : 2. The sages say it may be neutralized and then eaten, but if it is raised up, we do not say the *seʾah* which fell in is the one which is taken out. The principle is attested in earlier strata, in respect to mixtures of sacrificial materials, and we need not doubt this is an authentic ruling of our Eliezer. The attestation serves for M. Ter. 5 : 2, 4, 5, 6, all of which are closely related to this issue.

14. *Paying Back Heave-offering*

In M. Ter. 6 : 6 Eliezer says that if one has eaten Heave-offering in error instead of giving it to a priest, he may pay back from one kind instead of from another, with the proviso that he not pay back poorer for better food. This is consistent with Eliezer's view about giving Heave-offering from clean for unclean produce and should be regarded as an authentic tradition. ʿAqiba takes the opposite view.

15. *Protecting Heave-offering from Uncleanness*

M. Ter. 8 : 8, 9, 10, and 11 deal with the obligation to take action to prevent a transgression from taking place. Eliezer holds one must take affirmative action. Joshua says one is better off to do nothing, and let events take their course. The issue is already attested with reference to M. Pes., p. 107, and we may not doubt this is an authentic tradition.

16. *Tithing Olives from the Press*

Eliezer holds that if one takes olives from a clean vat, he has to give the tithes, but if from an unclean one, he does not. The anonymous rule is that if a person eats them one by one, he is not liable, but if he salts them and sets them down as a group, he is, so M. Ma. 4 : 3. The processing of the produce establishes the liability for tithes. But the anonymous rule qualifies this law: nibbling one by one is not regarded as processing, even if the man salts the olives. Eliezer then qualifies the rule, as is clear. This is consistent with his position in M. Ter. 11 : 2: the liquid renders susceptible to uncleanness. Since M. Ter. is well attested (above, p. 127), this pericope is likewise to be regarded as reliable.

17-19. *Tithing Dill, Caperbush, and Mustard*

Eliezer says (M. Ma. 4 : 5) that one tithes the seed, plant, and pods of dill; and (M. Ma. 4 : 6) that caperbush is tithed as to stalks, caperberries, and caper-flowers, against ʿAqiba, who says only the berries are tithed, because they are fruit. In Tos. Ma. 3 : 7, Eliezer says mustard-plant has been treated leniently. If a man planted it for the plant, one ignores his intention and regards it as planted for the seed, which then is tithed in all circumstances. This is entirely consistent with Eliezer's view that the plain sense of an action is taken as decisive, rather than an unstated intention. The rule certainly is reliable; along with it we accept the first two.

20. *Saffron Not Purchased with Tithe-Money*

Attested above, p. 158.

21. *Reliability for Second, First Tithes*

Tos. M.S. 3 : 16 has Eliezer's ruling that if a person separates Second Tithe, he is assumed to separate the First. The sages rule that he who gives the First is believed as to the Second, but not *vice versa.* Eliezer is in accord with the Shammaites. The same issue is faced by the

Houses (Tos. M.S. 3 : 15, *Phar.* II, pp. 116-117). Since the man has to take the trouble to bring the Second Tithe or its money-equivalent to Jerusalem, we do not take for granted that he will do so. Eliezer evidently is unwilling to investigate the unstated intention of the man. Since he does the right thing with regard to Second Tithe, it is assumed he will do the same with the First. But this may be a far-fetched interpretation of the basis for his ruling.

22. *Second Tithe and the Added Fifth*

In Tos. M.S. 4 : 5-6 we have a dispute between Liezer and sages. Liezer holds that if a man has given the principle of the Second Tithe but not the Fifth, he may eat the produce. The Fifth is no obstacle in eating the produce that has been redeemed. The sages say it is. Judah the Patriarch then comments that the law should follow Eliezer for the Sabbath, but the sages for the week-day. In the next pericope Yosah attests Liezer's opinion. These seem satisfactory attestations.

23. *Ḥallah for Produce from Palestine Sent Abroad*

Eliezer holds produce sent from Palestine to foreign lands is liable for Dough-offering. ʿAqiba differs. The dough was obligated when it was prepared, so Eliezer. ʿAqiba says the decisive principle is where the person is located: "Since you are not in the land, you are not liable." Judah attests the dispute in Sifré Num. 110. It should be our Eliezer's opinion and among the better traditions.

24. *Dough Prepared in Small Balls*

In M. Hal. 2 : 4, the anonymous rule is that a person who prepares his dough in small balls which then come into contact with one another is free of liability for Dough-offering. The liability comes only when they actually adhere. Eliezer says if they are in a common basket, that will render them liable to the Dough-offering, all the more so their adhering. According to the anonymous rule (elsewhere: Joshua), only the oven combines them.

25. *Israelite Farmers in Syria*

Eliezer holds Israelite sharecroppers for gentiles in Syria are liable for Tithes and for observance of the Seventh Year. Gamaliel says they are exempt. Accordingly, Eliezer regards Syria as part of the Land of Israel; Gamaliel does not. Judah, Simeon b. Gamaliel, and Rabbi treat the matter in different ways; in some respects, Syria is, in other respects, it is not, like the Land of Israel. So Eliezer is represented as laying claim in behalf of the Jews to Syria, just as in M. Yad. 4 : 3 he agrees that the (predominantly gentile) inhabitants of Ammon and Moab are liable to the Palestinian agricultural tithes. Gamaliel holds Syria belongs to the gentiles and therefore bears no liability for tithes. The pericope is not attested or later on alluded to until the time of Abbahu (y. Hal. 4 : 4). If Eliezer is accurately represented, then, as in M. Yad., he is a crypto-revolutionary. Tos. Orl. 1 : 8, well-attested, has Eliezer say *ʿorlah*-laws do not apply abroad; but Syria is not mentioned one way or the other.

26A. *Curdling Milk with ʿOrlah-Sap*

M. Hal. 1 : 7 says that milk curdled with the sap of *ʿorlah* is prohibited. Joshua says he heard explicitly that it is permitted to curdle with the sap of the leaves and roots, but not of the unripe figs. So Eliezer's tradition is not differentiated; Joshua distinguishes among the parts of the plant. Only the fruit is regarded as subject to the *ʿorlah*-taboo; therefore only the fruit cannot be used. Presumably Eliezer would differ in respect to leaves and roots as well.

26B. Note also M. Orl. 2 : 11/M. Orl. 2 : 13/Tos. Ter. 8 : 15: If leaven of unconsecrated food and leaven of Heave-offering fell into dough, but there is not enough in either to leaven the dough, while together they do leaven it—Eliezer says, "I decide according to the last to fall in."

This is more or less consistent with Eliezer's view that what has fallen into a mixture can be retrieved. It remains separate, as above, No. 15. The sages' view is that what is prohibited must be of sufficient quantity to prohibit by itself. M. Orl. 2 : 13 has to do with the vessels greased with unclean oil, then with clean oil, or *vice versa.* Eliezer says one decides whether the utensil is clean or not by which of them came first; the sages say, which came last. The issue here, as explained in Tos. Ter. 8 : 15, is that Liezer holds a man should first use unclean oil and afterward the clean, since when they take out the vessels, they take out from the first ones that come to hand, which will be clean.

27. *Baking before the Sabbath*

Eliezer rules, M. Shab. 1 : 10, that on the eve of the Sabbath, one may bake so long as there is time for the bottom surface to form a crust while it is still day. This rule accords with his principle in M. Ter. 8 : 1-3 that what begins licitly may be completed. Eliezer here is consistent with the lenient position of the House of Hillel.

28. *Weapons on the Sabbath*

The issue of wearing a weapon on the Sabbath is whether it is an ornament. Eliezer says it is, sages say it is not. We are not sure this is our Eliezer; the warrant is not strong. If it is our Eliezer, then he would differ from Yoḥanan b. Zakkai's view of war.

29. *Wick for the Sabbath Lamp*

In M. Shab. 2 : 13 Eliezer says a wick of cloth that has not been singed is not regarded as a wick and is unclean and is not used for the Sabbath lamp. ʿAqiba holds the opposite. The larger issue is probably how a man signifies his intention. Eliezer again holds that without actually doing what is required, one has not shown what his intention is. ʿAqiba just as consistently will rule that what is intended may be inferred from an uncompleted action. The principle therefore is the same as in other cases.

30. *Tiara on the Sabbath*

See above, p. 114. We have assigned this pericope to the best traditions.

31. *Scratching on the Sabbath*

Eliezer says, M. Shab. 12 : 4, that one who scratches on his flesh is liable for a Sin-offering on account of writing. Tos. adds the colloquy about Ben Saṭra's having done just that, which is evidence that writing is accomplished by scratching. Tos. reflects knowledge of the story, found only in the later strata, that Jesus had made notes on magic by scratching on his skin, so b. Shab. 104b, y. Shab. 12 : 4. Accordingly Eliezer may also have known, in connection with Simeon b. Sheṭaḥ's hangings, the story about Joshua b. Peraḥiah and Jesus in Egypt. But this is by no means sure; Tos. reflects knowledge of some such story.

32. *Weaving on the Sabbath*

M. Shab. 13 : 1 presents Eliezer's rule that one who weaves three threads at the beginning of the web or one on to what is woven is liable for a Sin-offering. The sages say there is no difference between beginning the weaving or adding to it; the measure is two threads. Tos. has Liezer say one is liable for even one. Tos. Y.T. 4 : 4 has the same rule.

33. *The Window-Shutter*

In M. Shab. 17 : 7 Eliezer says one may close a window-shutter if it is fastened and suspended on the window, but if not, one may not close it. The sages say one may do so one way or the other. The issue is adding to the house, hence building. Eliezer says if the window is not fastened, then the man is guilty of building. The sages say if this is done at random, it is not regarded as building. Tos. Shab. makes the issue 'adding on to a building'.

34. *Circumcision Overrides the Sabbath*

Eliezer's rule, M. Shab. 19 : 1, is that one may do anything at all in connection with circumcision on the Sabbath—hence a much stricter rule. Eliezer further is consistent with his opinion in regard to the Passover, M. Pes. 6 : 1-3, as we shall see. 19 : 2 is formulated according to ʿAqiba's viewpoint. Tos. Shab. 15 : 16 is surely an Ushan pericope, which would place the one before us among the better traditions. Eliezer's leniency here produces his strict rule in M. Shab. 19 : 4, again among the better traditions. We may therefore assign to Eliezer both the principle that the Passover and circumcision override the Sabbath, and the view that that principle is interpreted in a most lenient way.

y. 19 : 1 has an attestation for Rabbi; he ruled in accord with Eliezer. The pericope produces a whole series of other applications, *Sukkah*, a *lulav*, slaughtering, and so forth—all override the Sabbath. Various further proofs are adduced in support of these specific cases, e.g. the *Showbreads*, b. Shab. 131a. Isaac then says people in a certain town did according to Eliezer's rule and survived, while others who did not follow Eliezer suffered.

b. Shab. 130b has a saying of Simeon b. Laqish in the name of Judah the Patriarch, attested by Zera + Assi, "How could they abandon the opinion of the Sages (= ʿAqiba) and follow Eliezer—a Shammaite!" But this contradicts Rabbi's saying in y. Shab. 19 : 1.

35. *A Filter for Wine*

In M. Shab. 20 : 1, Eliezer says one may stretch out the filter on the festival, and on the Sabbath one may pour through one already stretched out. Sages say one may not do so on the festival and may not pour through one on the Sabbath. This pericope has Eliezer in the lenient position in regard to the filter. Eliezer says stretching out the filter is part of the preparation of food, which is permitted on the festival—even to the extent of preparing the necessary utensils, just as with circumcision on the Sabbath. If the filter is stretched out before the Sabbath, one may make use of it, and this is not regarded as winnowing. But stretching out the filter would be regarded as making a tent, which is forbidden, as above, in the case of the window.

36. *On that Day*

Eliezer and Joshua discuss the *on-that-day* sayings (*Phar.* II, pp. 127-130)—both from the viewpoint of the House of Hillel. Tos. Shab. 1 : 17 certainly takes for granted Eliezer is a Hillelite.

37. *Rendering an Alley Way Valid*

See above, p. 117.

38. *Passover Overrides the Sabbath*

M. Pes. 6 : 1-2/Tos. Pis. 5 : 1 has Eliezer in a position consistent with that in M. Shab. 19 : 1: The Sabbath is set aside by the performance of other commandments. In this instance the issue is slaughtering the Passover. Eliezer rules that things which can be done before or after the Sabbath nonetheless override the Sabbath: roasting the lamb and rinsing the entrails, carrying the offering to the Temple from outside the Sabbath limit, cutting off the wen from the carcass, etc. Eliezer argues that if slaughtering the animal overrides the Sabbath, the other practices, prohibited for a lesser reason than Sabbath-work, likewise will override the Sabbath. Joshua and ʿAqiba respond. Eliezer then introduces the argument attributed to Hillel (*Phar.* I, pp. 231-235), from *In its appointed time.* ʿAqiba's general rule that what can be done before the Sabbath will not override the Sabbath is introduced at the end.

The problem in the Hillel-story is, Does the Passover override the Sabbath? The story before us takes for granted that the Passover will override it. But the Hillel-pericope then introduces the problem of bringing the knives and Passover-offerings to the sanctuary, which Eliezer explicitly holds is permitted. The pericope thus leaves Eliezer closer than ʿAqiba + Joshua to the position attributed to Hillel. The principle of M. Shab. 19 : 1 and M. Pes. 6 : 1 is that the Sabbath will not stand in the way of performing other commandments. Since the stories of Hillel's rise to power focus on the issue of Sabbath + Passover and draw on materials from Eliezer's circle, they would supply an attestation, of a sort, that the Eliezer-materials come first, that is, before Usha. These pericopae then would fall among the best traditions.

39. *A Distant Journey*

If one is far from the Temple and has not kept the first Passover, he is to keep the second. A distant journey (Num. 9 : 9) is defined by ʿAqiba as further than Modiʿim. Eliezer says it is from the threshold of the Temple court. Yosi then attests Eliezer's opinion—one of the better traditions, so M. Pes. 9 : 2.

40. *If the Sacrificial Goat Falls Ill*

Tos. Kip. 3 : 14 has a story of a colloquy between "them" and Liezer. If the goat that has to be sent forth falls ill, what is the law as to its being carried away? Eliezer says, "He can carry others." The answers to this and the next questions are enigmatic. y. glosses: Eliezer knew the answer but would not say anything he had not heard from his master. Eliezer rules on other problems in connection with the Atonement rite, but this pericope is not attested as to its substance, only as to its theme, by the sayings of Judah in Eliezer's name. Eliezer's opinions will be that if the goat fell ill, it is not to be carried; if the agent is sick, another agent is not sent; if the goat does not die when pushed down the hill, it is not then slaughtered. Thus the rite is not completed, if circumstances intervene, by deliberate action. b. Yoma spins the story out to a number of other, unrelated matters, following the same form: a clear question followed by an obscure answer. Tos. Yev. 3 has the same sort of story, but with a different legal agendum.

41. *Spreading a Cloth over a Sukkah*

Tos. Suk. 1 : 9 has a story, related to the principle of No. 33, on making a 'tent.' Liezer says one does not do so on the festival or on the Sabbath. Then we have a story about Eliezer's sitting in a *Sukkah* and being asked, What is the law as to spreading a cloth over it? He replies enigmatically. But the story finally shows he holds one may not do so.

The story-technique is no different from that in No. 40. We have further stories about Eliezer's opinion on Sabbath- and festival-law, e.g., whether one is to study or spend the day with his family, so Tos. Suk. 2 : 1, b. Bes. 15b, etc. Perhaps among the strands of Eliezer's tradition was one consisting of stories about Eliezer's behavior, from which laws were to be inferred to guide others. Alongside such stories, obviously, apodictic laws were preserved. One cannot regard the story-form of law as more authentic than the generalized statement. Neither is attributable directly to Eliezer himself. But both take for granted that he is an important authority.

42. *Animal and Offspring in a Pit*

Tos. Y. T. 3 : 2 deals with an animal and its offspring which have fallen into a pit on the festival. Liezer says one raises the first for the purpose of slaughtering it and actually slaughters it, and feeds the second in its place. Joshua says one raises the first to slaughter it but does not then do so. Then he raises the second. In M. Bes. 3 : 4, Judah says one ascertains whether the animal is blemished or not; if not, then one may regard it as in readiness for slaughter from the preceding day, and it may be slaughtered—superficially in accord with Eliezer's rule. Judah's opinion may be explained otherwise, however, so does not necessarily attest Eliezer's. The difference between Eliezer and Joshua is whether one may practice 'deceit' in the matter. Eliezer says one may not.

43. *Powers of Rain*

See above, p. 151.

44. *A Eunuch and Ḥaliṣah*

Joshua has a tradition that a eunuch submits to *ḥaliṣah* and his brothers submit to the rite performed by his wife, and another that holds the contrary. ʿAqiba and Eliezer explain the tradition, distinguishing between the sources of the man's sterility. ʿAqiba says if the man is sterile by act of man, he submits to *ḥaliṣah*, because he was at one time normal. Eliezer says if the eunuch is so by nature he submits to *ḥaliṣah* because he can be cured, but one made so by a man cannot be cured and is exempt.

Joshua b. Batyra supplies a case in support of ʿAqiba's viewpoint. It may be that Joshua b. Batyra attests to the dispute. Clearly, the tradition on the subject antedated Joshua, ʿAqiba, and Eliezer and consisted of two contradictory statements. As often, Eliezer then solves the problem through reason; but in this instance ʿAqiba does so as well.

45-46. *Ḥaliṣah at Night, with the Left Foot, or without Spitting*

Eliezer says *ḥaliṣah* at night is invalid; *ḥaliṣah* done with the left foot is valid; and *ḥaliṣah* done without spitting is invalid. Eliezer glosses the anonymous rules. Eliezer's opinion is that *ḥaliṣah* is a court-action, and courts are in session only in the daytime. The opposite view is that it is not a court-action. But the anonymous rule, before its gloss, accords with Eliezer's opinion.

Judah seems to gloss Eliezer's opinion on a closely related matter in the same pericope (above, p. 84), so we may reasonably assign the theme to our Eliezer.

Eliezer says the woman must spit—hence closely following the Scriptural rule. ʿAqiba says not spitting will not invalidate the ceremony. ʿAqiba holds what involves the woman, if omitted, will not invalidate it.

47. *A Divorced Orphan-Minor*

In M. Yev. 13 : 6, Eliezer rules that once a woman has ceased to be subject to the Levir, she is never again permitted to him, and is not returned to be subject to him. Eliezer is consistent with the House of Hillel in M. Yev. 3 : 1. If the minor is divorced and remarried, her status according to Eliezer has not changed. She is like an adult woman in the same circumstances. This is not consistent with Eliezer's view that the minor is like one who has been seduced and therefore cannot contract legal changes in her situation. But the reason for this ruling differs, and the whole set of rulings is to be assigned to our Eliezer.

48. *A Woman Permitted to Marry the Levir*

Eliezer holds, M. Yev. 16 : 2, that once a woman is permitted to marry the Levir, when the Levir dies, she is permitted to marry anyone else. The contrary rule is that each wife of two sisters-in-law married to two brothers is prohibited to marry because of the husband of the other, her Levir. We cannot be entirely certain this is our Eliezer.

49. *A Woman's Remarriage on the Evidence of One Witness*

In M. Yev. 16 : 7 Eliezer and Joshua hold a woman may not remarry if a single witness testifies her husband has died. ʿAqiba shares this view. Gamaliel holds that a woman may remarry on the evidence of one witness. His opinion is based on a precedent attributed to his grandfather, Gamaliel the Elder.

50. *A Sin-Offering for Each Individual Action*

The issue of Tos. Yev. 1 : 4, whether a woman who has remarried upon evidence that her husband has died is liable for a Sin-offering for each and every act of intercourse with her second husband when it is learned that the first has not died, is well attested in M. Ker. 4 : 2-3, p. 153. The principle is simply applied to another case.

51-54. *Virginity-Claims*

M. Ket. 1 : 6-9 has a dispute between Eliezer and Gamaliel on the one side, and Joshua on the other, on believing a woman's explanation as to why she is not a virgin or how or when she has ceased to be a virgin. Gamaliel and Eliezer consistently accept the woman's account of her condition. Joshua with equal consistency says one does not rely on the woman's own word. She must prove her claim, or she will be regarded as a liar. The issue is not attested elsewhere. The ruling in favor of believing the woman does not accord with Eliezer's tendency in M. Sot. to take a negative view of a woman's sense of responsibility and his equally unfavorable view of educating a woman.

55-56. *Releasing Vows*

M. Ned. 10 : 5-6 deal with the annulment of the vows of a woman whose marriage has not been completed, but who is supported by the prospective husband. Eliezer says that since the husband is liable for the woman's maintenance, he may annul the vows. Eliezer likewise holds that a woman awaiting Levirate marriage may have her Levir annul her vows. Joshua says this is so when there is one brother-in-law, but not two—for then the Levir surely is going to marry the woman. ʿAqiba says neither one or two will be permitted to do so. Eliezer argues that since a man may annul the vows of a woman he has acquired for himself, he may also do so for a woman whom Heaven has acquired for him. But ʿAqiba replies others have a prospective right to the woman. Joshua says this argument supports his view. ʿAqiba says the same reasoning applies in opposition to Joshua's opinion.

Eliezer is consistent with the view of the House of Shammai that a declaration of betrothal effects acquisition of the woman. Here too there has been a declaration of betrothal on the part of one of the Levirs. This view (b. Ned. 74a), however, takes for granted the correctness of ʿAqiba's criterion.

57. *Annulling a Wife's Vows in Advance*

Eliezer rules, M. Ned. 10 : 7, that a woman may have her husband annul her vows in advance of her making them. The argument of Eliezer is that since the husband can annul prohibitions already in effect, he should be able to release prohibitions not yet in effect. The sages' reply is a Scriptural argument: What is to be confirmed is to be annulled. Since the husband cannot confirm the vows in advance, he cannot annul them in advance. Both are good arguments.

Eliezer's tendency, already well attested, is to rule in a lenient way in releasing vows, with the result that in this case he seeks to make it easy for a vow to be released even *before* it is made!

58. *Uncleanness of a Nazir during the Final Sacrifice*

M. Naz. 6 : 11 is not adequately attested by M. Naz. 3 : 3-5, above, p. 125. The issue here is what becomes of the offerings of a Nazir in whose behalf the blood has been sprinkled, if he suddenly contracts uncleanness. Eliezer says he loses all the offerings. This is more or less consistent with Eliezer's view that, if there is no sprinkling of the blood, there is no flesh, and *vice versa*. The sages say he can bring the rest of the necessary offerings when he will be clean.

The point here is that one cannot bring offerings piece-meal. Joshua in M. Naz. 8 : 1 holds the same view—indeed, takes it for granted in making his decision—and therefore would attest, in a general way, to Eliezer's law. But he does not allude to Eliezer as the authority for the law. So what he attests is the substance of the saying, but not the attribution of the opinion to Eliezer.

59. *The High Priest and the Nazir*

Eliezer says, M. Naz. 7 : 1, that if a Nazir and a High Priest have to choose which of them is to become unclean to take care of a neglected corpse, the High Priest should do so, because he does not have to bring a sacrifice on that account. But the Nazir would have to bring a sacrifice if he becomes unclean. The opposed sages say that the Nazir's sanctity is not perpetual, but the priest's is. This is the view of the House of Hillel (*Phar.* II, pp. 50-52), so in this instance Eliezer is consistent with the House of Shammai.

60. *Nazir and a Barleycorn's Bulk of Bone*

M. Naz. 7 : 2 says that a Nazir is made unclean by a half-*log* of blood. ʿAqiba then says he argued before Eliezer that the measure should be a *quarter*-log of blood. Eliezer says that a *qal veḥomer* argument is not acceptable in the analysis of the traditional rule. Joshua agrees that ʿAqiba has reasoned well, but the law is what it is. In this instance, Eliezer and Joshua are alluding to laws which come before them—not necessarily in the form in which we now have them; they say that the tradition is not to be interpreted. The pericope of M. Yev. on the eunuch (above, p. 182) is another instance of Eliezer's and Joshua's consideration of pre-70 laws; the same will be seen below, p. 193.

I see no reason to doubt that the early Yavneans did have pre-70 laws and did study them, and the substance of these rules furthermore seems beyond doubt. Had the Yavneans changed the laws, we should have not a discussion of the peculiarities of a tradition, but a completely new formulation of the original law in the language and substance approved by the Yavneans. Here, therefore, we may suppose the pre-70 law is in our hands.

61. *Not Teaching Torah to a Daughter*

M. Sot. 3 : 4D has Eliezer's saying, that one should not teach Torah to his daughter. Joshua expresses a similar attitude, against the view of Ben ʿAzzai. The statements do not attest to one another; they are different in form and reflect merely a common agendum. But the issue seems important at Yavneh.

62. *Testimony against a Wife*

M. Sot. 6 : 1 is adequately attested by M. Sot. 1 : 1, above, p. 159.

63-65. *The Neglected Corpse*

The set of rules on the neglected corpse, M. Sot. 9 : 2-4, involving ʿAqiba and Eliezer, is not attested by Eliezer b. Jacob's saying, which ignores the opinions of both masters. The legal problem is unattested.

66. *Purifying a Mamzer*

M. Qid. 3 : 13 presents Eliezer's view, that a *mamzer* cannot change the status of his progeny through marrying a slave. Ṭarfon says a *mamzer* who marries a female-slave produces off-spring who are slaves; when the *mamzer* frees his son, the son is a free man. We are not sure this is our Eliezer.

66A-E. *Eliezer's Rulings in M.-Tos. B.Q., B.M., Sanh.*

A. In M. B.Q. 6 : 4 Eleazar b. ʿAzariah, Eliezer, and ʿAqiba dispute the problem: If one lit a fire on his own property, how far may it spread for him to be accountable for the damages it causes? Eleazar says it is regarded as in the middle of a *bet kor*; Eliezer says sixteen cubits; ʿAqiba says fifty. Then Simeon rejects all three opinions. Tos. B.Q. introduces Judah b. Ilai, drops Eleazar b. ʿAzariah, but keeps the opinions of Eliezer and ʿAqiba as in M.

B. Tos. B.Q. 8 : 17 has Eliezer's ruling, which is in Tos. Yev. 3, that one who raises dogs is like one who raises pigs.

C. Tos. B.B. 2 : 11 presents the view of Eliezer that one may acquire a property by walking on it. This is consistent with the opinion of Eliezer in b. Eruv. 94a. But it is probable that neither Eliezer is ours, because of D.

D. M. B.B. 9 : 7 presents Eliezer's opinion that a real estate apportioned verbally may be acquired, whether the man is healthy or dying, by money, writ, or usucaption; movables may be acquired only by usucaption. The sages distinguish between the will given verbally on the Sabbath and one given on a weekday.

Tos. B.B. provides Eliezer with a precedent for his opinion; in M. the opposition has a precedent, which Eliezer has to reject. b. B.B. 157a has an attestation of Meir and Judah for the dispute, now assigned to Eliezer and Joshua, on the distinction between a weekday and the Sabbath. Eliezer according to Meir says on a weekday the verbal instructions are valid, and Meir's Joshua says that is the case both on the weekday and on the Sabbath. Judah's Eliezer says on the Sabbath the instructions are valid but not on a weekday, and Judah's Joshua rejects the distinction. Two disputes seem to be mixed up, one on the acquisition of property divided by a verbal will, the other on the effect of a verbal will made on the Sabbath as distinct from one made on weekdays. Joshua clearly does not distinguish between the two. Eliezer seems to have made some distinction, but Meir and Judah differ as to exactly what it was. A third issue, on acquiring real estate, lies in the background.

E. M. Sanh. 6 : 4, 1 : 4 has a dispute between Eliezer and ʿAqiba as to whether wild animals have to be given due process for capital crimes. Eliezer says they do not, and ʿAqiba—repeating the anonymous rule—says they do. We have no attestation for the pericope or for the issue.

67. *Sin-Offering and Guilt-offering*

In M. Zev. 1 : 1 Eliezer says the Guilt-offering follows the same law as the Sin-offering. Therefore just as the Sin-offering is unfit when offered not for it own name, so the Guilt-offering will be unfit if offered for some other purpose.

68. *A Bird Whole-Offering*

M. Zev. 7 : 4 provides another instance of Eliezer's legislating through logic in respect to the cult. The issue is whether the Whole-offering of a bird is subject to the law of sacrilege if it is offered after the manner of the Sin-offering and for the sake of the Sin-offering—that is, its blood is sprinkled below the red line though it should be sprinkled above.

Eliezer reasons from a *qal veḥomer*: If a Sin-offering, which is not subject to the law of sacrilege, comes under that law when it is offered not in the name of a Sin-offering, the Whole-offering, which *is* subject to the law of sacrilege, should *remain* under that law. Joshua rejects the logic of Eliezer. The problem of offering a sacrifice for some purpose other than what is called for is well attested, and the technique of finding the law regarding the cult from logical reasoning is equally well attested. We have no good reason, therefore, for rejecting the pericope.

69. *Slaughtering a Dying Animal*

In M. Hul. 2 : 6 Eliezer says that if a person slaughters a dying animal and the blood spurts forth, the slaughter is acceptable. Gamaliel says the slaughter is valid if the animal can jerk its leg. Simeon then attests Eliezer's opinion.

70. *The Cock-Partridge*

Eliezer holds the cock-partridge is like a female in respect to the prohibition against taking the eggs and the dam. The sages say the law does not apply to the male, even though it sits on the eggs. The issue is not attested and the pericope may not belong to our Eliezer at all.

71. *Redeeming a Firstling with a Hybrid*

Eliezer says one may redeem a firstling with a hybrid because it is a lamb, but not with a *koy*. The sages hold the opposite view with respect to the hybrid. I assume this is our Eliezer because the adjoining pericope, 1 : 6 certainly is his. Eliezer's opinion in 1 : 5 is a gloss of a rule in which he gives his reason for ruling against and with the foregoing.

72. *A Firstling of an Ass That Died*

See above, p. 112, M. Bekh. 1 : 6F-G.

73. *Slitting the Ear of a Firstling*

Eliezer says if one deliberately disfigures a firstling so as to render it available to non-priests, the firstling may never be slaughtered. The sages say that when a legitimate blemish appears, the animal may be slaughtered. Warrant for assigning the pericope to our Eliezer is ample, see M. Neg. 7 : 4-5, above, p. 128, where the same principle is applied strictly.

74. *Oxen as a Pledge for the Temple*

M. Ar. 6 : 3 has a gloss of Eliezer, that if one dedicates goods to the Temple and must give a pledge for them, he is not deprived of his ox. Warrant for assuming this belongs to our Eliezer is not strong.

75-76. *A Substitute of a Guilt-Offering*

M. Tem. 3 : 3 has Eliezer's view that if one separates a female beast as a Whole-offering, and it bore a male, the male is offered as a Whole-offering, rather than set aside and sold for the purchase of a Whole-offering. This rule does not seem to accord with Eliezer's view in M. Sheq., but the problem there is the language used by the man, not the facts of the case. Eliezer further holds that the substitute of a Guilt-offering and its progeny are left to die. The sages say they are left until blemished, then sold, and the price goes for a Free-will offering. These rulings are consistent with Eliezer's view that a Guilt-offering is treated like a Sin-offering, M. Zev. 1 : 1, above, No. 67, p. 188.

M. Tem. 6 : 5 gives Eliezer's view that the progeny of the *ṭerefah* may not be offered.

77. *How Many Sin-Offerings for Repeating One Type of Sin?*

M. Ker. 3 : 10 is well attested by M. Ker. 4 : 2-3, etc. See above, p. 153.

78. *Suspensive Guilt-Offering*

Eliezer's ruling in M. Ker. 6 : 1, 3, on offering a Suspensive Guilt-offering when one is not sure what sin he has done, is consistent with his position in M. Ker. 4 : 2-3 and is attested there. But Eliezer cannot be said to attest the story about Baba b. Buṭa, M. Ker. 6 : 3.

79. *See above, No. 66A.*

80. *See above, No. 66B.*

81. *See above, No. 66C.*

82. *Unawareness of Creeping Thing and Temple*

M. Shav. 2 : 5 is attested above, p. 121.

83. *The Comb of a Water-cooler*

M. Kel. 2 : 8/Tos. Kel. B.Q. 2 : 8 present Eliezer's opinion that the comb-shaped filter of the water-cooler is insusceptible to uncleanness. The air-space of the comb is not regarded as a receptable. The tradition certainly is to be assigned to our Eliezer.

84. *The Size of a Hole to Render a Lamp Clean*

If a lamp has a hole of sufficient size, it is regarded as insusceptible to uncleanness. Eliezer says the hole must be sufficiently large for a small coin to drop through. The pericope is otherwise wholly Ushan: Simeon, Judah, and Meir. But Eliezer's segment of it is independent of theirs. See below, No. 86.

85. *The Oven of ʿAkhnai*

If an oven is cut into rings, and sand is put between each ring, Eliezer says the oven is insusceptible to uncleanness. The sages say it is susceptible. The pericope is glossed, "This is the oven of ʿAkhnai." But M.-Tos. knows nothing of the debate between Eliezer and Joshua, to which the law is peripheral.

86. *The Size of a Hole to Render a Metal Vessel Clean*

M. Kel. 14 : 1 has Eliezer's opinion that, if the hole is big enough so that a small coin will fall through, the vessel is clean. The contrary view is that one assesses whether the vessel may still serve for some purpose: a bucket will remain susceptible if water can be drawn with it; a boiler, if water can be heated; a kettle has to be able to hold *selas*; jugs must be able to hold small coins, and so on. Eliezer says a single measure applies: if they can hold small coins, they remain susceptible. ʿAqiba has a separate, unrelated ruling. Tos. Kel. B.M. 4 : 2 brings further rulings in which Eliezer repeats a single measurement for different sorts of vessels.

87. *A Baker's Shelf Attached to the Wall*

M. Kel. 15 : 2/M. Ed. 7 : 7 present Eliezer's opinion that a baker's shelf attached to the wall is now clean, since it is fixed to the ground; M. Kel. 11 : 2 says what is fixed to the ground is clean. The sages say that even though it has been fastened, it is unclean, for it remains a vessel by itself.

88. *The Size of a Hole to Render a Wooden Vessel Clean*

Eliezer's rule in M. Kel. 17 : 1 is that the size of the hole depends on what the vessel is used for. It has to be big enough to allow objects normally kept in the wooden vessel to drop through. But this would seem inconsistent with Eliezer's reservation about assigning specific measurements according to the use to which a vessel is put, No. 86. Joshua occurs in the same pericope, which is why I assume it is our Eliezer; but the matter certainly is dubious. Eliezer should hold to a single measurement throughout, namely, small coins, unless he distinguishes between one sort of vessel and another. In this instance all we have is the ruling, without his reason.

89. *Throwing Out a New Cloth*

M. Kel. 27 : 12 presents Eliezer's opinion that a piece of new cloth is like purple or crimson cloth; it remains unclean even when thrown out, since it will continue to have value. The dispute is with Simeon, but M. Kel. 28 : 2 is ample warrant for assuming this is our Eliezer.

90. *A Small Rag*

A small rag is always unclean in Eliezer's opinion, because it can always be used. Joshua says it is always clean. Since it is a rag, it is not used for clothing; therefore, it is regarded as if it were thrown out, whether or not it is kept. ʿAqiba says what is set aside for use is unclean; what is not set aside is clean. He therefore compromises between the two opinions—but stands nearer Joshua's—M. Kel. 28 : 2.

91. *The Worm from a Corpse*

Eliezer says (M. Oh. 2 : 2) that the olive's bulk of worm from a corpse whether alive or dead is regarded as unclean, like the flesh of the corpse. The sages declare it clean. Eliezer says a quarter-*qav* of the ashes of a cremated corpse is unclean. The sages say it is clean. These are glosses of antecedent lists. Eliezer regards the worm as equivalent to flesh. Perhaps, therefore, he thinks the worm was generated by the flesh itself. The ashes are equivalent to the bones. The sages say neither substance renders unclean in a Tent.

92. *The Uncleanness of the Grave-stone*

In M. Oh. 2 : 4, Eliezer says that the grave-stone renders unclean when it is carried. Joshua says this is the case only if there is grave-dust underneath the stone—so the stone itself will not render something unclean. Tos. Ah. presents a debate, with Eliezer against Joshua and ʿAqiba. Tos. Ah. 3 : 8 has Simeon b. Yoḥai's continuation of the debate. Simeon's saying would have supplied an Ushan warrant had he alluded directly to Eliezer's opinion. But his knowledge of the issues of the debate seems of some importance.

93. *Uncleanness of Tomb*

The uncleanness of various elements of a tomb is further discussed in M. Oh. 9 : 15. Here we have a tomb carved out of rock. If the tomb is equally wide, top and bottom, Eliezer says touching the tomb anywhere makes a person unclean; the uncleanness is diffused throughout. Joshua says what is part of the earth is not going to make the man unclean.

94. *Projecting Window-sill*

In M. Oh. 12 : 3/Tos. Ah. 13 : 3, Eliezer rules that if there is a projection on a projecting window-sill, and the uncleanness was under the projection, it will not bring the uncleanness into the house. Joshua says one regards the window-sill as if it were absent; the projection is sufficient to bring in the uncleanness. So according to Joshua the projection does not protect against uncleanness.

95-96. *Wall Projections*

M. Oh. 14 : 4-5 deals with wall-projections surrounding a house, with an extension at the door of three fingerbreadths. If there is uncleanness in the house, what is under the projection is unclean. If there is uncleanness under the projection, Eliezer says that the house is unclean; Joshua holds that it is clean. If there are two wall projections one above the other, and one projects above the lower less than a handbreadth, uncleanness under them, between them, or under the overhanging part will produce uncleanness underneath and between them. Joshua says what is between and underneath the overhanging part is unclean, but what is underneath them is clean.

The masters are consistent with the views given in No. 94. Eliezer supposes that, even though the projection does not project a handbreadth out from the door, since it goes around the house, it brings the uncleanness into the house through the door. Joshua says uncleanness will exude from, but not enter, the house.

In the case in which the upper projection exceeds the lower in width, Eliezer says there is no intervention, and what is underneath will be unclean; they join together to form the Tent. Joshua says what is underneath the overhang is unclean, but what is underneath the lower projection is protected by it. So the lower projection intervenes. This is not consistent with his position in M. Oh. 14 : 4.

Tos. Ah. 13 : 12 has a better explanation: Eliezer says they raise up what is lower to complete one Tent with another; Joshua says they do not. The rulings on Tent are then more or less coherent with one another.

97. *Grave Area Produces a Grave-Area*

In M. Oh. 17 : 2 Eliezer rules a grave-area may make a grave-area, and Joshua says it sometimes does and sometimes does not do so. If one completed a whole furrow and continued, the continuation is not a grave-area. If one completed half a furrow and went back, the continuation will generate a grave-area. The view of Eliezer, by contrast, is that if a new furrow is begun anywhere within the hundred cubits of the grave-area, the whole is regarded as a grave-area, no matter how the man has ploughed.

98. *Bright Spot on the Palm of the Hand*

In M. Neg. 9 : 3 Eliezer is asked to explain why a man whose hand produces a bright spot is to be shut up. He is unable to explain the matter. Judah b. Batyra says he can explain the matter and does so, and Eliezer praises him for confirming the words of the sages. Judah b. Batyra is the hero of the pericope, but Eliezer does not seem to be represented as other than a great authority.

99. *Leprosy Signs on a Checked Garment*

M. Neg. 11 : 7 exhibits the same pattern. An anonymous rule, not attributed to Eliezer, holds that if a leprosy-sign spreads from a colored check to another, the garment is subject to the uncleanness, even though colored garments do not become unclean by reason of leprosy-signs. Judah b. Batyra again explains the tradition, which had been handed on without explanatory information.

100-102. *Rules on Selecting the Red Heifer*

M. Par. 1 : 1, 2 : 1, 3, and 5, have Eliezer's rules on the selection of the Red Heifer. He says it should be two years old; the sages, that it should be three or four years old. If it is pregnant, it is valid. It is not to be purchased from gentiles. It may be the hire or a harlot or the price of a dog. If it has fifty white or black hairs, they may be plucked out, and the heifer will be valid. These rules are given against the opinions of the sages or ʿAqiba or Joshua b. Batyra.

In general Eliezer rules that the Red Heifer is not subject to the laws governing normal Temple offerings; Tos. Par. 2 : 2B makes this clear: "This is not a 'coming to the House' "—that is, the sacrifice is performed outside of the Temple.

103-104. *The Red Heifer and the Temple Rules*

Eliezer again says the normal Temple sacrificial rules do not apply. Judah's view in 4 : 1 accords with Eliezer's. If, therefore, the slaughter took place with improper intention, it renders the sacrifice invalid—consistent with the rulings on intention in respect to sacrifices, above, p. 188. Judah may attest Eliezer's principle, but not his specific rulings. M. Par. 4 : 1, 3 certainly belong to our Eliezer.

105. *The Reed Pipe for the Heifer Ceremony*

M. Par. 5 : 4/Tos. Par. 5 : 6 has Eliezer's view that a reed pipe cut for the water or ashes of the Sin-offering is to be immersed immediately. Joshua says it should be made unclean and then immersed. Eliezer thus holds that the pipe is immersed while still clean. Joshua says it should be made unclean and then purified, so it will be in the status of the *Ṭevul-yom.* The Pharisees held that the rite should be carried out by the *Ṭevul-yom*, therefore by one in a lower state of ritual purity than would be necessary for the Temple cult. Eliezer's general principles in Nos. 100-104 are consistent, but the difference with Joshua is in a matter of detail. The consideration, he holds, simply does not affect the reed-pipe.

106. *Maddaf-Uncleanness*

M. Par. 10 : 1 contains Eliezer's view that what is susceptible to become unclean on account of corpse-uncleanness is not regarded as unclean with *maddaf*-uncleanness. Joshua says the contrary. The sages take an intermediate position; if it is unclean, it is regarded as unclean with *maddaf*-uncleanness. If not, it is not—not essentially different from Joshua's position.

The problem is the *Zab.* He conveys uncleanness to what is above himself, even though not actually touching the object. Eliezer's view is that what can be made unclean by the tread of a *Zab* is not regarded as unclean, for the one who prepares Sin-offering water, as if it were already unclean with *maddaf*-uncleanness. Eliezer's well-attested tendency in matters of Sin-offering water is to rule leniently.

107. *A Jar of Heifer-Ashes on Top of a Creeping Thing*

If one puts a jar containing the Sin-offering ashes on top of a creeping thing, the jar is still clean, so Eliezer in M. Par. 10 : 3. The sages rule contrariwise. Eliezer has already made a clearcut distinction between what is susceptible to corpse-uncleanness and what is susceptible to *midras*-uncleanness. The jar is made of stone, so is not susceptible. If it touches a creeping thing, it is clean. If placed on top of the creeping thing, the ashes still are clean in Eliezer's view. The jar is not susceptible, so what is in it also is safe. The sages say the ashes are not in a clean place, because they are on top of the creeping thing.

The tendency of leniency now is supported by Eliezer's interpretation of the requirements of Num. 19 : 9. To him a *clean place* means the jar; to the sages, the jar is *in* an unclean place. Tos. Ah. 7 : 11 has Joshua in the position of the sages.

108. *One Clean for the Sin-offering Rite*

If a person who is clean for the Sin-offering rite moved a creeping thing, Eliezer says he is still clean, so Tos. Par. 10 : 4.

109. *Loosely-Fastened Boards*

M. Par. 11 : 2 presents Eliezer's rule that loosely fastened boards are unclean in what concerns the Sin-offering water. They are susceptible to *midras*-uncleanness, and, even when clean, are therefore subject to *maddaf*-uncleanness, as in M. Par. 10 : 1. Tos. Par. 11 : 8 says the dispute concerns language, not law.

110. *Hyssop-Berries*

Eliezer says that one is not liable because of the berries of hyssop in regard to coming to the sanctuary. The rule is that one does not sprinkle with the young shoots or the berries. But if one has done so, Eliezer says it is an acceptable sprinkling; one who enters the Temple relying on such a purification rite is not liable for a Sin-offering. This is not an important gloss.

111. *First- and Second-Grade Uncleanness*

In M. Toh. 2 : 2 Eliezer rules that if a person eats food unclean at a first grade of uncleanness, he is unclean at a first level, and the same for the second and third levels. Joshua says the grade is one lower than the source of uncleanness. If one eats food unclean at a first or at a second grade of uncleanness, he is unclean at the second level; if at a third level, he is unclean at the second level for Holy Things, but not at the second level for Heave-offering. The practical difference is that, according to Joshua, the person who eats first- or second-degree-unclean food is unclean in the second degree, and so will render Heave-offering unfit by means of liquids.

111A. *The Uncleanness of Outer Parts of Vessels*

In M. Toh. 8 : 7 Eliezer rules that the outer parts of vessels made unclean by liquids will make unclean liquids but not food. Joshua says they make unclean liquids and food. Simeon brother of ʿAzaryah says both are wrong. The liquids made unclean by the outer parts of vessels (Eliezer) render unclean at one remove and render invalid at one remove (Joshua). The uncleanness is slight; but Joshua says they will make Heave-offering unclean. Eliezer's lenient tendency in these matters is consistent in a number of unrelated rulings.

Simeon's tradition is completely different from those of Eliezer and Joshua. For him the issue is the effect of uncleanness contracted from the outer parts of vessels. According to Simeon the liquid is a first-grade source of uncleanness. According to Eliezer's rule the food made unclean by the liquid says to the liquid, "What made you unclean would not have made me unclean, but you have done so." Tos. T.Y. 1 : 8 gives Joshua's argument. But here Simeon's *case* is based on Eliezer's view.

112. *Quarter-Log of Drawn Water in the Ritual Pool*

M. Miq. 2 : 4 has Eliezer's opinion that a quarter-*log* of drawn water at the outset renders the ritual pool invalid; or three *logs* on the surface do so. The sages do not distinguish between the outset and the end-result. In both cases the pool is made unfit through three *logs* of drawn water.

The sages' rule is consistent with M. Ed. 1 : 3, where Shemaʿiah and

Abṭalion say three *logs* render the immersion pool unfit. Eliezer's distinguishing when the drawn water is added is rejected by the sages. But the sages know nothing of the attribution to Shemaʿiah and Abṭalion.

113. *Water Caught in Jars*

M. Miq. 2 : 7 has a rule consistent with the above. Eliezer says empty wine jars left on the roof to dry, which have been filled with water, if left in the rainy season, may be broken, with the water allowed to flow into the pool. If not, they may not be broken. Joshua says they may be broken or turned upside down; one may simply not empty them directly into the pool.

The water certainly is rain-water. The pool has some valid water, so further water may be added. Eliezer says even a quarter-*log* of drawn water *at the outset* will render the pool invalid. Here too, if the water of the jar starts the pool, it renders it invalid. Joshua is consistent with the sages of M. Miq. 2 : 4, rejecting the distinction important there.

114. *Water Caught in a Pot in the Ritual Pool*

M. Miq. 2 : 8 deals with the case of a lime pot left in a cistern, which was filled with water. Eliezer says if the water floated over it in any amount, it may be broken; otherwise, not. Joshua rejects the distinction.

115. *Mud in the Ritual Pool*

M. Miq. 2 : 10 has Eliezer's rule that one may not immerse in mud. Joshua says one may do so in water and mud.

The pericope then contains Ushan and Yavnean opinions on the kind of mud of which "they spoke," with a rule for Eliezer. But this cannot be our Eliezer, for to him no sort of mud should be acceptable.

116-117. *Hard Labor Three Days out of Eleven*

M. Nid. 4 : 4 and 4 : 6 present Eliezer's and Joshua's view on the ritual status of a woman in hard labor who enjoys a respite. If she was in hard labor three days out of eleven, and there was a flow during the eleven days, it is regarded as a flux. If she then had relief for twenty-four hours and gave birth, she is regarded as one who gives birth while in a flux, and a *Zabah*, according to Eliezer. Joshua says the relief had to come for a night and a day.

If she is in hard labor during the eighty days of purifying of the female child, the blood that appears until the embryo is ejected is unclean, according to Eliezer. The sages say it is clean. This rule is based on logic.

118. *A Zab's Semen*

Eliezer rules, M. Maksh. 6 : 6, that a *Zab*'s semen is not a liquid such as to render susceptible to uncleanness. Eleazar b. ʿAzariah says the same of the blood of a menstruant. Simeon says the same of the blood of a corpse, but he does not attest the other two sayings.

119-120. *Carrying Carrion. The Flux of a Zab*

Eliezer says that what is carried on, or carries, carrion is clean, except for him that moves it or carries it, so M. Zab. 5 : 3. In 5 : 7 he says the same of one who touches or moves—Eliezer adds, *or carries*—the flux of a *Zab.* The point in both instances is that carrying is like moving. M. Kel. 1 : 2 is formulated according to Eliezer's view. Eliezer does not occur there.

121. *Decline after Temple Was Destroyed*

M. Sot. 9 : 15 contains Eliezer the Great's saying that when the Temple was destroyed, a decline began. No other saying of Eliezer alludes to the destruction of the Temple. Nor is he called "the Great" in sources heretofore considered.

122. *Three Wise Sayings*

The "three" wise sayings in M. Avot 2 : 10 are that one should be as concerned for another's honor as for one's own; one should be hard to provoke; one should repent a day before his death; and one should not get too close to sages. The repentence-saying elsewhere is highly developed; the others occur only here, though the fourth may relate to Eliezer's alleged excommunication, which would then have its first attestation here. But the allusion is not direct and explicit.

123. *The Temple Walls*

M. Ed. 8 : 6 presents Eliezer's tradition that the walls of the Temple were built outside the curtains and the walls of the court-yards were built inside the curtains. Eliezer says the builders stood outside the curtains when constructing the Temple walls, inside for the walls of the courtyard.

124. *Gathering Cucumbers by Sorcery*

Tos. Sanh. 11 : 5/y. Sanh. 7 : 13 have attributions to Eliezer of the law that one is liable for actually gathering cucumbers by sorcery, but is not liable if he only creates an allusion. M. Sanh. 7 : 11 has the tradition in ʿAqiba's transmission of Joshua's teaching. Eliezer is dropped.

125. *Eliezer Arrested for Minut*

Tos. Hal. 2 : 24 has the story of Eliezer's arrest for *minut.* Eliezer gets off by fooling the judge. Then, in a separate, appended story, ʿAqiba suggests Eliezer approved something a *Min* has said to him, and Eliezer then says that is indeed the case. The teaching Eliezer had approved finally is spelled out by the *baraita*-editor in b. A.Z. 16b-17a; Tos. knows no such details.

This would seem to me to reflect a negative opinion about Eliezer. But at the conclusion Eliezer says a man should flee from what is ugly or looks like something ugly—thus his own teaching is the antidote for his error. The story as it stands therefore cannot be regarded as constructed to present a negative view of Eliezer.

126. *Ammon and Moab Give Poorman's Tithe*

In M. Yad. 4 : 3 Eliezer says that he had learned from Yoḥanan, who had a tradition going back to Sinai, that Ammon and Moab give Poorman's Tithe in the Seventh Year—just what had been voted by the consistory after a debate among Ṭarfon, Eleazar b. ʿAzariah, and Ishmael. Ṭarfon advanced the view approved finally by Eliezer. The tradition is not represented as Eliezer's.

In b. Yev. 16a the teaching is attributed to Dosa b. Harkinas, stated to Joshua, Eleazar b. ʿAzariah, and ʿAqiba—and Eleazar then is supposed in M. Yad. to have the opposite view! b. Yev.'s story knows nothing about Eliezer's tradition *via* Yoḥanan b. Zakkai from Sinai.

127. *The Generation of the Wilderness*

M. Sanh. 10 : 3, above, p. 157.

128. *Gentiles in the World to Come.*

Tos. Sanh. 13 : 2 attributes to Eliezer the view that gentiles have no portion in the world to come. Joshua differs. Eliezer is in the "liberal" position in respect to the Generation of the Wilderness, but not in respect to gentiles.

iii. The Authenticity of Pericopae First Appearing in Mishnah-Tosefta

Of the approximately 130 pericopae surveyed, the following clearly represent extensions or applications of principles already attested in the Yavnean and Ushan strata or have some other sort of earlier attestation: Nos. 5-6: Judah rules in harmony with Eliezer; No. 7: Thorns in the vineyard; No. 8: Judah accords with Eliezer; No. 9; No. 11; No. 13: Mixture of prohibited and permitted substances; No. 14: Give better for worse Heave-offering; No. 15: Taking action to prevent a transgression; No. 16: Liquid renders susceptible; Nos. 17-19: Intention; No. 20; No. 21: Intention; No. 22: Rabbi and Yosah attest; No. 23: Judah; No. 25: Simeon, Judah, Rabbi attest the law, but not Eliezer's particular opinion; No. 26B: *ʿOrlah*—what is prohibited remains separate; No. 27: Licit action may be completed; No. 29: Intention; No. 30; No. 34: Circumcision on Sabbath (Usha + Rabbi); No. 35 = No. 34 (?); No. 37; No. 38 = No. 34 (pre-Usha?); No. 39: Yosi attests *re* distant journey; No. 43: Judah may attest; No. 43; No. 44 (may be Yavnean); Nos. 45-46: Judah may attest; No. 50: Sin-offering for each sin of a single type; Nos. 55-56: Releasing vows made easy; No. 57: Same principle as No. 56; No. 58: Sprinkling required for meat—Joshua may attest principle of Eliezer's ruling; No. 61: Woman regarded negatively; No. 62; No. 66D: Apportioning goods verbally—Meir, Judah attest; No. 67; No. 68; No. 69: Simeon attests; No. 72; No. 73; No. 75 = No. 67; No. 77; No. 78; No. 82; No. 92—Simeon; Nos. 100-104, 106-110: Red Heifer-rules show Eliezer's established tendency to rule leniently in this matter, and Judah rules consistently with Eliezer.

The following deal with legal *topics* already familiar in earlier strata: Nos. 5-6: Liability for *Peʾah* and defective clusters; No. 10: Seventh Year; No. 12: Heave-offering; No. 24: Liability for Dough-offering; No. 26A: *ʿOrlah*; No. 28: Sabbath-carrying; No. 31: Sabbath-scratching; No. 32: Sabbath-weaving; No. 33: Sabbath-building; No. 40: Atonement-rite; No. 41: Building on festival; No. 47: Female minor *re* divorce; No. 48: Levir-marriage; No. 49: Remarriage on testimony of one witness; Nos. 51-54: Virginity claims; No. 59: Nazir; No. 60: Nazir (may be Yavnean); No. 71: Redeem firstling; No. 76: Progeny of *ṭerefah*; Nos. 83, 84, 85, 86, 87, 88, 89, 90, 91, 93, 94, 95, 96, 97: Uncleanness; Nos. 98, 99: Leprosy signs; No. 105: Red Heifer rite; Nos. 111, 111A: Uncleanness; No. 112: Ritual pool; Nos. 113-115: Ritual pool; Nos. 116-117: Uncleanness of *Zabah*; Nos. 118-120: *Zab*; No. 126: Tithes from Ammon and Moab.

The following treat subjects heretofore not part of Eliezer's traditions: Nos. 1-4: The *Shema*ᶜ and the Prayer; No. 36: *On that day*; Nos. 63-65: Neglected corpse; No. 66: *Mamzer* (?); No. 66A: Fire-damage; No. 66B: Dogs; No. 66C: Acquire property through walking(?); No. 66E: Trial of animals; No. 70: Cock-partridge (?); No. 74: Oxen as pledge (?); No. 121: After Temple was destroyed; No. 122: Wise sayings; No. 123: Temple walls; No. 124: Sorcery; No. 125: *Minut*; No. 128: Gentiles in the world to come.

We therefore observe an astonishing continuity between the legal agenda and even of legal principles attested before Mishnah-Tosefta and those first represented in the final compilations. Of 130 items, only 21 are on entirely new legal or other problems—approximately 16.1 %. Of these, Nos. 36, 121, 122, 123, 125, and 128 are not on legal subjects at all. This leaves fifteen items for the theme of which we might have anticipated some sort of antecedent evidence. But of these fifteen, Nos. 66, 66C, 66E, 70, and 74 cannot be shown certainly to belong to our Eliezer; the warrant for each is unsubstantial. That leaves ten, or approximately 7.6 %—a negligible proportion of the total. Of these, the four traditions on the *Shema*ᶜ and the Prayer are part of a much larger set of Yavnean materials on that and related liturgical subjects. The problem is by no means alien to the circle of early Yavnean masters. We have no good reason based on theme alone to suppose Eliezer would not have issued rulings on such matters. As to the three on the neglected corpse (Nos. 63-65), the estimate on fire-damage, the rule against raising dogs, and the trial of animals, matters are not so clear.

The dominant tendency of the stratum marked by first appearance in Mishnah-Tosefta, strikingly, is *not* to invent for Eliezer rulings on issues not earlier considered in his legal traditions or principles formerly unrepresented in his laws. Just as we noticed (*Phar.* III, pp. 209ff.) that the Ushans did not appreciably expand the legal agenda on which rulings were issued in the names of the Houses, so with Eliezer we see that the earliest legal agenda in general remain normative later on. New specific problems will be worked out, to be sure, but if Eliezer in the Yavnean and Ushan strata has nothing to say on an important legal theme, the chances are excellent that nothing on said theme will be attributed to him in Mishnah-Tosefta.

The abundant evidence that a large proportion of materials first given in Mishnah-Tosefta represents nothing more than the extension of Eliezer's principles to new details supports this contention. Of the approximately 130 pericopae, we found no fewer than 60 attested by earlier masters either in detail or in the operative principle—46.1 %. The stability of the legal agenda is still further indicated by the final group; 51 pericopae, or 39.2 %, deal with already well-attested legal themes, though the specific problems and the same principles are not necessarily attested in the earlier strata. So approximately 86.1 % of pericopae whose themes or detailed laws first occur in Mishnah-Tosefta represent nothing more than the continuation of either the identical principles or the general concerns attributed to Eliezer in earlier strata.

What of the non-legal materials? Nos. 36, 121-123 (124), 125, and 128 are to be regarded as part of a tradition no less authentic than the other items. No. 36 has Eliezer and Joshua discuss *on-that-day* stories. The issue is simply, What went wrong? That they knew something of the pre-70 history of Pharisaism is hardly incredible. No. 121 is something a master after 70 might have said. The sentiment is perfectly commonplace. We are not certain, to be sure, that in the second century Eliezer b. Hyrcanus was called "the Great." The "three" sayings of M. Avot 2 : 10 are to be considered only in the context of the structure, attestations, and sources of M. Avot 2. They furthermore form part of the larger problem of Eliezer's relationship to Yoḥanan b. Zakkai, attested for the first time in M. Yad. 4 : 3, on the one wide, and in M. Avot, on the other. The stories spun out of the repentence-saying make clear that it is our Eliezer who is under discussion. But for M. Avot, no one can doubt it. I am unable to interpret the balanced sayings about the Temple in M. Ed. They would seem to be of legal importance. Joshua's, in the same place, asserts that it is permissible to sacrifice even without the Temple, an astonishing saying. But I do not see how Eliezer's is related.

The important items are Nos. 124 and 125. Both are complex, in the one case because of the attribution of the same saying to several masters; in the other, because of the complicated development of materials finally put together in Tos. But both seem of considerable historical interest.

No. 126 makes much of Eliezer's connection to Yoḥanan; but Eliezer contributes no independent tradition. Eliezer's saying that the gentiles have no portion in the world to come accords with the xenophobia characteristic of post-70 and post-135 times.

Excluding the "three" sayings and the connection to Yoḥanan, we may then observe that the sum of the biographical materials on Eliezer in the strata ending with Mishnah-Tosefta consists of a story connecting Eliezer to *minim*, on the one side, and to sorcery, on the other—and these are a commonplace combination, with rabbinic stories about Jesus as a sorcerer well attested by the time of Justin (*Phar.* I, p. 86).

Eliezer's relationships to the Houses figure directly or indirectly in the following:

1. Eliezer agrees with, or rules according to the principles attributed to, the House of Shammai: No. 7: Intention; No. 11: By favor/not by favor; No. 21: Intention; No. 34: In b. Shab. 130b—Rabbi says Eliezer is a Shammaite, but y. 19 : 1 says Rabbi ruled according to Eliezer; No. 26: Declaration of betrothal acquires woman; No. 59: Perpetual sanctity takes precedence.
2. Eliezer agrees with, or rules according to the principles attributed to, the House of Hillel: No. 27; No. 36: *On that day*; No. 38: Eliezer argues as does Hillel; No. 47: Divorced orphan.

Eliezer is thus represented as a Shammaite or rules according to Shammaite principles but is not explicitly so represented in six pericopae; he appears to be a Hillelite in four. The matter can hardly be said to have been settled in the Mishnah-Toseftan stratum. Indeed, in respect to No. 34, Rabbi says Eliezer is a Shammaite; but a later authority states that in the very same matter Rabbi ruled according to Eliezer. This would seem to cancel out No. 34. Eliezer's alleged connection to the House of Shammai figures not at all in 120 of the approximately 130 pericopae. To be sure, the Houses themselves are concentrated in only part of the same sections of law. But Eliezer's and the Houses' laws center upon agricultural, Sabbath-festival, and uncleanness law, so the possibilities for alleging Eliezer to have been a Shammaite greatly outnumber the actual instances of such allegations. In all one can hardly say the view that Eliezer was a Shammaite figured in the Mishnah-Toseftan stratum or consistently played a role in the formulation of the traditions before ca. 250.

Apart from the stories which represent Eliezer as a sorcerer or a *min*, not a single item in the tradition can be called hostile to him or not respectful of his authority and traditions. But the sorcery-stories in the first instance involve ʿAqiba and Joshua, so we cannot take it as an effort to denigrate Eliezer as a sorcerer, unless we suppose that accepted into the tradition was a similar view of ʿAqiba—whose students are ultimately responsible for the tradition. Hence it seems unlikely that the materials of Tos. Sanh. are so formulated as to reflect a hostile view of Eliezer. The *min*-stories are similarly told in a way respectful of Eliezer's authority. He is represented as having made a serious mistake. The *Hegemon* says the moral of the story: What is a sage like you doing in a place like this? And since Eliezer is represented as shrewd enough to get himself acquitted, the story should not be regarded as different in spirit from all that have come before it.

CHAPTER ELEVEN

SUPPRESSED TRADITIONS

i. Definition

A suppressed tradition is a teaching attributed to Eliezer in one corpus, normally Tosefta, which either occurs without such an attribution in another corpus, normally Mishnah; or does not appear at all; or the *opposite* of which is given without an accompanying, contrary opinion for Eliezer. The problem of what such pericopae mean can be dealt with only partially, for we do not yet have a thorough account of similar phenomena in relationship to other Yavneans and Ushans. Nor have the principles of the compilation of the Mishnah been sufficiently worked out so that we may say for sure that omission of the name of an authority normally is deliberate. It is entirely possible that for redactional reasons parallel traditions came down both in a specific master's name and without such attribution. We have already observed a similar tendency to give in one compilation to Eliezer or to Eliezer and Joshua what in another compilation is attributed to the Houses. We have no reason, on the face of it, consistently to suppose a hostile intent is present. There may well have been confused or duplicated traditions, deriving from different circles or different tradents, regarding the authority of a teaching held in common among those circles or tradents.

We furthermore are unable to assume that if Eliezer is said to hold an opinion, that opinion both originated with him and was unique to him, so its occurrence without his name must be regarded as noteworthy. The consistency of Eliezer's viewpoint with a rule in the Mishnah does not necessarily imply that Eliezer is the only master who held that opinion. It also does not have to mean that because Eliezer held an opinion consistent with a law given anonymously elsewhere, said law therefore originates with him. Various masters, guided by the same principles of logic and the same traditions, may well have independently reached the same conclusions. It therefore cannot be supposed at the outset that the absence of Eliezer's name always means that it deliberately has been suppressed. But the lists of Ilai and ʿAqiba clearly show that that possibility cannot be ignored.

Only through the examination of the specific pericopae shall we be able to assess the problem. But that assessment will not be easy, for we cannot be sure that what to us seems controversial at that time was so, and what to us seems routine in antiquity was received irenically. Whether or not the oven of ʿAkhnai is susceptible to uncleanness should not have been an issue of much controversy; yet, according to the story attached to the law, Eliezer was supposed to have been excommunicated for persisting in his opinion. To be sure, the point of the story has nothing to do with the facts of the case, which are ignored as soon as they are introduced. But to the storyteller it must have been perfectly sensible that such facts, and not, for instance, laws about releasing vows or making an *ʿeruv* or eating with Samaritans or consorting with *minim* or making cucumbers by sorcery, would produce heated debates and a tragic conclusion. So we shall have to preserve the awareness of the differences between our perceptions and those of the authorities responsible for the pericopae before us.

ii. The Laws

Pericopae are numbered according to the list above, pp. 83-84.

1. *Balsam Is a Fruit*

M. Shev. 7 : 6 says the rose, henna, lotus, and balsam are subject to Seventh Year taboos. In b. Nid. 8a Pedat says Eliezer says balsam is a fruit—the issue of M. So he would agree with the law, but that does not make Eliezer the source of M.

2. *Liquids*

M. Maksh. 6 : 4 lists seven kinds of liquids, including bees-honey. According to Tos. Ter. 9 : 8D, Nathan says Eliezer holds date-honey is a liquid only when water has been added—so date-honey itself is incapable of rendering something susceptible to uncleanness. We cannot say that the rule in Tos. even pertains to M.

3. *Second Tithe for Corpse-Shrouds*

M. M.S. 5 : 12 interprets Deut. 26 : 14, *Nor given thereof to the dead*, to mean, "I have not used anything thereof for a coffin or shrouds for a corpse." Sifré Deut. 303 has exactly the same words in Eliezer's name. ʿAqiba says *for the dead* means that "I have not exchanged it even for something clean." M. therefore omits only the attribution to Eliezer. Epstein says Judah b. Ilai, authority behind Sifra, is the source of Eliezer's law in M. Here is a case where M. omits attribution to Eliezer of what clearly is assigned to him elsewhere. The real problem is the source of Sifré's attribution, however, and it cannot be taken for granted that M. knew Judah's attribution of the law to Eliezer.

4. *Redeeming Fourth Year Fruits after 70*

Tos. M.S. 5 : 15-16 has a story that Eliezer had a vineyard whose fruits he did not want to redeem. Eliezer was told by his disciples he had to do so, and he did. b. Bes.'s version has the Fourth Year fruit to be renounced for the poor. The disciples tell him he does not need to do so. M. M.S. 5 : 2 says that fruit of a Fourth-Year Vineyard no more than a day's journey away from Jerusalem was taken up to the city; when this became burdensome, it was ruled that the fruit might be redeemed near the wall. Yosi then says this rule was made after the Destruction. Tos. therefore accords with Yosi. But M. does not attribute the law to Eliezer, who is alleged by both stories *not* to have known what to do. So we cannot say that M. has suppressed Eliezer's name.

To be sure, the stories may reflect a negative view of Eliezer's learning, for he had to rely upon his disciples' knowledge of the law. But it might also be argued—following Yosi's view of the history of the law—that Eliezer did not know that the law had been made, being absent from the consistory, etc. (!). For our present purpose it suffices to observe that Eliezer has not been represented as authority in one place for a law given anonymously in another, nor is the law supposed to have been made on his initiative.

5. *Cakes of Thank-offering of a Nazirite*

M. Hal. 1 : 6 gives exactly the opinion attributed to Eliezer in Tos. Hal. 1 : 6: Cakes of the Thank-offering of the Nazirite are exempt from Dough-offering if made for his own use, but liable if sold. Leazar b. ʿAzariah says Eliezer's law comes right from Horeb. M. omits saying that its tradition is Eliezer's, word for word—a curious situation.

6. *Leaven of Heave-offering and of Unconsecrated Food*

In M. Orl. 2 : 11 Eliezer says that one decides, according to the last to fall in, whether leaven of unconsecrated food and leaven of Heave-offering which fell into the dough have prohibited it. The sages say what matters is the *quantity* of the prohibited substance, not the *order* governing which substance has completed the leaven needed for the dough.

M. Orl. 2 : 4, 8, and 9, do not register Eliezer's contrary opinion. But it is given, finally, in 2 : 11, so his different ruling has not been suppressed; it simply has not been repeated in each place where it might have been included. This seems to me a stylistic or redactional consideration, nothing more.

7. *Wearing a Tiara on the Sabbath*

Tos. Shab. 4 : 6 gives Liezer's opinion that a woman may wear a tiara or other ornaments on the Sabbath. M. Shab. 6 : 1 says she may not do so. Eliezer's lenient opinion is omitted. But M. Ed. 2 : 7 says that very opinion was stated before ʿAqiba in Eliezer's name. So M. Shab. leaves out what M. Ed. includes. Meir says not only a woman should not do so, but if she does, she owes a sin-offering (y. Shab. 6 : 1). Perhaps he has left Eliezer out because he differs in an extreme way. But then M. Shab. 6 : 5 says a woman may wear other ornaments, as Eliezer states in Tos. M. Shab. 6 : 5 does *not* credit him as the authority for its teaching. So whether Eliezer's opinion is accepted or rejected, M. Shab. 6 will leave his name out. Further, in Tos. Shab. 4 : 11 Eliezer says a woman is not liable if she takes her spice-box out on the Sabbath. M. Shab. 6 : 3 says she may not go out with it, but if she does, Meir declares her liable for a Sin-offering. Eliezer's lenient rulings therefore are consistently excluded, or, when included, not given in his name.

This pericope involves three separate items, and in the light of Eliezer's general philosophy on the Sabbath—it may be set aside by other overriding considerations—we may suppose these rulings reflect a general philosophy that favored limiting the restrictions in respect to the Sabbath to matters covered by the thirty-nine prohibited sorts of basic work—not stretching out the wine-filter and not scratching/writing and the like. Then, as in Ilai's and ʿAqiba's lists, the exclusion of Eliezer would represent an effort to omit his lenient rulings, or, where they are accepted, to leave out his name, so that other lenient rulings may not be taken as normative too. Here the deliberate omission of Eliezer's name seems to be part of an effort to impose a stricter philosophy of Sabbath-observance than he had favored.

8. *The Difference between the Sabbath and the Festival*

In Tos. Y.T. 4 : 4 Eliezer distinguishes between the Sabbath-breaking penalty and the festival-breaking penalty. For the former a person is liable to bring a Sin-offering, for the latter, to be smitten forty stripes. The sages say whether one is guilty for Sabbath- or festival-breaking (weaving a knot, or writing a single letter—that is, not actually completing a prohibited action) he is liable on account of *Shevut.* M. Bes. says that an act culpable on the Sabbath is culpable on a festival day, without making such a distinction as Eliezer makes in the punishment. But the omission of Eliezer's distinction may mean that the pertinent issue—the punishment—was not relevant to M.

9. *Food for the ʿEruv*

In M. Eruv. 7 : 10A, Eliezer says one may make an *ʿeruv* with any sort of food except salt or water. Joshua says it must be a loaf. M. Eruv. 3 : 1 states explicitly that they make an *ʿeruv* with any food except water and salt—the exact words of Eliezer. y. Eruv. 3 : 1 confirms this observation. Eliezer's ruling on the *ʿeruv* clearly is more lenient than Joshua's, and it may be a pattern that where Eliezer's lenient rulings in respect to the Sabbath- and *ʿeruv*-laws are given, the attribution to his authority will be omitted, so that other of his lenient rulings will not likewise be accepted.

Then how was the rule preserved in 7 : 10? Perhaps 3 : 1 and 7 : 10 are to be assigned to different sources. 3 : 1 has a gloss of Judah. 13 : 3 has an Eliezer, but we were unable to show it is ours. 7 : 10 has Eliezer and Joshua, then 7 : 11 gives Eliezer and sages, finally Judah—so 7 : 10 stands apart from 3 : 1 or 7 : 11, which have Judah's glosses; 7 : 10 insists that what Judah has as a unanimous, but anonymous opinion is in fact a matter of dispute between Eliezer and Joshua, and the decision will not be Eliezer's. So behind 7 : 10 is an authority who rejects Eliezer's opinion and with it, his leniency in Sabbath-law, and behind 3 : 1 and 7 : 11 is Judah, who accepts it and approves his leniency.

10. *Burning Together Clean and Unclean Heave-Offering of Ḥameṣ*

M. Pes. 1 : 7C-C has a dispute about a dispute between Eliezer and Joshua. One version says they differed on burning clean and unclean Heave-offering-*ḥameṣ*; the other, unclean with *doubtfully* unclean. Eliezer says each is burned by itself; Joshua rules that both are burned together. The Ushans are Meir, Yosi, and, for C-E, Simeon. In M. Ter. 8 : 8 Eliezer holds that one must take steps to preserve the status of

Heave-offering whose cleanness is in doubt; in 8 : 8-11 he consistently rules one must do nothing to permit Heave-offering to become unclean. Joshua takes the opposite view in both instances.

But Simeon's record of the dispute between Eliezer and Joshua is simply a redefining of the issue at hand and does not lead to the inference that the dispute has been altogether suppressed. M. Ter. 8 : 8 indeed supplies all information necessary to reconstruct the materials of M. Pes. 1 : 7C-E, so we cannot regard this as a suppressed tradition at all.

11-14. *Atonement Opinions*

In Tos. Kip. 2 : 10, Judah says Eliezer holds both the high priest and the prefect take lots, one for each, in the right hand. M. Yoma 4 : 1 says the high priest takes two lots. Eliezer's contrary opinion is not recorded.

Tos. Kip. 2 : 16 has Judah in Liezer's name, that the counting was one, one and one, two and one, three and one. M. 5 : 3 says the counting was one, one and one, one and two, one and three. But Eliezer's opinion is not mentioned.

In Tos. Kip. 5 : 14, Eliezer says that if the one who is to lead the goat away falls ill, another one is not sent; if the goat falls ill, the agent does not carry it—these rulings given through a colloquy in story-form. M. Yoma 6 : 3ff. omits reference to the issues raised by Eliezer and the opposed sages. We cannot say the opinion of Eliezer has been suppressed. Left out are the *issues* on which he rules.

M. Yoma 7 : 3 does not refer to all of the sacrifices, the time of whose offering is debated by Eliezer and ʿAqiba in Tos. 3 : 19. As before M. simply omits part of the moot issue but then cannot be said to suppress only Eliezer's name or his opinions.

15. *Egg Born on Festival*

In Tos. Y.T. 1 : 1 Liezer says both the egg and the hen may be eaten. M. Bes. 1 : 1 has the House of Shammai's view that the egg may be eaten. Eliezer's opinion in Tos. actually explains the position taken by the House of Shammai—the hen is ready to be eaten, so the egg too is permitted. Lieberman says the pericope should stand as the conclusion to M. and follows the view of Meir. But we cannot say Eliezer's opinion has been suppressed. What is left out—if the passage belongs in M. but has been deliberately dropped—is simply Eliezer's amplification of the Shammaite viewpoint.

16. *Cooking on the Festival*

In Mekh. Vayassa 5 : 41-50 Eliezer says one may add to what is already baked and continue to bake or to cook. He provides an exegetical basis for M. Bes. 2 : 1, proving that in the case of a festival coming before the Sabbath one may prepare an *ʿeruv* to cover both days. M. does not necessarily suppress Eliezer's exegesis in particular; it simply does not normally present the exegetical arguments in favor of laws. We cannot conclude Eliezer's name has deliberately been left off a law which originates with him. We may say only that Eliezer concurs with the decided law and supports it by his exegesis.

17. *An Animal and Its Offspring in a Pit*

In Tos. Y.T. 3 : 2, Liezer and Joshua explain what to do if an animal and its offspring fall into a pit on the festival. M. Bes. 3 : 4 knows nothing of their dispute. Judah and Simeon deal with a firstling which fell into a pit. So the issue is not the same, though Judah concurs in Eliezer's principle that if the animal is regarded as ready for slaughter from the preceding day, it may be slaughtered. But this principle is not unique to Eliezer. We cannot regard it as a suppressed tradition at all. M. simply leaves it out.

18. *Fasting on Ḥanukkah*

Tos. Ta. 2 : 5 presents a story showing both Joshua and Eliezer (with the former in Lydda) agree one must not fast on *Ḥanukkah.* If one begins, he must even interrupt the fast. M. Ta. 2 : 10 has the rule that one does not fast. Gamaliel adds, if he begins, he does not interrupt it.

M. therefore leaves out the contrary opinion of Eliezer and Joshua in Tos. The opinion is never presented as a generalized statement, but only in the form of a story. Eliezer's and Joshua's difference from Gamaliel may be said to have been left out exactly where it should have been included. This may be regarded as an omitted difference.

Is it then a suppressed tradition? The rule is lenient, to be sure, but that by itself does not justify the view that it was left out so as to omit a viewpoint less strict than Gamaliel's. In any event if the tradition is suppressed, it is not Eliezer's alone and does not show deliberate and systematic exclusion of Eliezer's opinion.

19. *Spinning Blue Wool*

In b. M.Q. 19a, Judah says in Eliezer's name that a person may not spin blue wool with a spindle, though he may do so with a stone. Eliezer, cited without Judah's attribution, says one may do so on his thigh but not with a stone. Then in M. M.Q. 3 : 4 we have Eliezer's opinion that one may spin on his thigh—without reference to the stone or the spindle, also to Eliezer. M.'s Judah is thus b.'s Eliezer. But Judah in b. contradicts Judah in M. The confusion is complete: Judah's opinions contradict one another, and Eliezer's are inconsistent. But we cannot interpret confusion as deliberate suppression.

20. *Tefillin for Mourners*

M. Ber. 3 : 1 says one who is obligated to bury the dead does not have to put on *tefillin.* But after burial we are not told of the obligation. The presumption should be that he once again must do so. In y. Ber. 3 : 1 we have a dispute between Eliezer and Joshua on the matter. We cannot say the dispute is suppressed. Its *topic* is simply not included.

21. *Setting Up a Millstone*

A situation similar to No. 19 is in b. M.Q. 10a. Eliezer says one may set up a millstone but not complete its preparation. The sages say one may finish its preparation. Judah rules in Eliezer's name that one may set up a new, and compress an old one. M. M.Q. states one may set up an oven, stove, or mill during the festival week. Judah says a pair of millstones is not to be compressed for the first time.

Eliezer's distinction about not completing the work on the oven, stove, and mill is left out. His distinction between the new and the old mills is given—in Judah's name.

It seems that in the cases presented by the Tannaitic stratum of b., the problem is not suppression of Eliezer's name, but rather the confusion between traditions in Eliezer's name and those in Judah's.

22. *A Wooden Sandal for Ḥaliṣah*

M. Yev. 12 : 2 states a wooden sandal may be used for *ḥaliṣah.* Judah in Tos. Yev. 12 : 1 claims Eliezer would approve the sandals of his day. This suggests Eliezer would not have approved the wooden sandals of his own day. But it is hardly definitive evidence that Eliezer's view, contrary to that of M. Yev. 12 : 2, has been omitted. Perhaps M. Yev.

12 : 2 speaks of the sort of wooden sandal that would have met Eliezer's specifications.

23. *A Minor's Ḥaliṣah*

Tos. Yev. 12 : 12 has Eliezer's view that a minor who performed the ceremony of *ḥaliṣah* must do so again when she comes of age; if she does not do so, the first is regarded as null. M. Yev. 12 : 4 says a minor who performs *ḥaliṣah* must do so when she comes of age, and if not, the first is regarded as null—Eliezer's opinion in his exact words.

And this seems to me an important matter, since Eliezer's principle that a female minor can do nothing of legal effect is well attested in the best traditions and is here applied. Ishmael's comment and the opinions contrary to Eliezer's show the principle ought to originate with Eliezer. Why then supply Eliezer's rule and omit his name? It would seem that this is a case of deliberate suppression of the fact that Eliezer stands behind an accepted law. Perhaps authorities did not wish to accept a consistent application of his principle.

24. *Marriage on the Testimony of a Single Witness*

Eliezer's and Joshua's (and ʿAqiba's) opinion, contrary to Gamaliel's, is left in the form of a story, not stated as a general law. But the opinion registers exactly where it should and cannot be thought to have been suppressed.

25. *A Sin-offering for Each Sin*

Tos. Yev. 11 : 4 has Eliezer's opinion that a woman who remarries on word of her husband's death and finds he is still alive must give a Sin-offering for each act of intercourse with her second husband. The sages say one covers all. M. Yev. 10 : 2 ignores Eliezer's opinion and accepts that of the sages. But the omission of Eliezer's view here is of no consequence, since M. presents the consistent view in different cases—M. Ker. 4 : 2-3 and M. Shav. 2 : 5. We cannot therefore suppose that Eliezer's opinion has deliberately been suppressed. It may not have been thought pertinent to M. Yev. 10 : 2, which concentrates on the issue of whether the court has consented to the remarriage, and to which the *number* of Sin-offerings to be brought is not central.

26. *An Orphan's Right to Melog*

M. Ket. 11 : 4 presents two rulings of Liezer, first, that an orphan has a right to worn-out articles; second, Judah in Liezer's name says that the orphan has the right to usufruct on her *melog*-property.

M. Ket. 11 : 6 has the rule that a minor-orphan who has exercised the right of refusal is *not* entitled to these benefits. Eliezer says the orphan has such a right, because her deeds are of no consequence. Thus his opinion, contrary to M. Ket. 11 : 6, has not been allowed to register.

One recalls that in No. 23 when Eliezer's principle is accepted, his name is dropped. Now, when it is not, his contrary view is not allowed to register. So here we have a tradition to be regarded as suppressed, evidently because Eliezer's consistency in the matter was admired but rejected by others. It has to be regarded as a controversial issue.

27. *The Neglected Corpse*

In Sifré Deut. 206 Eliezer says if a corpse is found between two towns, both bring heifers. The sages say only one does so. M. Sot. 9 : 2 has Eliezer's opinion, but not that of the sages, so Eliezer rules without opposition. This is the opposite of a suppressed tradition. What probably happened is that Sifré Deut. has taken Eliezer's opinion in M. Sot. and supposed that a contrary opinion must have existed. Since Eliezer says if it is found exactly between two cities, both bring heifers, the only possible alternative is that both do *not* bring heifers. So an opposed opinion has been spun out of Eliezer's.

28. *Agricultural Taboos Abroad*

M. Qid. has Eliezer say that the taboo about new produce applies abroad. This glosses the antecedent list that *ʿorlah* and mixed seeds apply abroad, so it would seem Eliezer agrees that *ʿorlah* applies abroad. But in Tos. Orl. 1 : 8 Yoḥanan b. Nuri says in the name of Eliezer the Great that *ʿorlah* does not apply abroad. Accordingly, the ʾP must be dropped from Eliezer's saying in M. Qid; or this is not our Eliezer; or the traditions conflict, in which case Yoḥanan b. Nuri's is preferable to M. Qid.'s. But we cannot call it a set of "suppressed" or even distorted traditions. My view is that the real problem is ʾP, used as a joining word in such a way as to distort the meaning of the passage.

29. *An Ox That Gores*

b. B.Q. 41b-42a assigns to Eliezer an exegesis that an owner is free of liability for ransom in the case of the *tam*-ox. He therefore agrees with M. B.Q. 4 : 5. But he is not necessarily the authority for that rule, and we cannot say for sure his name has deliberately been dropped from M.

30. *Dedicating Goods and Paying the Ketuvah*

M. Ar. 6 : 1 has Eliezer's opinion, together with Joshua's, about a man's dedicating his goods and paying the wife's *Ketuvah.* Tos. Ar. 4 : 5 then gives a further point of difference: Once the *Ketuvah* has been paid, may the couple remarry? Eliezer says the couple may remarry; Joshua says they may not; and the House of Hillel say they may not; then the subscription draws the obvious conclusion that Eliezer follows the House of Shammai, and Joshua, the House of Hillel.

M. Ar. has not omitted Eliezer's opinion. It has dropped the issue disputed by both Eliezer and Joshua, both the House of Shammai and the House of Hillel, and simply ignored the question of whether the couple may remarry. This is hardly a suppressed tradition.

31. *Flesh and Blood in the Cult*

In Tos. Zev. 4 : 1-2 Eliezer and Joshua differ. Eliezer says if the sprinkling of the blood has not taken place, the sacrifice of the flesh is invalid. If the sacrificial flesh is invalid, the sprinkling of the blood still is valid. Joshua says if the one is unacceptable, so is the other under all circumstances. M. Zev. 2 : 4 accords with Joshua's opinion. But Joshua is not named, nor is Eliezer's opinion given. What is suppressed, therefore, is the fact that earlier masters have debated the issue. But it is Eliezer's view that is wholly left out; Joshua's name alone is dropped.

Still, Eliezer and ʿAqiba debate a different case involving the same principle in M. Me. 1 : 2, so we cannot say Eliezer's opinion has been suppressed at all. It simply occurs in one way in Eliezer + ʿAqiba problems, in another, or not at all, in those involving Eliezer and Joshua. This would seem to me a consideration of transmission or redaction.

32. *A Torn Cushion*

M. Kel. 23 : 1 says a torn-cushion is unclean, but what is in it is clean. In b. Sanh. 68b Eliezer is given the opposite opinion: The contents are in the same ritual condition as the container. M. Kel. does not list Eliezer's opposed position.

The story, however, cannot attest to the existence of such an opinion by the time of M.-Tos.'s final redaction. It could as well have been drawn out of M. Kel. 23 : 1 to provide a detail for the story, or perhaps to make clear that a contrary opinion was possible. No tradition attributes the rule to Eliezer, but Tos. Kel. B.B. 2 : 6 does give it to Eleazar b. ʿAzariah(!).

33-35. *Tent*

In Tos. Ah. 7 : 3, Judah rules in Eliezer's name that if the door is open, the house is clean, because the lock is unclean. M. Oh. 6 : 2 ignores Eliezer's view in the case (above, Vol. I, p. 290, for details). Eliezer thus has not been allowed to register his contrary opinion. I am not clear why this should be the case. The formulation in M., however, is such that Eliezer's opinion is not directly pertinent to matters as stated.

Tos. Ah. 9 : 7 has a dispute between Eliezer and Joshua in Judah's name. M. Oh. 8 : 6, to which the dispute is pertinent, gives no hint of the matter. But the passage follows Eliezer's opinion. Here is a case in which Judah's allegation of Eliezer's opinion does not register; the opinion itself is given anonymously.

Tos. Ah. 13 : 10 has a dispute, well attested by Yavneans, between Eliezer and Joshua about an olive's bulk of corpse cleaving on to a treshhold in various positions. M. Oh. 12 : 8D divides the threshhold so that both parties are correct—a compromise. The dispute itself does not register in M.

36-37. *The Heifer-Rite*

Tos. Par. 5 : 9 has Judah's tradition in Eliezer's name that if a crown of mud is made for the water, it is valid. M. Par. 5 : 7 says if the vessel was crowned with a brim of clay and the water reached it, such of the water as reaches the clay brim is invalid. But if the brim was firm, it is valid. Eliezer makes no such distinction; the water is valid under all circumstances. Eliezer's lenient principle and ruling are thus ignored in M., and Judah's record of his law in Tos. is bypassed.

In M. Par. 9 : 3 Eliezer says a mouse will make the water invalid. M. Par. 11 : 1 omits both Eliezer's opinion and the mouse. But Gamaliel is included. I do not know why.

38. *Doubt in Matters of Uncleanness*

In Tos. Toh. 7 : 9 Eliezer distinguishes between public and private property, thus qualifying the pertinent Mishnah. His qualification is ignored by M. But M. frequently will give a gross definition for a dispute, which then is refined by Tos.'s redefinition of the same point of conflict in narrower and more subtle terms. This would not constitute a suppressed tradition specifically of Eliezer.

39-40. *Pigeon-Racers' Testimony*

M. Sanh. 3 : 3 has Eliezer's opinion, in his exact words, that pigeon-racers cannot give testimony, so M. Ed. 2 : 7's report before ʿAqiba. M. has a version omitting Eliezer's name. M. Ed. presents a tradition that assigns the teaching to Eliezer and has the matter stated before ʿAqiba. This would seem to me a conflict merely of redactional forms, not of the acceptability either of the rule—no one holds otherwise—or of Eliezer as authority behind a rule.

M. R.H. 1 : 8 likewise states that a pigeon-racer cannot give testimony about the New Moon, without crediting the rule to Eliezer.

41. *The Creeping Thing in the Mouth of the Weasel*

M. Toh. 4 : 2 says that if a weasel had a dead creeping thing in its mouth and passed over loaves of Heave-offering, and one is not sure whether it touched them or not, the condition of doubt is deemed clean. Tos. Ed. 1 : 10H–K has the same ruling in Eliezer's name. Joshua says they are unclean. So M. has given as an anonymous, unanimous opinion what Tos. Ed. knows only as Eliezer's disputed ruling. This would seem simply a case of different traditions about the attribution of the same rule, as seems common with M.–Tos. Ed.

42. *An Olive's Bulk of Flesh from the Limb of a Living Person*

In Tos. Ah. 2 : 7, Eliezer says it is clean; note also M. Ed. 6 : 2-3/Tos. Ed. 2 : 10. M. Oh. 2 : 6 does not know Eliezer's opinion.

43. *Cucumbers by Sorcery*

Tos. Sanh. 11 : 5 has ʿAqiba attribute M. Sanh. 7 : 11, making cucumbers by sorcery, to Eliezer. But M. Sanh. is in Joshua's name.

44-47. Not Proved.

Our original catalogue of allegedly suppressed traditions proves far too long. Three items, Nos. 19, 21, and 43, simply are confused traditions, in which, for one reason or another, different authorities are cited for the same teaching. The following are either not suppressed traditions or not suppressed traditions attributed only to Eliezer; or they turn out to be irrelevant to the problem: Nos. 1, 2, 4, 6, 8, 10, 13, 14, 15, 16, 17, 18, 20, 22, 24, 25, 27, 28, 29, 30, 31, 32, 33, 35, 37, 38.

That leaves Nos. 3, 5, 7, 9, 11, 12, 23, 26, 34, 36, 39, 40, 41, and 42. Of these, Nos. 7 and 9 concern Eliezer's leniency in respect to the Sabbath. Nos. 23 and 26 involve Eliezer's consistency in respect to the minor female's legal status.

The following are cases in which M.-Tos. Ed. has one chain of tradition while another part of M.-Tos. has a different chain, therefore probably a problem of transmission or redaction, rather than of deliberate suppression: Nos. 39, 40, 41, 42.

The important problems are in Nos. 3, 5, 11-12, 34, and 36. I am not sure why Eliezer's name is omitted in No. 3, M. M.S. 5 : 12; Eliezer and ʿAqiba are presented as opposed to one another many times. The omission of ʿAqiba's disagreement *and* of Eliezer's name for his contrary view seems puzzling. Leazar b. ʿAzariah has clearly approved Eliezer's opinion in No. 5, so why drop Eliezer's name in M.? I cannot say. I see no reason that M. Yoma has dropped Judah's contrary view in Eliezer's name in Nos. 11-12. The same applies to M. Oh.'s omission of the fact that it gives Eliezer's opinion as the law. M. Par. 5 : 7 has dropped Eliezer's lenient opinion; but his tendency to rule in a lenient way in the heifer-sacrifice certainly is noted, and several of those rulings do occur in M. Par. So we cannot say that the ruling was omitted because of a bias against Eliezer's opinion or traditions in this matter.

We find ourselves able to propose an explanation for the revision or omission of Eliezer's traditions in respect to the Sabbath—he was too lenient; and to the minor-female—he was too consistent. The other items of suppressed traditions met our original criteria but elude a reasonable explanation.

Strikingly absent from the consideration of suppressed traditions is Eliezer's relationship to the House of Shammai. While it is commonly alleged that traditions were either revised or otherwise tampered with because of Eliezer's having been a member of the House of Shammai, in fact none of the pericopae before us deals with an issue disputed by the Houses. In no case is it alleged that because of that relationship a tradition assigned to Eliezer in M. has reversed his real opinion, given in Tos.; or that Eliezer's authority behind a tradition in Tos. has been ignored in M. It goes without saying that Eliezer's discipleship to Yoḥanan b. Zakkai plays no role whatever in the suppression or revision of his traditions.

What is striking is that of 43 possible "suppressed traditions," 26, or 60.4 %, turn out not to conform to our definition of a suppressed tradition. If we add the confused traditions involving Judah b. Ilai, possibly also Nos. 11-12, we exclude five more, or 11.6 %. It would then seem that as many as (approximately) 12 pericopae reveal a tendency to suppress either Eliezer's name or even what Eliezer had actually said. That figure seems of no great consequence when measured against the minimum of 220 teachings in Eliezer's name which are well attested at Yavneh (20 or 21), Usha (62), the circle of Rabbi (8), and in Mishnah-Tosefta (130). All these teachings have *not* been suppressed.

We have only a little evidence—Ilai's and ʿAqiba's lists—that Eliezer's opinions have been tampered with. That evidence is probative in two respects: first, for itself; second, for the numerous pericopae for which *no* such allegation is made in regard to the accuracy of the representation of Eliezer. Of course we know nothing about what has been suppressed so successfully that not a trace remains. But we know nothing, too, about all the sayings and doings of Eliezer which never found their way into the processes of rabbinic preservation, formulation, transmission, and recension. In point of fact, the tradition in our hands gives strikingly little evidence of having been tampered with, either through suppression of things Eliezer did say, or through attribution to him of opinions he did not hold, or through exclusion of his name from the report of his sayings. Clearly, these things happened. But for the most part no one alleged of the vast majority of Eliezer's pericopae that he had said something not recorded, or that he said the opposite of what is claimed for him, or that he said something now given either in someone else's name or anonymously.

iii. Sayings about the Value of Eliezer's Traditions

The internal evidence just surveyed may now be compared with the explicit references listed above (p. 86) to the revision or suppression of Eliezer's traditions:

1. M. Shev. 8 : 9-10: ʿAqiba will not report Eliezer's real opinion, which is that a hide anointed by Seventh Year oil is permitted, and, probably, that it is permitted to eat Samaritan cooking.
2. Tos. Hal. 1 : 10/M. Hal. 2 : 8: Ishmael's students do not tell Ishmael that Eliezer is behind the view that Dough-offering is taken from the

clean for the unclean dough. After Ishmael agrees, then the students reveal "so-and-so in the south," Eliezer, is the authority.

3. M. Eruv. 2 : 6: Ilai can find no one to confirm his traditions in Eliezer's name which involved a considerable leniency in two rulings on the *ʿeruv*, and what probably is a lenient opinion in a minor matter on the observance of Passover. No other disciple of Eliezer admitted to having these same traditions.

10. M. Toh. 8 : 7: Simeon brother of ʿAzaryah says both Eliezer and Joshua have false traditions on the capacity of outer parts of vessels to convey uncleanness.

12. b. Nid. 9b: Rabbi ruled according to Eliezer's opinion and had to defend his action, saying it is all right to do so in an emergency —implying that otherwise it is not.

14. Tos. Ed. 1 : 4: Judah says the opinion of the individual is mentioned along with that of the majority so that, if necessary, people may rely upon the individual. The sages say it is done so that in the case of contradictory traditions people may known which one to accept —namely, that attributed to the majority.

16. Tos. Hul. 12 : 24: Eliezer accepted a teaching of the *minim*.

17. Sifré Deut. 188: It is prohibited to mix up the opinions of Eliezer and Joshua and to report that, if one says, 'clean,' his opinion is, 'unclean.'

18. y. M.Q. 3 : 1: Qerispai + Yoḥanan + Rabbi: If someone tells me that Eliezer teaches so-and-so, I should accept his opinion, but the Tannaim exchange his teachings with those of others. This appears in y.'s version of Eliezer's excommunication.

These sayings do not greatly change the impression left by the internal evidence reviewed earlier. A few of Eliezer's teachings may have been subjected to tampering, but the great bulk of them cannot be declared inauthentic on that account. No. 1 clearly is one of those few—but we are told, in the Mishnah of all places, that Eliezer's teaching has been misrepresented, and ʿAqiba is presented as the authority for the matter. So the *revision* of Eliezer's opinion has not been suppressed. Ishmael clearly is represented as hostile to Eliezer; we are not told why; and we have only this story as evidence of the fact. But No. 2 makes it equally clear that Ishmael's own students knew Eliezer's tradition and passed it on. Ishmael accepted it despite Eliezer's sponsorship. Further, Ishmael praises Eliezer's consistency in another evidently moot point, the legal nullity of a female-minor's deeds.

No. 3 indicates only that Ilai had difficulty finding others who had the same traditions as he did in Eliezer's name. It does not tell us that the reason for the difficulty was the controversial character of those rulings; while we may so interpret the matter, the story itself—again in the Mishnah—does not say more than that the traditions were unique to Ilai.

No. 10 represents merely a disagreement in the interpretation of moot traditions.

No. 12 clearly shows that the *baraita*-redactor claimed Rabbi would not routinely rule according to Eliezer's opinion.

No. 14 uses Eliezer's name as an example, but does not say it is specifically Eliezer's opinions that are to be rejected. Eliezer simply stands here for the minority over against "the sages" or an anonymous rule—as in the story of the excommunication.

No. 16 does not say Eliezer "follows" the *minim*, but, at worst, has approved a single (in b. A.Z., innocuous) teaching.

No. 17 seems to use Eliezer and Joshua as examples, as in No. 14. But then No. 18 puts into Rabbi's mouth the assertion that people deliberately confuse Eliezer and someone else, so, as stated, perhaps the intent of Sifré Deut. is to claim exactly that. On the other hand Sifré Deut, might be shaped out of, and after, Qerispai's saying, so the matter cannot be certainly resolved one way or the other. Internal evidences that the opinions of the one have been exchanged for those of the other—Eliezer and Joshua, or Eliezer and the sages—are not many. Ilai's and ʿAqiba's seem most pertinent. And Ilai does not claim others have the opposite of his tradition. Only ʿAqiba does claim Eliezer's position is the opposite of what is alleged in his name.

Sayings favorable to Eliezer and to his traditions are as follows:

5. M. Sheq. 4 : 7: Pappyas has traditions supporting the opinions *both* of Eliezer and of Joshua.

6. b. Suk. 28a: Eliezer never said anything he did not hear from his masters. This is further glossed into the stories, e.g., b. Yoma 66b adds it to Tos. Kip. 3 : 14. But Tos. Yev. 3.M includes the saying. If this too is not a gloss, then the allegation comes fairly early.

7. Tos. Yev. 13 : 3-5: Eliezer alone is fully consistent in regard to the legal in capacities of minor-females, so Ishmael.

M. Sheq. 4 : 7: ʿAqiba says the same of Eliezer: "I prefer the opinion of Eliezer to the opinion of Joshua, for Eliezer has applied his rule equally in all cases, and Joshua has made distinctions in its application."

8. M. Neg. 9 : 3, 11 : 7: Judah b. Batyra supports Eliezer's tradition.

9. M. Par. 1 : 1/Tanḥuma Ḥuqat 24: God praises Eliezer.

11. Tos. Nid. 1 : 9/b. Nid. 7b: When Eliezer was alive, people followed his ruling (with variations).

13. M. Yad. 4 : 3: Eliezer has an accurate record of the teachings of Yoḥanan b. Zakkai, which go back to Sinai.

15. Tos. Sot. 15 : 3: When Eliezer died, the Scroll of the Torah was annulled (BṬL).

19. b. Sanh. 68a-b: Much learning dies with me, for no one asked me questions.

20. y. A.Z. 3 : 1: Jacob b. R. Idi + Joshua b. Levi: Eliezer would have received the holy spirit, but the generation in which he lived prevented it by being unworthy of the honor.

21. b. B.M. 59b: Heaven announced that the law follows Eliezer.

22. y. Sanh. 1 : 2: Yoḥanan b. Zakkai ordained Eliezer.

The allegations that Eliezer carefully reported only what he had learned from his masters, and that Eliezer had studied with and been ordained by Yoḥanan b. Zakkai (Nos. 6, 13, 14, 22) seem to me intended to support the acceptability of Eliezer's traditions. They depend upon the prior assertion that Eliezer was a disciple of Yoḥanan (= Hillel!), so probably depend upon the stemma beginning with Avot. But the careful imitation of the master has a second meaning: Anything Eliezer might have said on his own is unacceptable. Indeed, the favorable allegations seem to me a reflection of a contrary view—and not much of a defense. This view comes in particular in Nos. 12, 17-18. It would seem that the question was important in the third century. To Rabbi were assigned conflicting opinions about the usefulness of Eliezer's materials.

Nos. 5 and 8 are more favorable than No. 10 is unfavorable.

Praise of Eliezer's consistency, No. 7, coming from both Ishmael and ʿAqiba, seems to me not part of a larger, favorable polemic, but a neutral observation of a fact.

The important sayings are Nos. 9, 20, and 21. No. 9 is a late *aggadah*, of no historical weight in the analysis of the formation of Tannaitic traditions. But in both No. 20 and No. 21, we have the sanction of Heaven invoked in Eliezer's behalf. As noted, both stories make Eliezer into a Hillelite. No. 20 is explicitly within a Hillelite structure. Hillel would have received the holy spirit, but the generation's poor character prevented it; then the same is said about Eliezer, in exactly the same way. No. 21 is closely related; the holy spirit *did* announce that the law follows Eliezer. To be sure, the story then goes on to stress the opposite is desirable. But both stories make the same, highly favorable point about Eliezer. In both instances it is taken for granted that Eliezer was a Hillelite. The assertion to the contrary becomes important in the first Amoraic stratum, and is already clear. It is not explicitly stated before the generation involved in the formation of Mishnah-Tosefta that Eliezer was a Shammaite.

The contrary view emerges as often as not in the analysis of internal evidences of discrete pericopae.

Praise of Eliezer in Tos. Sot. 15 : 3 seems to me routine. The story about Eliezer's death, b. Sanh. 68a-b, obviously is a favorable account, but stress on Eliezer's formidable learning forms part of no larger argument in his behalf, so far as I can see.

iv. Conclusion

While some traditions about Eliezer may have been suppressed, one cannot say we have found much evidence of that fact. And what evidence there is (by definition) has not been suppressed at all. We should know nothing of the matter without the preservation of stories and sayings that say so. These occur as an integral part of the normative tradition of the Mishnah itself. Nor have we much evidence that Eliezer's opinion has been revised, for one purpose or another, for that allegation occurs only seldom, and, when it does, it is accompanied by ample testimony as to what Eliezer had actually said. While it is further alleged that Tannaite tradents give Eliezer's opinion for Joshua's and *vice versa*, this does not seem to have happened in a large proportion of the materials before us, and when we do find it, it shows not deliberate falsification, but the difficulty of establishing firm traditions as to what one or another master had actually stated, e.g., whether or not handkerchiefs are subject to the law of 'mixed seeds.' Strikingly, few such pericopae occur in matters of uncleanness and cleanness, to which Sifré Deut. specifically refers. And there the difficulties occur chiefly in the definition of the protasis of the pericope, not the apodosis.

The evidence of favorable or unfavorable judgments about Eliezer's traditions adds up to very little. Many such judgments seem in the end mere disagreements on points of law, and, if regarded as motivated by a general hostility to Eliezer's philosophy or person, they then would have to be supplemented with the whole corpus of legal disagreements. It would seem that toward the completion of the Mishnah, problems in respect to Eliezer's laws were raised. But M. itself, along with Tos., provides the most definitive possible testimony as to the facts of the case. It cannot be regarded as revealing other than considerable respect for the importance of Eliezer's opinions.

Favorable sayings testify to the presence of a hostile polemic, but no more decisively than unfavorable ones. The most important is the assertion that Eliezer always imitated his master, along with the correlative claim that Eliezer's master was Yoḥanan b. Zakkai. These assertions seem to be part of the third-century inquiry, once the document was completed, into the history of the Mishnah and its masters. Avot is the most important evidence of the result of the inquiry, and in Avot Eliezer's relationship (along with others) to Yoḥanan is of course taken for granted. Other affirmative opinions on Eliezer and his traditions do not appear to be part of a systematic polemic in Eliezer's behalf.

CHAPTER TWELVE

THE POOR TRADITIONS

i. Definition and Criteria

While for the best, better, and fair traditions one may trace the growth of materials from Eliezer's own circle and those of his contemporaries and their continuators to final appearance in M.-Tos., for the poor traditions one cannot. They not only appear in compilations completed long after Eliezer's life, but also exhibit no important connections, or none at all, to traditions about, and sayings earlier attributed to, Eliezer. We were able to demonstrate that most pericopae first appearing in Mishnah-Tosefta constitute either extensions of principles attributed to Eliezer by earlier masters and reasonably well attested in his name, or, at least, sayings on problems already well attested within Eliezer's legal agenda. If, therefore, a topic does not occur in the best and the better traditions, it is highly unlikely that it will appear in the fair ones. The poor traditions, on the contrary, present a strikingly new agendum for Eliezer's consideration and dispose of that agendum without much reference to already attested principles.

Criteria for the evaluation of the historical reliability of the poor traditions are difficult to establish. One criterion, which can hardly be thought decisive, is thematic appropriateness. If we know on the basis of other evidences that some issues were particularly urgent after 70, we may imagine that attribution to Eliezer of a saying about, or a story pertinent to, such issues is not completely without foundation. The reason is that Eliezer *might* have ruled about such a matter or addressed a saying to such a situation as demonstrably confronted others of his time. But such a criterion distinguishes merely between likelihood and unlikelihood. It helps us very little to show what *probably* is Eliezer's. Since we can hardly claim to *know* about Eliezer more than we can *show* to be probably correct, this criterion is of limited usefulness. Still, Eliezer might have alluded to the effects of the destruction of the Temple; he might have commented on the issues of sin and atonement, suffering and redemption, punishment and forgiveness, atonement and salvation, which seemed important to other rabbinic masters and moreover occupied an important place in the literature produced by other Jewish groups, e.g., the pseudepigraphs after 70. The modest historical value of the poor traditions is illustrated by the obvious limitations of such a criterion, for, because we may say someone might have said or done what is claimed in his behalf, we should hardly go on to say that he actually did do so.

A second, not much less unsatisfactory criterion, though of somewhat greater usefulness, is appearance of a tradition in a corpus attributed to Tannaitic authorities, such as one of the Mekhilta's, Sifra, Sifré, and related compilations. While it seems clear that these compilations come after Mishnah-Tosefta, the editors have limited themselves to attributions to Tannaitic authorities; sometimes the sayings are not much different from materials familiar in Mishnah-Tosefta or are variations or developments of such materials. Pericopae first occurring in such compilations therefore have a somewhat stronger *prima facie* claim to have taken shape within the century of Eliezer's death than those first occurring in compilations of *midrashim* first attested well after the third century or not attested at all in cognate Talmudic literature.

But a Tannaitic attribution in the *Gemarot* of Palestine or Babylonia is not of the same order, for, as is readily seen, stories attributed to named Amoraim in the Palestinian tradition appear in the Babylonian with the claim of Tannaitic origin, TNY' and its equivalents. We therefore cannot take at face value the attribution of the Babylonian *beraitot* to origin before ca. 200 or to an authority with first-hand knowledge of Tannaitic traditions.

A third criterion, which is already familiar but here is of very slight application, will be consistency with what has gone before. If we are able to show that a better or fair tradition maintains that Eliezer's opinion is the opposite of what is attributed to him in a poor tradition, we obviously will stand by the earlier allegation and reject the later one.

These three criteria do not carry us very far into the analysis of the traditions before us, for they simply are not pertinent to the larger number of the poor traditions.

ii. Traditions First Appearing in Tannaitic Exegetical Compilations

We follow the list given above, pp. 77-82.

4. Mekhilta Beshallaḥ 4 : 1-9: There is a time for a brief prayer, and a time for a lengthy one (Mekhilta Vayassa 1 : 93-105, Mekhilta deR. Simeon b. Yoḥai, p. 57, ls. 4-8, Sifré Num. 105, Mekhilta deR. Simeon b. Yoḥai, p. 103, ls. 19-23). The sayings and stories on this theme may relate to Eliezer's view that one should not make his prayer routine or follow a fixed text. It then follows that sometimes a long prayer is called for, sometimes a short one. The sayings and stories recur in the several Tannaitic collections, which seem to draw on one another's materials. The teaching is consistent with an established saying and may be regarded as an extension and development of the law, hence authentic.

7. Sifré Deut. 303: This is attested, but not in Eliezer's name, in M. M.S.

10. Mekhilta deR. Simeon b. Yoḥai, p. 39, ls. 7-14: One may not bring the Passover from Tithes, just as the Passover in Egypt did not come from Tithes. ʿAqiba says the analogy is irrelevant as stated but should produce the rule that the Passover is to come from unconsecrated beasts. The principle under discussion, namely, drawing analogies from what is impossible for what is possible, occurs in several different cases. The principle that tithes are not used for other holy obligations also appears in respect to shrouds from Second Tithe (No. 7), so in a general way the rule is consistent with what is already established.

11. Mekhilta Pisḥa 6 : 88-91: Probably not our Eliezer.

12. Sifré Deut. 133: Eliezer and ʿAqiba differ on the interpretation of Scripture. Eliezer and ʿAqiba both say one sacrifices in the evening and eats at sunset. But Eliezer says one burns the remainder at midnight, and ʿAqiba says one eats until midnight.

The problem is analogous to M. Ber. 1 : 1, with ʿAqiba in the position of Gamaliel. The specific issue is unattested, but the opinion of ʿAqiba seems to be consistent with Gamaliel's.

13. Mekhilta Vayassa 5 : 41-50: Eliezer proves that one may effect *ʿeruv-tavshilin*: "Adding to what is already baked, you may bake." The legal principle occurs in M. Bes. 2 : 1, but not in Eliezer's name. He supplies an exegesis in support of the established principle.

14. Sifra Tazriʿa 12 : 6: Eliezer says Scripture rules the leper should let his hair grow loose. ʿAqiba says the exegesis should prove the leper is not to wear *tefillin*.

17. Sifré Deut. 212, 213: Eliezer and ʿAqiba debate the interpretation of Deut. 21 : 12. Eliezer says the captive should cut her

nails. ʿAqiba says she should let them grow. Eliezer says she weeps for her father and mother. ʿAqiba says these refer to idolatry.

20. Mekhilta Neziqin 9 : 29-30: We are not sure this is our Eliezer.

22. Sifra Vayiqra 13 : 4: Eliezer and ʿAqiba prove that the *ʿomer* is brought from barley, not from wheat. Eliezer's proof is a *heqqesh* based on *Aviv.* ʿAqiba's is based on logic.

23. Mekhilta Baḥodesh 10 : 58-86 = Sifré Deut. 32: The story about Eliezer's illness uses Eliezer's name as the setting for ʿAqiba's sermon that chastisements are precious. The story should be regarded as part of the tradition about ʿAqiba, not Eliezer. It seems to me to produce the well-attested fact that Joshua, ʿAqiba, Ṭarfon, and Eleazar b. ʿAzariah survived Eliezer, nothing more. b. Sanh. 101a-b assigns the story to Rabbah b. Bar Ḥana.

24. Sifré Deut. 38: Gamaliel's son's wedding has Eliezer ask a leading question for Joshua, who supplies the sermon that it is appropriate for Gamaliel to serve as host, just as did Abraham. Ṣaddoq improves on the sermon. The story belongs to Joshua's traditions.

25. Sifré Deut. 144: Yoḥanan b. Zakkai's and Eliezer's courts are good ones. Since Eliezer is linked to Yoḥanan, the saying depends upon Avot. But then it ignores the other disciples, including Eleazar b. ʿArakh, so does not know the version of Yoḥanan b. Zakkai's saying according to Abba Saul—which should attest a remarkably early version of the Eliezer + Yoḥanan stemma.

32. Mekhilta Pisḥa 1 : 114-118: Eliezer says Ex. 12 : 1, *saying,* means, "Say it and bring me back word." Ishmael says it means to tell it immediately.

33. Mekhilta Pisḥa 14 : 11-22 (+ Sifra Emor 17 : 11): Eliezer says *Succoth* (Ex. 12 : 37) means, literally, a place where the people put up booths. Others give more imaginative explanations.

34. Mekhilta Pisḥa 14 : 95-97: Eliezer says an idol passed through the sea with the Israelites. This is not demonstrably our Eliezer.

35. Mekhilta Pisḥa 14 : 113-117: Eliezer says the redemption will take place not in Nisan, as in Egyptian times, but in Tishri. See also Mekhilta deR. Simeon b. Yoḥai, p. 35, ls. 18-21, b. R.H. 10b-12a.

36. Mekhilta Beshallaḥ 1 : 57-69: Eliezer says God tired the people out so as to refine and test them. Joshua says he took a roundabout way in order to give them the Torah.

37. Mekhilta Beshallaḥ 2 : 8-15: *Ḥirot* is defined by Eliezer. Joshua regards it as a place name.

38. Mekhilta Beshallaḥ 7 : 109-121: The Egyptians were smitten at

the sea by 200 plagues, so Eliezer, as against Yosi the Galilean, ʿAqiba, etc.

39. Mekhilta Vayassa 6 : 47-9: The *manna* tasted like fine flour. Joshua says it was like a stew.

40. Mekhilta Vayassa 1 : 1-12: Eliezer says all journeys in the wilderness were at the divine command and reflected faith in God. Joshua says only that referred to in Ex. 15 : 22 was at the command of Moses. All the rest were at the divine command.

41. Mekhilta Amalek 2 : 186-192: Eliezer says the generation of the Messiah consists of three generations.

42. Mekhilta Amalek 1 : 173-175: The Israelites made war on Amalek only because of the divine command.

44. Mekhilta Amalek 3 : 127-140: Joshua and Eliezer describe how God saved Moses at the court of Pharaoh.

45. Mekhilta Baḥodesh 2 : 43-5: The covenant referred to in Ex. 19 : 5 means that of the Sabbath. Mekhilta deR. Simeon b. Yoḥai, p. 41, ls. 16-17, has Passover; *idem.* p. 139, ls. 3-5, has circumcision for Eliezer's opinion, and *ʿAqiba* says it is the Sabbath.

46. Mekhilta Baḥodesh 4 : 36-44: God spoke to Israel only after the people had accepted his commandments.

47. Mekhilta deR. Simeon b. Yoḥai, p. 1, ls. 12-18: God revealed himself in the bush to signify that redemption comes when Israel is at its lowest point.

48. Mekhilta deR. Simeon b. Yoḥai, p. 38, ls. 22-25: Eliezer says Ex. 13 : 5 refers to fruit-milk and date-honey. ʿAqiba says it is regular milk and bees-honey. Perhaps the exegesis relates to the issue of whether date-honey is a liquid.

49. Sifra Mekhilta de Miluʾim 2 : 35: The sons of Aaron died outside. ʿAqiba says they died within. I see no relationship between this exegesis and M. Sheq. or M. M.S.

50. Sifra Beḥuqotai 5 : 1: God punishes the people only after testifying against them first, so they are forewarned.

51. Sifré Deut. 29: God was angry at Moses on Israel's account.

52. Sifré Deut. 32: Some people like life more than money, others money more than life, so they both are told to love God more than anything else.

54. Sifré Num. 136, Sifré Deut. 338: Moses saw the whole of the Land of Israel.

55. Midrash Tannaim to Deut. 14 : 22: Going to the Temple moves a person to study Torah.

56. Sifré Zuṭṭa 13 : 34: A man's agent is like himself—proofs from ʿAqiba, Joshua, and Eliezer.

69. Midrash Tannaim to Deut. 6 : 6 (b. Ber. 13a): Eliezer says *kavvanah* is required only for the first sentence of the *Shemaʿ*. ʿAqiba says the whole passage requires it. The theme is well attested at Yavneh.

70. Sifra Shemini Mekhilta deMiluʾim 2 : 32-3: Nadav and Abihu were killed because they taught law in the presence of their teacher Moses, and whoever does so is liable to death. Eliezer predicted exactly the same fate for a disciple of his who did so, and the disciple died. The saying and story develop the principle that one should say only what he has heard from his master; now one should do so only under the master's direct supervision.

71. Sifré Deut. 140: A person must have his own *Sukkah* and cannot fulfill his obligation with someone else's. ʿAqiba differs.

72. Sifré Zuṭṭa 24: A woman may be forced to drink the waters of cursing. ʿAqiba says one does so only after the Divine Name has been erased. So he agrees on the principle.

73. Sifré Num. 153: Num. 30 : 2 proves, according to Eliezer, that an utterance is like an oath. ʿAqiba says no Scriptural proof is required for the proposition.

74. Sifré Deut. 61: Eliezer says Deut. 12 : 3 proves that one must uproot an *asherah*. ʿAqiba says no Scriptural proof is necessary; the passage proves, rather, one must change the name of the place where the *asherah* was planted.

75. Sifra Shemini 10 : 5-6: Eliezer and ʿAqiba dispute the extent to which an oven has to be heated in the completion of its manifacture. M. Kel. 5 : 1 has Judah within the framework of Eliezer's opposition, holding the oven has to be heated, against Eliezer's judgment that it is completed without heating. The tradition seems a strong one, because of Judah's presence, despite his differing from Eliezer.

76. Mekhilta deR. Simeon b. Yoḥai, p. 106, ls. 23-26: Eliezer says Ex. 16 : 4 means a man should not gather today for tomorrow. This is parallel to his saying, b. Sot. 48b, that one who wonders what he will eat the next day is a person of little faith—the view of Hillel.

77. Mekhilta Vayassa 7 : 68-74: Eliezer says the people in the wilderness obeyed God only on condition that he supply all their needs. Their faith was on account of material considerations.

78. Mekhilta deR. Simeon b. Yoḥai, p. 143, ls. 3-8: Eliezer praises the faith of the people at the sea, aplying to Ex. 14 : 13-14 the Song

2 : 14. ʿAqiba says the Scripture refers to their faith at Mount Sinai.

79. Mekhilta Neziqin 18 : 9-16: Scripture warned about the stranger because there is a bad streak in him. The same teaching is appended to b. B.M. 59b.

The pericopae first appearing in the Tannaitic compilations ignore biographical and legal issues and concentrate, as is to be expected, chiefly on exegetical problems. The alleged relationship between Eliezer and the House of Shammai makes no appearance, nor does his discipleship to Yoḥanan b. Zakkai play any important role. None of the pericopae reveals the slightest measure of hostility to Eliezer, and in none is it stated that because Eliezer is a Shammaite, one must not follow his teachings.

Sifra's and Sifré's traditions stand apart from those of the Mekhilta. No. 7 is attested; No. 12 seems to have a claim on authenticity. In Nos. 13 and 14 Eliezer and ʿAqiba debate whether a verse is to be interpreted literally or figuratively. This issue never occurs in Mekh. No. 22 simply provides Eliezer and ʿAqiba with different proofs for the same proposition. No. 23 depends upon Eliezer's having studied with Yoḥanan, linking the two. Nos. 49, 54, 55 are anomalous. Nos. 50 and 51 are entirely appropriate to the Yavnean situation, with its stress on divine punishment and forewarning. Nos. 52 and 69 accord in a general way with Eliezer's involvement in the matter of the *Shemaʿ*. No. 56 has the early Yavneans prove the position of Shammai. No. 70 is consistent with Eliezer's established views on the necessity of the disciple to be submissive to the master. No. 71 is a well-attested legal principle. No. 72, 73, 74 all deal, along the lines of No. 22, with the problem of how Scripture is to be interpreted. No. 75 presents a commonplace dispute about logic and falls well within the framework of Eliezer's legal interests; Judah provides an attestation for the issue, but not for Eliezer's opinion.

If we now leave out all but Sifra and Sifré, we find, on the whole, a corpus of materials not far outside what is already familiar. Nos. 7, 12, 24, 52, 56, 69, 70, 71, 72, 75 are relatively well attested. Nos. 13, 14, 17, 22, 33 (Sifra), 73, 74 exhibit a fixed difference between Eliezer and ʿAqiba on exegetical matters. Nos. 50 and 51 are on topics important in Yavnean times. That leaves as anomalies Nos. 49, 54, and 55.

By contrast, the materials in Mekhilta deR. Ishmael and those in Mekhilta deR. Simeon b. Yoḥai not borrowed directly from Sifré,

Sifra, or the *Gemarot* stand wholly by themselves, with scarcely any relationship to other materials of Eliezer. While nothing before us is attested, Mekhilta has not even the sort of antecedents one may claim to find for Sifra and Sifré. The exegetical principle dividing Eliezer and ʿAqiba—whether one interprets a passage literally or fancifully—makes no appearance. Rather, we have a Scripture and then differing interpretations, assigned in no perceptible pattern, revealing no clear and consistent difference, to two names, Eliezer and Joshua, or Eliezer and ʿAqiba. But nothing in the already-familiar corpus of materials pertinent to Eliezer has prepared us for these pericopae. The concentration of the materials in a few specific themes, e.g., the war against Amalek, the events at the Red Sea and at Sinai, however, suggests the assignments of materials are not random.

Among the materials in Mekhilta deR. Ishmael the following seem to relate to themes or problems attested earlier: Nos. 4 (prayer); 10 (the possible from the impossible); 13 (*ʿeruv tavshilin*). In No. 23 Eliezer is irrelevant. The following seem to exhibit no antecedent roots of any sort: Nos. 32, 34, 36, 37, 38, 39, 40, 41, 42, 44, 45, 46, 47 which contradicts 78, and 79. Nos. 35 and 47 pertain to the problem of redemption, a Yavnean concern. No. 48 may relate to a legal problem. No. 76 certainly relies on b. Sot. 48b, and Hillel gets the same teaching in a dispute with Shammai, so again Eliezer is represented as a Hillelite.

Of the 22 pericopae in Sifra and Sifré, ten seem related to already familiar materials, while an additional seven deal with a fixed problem in exegetical techniques employed by Eliezer and ʿAqiba, respectively, and two *might* have been stated by Eliezer. Of the approximately 25 pericopae in the Mekhiltas, fifteen are quite new. Two pertain to a Yavnean concern and *might* have been said by Eliezer, and two more may be related to materials known elsewhere. It is striking that remarkably few pericopae in Mekhilta deR. Ishmael exhibit parallels in the other compilations of Tannaitic Midrashim or in the *Gemarot.* By contrast, a great number of pericopae in Sifra and Sifré—not listed here but cited in the appropriate legal contexts—depend upon or supply exegetical bases for opinions of Eliezer in Mishnah-Tosefta.

Mekhilta deR. Ishmael certainly must be regarded as a quite separate body of traditions. Whether these are early or late we cannot say. They are nearly entirely autonomous. But they assign to Eliezer an exegetical interest in Amalek, an appropriate theme for a Yavnean exegete who had survived a war with Rome, and a concern for the spirit of the people in the time of redemption from Egypt (though with contradictory views of that spirit), again an appropriate theme for an exegete contemplating the redemption everyone hoped would soon come. Similarly, in No. 38, Eliezer comments on how the Egyptians were punished, perhaps with Rome in mind (?). We cannot, therefore, reject Mekhilta's exegeses out of hand. In their general concerns they reflect interests relevant at early Yavneh. We cannot assume Eliezer did not provide exegeses of non-legal Scriptures, though these cannot often be found in the earlier compilations. If he did, this is—more or less—what he ought to have said. But that is a very weak argument indeed in behalf of the essential authenticity of the Mekhiltan materials. The best one may say is that while one cannot demonstrate their probable authenticity, one also has no good reason to reject the whole corpus.

iii. The Tannaitic Stratum of the Gemarot

The traditions marked TNY in y. and TNY' (or equivalent) in b., without attestation or antecedents in Mishnah-Tosefta or in the Tannaitic Midrashim, follow (numbered according to the list on pp. 70-73).

1. b. Ber. 3a: The night is divided into three watches, at each of which God mourns the destruction of the Temple. The saying develops M. Ber. 1 : 1.

2. See above, No. 69.

3. = Tos. Ber. 3 : 7.

5. b. Ber. 47b: Who is an *ʿam haʾareṣ*? Whoever does not read the *Shemaʿ* evening and morning. Joshua says it is one who does not put on *tefillin.* These certainly are important Yavnean issues. Meir says it is one who does not eat his unconsecrated food in ritual cleanness. The saying attributed to Eliezer therefore is thematically appropriate.

6. b. Ber. 62a: One should wipe with the left hand because one eats with it. Joshua, ʿAqiba, or Gamaliel appear in other recensions of the pericope. This is a peculiarly "rabbinical" teaching.

8. b. Shab. 12a, 107b: Eliezer says one may not kill vermin on the Sabbath or catch a flea. He rules in accord with M. Shab. 1 : 3 and with the House of Shammai. This is certainly our Eliezer. But Eliezer's tendency in M. Shab. 1 : 10 seems closer to that of the House of Hillel. Simeon b. Eleazar attests the saying, though not the attribution to Eliezer.

9. b. Pes. 36a, y. Pes. 2 : 7: ʿAqiba says he kneaded dough for Eliezer

and Joshua with wine, oil, or honey; or, y. Pes. 2 : 7: fruit-juice. This is in connection with Passover. The story relates to Tos. Ter. 9 : 9.

15. b. Yev. 70a: Eliezer proves an uncircumcized priest may not eat Heave-offering from Ex. 12 : 45 and Lev. 22 : 10. ʿAqiba says such a proof is unnecessary.

16. b. Yev. 46a: Eliezer says a proselyte who was circumcized but not baptized is acceptable. Joshua says a proselyte who was baptized but not circumcized is acceptable. Sages require both rites.

18. b. Yev. 34b, y. Ket. 5 : 6: An infant is nursed for twenty-four months. Joshua says nursing may go on four or five years.

19. b. Hag. 10a: Eliezer and Joshua supply biblical precedents for the release of vows, M. Hag. 1 : 1. The proofs certainly pertain to current practice.

21. b. Qid. 18b: ʿAqiba interprets Ex. 21 : 8 to mean once the female captive has been taken as a wife, she cannot be sold. Eliezer agrees, but interprets the Scripture according to its simple meaning for this purpose. The difference is the interpretation of BGD.

26. b. Sanh. 68b, y. Shab. 2 : 7: y. does not assign Eliezer's death scene to Tannaitic authority. b. Sanh. introduces it with TNYʾ. b. Ber. 28b has a separate death-scene, tied to that of Yoḥanan b. Zakkai, with a completely different story; it depends upon M. Avot in linking the two. ARN then unites the two deathbed messages. y. Sot. 9 : 16/A.Z. 3 : 1 has still a third death-scene, this time in the name of Jacob b. R. Idi + Joshua b. Levi, also linking Eliezer to Yoḥanan.

27. b. Sot. 48b: See above, No. 76.

28. b. B.M. 59b: Oven of ʿAkhnai-debate "explains" why Eliezer was excommunicated. y. M.Q. 3 : 1 does not know this as a Tannaitic tradition. Interpolations or additions come from Ḥanina, Jeremiah, Qerispai + Yoḥanan + Rabbi.

29. b. B.B. 74b: Eliezer and Joshua aboard ship saw the eye of Leviathan.

30. b. B.B. 121b: The 15th of Av marks the end of gathering wood for the wood-offering, so Eliezer.

43. b. Bekh. 5b: Rephidim was the name of a place, so Eliezer. Joshua interprets the name in a figurative way. The same is repeated for Shiṭṭim. b. Sanh. 106a does not have a Tannaitic attribution. The first passage involves the interpretation of the Amalek story; the second relates to the Moabites.

56. y. Shab. 9 : 3: Eliezer and Joshua on Is. 1 : 18 say that the sins will be forgiven.

57. y. Ta. 1 : 1: Eliezer says redemption depends upon repentence. Joshua says Israel will be redeemed no matter what.

58. b. Ber. 6a: Deut. 28 : 10, *All the peoples of the earth shall see* means the peoples will see the *tefillin* on the Jews' heads. See No. 5.

59. b. Shab. 55b: Eliezer and Joshua refer to Gen. 49 : 4. Reuben was a bad man.

60. b. Pes. 117a: Eliezer says Psalms were said by David with reference to himself. Joshua says they refer to the Jewish people.

61. b. Ta. 9b: Eliezer says the world draws its water-suply from the ocean.

62. b. Sanh. 92b: The dead raised by Ezekiel sang I Sam. 2 : 6.

63. b. B.B. 25a-b: The world is like an *exedra.*

64. b. Yoma 54b: The world was made from the center.

65. b. Yoma 54b: The heaven was made from heavenly material, earth from earthly material.

66. b. B.B. 16a: Eliezer says Job sought 'to turn the dish upside down.'

67. b. Ar. 17a: The patriarchs would not have been able to survive divine reproof. Even they were imperfect.

68. b. Hul. 92a: Eliezer says Gen. 40 : 10 refers to the patriarchs and the tribes. Joshua says it refers to the Torah, Moses, the Sanhedrin, and the righteous people of every generation. Eleazar the Modite says the verse refers primarily to the Temple and priesthood. Joshua b. Levi also interprets the Scripture.

80. b. A.Z. 7b: Eliezer says one should first ask for his own needs, then recite the Prayer. Joshua says the opposite. The issue is attested at Yavneh.

81. b. Eruv. 54b: Eliezer says one should repeat a tradition to his disciple four times. ʿAqiba says it is to be repeated as many times as necessary for it to be learned. The issue of how to master oral traditions is well attested at Yavneh; this pericope has an Ushan interpolation.

82. b. Ta. 25b: A story about Eliezer's failure to produce rain. ʿAqiba succeeded in doing so—a second, attached story.

83. y. Ber. 2 : 8: Story about the death of Liezer's maid. He would not accept consolation, for a slave-girl is no different from any other piece of property. [vs. Gamaliel.]

84. y. B.Q. 4 : 5, b. B.Q. 41b-42a: Eliezer provides an exegesis to prove that the owner of the *Tam*-ox is free of paying half the ransom. ʿAqiba says an exegesis to prove that proposition is unnecessary. The

issue is attested in M. B.Q. 4 : 5, for which the two masters provide proof.

Nos. 1, 8, 9, 18, 27, 80 seem to relate to already-attested teachings of Eliezer. In addition, Nos. 5, 19, 58, 81, and 84 pertain to concerns already exhibited in legal or other pericopae. No. 15 has Eliezer and ʿAqiba differ on whether an exegesis is needed to prove a stated proposition, with Eliezer of the view that it is. Nos. 21 and 43 relate to literal *vs.* figurative exegesis.

Completely new are No. 6—why wipe with the right hand?—and No. 16—does a proselyte have to be circumcized? (a problem familiar in the writings of Paul). New exegetical items in addition are Nos. 59, 60, 61, 62, 63, 64, 65, 66.

Biographical materials unfamiliar until now are in No. 26, the several death scenes; No. 28, Eliezer's excommunication; No. 82, Eliezer could not produce rain; and No. 83, Eliezer regarded slaves as property.

Teachings on redemption and forgiveness include Nos. 56, 57, 67, possibly No. 68.

Thus of approximately 33 items first appearing in the Tannaitic stratum of the *Gemarot*, eight are new exegetical pericopae, focused upon a fixed methodological difference between Eliezer and his opponent. Six seem based upon known teachings of Eliezer, and five more fit into the established legal and theological agendum, one a third of the whole. In addition, three or four items pertain to the issues which ought to have been important at Yavneh, so nearly half of the new materials in theme if not in detail might appropriately derive from the times of Eliezer. As stated, three exegeses deal with already familiar methodological disagreements. The biographical items are wholly new, but at least one, No. 6, relates to M. Kel. One set of death-scenes juxtaposes Eliezer to Yoḥanan, by now an important concern in the Avot-stemma. But the other set knows nothing of that relationship and depends upon No. 26. Except for the exegetical pericopae, Nos. 50-66, the bulk of the materials first appearing in the Tannaitic strata of the *Gemarot* seems as authentic as the equivalents in Sifré and Sifra, not to mention the two Mekhilta's.

iv. Amoraic and Later Contributions to the Traditions about Eliezer

Our survey of the several stages in the formation of the traditions about Eliezer concludes with the items first appearing in the Amoraic strata of the *Gemarot* and in the various collections of Midrashim compiled in and after Amoraic times. ARN is included, since it certainly derives from the same period as that in which the *Gemarot* took shape and serves as *Gemara* for Avot. As observed, its account of Eliezer's death depends upon the death-scene linking Eliezer to Yoḥanan b. Zakkai, and that story derives from late third-century Palestinian Amoraim, so we need not pay further attention to the theory that ARN, so far as Eliezer is concerned, is a compilation of materials deriving in their present state from pre-Mishnaic times.

1. *Eliezer Despised ʿAqiba*

y. Pes. 6 : 3 attaches to the debate between Eliezer and ʿAqiba about the Passover's overriding the Sabbath the story that ʿAqiba had studied with Eliezer for thirteen years, but when he entered the debate, Eliezer did not know him (!). Joshua told Eliezer who he was, saying that he had despised ʿAqiba and now he had to do battle against him. b. Pes. 69a has a story, marked TNYʾ, that Eliezer told ʿAqiba he would be slaughtered, and ʿAqiba said that Eliezer should not deny him, for he merely repeated what he had learned from Eliezer. Both stories look like dramatizations of the debate.

2. *Imposing the Soṭah-Rite*

In y. Sot. 1 : 1 we find a debate between Eliezer and Joshua on whether one is obligated to impose the *Soṭah*-rite on his wife if he has reason to be jealous of her. Eliezer says it is an obligation to do so; Joshua says it is an option. Leazar b. R. Yosi before R. Yasa says Eliezer follows the House of Shammai, Joshua of Hillel. Num. R. spells out this last comment. Eliezer agrees with the House of Shammai that divorce is possible only on account of adultery. Therefore it is one's duty to warn the wife. Joshua agrees with the House of Hillel that divorce is possible on any account, therefore one may as well divorce the wife as warn her. Thus y.'s dispute may begin in the association of Eliezer with the House of Shammai, Joshua with the House of Hillel, then extrapolating from that normal pattern the results, for the *Soṭah*-rite, of the debate between the Houses on divorce. The passage then depends upon two facts: first, the involvement of Eliezer and Joshua in M. Sot. 1 : 1; and second, the relationship between the masters and the Houses.

3. *The Date of Pentecost*

In b. Men. 65b Yoḥanan b. Zakkai debates with the Sadducees on the debate of Pentecost. Then Eliezer, Joshua, Ishmael, and Judah b. Batyra supply further proofs for Yoḥanan's proposition. Eliezer says the foregoing proof is unnecessary; Scriptural evidence requires no further exegesis. Deut. 16 : 9 says one must count for himself—and therefore not according to the Sabbath of creation. Judah b. Batyra has the best proof—not much different from Yoḥanan's. The pericope depends upon the late account of Yoḥanan and the Sadducees.

4. *Eliezer Descends from Moses*

Aḥa in the name of Yosi b. R. Ḥanina tells the story in Midrash Tanḥuma Ḥuqat 24 that Moses heard in the heavenly academy the saying of Eliezer that a heifer has to be a year old and a Red Heifer has to be two years old. He was impressed with Eliezer and asked why did not God use him as his prophet. God explains his choice, and Moses asks that Eliezer be made his descendant. God agrees. The story depends upon M. Par. 1 : 1 and on the fact that Moses named his son Eliezer. It is not part of a developing tradition dealing with Eliezer himself.

5-6. *Prepare a Throne for Yoḥanan b. Zakkai. Eliezer Deserved the Holy Spirit.*

Jacob b. R. Idi + Joshua b. Levi's death scene for Yoḥanan introduces concern for ritual uncleanness and the Messiah: "Prepare a throne for Hezekiah." Then, when Eliezer died, he said the same thing, except that he asked for a throne for Yoḥanan—so y. Sot. 9 : 16.

The same masters further combine Hillel and Eliezer. Hillel and Samuel the Small would have received the holy spirit—thus a heavenly voice told the elders—but the generation's unworthiness prevented it. Then, "There are among you *two* who are worthy of the holy spirit, and Samuel the Small is one of them, and they set their eyes on Eliezer. And they were rejoicing that their opinion was the same as heaven's."

Joshua b. Levi thus regarded Eliezer as Yoḥanan's disciple and Hillel's equal; he certainly knew M. Avot and regarded Eliezer as the best of the disciples of Yoḥanan, therefore next in the line from Hillel. But then he ignores Abba Saul's downgrading of Eliezer in favor of Eleazar b. ʿArakh.

7. *Eliezer Was a Prodigy*

Eliezer was one of the two children, along with Joshua, glossed into a story about a wonderful saying of children about the meaning of the duplication of the letters M N Ṣ P K, so y. Meg. 1 : 9. Gen. R. expands the story by adding appropriate Scriptures and adds the name of ʿAqiba to those of Eliezer and Joshua. The story of Eliezer's origins is ignored.

8. *Eliezer Copied Yoḥanan b. Zakkai's Deeds*

y. Ber. 2 : 3 has the saying that Yoḥanan wore his *tefillin* all the time, and so did his disciple, Eliezer, a familiar theme, developing the idea that one should say only what his master has stated.

9. *Eliezer and Joshua Approved the Targum*

y. Meg. 3a has Jeremiah + Ḥiyya b. Ba's saying that ʿAqilas's *targum* was done 'before' Eliezer and Joshua, and they approved it. b. Meg. 3a says they dictated it.

10. *Eliezer and Joshua at the Circumcision of Aḥer*

y. Hag. 2 : 1 presents Elisha b. Abbuya's account of his circumcision, at which ceremony it was already clear that he would turn out badly. Most people who came celebrated by drinking and dancing. Eliezer and Joshua studied Torah, with the result that fire came forth from heaven and licked about them. Abbuyah said that he was impressed with the supernatural power of Torah, and he therefore would see to it that his son became a master of Torah. But this is not regarded as study of Torah for the sake of heaven; therefore his intention was not fulfilled, and Elisha became an apostate. Eliezer and Joshua are included because they presumably lived in Jerusalem before 70 and are the most important Yavnean names associated with the pre-70 city. But Eliezer plays no role in Yoḥanan b. Zakkai's *Merkavah*-materials, so the detail drawn from the *Merkavah*-stories has not generated the inclusion of his name.

11. *ʿAqiba Studied with Eliezer and Joshua*

y. Naz. 7 : 1 presents ʿAqiba's story about how he began to study Torah. He learned a law from Eliezer and Joshua which contradicted his understanding of his obligations to the neglected corpse, so he realized that even the best intentions, unaided by knowledge of Torah, will not produce merit. Eliezer and Joshua are routinely cited as his masters. They play no differentiated role in the story, nor are they credited with enunciating the law they taught to ʿAqiba. On the contrary, it is a standard tradition.

b. Ned. 50a likewise takes for granted that ʿAqiba studied with Eliezer and Joshua.

12. *Yoḥanan b. Zakkai Ordained Eliezer*

Ba, y. Sanh. 1 : 2, says Yoḥanan ordained Eliezer and Joshua. Joshua *alone* ordained ʿAqiba.

13. *Eliezer Collected Funds*

The names of Eliezer, Joshua, and ʿAqiba are used in the story of Abba Judah and the miraculous reward Heaven bestowed upon him for donating half of his meagre funds to the support of the rabbis. But they play no differentiated role in the story.

14. *Eliezer Helped Yoḥanan b. Zakkai's Escape*

b. Git. 56a and all related accounts of Yoḥanan b. Zakkai's escape from Jerusalem place Eliezer in the city as his disciple and give him a minor role in the escape. He, along with Joshua, carried the master out of the city. Neither disciple plays a part thereafter.

15. *Eliezer and the Widow's Son*

Eliezer is asked by a widow's son which takes precedent, the father or the mother. He says one must honor the father first. Joshua gives the same answer, but then discovers the question is not sincere, so he insults the boy, so b. Qid. 31a.

16. *Producing (Male) Children*

b. B.B. 10b has Eliezer advise one to give generously to the poor in order to have sons. Joshua says he should be considerate of the wife's sexual pleasure.

17. *Eliezer's Sexual Behavior*

Imma Shalom reports that Eliezer has sexual relations at midnight and does so enthusiastically, so b. Ned. 20b. Kallah Rabbati combines Nos. 16 and 17 in a set of variations.

18. *Eliezer Spoke Seventy Languages*

b. Sanh. 17b contains Rav Judah + Rav's saying that a Sanhedrin is set up only in a city with two people who can speak seventy languages. At Yavneh were four such, Eliezer, Joshua, ʿAqiba, and Simeon the Temanite.

19. *Eliezer's Origins*

The stories about Eliezer's origins, beginning in ARN, take for granted that he studied in Jerusalem with Yoḥanan b. Zakkai, as is to be expected on the basis of Avot. ARN stresses that Eliezer had no means of support in Jerusalem and so starved. The chria about bad breath and Torah recurs in all versions, with minor variations in the chriic settings. A further detail in common is the effort of the father to disinherit Eliezer. Gen. R. 42 : 1 adds that Eliezer's sermon before the father was on Gen. 14 : 15.

20. *Eliezer Among Yoḥanan's Comforters*

ARN Chap. 14's story about Yoḥanan b. Zakkai's son's death, with Eleazar b. ʿArakh as the hero, includes a witless saying attributed to Eliezer, who, along with Joshua, Yosi, and Simeon, is rebuked by Yoḥanan. Only Eleazar b. ʿArakh has something worthwhile to say—so Abba Saul in Avot lies in the background of the story.

21. *Eliezer and the Proselyte*

ʿAqilas asks Eliezer whether the benefit of the proselyte consists merely in bread and clothing. Eliezer says it is enough. Joshua then assures ʿAqilas that bread means Torah, and clothing means the rabbi's cloak. The account has Eliezer behave like Shammai in dealing harshly with the proselyte; Joshua offers more welcome counsel, as in b. Shab. 30b-31a. Qoh. R. 1.8.4 has a still closer parallel to b. Shab.

22. *Eliezer and the Roman Lady*

Eliezer is asked by a Roman lady about Num. 5 : 27. He says the woman's only wisdom is at the distaff (Ex. 35 : 25), a saying congruent to Eliezer's sentiment in M. Sot.

23. *Qoh. 11 : 2*

Eliezer interprets the reference to seven and eight in Qoh. 11 : 2 as representing the days of the week and the eight days of circumcision. Joshua says the reference is to the seven days of Passover and the eight days of Sukkot, so b. Eruv. 40b.

24. *Prov. 14 : 34*

In the colloquy of Yoḥanan b. Zakkai and the disciples on Prov. 14 : 34, Eliezer, like all the others except for Neḥuniah b. HaQanneh/Eleazar b. ʿArakh, says that whatever kindness is done by the gentiles is really sinful, because they do it with the wrong motives. Neḥuniah/Eleazar says the gentiles do no kindness at all. Eliezer is simply part of the chriic structure, leading to the "best saying" of someone else, as in No. 20 and elsewhere.

25. *I Kings 21 : 10, 13*

In b. Shav. 35b Eliezer says all the names mentioned in connection with Naboth are sacred, but those mentioned in regard to Micah (Judges 17-18) are sometimes secular and sometimes sacred. Then Eliezer and Joshua debate the divine names mentioned in connection with Gibeah of Benjamin, Judges 20 : 18-28.

26. *The Flood*

In Gen. R. 5 : 3, Eliezer says the waters of the flood were absorbed by the sea, consistent with his view of the ocean as the receptacle and source of all water. Joshua says they went to the receptacle of the sea.

In Gen. R. 25 : 2, Joshua says the planets did not function during the flood, and Eliezer says they did. The Yavneans' opinions are given by Yoḥanan and Jonathan as well.

27. *Other Midrashim*

A. Eliezer says one should sow, meaning to have children, early and late. Joshua says one should help the poor morning and evening, so Gen. R. 61 : 3, *re* Qoh. 1 : 6.

B. In Gen. R. 98 : 4 Eliezer and Joshua agree on the meaning of Gen. 49 : 3, "So have you left nothing for yourself." Eleazar of Modiim has a different explanation. The same pattern is repeated in connection with subsequent element of the same verse.

C. Eliezer says there was wickedness where the Great Sanhedrin met. Joshua interprets Lev. 4 : 2/Qoh. 3 : 16 along the same lines, but introduces the Golden Calf, so Lev. R. 4 : 1.

D. In Lev. R. 14 : 4 Eliezer says Lev. 12 : 2/Job 38 : 8 mean that a woman has doors as a house has doors. Joshua says the woman has keys as a house has keys. ʿAqiba says that as a house has hinges, so a woman has birthpangs.

E. Lev. R. 19 : 1 has Eliezer and Joshua saying that Song 5 : 11, *curls*, refers to piles and piles of legal teachings, which are preserved by people who study early and late.

F. Eliezer and Joshua discuss the meaning of Ps. 139 : 16, in Tanḥ. Bereshit 28 = Pes. R. 23 : 1. Eliezer says that the meaning is that God is faithful to keep his promises according to schedule. Joshua says it means God prefers the Day of Atonement.

G. In Num. R. 9 : 25, Eliezer says the compensation for the woman falsely accused of adultery is that she will have a child. Joshua says she will no longer suffer in childbirth or will have males instead of females, and the like.

H. An angel spoke through Balaam, so Eliezer. Joshua says it was God himself, in Num. R. 20 : 18.

I. Eliezer and Joshua discuss the meaning of Ruth 4 : 1, in Ruth R. 7 : 7. In Midrash on Psalms to 22 : 12, both Eliezer and Joshua say Song 6 : 10 refers to the appearance of Israel. Eliezer says they looked like ministering angels. Joshua says they looked like troops arrayed under their banners.

J. In Midrash on Psalms to 90 : 4, Eliezer says the day of the Messiah lasts a thousand years. Joshua says it is two thousand.

v. Conclusion

Of the materials first appearing in Amoraic and later strata of the rabbinic tradition, only two pertain to legal matters, No. 2, which deals with a subject already on Eliezer's agendum and may represent a development of earlier materials; and No. 3, which is wholly new. The date of Pentecost was at issue between Pharisees and Sadducees, but the pericope assigning a proof for the Pharisaic position to Eliezer seems to me artificial and unrelated to the tradition formed in Mishnaic times.

Eliezer's relationship to Yoḥanan b. Zakkai produces two sorts of pericopae. First, since Eliezer appears on the list in Avot, stories relying upon that list for a narrative structure naturally will include his name in a subordinated position. In such stories he occurs as merely one among several disciples whose opinions are rejected, as in Nos. 20 and 24. In other such stories Eliezer appears only alongside Joshua. Neither master is differentiated from the other, and both form part of the narrative background, as in Nos. 12 and 14.

The second sort of pericope will stress Eliezer's unique relationship to Yoḥanan, as the leading disciple, in particular, Nos. 5-6, which represent Eliezer as the continuator of the line from Hillel through Yoḥanan; No. 8, in which it is said Eliezer did whatever Yoḥanan did (a theme already familiar, e.g., b. Suk. 28a); and No. 19.

Eliezer is routinely linked to Joshua, as part of the narrative structure, in No. 7, where both names are added to a story about wonder-working children; No. 9, Eliezer and Joshua approved ʿAqilas's *Targum* or actually dictated it (in unison?); No. 10, both masters attended the circumcision of Aḥer and did wonders; No. 11, ʿAqiba studied with Eliezer and Joshua; No. 13, Eliezer, Joshua, and ʿAqiba collected money; and in a considerable number of midrashic pericopae, Nos. 23, 25, 26, and the group listed in No. 27, ten examples. In No. 18, Joshua, ʿAqiba, and Eliezer, along with Simeon the Temanite, exemplify the Yavnean masters. In none of these pericopae is Eliezer presented as a differentiated personality. Nos. 15 and 21 contrast Eliezer's virtue to Joshua's.

Eliezer's individual relationship with ʿAqiba is important only in No. 1, which is a dramatic embellishment of M. Pes. 6 : 3.

Eliezer as an individual is significant only in Nos. 4, 16-17, 19, and 22. No. 4 contains a story on the fact that Moses's son was named Eliezer. I see no close connection to M. Par. 1 : 1. Any other legal saying of Eliezer would have served as well. Eliezer's sexual counsel and behavior are reported in Nos. 16 and 17. But No. 17 contradicts No. 16. Eliezer should in No. 16 stress the sexual side of things. The single most interesting group of stories is contained in No. 19, about Eliezer's origins. No. 22 is not wholly new, and the narrative is confused.

The last stratum, therefore, supplies by far the greatest quantity of biographical materials, but only a few focus on Eliezer as an individual, and among these few, only No. 19 is important.

The second dominant trait of the final stratum is the stress on relationships with Yoḥanan b. Zakkai, but most of these sayings, too, simply take for granted that Eliezer was a disciple, without giving much detail or setting forth his individual traits. Only three items, Nos. 5-6 and 8, are important in revealing the relationship to Yoḥanan. They make two points. First, Eliezer copied the master faithfully—a point already familiar in the Tannaitic stratum, since it first occurs in Tos.—without reference to Yoḥanan in particular!—though there it may be a gloss. Second, Eliezer really continues the Hillelite line. This last allegation is especially important, for it makes explicit what is implicit in pericopae first occurring in much earlier strata, that Eliezer accurately preserved the traditions of Hillel and his House.

The rest of the contributions of the final stratum is of little historical use. Where Eliezer's name is introduced as part of a narrative which deals with events in which he plays no part or of discussions in which he makes no contribution, we may assume that his presence at Yavneh and place on Avot's list of Yoḥanan's disciples have led to the inclusion of his name. But such pericopae provide no independent details about him. It is taken for granted that Eliezer + Joshua taught ʿAqiba. But this fact yields virtually no details about their relationship, other than in No. 1.

The later Midrashim evidently drew freely upon the dispute-form produced by Eliezer's and Joshua's names: Scripture... Eliezer says... Joshua says.... But I discern in the succession of differences no clearcut pattern; the whole seems to me random, an artificial construction based on redactional considerations and not a living tradition of what Eliezer and Joshua had actually said or even of Scriptures on which they had (collectively) commented. Nor do I see even the pertinence of the themes of the exegeses to the situation after 70, as seemed to be evident in the stress of the Tannaitic Midrashim on redemption, on the punishment of the Egyptians and the war against Amalek, on the conditions under which Israel would be redeemed, on the need for penitence, and similar themes particularly relevant to the period after 70 in general, if not to Eliezer in particular. Why Eliezer's and Joshua's names should have been used for just the items in which they occur in Gen. R. and Lev. R, not to mention the medieval compilations, I cannot say. But I see no connection whatever to the times in which they lived. In all, therefore, apart from the relationship of Eliezer to Yoḥanan, which seems important to Jacob b. Idi + Joshua b. Levi, as it was to redactors represented both earlier and in No. 8, and apart from the stories about Eliezer's origins, we find nothing of much historical or biographical interest in the Amoraic and later strata.

THE MAN

CHAPTER THIRTEEN

EARLIER VIEWS OF ELIEZER BEN HYRCANUS

i. Introduction

Earlier accounts of the life of Eliezer have in common a wholly uncritical approach to the sources. First, while the problem of *which* Eliezer is referred to in various pericopae is raised, it is never systematically dealt with, except, as noted, by Y. N. Epstein (and then without regard to the contents). Nearly everything attributed to any Eliezer is normally assumed to derive from ours in virtually every scholarly account before us. Second, it is always taken for granted that whatever is attributed to Eliezer is what he actually said. Stories about him, moreover, relate what really happened. While former students of Eliezer have done much to elucidate various specific traditions, in the main they take everything at face value. They make composites of various tales into a single coherent narrative and organize the legal materials around a few basic issues—e.g., Eliezer as conservative or as a Shammaite or as a patrician or as a logician.

Comments on specific problems nonetheless are sometimes interesting, if seldom conclusive. And a few studies on special topics, e.g., Urbach on Eliezer within the structure of rabbinic theology, Lieberman on Sifré Zuṭṭa as a document beginning in Eliezer's circle at Lud, Gilat on the exposition, in a traditional spirit, of the *content* of legal pericopae, constitute important contributions. But in the main, the former efforts to examine the traditions about Eliezer add up to little more than compilations of those traditions, distinguished from one another by the episodic insertion of friendly or hostile homilies.

While the earlier students of Eliezer take for granted the equal historical veracity of pretty much everything they find in all sources, early, late, and medieval, they do tend to select what they like and omit what they do not. For instance, the matter of the excommunication of Eliezer and his involvement with *minim* is apt to be bypassed or dealt with in a cursory manner. Only a few have admitted their selectivity; none has justified it.

It is futile to attempt to refute theses on Eliezer which consist of nothing more than composites of sources, sometimes, as with Jawitz, greatly embellished with homilies and pious thoughts, other times, as with Gilat, carefully and critically sifted. I find it curious that no one has shown, on the basis of the prevailing conception of a unitary tradition, what really must lie at the bottom of things. Eliezer was a Shammaite. He never said anything he had not learned from his master. His master was Yoḥanan b. Zakkai. Therefore, Yoḥanan ben Zakkai was a Shammaite. But Yoḥanan's master—always imitated by Yoḥanan—was none other than Hillel. So Hillel too must have been a member of the House of Shammai. Or Hillel really was Shammai. This and similar propositions may be proved as readily as many of those we shall now review. It is not our task to attempt to "disprove" what obviously cannot stand up under critical examination or to point out the recurrent gullibility or pseudocritical spirit of earlier accounts. Nor shall we underline the numerous points on which scholars on the basis of the same evidence contradict either themselves or one another or both. The reader has in hand the bulk of the traditions and may now review and assess for himself what is of value and what is merely a curiosity in antecedent inquiries.

ii. Compilations of Stories and Sayings

Zekhariah Frankel, *Darkhé HaMishnah, HaTosefta, Mekhilta, Sifra, veSifré* (Repr. Tel Aviv, 1959), pp. 78-87, points out that Eliezer rules on matters, such as sacrifices, ignored by the Houses. In fact Eliezer made rulings on the basis of logic, not only of what he had heard from his teachers. The Palestinian Talmud regards him as a Shammaite, and the Babylonian Talmud calls him one who has been excommunicated. But when he was excommunicated, Eliezer proved his point and did not rely merely upon heavenly support. One can tell Eliezer apart from Eleazar b. Shammuʿa on the basis of other parties in the same pericope, e.g. Joshua, rather than Judah and Meir. But most pericopae involving an Eliezer and "the sages" are those of Eliezer b. Hyrcanus. References of Ilai to an Eliezer are to Eliezer b. Hyrcanus as well. Eliezer favored the plain meaning of Scripture. In legal matters his method was to judge all details according to a single principle. He was consistent in his rulings: "In some places he rules strictly, and in some places he rules leniently"[!]. He began his studies at the age of twenty-two, against his father's wishes. He helped Yoḥanan b. Zakkai escape from Jerusalem. He went with Gamaliel and Joshua to Rome. He was arrested for *minut.* He was excommunicated before Gamaliel's deposition, therefore was not present at the consistory which accomplished the act.

J. Brüll, *Mavo HaMishnah. Kollel Toledot Gedolé Torah Mimot ʿEzra ʿAd Sof HaMishnah veDarkhé Limudēhem* (Frankfurt a/M, 1876), pp. 75-82, points out that Eliezer was praised as Yoḥanan's best student. (He and others of the same view do not cite the revision of Abba Saul in favor of Eleazar b. ʿArakh!) Eliezer was excommunicated by Gamaliel and his court. The reason was that he opposed the ruling of the majority. He was a Shammaite. And this too contributed to his excommunication. He rejected the tendency of Gamaliel and his contemporaries to produce new laws on the basis of logical generalizations and to extend old principles to new cases. Eliezer stuck by the old law. He taught only what he had learned from his master, Yoḥanan b. Zakkai. Since Eliezer rejected the heavenly voice which announced that the law follows the House of Hillel, his contemporaries likewise rejected the heavenly voice which announced that his opinion was correct. Sometimes an Eliezer will be *ben Shammuʿa*, particularly when he occurs with Meir. Eliezer was consistent in his rulings. Most of the disputes between ʿAqiba and Eliezer, or Joshua and Eliezer, took place before the excommunication.

J. Derenbourg, *Essai sur l'histoire et la géographie de la Palestine d'après les thalmuds et les autres sources rabbiniques* (Paris, 1867), pp. 323-325, portrays Eliezer as intransigeant and a rationalist. He based his opinions on the plain sense of Scripture. He had a prodigious memory and remembered many old laws. He replied to new questions only in terms of what he had already learned. He would, to be sure, use logical means to extend a known law to an unknown situation. But he would invent nothing new. He was excommunicated and lost touch with the formation of the law. Eliezer was arrested (pp. 357ff.) on suspicion of being a Christian; the story is authentic.

H. Wassertrilling, "Die halachische Lehrweise des Rabbi Elieser ben Hyrkanos," *Jüdische Literaturblatt*, No. 22, 1877, pp. 26ff., reviews the traditional sayings on the history of the legal tradition. He stresses the rational and logical traits of the exegeses of legal passages of Scriptures.

J. Hamburger, *Real-Encyclopädie für Bibel und Talmud* (Strelitz, 1883), Vol. II, pp. 162-168, alludes to the various stories about Eliezer's life, beginning with his leaving his father to study with Yoḥanan in Jerusalem, ending with the death-scene(s).

Emil Schürer, *A History of the Jewish People in the Time of Jesus*

Christ. II. The Internal Condition of Palestine and of the Jewish People, in the Time of Jesus Christ (Edinburgh, 1885), Part i, pp. 370-372, claims that Joshua, and not Eliezer, had relationships with Gamaliel, because of Eliezer's excommunication. Eliezer "was of a firm, unbending character, and a very strict adherent to tradition, over which, by reason of his faithful memory and extensive scholarship, he had more influence than any other... He was not to be moved by any reasons or representations from what he knew as tradition." This produced strained relationships with Gamaliel. The legend that he was secretly a Christian proves the contrary. His trial was seen by him as just punishment for his pleasure with a Jewish-Christian's legal opinion, represented as having been derived from Jesus.

Heinrich Graetz, *History of the Jews* (Repr. Philadelphia, 1949, trans. by H. Szold), Vol. II, pp. 337-339, states that Eliezer refused to submit to the "universally binding enactments." He relied, instead, on traditions he had received from earlier authorities, in particular Yoḥanan b. Zakkai. He was conservative, "the organ of tradition." He was isolated on that account. He was excommunicated for refusing to submit to others and for the expression of his opinions in harsh terms. He had no influence over affairs and took no part in "the development of the Law."

M. Braunschweiger, *Die Lehrer der Mischnah. Ihr Leben und Wirken* (Frankfurt a/M., 1890), pp. 10-19, gives Eliezer's dates as 50-120 A.D. His father, a rich man, opposed his going to study with Yoḥanan. He had a very good mind and never forgot what he was taught. Various teachings are reviewed, e.g., on saying the *Shema*ʿ, on honoring parents, on who is an *ʿam haʾareṣ*. Eliezer approved a teaching of the *minim*. His death ended his excommunication.

J. Bassfreund, "Der Bann gegen R. Elieser und die veränderte Haltung gegenüber den Schammaiten," *MGWJ* 42, 1898, pp. 49-57, reviews the pertinent sources.

J. H. Weiss, *Dor Dor veDorshav* [*Zur Geschichte der jüdischen Tradition*] (Vilna, 1904), Vol. II, pp. 74-80, sees Eliezer as a person of controversy, from his youth, when he abandoned his father's house, to his old age, which was spent in excommunication. He learned traditions and never forgot them; he taught only what he had learned. But he was prepared to generalize on the basis of the traditions in hand. The stress on received traditions derives from the House of Shammai, of which he was a member. The excommunication was unfair because Eliezer's logical arguments were ignored; the consistory followed its own will, rather than reason. A factor in his excommunication may have been his involvement in *minut.*

Eleazar Tsarkes (Zarkes), "Dor Lefi Dorshav," *Kenesset Hagedolah* 4, 1891, pp. 65-71, severely criticizes I. H. Weiss's negative judgment on Eliezer. The defense is appropriate to the indictment.

S. Mendelsohn, "Eliezer (Liezer) ben Hyrcanus," *Jewish Encyclopedia*, Vol. V, pp. 113-115, states that Eliezer was a disciple of Yoḥanan ben Zakkai. "His earlier years are wrapped in myths; but from these latter it may be inferred that he was somewhat in advanced in life when a desire for learning first seized him, and impelled him, contrary to the wishes of his father, to desert his regular occupation and to repair to Jerusalem... Eliezer was at Javneh but conducted his own academy at Lydda." Once he accompanied Gamaliel and Joshua on an embassy to Rome. He was severe with his pupils and colleagues. The main feature of his teaching was strict devotion to tradition. He objected to allowing midrash or "the paraphrastic interpretation to pass as authority for religious practice." In this respect he sympathized with the "conservative" House of Shammai. Hence the assertion that he was a Shammaite, though he was a disciple of Yoḥanan, one of Hillel's most prominent pupils. In opposing the majority, he had to be made into an example. During the persecutions of the Jewish Christians, he was charged with being a member of that sect. When he lay dying, at Caesarea, he answered many questions. Then Joshua revoked the sentence of excommunication. He was buried at Lydda.

Z. Jawitz, *Sefer Toledot Yisra᾿el* (Cracow, 1908), Vol. VI, pp. 31-34, sees Eliezer as a Levite, because he is descended from Moses. He was son of a rich man, who opposed his studying Torah. He was acquainted with Agrippas II and discussed circumcision with him. Eliezer never said anything new, but only what he had heard from his teachers. He was the brother-in-law of the patriarch, whose sister he acquired through Levirate marriage (!). He had many slaves and beautiful children, etc.

Benjamin Ze᾿ev [Wilhelm] Bacher, *Aggadot HaTanna᾿im* (Hebrew: A. Z. Rabinovitz) (Berlin, 1922), Vol. I, part i, pp. 72-114, surveys the non-legal pericopae, citing them in full, with brief notes. Eliezer was one of the great disciples of the House of Hillel, but his harsh principles and conservative tendencies made him appear to be a Shammaite. The tradition, particularly stories, preserves *his exact words as spoken in real life.* It shows a very sharp mode of self-expression. He was exact in memorizing and preserving the teachings of his masters. He saw the destruction of the Temple as the beginning of a spiritual decline for Israel. He did not like proselytes. His tendency in the interpretation of Scripture was to exaggerate the miracles in those stories, e.g., two hundred plagues against the Egyptians at the sea. He stressed the importance of Sabbath rest, which was the main expression of the Covenant. He likewise laid special importance to honoring one's father and mother. He is not credited with knowledge of mystical sciences, but post-Talmudic literature attributed to him various mystical texts.

Eliezer and Joshua debate the interpretation of various Scriptures. Mekhilta deR. Ishmael contains the larger part of these. Some of these are transmitted by Abba Ḥanin, known to us primarily in this connection. The sayings on the creation of the world are seen as within the *Maʿaseh Bereshit*-mystical tradition. In all, it is hard to see much difference between Bacher's collection and Konovitz's (below), except that Bacher concentrates on *aggadic* materials and supplies a few philological footnotes, of questionable value.

Another, fuller collection is given by A. M. Hyman, *Sefer Toledot Tannaʾim veʾAmoraʾim* (London, 1910), Vol. I, pp. 161-175. Hyman says Eliezer was a Levite, descended from Moses. He differs from I. H. Weiss's view that Eliezer was a harsh and contentious person. Eliezer in fact was a kindly person, modest and irenic. Eliezer knew many languages. He was Yoḥanan's leading disciple and successor. When he was excommunicated, he settled in Lydda. Brüll maintained that Eliezer refused to accept the opinion of the majority, but the issue is what is true, not what the majority wants. Among Eliezer's disciples were ʿAqiba, Onqelos, Ilai, Abba Ḥanin, Dosetai b. R. Yannai, Ḥanina b. Teradion, Judah b. Gaddish, Yoḥanan b. R. Ilai, Yosi b. Durmasqit, and so forth. Eliezer lived from before the destruction of the Second Temple to the end of the Bar Kokhba War, about ninety years.

George Foot Moore, *Judaism in the First Centuries of the Christian Era. The Age of the Tannaim* (Cambridge, 1927), II, p. 250, says that Eliezer was arrested on a charge of being a Christian.

Z. Baroshi (BRWŠY), *R. Eliezer HaGadol. Toledot Ḥayyav uMishnato* (Tel Aviv, 1965), provides a kind of historical novel, in which stories about Eliezer are strung together and retold in a simple narrative.

Yisraʾel Konovitz, *Rabbi Eliezer. Ossaf Shalem shel Maʾamarav baSifrut HaTalmudit veHaMidrashit* (Jerusalem, 1965), claims to collect *all* stories and sayings attributed to Eliezer. These are divided according to subject: biography, then Scriptures, faith; society; agricultural, festival, family law; vowing; judges; the sanctuary; cleanness rules. Konovitz makes virtually no comments whatever, evidently perceiving no difficulties even in the exposition of the various pericopae.

iii. Special Studies

Ḥayyim Oppenheim, "Rabbi Eliezer ben Hyrcanus," (Hebrew) *Bet Talmud* (Vienna, 1885), Vol. IV, pp. 311-316, 332-338, 360-366, places Eliezer's death at 110 A.D. He was excommunicated because of his stubbornness in legal disputes. His legal position was based on extreme conservatism. He never said anything he had not heard from his master. This, to be sure, is not possible, for he has more than three hundred laws, and not all of these came from his master. Other contemporaries, moreover, differed with him, so he could not have received all his teachings from tradition. He was a Shammaite, though at times he differs from the House of Shammai. So his laws, in part, derive from his own reasoning. What he meant in claiming he always quoted his teacher was that he cited his masters when he had traditions or principles from them. He would extend those principles to new cases. The laws he himself originated were as follows: laws which he derived from the plain meaning of Scripture; laws which he derived from principles revealed in Scripture or from the context of Scripture; laws which he found revealed in the setting of biblical stories; laws developed from analogous situations or rulings; laws produced by generalization on the basis of existing principles; laws based on the exegesis of Scriptures, e.g., from *gezerah shaveh, qal veḥomer, heqqesh*, and so forth. Other laws were produced by him on the basis of stories which he had heard and incidents which he had witnessed; or of the explanations for ancient laws; or of conflicts between received laws; or of logic and reason. Eliezer expounded the 'reasons' for various laws and on that basis, produced new ones. He also made the effort to harmonize his exegesis of Scripture with traditions he had received. He would try to relate the old laws to Scriptural exegesis. It is not correct to claim that Eliezer opposed the majority and was stubborn. He was opposed to excessive disputes. Oppenheim's essay is the best effort before Gilat (below) to systematize the legal legacy.

C. Augustus R. Toetterman, *R. Eliezer ben Hyrcanos. Sive de vi qua doctrina Christiana primis seculis illustrissimos quosdam Judaeorum attraxit* (Leipzig, 1877) thinks that Eliezer really was a Christian. Toetterman rapidly surveys the various *aggadot* about Eliezer's origins and studies with Yoḥanan. The question about *so-and-so* in the world to come (Tos. Yev. 3) refers to Jesus. Various other elements in the same pericope are interpreted in the same way. The arrest on charges of *minut* completes the case for Eliezer's crypto-Christianity. The inevitable result was the excommunication: "Inde quoque conspicitur, quam longe R. Eliezer a moribus Pharisaeorum quam que prope a Christianismo abfuerit."

H. Graetz, "Historische und topographische Streifzüge. Die Römischen Legaten in Judäa unter Domitian und Trajan und ihre Beziehung zu Juden und Christen," *MGWJ* 34, 1885, pp. 17-34, says the arrest of Eliezer shows that there was a persecution of Christianity under Domitian. This event took place before Eliezer's excommunication. The *hegemon* can "only" be Pompeius Longinus, who was Legate under Domitian in Judea. All the details of the story "have the character of historicity."

H. M. Horowitz, "Maʿaseh Rabbi Eliezer b. Hyrcanus," (Hebrew) *Bet ʿEqqed HaAggadot*, Vol. I, 1881, pp. 1-16 [German: *Bibliotheca Haggadica. Monatsschrift*, M. Horowitz. Frankfurt a/M.], presents the seven versions of the story of Eliezer's coming to Yoḥanan b. Zakkai. He does not add much to the elucidation of the relationships among them. His comments are unimportant.

R. Travers Herford, *Christianity in Talmud and Midrash* (Clifton, 1966, repr. of 1903 ed.) refers to the Ben Stada passage, which he regards as alluding to Jesus. The *certain person* of b. Yoma 66b also refers to Jesus, and Eliezer regards him as a *mamzer.* As to the arrest of Eliezer and his interview with Jacob the *Min*, Herford doubts this took place in the persecution of Nero. But there was another in 109, in Trajan's time, to which the passage may refer (pp. 140ff.) Eliezer was not a Christian, but did not deny it in court. The incident could have happened in Caesarea. As to Jacob, Herford sees no reason to doubt his involvement in the story. Jacob lived in Galilee in 130. Herford assumes all details of all versions are equally "historical."

Ludwig A. Rosenthal, *Über den Zusammenhang, die Quellen, und die Entstehung der Mischna* (Berlin, 1918), Vol. II, pp. 31-42 (54-72) uncovers a *JE–Quelle*, meaning Joshua + Eliezer. Rosenthal reviews the usual *aggadot.* He sees Eliezer as a Shammaite, giving various (dubious) examples to prove it, e.g., M. Suk. 2 : 6, which may not refer to our Eliezer at all. "JE" is located primarily in *Qodashim* and

Ṭoharot. Nota the same author's *Über den Zusammenhang der Mischna* (Strassburg, 1890), I. *Die Sadduzäerkämpfe und die Mischnasammlungen vor dem Auftreten Hillel's.*

Isaak Halevy, *Dorot HaRishonim* [*Die Geschichte und Literatur Israels*], Ie. *Umfasst den Zeitraum von der Zerstörung des Tempels bis zum Abschluss des Mischnah* (Berlin and Vienna, 1923), pp. 293-302, 372-386, sees Eliezer as "the sage of the council in Yavneh." He explains M. Nid. 1 : 4, *re* four women may rely upon their normal period. The *Gemara* on the passage states that after Eliezer's death, Joshua ceased to follow Eliezer's rule and instead restored the hegemony of his own. This must mean that there was no final decision on the matter. The council of Yavneh was constituted by only a minority of the sages of the day. When Eliezer was "sage of the council," he was able to determine matters, but after he was banned, he could not make final decisions. Before the excommunication, he had already influenced many to follow his rule. Eliezer was not a strict, but a lenient judge. His rulings tended to ease the burden of the law. He was not a Shammaite. Halevy rejects Weiss's assertion that Eliezer was mean-spirited and a controversial figure. He also holds that Eliezer was learned when he came to Yoḥanan. He further discounts I. H. Weiss's view that Eliezer was a person of ill-will toward his disciples, and that he cursed them. His critique of Weiss is vituperative. His defense of Eliezer is pious. But his analysis of the legal materials is always careful and critical.

Morris Goldstein, *Jesus in the Jewish Tradition* (N.Y., 1950), pp. 39-51, deals with Eliezer's arrest for *minut.* There is a definite reference to Jesus in b. A.Z. 16b-17a. Goldstein conveniently summarizes earlier opinion. Edershem, Friedlander, and Zeitlin do not regard the story as reliable; Herford, Strack, and Klausner do. Klausner dates the incident at 60 and sees Jacob as James, Jesus's brother. H. P. Chajes puts the incident in 95, in Domitian's persecution of Christianity. But 109 or 110 is the commonly accepted date. Eliezer was arrested because, deprived of the companionship of the sages by his excommunication, he had no one to talk with but sectarians (!). The *minim* certainly were Christians, at least in this instance. Goldstein's survey of earlier opinions is very convenient.

Karl Georg Kuhn, "Giljonim und sifré *minim*," in Walter Eltester, ed., *Judentum, Urchristentum, Kirche. Festschrift für Joachim Jeremias* (Berlin, 1960; ZNW Beiheft No. 26), pp. 24-61, deals with the problem of *minim*, pp. 35-38.

Salo W. Baron, *A Social and Religious History of the Jews*, 2nd ed., revised and enlarged, I. *Ancient Times*, Parts I-II (Philadelphia, 1952), sees Eliezer as a "mouthpiece" of older traditions (I, p. 294, n. 2). He as "cantankerous and unable to get along with people" (II, p. 120). He thought converts were unreliable (II, p. 148) and had a bad streak. He engaged in protracted celibacy (II, p. 221). He was the heir of the House of Shammai at Yavneh (II, p. 228). He praised even unreasonable extremes of filial piety (II, p. 239). He was one of country's richest [!] landowners (II, p. 276). In so stating, Baron may have confused our Eliezer with Eleazar b. Ḥarsom. Baron's account is wholly derivative, therefore uncritical. The legal materials are virtually ignored in favor of trivialities.

Hugo Mantel, *Studies in the History of the Sanhedrin* (Cambridge, 1961), pp. 110-115, sees Eliezer's excommunication as the result of his refusing to accept the opinion of the majority. Eliezer issued practical rulings contrary to the accepted opinion. He was a strict traditionalist, one of the foremost disciples of Yoḥanan. There is evidence that Eliezer was ʿAqiba's teacher (pp. 123ff.), but he did not ordain ʿAqiba because of antagonism. He was one of the emissaries sent to collect funds for the Palestinian schools. Eliezer is not the subject of a major study in Mantel's book, but, wherever he appears, Mantel supplies a full account of the scholarly literature dealing with him. Mantel's is by far the best researched study in Talmudic historical problems known to me.

Geza Vermes, "The Decalogue and the Minim," in Matthew Black and George Fohrer, ed., *In Memoriam Paul Kahle* (Berlin, 1968), pp. 232-240, provides the clearest picture of the problem of the *minim.*

Saul Lieberman, *Siphre Zuṭṭa (The Midrash of Lydda*). II. *The Talmud of Caesarea* (Hebrew) (N.Y., 1968), pp. 92-96, observes that many teachings in Sifré Zuṭṭa given without the name of the authority behind them in fact derive from Eliezer b. Hyrcanus, who lived in Lydda. He gives seven instances. The collection derives from a Tanna who stood in opposition to the school of Judah the Patriarch. Bar Qappara, Eleazar b. R. Simeon's disciple, is the best candidate for the final redactor of the compilation, which derives from Lydda (pp. 114-116).

Ephraim E. Urbach, *The Sages. Their Concepts and Beliefs* (Hebrew) (Jerusalem, 1969) alludes many times to teachings of Eliezer (s.v., in his index). The teachings are integrated into his discussions of theological issues and the comments do not focus upon the figure of Eliezer in particular. Among many points of interest, Urbach notes (pp. 603-604) that the difference between Eliezer and Joshua on the date of the redemption—Tishri or Nisan—reflects a more fundamental disagreement on the nature of the final redemption. Joshua says it is going to be like the redemption from Egypt, therefore will take place in Nisan. Eliezer says it will be on the first day of Tishri, a day of penitence; the larger issue is the nature of the final redemption, the end of time, the activity of the Messiah, and so on.

R. Freudenberger, "Die delatio nominis causa gegen Rabbi Eliezer ben Hyrkanos," *Revue internationale des droits de l'antiquité* 15, 1968, pp. 11-19, places Eliezer's arrest in Trajan's time, or, less likely, Hadrian's. Tos. and b. are independent of one another (*unabhängig*) but go back to the same tradition. *Minut* means heresy, normally Jewish-Christianity. The story is important, for "ihre Historizität kaum bestritten werden kann."

iv. Ben Zion Bokser and Louis Finkelstein

Ben Zion Bokser, *Pharisaic Judaism in Transition. R. Eliezer the Great and Jewish Reconstruction after the War with Rome* (N.Y., 1935), sees Eliezer (p. 5) as "a member of the upper class, a landed aristocrat... rigidly conservative in his conception of Jewish piety, social doctrine, and the champion of a static jurisprudence." He was repudiated as were the conservative Shammaites. He defied the majority and so was excommunicated.

To isolate Eliezer's sayings, one has to seek pericopae involving Joshua; if a scholar in a discussion is not a contemporary of our Eliezer, one must eliminate the material.

Eliezer studied with Yoḥanan despite his father's protests. The story of his origins proves Eliezer came from a family of landowners, began his studies as a mature man, and studied with Yoḥanan. Yoḥanan himself testifies to Eliezer's good memory. Eliezer was a great linguist and certainly was familiar with Greek. He was informed on subjects of a scientific nature. Eliezer was deeply attached to Yoḥanan. He was a Levite. He married Imma Shalom, Gamaliel's sister. His children were famous for their beauty. He also married his minor niece at his mother's insistence. He was wealthy and owned much land. He lived in Lydda, a town "particularly popular with the emigré aristocracy." During the anti-Christian persecutions, he was arrested on suspicion of heresy. Some see the reference to Jesus in the question about "a certain one" and his place in the world to come, b. Yoma 66b. But this is unsupported. It could as well be an allusion to Solomon.

Eliezer participated in the Yavnean school and also conducted his own. ʿAqiba began his career with Eliezer and Joshua. Eliezer also instructed Ilai, Nathan, Joseph b. Perida, Yosi, Abba Ḥanin, Yoḥanan b. Nuri, Judah b. Batyra, Ḥaninah, and Judah b. Gaddish. Eliezer also collected funds for the rabbis, proclaimed fast days, and went to Rome with Gamaliel. This was in 116-117, in connection with the war against Trajan; the rabbis went to prevent retaliation. At his death people lamented that a scroll of the law had been destroyed.

He had unpolished manners, was crude of speech, and engaged in "bullying at the slightest provocation." When Yoḥanan's son died, he told him to have another one. He told ʿAqiba he would be slaughtered. He praised himself.

He was a Shammaite and a dissenter at Yavneh. While he was a disciple of "an ardent Hillelite, R. Yoḥanan b. Zakkai," he also was a wealthy landowner and insisted on the status quo. At first his views were "repudiated as Shammaitic." But there was an open break on account of the oven of ʿAkhnai. The opposition did not want the priests to evade the laws of Levitical uncleanness and objected to his ruling that the stove was clean. It was not broken, for the owner intended to continue to use it. The intention thus put it into the category of a whole vessel. Eliezer was more friendly to the priests and regarded the stove as actually broken. The rabbis not only excommunicated him but also burned all the types of priestly food he had regarded as ritually pure. He was in Rome in 117-118, so must have died thereafter, in Caesarea.

Eliezer opposed individualism and universalism in theology, defending the "more conservative" viewpoint. Likewise in matters of social doctrine: "His colleagues endeavored to continue the development in the direction of individualism and universalism, to reach out after a greater measure of social equality, a more thorough-going pacificism, and a more inclusive humanitarianism. He... dissented, representing the more conservative point of view." Similarly, his colleagues represented the forces of social change. They facilitated change and emphasized individualism. Eliezer opposed change and defended the status quo, emphasizing uniformity and stability: "The law is to him a great impersonal fact, a body of eternal and immutable formulae. The applications of the law are mechanical, in accordance with the dictates of a rigorous logic. Conditions under which the law has to be carried out are disregarded. Individualization is minimized." The conclusion is as follows:

> R. Eliezer was the disciple of an ardent Hillelite... He apparently accepted the formal repudiation of Shammaism. But we know that he was a great landowner, a member of the upper class. It was consequently inevitable that, wherever Pharisaism was still flexible, he reasserts the point of view related to his class interests—the old point of view of the Sadducees and the Shammaites. It was the common rural background which made him, like the Sadducees, 'boorish in behavior'... It was fully in consonance with his class traditions that he taught a theology in which there was very little concern for the individual; that he was hostile to the non-Jewish world and unfriendly to proselytizing propaganda; that he emphasized the Temple, the cult of sacrifices, and the priesthood; that he championed the interests of agriculture and defended the rights of property; that he was unsympathetic to the women, the poor, the lowly born, the slave, and the criminal. Conservative in his attitude toward piety and social doctrine, he like the Sadducees and the Shammaites was very naturally moved to develop a system of jurisprudence which emphasized stability, uniformity, and opposed change. That, like the Sadducees and the Shammaites, R. Eliezer too was finally repudiated is only an indication of the extent and the direction of the class struggle—a struggle of which the combatants may not have been fully conscious, but which every utterance of theirs betrays.

Louis Finkelstein, *The Pharisees. The Sociological Background of Their Faith* (Philadelphia, 1962[3]), Vol. I, p. 78, sees the excommunication as the result of Eliezer's stubborn insistence on his views, although he was outvoted. Eliezer was a descendant of provincials and (p. 84), was "noted for his ill-breeding. He was wont to utter the most lurid curses against those who disagreed with him."

Louis Finkelstein, *Akiba. Scholar, Saint, and Martyr* (Philadelphia, 1936; repr. 1962), sees Eliezer as "a nationalist," in contrast with Joshua, "a peace-lover" (p. 65). He calls Eliezer "foppish" (p. 77). Eliezer was a Shammaite, and ʿAqiba would "lie in wait for any expression of Shammaitic opinion which he might need to refute." As to the ritual status of liquids, Finkelstein writes as follows (pp. 97-100):

> The interest of the patricians in the cultivation of olives, which had led to one of Akiba's earliest controversies with Tarfon, formed the basis of an even more prolonged and bitter discussion with Eliezer. Since the olive had become the fruit par excellence of Galilee, the production of its oil in the prescribed "purity" involved serious difficulties. Living at a distance from Jerusalem and the Temple, the Galileans could hardly arrange to "cleanse" themselves when they became defiled by contact with the dead, for that particular form of "impurity" could be removed

only with the ashes of the red heifer which were kept in the Sanctuary (Num. 19 : 1ff.). The Galileans, apparently, did bathe to wash away minor impurities, but in the eyes of the scholars this did not mitigate the effects of the major impurity. Legally they were "impure" and their touch contaminated. What, then, was to be done about the olives which they garnered? The Shammaites, who were especially concerned with this question, had an easy solution. They pointed to the verse in Leviticus (11 : 34) which denies that food can become impure unless it is moistened. The plucked olives were moist only with their own juice and, said the Shammaites, that liquid is not sufficient to render them susceptible to impurity. The Hillelites asked why the juice of grapes and all other fruits should be considered "preparation" for defilement and not the juice of olives. No satisfactory answer was given to this question, but the Shammaites insisted on their position.

This convenient rule did not, however, solve the whole problem. What was the status of the oil derived from the olives? The question was not merely academic and theoretical; nor did it concern only the super-pious who observed the laws of purity after the Temple was destroyed. It had a very practical importance, and involved vast property interests. The Heave-offering which every Jewish farmer in Palestine gave to the priest could be eaten only if it was pure. Obviously, if it was held that most of the olive oil produced in Galilee was impure, the priests would lose a large fraction of their income.

The situation was aggravated rather than mitigated by the destruction of the Temple. While the ashes of the last red heifer had somehow been saved and were available for purification, they could be used only sparingly. Levitical impurity thus became so widespread that the priests had to reconsider the status of the Heave-offering of wine and other fruit juices, as well as of olives.

Eliezer solved the whole problem with a sweeping declaration that "liquids are not susceptible to any form of impurity." The urgency which led to this decision is obvious from the fact that it runs counter to a specific statement in Scripture (Lev. 11 : 34) and certainly was opposed to the tradition of the day. It is especially noteworthy that Eliezer ben Hyrkanos, who boasted that he never gave an opinion which he had not received from his masters, should have been the author of this remarkable, and in a sense revolutionary, innovation. The proof he offered as basis for his interpretation of the Law effectually refutes him, as he himself must have recognized. He maintained that his rule was a corollary of a pronouncement made more than two hundred years earlier by Jose ben Joezer, one of the earliest Pharisaic teachers, who declared that the "liquids of the Temple slaughter-house are pure." Eliezer insisted that legally no distinction could be drawn between the liquids which Jose ben Joezer mentioned and others; if the old Pharisaic sages was correct so far as his rule went, then all liquids were pure.

It is obvious that an opponent of Eliezer might argue with equal, if not with greater cogency that Jose ben Joezer's words imply that other liquids *are* impure. But Eliezer, like the earlier Shammaites, did not listen

> to objections. Convinced, doubtless, that the ruling was indispensable and justified, he offered it to those who would follow him.
>
> Akiba, however, was unmoved by the plight of priest or provincial farmer. He knew that liquids had always been considered impure, and he could see no great reason for making a change in the tradition. On the contrary, he opposed even the attempt made by his colleagues to effect a compromise declaring liquids subject only to "rabbinical impurity."

Eliezer is described (p. 122) as a leading patrician figure: "His insolent bluntness, his stubborn insistence on his own infallibility, his total disregard of the rights of others, made him, in spite of his briliant record, especially vulnerable." Therefore Joshua and ʿAqiba were able to have him excommunicated on the issue of "The Stove of the Serpent Rings":

> Biblical law demands that earthenware pots and ovens which have become defiled, as, for instance, by contact with a dead insect, be broken (Lev. 11 : 33). To circumvent this law, the prosperous had invented a "serpent stove," i.e., an oven which—made of tiles, joined together by loose layers of earth—could be taken apart and put together again. This procedure they called "breaking the oven." Eliezer, speaking for the wealthy farmers, who could afford such complicated utensils, defended the legal fiction. But the poorer scholars, who had to be satisfied with ordinary ovens, resented the subterfuge. They said that the oven would remain defiled unless it was actually broken. This view was defended by Joshua and adopted by the conclave. Eliezer continued to declare these ovens pure. When the conclave assembed to hear charges against Eliezer, Gamaliel found himself in a dilemma. He could not defend in his brother-in-law the defiance he had repressed in others. Moreover, Eliezer made no attempt to deny or mitigate the accusation; he merely insisted that he was right and all the others were wrong. Whatever may have been the original intention of Eliezer's accusers, his attitude drove them into a frenzy of anger, and they not only ousted him from the Sanhedrin, but expelled him from the Pharisaic order. Not for half a century had this punishment been meted out to a scholar.

v. Alexander Guttmann

Alexander Guttmann, "The Significance of Miracles for Talmudic Judaism," *Hebrew Union College Annual* 20, 1947, pp. 363-406, notes that the House of Hillel accepted the message of the echo (*Bat Qol*), the House of Shammai rejected it. The echo decided that law should follow the House of Hillel. Frankel had asserted that the excommunication of Eliezer ended the existence of the House of Shammai, and the demotion of Gamaliel II ended that of the House of Hillel. But the evidence is inadequate to support that allegation. Eliezer was not a Shammaite. The stories about Eliezer's excommunication, y.

M.Q. and b. B.M., do not wholly correlate. They differ in many respects. The sequence of each passage is essentially different from that of the other. y. has fewer miracles, and these are "less miraculous." But as to the *Bat Qol* both passages are in agreement. And both represent the sages as rejecting the role of miracles in deciding the law. The echo agreed with Eliezer, and Joshua rejected it.

Gamaliel is not mentioned, but "he appears to be officially responsible for the ban." His name is omitted because he did not play as eminent a role as Joshua, or he might not have been at the consistory. He might have attended the session subsequent to the controversy in which "R. Eliezer's personality had been discussed and which resulted in the ban." We do not know why Eliezer was banned. "R. Eliezer's *Bat Ḳol* must have had at least some influence upon the decision to put him under a ban."

Then what was the difference between this echo and the one which decided the basic legal issue in favor of the House of Hillel? In the latter case the echo supported the majority opinion, while here it supported the minority. The echo in the case of the Houses came when the controversies were still open, between 70 and 90. The one in connection with Eliezer and Joshua came after 90.

The fact is that after 90 the rabbis engaged in polemics against Christianity. Before then they did not realize the danger of Christianity. The echo could be accepted before then, but miracles were so important to Christianity that the rabbis had to reject them. We know that Eliezer was a specialist in "the halakhic branch of sorcery," yet, had all the sages opposing Eliezer heard the echo, "they certainly would not have opposed it, since all their efforts were concentrated on the strengthening of God's will." Eliezer appeared to be friendly to Christianity: "Suspicion of Christian leanings combined with the employment of a device which, at this time, was fundamental and successful for Christianity, might have worked almost automatically against R. Eliezer as circumstantial evidence of his pro-Christian sympathies." Joshua was an outstanding polemicist against Christianity.

Why was Eliezer questioned in the hour of his approaching death? Did the sages wish to secure information from him to in order to increase their knowledge? The subject was ritual purity: "They wanted to ascertain that R. Eliezer was in accord with the sages as regards the attitude toward ritual purity." The Christians were opposed to the whole concept, so the opinion of Eliezer was taken as evidence of his true loyalty. He was shown to agree "in principle with the Pharisees." After the ban, Eliezer had done nothing to indicate sympathy for Christianity, so he was exonerated.

Alexander Guttmann, "Eliezer ben Hyrcanus—a Shammaite?", in Samuel Löwinger, Alexander Scheiber, and Joseph Somogyi, eds., *Ignace Goldziher Memorial Volume* (Jerusalem, 1958), Vol. II, pp. 100-110, says that in only one instance in the Palestinian Talmud can the reference to Eliezer as a Shammaite be understood as meaning he was a member of the House of Shammai. But *Shammuti* means "under ban," not "Shammaite." In numerous discussions he is not designated as a Shammaite. While Frankel and others interpreted the excommunication of Eliezer as punishment for his adherence to the House of Shammai, this is not so. There is no indication in the sources that Eliezer was associated with Shammaites. Indeed, shortly after the destruction in 70 the House of Shammai was outlawed and did not continue as a separate school.

Alexander Guttmann, *Rabbinic Judaism in the Making. The Halakhah from Ezra to Judah I* [Detroit, 1970), pp. 117-118, 203, and 263, says that Eliezer occasionally followed Shammaitic views, but was not a Shammaite. He could not have been, for the Houses came to an end very early in the Yavnean period, right after 70. Gamaliel excommunicated Eliezer, his own brother-in-law, to prevent the spread of dissent and sectarianism.

vi. Yitzhak D. Gilat

Yitzhak D. Gilat, *The Teachings of R. Eliezer b. Hyrcanos and their Position in the History of the Halakha* (Hebrew) (Tel Aviv, 1968), concentrates on the legal materials, all of which he interprets in the light of allegations of Eliezer's extreme conservatism. He provides an English summary, [1] as follows:

> This monograph deals with the teachings of R. Eliezer and his place in the history of the *Halakha*, according to his manifold *halakhic* dicta which have been preserved in Talmudic litterature. These teachings present us with a portrait of *halakhic* tradition during the period of the Second Commonwealth. They enable us to reconstruct the historic

[1] Reprinted by permission. © 1968 by Dvir Co. Ltd., Tel Aviv, in *Bar-Ilan University Series of Research Monographs in Memory of the University's Founder and First President, Professor Pinḥas Churgin, No. 3.* I am grateful both to the Dvir Co. and to Professor Gilat for permission to reprint the English summary of *Mishnato shel R. Eliezer ben Hurqanos uMeqomah beToledot HaHalakhah,* pp. ix-xxii.

halakha as it actually flourished during the Temple period and compare it with its later development during the lifetime of R. Eliezer after the Destruction. In this manner, the history of the *halakha* and its evolution may be carefully studied.

R. Eliezer's teachings superseded those of all his contemporaries: "If all the scholars of Israel were to be on one side of the balance, and R. Eliezer ben Hyrcanos on the other, he would outweigh them all." His superb memory made of him a rich storehouse of oral traditions. R. Eliezer himself testified: "If all the seas were ink, and all the reeds writing instruments, and all the people of the world scribes, they could not possibly write down all the teachings that I learned and studied in the Academy" (Avot de Rabbi Nathan XXV). Rabban Yoḥanan ben Zakkai, who showered praises upon his disciple's phenomenal memory referring to him as "a watertight well which loses no water" (Avot *ibid*), "a tarred flask which preserves its wine" (Avot de Rabbi Nathan XIV).

The complete dependence of R. Eliezer on the early *halakha* is amply stressed by his declaration: "and I never said a *halakha* which I did not hear from my master" (Sukka 28a).

Chapter One is devoted to four special fields in which R. Eliezer's unique attachment to ancient tradition and early *halakha* comes to light.

1. *Sabbath* — Accepted *halakha* differentiates on the one hand between primary labors and secondary acts, and on the other hand, between both these types of labors and other acts forbidden by the rabbinical injunction of *shevut* (the requirement to rest). The thirty-nine primary labors are listed in the Mishnah (Shabbat VII, 2); the secondary acts are therefore those which closely resemble them. There is practically no difference between the former and the latter, as may be seen by the fact that the punishment prescribed for the commission of primary labors is exactly the same as that meted out for the commission of secondary acts. The only distinction between them occurs in the case where a person committed a number of primary labors unintentionally, due to a singular case of ignorance, and is required to bring an offering for each labor, whereas the commission of a primary and secondary labor of like nature, on similar grounds, requires merely a single offering. On the other hand, those who perform labors forbidden because of *shevut* do not face the above penalties, since the prohibitions are by rabbinical injunction only. According to the accepted ruling, a labor performed on Sabbath is not punishable if done either in a manner different from that in which it is usually done, or if it is not necessary in itself.

R. Eliezer's decision on these questions is quite to the contrary, for he ruled that no distinction is to be made between a primary labor and a secondary act. In other words, a person performing several labors of related nature, due to a singular state of ignorance, is held responsible for each and every labor. Moreover, it may even be proper to assume that R. Eliezer's dictum pertains to the performance of recurring transgressions, e.g., one who reaps over and over again, in a singular state of ignorance is responsible for each act of reaping.

R. Eliezer also holds a person liable for the performance of unnecessary labors and labors performed in an unusual manner or by misconstruction. In other instances, labors which have been rendered as *Shevut* by the sages are understood by R. Eliezer as biblical injunctions.

R. Eliezer's approach follows in the footsteps of the early *halakha*; during the period of the Second Commonwealth, which demanded a stringent observance of the Sabbath, a fact well-evidenced by apocryphal literature. In that period, any labor which could be fitted into the category of "thou shalt not do any work whatsoever" was outlawed and no distinction whatsoever was practiced in relation to the various types of labors. However, as a result of R. ʿAqiva's ruling that the performance of several labors of related nature required only a *single* offering, similar labors were grouped into similar categories. The prime labors in these categories received the title *Avot Melakhot* and the secondary acts which resembled them were defined as *Toledot.* As has been shown, the distinction between the two did not yet exist during the time of Rabbi Eliezer.

In addition, the early *halakha* dealt with particular concrete cases and was quite divorced from the usage of generalizations, abstract principles, and concepts. Only after the Destruction, a period marked by the development of scholarship in the Academies, did the generalized *halakhot* and abstract concepts make their initial appearance, a process which was continued and further developed in the Amoraic period.

It is thus apparent that the abstract concepts which were used to define the various labors were actually the fruition of systematic inquiry which took place during the later generations. These concepts had not been defined or recognized prior to R. Eliezer.

Many labors, although designated as *shevut*, are also of early origin. However, after the acceptance of the thirty-nine primary labors as the recognized definition of work according to the biblical passage, and the limitation of the original concept, the sages could offer no substantial reason to outlaw these acts which had absolutely no resemblance to the primary labors. They were therefore relegated to the special category of *shevut* and their transgression was exempt from the severe penalties of death or of the Sin-offering.

R. Eliezer's ruling that each labor and act was forbidden *per se* and not because of any relationship with other labors anteceded the distinction between *Avot Melakhot* and *Toledot* and required punishment for many of those acts defined as *Shevut* as if they were actual labors.

2. *Measurements*—Even though the Talmud records the tradition of Rav, that the various measurements were part of the oral law given to Moses during the Revelation at Sinai, it can be shown that many Tannaitic and Amoraic sources are based on the assumption that the sages themselves originated the measurements. An inspection of the measurements and specifications mentioned in connection with the laws of uncleanliness, the Sabbath, etc., illustrates the fact that R. Eliezer adopts his measurements and standards according to the natural-individual status of the objects, or the smallest individual unit (provided that such a unit exists). On the other hand, the sages maintain

a strict and unfluctuating system of measurements for the various cases.

There were thus three systematic approaches to the fixation of measurements: a) the minimum measurement b) the individual instance c) the standard measurement as a compromise between the extremes.

R. Eliezer's *halakhot* concerning measurement reflect ancient traditional *halakha* in opposition to the tendency of the sages towards standardization and contrary to the differentiation, which characterizes later renewed *halakha.*

3. *Intention and Execution*—Two major approaches mark the *halakhic* concepts in the system of obligations and punishment, as well as the classification of various objects. One school of thought sees the execution of an act as the guiding factor, while another places intention above all other qualifications.

In many of his *halakhot*, R. Eliezer's principle is that the commission of a deed alone serves as a basis for a person's indictment, whereas other sages (e.g. R. Joshua) stipulate that guilt may be ascertained only after an examination of the intent and mental state of the transgressor. R. Eliezer also limits the ability of a utensil to receive impurity according to its present objective state, without regarding the owner's intention. According to his teachings, the *halakhic* state of different objects in questions of Impurity and Cleanliness, Civil law, and Sabbath prohibitions, is determined according to their temporary condition, thus completely disregarding their previous status, or the possibility of their regression.

The source of R. Eliezer's approach, which places matter over mind, lies in the teachings of the School of Shammai, and is based on the ancient *Weltanschauung* of natural law which weighs the rights and duties of man mainly according to his actions, and which thus evaluates and judges him *a propos.*

It may be noted that the above approach guided R. Eliezer as a theoretical and logical principle in the settling of legal problems. However, a study of his personal acts, of his religious and moral teachings, stresses the *hassidic* elements of thought and intention as the supreme measure of things. It is his belief that, by virtue of these spiritual values, a person achieves "the world to come."

4. *The Severity of the Early Halakha*—A prime characteristic of early halakha is the utter lack of any distinction between tradition and oral law originated by the exegesis or dicta of the sages. The rabbis of the early period viewed the traditions which had passed down from their ancestors as a single complete unit. This approach led to the view that strict observance of lenient rules (as defined by the later *halakha*) was equal to the more severe practices. The careful discrimination between biblical and rabbinical injunctions is the product of the Tannaitic period, commencing a generation prior to the Destruction of the Temple. This distinction saw its development in the Academies in the wake of inquiries into the methodology of study, which brought about the arrangement and alignment of the various *halakhot* and the creation of rules and concepts to define them.

An additional cause for the development of this distinction between biblical and rabbinical injunctions was the tendency towards leniency which emerged during the Post-Temple period. The "devaluation" of a prohibition by defining it as rabbinical, and by granting it a minor status, opened up new avenues towards dispensations in certain circumstances.

The *halakhic* developments mentioned above are evidenced through a study of R. Eliezer's dicta in relation to the Sabbath, Passover, Sukka, the Intermediate Days, Mourning, etc.

R. Eliezer usually explains biblical passages according to their simple meaning. This method serves as his criterion for the clarification of the *halakha* and as the basis for his decision. On the other hand, he was opposed to a pedantic inspection of the language and form of the passages which, while pretending to be simple interpretation, actually curtailed the extent of the *halakha* and its meanings. R. Eliezer's method of scriptural explanation is identical to his treatment of ancient *halakhot.*

R. Eliezer's mode of biblical interpretation, which is basically exegetical in nature, was in effect the same method as that employed by the early Midrash. However, the necessity to solve questions which arose from an exacting study of the Pentateuch, and the everyday problems posed by life itself, steadily widened the *midrashic* method, its rules and hermeneutic elements. This trend, which began during the period of the Second Commonwealth, reached its climax after the Destruction. R. Eliezer's method, like that of the early Midrash, remained in complete seclusion.

This method in a more radical form, which included explanation of the passage according to its actual written form (and not only according to its sense), was held in esteem by the School of Shammai. R. Eliezer adopted this method in its limited mode and explained biblical passages and *halakhot* accordingly.

R. Eliezer was extremely precise in his study of the words of each passage. He expounded them exegetically and thereby assured the stability of various *halakhot.* This result was achieved by closely inspecting each word and its meaning, or by showing its redundancy, which consequently permitted the inclusion of an additional *halakha.* R. Eliezer also placed no limit on the number of *halakhot* which might be derived from the close examination of a single word or passage.

In olden times, it was an accepted rule that several *halakhot* could be derived from each passage, especially if they were derived from contemplation of the passage's simple meaning. The general principle arising from R. Ishmael's ruling in *Sifra, Tazri'a* chap. XIII, 2, was apparently adopted in reaction to the extensive usage of exegetical techniques in the Academies after the Destruction. The free character of the Midrash, which reached its zenith in the Academy of R. 'Aqiba who was said to have explained "each and every crown of a letter exegetically" and to have derived from them "piles and piles of *halakhot,*" was responsible for the demand for restraint in biblical exegesis. Among the various reactions was the inception of the rule that no more than one *halakha* might be derived from a single passage. The exact explanations of R. Eliezer offer an intensive insight into the simple meaning of the Bible. They are a direct outcome of his method which was a continuation of the early Midrash and R. Eliezer therefore placed no limit on the number of *halakhot* derived from a single word.

In his dealings with other sages, R. Eliezer employed the hermeneutic rules in order to ensure his *halakhic* traditions and occasionally as a means for the deduction of a new *halakha.* His teachings exhibit exegetical rules, which generally reflect ancient "Talmudical" modes of exegesis.

Frequent use was made of the inference *a minori.* However, he placed great stress on the limitation of the "*dayo*." The exegetes attempted to widen the scope of the inference *a minori* and also to diminish the limitations posed by the "*dayo*" to minimal proportions. R. Eliezer, whose teachings were mainly based on oral traditions, was therefore quite vehement in stressing the limiting power of the "*dayo*" in deciding new *halakhic* questions. He is quoted as saying: "Even if you refute my arguments the whole day long, the result of the inference *a minori* must suit the original hypothesis" (Sifra *ibid*, chap. II, 4).

Inference by analogy is also very widespread in R. Eliezer's *halakhic* system and enables us to trace the original connotation of the term, i.e. a logical analogy between two equal elements. R. Eliezer thus used the term not as a mere combination of two distant words on a formal-literal basis, but rather as a logical comparison based on the inner content of the two subjects under discussion or as an exegetical analogy which derived the obscure from the distinct.

During the epoch of R. Eliezer, the various limitations of the inference by analogy, namely the rule that a person may not originate such an inference of his own volition, or that the biblical word had to be available for exegetical exposition were completely unknown. Only with the further development of this hermeneutic principle, in the identification of words in different contexts on a lexical basis, do we find it used as a method for establishing new *halakhot* on linguistic grounds. The rules limiting inference by analogy were thus enacted as a reaction to this method. At first, R. Ishmael ruled that it might be utilized only for "available" words. When this limitation did not suffice, it was afterwards declared that a person might not originate such an inference of his own volition and that only one based on tradition received from his master was acceptable.

R. Eliezer's system of Pentateuchal exegesis made use of the principles of "inclusion" and "exclusion" instead of "the general" and "the particular." He also employed special rules such as: a) "A law included under a generality which has become a particularity, in dealing with a new case, may not be returned to the generality, unless the passage specifically does so." b) "Preference is granted to that passage which validates itself and another passage, over that which validates itself and invalidates another pasage."

R. Eliezer utilized the principle of *Notarikon.* He also assumed "the possible from the impossible," in the same manner in which it is employed in the early Midrash.

R. Eliezer attempted to limit the use of scriptural exegesis as a basis for the development of the *halakha* (which achieved popularity in the wake of the diminishing authority of the Great Sanhedrin and eventual Destruction of the Temple). This is also seen from his inclusive rule that "Biblical enactments may not be derived from Rabbinical ones, and *vice versa.*"

R. Eliezer's reliance on age-old oral tradition did not prevent him from employing logic and reasoning not only for the clarification of ancient *halakhot*, but also in the widening of their scope. It is suggested that some of R. Eliezer's *halakhot* whose reasons are clearly stated were the product of logical examination of problems which arose from time-to-time, and were therefore not based exclusively on traditional teachings.

R. Eliezer's declaration: "And I never said a *halakha* which I did not hear from my Master" cannot be taken *per se.* In truth, R. Eliezer made use of logic and reasoning as decisive factors in rendering *halakhic* decision. However, this does not detract from the fact that oral traditions and previous studies were considered by this great Tanna to be the pinnacle of scholarship and he devoted himself to their study and dissemination. As a result, his teachings are replete with ancient *halakhot* set in the style of the early Midrash and their value for the clarification of the sources of the *halakha* and its foundations is inestimable.

Various Tannaim, among them contemporaries of R. Eliezer, commented on his method of equalization, i.e., judgment of the particulars of the *halakha* according to a single standard. These sages even praised R. Eliezer on this point, and in certain *halakhic* controversies rendered decisions in favor of R. Eliezer rather than his colleagues.

R. Eliezer's concept of *halakha* is therefore of an all-inclusive nature, wherein he visualizes the law and all its intricacies homogeneously, and systematically compares and equalizes the *halakhot.* This was also apparently the method of the early *halakha* which had no knowledge of the differentiation which was the product of later development.

The method of equalization served as the basis for many of R. Eliezer's *halakhot*, even though the Talmud explained them according to biblical exegesis, logical reasoning, or other modes of interpretation. R. Eliezer himself did not openly acknowledge this system as a measuring rod for rendering *halakhic* decisions. He generally employed the accepted methods of learning and debate then current in the academies. However, the fact that Mishnaic and Talmudic sages, as well as the medieval Commentators, emphasized this method as the underlying principle of R. Eliezer's *halakhot* proves that we indeed have here a basic rule in R. Eliezer's study of the various aspects of *halakha.*

The system of generalization in relation to particular *halakhot*, which delves into their innermost meaning and elucidates their common factors which are so decisive in the establishment of a unified and consistent *halakhic* system, guided R. Eliezer in his method of equalization, serving as the substratum which guided him in the acceptance of various *halakhot* as binding.

In the six chapters of Part Two entitled "The *Halakhot* of R. Eliezer," the *halakhot* of this immortal Tanna concerning Blessings, Sabbath, Erubin (enclosures), Passover and its sacrifices, the festivals, mourning, impurity and purity are dealt with in close detail. In the course of this exposition of his teachings, his *halakhic* outlook as well as the abstract principles underlying his decisions, the influence of political, social and economical conditions upon them and their relationship to the early *halakha*, to the School of Shammai and to his *halakhic* opponents are all clarified and elucidated.

The personal traits and actions of R. Eliezer bring to light customs and *halakhot* whose source lies in the teachings of "the Early Pious." Typical of these is the extreme severity of the laws of menstruation and abstinence from sexual relations. In the spirit of "the Early Pious," who were wont to dedicate a daily guilt offering for doubtful transgression and desirous of bringing a sin offering, R. Eliezer permitted the bringing of such a guilt offering at any time of the day and widened the scope of those required to bring the sin offering. He himself was strictly observant of the laws of booths (*Sukka*) and he wore phylacteries the whole day long. Tradition has attributed to him the holy spirit and the power of prophecy. His piety and sanctity have served as the subject of various Aggadic-Midrashic treatises.

The opinions and *halakhot* of R. Eliezer reflect the *halakha* as it actually existed in Israel's past, and dealt with practical problems. Theoretical *halakha* began making inroads into the academies on the eve of the Destruction.

The flourishing of Midrashic techniques and the fact that the sages continued to occupy themselves with precepts pertaining to the Temple, which were now inapplicable, lent impetus to the development of abstract-theoretical *halakha* which became part and parcel of the teachings of the sages.

The *halakhot* of R. Eliezer were thus based on reality and are generally indicative of the social conditions of the Temple period. Several examples may be offered:

(1) From several of R. Eliezer's dicta concerning the public road and private ground, it is possible to detect the prevalent reality during the pre-Hasmonean period (or that of the Society of Hassideans). Social organization was then based on cooperative values, and the power of "the public domain" over individual property was greatly felt. Land belonged to the entire community, whose members, being mainly agriculturists, received parcels for filling and earning a livelihood. However, if "the public" (= the populace) began to make use of a section of the parcelled land, the ground was automatically converted into a public road and returned to the status of "public property" without the necessity of a court order or a legal act of possession.

(2) The *halakhot* of R. Eliezer, by which one is required to tithe grain and fruits whose final preparation has not been completed (in contrary

to the opinion of the sages), is derived from the positive attitude toward the setting aside of tithes and heave-offerings during the days of the Second Temple. However, concurrent with the Destruction, the sages showed a marked tendency towards leniency and exemption from tithing wherever possible. With this background, one may understand more clearly the demands of R. Eliezer and the early *halakha* for tithes on fruit juices etc., contrary to R. Joshua and other sages who exempted them.

(3) The decline of agriculture and the difficult economic situation after the Destruction influenced the *halakhic* controversies between R. Eliezer and the sages on such assorted questions as: measurement of gardens, consideration of fruit juices as fruit and permission to carry on work during the Intermediate Days of Festivals or while in a state of mourning, etc. In all instances, R. Eliezer reflects the early *halakha* or its intermediary stages before the Destruction, whereas the sages represent later *halakha*.

(4) A tendency towards stringency in the laws of menstruation (unlike the early *halakha*), stemming from Hassidic and Sectarian circles, underwent widespread development after the Destruction. The abolition of laws concerning ritual purity, which were so closely attached to the Temple, was responsible for the great emphasis placed on types of impurity derived from the individual corpus. Because of the lack of means for the purification of a person defiled by contact with a dead body (due to the shortage of ashes from a red-heifer), many Jews adopted sexual abstention. These austere measures blended with the general movement towards abstinence which saw its development in the days following the Destruction. The abstainers mourned for Zion and the Temple and desired to find a substitute for the expiatory sacrifices.

The above developments are evident from various *halakhot* of R. Eliezer.

(5) After the Destruction, the general trend as to limit the scope of sacrifices and diminish the expiatory powers of those methods which had been practiced in the Temple. On the other hand, those methods of expiation which had subsisted after the Destruction were appropriately emphasized.

In this manner, the differing opinions of R. Eliezer and the sages concerning the Sin-offering, the Guilt-offering, and the broken-necked heifer are interpreted.

(6) R. Eliezer was outstanding in his *halakhic* and *aggadic* statements expressing his hostile attitude towards the Gentiles, and tended towards the negation of all dealings and economic cooperation with them.

However, the economic and administrative reality after the Destruction actually pointed towards Jewish-Gentile relations. The latter were, in effect, landlords who rented out lands to the Jews who received them as tenant-farmers. Common living quarters in the large towns created the basis for cooperation in economic matters. Several lenient practices which were furthered by later *halakhic* rulings may better understood as part of the positive scheme of the sages to cope with the new reality.

(7) A zeal for Jerusalem, its honor and its sanctity, the superiority of

Eretz-Israel, an impatient expectation for the Kingdom of the Davidic dynasty (= that of the Messiah), and the firm belief that the Temple would be rebuilt immediately, are evident in the *halakhot* of R. Eliezer. His nationalistic inclinations and his close relationship with the Zealot cause induced him to permit the carrying of weapons on the Sabbath, in opposition to early *halakha*.

Talmudic tradition has attributed to R. Eliezer the epithet *Shammaite*, which has been interpreted by the Gaonim and medieval writers of Novellae as "a pupil of the House of Shammai."

In fact, this appellation was adopted by the editor of the Tosefta, who included R. Eliezer's *halakhot* in a list of "leniencies of the House of Shammai," even though they were not specifically mentioned as belonging to that school. Accordingly, the Palestinian Talmud assuming that the *halakhot* of R. Eliezer are identical with those of the House of Shammai, utilizes this factor in the solution of different problems, and even raises a question when the two opinions clash with one another.

Tannaim and Amoraim often commented on the fact that R. Eliezer's opinion is that of the House of Shammai. In the present work, many additional sources have been offered showing his identification with the Shammaitic system of clarification of the *halakha*, its exegesis and final decision.

Nevertheless, there are also instances in which R. Eliezer disagreed with the schools of both Hillel and Shammai. Sometimes, his system was a sort of compromise between them, but usually it represented a third opinion. There are also a number of instances where R. Eliezer's ruling was strictly in accordance with the House of Hillel and was openly opposed to the House of Shammai.

However, these slight deviations from the Shammaitic system have been found in the teachings of other famous disciples of the House of Shammai. On the other hand, many of the well-known disciples of the House of Hillel adopted certain *halakhot* according to the House of Shammai and so the above-mentioned deviation may not be brought as an argumentation against the relationship of R. Eliezer to the House of Shammai.

According to accepted tradition, R. Eliezer's chief master was Rabban Yoḥanan ben Zakkai, who received instruction from both Hillel and Shammai (Avot II, 8). Rabban Yoḥanan ben Zakkai apparently acquainted R. Eliezer with the doctrines of both Hillel and Shammai, and he preferred the teachings of the latter to those of the former.

The *halakhic* system of Rabban Yoḥanan ben Zakkai as well as his relationship with contemporary *halakha* is still largely unexplored. However, the sources mention the tremendous volume of Tora and wisdom which he acquired from his ancestors (cf. the tradition regarding R. Eliezer). Rabban Yoḥanan ben Zakkai, like his star pupil, is also credited with the statement that "he never said a *halakhic* statement which he had not heard from his master." Rabban Yoḥanan ben Zakkai is also known as an opponent of the use of biblical exegesis as a means of renewing the *halakha* and was a staunch supporter of ancient oral tradition. He expressed the fear that the coming generation would override the early *halakha*, since it was not supported by biblical exegesis. Rabban Yoḥanan ben Zakkai also preferred a decision based on authority to theoretical consideration. One may thus conjecture that Rabban Yoḥanan ben Zakkai was a Tanna who based *halakha* on oral tradition, instead of upon exegesis, and whose teachings were those of the ancients and thus with early *halakhot*.

It is quite possible that Rabban Yoḥanan ben Zakkai's stern relationship towards early *halakha* and his reservations regarding the midrashic methods which underwent great development around the time of the Destruction are able to explain the somewhat puzzling fact that many scholars who were active before and after the Destruction were absent from the Academy of Rabban Yoḥanan ben Zakkai in Yavne. These sages apparently objected to the ruling of Rabban Yoḥanan ben Zakkai that "he never said a *halakha* etc," which stood in direct opposition to the accepted system of the sages of his generation. The latter, who mainly included the pupils of the school of Hillel and the Patriarchate, strove for an extension of the *halakha* and the discovery of new methods to resolve questions by everyday problems, according to theoretical introspection, and the recognition that exegesis and oral tradition were equivalent.

The withdrawal of the sages from Rabban Yoḥanan ben Zakkai and the latter's retirement to Beror Hayil may be depicted as a struggle for the true character of the *halakha* and its methods of development between those who stood for upholding oral tradition and those who favored the extensive usage of biblical exegesis. This struggle reached its climax several years after the death of Rabban Yoḥanan ben Zakkai, in the stormy encounter between R. Eliezer, Rabban Yoḥanan ben Zakkai's principal disciple and faithful exponent of his teachings, and the members of the Yavneh Academy, under the leadership of the Patriarch, which led to R. Eliezer's excommunication.

The Babylonian Talmud made use of the tradition associating R. Eliezer with the House of Shammai as a basic reason against *halakhic* decisions in his favor. However, it may be proven from Tannaitic and Amoraic sources that many *halakhot* were decided according to R. Eliezer.

Rashi's ruling that, since he was "blasphemed" in the case of "the oven of ʿAkhnai, his opinions are unacceptable as *halakha* is quite surprising, since the question of "blasphemy" is not at all relevant to the argument that his opinions are not acceptable as *halakha.* "Is it for that reason alone that *halakha* should not be according to his dictum, in every instance?" is a question pondered by the medieval novellaeists.

Moreover, R. David Luria proved that the ban on R. Eliezer was not complete in all its *halakhic* aspects and did not include actual excommunication. Its solitary aim was to separate him from the sages and remove him from the Academy, so that "strife may not multiply in Israel."

The fact of the matter is that, on the day of the ban, the only question under discussion in the Academy was "the oven of ʿAkhnai, which in the ensuing debate was eventually declared unclean by majority vote. According to the Palestinian Talmud, R. Eliezer would not have been too upset had this been the only action taken. However, "on that day, all objects which R. Eliezer had declared clean were brought and burnt in fire." The burning of all objects upon which R. Eliezer had passed positive judgment *up to that day*, was a breach of accepted procedure and a direct blow at the academic right of a Rabbi to render a decision. During the Temple period and the first years after the Destruction, there had been no development of unanimity in the field of *halakha*. Each sage rendered decisions in his town and neighborhood according to the traditions he had received and his *halakhic* speculations. The burning of the objects had a demonstrative motive: open objection to the *halakhic* decisions of R. Eliezer and the negation of his teaching and tradition.

In the argument over "the oven of ʿAkhnai," the long drawn-out struggle reached its climax. This argument was actually a battle between the early *halakha* based on oral tradition, which R. Eliezer considered as the basic foundation, and the later *halakha*, which based itself on theoretical study and exegesis in order to meet day-to-day problems.

These varied approaches are also typical of the School of Shammai and the School of Hillel. The former generally represented the early conservative *halakha*, while the latter reflected the later *halakha*. The *halakhot* of R. Eliezer are thus coupled with those of the House of Shammai. However, this relationship is not a direct one, but is secondary in nature. It derives from his system which visualizes early *halakha* and tradition as the main pillars of *halakha*.

As long as there was complete freedom to render decisions, the discussions and debates did not depart from accepted procedure and there was no requirement for special sanctions. However, certain limitations were placed on this freedom in order to crystallize the *halakha* and lead to its unification. The scope of activity of the Academy as a judicial body empowered to render decisions on questions under argument and even dismissal of age-old traditions and customs was widened, and a crisis ensued. The results were tragic: the ban, and the burning of the objects declared clean by R. Eliezer. His position in society and his *halakhic* influence were completely destroyed.

Together with the ban, his *halakhot* were outlawed in the Academy. The Rabbis were careful not to mention his name, fearing that this would lead to opposition towards the particular *halakha* concerning "the oven of ʿAkhnai." At times, R. Joshua's name was substituted for R. Eliezer's, in order that his opinion be accepted without reference to its true author. Attempts were made to conceal his decisions, even those based on ancient custom and time-honored tadition.

However, R. Eliezer did not yield. Up to the day of his death he refused to recant, even though his colleagues foresook him, and would not study his *halakhot*.

Only after his death did the attitude towards him change. With the lifting of the ban, his *halakhot* again found their way into the circles of the sages and the Mishna. There are several examples where the anonymous Mishna represents the opinion of R. Eliezer. In some places, the populace adopted his opinion as its custom. *Halakhic* decisions were openly accepted according to R. Eliezer in several instances.

After his death, when the fear of his negative influence subsided, R. Joshua and the other sages returned the *halakhot* of R. Eliezer to their former status and in certain cases decided in favor of his opinion.

The resentment towards R. Eliezer's *halakhot* which was expressed by the Amoraim and later authorities was usually motivated by his Shammaitic leanings. As has been shown above, R. Eliezer followed the system of the School of Shammai, and it is quite possible that they were never brought before them for discussion. In addition, it is most certain that R. Eliezer occasionally rendered decisions in opposition to the *halakha* of the School of Shammai, for no single issue alone served as the basis for the *halakhic* disputations, but rather several issues. In the course of time, however, the identification of R. Eliezer with the House of Shammai became strengthened and led several of the Amoraim to the conclusion that "*Halakha* is not decided according to R. Eliezer's opinion" in keeping with the general rule that "*Halakha* is always decided according to the School of Hillel."

vii. The Eliezer of History and the Eliezer of Biography

We cannot recover much of the biography of Eliezer b. Hyrcanus, even though materials purporting to relate his life-story are in our hands. The reason is that the most reliable traditions do not center upon Eliezer's life, but rather upon his legal opinions. Of the earlier accounts, only Gilat and Oppenheim take full account of that fact and focus on law. But the limitations of their method and the consequent unsatisfactory results are self-evident. Like Bokser and Finkelstein, Gilat and Oppenheim bring to the traditions a hermeneutical approach inappropriate both to the data and to the problems of historical inquiry. By taking for granted the veracity of all allegations about Eliezer, they begin with the supposition that he never said anything he had not learned from his masters. It follows that his sayings constitute the "old" law, and any difference with Eliezer's position will represent an innovation. On that basis their analyses follow, as if we had a clear picture of the old law and therefore could verify the allegations concerning his relationship to it. But we cannot, so their interpretation of the legal materials is, at best, dubious, but more often, pointless. Still, their expositions of discrete pericopae are not uninteresting.

With Bokser and Finkelstein it is obvious that contemporary concerns of the 1930's have shaped their understanding of the traditions of late antiquity and produced the faults of serious anachronism, of drastic over-interpretation of the sources, and of the imposition of categories of interpretation entirely inappropriate to the data. But Gilat, Oppenheim, and the other traditionalists likewise have allowed later concerns—those of the later Talmudic literature—to determine their choice of worthwhile issues. Gilat's stress on Eliezer as a legal conservative depends upon nothing more than the assertion that Eliezer never said or did anything not already said or done by his masters—a theme quite absent in the earliest strata of the Eliezer-materials and evidently introduced as part of a polemic in favor of his traditions at a point at which they were under attack, evidently toward the end of the second century and the beginning of the third.

In the main, however, earlier accounts of Eliezer tend to ignore the legal materials, which permit a considerable study of Eliezer as a historical figure, in favor of those which purport to reveal his biography or philosophy. These have been strung together, according to the natural requirements of biography, into stories about his origins, education, active life, excommunication, melancholy old age, and his death. Were we to accept the biographical agendum, we should have to formulate *ad hoc* arguments about what is, and what is not, credible in the various legends about Eliezer told for many centuries after his life. Such arguments would constitute nothing more than the objectivization of intuitions. In the absence of solid evidence one can do little more than posit "reasons" for believing or disbelieving, in detail or in general, materials which to begin with exhibit no close connections to the historical character they claim to describe.

We have a substantial corpus of legal materials produced in the circles of Eliezer's disciples and associates, the existence of which seems adequately attested within decades of his death. These materials do not pertain to Eliezer's biography. To be sure, one may derive from them details, not all of them inconsequential, about where Eliezer lived, his station in life, his associates and his disciples. But were we to concentrate upon biographical details, we should neglect the primary and important historical facts before us, which consist of a small but a genuine account of some of Eliezer's opinions and rulings. Our study of the traditions cannot, therefore, be ignored in the formulation of a life of Eliezer. It must, on the contrary, impose the main outline of our inquiry. To the traditions about Eliezer we may then add other fairly dependable, independent evidence about the times in which he lived. Together these materials cannot produce a comprehensive history of the Yavnean period. But they do allow the formulation of a number of reasonably reliable statements about Eliezer as a historical figure.

The Eliezer of history is revealed by the best, the better, and the fair traditions. These are to be divided into two parts. The best pericopae tell us what Eliezer actually thought about a number of discrete legal issues. The better and the fair ones provide a picture of the legal issues he faced, but not necessarily of his actual opinions about them. One must therefore distinguish between the best and better materials, which reveal whatever we are likely to know about the Eliezer of history, and the fair ones, which constitute an extension of the former and give a picture of the Eliezer of living traditions. That is, the fair traditions portray the Eliezer seen by people in close touch with the evolving traditions begun in Eliezer's own circle of disciples and associates and their continuators.

The poor traditions of various sorts portray the Eliezer of legend. They do not relate materials evolving out of Eliezer's life and circles of disciples and associates and their successors and continuators, but tell us only what later masters thought important to say about Eliezer. As noted, one may argue that these materials are appropriate to the times of Eliezer and congruent to the range of problems he ought to have confronted. They report things he might have said and should have done. They not merely fill in gaps in his portrait; they supply a full-length picture, giving a private life and a biography to a man hitherto known through policies and programs, but not revealed as a personality in his own right. To this affirmative—if weak—argument in behalf of their authenticity we may add a negative, slightly better one. The poor traditions tend not to attribute to Eliezer things which he ought not to have said; they do not tell us that he taught ideas important only later on. They exhibit little trace of the rabbinism developing in other circles in his own time and flourishing in all circles later on. The absence of "rabbinical" sayings (below, pp. 298-307), is striking evidence that the later tradents did not normally hand on in Eliezer's name materials they certainly could not have received from his living traditions. That does not mean what they did hand on certainly were things he actually said and stories redacted in his own day and under the hand of his disciples (or enemies). But it strongly suggests that the tradents normally did not deliberately anachronize in telling about Eliezer and in attributing sayings to him.

Until Eliezer, rabbinic heroes are known through traditions and legends, but not through historically reliable materials. Of the historical Hillel nothing may be said. But the Hillel of later rabbinic legend is a fully developed figure. The other pre-70 Pharisaic masters are primarily figures of legend. The Houses of Shammai and Hillel produce legal traditions, many of them quite reliable, but do not constitute historical actors at all. They testify to the state of Pharisaic law but report little about the activities of the Pharisaic group.

Yoḥanan b. Zakkai is the subject of legends but in addition stands behind traditions of considerable interest. If we take for granted—and we must—that Yoḥanan was the major figure in the transition of Jerusalem Pharisaism to Yavneh and in the establishment of the Yavnean institution after 70, then we must be astonished at how little we have about him from Yoḥanan's own associates and successors. The first important attestations of Yoḥanan's materials come from Usha, chiefly from Judah b. Ilai (but show no relationship to Eliezer). It is only with the few appearances of Yoḥanan in Mishnah-Tosefta that we see the beginning of a significant corpus of materials about him. Then, in the legendary stage, Yoḥanan is given a full repertoire of sayings and stories. He gets the major role in the siege of Jerusalem and the later negotiations with the Romans. He is made into a dominant historical figure. The silence of the Yavneans and most Ushans should tell us the historical Yoḥanan b. Zakkai was an unimportant figure at best. But the facts of history require a quite contrary view, even though the legends which purport to describe the course of events have little to recommend them, beyond their *prima facie* plausibility. While, therefore, with reference to Yoḥanan b. Zakkai, we could speak of a figure as revealed chiefly by *tradition* (of varying worth) and a character portrayed primarily by *legend* (mostly late and imaginary), in Eliezer we perceive in addition a historical actor, and one of the first importance.

It remains to compare the results based on historically more reliable traditions with the accounts of Eliezer given by earlier biographers. As stated, the most important difference is that until now all sayings attributed to and stories about Eliezer have been combined into a single picture, though details may vary from one modern authority to the next. All earlier accounts maintain the pretense that everything Eliezer is supposed to have said was actually stated by him, and everything he is alleged to have done actually happened. Since we have no grounds whatever for accepting these suppositions, we have to reject out of hand virtually every biographical statement in antecedent accounts, though interpretations of specific pericopae are not thereby rendered wholly valueless.

Frankel's view that Eliezer made rulings on the basis of logic and not only of what he had heard from his teachers seems to me generally correct, though the application of logic appears to have been limited chiefly to matters of cultic law and purity rules. His view of Eliezer as a Shammaite is unfounded and probably incorrect. As to the excommunication, we have no strong evidence to affirm the story. Clearly, something has gone wrong with the transmission of a few of his teachings, and those teachings seem to have been particularly controversial—not only because the contemporary authorities say so, but also because of their content. As to Eliezer's interpretation of Scripture, we cannot say for sure that he invariably favored the plain meaning, though this would appear in later strata to have been a widely-held opinion. As to Eliezer's beginnings his studies at the age of twenty-two (or twenty-seven, or some other age, depending on the version of his origins), his work with Yoḥanan b. Zakkai, his place in Jerusalem before 70, his helping Yoḥanan in the escape, his excommunication (before Gamaliel's deposition), and similar matters, we know nothing at all. The most important of these matters is his alleged discipleship with Yoḥanan. Here the legal traditions exhibit strikingly little evidence in support of that allegation. Apart from Abba Saul, it seems unlikely that anyone before the early third century, when the list was promulgated, knew about Eliezer's relationship to Yoḥanan. Thereafter, however, as stories about Yoḥanan were spun out, Eliezer would routinely be included. In the Yoḥanan-stories, however, Eliezer rarely, if ever is given a differentiated role or an individual personality. He is simply a name, along with Joshua, to serve when needed for detail.

Brüll's Eliezer is modeled on Frankel's. His stress on Eliezer's conservatism and opposition to the development of new laws on the basis of logical considerations seems to me entirely the opposite of the case. As to the heavenly voices which announced that the law follows the House of Hillel and Eliezer and so on, nothing needs to be said.

Hamburger and Derenbourg have not improved on the picture of Frankel. Indeed, since Frankel questions the allegation about Eliezer's saying only what he had heard, and Hamburger and Derenbourg (and Gilat nearly a century later) take for granted that the allegation to that effect must be correct, the latter represent a retrograde tendency in studying Eliezer, ignoring even such critical considerations as had been introduced before their time. Schürer's picture of Eliezer's "firm, unbending character" and so forth relies on little more than the accounts he cites, particularly Hamburger. Graetz's subjectivism and homiletics require no comment; as in most aspects of 'Talmudic history,' in this too he exercised a deleterious influence because of his popularity. Braunschweiger's allegation that Eliezer approved a teaching of the *minim*, depending on b. A.Z.'s embellishment of Tos. Hul., is an indication of his (and others') uncritical combination of all versions of a story into a single harmonious account, as was customary in the aftermath of Graetz. Weiss's picture emphasizes Eliezer's membership in the House of Shammai, so Weiss did not bother even to notice the many points of difference and of Eliezer's consistency with the House of Hillel; that is to say, his use of sources was episodic, unsystematic, and not very thoughtful. In this regard, he did not meet the modest standards even of his own time, as represented, for example, by Oppenheim.

S. Mendelsohn makes a brave show of criticism: "His earlier years are wrapped in myths." Yet these "myths" forthwith produce exactly the historical allegations they are meant to convey. Mendelsohn is not bothered by Eliezer's relationship both to Yoḥanan and to the House of Shammai.

Jawitz is noteworthy for the use of the latest and worst possible materials; he has not even missed Eliezer's conversation with Agrippas and his sayings about producing beautiful children. Bacher's assembly of *aggadic* and *midrashic* sayings, Hyman's collection of biographical and legal ones, and Konovitz's complete (too complete) array of everything attributed to any Eliezer make no important points and therefore require no comment.

Oppenheim seems to me to have produced an original and valuable effort thoroughly to investigate the legal materials. Except for Gilat, he stands quite by himself in his effort to organize and systematize materials in a manner appropriate to the critical standards of his own time. Oppenheim to be sure takes for granted Eliezer's 'conservatism,' but he then makes the effort to account for laws which clearly originate with Eliezer and to show how these laws go back to revealed principles or ideas already attributed to Eliezer's predecessors.

Halevy's treatment of Eliezer is less elaborate than one might have expected. His long attack on Weiss's negative opinion of Eliezer's personality seems to have exhausted his interest in the subject of Eliezer himself. Halevy's conception of the organization of the "sages'" government at Yavneh furthermore imposes a quite fantastic interpretation on various details. His views, however, that Eliezer tended to ease the burden of the law, that he was not a Shammaite, that he was apt to be lenient—all arise from a closer reading of the sources than was attempted by others.

The sociological and economic interpretations of Eliezer seem the most curious element in the legacy of earlier scholarship. They are frequently plausible, but never conclusive and compelling, and the mode of argument, in both Bokser's and Finkelstein's cases, consists of colorful narrative, accompanied by frequent reiteration of what is to begin with alleged, instead of an effort to show that what is alleged is not only plausible but also the best of many possible interpretations. The whole approach therefore is to be regarded as a deductive mode of argument, in which an antecedent "principle" is illustrated through many cases, but independently demonstrated in none of them. As to the principal allegation, we have no decisive evidence that Eliezer was rich or that he was poor. His sayings, seen without preconceptions about his economic interests, seem to me to show neither that he was an aristocrat or patrician nor that he was a plebian or a commoner. That Lydda was "particularly popular with emigré aristocracy" was because Eliezer lived there. He lived there because he was an emigré aristocrat. Eliezer's role as a Shammaite is taken for granted, also his conservatism in law—which proves his conservatism in everything else. Halevy's piety about Eliezer's saintliness finds its counterpart in Bokser's and Finkelstein's impiety about his boorishness. The dramatic language employed in this connection—"bullying at the slightest provocation"—seems particularly odd. The issues of Eliezer's opposition to individualism and universalism in theology are totally extraneous to the materials before us and seem, moreover, to be irrelevant even to the poorest traditions. Indeed, if we had not known that Eliezer was supposed to be opposed to individualism and universalism, we might not have grasped that these issues were implicit in his sayings, though admittedly, they possibly occur in a few of them. Eliezer's espousal of uniformity and stability seems exactly contrary to the tendencies we discern. As to his "mechanical application of the law," it is difficult to find evidence that he ever actually applied the law, mechanically or otherwise. The allegation as to Eliezer's class sympathies and the class struggle of his day is, to be sure, an important datum for the study of the history and sociology of Talmudic scholarship in the first half of the twentieth century.

Finkelstein likewise sees Eliezer as "ill-bred" and a provincial, "wont to utter... lurid curses..." This colorful language is enriched with such adjectives "foppish." Finkelstein's plausible explanation of the problem of the ritual cleanness of olive oil and so on seems to go far beyond the limits of the evidence. Eliezer's opinion that liquids are not susceptible to uncleanness is interpreted by itself, without the detailed consideration of all other pericopae in which the problem arises. Instead, we are told that like the earlier Shammaites, Eliezer did not "listen to objections." The treatment of the problem would be more helpful if, instead of personal criticism of Eliezer, Finkelstein had raised the problems and "objections" to be considered in Eliezer's own pericopae. The interpretation of the ʿAkhnai-oven is equally plausible, but also without the support of more evidence than the allegation that such *might* have been the case.

Guttmann's stress is on the *aggadic* stories of the later strata. His view that Eliezer was not a Shammaite because the House of Shammai "was outlawed" after 70 depends upon the allegation that the House of Shammai was outlawed after 70 and therefore Eliezer could not have been a Shammaite. Legal traditions in support of his view are not assembled. Oppenheim's example should have been followed.

Gilat's fundamental allegation, that Eliezer's traditions are old—because of his good memory—and that they allow the reconstruction of the law of his and earlier times, is utterly without foundation. In point of fact we do not know how the law was applied within pre-70 Pharisaism, and the details in our hands are trivial, not of broad and probative value. And unless we take for granted that Eliezer represents the old law, we also do not know that his sayings relate to the earlier situation. It follows that the bulk of Gilat's specific allegations likewise is false. It certainly cannot be shown, in general or in detail, that Eliezer was completely dependent on the early *halakhah.*

This does not mean that Gilat's interpretation of the principles of Eliezer's rules is without interest. The explanation of some of the legal pericopae seems valuable; his effort to interpret the legal materials in a traditional framework is not uninteresting. But the "historical" framework so important to Gilat's larger allegations is based on nothing more than a superficially plausible, but unsupported notion. Therefore at every point even the interpretation of the law may be called into question.

That Sabbath-law was strictly interpreted in Second Temple times may be attested by Apocryphal literature. But then we do not know the situation of *Pharisaic* sectarian law in this matter, unless we assume that the Apocryphal books cited in evidence derive from or portray Pharisaism.

I do not follow Gilat's point about measurements "according to the natural-individual status of the object." Eliezer's own inconsistencies in the matter suggest that whatever "ancient tradition" he represented was internally contradictory.

As to Eliezer's consistency with the House of Shammai in respect to intention, this seems to me well-established in some areas of law, not in others (the cult in particular). But the "ancient *Weltanschauung* of natural law which weighs the rights and duties of a man mainly according to his actions and which thus evaluates and judges him *a propos*" is either fantasy or gibberish. It goes without saying that the statements about Eliezer's Scriptural interpretation cannot be verified by reference to the historically most useful materials. A number of issues introduced by Gilat derive from hermeneutical principles not revealed in, or not integral to, Eliezer's sayings at all. Some of the pericopae involving Ishmael with an Eliezer may not pertain to our Eliezer at all.

Gilat's view of Eliezer's personal traits and actions as reflective of the teachings of "the early Pious" is never demonstrated. Eliezer's relationship to such teachings is assumed, then used to demonstrate that he was an exemplar of the teachings of "the Early Pious." The allegation that Eliezer's dicta concerning the public road and private ground reflect the "prevalent reality during the pre-Hasmonean period" is original. We are supposed to concede that before the Hasmoneans, "social organization was based on cooperative values," but Gilat does not allude to a shred of *usable* evidence on that point. As to the "positive attitude" towards the setting aside of tithes exhibited in earlier times, the picture seems hardly so clear. According to the rabbinic traditions about the Pharisees, some of the tithes were normally given by everyone, but most were not—and that is one of the reasons Pharisees were different from ordinary folk. Gilat's references to economic conditions after the destruction are plausible. In general one cannot deny that there was a period of difficulty. But how this theory necessarily helps one to interpret specific opinions of Eliezer, apart from its theoretical plausibility, is hardly demonstrated. Eliezer's hostility to gentiles occurs in some sayings, but in others he seems not to have been hostile at all. The zeal for Jerusalem, etc., may be located in *aggadic* sayings, but I do not see where Gilat finds it in Eliezer's laws. Nor is his "close relationship with the Zealot cause" revealed by his ruling about weapons on the Sabbath. Not everyone who carried a sword was a Zealot, and most were not. (Some were Romans.) Gilat's view that Eliezer was really a Shammaite, who sometimes differed from both Houses, and at times ruled strictly in accord with the House of Hillel, but was really a Shammaite all along, is a mess of contradictions.

As to Eliezer's supposed relationship to Yoḥanan b. Zakkai, Gilat relies upon the "sources" which mention the "tremendous volume of Tora and wisdom which he [Yoḥanan] acquired from his ancestors" and handed on to Eliezer. The purported view of Yoḥanan that biblical exegesis should not serve as "a means of renewing the *halakha*" and his "staunch support of ancient oral traditions" merely repeats what some (few) pericopae have to report about Yoḥanan. Others say no such thing. And of course, what we know about the "ancient oral tradition" cannot be gainsaid. In all, Gilat exhibits the virtue of supplying a detailed account of much of the legal literature produced in Eliezer's name. But it is difficult to find in his work a single acceptable historical or biographical allegation.

CHAPTER FOURTEEN

THE ELIEZER OF HISTORY

i. Introduction

Having distinguished the more from the less useful traditions, we now seek to recover the picture of Eliezer drawn by his contemporaries and immediate disciples. That picture is composed of what several individuals who ought to have known what they are talking about said about Eliezer either in the course of his lifetime or shortly after his death. Our assumption (p. 94) is that those individuals or circles were not in collusion, but approached the Eliezer-materials from varying perspectives. Their sayings and stories, handed on in different ways to different circles, produce points of agreement among disparate authorities which allow us to construct a reasonably reliable account of the historical Eliezer. They further permit us to raise questions, not necessarily elicited by Eliezer's actual sayings, about his place in the larger historical setting. We shall rapidly review the positive results of our inquiry into the best and better traditions and then use those results to answer a number of questions.

1. *Agricultural Rules, Tithes, and Taboos*

One may give Heave-offering from what is clean for what is unclean, and Dough-offering from clean for unclean dough. To prevent abuse of the rule, one may not give worse produce (unclean) for better (clean), for this would diminish the return to the priests. The established rule, to which Eliezer takes exception, however, rigidly distinguishes among various sorts of closely related produce or of the same produce in different states, i.e., liquids and solids. In permitting an exception to the rule, Eliezer made it considerably less complicated to give the requisite produce. He stands close to the position of the House of Shammai, which ruled that if a man gave Heave-offering of grapes intended for eating but later on made them into raisins, it is valid Heave-offering, and the gift does not have to be duplicated.

If one has to burn Heave-offering of *ḥameṣ* that is clean with the same that is unclean, one must keep them separate. (Joshua says they may be burned together.)

With Heave-offering which has fallen into a large quantity of secular produce, if one knows what has fallen into what, then one may not regard the Heave-offering as neutralized. But if one cannot distinguish the holy from the secular produce, the whole mixture will neutralize the Heave-offering. This is Meir's, and the Mishnah's, view of Eliezer's opinion on the matter. Judah places Eliezer in a still more lenient position. We may take for granted that Eliezer and Joshua discussed the principles of the neutralization of Heave-offering, but we are not entirely sure of Eliezer's exact opinion. Clearly, he took the lenient position *vis à vis* Joshua.

The cakes of Thank-offering and wafers of the Nazirite are not liable for Dough-offering if they are made for the Nazirite's own use, but are liable if made for sale.

ʿOrlah-laws do not apply outside of Palestine. We may generalize that the application of agricultural taboos is thereby suspended for foreign countries—a major reform, if the rule was originated by Eliezer.

In respect to a hide anointed by Seventh Year oil, one may make use of it, and by extension one may use Seventh Year oil for that purpose. It is entirely legitimate to do so. The opposition held the hide should be burned—and attributed that opinion to Eliezer. Eliezer wanted the enforcement of the laws of Seventh Year produce to be lenient. The same applies to the *ʿeruv*, a law evidently unique to pre-70 Pharisaism. His rules would make it easy for non-Pharisees to take up the Pharisaic discipline, just as he (theoretically) removed that discipline from the concern of Jewries abroad.

One may not purchase saffron with the money of Second Tithe, because it is not a food, merely a coloring.

The *etrog* is like a tree in all respects, contrary to the view of Gamaliel that it is like a tree in three ways and like a vegetable in one.

2. *Sabbaths and Festivals*

One may do anything necessary for circumcision on the Sabbath. ʿAqiba ruled that on the Sabbath one may do only the thing which cannot be done before the Sabbath—the actual act of circumcision itself. Conversely, in Eliezer's view, if one circumcizes on the Sabbath a child who does not have to be circumcized on that day, he will be liable for an appropriate Sin-offering.

However big a field, if it is surrounded by a fence, it is regarded as a single courtyard and requires no *ʿeruv* and one may carry therein on the Sabbath. This is the most lenient possible ruling on the subject. ʿAqiba presents a stricter law. Likewise, if one party forgot to participate in the *ʿeruv* for a courtyard, he is prohibited from using it, but all others in the courtyard may continue to do so, a lenient opinion which removes social pressure from the man who failed to participate in the rite, and, by extension, from the dissenter who does not believe in it to begin with. One may furthermore purchase a share in an *ʿeruv* from a storekeeper or baker. The sages hold one may not do so by means of coins. One may make an *ʿeruv* with any kind of food except water and salt. Joshua says it has to be a loaf of bread only. These are consistent with Eliezer's general leniency in regard to the *ʿeruv* in particular, and Sabbath-law in general.

The 'Powers of Rain' prayer is said from the first day of Sukkot. A *Sukkah* must have some sort of a roof. One may carry out his obligation to consume bitter herbs on Passover by eating an herb which others regarded as not appropriate—evidently a lenient opinion. Judah in the name of Eliezer gives three rulings on the conduct of the Temple rite on the Day of Atonement: how the high priest drew lots, where he would stand, and how he would count as he sprinkled the blood. Eliezer held, consistent with the House of Hillel, that one may make use of a splinter with which to pick his teeth on the festival, even though the wood was not set aside for that purpose before the festival. One may set up a new millstone in the festival week. A woman may go out on the Sabbath wearing a tiara.

3. *Family Affairs*

Eliezer greatly facilitated annulling vows. One may release a man from his vow by referring to the honor of his parents. Ṣaddoq drew the conclusion that, if so, one may do so also with reference to the honor of God, and so vows are no longer going to be effective. One may release a man from his vow even by reason of what happens unexpectedly. Ṣaddoq certainly would have to point out that vows can never again be taken seriously, for on any pretext whatever they may be rendered null and void.

A female minor can do nothing of legal effect. Eliezer therefore would rule out the possibility of the marriage of a minor under any circumstances.

A conditional writ of divorce, permitting a woman to marry anyone except one particular person, is valid. This ruling limits a woman's freedom in the situation of divorce. It is more or less consistent with Eliezer's view that one is obligated to carry out the rite of the *Soṭah* if he has any reason whatever—any sort of evidence satisfies Eliezer—to suspect she has been unfaithful. It is likewise consistent with his opinion that a woman is not to study Torah, but that her sole occupation should be home-making. Eliezer's view of divorce with a limiting condition may be regarded as parallel to the opinion of the House of Hillel, that any sort of grounds will justify a divorce. But it is not a close parallel, and distinctions between the two rulings may easily be introduced. A writ of divorce brought from one village to another—not merely from a foreign country—must have the verification of the agent that in his presence the writ was written and sealed. One warns his wife in regard to the *Soṭah*-rite on the evidence of a single witness or on his own evidence, but causes her to drink on the evidence of two—or the opposite.

4. *Theoretical Problems*

If a person has begun a deed licitly, he may complete it, even though in the meantime it is no longer permitted to undertake such an action.

Eliezer rules in a lenient way on the possibility of restoring to their original condition mixtures of sacred and secular substances. If a *se'ah* of unclean Heave-offering fell into a large quantity of clean, it may be removed, "for I say, the *se'ah* which fell in is the one which is lifted out." Likewise in a mixture of valid Whole-offering limbs with those which were blemished, if the head of one is offered, the others are all acceptable, because the one which was offered is assumed to be that of the blemished animal; the rest are thereby rendered valid. If various sacrificial bloods are mixed together, it is possible to sprinkle them. The sages say the whole has to be poured out, which will require a new sacrifice.

On the question of intent, Eliezer says that outside of the cult one judges only from what one actually does, rather than attempting to work out a person's intent without an explicit statement of what he actually proposed to do. Joshua says one may indeed interpret a man's intention. Eliezer's view of the problem of intention is consistent with opinion of the House of Shammai, that unstated intention is not taken into account in assessing the effect of a person's actions. The wrong intention, however, can render a sacred act or cultic object invalid. Thus if a man intended to do something wrong with the handful of the Meal-offering, whether or not he actually carried out his intention, he has rendered the offering invalid. If a man intended to eat something not ordinarily eaten or do something improper with a sacrifice, he has invalidated it. In respect to Sin-offering-water, the wrong intention, without any action, will render the water unfit. Joshua says not the intention but the actual action is what will render the water unfit. Likewise a sacrifice must be offered only for the purpose for which it may appropriately be designated, thus with exactly the right intention. If one sacrifices on the Passover coinciding with the Sabbath an animal eligible for the Passover sacrifice, but for a purpose other than the Passover, he is liable for a Sin-offering. This is the converse of Eliezer's view that one may actually do all that is needed in connection with such a sacrifice: One must be sure that the sacrificial process is absolutely required. Similarly in respect to the circumcision necessary on the Sabbath, one may do all the required preparations on that day; but if the circumcision is not necessarily done on the Sabbath, then Eliezer will rule in a strict way as to the appropriate penalty. One must do the right thing in the right way with the correct intention. Joshua says doing the right thing is sufficient, even with the wrong intention. The case of the Passover underlines the view of Eliezer that for sacrifices and the cult in general one's intention must be fully and correctly spelled out.

Eliezer and ʿAqiba, Eliezer and Joshua, and Eliezer and Judah b. Batyra are represented in three unrelated cases as disputing the identical legal principle, namely, whether a man must exert himself to forestall the development of an illegal situation, or whether he may simply stand by while such a situation takes shape on its own. Judah b. Batyra is of the same view as Eliezer. Joshua and ʿAqiba both differ from Eliezer; the differences are in separate pericopae. One should undertake no action which will produce a violation of the law. Therefore, in giving Dough-offering on the fifteenth of Nisan, a woman should not designate the offering until the dough is baked. Joshua says she should not worry about the problem of leaven on Passover in this connection. One therefore has, according to Eliezer, to take affirmative action in order to avoid violating the law. Joshua says one needs to do nothing, one way or the other; if the law is broken of itself, that is no one's problem. Eliezer likewise rules in respect to a mixture of blood to be sprinkled once with blood to be sprinkled four times that one must sprinkle the whole four times, lest he diminish the required number of sprinklings and so violate the law. Joshua says one should do no such thing; he should sprinkle just once.

5. *The Theory of the Cult*

If one does many individual transgressions of a single category in a single period of unawareness, he must bring a Sin-offering for each transgression. ʿAqiba says one Sin-offering suffices for all such acts. ʿAqiba on the one side, and Joshua and Gamaliel on the other, all are involved with the issue of how to atone for several actions of the same sort done in the same spell of unawareness. Joshua, Gamaliel, and Eliezer respond to the issue. Gamaliel and Joshua say they have no tradition. Eliezer supplies a ruling based upon logic. Then Gamaliel and Joshua cite an appropriate case which turns out to accord with the conclusion produced by Eliezer's logic. A man also must give a Sin-offering when he is not certain just what sin he has done, when he has done it, or indeed whether he has sinned at all. If the Sin-offering is not for the sin the man thinks he might have done, it will serve for some other. Similarly, one may bring a Suspensive Guilt-offering every day except for the day after the Day of Atonement.

6. *The Temple and Sacrifice*

One may dedicate to the Temple part of his property, but not all of it. Eliezer and Joshua rule on the question of what to do with a man who has dedicated his property to the Temple while liable for his wife's *Ketuvah*, but we are not sure exactly what each authority stated in such a case.

If a person has set aside a redemption-lamb for the firstling of an ass, the owner is liable for that lamb and must make it up if it dies. The sages say the owner is not liable to restore the lamb. Joshua and Ṣaddoq support the latter position. The progeny of Peace-offerings may not be brought as Peace-offerings. Joshua and Pappyas have a tradition that the progeny may be given as Peace-offerings.

The 'blood without the meat' is ineffectual. That is, if the sprinkling of the blood has been carried out, but the sacrifice itself is proved to be impaired, the whole thing must be done again. ʿAqiba says the opposite also is the case. According to Eliezer, however, if the proper sprinkling of the blood does not take place, then the meat is not retrospectively rendered unfit.

If one slaughters at night and in the morning finds the walls of the neck filled with blood, the slaughter is valid.

7. *Sources of Uncleanness*

Joshua and Eliezer debate the definition of liquids which are capable of becoming unclean and rendering produce susceptible to uncleanness. We are not certain about the exact details of the discussion.

Eliezer says the sap of crushed olives is not capable of receiving or rendering susceptible to uncleanness.

Eliezer and Joshua deal with the case of two jars, each containing a half-olive's bulk of corpse, which are stopped up. In a house they together serve to render the house unclean. But the jars themselves are clean. If one is open, it and the house are unclean, the other remaining clean. Judah refines the dispute. Eliezer and Joshua likewise discuss the case in which an olive's bulk of corpse cleaves to the outer Joshua of the door jamb of the threshhold. Eliezer says it renders the house unclean. Joshua says the house remains clean. An olive's bulk of flesh from the limb of a living person is unclean. The dirt of a grave area and that which comes from abroad join together to make up the quantity capable of rendering something unclean. The sages say that quantity can be composed only of a single sort of dirt—therefore a lenient rule.

8. *Persons Subject to Ritual Uncleanness*

If a person deliberately removed the tokens of uncleanness in respect to an attack of leprosy, he can become clean only after the purification of another sign of leprosy which afterward occurs on his flesh. Judah b. Ilai claims Eliezer and the sages hold that such a person can never be purified. They differ as to one who cut off the sign as dead flesh.

If a Nazir contracts uncleanness at the very end of his spell, he need not lose the whole of the period he has already properly observed. He loses only a small part of the period.

A *Zab* who examined himself only on the first and seventh days of his period is regarded as having been clean on the intermediate days, a lenient ruling.

9. *Objects Subject to Ritual Uncleanness*

A shoe on the last is insusceptible to uncleanness, because it is not completed. This represents the application of an old principle to a new case. The beehive will save from uncleanness what is in an earthenware vessel, since it has the capacity to preserve its contents from severe corpse-uncleanness. The sages hold that partitions afford protection in a 'Tent,' but not in earthenware vessels; considerations of logic do not change the situation. Eliezer proposes to extend by logic an established decision, and the sages stand pat. A beehive is like immovable property. The sages hold the opposite opinion. A money-bag or a pouch for pearls is unclean. We are not sure which object was subject to Eliezer's ruling. When broken, a metal vessel may both contract uncleanness and be rendered clean. Eliezer rules on whether a handkerchief, a wrapper for a Torah-scroll, and a towel are subject to the law of diverse kinds, but we do not know what he said. Judah claims he said they are not subject to the taboo.

10. *The Courts*

A pigeon-racer may not give testimony. A woman is covered up before her body is hung.

11. *The Schools*

One must repeat a lesson to his disciple four times. ʿAqiba said one must do so as many times as are necessary for the disciple to master the tradition.

12. *The Age*

The generation of the wilderness is destined to enjoy the world to come. ʿAqiba denies it.

ii. Origins, Early Life, Education

We do not know where Eliezer came from, who his parents were, how he was educated, at what point in life he became a Pharisee, whom he married, when or where he died. The historical Eliezer lacks a personal biography. But the information in our hands permits a number of likely surmises.

First, he certainly was a Pharisee. The topics of his best-attested legal rulings leave no doubt on that question, for they focus upon the two areas of everyday life—agricultural taboos and ritual purity—which constitute the primary interests of Pharisaism. The third important interest in his legislation, the cult, follows from the first two. The Pharisees before 70 did not control the Temple and did not make laws to govern its cult. But afterward, they made plans for the conduct of the Temple when it would be restored. The reason for their strong interest in the matter was that their piety had earlier centered upon the priesthood, cult, and Temple; they had stressed the proper provision of the priestly taxes—though they did not necessarily benefit—and the appropriate, domestic application of the purity-laws of the Temple. It therefore was important to Eliezer, as a representative of pre-70 Pharisaism, to continue the earlier trend to make laws affecting the governance of the cultic life. Nothing in Eliezer's legal legacy suggests that he anticipated the Temple would be subordinated in the spirituality of his day or later times; nothing replaced the offerings, no one took the place of the priest, no new forms of piety were evolved to substitute for those that had depended upon the Temple's sanctity.

Among the Yavnean authorities ought to have been others not likely to have been Pharisees before 70—priests, Sadducees, apocalyptics and mystics, adherents of other groups, rich men, common folk. We need not doubt that Gamaliel was a Pharisee, for his father, Simeon, is explicitly named as one by Josephus, and his grandfather, Gamaliel, is likewise so characterized by Acts' version of Paul. But Simeon's daughter married a disciple of Yoḥanan b. Zakkai said not to have been a Pharisee; it is difficult to demonstrate that Yoḥanan himself was a member of the sect before 70 (p. 140). His legal rulings hardly supply decisive evidence that he was; Eliezer's do.

Second, he probably was born and educated before the destruction of Jerusalem. On this question we can be less certain. It is only an assumption, based on the surviving materials, that Eliezer, along with Joshua, Gamaliel, Ṣaddoq, Ṭarfon, and a few others, constituted the first group of important Yavnean authorities, after Yoḥanan himself. If this assumption is sound, then Eliezer, among the others, presumably was a mature man at the beginning of the Yavnean period. He certainly was well informed about Pharisaic law, so probably learned it before 70.

This must mean, third, that before 70 he was inducted into the sect. We do not know how the Pharisees taught neophytes, though the legal traditions on the subject are clear that a gradual process of absorption marked entry into the sect. The beginner was taught simple, then more complex rules; he began by tithing, then went on to the larger and more difficult matter of learning to preserve the ritual purity of secular food. But whether this process was carried out by formal education, discipleship or in some other way is hardly clear. Nor do we have evidence of his education in other subjects, such as philosophy, science, mysticism, or Greek language, not to mention Scripture and other sacred subjects. To be sure, much may be taken for granted about the education of any Jewish male in first-century Palestine, for knowledge of Scriptures—but what books and in what recensions who can say?—and the rites and liturgy of the country's Jews may be presumed to have been widespread. But we find in the traditions pertinent to the historical Eliezer no information whatever about educational institutions, curricula, techniques, or goals.

Fourth, he certainly does not appear to have been a priest or a Levite. Nothing in his sayings indicates much interest in priestly or Levitical affairs as such, apart from those aspects that impinged upon the Pharisaic piety.

We know nothing about the master whom he might have served as a disciple or whether he was part of a master-disciple circle at all. Nothing in the materials before us permits speculation about his station of life, his personal wealth, his family's occupation, his class sympathies. His personal traits are revealed, if the saying is genuine, only by the counsel to repent before death—a commonplace of the time, meant to inculcate not a morbid spirit but ethical behavior.

If his view that the generation of the wilderness will enjoy the world to come means more than it says, then Eliezer also believed in the power not only of penitence but also of divine grace. This belief does not imply personality-traits of one kind or another. But it does permit the guess that in his time the issues of penitence and grace were important. This, to be sure, we might have surmised without such a saying, for with the destruction of the Temple, it was natural for people to speculate about reconciliation with God and its means—penitence on man's side, grace on God's.

iii. Eliezer's Active Career

We do not know where Eliezer lived in the years after 70 or what he did for a living. We do not know much about how he spent his time, though the legal record requires the surmise that he gave great effort to legal study and legislation. He was associated in this connection chiefly with Joshua and ʿAqiba, secondarily with Gamaliel and Ṣaddoq, and practically not at all with other important masters of his own day. Ilai has legal traditions in his name, so Eliezer presumably taught Ilai as a disciple, but we do not know for what purpose—whether to train him for a career in public administration or merely to educate him as an observant Pharisee. The latter would seem more likely; the bulk of Ilai's chains have to do with religious observance, not the administration of justice, on which, from Eliezer, we have almost no sayings.

The best traditions make one thing clear: at some point in his life Eliezer fell under a shadow, so that it was necessary to preserve his traditions in a peculiar way—by saying he said the opposite of what was his true opinion. It was difficult for Ilai to find others to verify that Eliezer had said what his best disciple had as the record of his teaching. We do not know what happened. Since the two lists of evidently controversial teachings place Eliezer in a lenient position *vis à vis* Pharisaic law, it stands to reason that he had proposed a considerable revision of earlier Pharisaism. This revision would have included a lenient approach to the application of the *ʿeruv*-laws and of the laws on the Seventh Year. It further involved a rapproachment with the Samaritans—not a matter of concern only to Pharisees. According to him Jews might now enter social relations with Samaritans.

The revision of Eliezer's traditions by ʿAqiba therefore reflects some public event which changed the relationship between Eliezer and the larger body of the sages. His opinions were no longer acceptable. Then ʿAqiba, who agreed with Eliezer's views, claimed in Eliezer's name the exact opposite of what he had originally said so as to secure the acceptance of his opinions. Ilai had the same problem, but he simply preserved the traditions as best he could. He hoped to find others who might support his allegation of Eliezer's real opinion and perhaps also testify that these should be the normative law. Ilai's list of lenient rulings of Eliezer had to do with *ʿeruv*-laws and a bitter herb for Passover. But while he was unable to find others who knew equivalent lenient rulings in Eliezer's name, his list *was* preserved in the appropriate context. ʿAqiba's little list of traditions in Eliezer's name, which contained lenient rulings in respect to the Seventh Year—one may use a hide anointed with the oil of the Seventh Year, and in regard to the relationships with Samaritans—one may have social intercourse with them ("eat their bread"), likewise was preserved. At some point both traditions were taken into the normative compilations, so in time the reasons for suppressing them ceased to be important or were forgotten. I should suppose this came with the predominance of ʿAqiba's disciples, at Usha. But we must also postulate that Ishmael, who clearly disapproved of Eliezer's teachings, must have stood among Eliezer's opposition. His virtual absence from Eliezer's corpus, rather than anything he actually is claimed to have said, represents the best evidence of the state of affairs. Eliezer's pericopae place him in relationships chiefly with Joshua and ʿAqiba, so his disciples and theirs are apt to be responsible for the formation of the larger part of the corpus of the best and—it goes without saying—the better traditions. That is why we have them. Perhaps the reason for ʿAqiba's favorable attitude toward Eliezer is what the later stories allege: he was Eliezer's disciple. But Joshua's place is much less clear. We cannot take for granted that Joshua and Eliezer studied with the same master; on the contrary, if they had, they should have stood together on a wide range of moot issues. It seems more likely that they were associated because they shared a common agendum of legal concerns and differed on minor details, indicating a broad range of agreement on fundamental principles.

Of other alleged disciples of Yoḥanan b. Zakkai we hear nothing at all. Simeon b. Natanel was married to Gamaliel's daughter; Eliezer was married to his sister. So the two should have come in contact. We have no evidence of that fact. Yosi the Priest is quite unheard of in Eliezer's (or others') traditions. Eleazar b. ʿArakh, a mystic, plays no role whatever. Among contemporaries, Ṭarfon and Eleazar b. ʿAzariah seem important. The former is supposed to have been another teacher of ʿAqiba, the latter is given an important place in the consistory of Gamaliel. Ṣaddoq comes in chiefly through Joshua, with whom he is repeatedly associated, though he has some independent sayings or interpolations as well. In all, therefore, the traditions about Eliezer place him into close relationships with the figures of greatest importance in the surviving materials of early Yavnean times.

iv. Eliezer's Historical situation. Pharisaism and Rabbinism

We do not know where Eliezer spent the years before the War of 66 or how he reached Yavneh. Nor have we evidence on his attitude to either the War of 66 or war in general. He cannot certainly be called either a nationalist and zealot or a pacifist. We do know that in his time the Temple was destroyed. His attitude toward the destruction of the Temple is not difficult to recover. He clearly devoted his best energies to working out the laws of the Temple cult, so he believed in the cult and presumably regretted the Temple's destruction and the consequent cessation of animal sacrifices. The cultic rules obviously are matters of legal theory; they do not derive from Eliezer's actual knowledge of how the Temple had been run before 70, nor do they indicate much interest in the question. Precedents are seldom cited in Eliezer's discussions. To be sure, he has a number of sayings about the conduct of the cult on the Day of Atonement; these are matters of generally unimportant detail and do not add up to much.

Clearly, Eliezer expected the Temple to be rebuilt. Since he made up laws for the rebuilt sanctuary, he presumably wanted to see the reconstruction and anticipated that in the new Temple his laws would be enforced. Hence he believed in the efficacy of the cult and did not doubt it would be restored. We have no hint that he disapproved of the former Temple. The absence of traditions on that subject is because he was not a priest and had no clear knowledge of what had been done. When he did, he gave it—that much emerges from Judah's sayings in his name. So presumably he thought what had been done in general should be repeated in the future, with modification of details. These he figured out on the basis of logic. His concern for the Temple marks him once again as a Pharisee, for, as stated, Pharisaic piety was based upon the Temple and its laws of uncleanness; the Pharisees simply enlarged the area in which those laws were to be observed and enforced. Whether or not they liked the particular Temple administration, the Pharisees certainly revered the cult itself and took most seriously the laws surrounding its conduct, including, first and foremost, purity laws. Later on the cult and its law would be considerably less interesting, in particular to generations entirely unfamiliar with its appeal. The theory of the cult, to be sure, would occupy the lawyers for a long time to come.

In Eliezer's time Rome ended its former experiments with the government of the Jews and established direct rule. We know nothing about Eliezer's attitude toward Rome and the new regime in Palestine. Gamaliel had to negotiate with it; Eliezer evidently did not. This must mean that in Yavneh he did not enter into direct relationships with the Roman regime; but we do not know whether other masters of the day, except for Gamaliel, had any more direct contact with the Romans than he evidently did.

The larger problems faced by the Jews deprived of their cult and its celebrations, including the observance in the Temple and in Jerusalem of the pilgrim-festivals, not to mention the bringing of first fruits and of the Second Tithes or equivalent funds to the city of consumption—none of these seem to have elicited his attention. He does not legislate about the observance of Sukkot after the destruction, as did Yoḥanan b. Zakkai, though we have two rulings pertinent to the festival. He has nothing to say about the New Year or the use of the *shofar* on the Sabbath that coincides with the New Year, as did Yoḥanan; also omitted are the use of new produce and the waving of the *ʿomer*. The various Temple-oriented festival celebrations subject to Yoḥanan's *taqqanot* are ignored in Eliezer's legislation. This is striking, for Eliezer, as an early Yavnean master, ought to have had more to say about the sacred rites now no longer possible to effect than we can discern in respect to these lively issues.

Eliezer certainly did not anticipate that the Temple would never be rebuilt. He had no program for any considerable time before the reconstruction. Perhaps it was hoped that the Romans would not delay in permitting the buildings to be restored. No one in his time could foresee the disastrous Bar Kokhba War or the definitive prohibition of the Jews from Jerusalem in its aftermath.

Eliezer's legislation therefore suggests he presumed life would soon go on pretty much as it had in the past. Issues important to pre-70 Pharisaism predominate in his laws; issues absent in the rabbinic traditions about the Pharisees are—except the cult—mostly absent in his as well. Eliezer therefore comes at the end of the old Pharisaism, not the beginning of a new rabbinism—traces of which are quite absent in his historically usable traditions. Indeed, on the basis of his laws and sayings we can hardly define what this rabbinism might consist of. The centrality of the Oral Torah, the view of the rabbi as the new priest and of study of Torah as the new cult, the conception of piety as the imitation of Moses "our rabbi" and the conception of God as a rabbi, the organization of the Jewish community under rabbinic rule and by rabbinic law, and the goal of turning all Israel into a vast academy for the study of the (rabbinic) Torah—none of these motifs characteristic of latter rabbinism occurs at all. Since by the end of the Yavnean period the main outlines of rabbinism were clear, we may postulate that the transition from Pharisaism to rabbinism or the union of the two took place in the time of Eliezer himself. But he does not seem to have been among those who generated the new viewpoints; he appears as a reformer of the old ones. His solution to the problem of the cessation of the cult was not to replace the old piety with a new one, but rather to preserve and refine the rules governing the old in the certain expectation of its restoration in a better form than ever. Others, who were his contemporaries and successors, developed the rabbinic idea of the (interim) substitution of study for sacrifice, the rabbi for the priest, and the Oral Torah of Moses "our rabbi" for the piety of the old cult.

Indeed, the virtual absence of rabbinic ideas not only among the best and better traditions, but even among the poorest ones, shows, as observed, that Eliezer has not been anachronistically 'rabbinized.' To be sure, the tradents and compilers later on assumed everyone before them—back to Moses—was a rabbi. But they did not regularly attribute to Eliezer sayings to link him specifically to the rabbinic system of symbols, and this suggests that, just as with the laws, a limited agendum defined topics appropriate for attribution to Eliezer, so with theological matters, ideas originally not within Eliezer's agendum were not commonly added afterward. If so, we may take seriously the attribution of rabbinic ideas to others of his contemporaries. Where do we first find them?

Clearly Yoḥanan b. Zakkai—whom we could not conclusively show to have been a Pharisee—appears to have been a rabbi. It is in his sayings, admittedly first occurring in late compilations, that we find the claim of replacing the cult with something—anything—as good. He is alleged to have told Joshua that deeds of loving kindness achieve atonement, just as did the cult. He is further made to say that man was created in order to study the Torah. When Israel does the will of their father in heaven—which is contained in the Torah and taught by the rabbi—then no nation or race can rule over them. The cult is hardly central to his teachings and seldom occurs in his laws. The altar to be sure serves to make peace between Israel and the father in heaven—but is not so important ("how much the more so") as a man who makes peace among men or is a master of Torah. Yoḥanan's *taqqanot* are even better testimony, for they take account of the end of the cult and provide for the period of its cessation. The Temple rites may be carried on ("as a memorial") *outside* of the old sanctuary. The old priesthood is subjected to the governance of the rabbi. The priest had to pay the *sheqel* and ideally should marry anyone the rabbi declares to be a fit wife. Eliezer says nothing of the sort; what Yoḥanan has to say about the situation after 70 is either without parallel in Eliezer's sayings or contradicted by their tendency. To be sure, we are scarcely able to claim that rabbinism begins with Yoḥanan or that Pharisaism ends with Eliezer. But Yoḥanan's tradition certainly reveals the main theological themes of later rabbinism—though these themes are more reliably attributed to later Yavneans and still more adequately spelled out in their sayings. And Eliezer's laws and theological sayings are strikingly silent about what later on would be the primary concern of the rabbinic authorities, the Oral Torah in all its social and political ramifications, and remarkably narrow in their focus upon the concerns of pre-70 Pharisaism.

Further investigation may show that the list of M. Avot of Yoḥanan's disciples represents a composite of the five components of the Yavnean group: Eliezer clearly was a Pharisee; Yosi was a priest; Simeon b. Nathaniel was an *ʿam haʾareṣ*, not observant of the purity laws; Eleazar b. ʾArakh was a mystic; and Joshua b. Ḥananiah should represent rabbinism. But this remains to be studied.

If Eliezer stands for the old Pharisaism, who stands for the scribes? The scribes form a distinct group—not merely a profession—in the Gospels' accounts of Jesus's opposition. Scribes and Pharisees are not regarded as one and the same group. To be sure, what scribes say and do not say is not made clear. One cannot derive from the Synoptic record a clear picture of scribal doctrine, if any, though one certainly finds an account of the Pharisaic law on ritual uncleanness and tithing. Since the materials now found in the Synoptics certainly were available in Palestine between 70 and 90, however, they may be presumed accurately to portray the situation of that time, because their picture had to be credible to Christians of the period. (Even the Fourth Gospel contains traditions that go back to Palestine before 70, but we concentrate attention on the picture presented by the Synoptics.) If so, we have in the Synoptics a portrait of two groups at Yavneh (and possibly earlier) in close relationship with one another, but not entirely unified.

Now, having seen in Eliezer an important representative of the old Pharisaism, we find no difficulty in accounting for the Pharisaic component of the Yavnean situation. It likewise seems reasonable to locate the antecedents of the ideological or symbolic part of the rabbinic component at Yavneh in the scribes. Admittedly, our information on scribism in the rabbinic literature is indistinguishable from the later sayings produced by rabbinism. But if we consider that scribism goes back to much more ancient times than does Pharisaism, with its main outlines clearly represented, for instance, by Ben Sira, we may suppose that what the scribe regarded as the center of piety was study, interpretation and application of the Torah. To be sure, what was studied and how it was interpreted are not to be identified with the literature and interpretation of later rabbinism. But the scribal piety and the rabbinic piety are expressed through an identical symbol, *Torah.* And one looks in vain in the rabbinic traditions about the Pharisees before 70 for stress on, or even the presence of the ideal of, the study of Torah. Unless rabbinism begins as the innovation of the early Yavneans—and this seems to me unlikely—it should represent at Yavneh the continuation of pre-70 scribism.

But it continued with an important difference, for Yavnean and later rabbinism said what cannot be located in pre-70 scribal documents: The Temple cult was replaced by study of Torah, the priest by the rabbi (= scribe); and the center of piety was shifted away from sacrifice entirely. So Yavnean scribism-rabbinism made important changes in pre-70 scribal ideas. It responded to the new situation in a more appropriate way than did Yavnean Pharisaism represented by Eliezer. Eliezer could conceive of no piety outside of that focused upon the Temple. But Yavnean and late scribism-rabbinism was able to construct an expression of piety which did not depend upon the Temple at all. Eliezer appears as a reformer of old Pharisaism; the proponents of rabbinism do not seem to have reformed old scribism. What they did was to carry the scribal ideal to its logical conclusion. If study of Torah was central and knowledge of Torah important, then the scribe had authority even in respect to the Temple and the cult; indeed, his knowledge was more important than what the priest knew. This view, known in the sayings of Yoḥanan b. Zakkai, himself an opponent of the priesthood in Yavnean times, is not a matter only of theoretical consequence. Yoḥanan also held that he might dispose of Temple practices and take them over for the Yavnean center—and for other places as well—and so both preserve them ("as a memorial") and remove from the Temple and the priests a monopoly over the sacred calendar, festivals, and rites. Earlier scribism thus contained within itself the potentiality to supersede the cult. It did not do so earlier, because it had no reason to, and because it probably could not. The later rabbinism, faced with the occasion and the necessity, realized that potentiality. By contrast, earlier Pharisaism invested its best energies in the replication of the cult, not in its replacement. After 70 it could do no more than plan for its restoration.

Scribism as an ideology, not merely a profession, begins with the view that the law given by God to Moses was binding and therefore has to be interpreted and applied to daily affairs. That view must go back to the fourth century B.C., by which time Nehemiah's establishment of the Torah of Moses as the constitution of Judea had to have produced important effects in ordinary life. From that time on those who could authoritatively apply the Torah constituted an important profession. The writings of scribes stress the identification of Torah with wisdom and the importance of learning. Ben Sira's sage travels widely in search of wisdom and consorts with men of power. Into the first century, the scribes must have continued as in identifiable estate, high in the country's administration. Otherwise the Synoptics' view is incomprehensible. So those who were professionally acquainted with the Scriptures—whether they were priests or not—formed an independent class of biblical teachers, lawyers, administrators, or scribes, alongside the priesthood. We do not know what they actually did in the administration of the country. Perhaps Yoḥanan b. Zakkai's reference to decrees of Jerusalem authorities (M. Ket. 13 : 1ff.) alludes to the work of scribes, who therefore were involved—as the Pharisees certainly were not—in the determination of family law and in the settlement of trivial disputes.

The NT references support this supposition. The scribes occur in association with the high priests in Matt. 2 : 4, 16 : 21, 20 : 18, 21 : 15, 27, 27 : 41, Mk. 8 : 31, 10 : 33, 11 : 18, 27; 14 : 1, 43, 53; 15 : 1, 31, etc.; with the Pharisees in Mt. 5 : 20, 12 : 38, 15 : 1, 23 : 2, 13, ff.; Mk. 2 : 16, 7 : 1, 5. But they are not the same as the one or the other. The scribes are called 'learned in the law' and jurists (Matt. 22 : 35, Luke 7 : 30, 10 : 25, 11 : 45, 52, 14 : 3). They are teachers of the law (Luke 5 : 17, Acts 5 : 34).

Mishnaic literature—except Eliezer's saying in M. Sot. 9 : 15—obviously will miss the distinction between Pharisees and scribes, both of whom are regarded as ḤKMYM, sages. But we have no reason to suppose all scribes were Pharisees, any more than that all Pharisees were scribes. Indeed, as Schürer points out (*A History of the Jewish People*, etc., Division II, Vol. I, pp. 319f.), "Inasmuch ... as the 'scribes' were merely 'men learned in the law,' there must have been also Sadducaean scribes. For it is not conceivable that the Sadducees, who acknowledged the written law as binding, should have had among them none who made it their profession to study it. In fact those passages of the New Testament, which speak of scribes who were of the Pharisees (Mark 2 : 16, Luke 5 : 30, Acts 23 : 9) point also to the existence of Sadducaean scribes." The scribes therefore represent a class of men learned in Scriptures, perhaps lawyers in charge of the administration of justice. They had to develop legal theory, teach pupils, and apply the law.

Naturally, such people would come to the center of the administration of government and law, so they could not have remained aloof from Yavneh. Some of them may, to be sure, have come because they were Pharisees. But others, whatever their original ritual practices, would have come because Yavneh represented the place in which they might carry on their profession.

The latter rabbinic history of the Second Temple assigns to the scribes the period from Ezra to Simeon the Just—that is, the period before the (imaginary) existence of Pharisaism itself. It assumes of course that all scribes were Pharisees and all Pharisees were scribes, so it need not set aside a "scribal period" after Simeon, from whose time it traces the history of the Pharisaic-rabbinic party itself.

Josephus—himself a new adherent of the Pharisees—does not confuse the scribes with the Pharisees. In none of his allusions to the Pharisees does he also refer to the scribes (*grammateīs*). In *Life* 197-8, he refers to a delegation of Jerusalemites to Galilee. Two were from the lower ranks of society and adherents of the Pharisees, the third was also a Pharisee, but a priest; the fourth was descended from high priests. These were all able to assert that they were not ignorant of the customs of the fathers. To be sure, the Pharisees are referred to as knowledgeable in the Torah; and they have traditions from the fathers, in addition to those that Moses had revealed. But they are not called scribes. They were (*War* 1 : 107-114) exact exponents of the laws. They also were (*War* 2 : 162-166) the most accurate interpreters of the laws. But they are not called scribes. The long 'philosophical school' account in *Antiquities* 18 : 11-17 describes the Pharisees as virtuous and says that "all prayers and sacred rites of divine worship are performed according to their exposition"—but they too are not scribes.

When Josephus does refer to scribes, he does not refer to Pharisees. For example, in *War* 1 : 648ff. = *Antiquities* 17 : 152, he refers to two *sophistai* who ordered their disciples to pull down the eagle that Herod had set up in the Temple. They are Judah son of Sepphoraeus and Matthias son of Margalus, men who gave lectures on the laws, attended by a large, youthful audience. If these are scribes, they are not said also to be Pharisees, who do not occur in the account. We find also *hierogrammateīs* and *patriōn exēgētai nomōn*—not in the context of the passages about the Pharisees. While, therefore, the Pharisees and the scribes have in common knowledge of the country's laws, the two are treated separately. Josephus does not regard the scribes as wholly within the Pharisaic group; he presents the scribe as a kind of authority or professional teacher of law. Josephus's further references to *grammateus* (sing. or pl.) are as follows:

> *Apion* 1 : 290: The sacred scribe Phritobeuates; *Antiquities* 6 : 120: It was reported to the king by the scribes that the host were sinning against God; 7 : 110: He made Seisa scribe; 7 : 293 = 7 : 110; 7 : 219: Joab took the chiefs of the tribes and scribes and took the census; 7 : 364: David appointed six thousand Levites as judges of the people and as scribes; 9 : 164: When the scribe and priest of the treasury had emptied the chest; 10 : 55: When the money was brought, he gave superintendence of the temple . . . to the governor of the city [and] Sapha the scribe, etc.; 10 : 94f.: Baruch, scribe of Jeremiah; 10 : 149: the scribe of Sacchias; 11 : 22, 26, 29: Semelios the scribe, etc.; 11 : 128: On the scribes of the sanctuary you will impose no tribute; 12 : 142: The scribes of the Temple; 11 : 248, 250, 272, 287: scribes of the Persian kings; 16 : 319: the scribe Diophantus had imitated his manner of writing; 20 : 208f.: The *sicarii* kidnapped the secretary of the captain; *War* 1 : 479: village clerks; 5 : 532: Aristeus, the secretary of the council—

so H. Thackeray, *Josephus Lexicon*, Fascicle II, pp. 117-118. The entry for *hierogrammateus* is not yet available, nor for *sophistēs*. It is clear, however, that Josephus does not associate scribes with Pharisees; no scribe is a Pharisee; and no Pharisee is described as a scribe. The two are separate and distinct. One is a sect, the other is a profession.

Since later rabbinism found pre-70 scribism highly congenial, it is by no means far-fetched to trace the beginnings of Yavnean rabbinism to the presence of representatives of the pre-70 scribal class, to whom the ideal of study of Torah rather than the piety of the cult and the replication of that cultic piety in one's own home, was central. Yavneh therefore incorporated these two important strands of pre-70 religion—the one the piety of a sect, the other the professional ideal of a class—and others as well. Among them, as we have seen, Eliezer's teachings made for pre-70 Pharisaism an important place in the Yavnean synthesis.

Thus far, our definition of rabbinism has focused upon its central symbols and ideas. These seem to continue symbols and ideas known, in a general way, from 'scribism'—if not from individual scribes, who, as I have stressed, formed a profession, not a sect. But what of the later, and essential, characteristic trait of rabbinism, its formation as a well-organized and well-disciplined movement, its development of important institutions for the government of the Jewish communities of Palestine and Babylonia, its aspiration to make use of autonomous political instruments for the transformation of all Jews into rabbis? Of this, we have no knowledge at all in the earliest stratum of the Yavnean period. Clearly, Yoḥanan b. Zakkai worked out the relationship between the synagogue and the Temple. But the nature of the "gathering" at Yavneh—whether it was some sort of 'academy,' or a nascent political institution, or merely an inchoate assembly of various sorts of sectarians, professionals, pre-70 authorities, and whatever—is simply unilluminated. Eliezer's historical record is strikingly silent on this very point. From his materials we have no evidence on either how he enforced or applied the law outside of his own household or disciple-circle, or how anyone else did. We have no hint about the evolution of an institution one might regard as a nascent political authority—a government—in any terms. Eliezer's laws omit reference even to the legal theory behind such an authority. And they are strikingly silent about the whole range of laws to be applied in civil life. Whence such laws reached the Yavneans we do not know. They cannot have come from Eliezer, and, given the nature of the rabbinic traditions about pre-70 Pharisaism, they also did not derive from other Pharisees. So in all the 'rabbinism' possibly present in Yoḥanan's corpus and remarkably absent in Eliezer's is simply the symbolic and ideological element represented by the study of Torah as the central expression of piety.

v. Eliezer and the Houses

To understand how Eliezer represented pre-70 Pharisaism at Yavneh, we must consider four closely related questions. First, what was his relationship to the pre-70 Houses? Second, what may be learned from him about the old Pharisaic law? Third, what were his own contributions to, and innovations in, the law? Finally, did Eliezer actually apply or enforce the law?

Not only did Eliezer issue legal opinions on issues important to the general concerns of pre-70 Pharisaism, but he also ruled on specific matters decided by the Houses, and in some instances was held responsible for the formulation of Houses' pericopae or represented as participating in those same pericopae. For example, Eliezer and ʿAqiba are portrayed (M. Sheq. 8 : 7) as debating an issue before the Houses: What is the criterion in determining where something which has contracted uncleanness is to be burned? Eliezer says what is decisive is the nature of the impurity which has imparted the uncleanness. What comes from a primary source of uncleanness is burned outside the Temple court, what is unclean from a secondary source is burned inside. ʿAqiba says what is decisive is the location in which the uncleanness was contracted. Judah (M. Tos. Sheq. 3 : 16/M. Sheq. 8 : 7) states that Eliezer ruled in a way consistent with the opinion of the House of Shammai, ʿAqiba with the House of Hillel. But in fact the rulings of both Houses depend upon the principle Eliezer declared to be decisive, namely, the nature of the impurity which has imparted the uncleanness, rather than the location in which the uncleanness has been contracted. M. M.S. 3 : 13 turns out to focus upon the same issue, with the Houses' rulings determined according to the underlying principle attributed to Eliezer. ʿAqiba's formulation of the issue never produces a Houses' dispute. But the superscriptions of the pertinent pericopae then explicitly allude to ʿAqiba's principle. Judah b. Ilai assures that Eliezer's opinion predominates in the definition of the Houses' dispute.

Eliezer differs with Gamaliel on the status of the *etrog.* Ilai's grandson then claims ʿAqiba followed the opinion of both Gamaliel and Eliezer; Eliezer rules in conformity to the opinion of the House of Hillel.

Judah represents Liezer as a member of the House of Hillel in Tos. Y.T. 1 : 3.

Ilai (Tos. Dem. 1 : 3) gives clear evidence that Eliezer ruled in a way consistent with the view of the House of Shammai. He says the first fruits of the garden are always liable, for they are taken account of—therefore are viewed as guarded and of value. We have already observed that Eliezer's view that one may give Heave-offering from what is clean for what is unclean is more or less consistent with the principle of the Houses of Shammai, but still more lenient. Eliezer's view of intention, except in respect to the cult, is congruent with that of the House of Shammai: One does not take account of what is not either done or made explicit in respect to a person's intentions.

Eliezer's opinion on the *seʾah* of unclean Heave-offering which has fallen into a hundred of clean Heave-offering is related by the redactor to the view of the House of Shammai. But, as observed, without the redactor's intrusion, one might readily reconstruct the pericope as an argument on the same issue between Eliezer and "the sages," and in this case—as the traditional commentators observed in regard to "who agreed with whom" (*Phar.* II, pp. 89-92)—Eliezer either holds the exact opinion of the House of Hillel or is consistent with it. Eliezer further agrees with the House of Hillel about how much one may drink on the day of Atonement before being culpable for violating the fast. He is consistent with the House of Hillel that a husband inherits his minor-wife only after sexual relations have taken place.

In some instances, e.g., Tos. Ar. 4 : 5, Eliezer and Joshua will stand for the House of Shammai and the House of Hillel, respectively. The evidence deriving from the better traditions does not change the picture. Redactional considerations evidently tended to put Eliezer's and Joshua's names in place of those of the Houses; or there will be disputes between them on subjects parallel to those of the Houses' disputes; or Eliezer will rule consistently with the tendency of the House of Hillel. The better traditions do not represent Eliezer as a Shammaite at all, and only once as a Hillelite. But there the issue of Eliezer's relations to the House is unimportant.

We certainly cannot claim that Eliezer was a member of the House of Shammai or that he always, or normally, agreed with them. In some instances he is consistent with the Shammaites, in others, with the House of Hillel, and in still others he disagrees with both Houses. The best traditions place him among the Shammaites in about as many pericopae as among the Hillelites; no systematization of the matter is discernible. I assume there was none because Eliezer came after the Houses and was independent of both of them. He ruled on the common agenda of laws, but when he dealt with the same specific issues as the Houses did, he did not consistently follow one or the other of the Houses. Furthermore, the great majority of his rulings are on specific details not dealt with by the Houses at all. The most reliable conclusion is that Eliezer had traditions on subjects of importance to the Houses, but these were seldom the same in detail. Eliezer cannot have been a member either of the House of Shammai or of the House of Hillel.

If so, how did he relate to the divisions of pre-70 Pharisaism? Either Eliezer was not in Jerusalem, where the Houses were evidently located, and so did not side with one party or the other, but had his own, closely related, traditions on specific, moot points. Or Eliezer was in Jerusalem, but associated with other circles of Jerusalemite Pharisaism than the Houses. They appear to have been relatively small groups—later on, it was conceived that the Houses could meet together in a single room!—and therefore would not have predominated, as they did in the early Yavnean period, in the definition of the legal agenda. Between these two possibilities, the choice is unimportant, for according either theory, it is plain that within pre-70 Pharisaism there was complete agreement on an immense number of principles. Groups or individuals differed on only a few trivial details.

vi. Eliezer and the Old Law

Eliezer's historically useful sayings provide good evidence about the main outlines of the Pharisaic legal tradition at the last half of the first century. By reviewing the several concrete legal opinions, we may assess Eliezer's part in the general state of affairs prevailing in early Yavnean times. Pericopae are enumerated according to the lists in Chapters Eight and Nine.

VIII.ii.1-2. Tos. Ter. 3 : 18/M. Ter. 2 : 1; Tos. Hal. 1 : 10/M. Hal. 1 : 10: Giving Heave-offering certainly was closely regulated by Pharisaic law. The tendency had been carefully to restrict offerings to cover only the exact species from which they were taken.

VIII.ii.3. Tos. Hal. 1 : 6/M. Hal. 1 : 6: One need not give a Dough-offering from cakes for the Thank-offering of a Nazirite. We have no idea about the prior situation. The question seems to arise first in Yavneh.

VIII.ii.4 = 15. Tos. Orl. 1 : 8: *ʿOrlah*-laws do not apply abroad. The opposite view must be that they do. Such a view should extend to the diaspora other agricultural taboos as well—for how can one distinguish between one and another?—and presumably will apply the tithing-laws as well. Eliezer is consistent on these. We cannot be sure about the prior state of Pharisaic opinion.

VIII.ii.5. Tos. Shev. 4 : 21/M. Bik. 2 : 6: The dispute between Gamaliel and Eliezer about the status of the *etrog* indicates that no firm view of the matter existed before this time.

VIII.ii.6. M. Eruv. 2 : 5-6. M. Shev. 8 : 9-10: Ilai's list shows that Pharisaism before Eliezer accepted the efficacy of the *ʿeruv*. It presumably required the *ʿeruv* in circumstances Eliezer regarded as exempt, however, and strictly enforced the use of the *ʿeruv* upon all parties to a given courtyard or alley-way. This last view is virtually certain (*Phar.* I, pp. 379-385) for Simeon b. Gamaliel held that opinion, and it was taken for granted as law.

ʿAqiba's report about Eliezer's view in regard to the use of a hide anointed by the oil of the Seventh Year suggests that prior to Eliezer the rule was strict; such a hide had to be burned.

Likewise prior to his time Pharisaism almost certainly forbade Samaritans' cooking, thus intercourse with them.

VIII.ii.7. M. Pes. 3 : 3: Earlier law does not seem to have decided how to separate Dough-offering on the fifteenth of Nisan. Nor had anyone settled the issue raised in this connection, as well as in M. Zev. 8 : 5-12 and M. Ter. 8 : 8-11, about whether one must take action to prevent a transgression of the law from taking place. The issue evidently was first raised by Eliezer and Joshua.

VIII.ii.8. M. Sheq. 4 : 7: The disposition of cattle found among property sanctified for the Temple's use introduces the issue of intention. Eliezer is in accord with the House of Shammai's view that without an explicit statement of intention, one goes only by what is actually done. Joshua is consistent with the House of Hillel's opinion: one may interpret the intention that underlies a deed. The earlier authorities debated the same principle, for instance in M. Naz. 5 : 1-5.

VIII.ii.9. M. Sheq. 8 : 6: What is decisive in determining where to burn sanctities that have contracted uncleanness is the degree of uncleanness of the source of the uncleanness, rather than the place in which it was contracted. The Houses debate the same issue. But while in No. 8 the principle is attested, here the actual facts of the case seem to have elicited attention before Eliezer's time.

VIII.ii.10. M. Yev. 13 : 2: The deed of a female child is of no legal effect. The consequences for the right of refusal, betrothals, inheritances, and the like are considerable. We have no precedent for Eliezer's opinion.

VIII.ii.11. M. Yev. 13 : 7: Not usable.

VIII.ii.12-13. M. Ned. 9 : 1-2: Eliezer makes it easy to release vows. The antecedent law certainly held one may not release vows by reference to the honor of parents or to the honor of heaven or to what happens unexpectedly. The innovation would, as Ṣaddoq rightly points out, end the practical effect of vowing.

VIII.ii.14. M. Git. 9 : 1: Eliezer permits conditional writs of divorce. It is difficult to see that the question had earlier been settled one way or the other. But Eliezer's opinion was highly controversial, so perhaps earlier practice was not to admit such a condition into the writ of divorce.

VIII.ii.16. M. Bekh. 1 : 6: The owner is liable for the redemption lamb set aside for the firstling of an ass. The earlier law cannot have settled the question. It was formerly either ambiguous or not dealt with at all.

VIII.ii.17. M. Ar. 8 : 4: One may dedicate part of his property but not all of it. We have no idea whether the opposite opinion represents the antecedent situation.

VIII.ii.18. M. Kel. 8 : 1: Eliezer says food in a bee-hive hung in the air-space of an oven will not be made unclean on account of the presence of an insect in the oven. Here it is clear that Eliezer's opinion was based on logic; the issue was new.

VIII.ii.19. M. Kel. 26 : 4: A shoe on the last is insusceptible to uncleanness because it is not completely manufactured. The principle is old, the application new.

VIII.ii.20. M. Ed. 2 : 7: A woman may wear a tiara on the Sabbath, a pigeon-racer may not testify in court. The principle of the Sabbath was established; the application is new. As to the pigeon-racer, matters are not clear.

VIII.ii.21. Repent before death: this cannot be new to Eliezer, except perhaps in the formulation of the principle.

VIII.iv.1. Sifré Deut. 221/M. Sanh. 6 : 4: A woman is hanged with her face away from the people, or her body is covered up. We cannot be sure of antecedent opinion. It hardly matters. Pharisees had no authority to hang anyone.

VIII.iv.2. M. Ker. 6 : 3: Not usable.

VIII.iv.3. Sifra Shemini 8 : 5/M. Ed. 8 : 4 (*Phar.* I, pp. 61-2): Uncleanness does not pertain to liquids. Antecedent opinion has to have been according to ʿAqiba, that it does.

VIII.vi.1. M. Ker. 3 : 10 (M. Shav. 2 : 5): If one does many individual acts of work of a single category in a single period of unawareness, he brings a Sin-offering for each act. The question does not seem to have been settled in antecedent Pharisaic legal theory.

VIII.vi.3. Tos. Dem. 1 : 3: The first fruits in the garden are always liable to tithes, for they are guarded. Antecedent opinion was divided. Eliezer is in accord with the position of the House of Shammai.

VIII.vii.2. Sifré Num. 110/M. Hal. 2 : 1: Eliezer says fruit from abroad is free of liability to the Dough-offering. Thus just as fruit grown abroad is not subject to agricultural taboos (*ʿorlah*), so it will not be subject to the tithes if it is brought back into Palestine. The antecedent rule is not clear, though it ought to have held the opposite of Eliezer's opinion.

VIII.vii.5, 6, 7, 8. Tos. Kip. 2 : 10, 16, 3 : 1, 3 : 19: Eliezer's rules about the conduct of the cult on the Day of Atonement do not suggest whether other, contrary rules come before his time.

VIII.vii.9. Not usable.

VIII.vii.10. Tos. R.H. 2 : 10: Eliezer and ʿAqiba discuss the Scriptural warrant for the Additional Services on the New Year. It is difficult to postulate an antecedent rule.

VIII.vii.11. b. M.Q. 19a: Eliezer's rule on spinning the blue-wool for the fringe does not give an indication of an antecedent opinion.

VIII.vii.12. b. M.Q. 10a/M. M.Q. 1 : 9: We cannot say whether Eliezer's rule that one may set up a new millstone in the festival week contradicts an earlier law.

VIII.vii.13. Tos. Ket. 11 : 4/M. Ket. 11 : 6: See above, VIII.ii.10.

VIII.vii.14-16. Tos. Nez. 2 : 12-13/M. Naz. 3 : 3-5: Eliezer's opinion about the Nazir's losing thirty or seven days in the event of his contracting uncleanness at the last minute does not give evidence of an antecedent tradition on the subject. The opposition evidently consisted of contemporaries.

VIII.vii.17. b. B.B. 157a/M. B.B. 9 : 7: Eliezer's opinion about an oral will is opposed by a precedent, which Eliezer rejects. Then an alternative set of distinctions is introduced. The availability of an old law seems unlikely.

VIII.vii.18. Tos. Sanh. 9 : 6/M. Sanh. 6 : 4. See above VIII.iv.1.

VIII.vii.23. Tos. Ah. 7 : 3/M. Oh. 6 : 2: Eliezer's opinion is on a minor detail of the laws of Tents and takes for granted a considerable antecedent corpus of law. But we cannot be sure the detail he contributes represents an innovation.

VIII.vii.27. Tos. Par. 5 : 9/M. Par. 5 : 7: Eliezer's opinion on collecting the water for the heifer-ceremony deals with a minor detail of what seems to be an established law, but we cannot say whether his opposition affirms the contrary detail of that established law.

VIII.vii.28. Tos. Par. 7 : 7/M. Par. 7 : 10: The same situation pertains to guarding the water.

VIII.vii.1. Tos. Ter. 9 : 9C/M. Ter. 11 : 2: On the various versions of the dispute between Joshua and Eliezer about making olives and grapes into oil and wine, respectively, we do not have a clear picture of the antecedent rule, if any, and cannot ascertain whether Eliezer and Joshua have innovated in a minor detail of a considerable corpus of decided law.

VIII.vii.4. M. Eruv. 7 : 11: Judah says Eliezer holds that one may give money to a storekeeper to secure a share in an *ʿeruv.* The sages say one may do so only by making a formal act of acquisition. Certainly Eliezer's is the more convenient way. But we do not know for certain that the earlier law held the opposite.

VIII.vii.20. Tos. Zev. 8 : 15/M. Zev. 8 : 4: If limbs of a Sin-offering are mixed up with the limbs of a Whole-offering, one may put them above the altar-fires, and the flesh of the Sin-offering above the fire is regarded as if it were wood. We do not know the antecedent opinion.

VIII.vii.21. Tos. Zev. 8 : 20/M. Zev. 8 : 8A: If a bowl of blood of unblemished offerings is mixed with bowls of blood of blemished offerings, and if one bowl is offered, then all may be offered, because it is assumed that the unfit blood has been offered, and the rest is fit. We do not know the earlier situation, but Eliezer's opinion is well attested, and it looks like an application of his own principle.

VIII.vii.22. Tos Men. 2 : 17/M. Men. 3 : 1: In respect to intent in the invalidation of the Meal-offering Eliezer's views seem to represent a considerable innovation. But we cannot be sure that the opposition drew upon established Temple-law.

VIII.vii.24. Tos. Ah. 9 : 7/M. Oh. 8 : 6: In the case of the two jars, each of which contain a half-olive's bulk of a corpse and tightly stopped up, if lying in a house, they render it unclean but themselves remain clean. If they open into two rooms of a house, the rooms are unclean. We have no idea how the earlier law might have ruled.

VIII.vii.25. Tos. Ah. 17 : 6/M. Oh. 17 : 5: Dirt from a grave area and dirt from abroad join together to make up the bulk sufficient to convey uncleanness. The sages differ. We do not know whether Eliezer originates a new rule.

VIII.vii.26. Tos. Neg. 3 : 5/M. Neg. 7 : 4-5: If a man deliberately plucked out the tokens of uncleanness, Eliezer says he may become clean again after a sign of leprosy appears and has been cleansed. We do not know the earlier law, if any.

VIII.vii.29. Tos. Uqs. 3 : 15/M. Uqs. 3 : 10 = M. Shev. 3 : 10: We do not know whether or not the opinion of Eliezer on the status of honeycomb as real estate depends upon earlier law.

IX.ii.1. Tos. Peʾah 3 : 3/M. Peʾah 6 : 2: Eliezer defines a dispute between the Houses with respect to the law of the Forgotten Sheaf.

IX.ii.3. M. Kil. 9 : 3/Tos. Kil. 5 : 18: Eliezer says either that handkerchiefs, Torah-wrappers, and towels come under the law of diverse kinds, or that they do not. The antecedent rule also is unclear.

IX.ii.4. Tos. Ter. 5 : 10-11/M. Ter. 4 : 8-11: Eliezer and Joshua dispute about the laws of neutralizing Heave-offering which has fallen into a much larger quantity of secular produce. We do not know for sure what they said, not do we have evidence of the antecedent rule, if any.

IX.ii.5. Tos. Ter. 7 : 10C/M. Ter. 8 : 3: Eliezer rules a deed begun licitly may be completed even though in the meantime it has become illicit. This was the view of the House of Hillel and should not be regarded as an innovation of Eliezer.

IX.ii.6. M. Ter. 11 : 2/Tos. Ter. 9 : 9: On whether date-honey, cider, and vinegar from winter-grapes are liquids capable of becoming unclean, Eliezer regards them as liquids. Joshua does not. We do not know the earlier rule, if any.

IX.ii.7. Tos. Shab. 15 : 10/M. Shab. 19 : 4: Whatever needs to be done in carrying out a circumcision on the Sabbath may be done. ʿAqiba said only the actual operation may be done. The earlier rule cannot have been clear, either as to details or in principle. In general, however, Eliezer is consistent with stories about Hillel on this point.

IX.ii.8. Tos. Eruv. 4 : 1-2/M. Eruv. 3 : 6-7: The Sabbath and the festival form two separate 'sanctities,' each to be observed by itself. We do not know the antecedent theory.

IX.ii.11. b. Eruv. 54b: One repeats a lesson four times. ʿAqiba says one does it over and over again until it is learned. We do not know the earlier rule, if any.

IX.ii.12. M. Pes. 1 : 7/Tos. Pis. 1 : 5: Eliezer says clean Heave-offering of *ḥameṣ* is to be burned apart from unclean Heave-offering of *ḥameṣ* We do not know the earlier law.

IX.ii.14. M. Pes. 6 : 5/Tos. Pis. 5 : 4 (+ M. Zev. 1 : 1, Tos. Zev. 1 : 1, Tos. Pis. 4 : 5-6): Regarding the Passover slaughtered for some other purpose, Eliezer's principle is that the wrong intention may impair an act of the cult. We do not know the preceding legal viewpoint(s).

IX.ii.19. b. Suk. 19b/M. Suk. 1 : 11/Tos. Suk. 1 : 10: A cone-shaped Sukkah is unfit, because it has no roof. The earlier law is not clear.

IX.ii.23. M. Ta. 1 : 1/b. Ta. 2b: The 'Powers of Rain' prayer is said on the first day of Sukkot and following. We do not know the earlier custom, if any.

IX.ii.26. Tos. Yev. 12 : 11: Eliezer would have permitted the wooden sandals of Judah's time for the *ḥaliṣah*-rite. We do not know either Eliezer's opinion or the earlier law.

IX.ii.32. M. Git. 1 : 1-2: An agent must testify as to the writing and testimony of a writ of divorce when he brings it from one village to another nearby. The earlier law is not represented, but it ought to have required such testimony only for writs originating abroad.

IX.ii.33 [= 37]. Tos. Zev. 4 : 1-2/b. Pes. 77a/M. Me. 1 : 2-3, etc.: Eliezer held that sprinkling the blood when the sacrifice is impaired is of no effect. ʿAqiba says sprinkling the blood when the sacrifice is impaired is effectual. We do not know the earlier rule, certainly not for the Temple. Eliezer's is internally consistent.

IX.ii.38. M. Ar. 6 : 1: A man who dedicated his property to the Temple and owes his wife's *Ketuvah* has to make the wife vow to yield no benefit to him when he divorces her. We do not know the earlier requirement, if any.

IX.ii.40. M. Ker. 4 : 2-3/Tos. Ker. 2 : 12-15, 3 : 5-8: A person must give a Sin-offering when he is not certain exactly what sin he has done. The earlier rule is not given.

IX.ii.44. Tos. Kel. B.M. 4 : 14/M. Kel. 14 : 7: A broken metal vessel may be rendered unclean and then clean again. Joshua says only when it is whole does it undergo these processes. We have no idea of the antecedent law.

IX.ii.45. Tos. Kel. B.B. 4 : 3/M. Kel. 26 : 2: A money-bag or a bag for pearls is unclean. The antecedent rule is not given.

IX.ii.53-56. M. Par. 9 : 4, etc.: The wrong intention in respect to Sin-offering-water will render the rite unacceptable, even though nothing wrong has actually been done. Joshua differs. The earlier rule is not before us.

IX.iii.1.1. Tos. M.S. 1 : 14: Saffron is not food, therefore is not to be purchased with Tithe-money. The principle is old. The application may or may not reflect a new issue.

IX.iii.1.8. Tos. Kel. B.M. 8 : 8/M. Kel. 18 : 9: A connector serves to bring uncleanness in respect to the piece of a bed and to render clean both parts of a bed in a ritual pool.

IX.iii.4.1. Tos. Sot. 1 : 1/M. Sot. 1 : 1: One warns a wife on his own evidence or before one witness but causes her to drink on the evidence of two. The earlier rule is hardly evident.

It seems difficult to determine Eliezer's general relationship to antecedent Pharisaic law. The cases before us do not permit speculation on the question. Unless we assume at the outset that all of his opinions represent the former law, in most cases we cannot say for sure what is new and what is not. The few instances in which we may be certain he relates to former legislation—either because he affirms it or because he changes it—are those in which his rulings are related to those of the House of Shammai or the House of Hillel. Otherwise, only in the instances in which his rulings evidently were controversial are we reasonably sure that he has said something new. These instances, therefore, will have to provide the bulk of evidence as to Eliezer's own plans for the reconstruction of the faith after 70.

Nonetheless, as we survey the areas in which he gave rulings at all, we observe little significant difference from the agendum earlier considered by the Houses. As we have shown (pp. 134-138, 161-167), no type of law important to the Houses' agendum is neglected by Eliezer; no type of law, except that pertaining to the cult, neglected by the Houses is dealt with extensively, or at all, by Eliezer. And the additional interest in the cult is for obvious reasons. Agricultural tithes and taboos, uncleanness laws, and, to a much less extent, festival and Sabbath laws form the center of his interests, as they did of the Houses. Clearly, Eliezer in general stands wholly within the established legal tradition of Pharisaism. It is considerably less clear in what way his detailed rules relate to that tradition. Perhaps each and everyone of them constitutes a major innovation in the earlier law. But even so, all together those innovations add up to very little. They concern trivial details of already decided laws; or they raise theoretical issues of no workaday importance whatever; or they raise issues not formerly considered, probably because even in theory they were not interesting or significant to begin with. Or perhaps Eliezer does, as is commonly alleged, really give the old law, standing against innovations on the part of others. But if this were true—and in some important matters it certainly is not—then the old law for which he stood is of slight interest. It still constitutes nothing more than minor and unimportant details of a legal system which no one evidently attempted to overturn or significantly to reform. Whichever way, therefore, we see Eliezer's relationship to the old law, we can learn about the old law only what we already knew, and that is about the chief areas of everyday life with which it was concerned. And these already were abundantly clear from the evidence both of the Synoptic Gospels and of the rabbinic traditions about the Pharisees. Eliezer at best supplies ample evidence about the larger, but already familiar, configuration of pre-70 Pharisaic law.

vii. Eliezer's Own Contribution

The problem of what Eliezer himself contributed is important in helping to determine his larger policy for the reconstruction of Judaism after the destruction of the Temple. As is clear, it will not be easy to isolate his own laws from possibly earlier ones. It cannot be doubted, to be sure, that Eliezer assumed Pharisaism would continue as before. It would be a liberalized Pharisaism, with more cordial relations to the Samaritans, on the one side, and to the non-Pharisees, on the other. He evidently planned that observant Pharisees would enjoy more of the Seventh Year produce, and in more ways, than was hitherto deemed appropriate. Since these specific rulings were controversial, they were important, and others, we do not know who, so strongly rejected Eliezer's opinions that it became necessary to suppress even his name. But how serious an 'incident' was produced we cannot say; the bulk of the preserved traditions reveals no hostility or systematic opposition, and I assume there was none. It was the convention of rabbinic historiography to invent dramatic "incidents" out of the evidence of conflict, and so to represent as a clash of personalities what was originally a difference, of some seriousness to be sure, in matters of law. In the case of Eliezer the story was told that he had rejected the will of the majority and had preferred the opinion of Heaven; in the case of Gamaliel, his indifference to the poverty of the other sages and his disrespect for his colleagues were made into the occasion for his deposition. In both instances the stories follow long after the fact, which was, at least in respect to Eliezer, nowhere represented accurately, except in the laws.

We shall now resurvey the cases already considered, to ascertain what evidence may be assembled on Eliezer's innovations in law. Pericopae are enumerated according to the lists in Chapters Eight and Nine.

VIII.ii.1-2. Tos. Ter. 3 : 18/M. Ter. 2 : 1; Tos. Hal. 1 : 10/M. Hal. 2 : 18: One may give Heave-offering from what is clean for what is unclean—a considerable liberalization of what evidently was antecedent practice.

VIII.ii.3. Tos. Hal. 1 : 6/M. Hal. 1 : 6: Eliezer's rule that the Nazir's Thank-offering is free of the obligation to the Dough-offering if the cakes are made for his own use should be his own. Eliezer distinguishes between what is made for sale and what is made for one's own use.

VIII ii.4 = 15. Tos. Orl. 1 ; 8: Eliezer holds that *'orlah*-laws do not apply abroad. This represents a major change. It means that the whole system of agricultural tithes and taboos will ultimately have to be declared in abeyance for the diaspora. We cannot suppose the foreign communities much cared what a Palestinian Pharisee had to say. They will have had their own customary practices for many centuries, though for Babylonia we do not know what they were.

Perhaps, like Eliezer, they supposed the biblical agricultural legislation pertained only to the holy land, but had nothing to do with the (unholy) diasporan territories. But for Eliezer to say so meant that in his view such authority as the Yavneans might inherit from the Temple over the governance of the diaspora would not be used to enforce the application of the laws of agricultural tithes and taboos.

Since the foreign countries were by definition ritually unclean, the Pharisaic rules on that subject could not apply. So Eliezer is prepared to admit that the Pharisaic laws affect only the Palestinians and have no relevance to the diasporan communities.

We do not know what other legislation Eliezer would have thought did apply to the diaspora; of the legal topics on which he had opinions, agricultural and uncleanness themes predominate, along with the Temple cult. His teachings about family law and the few items on the Sabbath and festivals remain—not much of a legacy for the foreign communities. It is therefore difficult to see that he had much to say to the exiles, and this in a time in which the numbers of Jews living abroad had been vastly expanded by the Roman conquest. Perhaps from Eliezer's viewpoint the legislation was meant to ease the burden of the exiles. They should be permitted to enjoy the gifts formerly owing to the priests of the Temple and to make use of their lands in the Seventh Year and their fruit trees in the fourth. But it is clear that the Pharisees among the exiles, no longer able to eat their secular food in ritual purity, would have been aided by the removal of the discipline of the agricultural laws. The special dietary restrictions they had observed in Palestine would thereby have been abrogated, and not only by circumstances.

VIII.ii.5. Eliezer's view that the *etrog* is in all respects subject to the law of a tree has the virtue of consistency. But it does not seem an important innovation.

VIII.ii.6. M. Eruv. 2 : 5-6, M. Shev. 8 : 9-10: Eliezer certainly applied the laws of the *ʿeruv* in as lenient a manner as possible, saying that not all parties to a courtyard in which an *ʿeruv* was located needed to participate in it, and that an ordinary fence, around however big a field, sufficed so that an *ʿeruv* in addition was not required.

His opinion on hart's tongue may be original but does not seem important.

ʿAqiba's report in M. Shev. contains two major innovations. First, the laws of the Seventh Year will not be strictly enforced, at least in respect to the hide anointed with Seventh Year oil.

Second, social intercourse is permitted with Samaritans. It would be difficult to exaggerate the novelty of this last rule. Eliezer evidently would reject the hostility evident among the Zealots toward non-Israelite populations in Palestine and the surrounding countries. Just as Jews in those countries will not be required to obey Palestinian agricultural laws and taboos, so the gentiles—for the Jews regarded Samaritans as no better than gentiles—may be treated with cordiality.

VIII.ii.7. M. Pes. 3 : 3, M. Zev. 8 : 5-12, M. Ter. 8 : 8-11: Eliezer certainly seems to have contributed the view that, if faced with a choice of taking action in order to prevent a transgression of the law or of doing absolutely nothing, one must take action.

VIII.ii.8. M. Sheq. 4 : 7: The debate between Eliezer and Joshua is not original; the same principle separated the Houses.

VIII.ii.9. M. Sheq. 8 : 6: Eliezer's principle that the degree of uncleanness is decisive in determining where to burn the unclean holy objects is not new to him.

VIII.ii.10. M. Yev. 13 : 2: Eliezer's principle that the deed of a female minor is of no legal effect produces considerable results, for it means that the hitherto ambiguous status is resolved. The female minor no longer contracts marriages, inherits, exercises the right of refusal—she no longer has to—or enjoys the perquisites of a wife in respect to the *Ketuvah* and writ of divorce. Eliezer's contribution greatly simplifies matters, but the female minor enjoys little legal protection and has no rights whatever.

VIII.ii.11. M. Yev. 13 : 7: Not usable.

VIII.ii.12-13. M. Ned. 9 : 1-2: Eliezer's view about releasing vows certainly is his own contribution.

VIII.ii.14. M. Git. 9 : 1: Eliezer's acceptance of conditions in the writ of divorce very likely is his own view.

VIII.ii.16. M. Bekh. 1 : 6: Eliezer's opinion that the owner is liable for the redemption lamb set aside for the firstling of an ass settles the question of the status of the ass. It should be his own.

VIII.ii.17. M. Ar. 8 : 4: Limitations on the extent of gifts to the Temple may be Eliezer's.

VIII.ii.18. M. Kel. 8 : 1: Eliezer's own logic has produced his opinion about the bee-hive's protecting the food within it from the uncleanness imparted by an insect in the airspace of an oven.

VIII.ii.19. M. Kel. 26 : 4: The opinion of Eliezer does not introduce a new principle. The application is of no importance.

VIII.ii.20. M. Ed. 2 : 7: The principle in respect to the Sabbath is not new. As to the pigeon-racer, we cannot say whether or not Eliezer has introduced the rule.

VIII.ii.21. Repent before death—a commonplace.

VIII.iv.1. Sifré Deut. 221/M. Sanh. 6 : 4: Eliezer's view about protecting the woman from public disgrace certainly is his own.

VIII.iv.2. M. Ker. 6 : 3: Not usable.

VIII.iv.3. Sifra Shemini 8 : 5/M. Ed. 8 : 4 (*Phar.* I, pp. 61-2): Eliezer attributes his opinion that uncleanness does not pertain to liquids to Yosi. But it may be his own conclusion, based upon Yosi's precedent, and, if one excludes the liquids specified in Scripture, we may say that it represents a major leniency in the application of the purity laws, for it will mean that dry produce becomes susceptible to ritual uncleanness only in relatively infrequent circumstances, and then by deliberate action.

VIII.vi.1. M. Ker. 3 : 10 (M. Shav. 2 : 5): Eliezer's theory that each sin will impose the requirement of its own Sin-offering is his own.

VIII.vi.3. Tos. Dem. 1 : 3: Eliezer is consistent with the House of Shammai that first fruits are regarded as guarded, therefore of value and subject to tithes. He does not originate the principle, but neither do the House of Shammai; both simply apply to a disputed case the view that what is of value is subject to tithes.

VIII.vii.2. Sifré Num. 110/M. Hal. 2 : 1: Eliezer's opinion is consistent with his view about *ʿorlah*, and, if carried through, would lead to the suspension in the exilic communities not only of the agricultural taboos, but also of the agricultural tithes.

VIII.vii.5-8. Tos. Kip. 2 : 10, 16, 3 : 1, 19: Eliezer's theories about the conduct of the high priest on the Day of Atonement presumably are new to him, but I cannot say what they implied.

VIII.vii.9. Not usable.

VIII.vii.10. Tos. R.H. 2; 2 : 10: Eliezer certainly is not credited with the composition of the New Year Additional Service or of any clause within it.

VIII.vii.11-12. b. M.Q. 19a and b. M.Q. 10a seem to represent a lenient approach to the problem of working in the festival week, but the data are unclear as to exactly what is to be attributed to him.

VIII.vii.13. As stated.

VIII.vii.14-16. Tos. Nez. 2 : 12-13/M. Naz. 3 : 3-5: Eliezer's opinion looks like an effort on his part to ease the burden on the unfortunate Nazir. But it is difficult to claim that he thereby originated a new viewpoint on the application of the law to the Nazir. It certainly is not comparable to his innovations in respect to vowing.

VIII.vii.17. b. B.B. 157a/M. B.B. 9 : 7: We do not know exactly what Eliezer suggested or why. Whether he is credited with innovating rules on the division of estates according to an oral will cannot be certainly decided.

VIII.vii.18. As stated.

VIII.vii.23. Tos. Ah. 7 : 3/M. Oh. 6 : 2: I do not see evidence that Eliezer's opinion represents an important innovation in the law.

VIII.vii.27. Tos. Par. 5 : 9/M. Par. 5 : 7 and Tos. Par. 7 : 7/M. Par. 7 : 10: Eliezer supposedly ruled in a lenient way on laws about the preparation of the Sin-offering-water, but these cases do not suggest so. In any event we are not sure that the old law was strict; it may have been that the issues first arose in Eliezer's time and that the opposition took a different view, without Eliezer's rule's representing a major innovation in the decided law. One recalls that the lenient application of purity laws in respect to the heifer-ceremony is represented as an important issue between Yoḥanan b. Zakkai and the Sadducees. Eliezer's tendency certainly is consistent with Yoḥanan's, but the specific issues are quite unrelated, and no one observes that Eliezer in this matter did precisely what his master had done.

VIII.vii.1. Not usable.

VIII.vii.4. As stated.

VIII.vii.20, 21. As stated.

VIII.vii.22. Tos. Men. 2 : 16/Men. 3 : 1: Eliezer held that intention without an accompanying action would serve to invalidate the Meal-offering and other aspects of the cult, as appropriate, and this view was opposed by his contemporaries. But if the issue was faced by Pharisees before 70, it was not in the Temple. Perhaps Eliezer's opinion, part of his larger, theoretical reconsideration of cultic law, represents an effort at revising the former situation, but we cannot be sure.

VIII.vii.24, 25, 26. As stated.

VIII.vii.29. Tos. Uqs. 2 : 15/M. Uqs. 3 : 10 = M. Shev. 3 : 10: I cannot see that Eliezer's opinion marks a major innovation in the law.

IX.ii.1. Tos. Pe᾽ah 3 : 2/M. Pe᾽ah 6 : 2: Eliezer contributes a definition of a Houses' dispute.

IX.ii.3. M. Kil. 9 : 3/Tos. Kil. 5 : 18: If we knew for sure which opinion was Eliezer's, we should be able to suggest what he contributed.

IX.ii.4. Tos. Ter. 5 : 10-11/M. Ter. 4 : 8-11: As above.

IX.ii.5. Tos. Ter. 7 : 10C/M. Ter. 8 : 3: The principle of Eliezer is consistent with the opinion of the House of Hillel, so we cannot say he contributed the view that what has begun legally may be completed even after it has become illegal.

IX.ii.7. Tos. Shab. 15 : 10/M. Shab. 19 : 4: Eliezer's view that the Sabbath may be set aside in order to do anything connected with the performance of *any* other commandment to be done on that day—not only the cult—must represent a major innovation in the law, and one which greatly limits the restrictions imposed by the Sabbath. In effect a different 'philosophy' of the Sabbath is represented in Eliezer's opinion. It is holy day, to be sure, but it is not going to affect the performance of other, equally sacred actions, which may proceed unimpeded on that day. ʿAqiba's rule would give the Sabbath precedence over other commandments to be carried out that day. In this matter Eliezer must be regarded as very lenient *vis à vis* the Sabbath.

IX.ii.8. Tos. Eruv. 4 : 1-2/M. Eruv. 3 : 6-7: This rule is consistent with the foregoing, in a general way, for it treats the Sabbath quite apart from the following festival day; the observance of each is of equivalent importance, and each is to be preceded by equal preparations.

IX.ii.11. b. Eruv. 54b: Eliezer cannot be said to have initiated the practice of oral formulation and transmission of teachings.

IX.ii.12. M. Pes. 1 : 7/Tos. Pis. 1 : 5: Eliezer's view that one must under no circumstances permit Heave-offering to become unclean is consistent with his opinion that one must make strenuous efforts to permit no such thing to happen.

IX.ii.14. M. Pes. 6 : 5, etc.: The principle of Eliezer that the wrong intention in a sacrifice is retroactively of grave importance *may* be his own contribution.

IX.ii.19. b. Suk. 19b/M. Suk. 1 : 11/Tos. Suk. 1 : 10: The principle that a *Sukkah* requires a roof cannot begin with Eliezer.

IX.ii.23. M. Ta. 1 : 1, etc.: Eliezer and Joshua evidently were attempting to solve a problem hitherto not treated at all. But I see no important principle underlying his rule.

IX.ii.26. Not pertinent.

IX.ii.32. M. Git. 1 : 1-2: Eliezer and Gamaliel both agree on the new rule, which therefore cannot originate with Eliezer.

IX.ii.33[= 37]. Tos. Zev. 4 : 1-2, etc.: Eliezer's view that sprinkling the blood when the sacrifice is impaired is of no effect may begin with him. But we do not know how things were done in the Temple, so cannot say whether Eliezer here has introduced a new principle.

IX.ii.38. M. Ar. 6 : 1: As above, No. 33.

IX.ii.30. M. Ker. 4 : 2-3, etc.: Eliezer's opinion that one may bring a Sin-offering even in a situation of doubt may be original to him, but we do not know what the Temple authorities had decreed.

IX.ii.4. Tos. Kel. B.M. 4 : 14, etc.: We do not know the earlier rule, so cannot tell whether Eliezer has made up a new one.

IX.ii.4, 5. Tos. Kel. B.B. 4 : 3/M. Kel. 26 : 2: We do not know what object was the topic of Eliezer's rule. He does not seem to have innovated a basic principle.

IX.ii.53-56. M. Par. 9 : 4, as above, No. VIII.vii.27.

IX.iii.1.1. Tos. M.S. 1 : 14: We cannot be sure Eliezer has done more than apply an old principle.

IX.iii.1.8. Tos. Kel. B.M. 8 : 8/M. Kel. 18 : 9: No new principle emerges from Eliezer's ruling, so far as I can see.

IX.iii.4.1. Tos. Sot. 1 : 1/M. Sot. 1 : 1: Eliezer defines a detail of the *Soṭah*-rite.

viii. Eliezer and the Application of the Law

Evidence that Eliezer was able to enforce the laws as he taught them is difficult to locate. We shall review the information to be derived from the best and better traditions. Pericopae are enumerated according to the lists in Chapters Eight and Nine.

VIII.ii.1. Tos. Ter. 3 : 18/M. Ter. 2 : 1; Tos. Hal. 1 : 10/M. Hal. 1 : 8: No evidence of enforcement. In Tos. Ter. 3 : 18, Eliezer cites a precedent in accord with his own view, but he does not claim the people acted on his instructions. The precedent would indicate only that people gave Heave-offering.

VIII.ii.2. Tos. Hal. 1 : 6/M. Hal. 1 : 6: Temple law. No practical consequences.

VIII.ii.4 = 15. Tos. Orl. 1 : 8: No evidence of enforcement.

VIII.ii.5. Tos. Shev. 4 : 21/M. B.K. 2 : 6: ʿAqiba kept the law as enunciated both by Eliezer and by Gamaliel.

VIII.ii.6. M. Eruv. 2 : 5-6, M. Shev. 8 : 9-10: No evidence of enforcement; contrast Gamaliel, *Phar.* I, pp. 379ff.

VIII.ii.7. M. Pes. 3 : 3, M. Zev. 8 : 5-12, M. Ter. 8 : 8-11: No evidence of enforcement. M. Zev. is Temple law, without practical consequences.

VIII.ii.8. M. Sheq. 4 : 7: No evidence of enforcement. The debate is about a principle, but no cases or precedents are brought in evidence.

VIII.ii.9. M. Sheq. 8 : 6: Temple law. No practical consequences. The same is so for M. M.S. 3 : 13.

VIII.ii.10. M. Yev. 13 : 2: No evidence of enforcement.

VIII.ii.12-13. M. Ned. 9 : 1-2: No evidence of enforcement.

VIII.ii.14. M. Git. 9 : 1: The story about the meeting to rescind Eliezer's rule suggests but does not prove that it would have been an enforceable clause had Eliezer's view prevailed.

VIII.ii.16. M. Bekh. 1 : 6: Temple law, no practical consequences.

VIII.ii.17. M. Ar. 8 : 4: Temple law, certainly without concrete results after 70.

VIII.ii.18. M. Kel. 8 : 1: No evidence of enforcement.

VIII.ii.19. M. Kel. 26 : 4: No evidence of enforcement. But for Nos. 18 and 19 the stories about the importance of theoretical rulings on cleanness-questions suggest that practical consequences were to be anticipated, at least for Pharisees.

VIII.ii.20. M. Ed. 2 : 7: No evidence of enforcement. We have no stories about Eliezer's "court."

VIII.ii.21. The chriic expansions place the matter in the master-disciple circle. The counsel cannot have produced evidence of practical application.

VIII.iv.1. Sifré Deut. 221/M. Sanh. 6 : 4: Pharisees did not hang anyone. The rule is purely theoretical.

VIII.iv.2. M. Ker. 6 : 3: Not usable.

VIII.iv.3. Sifra Shemini 8 : 5/M. Ed. 8 : 4 (*Phar.* I, pp. 61-2): No evidence of enforcement of this particular rule.

VIII.vi.1. M. Ker. 3 : 10 (M. Shav. 2 : 5): Temple law, no practical consequences.

VIII.vi.3. Tos. Dem. 1 : 3: No evidence of enforcement.

VIII.vii.2. Sifré Num. 110/M. Hal. 2 : 1: No evidence of enforcement. We do not know how the diasporan communities settled the question before 70.

VIII.vii.5-8. Tos. Kip. 2 : 10, etc.: Temple laws, no practical consequences.

VIII.vii.9. Not usable.

VIII.vii.10. Tos. R.H. 2 : 10: No evidence suggests Eliezer's exegesis produced practical results or was meant to.

VIII.vii.5-8. Tos. Kip. 2 : 10, etc.: Temple laws, no practical consequences.

VIII.vii.9. Not usable.

VIII.vii.10. Tos. R.H. 2 : 10: No evidence suggests Eliezer's exegesis produced practical results or was supposed to.

VIII.vii.11, 12. b. M.Q. 19a, 10a: No evidence of enforcement.

VIII.vii.13. Tos. Ket. 11 : 4/M. Ket. 11 : 6: No evidence of enforcement.

VIII.vii.14-16. Tos. Nez. 2 : 12-13/M. Naz. 3 : 3-5: No cases are cited in which the law was applied. Since these are Temple laws, no practical consequences in any case were possible.

VIII.vii.17. b. B.B. 157a: A precedent is cited, but not according to Eliezer's opinion.

VIII.vii.18. M. Sanh. 6 : 4: No evidence of enforcement.

VIII.vii.23. Tos. Ah. 7 : 3/M. Oh. 6 : 2: No evidence of enforcement.

VIII.vii.27-28. Tos. Par. 5 : 9/M. Par. 5 : 7; Tos. Par. 7 : 7/M. Par. 7 : 10: Temple law, purely theoretical.

VIII.vii.1. Tos. Ter. 9 : 9C/M. Ter. 11 : 2: No evidence of enforcement.

VIII.vii.4. M. Eruv. 7 : 11: No evidence of enforcement.

VIII.vii.20-22. Tos. Zev. 8 : 15/M. Zev. 8 : 4; Tos. Zev. 8 : 20/M. Zev. 8 : 8A, Tos. Men. 2 : 16/M. Men. 3 : 1: Temple law, purely theoretical.

VIII.vii.29. Tos. Uqs. 3 : 15/M. Uqs. 3 : 10 = M. Shev. 3 : 10: No evidence of enforcement or that a live issue was at hand.

IX.ii.1. Tos. Pe'ah 3 : 2/M. Pe'ah 6 : 2: Not relevant.

IX.ii.3. M. Kil. 9 : 3, etc.: No evidence of enforcement.

IX.ii.4. Tos. Ter. 5 : 10-11/M. Ter. 4 : 8-11: No evidence of enforcement.

IX.ii.5. Tos Ter. 7 : 10C, etc.: We have no data to suggest the problem came up at just this time or that Eliezer's decision produced practical results.

IX.ii.6. M. Ter. 11 : 2. As above.

IX.ii.7. Tos. Shab. 15 : 10, etc.: This is not necessarily a theoretical matter, for the latter strata contain allegations that in Eliezer's village people did things according to his opinion in respect to circumcisions on the Sabbath. If so, he was consulted as the local authority.

IX.ii.8. Tos. Eruv. 4 : 1-2/M. Eruv. 3 : 6-7: No practical application is reported.

IX.ii.11. b. Eruv. 54b: We have no stories to tell us exactly what was done, but we may suppose Eliezer taught the way he said one should.

IX.ii.12. M. Pes. 1 : 7: No evidence of enforcement.

IX.ii.14. M. Pes. 6 : 5, etc.: No evidence of enforcement.

IX.ii.19. b. Suk. 19b/M. Suk. 1 : 11: No evidence of enforcement.

IX.ii.23. M. Ta. 1 : 1: No evidence of enforcement.

IX.ii.26. Tos. Yev. 12 : 11: Not relevant.

IX.ii.32. M. Git. 1 : 1-2: No evidence of enforcement.

IX.ii.33 [37], 38, 50. Tos. Zev. 4 : 1-2; M. Ar. 6 : 1; M. Ker. 4 : 2-3, etc.: Temple law, of theoretical interest only.

IX.ii.44-45. Tos. Kel. b. B.M. 4 : 14, Tos. Kel. B.B. 4 : 3, etc.: No evidence of enforcement.

IX.ii.53-56. M. Par. 9 : 4: Temple law, theoretical issue.

IX.iii.1.1. Tos. M.S. 1 : 4: No evidence of enforcement.

IX.iii.1.8. Tos. Kel. B.M. 8 : 8/M. Kel. 18 : 9: No evidence of enforcement.

IX.iii.4.1. Tos. Sot. 1 : 1/M. Sot. 1 : 1: Temple law, theoretical issue.

All laws pertaining to the Temple are matters of legal theory and cannot have been enforced in Eliezer's time or afterward. But it is striking that other important sorts of law, for instance, tithing, agricultural taboos, and uncleanness rules, produce no evidence of how or even whether they were applied. In fact, on the basis of evidence before us we do not know that Eliezer exercised any kind of practical authority at all, except, possibly, in the matter of permitting circumcision on the Sabbath—and this was in his own village. Nor does the evidence before us permit the description of the sort of institution—whether civic or academic—which Eliezer conducted (at Lydda?), the range of its authority, or the type of activity that took place within it. So far as we know, Eliezer's laws represented his own opinion, perhaps also that of other sages, but as to the nature of his and their authority after 70, we here have no information whatsoever. The later strata do not greatly change the situation, for only rarely do they even claim to supply evidence on Eliezer's practical activities, though they assume he applied the law as he taught it. In point of fact the considerable efforts on the part of Eliezer and others to preserve and reshape the Pharisaic law appear to have been chiefly, perhaps wholly, theoretical. If such was not the case, we are unable to demonstrate it.

But Eliezer's laws are strikingly silent about the sorts of public affairs that ought to have produced cases, precedents, and evidence that laws were enforced and how this was done. The most important kinds of law should have been civil law, torts and damages, conflicts over property, real estate litigations; criminal actions (unless the Jewish population produced no thieves, robbers, murderers, and the like, and this seems unlikely); the collection of taxes, the establishment of local courts and their conduct, including rules of evidence (on which we have one saying); practical Sabbath and festival law, involving questions other than whether one brings a Sin-offering to a non-existent Temple in the case of some minor violation; the application of the laws of family life, e.g., *ḥaliṣah* (later on important in Babylonia), divorce-settlements, collection of the marriage-contract's specified dues; the rights of orphans and the division of estates; the regulation of the dietary laws observed by the bulk of the Jewish population (if there were numbers of such laws, and we cannot show that there were); and a wide range of similar, practical affairs. The sorts of laws which, for Babylonia, produced an abundance of cases are virtually ignored in Eliezer's preserved corpus. This constitutes probative evidence that Eliezer did not administer the affairs of the community and had no authority over them. He contributed little, if at all, to the formulation of laws now codified in *Neziqin* and much of *Nashim* as well as the practical tractates of *Qodashim, Ṭoharot (Niddah)*, and much of *Mo'ed*, because, like earlier Pharisees, he had no traditions on these subjects and now had no reason to deal with matters wholly outside the range of his practical authority and concern. In no way, therefore, can Eliezer's civil authority be compared to that of a later rabbi. Not only was his view of law purely Pharisaic, but so too was his conception of its enforcement. His possibilities of carrying out even the trivial laws he thought important were inconsequential. Whatever the situation of other Yavneans, Eliezer cannot be seen as a political or a civil authority.

ix. Eliezer's Program for Yavneh

While we may trace the main outlines of Eliezer's plans for the interim-period in which the cult would not be carried on, we are unable to show how, if at all, he effected these plans. It presently would seem that they were matters of legal theory, without practical consequence for the larger part of the Jewish population. That picture may change with the detailed examination of traditions attributed to other contemporaries. But it will not change for Eliezer himself, for it simply cannot be shown that he ever was able to tell others what to do, nor have we evidence about the basis in practical politics on which he might have attempted to take charge of the life of the larger community.

Perhaps his influence extended beyond the doors of his own house or the limits of his own circles of disciples and like-minded colleagues. But we cannot show it and had best not assume it. In point of fact whatever happened at Yavneh to yield evidence on the practical effects of rabbinical administration of the life of the ordinary Jews leaves no mark whatever on Eliezer's sayings. By contrast, while we do not know how Yoḥanan b. Zakkai effected his Yavnean decrees—if he carried them out at all—at least the substance of the decrees pertains to the life of common people. Eliezer legislated, in theory if not in practice, primarily for people subject to Pharisaic discipline and mainly about matters important to Pharisaic piety.

This fact underlines the conclusion already reached, that Eliezer's program for the Yavnean period concerned Pharisaism and little else. We simply do not know what, if anything, he might have had to say to non-Pharisaic Jews at Yavneh and in other parts of the country. Perhaps the saying to repent before death then would have seemed more important than it does now; but it hardly constitutes much of a program for a country which had just lost its autonomous government and capital and a people suddenly without a sanctuary or a cult.

In the aftermath of the destruction, Eliezer evidently intended to liberalize the application of the Pharisaic discipline. I see no necessary connection between his intent and the recent events. Perhaps he simply thought that by making it easier for large number of Jews to take on the Pharisaic way of living, he might win over people who aforetime were not Pharisees. Since, moreover, the Pharisaic laws enabled Jews outside of the Temple to participate in its cult in their own homes and so to share in its sanctity, he may have posited the Pharisaic way as a means of preserving both the sanctity and the symbolic presence of the cult during the interim in which they were no more. Hence it may have seemed wise to formulate the Pharisaic laws in as lenient a way as possible. But if this was Eliezer's intent—and we cannot show that it certainly was—I doubt his motive was purely propagandistic. He gives no evidence that his interest was to win as many Jews as possible to the Pharisaic way and by subterfuge to make it easier for them to undertake the sect's discipline. It is inconceivable to me that he stated a law contrary to his real opinion merely to make it more acceptable to outsiders.

The main outlines of his policy for the present age are already clear and require only brief summary. From the Jews outside of Palestine, obedience to neither the laws of tithing nor the laws of ritual purity nor the agricultural taboos would be required. For the Pharisees among them the conditions of life in exile were made considerably easier. But this was done by effectively destroying the form of their earlier piety. We have no evidence of what, if anything, was offered in its stead.

For Pharisees in Palestine the application of the primarily sectarian laws was to be done in a more lenient way than earlier. Giving Heave-offering was simplified. One no longer would have to distinguish between clean and unclean produce of the same species in the same state but might give from the one for the other. Presumably other distinctions formerly operative in the giving of Heave-offering would likewise be obscured. The laws of the Seventh Year similarly would be applied less rigidly than earlier, if the case of the hide anointed by Seventh-Year oil signifies a broader policy. Hence greater benefit from the produce of the Seventh Year would be enjoyed by the pietists. It may be that the more difficult conditions of economic life required some such lenient ruling, but we have not a shred of evidence that economic considerations figured in Eliezer's enactments.

The Pharisaic custom of providing an *ʿeruv* for carrying on the Sabbath was extended, so that, first, a fence would be sufficient to establish a single courtyard, however large; second, a person might simply buy a share in an *ʿeruv* from a storekeeper; third, for *ʿeruv-tavshilin* any sort of food, not merely bread, might be used; and fourth, dissenters or forgetful people would not be subject to pressure from their neighbors.

This last point suggests that Eliezer hoped to improve relationships between Pharisees and other Jews, on the one side, and between Jews and Samaritans, on the second. Eliezer allowed Jews to eat with Samaritans. Hence the xenophobia characteristic of the recent war was rejected in favor of a more irenic approach to relationships within the

Jewish community, formerly characterized by heated sectarian and civil strife, and between Jewry and its neighbors, earlier marked by Jewish hostility toward closely kindred groups.

The Sabbath rules were set aside in favor of other, equally important religious duties. The tendency to erect ever higher walls around the Sabbath was thus countered by Eliezer's view that the Sabbath was to be no more important than other religious requirements. Its sanctity was separate and distinct from, and no greater than, that of the coincident festival. Eliezer may have planned also to liberalize the rules governing work on the intermediate days of a festival.

Vows were to be virtually excluded from the pious life. To be sure, temperamental people would continue to make them. But Eliezer would render the nullification of a vow a routine and simple matter. One might, on any pretext whatever, simply express regret that he had vowed, and the matter was done with. The dedication of one's property to the Temple—which now would mean its destruction—was limited. An oath to give the whole of one's property to the sanctuary was null. Presumably anyone in sufficient command of his senses to refrain from giving the whole lot would be unlikely to make such a gift to begin with. Likewise, a Nazir, subject to his earlier vow, would not be forced by last minute accidents into a perpetual renewal of the binding rules. His liability was limited to a few days, rather than to the repetition of the whole spell of Naziriteship.

Consistent with his leniency in the giving of tithes and Heave-offerings, Eliezer may have intended to limit the effect of the uncleanness rules by ruling that uncleanness pertains to no liquids, except, presumably, those specified in Scriptures. Here matters are less certain; we have a number of conflicting details which seem not wholly in accord with one another or with this basic principle. Certainly Eliezer wanted to make it easy to neutralize the prohibiting effects of holy materials which have fallen into secular produce or of impaired materials of the cult mixed with acceptable materials. The rules of neutralizing Heave-offering which has fallen into secular produce are enforced in a lenient way. Mixtures of bowls of blood or of blemished and unblemished sacrificial parts will be readily rendered fit for use on the pretext that one may easily remove the prohibited substance.

Eliezer's rules on the rights of women are at variance with these lenient tendencies. He seems to have consistently applied laws to the disadvantage of females, young and mature. A minor had no legal rights of protection. A woman might be divorced and yet not wholly free to remarry anyone she wanted. A woman was not to participate in the study of the law. Her husband theoretically might impose upon her the *Soṭah*-rite for the slightest pretext or none at all. Eliezer's reforms stopped short of improving the situation of women, who, like the diasporan Jews, were given no important role in Pharisaic piety.

Eliezer evidently proposed for the cult to be ruled in accord with an orderly logic, which would settle all manner of details. What may have seemed to him illogical or inconsistent was to be rationalized. I do not see what practical consequences for the Yavnean situation were to be anticipated. Eliezer continued the earlier Pharisaic tendency to apply to the *Parah*-ceremony a less strict rule as to purity and other questions than was regarded by the Sadducees as proper. But this is not original to him and therefore has nothing to do with his Yavnean program.

One ethical issue seems important. Eliezer held that, faced with a choice of taking affirmative to prevent a possible violation of the law or of doing nothing at all, a person should assume responsibility and therefore take action. It would not be proper to disclaim responsibility and to stand aside. The contrary view was that one needs do nothing at all, so long as his own hands are not sullied.

In general, therefore, the tendency of Eliezer's own rulings seems to have been in a single direction, and that was toward the rationalization and the liberalization of the application of Pharisaic law. We cannot, to be sure, take for granted that all or even the very best attested traditions derive from Eliezer and have been formulated in his exact language. Nor is our interpretation of each detail necessarily the only possible way of seeing things. But if this view of Eliezer's own contribution is in the main valid, then it follows that what is asserted by the later tradition is absolutely correct: Eliezer really said nothing he had not heard from his masters. In an exact sense he was profoundly conservative. By attempting to reform details and to ease the strictness of the law, he hoped to conserve the Pharisaic way of piety substantially unchanged and unimpaired, essentially intact. This must mean that for Eliezer the destruction of the Temple did not mark a significant turning in the history of Judaism. Just as the destruction of the first Temple was followed, in a brief period, by the construction of the second, so he certainly supposed the same would now happen. He would see to it that the third Temple would be different from the second only in the more logical way in which its cult would be carried on, on the one side, and in the slightly simpler requirements of the application of the cult's purity rules to daily life and of the enforcement of the priestly taxes, on the other.

x. Eliezer and the Christians

The comparison of Eliezer's legal agendum with that of the Synoptic Gospels will show a number of points at which Eliezer and the Christians were concerned with the same problems. In some of these both posited the same policy; in others they followed the same tendency; at still others they were diametrically opposed. The differences show what is already obvious: that the Christians knew and rejected Pharisaic piety, while Eliezer accepted and advocated it. Since the Synoptic picture reveals the situation prevailing after 70—whether or not its portrait likewise conforms to conditions before that time is not our problem—we may make use of materials from all legal traditions attributed to Eliezer, in the theory that the Synoptics supply attestation for the issue contained in those traditions, if not for Eliezer's exact opinion on it.

1. Christian fasting: Pharisees and disciples of John fast, but Jesus's disciples do not—Matt. 9 : 14-17 (Lk. 5 : 33-39, Mk. 2 : 18-22)	1. No equivalent. The question does not occur in Eliezer's sayings, and he has no rulings on fasting, except in connection with rain.
2. Picking grain on the Sabbath—Matt. 12 : 1-8 (Lk. 6 : 1-5, Mk. 2 : 23-28)	2. No equivalent. Nor is the issue of healing on the Sabbath raised. But Jesus's stress that the sacrifices are done on the Sabbath is taken for granted in Eliezer's case of permitting the Passover and all its appurtenances to be carried out on the Sabbath, also circumcision. Eliezer's principle that the Sabbath is set aside by other religious considerations is consistent with the view attributed to Jesus that the Sabbath is no more important than other religious considerations—in this case, the presence of the son of man.
3. You have heard ... you shall not swear falsely, but shall perform to the Lord what you have sworn. But I say to you Do not swear at all, either by heaven ... or by earth ... or by Jerusalem ... or by your head—Matt. 5 : 33-7.	3. Eliezer's view of swearing is different in form, but not much different in substance. He does not say one should not swear. But he says if one does, the oath is easily rendered of no effect.

4. Do not say, What shall we eat.... Your heavenly father knows that you need them all—Matt. 6 : 25-33 (Lk. 12 : 22-23).

4. The identical viewpoint is in b. Sot. 48b: One who worries about what he will cat on the morrow is among those of small faith.

5. A disciple is not above his teacher, but everyone when he is fully taught will be like his teacher—Lk. 6 : 40 (Matt. 10 : 24-5).

5. Eliezer is said to have taught nothing but what he learned from his teacher. The (probably earlier) stories about his remaining silent when asked what he had not heard (or did not wish to tell) may be still more pertinent.

6. You say, If any one tells his father or his mother, What you have gained from me is given to God, he need not honor his father.
So for the sake of your tradition you have made void the word of God—Matt. 15 : 1-6 (Mk. 7 : 9-13; Lk. 11 : 37-41).

6. This is a point of directly pertinent comparison, for Eliezer holds the same view in respect to the annulling of vows. He regards the honor of parents as sufficient grounds for releasing a man from his vow. Therefore one *cannot* deprive the father of his honor by means of a vow. Mk. is still more pointed: "If a man tells his father or mother, what you have gained from me is *Corban* ..."

7. Not what goes into the mouth defiles a man, but what comes out of the mouth, this defiles a man—Matt. 15 : 10-12 (Mk. 7 : 14ff.)

7. This has no equivalent in Eliezer's sayings. He would have disagreed with the first statement, not necessarily with the second.

8. Scribes and Pharisees tithe mint and dill and cummin and neglect weightier matters of the law—Matt. 23 : 23 (Lk. 11 : 42: mint and rue). But dill is merely illustrative, not significant in itself.

8. M. Ma. 4 : 5: Dill's seed, plant and pods are tithed, so Eliezer. Eliezer therefore will differ in respect to the exact detail.

9. Scribes and Pharisees cleanse the outside of the cup and of the plate—Matt. 23 : 25 (Lk. 11 : 39; Mk. 7 : 3-4).

9. M. Toh. 8 : 7: The outer parts of vessels made unclean by liquids make the liquids unclean but do not make food invalid, so Eliezer. Joshua says they do. Simeon says liquids made unclean by the outer parts of vessels make other things unclean, etc. Accordingly, Jesus's saying that the outer parts of the cup and plate may convcy uncleanness is in general congruent to the opinions of all three Yavneans, who hold that the outer parts can convey uncleanness, therefore have to be cleaned (purified).

10. Pharisees fast twice a week and give tithes of all that they get—Lk. 18 : 12	10. The first point is without parallel, but the second certainly is to be taken for granted. To be sure it is not unique to Eliezer.

Eliezer's general tendency, which was in some details to ease the discipline of Pharisaic law, furthermore corresponds in a superficial way to the allegation that Jesus's burden is easy, while that of the Pharisees is difficult. But the issue seems to me external to the traditions about Eliezer, and for the Christians, what eased the Pharisaic discipline was its abrogation, not its lenient application.

The most striking points of contact are Nos. 2, 3, 4, 6, 8, and 9. The principle of Eliezer on the Sabbath's being set aside by the sacrifices is the same as the presupposition underlying Jesus's argument. It does not begin with either authority, to be sure. But they have in common the opinion that the Sabbath is no more important than various other commandments, and this is by no means clear to Eliezer's opposition. A second, and even more important point in common is the view that vowing is not to be encouraged. Jesus's instruction is not to vow at all. Eliezer's is to make vows of no effect. Both agree that a sign of faith is lack of anxiety about material things; Eliezer (like Yoḥanan b. Zakkai, b. Ber. 28b) would substitute anxiety about death, Jesus, about the coming of the kingdom. No. 6 is a more concrete illustration of the general idea of No. 3. Eliezer's revision of the law of vowing takes account of the sort of critique attributed to Jesus and vitiates its force by changing the rules of vowing so that one simply cannot in that way make void the word of God. The tithing of dill is important specifically to Eliezer; here is a point of contact and opposition. The same is so for cleansing the outsides of vessels, No. 9, but the tradition cannot begin with Eliezer. So on those points important to the Pharisaic discipline—Nos. 7, 8, 9, 10—the two authorities will take opposite positions, for Eliezer was a Pharisee, and Jesus was not. But the two are in accord in respect to the 'philosophy' of the Sabbath (No. 2), vowing (Nos. 3, 6), faith (No. 4), and discipleship (No. 5). The Sabbath and vowing, moreover, represent important innovations on Eliezer's part and are central to Jesus' critique of the Pharisees; his third point, about a conflict between ritual and ethics, of course cannot have been taken seriously by people who saw no contradiction between the two.

One cannot derive from these facts the conclusion either that Eliezer was sympathetic to Christian viewpoints or that he was aware of, and opposed to, Christian criticism of Pharisaism. It seems, as to the former, that he too recognized anomalies perceived by the Christian Jews responsible for the pericopae in which those anomalies are important. The perpetual priority of the Sabbath certainly seemed to him dubious; the disruptive effects of vows for family life cannot have been unfamiliar, and his ruling is to be seen as an effort to counter a pernicious phenomenon. As to the latter, Eliezer took for granted the importance of tithing in general, and his ruling on dill represents nothing more than the application of well-established principles to trivial matter. All authorities in M. Toh. 8 : 7 take for granted that ritual uncleanness pertains to the outer sides of vessels; the point is not moot. But no one is entirely sure what effects follow from that fact—and Jesus certainly is not clear on the point—so the issue may be new to the Yavnean Pharisees or an old tradition may have required more careful definition. So the two striking points of conflict—dill and the outer sides of vessels—seem to represent matters of some, though modest, importance in the Yavnean period. Both points of noteworthy agreement—Sabbath and vowing—reveal Eliezer as unique among the early masters of Yavneh. While the view of the subordinated position of the Sabbath is attributed also to Hillel, the stories about Hillel and the Passover on the Sabbath first surface at Usha, while Eliezer's principle for circumcision on the Sabbath is well-attested at Yavneh and cannot be regarded as something he learned through the House of Hillel.

In this connection we may reconsider the allegation of W. D. Davies, *The Setting of the Sermon on the Mount* (Cambridge, 1964), p. 315:

> ... one fruitful way of dealing with the SM [Sermon on the Mount] is to regard it as the Christian answer to Jamnia [Yavneh]. Using terms very loosely, the SM is a kind of Christian, mishnaic counterpart to the formulation taking place there ... It was the desire and necessity to present a formulation of the way of the New Israel at a time when the rabbis were engaged in a parallel task for the Old Israel that provided the outside stimulus for the Evangelist to shape the SM ...

The striking points of contact between Eliezer's legal agendum and that of the Synoptic Gospels—which center, as is to be expected, on the Pharisaic pericopae and therefore on Matt. 23/Matt. 7 and parallels—support Davies' interpretation. Naturally, the Synoptic view of Jesus focuses upon the Temple period and its issues. The Synoptics' Pharisaism is the pre-70 Pharisaism of tithing, ritual purity, and related matters. Their critique is that these are not so important as ethical actions. The points of congruence with Eliezer underline the larger similarity, for he too is a figure out of pre-70 Pharisaism, rather than of scribism or post-70 rabbinism.

Jesus is portrayed not only as an anti-Pharisee, but also as a kind of scribe-rabbi, who teaches the Torah of Moses and is an authoritative interpreter of Scriptures—a role in which the Synoptic writers never cast a Pharisee. The Synoptics' Pharisees are not represented as teachers of Torah or preachers in synagogues or lawyers in charge of the application of law or the administration of justice. Those sorts of scribes or "rabbis" also exhibit important activities in common with Jesus. Accordingly, the Synoptics' Jesus stands in close relationship both with Pharisees and with scribes. He is opposed to the piety of the one and stands against the authority of the other. But his teachings in important ways take for their detailed agenda the legal issues and problems of Pharisaism—and not all of these are resolved in a negative way—and he stands very close indeed to the conceptual world of Pharisaism. And his activities evidently were seen as the sorts of things a scribe, at least of the lower class, would have done. In a general way, therefore, the Synoptics' Jesus constitutes an amalgam of the formerly separate and distinctive traits of Pharisaism and scribism—a peculiarly Yavnean phenomenon.

CHAPTER FIFTEEN

THE ELIEZER OF TRADITION

i. Introduction

The Eliezer of tradition emerges from pericopae which cannot be shown to have been redacted either close to Eliezer's own times or among his disciples and contemporaries or their direct successors. But the themes and often the principles and detailed opinions of those pericopae are closely related to materials deriving from authorities who, for various reasons, ought to have known what they were talking about. The materials before us are called *traditions* because they represent either a later stage in the evolution of historically valuable pericopae or an addition to those pericopae which may well have begun in the earlier stages of the formation of Eliezer's materials. We certainly do not suppose that materials unattested by Yavneans or Ushans cannot have been known in Yavnean or Ushan times. We maintain only that such materials cannot be regarded as of the same order of reliability. When, however, we know for sure that themes, principles, or even detailed opinions in unattested pericopae first occurring in Mishnah-Tosefta relate closely to what has already been attested in earlier strata, we may claim sound reason to introduce such pericopae into an account of the historical Eliezer. In regard to numerous pericopae the new materials have been developed on the basis of established ones; and in regard to others new materials are consistent in theme with the already attested agenda.

1. *Agricultural Rules, Tithes, and Taboos*

Land in which one may sow a quarter-*qav* of seed—ten and a fifth *amot* square—is liable for the *Pe'ah*-gift. ʿAqiba says a much smaller plot is liable. A vineyard wholly made up of defective clusters belong to its owner. ʿAqiba says it belongs to the poor. Both rulings on Eliezer's part favor the landowner. One who keeps thorns in a vineyard forfeits the adjacent vines. Since the man has kept the thorns, it is assumed he wants them. They therefore are of value, and the taboo against mixed seeds will apply.

Arum which has grown in the Seventh Year belongs to the poor. Joshua says the poor have no claim on it. Eliezer's view is that the poor alone may eat after the beginning of the Seventh Year taboo. If one has three kinds of vegetables pickled in a single jar, as soon as one of them becomes prohibited by reason of the advent of the Seventh Year, the others may not be used either. Joshua says the opposite, and Gamaliel says one goes by the species, and their being pickled together is of no account. If one receives Seventh Year fruits as a gift or inheritance, he has to give them to people who eat Seventh Year produce. The sages say they are to be sold, not given away, and the money is then to be divided among everyone. The difference is that the sages do not want to reward the sinner. Eliezer will regard the money as prohibited, just like the fruit; the sages say it is in effect to be left ownerless.

If a person wants to give more than the required minimum of Heave-offering, he may give as much as a tenth of the crop. Ishmael says he may give as much as a half. Ṭarfon and ʿAqiba say he may give virtually the whole crop. If a *seʾah* of unclean Heave-offering fell into a hundred of clean unconsecrated food, one may raise up that unclean *seʾah*, for the one which fell in is raised up, then burned. The sages say one needs to do nothing, for the unclean *seʾah* is neutralized and may be consumed. If a hundred of unclean Heave-offering fell into a hundred of clean Heave-offering, it is taken up and burned. The sages say it is neutralized. If a *seʾah* of Heave-offering fell into a hundred of unconsecrated food and a new *seʾah* has been raised up and then has fallen elsewhere, Eliezer rules it is treated like certain Heave-offering, and the sages say it is not, unless it is in the prescribed proportion. If a *seʾah* of Heave-offering fell into less than a hundred of unconsecrated food, and the whole was then subjected to the law of Heave-offering, and some of the mixture fell elsewhere, Eliezer holds the new mixture is regarded as certain Heave-offering, and sages say it is not, except in prescribed proportion. If a person by mistake ate Heave-offering, he has to repay its value and an added fifth. Eliezer says he may pay back from one kind instead of from another, consistent with his opinion that one may give from clean for unclean produce. ʿAqiba says one pays back the same kind.

If a person takes clean olives from the press, he is liable to tithes when he nibbles on them. But if they are unclean, he is not liable. Salting them acts as the completion of their processing, so they are liable to tithes. But if they are possibly going to be returned to the vat, they are not finished. One tithes dill, caperbush, and mustard. He who separates Second Tithe is presumed to have separated the First. The sages say the opposite is the case. If a man has given the principle of the Second Tithe but not the added Fifth, he may eat the produce; the sages say he may not. Judah the Patriarch agrees with Eliezer for the Sabbath, but not for the weekday. After the destruction of the Temple, Eliezer was told that he had to continue to bring up the produce and redeem it in, or near, Jerusalem (but that law is not attributed to Eliezer in Tos., and in b. Bes. 5a/b. R.H. 31b it is explicitly attributed to Yoḥanan b. Zakkai).

Produce from Palestine which is taken abroad is liable for Dough-offering, for it was obligated as soon as it was prepared. ʿAqiba holds that the person is not liable when abroad. Small bits of dough adhere together to form the quantity liable for the Dough-offering.

Israelites who are sharecroppers for gentiles in Syria must give Tithes and are liable to observe the Seventh Year. Syria is therefore regarded by Eliezer as Jewish property, no different from Palestine. Gamaliel differs.

One may not curdle milk with the sap of *ʿorlah*-fruit. Joshua says one may do so with the sap of leaves and roots, but not of unripe figs, and all take for granted one may not use the fruit (as the Scripture makes clear). If leaven of unconsecrated food and of Heave-offering have fallen into dough, but in each was an insufficient quantity to leaven dough, while together they do so, Eliezer says the part that completed the quantity sufficient to leaven the dough will be decisive. If it is the Heave-offering, the whole is prohibited; otherwise the whole is permitted. The sages say it does not matter; the prohibited species only is taken into account if by itself it can produce the leavening. If one has anointed dishes with unclean oil and then done so with clean, or *vice versa*, Eliezer says one decides whether the vessel is clean or unclean by which oil was applied first. The sages say one decides according to which was applied last. Eliezer says one should use the unclean oil first, then the clean.

2. *Sabbaths and Festivals*

One may put bread into the oven at dusk on the Sabbath if there is time for the bottom surface to form a crust. It is permissible to carry a sword, spear, or club on the Sabbath, for these are adornments. A wick of cloth which has been twisted but not singed is not used for the Sabbath-lamp; it is necessary by an actual deed to demonstrate its purpose as a wick for the lamp, not merely by twisting. A woman may wear a tiara on the Sabbath; it is regarded as an ornament. On the

Sabbath one may not write on his flesh by scratching. One may not weave three threads at the beginning of a web or one onto what is woven. If a window-shutter is not fastened to the window-frame it may not be used to close the window on the Sabbath. Similarly, one is not to spread a cloak over a *Sukkah.* But he may stretch out the filter on the festival day and may on the Sabbath pour wine through a filter which is already stretched out. In order to render an alley-way valid, one must erect two side-posts.

Passover overrides the Sabbath in all respects—a point consistent with Eliezer's view of circumcision on the Sabbath. A person is exempt from keeping the first Passover if he is on a distant journey, which is anywhere beyond the threshold of the Temple court (an opinion attested by Yosi).

If the goat used for the Atonement rite fell ill, it is not to be carried. If the one who is to send him forth fell ill, another is not appointed in his place. If the goat was pushed down the hill and did not die, the agent is not to go down and kill it. Thus if the rite cannot be carried out under normal circumstances, it is not to be fulfilled by extraordinary means.

On the festival a disciple is to stay home with his family.

If an animal and its offspring fell into the pit on the festival, one may raise the first on condition of slaughtering it for use on the festival, and one slaughters it, but leaves the first in the pit and feeds it there.

If the community fasted and rain fell before noon, the fast is not to be completed. Others say only if the rains came before dawn is the fast cancelled.

In respect to the rules of mourning, *Aṣṣeret* is regarded as the Sabbath, Gamaliel says the New Year and Day of Atonement are treated as festivals. According to Eliezer, *Aṣṣeret* counts in the required seven and thirty days of mourning, but does not interrupt the count; it is added to the total.

3. *Family Affairs*

A eunuch sterilized by exposure to the sun submits to *ḥaliṣah*, and his brothers do so with his wife, because he may be healed. But one made so by man may not, since he can never have a remedy for his condition. Eliezer's interpretation of the old tradition, which held that a eunuch both does and does not submit to *ḥaliṣah*, competes with ʿAqiba's, who interprets matters contrariwise. *Ḥaliṣah* is not to be done at night. It may be done with the left foot. If the woman drew off the shoe and pronounced the required formula but did not actually spit, the act is invalid. If two sisters who were deaf-mutes, one of age and the other a minor, married brothers, and the husband of the minor died, his wife is exempt from Levirate marriage by virtue of being 'the sister of his wife.' Eliezer says that if the husband of the adult wife died, the minor is instructed to exercise the right of refusal against him. Gamaliel says it is better if she comes of age, and then the other will be exempt as the sister of his wife. Joshua takes a still more stringent position. Once a woman is permitted to the Levir, if he then dies, she may marry anyone at all. That is, once free of the Levirate connection, a woman permanently remains so.

A woman may marry on the evidence of a single witness that her former husband has died.

A woman's claims as to the cause of her sexual status are to be accepted. Thus if a woman says that after her betrothal she was raped and therefore has not lost her rights, she is to be believed.

A woman past puberty, or one who has waited twelve months after betrothal, or a widow thirty days from when the betrother has sought to complete the marriage may rely upon her prospective husband to annul her vows. One who awaits Levirate marriage may have her vows annulled by her prospective brother-in-law even when there is more than one Levir. Vows may be annulled in advance by a husband for his wife—that is, even before they have been made. In all three rulings, Eliezer continues the policy of rendering vows of no account.

One should not teach Torah to his daughter.

The most casual testimony is sufficient to warrant a man's divorcing his wife and paying her *Ketuvah*, if he has already warned her not to 'go aside in secret,' that is, not to commit adultery.

Four types of women may rely on their normal period in determining whether they are unclean by reason of the menstrual period: the virgin, the pregnant woman, the nursing mother, and the old woman. Joshua says he heard only the virgin may do so. The dispute of Eliezer and Joshua deals with a point at issue between Shammai and Hillel, but while the language of Eliezer is the same as the formulation given to Shammai, the opinion is different. Shammai says all women may do so, and Hillel says all women have to rely upon their examination. Yosi then differs from both, specifying only the pregnant woman and the nursing mother who have missed three periods. The attestation derives from Judah the Patriarch, who is said to have ruled according to Eliezer. M. states that the law follows Eliezer. Tos. supplies: "In Eliezer's lifetime, people would follow his opinion, but after he died, Joshua restored matters to their former condition"—meaning, to his version of the law. y. has just the opposite. Presumably because M. claims Eliezer's opinion is normative, y. has reversed the situation with Joshua.

There is no way for a *mamzer* to purify himself from his *mamzerut.*

4. *Theoretical Problems*

A high priest must make himself unclean with a neglected corpse, if the only alternative is a Nazir's doing so. If a Nazir suddenly contracts uncleanness during the final sacrifice, he loses those sacrifices which have already been made. The whole thing is to be done over again, because the sacrifices must be offered all together.

If a neglected corpse is found exactly between two cities, both cities bring heifers. If the head is found in one place and the body in another, the head is brought to the body. For measuring the location of the neglected corpse, one begins from the navel.

5-6. *Theory of the Cult. The Temple and Sacrifice*

A Sin-offering and a Guilt-offering are subject to the same rules, because both are brought in expiation of sins. The Whole-offering of a bird offered below the red line after the manner of the Sin-offering and for the sake of the sin-offering is subject to the law of sacrilege—an opinion based on a logical argument.

The substitute of a Guilt-offering is treated like the substitute of a Sin-offering. The progeny of a *ṭerefah* may not be offered on the altar. A firstling may be redeemed with a hybrid, but not with a *koy.* If one deliberately rendered a firstling unfit by slitting its ear, it may never be slaughtered, even though some other blemish may later occur in it.

The means of man's livelihood—his ox or his tools—may not be taken as a pledge for the vow of Valuation. This is consistent with the rule that one may not give to the Temple his whole property.

A heifer whose neck is broken should be in her first year, and the Red Heifer should be two years old. A Red Heifer for the Sin-offering rite that was pregnant is valid. It may not be purchased from gentiles. It may be born of Caesarean section or may be purchased with the hire of a harlot or the price of a dog. It may have as many as fifty scattered black or white hairs. It is not subject to ordinary Temple rules. Therefore one does not require the appropriate intention. It may be slaughtered by a priest with unwashed hands and feet. Intention in no respect will render invalid the Red-Heifer sacrifice. A reed pipe cut freshly from the ground for holding the water or ashes of the Sin-offering should be immersed immediately. Whatever is susceptible to become unclean on account of corpse-uncleanness, whether unclean or clean, is not regarded with respect to one occupied with the Sin-offering water as unclean with *maddaf*-uncleanness. If a jar containing the ashes of the Sin-offering is placed on top of a dead creeping thing, it remains clean. One clean for the Sin-offering rite who moved a creeping thing is regarded as still clean. Loosely-fastened boards are unclean in what concerns Sin-offering water. If one has been sprinkled by means of hyssop-berries, he is regarded as clean in respect to coming to the sanctuary.

7. *Sources of Uncleanness*

An olive's bulk of worm from a corpse, whether alive or dead, is unclean, like the corpse's actual flesh. The ash of a cremated corpse renders unclean if it is a quarter-*qav* in quantity, just like a bone. A grave-stone renders unclean by carrying. A tomb which is equal, top and bottom, renders unclean him who touches it on any spot. If there was a projection on a projecting window above the window, and uncleanness is under the projection, it does not bring uncleanness into the house. A grave-area may make a grave-area.

The semen of a *Zab* does not render something susceptible to uncleanness as a liquid. Whatever is carried on carrion is unclean. One who carries the flux of a *Zab* is unclean.

8. *Persons Subject to Ritual Uncleanness*

He who eats food unclean at a first-grade uncleanness is regarded as unclean at a first level of uncleanness, and so with second and third.

If a woman was in hard labor for three days out of eleven and had relief from her pains for twenty-four hours and then gave birth, she is regarded as a *Zabah*. If she had hard labor during the eighty days of purifying of the female child, all the blood she sees until the abortion comes out is unclean.

9. *Objects Subject to Ritual Uncleanness*

The comb-shaped filter of the water cooler is insusceptible of receiving uncleanness. If a small coin can drop through a hole in a lamp, the lamp is no longer susceptible of uncleanness. An oven cut up into rings is regarded as broken, and even though it is then reconstructed with sand between each ring, it is still broken and therefore clean. If a bucket, a boiler, a cauldron, a jug, or a wine- or oil-measure is broken so that it can no longer hold a small coin, it is clean. But if it can hold a small coin, it is capable of becoming unclean. A baker's shelf fixed to a wall is clean. A wooden vessel becomes clean if the objects usually kept in it can drop through a hole which has been made in it. A patch of new cloth which is thrown out is rendered insusceptible to uncleanness.

A quarter-*log* of drawn water at the outset invalidates the ritual pool. If a person has left wine-jars on the roof to dry out, and they were filled with rain-water, during the rainy season they may be broken into the cistern which contains a little water. But if there is no water in the cistern, they may not be broken. If a plasterer forgot his lime-pot in the cistern, and it was filled with water, if the water of the pool floated over it in any amount, it may be broken, so that its water may replenish the pool. But if not, it may not be broken. One may immerse himself in the water of an immersion pool which has in it water and mud, but not in the mud of such a pool.

10. *The Courts*

Wild animals do not have to be tried. They may be killed at random. But an ox which has killed a man is tried by a court of twenty-three judges.

12. *The Age*

On that day the sages overfilled the measure,—that is, the Shammaites' decrees were excessive.

The destruction of the Temple marked the decline in the generations. Sages became like scribes. No one now seeks (wisdom). One can rely only on God.

While excommunicated, Eliezer approved a decision of the assembly of sages that Ammon and Moab give Poorman's Tithe in the Seventh Year, attributing it to Yoḥanan and thence to Moses.

Eliezer was arrested on suspicion of being a *min.*

Gentiles have no portion of the world to come.

13. *New Subjects*

One reads the *Shemaʿ* in the evening until the end of the first watch. In the morning, one may do so from the time that it is possible to distinguish between blue and green. One should not follow a fixed text in prayer but should make up something new every day. This rule produces the further observation that there are times that a brief prayer is called for, and times that one should pray at length. The *havdalah*-prayer, "Favors man with knowledge," should be inserted in the Thanksgiving-blessing and not be said as a blessing by itself. Evidently Eliezer qualified his rule about not having a fixed liturgy; this would apply to the supplications but not to the introductory and concluding blessings of the Eighteen Benedictions. Or he contradicts himself with respect to the *havdalah.*

One is prohibited from doing a magical deed but is permitted to create the illusion of having done a magical deed.

If a man kindles a fire in his own property, it may spread sixteen cubits in every direction for him to be accountable for the damages it causes.

It is forbidden to raise dogs in Palestine.

Merely walking in a property constitutes an act of acquisition. One may make a verbal will, whether healthy or dying; real estate is thereby to be acquired by money, writ, or usucaption, and movables are acquired only by usucaption—thus a verbal will in and of itself will not be of effect. But the real issue before Eliezer should be whether there is a distinction between acquiring real estate and movables, and he says there is. Then "walking" is insufficient for real estate, so Eliezer has contradictory opinions.

If one slaughters a dying animal and the blood spurts forth, it is valid slaughtering; the animal need not jerk a leg. A cock-partridge is functionally the same as the dam, and therefore one may not take both the partridge and the eggs.

Eliezer had a good memory.

Eliezer said one should be as concerned for his fellow's honor as he is for his own, should be patient, should repent a day before dying, and should not get too close to the sages.

ii. Origins, Early Life, Education

While the Eliezer of tradition is given little more of a biography than the Eliezer of history, two important biographical themes first occur in the materials before us. To be sure, no one alludes to his station in life or to his beginnings as an ignorant man. But the relationship to Yoḥanan is made explicit in M. Avot and is central in M. Yad. Furthermore, some sort of excommunication is alluded to in

M. Yad. A story about Eliezer's excommunication therefore ought to have circulated before ca. 250 A.D. It may be that the reference to the "oven of ʿAkhnai" in M. Kel. 5 : 1 is not a later gloss, in which case the introductory element of the story of the excommunication was already settled. But the details of the story are hardly attested in this stratum of traditions.

The relationship to Yoḥanan is another matter. Yoḥanan originally is presented as praising Eliezer: "If all the sages in Israel were in one scale of the balance, and Eliezer ben Hyrcanus in the other, he would outweigh them all." That this saying is primary to the primitive structure of the pericope is proven by the list of disciples in M. Avot 2 : 9, which places Eliezer at the head of the list. It is further demonstrated by Abba Saul's correction of Yoḥanan's saying, which explicitly alludes to the primary form and rejects it: "If all the sages of Israel were in one scale ... *and Eliezer with them*, and Eleazar b. ʿArakh were in the other, he would outweigh them all." If Abba Saul's saying is authentic, then he would supply an important attestation both to the original list and to the tradition of Eliezer's discipleship with Yoḥanan. In that case, the tradition goes back to late Yavneh or early Usha. The purpose of the correction—to replace Eliezer by Eleazar—is served also by the *Go forth*-sayings, which reflect the original sequence of disciples, with Eliezer first, and then contradict it by turning the last saying into a climax, so that the first is made least and the last is made greatest. The same hand which inserted this may also have reversed the attributions of Eliezer and Eleazar, for it is better to be a flowing spring than a plastered cistern. (That it is better to come first than last is shown by the question, "Why did the House of Hillel merit having the law following their opinion? ... Because they were kindly and modest, and placed the opinion of the House of Shammai ahead of their own." So they gave the advantage to the opposition—a sign of modesty.)

It seems that the downgrading of Eliezer, which breaks the symmetry of the form, reflects the (still mysterious) event involving his disgrace and excommunication. The sayings which put him first ought to antedate these events. But if they do, they establish very early what no internal evidence even hints at, namely the discipleship with Yoḥanan. They possibly come from Eliezer's own circle and probably would have surprised Yoḥanan himself. At any rate we have no reason to suppose the highly stylized materials in M. Avot 2 : 8-9 derive from Yoḥanan himself.

M. Yad. 4 : 3 is firm on Eliezer's having studied with Yoḥanan. It is an equally peculiar pericope. It represents Eliezer as living in isolation from the other masters, though it does not explain why. Still, the story is further evidence that something has happened to set Eliezer apart, though the details have not yet been made definite. Yosi the son of the Damascene is then asked, "What new thing came up in the house of study today"—the first indication that the Yavnean gathering constituted a "house of study." Yosi then tells Eliezer that the group has voted that Ammon and Moab give Poorman's Tithe in the Seventh Year. Eliezer says that is exactly what he heard from Yoḥanan. The original debate involves Ṭarfon, who says they must give Poorman's Tithe, and Eleazar b. ʿAzariah, who assigns them Second Tithe, with Joshua and Ishmael siding with Ṭarfon. Gamaliel is not included in the pericope, but he does appear in M. Yad. 4 : 4. And in M. Yad. 4 : 2, Eliezer himself occurs, to be sure, in an interpolation irrelevant to the pericope. The larger setting therefore is puzzling.

Still more curious is the representation of the whole assembly as imposing on the lands of Ammon and Moab the Jewish agricultural taxes. These would presumably have to be paid over the dead bodies of the predominantly gentile inhabitants of Ammon and Moab. So Yoḥanan is now discovered to have been a crypto-revolutionary—not alone, but along with the whole of the *on-that-day* consistory, which now includes, in redactional context, both Eliezer (explicitly) and Gamaliel (implicitly)! The inclusion of Eliezer is impossible, for M. 4 : 3 forthwith excludes him; Gamaliel can be accounted for in the theory that he participated as a private person, no longer as *nasi*.

But the content of the saying attributed to Yoḥanan *via* Eliezer is as suspicious as its form; both are probably fraudulent. The secret teaching was revealed by Eliezer only when he was in a state of excommunication, so that he never is given the opportunity to deny the reported revelation at the actual consistory. The story is incredible. But the problem of who made it up cannot be neglected (see below, section iv).

The pericopae before us therefore lead to the supposition that Eliezer was a disciple of Yoḥanan. His early life is still unilluminated. But no one now doubts Eliezer was a student of Torah and derived his traditions from the first master of Yavneh. The traditions moreover underline the already-evident motif that something has happened to isolate Eliezer from his colleagues but are not clear on exactly what might have happened. It is taken for granted, however, that he was by himself. Had he been excommunicated, Yosi should not have had to come to him—later stories say even ʿAqiba kept his distance—so perhaps the excommunication was not yet part of the account of Eliezer's "estrangement." But we have no better idea of what might have been alleged.

iii. Eliezer's Active Career

We have no evidence about what Eliezer actually did either for a living or within the Yavnean gathering. To be sure, the problem of what to do with fruits of the Second Tithe suggests he possessed some sort of land and farmed it. But we do not know how large were his possessions or how much of an income was yielded by them. The same source says they were at Lydda, and since most materials —except the ʿAqiba-centered death-scene—are firm on placing Eliezer there, we do not have to wonder where he lived. His reference in M. Git. 1 : 1 to Lydda further suggests, but does not confirm, that he spent time there.

This means he was not domiciled at Yavneh. Indeed, no available tradition places him in Yavneh at any point in his career, so we do not know his relationship to the gathering there. Perhaps a number of local authorities (but we do not know what their authority consisted of) were in communication with the Yavnean gathering or with Gamaliel himself but spent the bulk of their time in their own towns.

The story about the fast in Lydda further suggests that Eliezer exercised some sort of religious authority in the town; we do not know upon what basis or for what areas of ordinary life. The view that he was able to effect his view of what to do in connection with circumcision on the Sabbath reenforces the theory that in Lydda he was an authority in minor matters of religious practice. He is not represented as a civil administrator; he did not judge cases of torts, damages, or other domestic conflict; he had no place in the administration of justice, criminal (except for homicidal oxen) or otherwise.

To be sure, he would now seem to have had disciples in attendance, but we still do not know for what purpose he gathered and educated them, nor are we certain he bestowed upon them any form of certification or rabbinical recognition. The stories about relationships to disciples concern festival behavior—covering the *Sukkah* with a cloak, spending *Sukkot* at home, and domestic matters—mourning practices and the like. He is further represented as being asked a series of questions about the Day of Atonement, and these questions, reenforced by the traditions in quite different form handed on in Eliezer's name by Judah, strongly suggest he taught laws about the Temple's rites on that day.

In all, therefore, we may safely suppose Eliezer did teach some laws, and, so far as the disciples' involvement is concerned, they were about festival behavior and Temple rites on the holy day—not much of a legacy. The stories in M. Neg. 9 : 3 and 11 : 7 further portray him as explaining inherited traditions and approving the explanation of disciples. We need not doubt, therefore, that he held and handed on antecedent traditions of some sort; they need not have been limited to the cult and the sacred calendar. But it is difficult to demonstrate what other topics were included.

iv. Eliezer's Historical Situation. Pharisaism and Rabbinism

The established view of Eliezer as a Pharisee certainly is confirmed by the topics and substance of the materials before us. He still has no "rabbinical" sayings about study of Torah and the like. Strikingly, he does say it is better to stay home on the festival than to come to the master. Later versions of the saying produce a sermon making the opposite point, now in accord with the rabbinical view about the priority of study of Torah, therefore of the master over the family. Perhaps the first instruction was thus revised to make Eliezer conform to later opinion on the subject. While a large number of sayings pertains to the Temple, none affirms that study of Torah is equivalent to sacrifice or that the rabbi is the new priest or similarly important rabbinical allegations.

What is strikingly new in the traditions is the claim that Eliezer was in favor of war in general and of the expansion of the Jews' territories in and around Palestine in particular. To be sure, the whole of the Yavnean consistory is represented as imposing upon Moab and Ammon the Jewish agricultural taxes, so in this respect Eliezer does not stand alone. But Eliezer is supposed to have contributed the approval of Yoḥanan b. Zakkai, a remarkable and incredible claim. To that claim one must add Eliezer's own view that Syria is to be regarded as no different from Palestine. What this means is that the Jews are regarded by him as rightful owners of Syria, as much as of Palestine, and therefore must pay the same taxes they would pay if living within the borders of Jewish Palestine. To effect such a claim obviously would involve the Jews in a greater war than that of 66-73. Gamaliel is further represented as opposing Eliezer on this question, and well he might, for he was supposed to have been the Jews' delegate to the Roman government and could hardly have joined those who would foster a new war against Rome and extend the limits of the war to include the nearby diaspora communities. Eliezer's opinion on war—expressed in the rule that a sword is an ornament—is consistent. To these laws one may add the sentiment that gentiles have no portion in the world to come. The *mamzer* likewise may not improve his status—so a generalized xenophobia, appropriate to the laws about the status of Syria and carrying a sword on the Sabbath, extended to the excluded caste of Israel itself.

These allegations, first occurring all at once in the stratum of traditions about Eliezer, do not necessarily contradict the quite contrary allegations of the historically reliable stratum composed of the best and better traditions. It may be argued that approving an alliance with the Samaritans was meant to correct a major error in the earlier war, for it was now clear that the Jews could do nothing without reliable allies. The liberalization of the Pharisaic discipline and the mitigation of its effects on non-Pharisees likewise might constitute an effort to unify the local population and to limit the decisive effects of the peculiar practices of what was now the regnant, or at least, a highly influential, sect. The declaration that the whole discipline would not apply to the diasporan communities would produce the same effect. In the event of Pharisaic domination of a reconstituted, and greatly enlarged, Jewish state, it would be unnecessary for the diasporan Jews to undertake the expensive tithes and the onerous uncleanness-taboos of the Pharisees. Their Sabbath rule would, moreover, be imposed lightly. But, to be sure, this concession would not effect the immediately surrounding countries—Syria, Moab, and Ammon—which would be incorporated into the greater state. I see no connection, to be sure, between this proposed interpretation of the new materials and Eliezer's opinion that the generation of the wilderness will inherit the world to come; I cannot imagine any special group of Jews of the first century who traced their lineage back to that generation in particular.

It therefore seems possible to harmonize the portrait given by the best and better traditions with the sharply different one presented in the fair ones. But the two are so clearly at variance with one another, and each is so strikingly limited to its own stratum, that an alternative explanation may be called for. The historical Eliezer, like his alleged master, Yoḥanan, indeed did oppose war in general and (possibly) the war against Rome in particular; he did seek to alleviate the burden of the Pharisaic discipline on non-Pharisees and to limit its demands upon Pharisees and did propose a more tolerant attitude toward non-Jews in Palestine and Jews in the diaspora. Then the Eliezer of history is misrepresented in the stratum of traditions. He is now alleged to have advanced the opposite of his former policies. So the new materials come later and strikingly revise and contradict the old.

At what point in the evolution of the tradition would such a complete revision of his former attitudes have been introduced? It cannot have derived either from ʿAqiba or from Ilai, both of whom play important parts in the earliest portrait. Then it should have either come from a different set of Yavneans or, more likely, appeared after Yavneh, some time between ca. 120 and ca. 180. In that case the predominant party in the production of traditions will have been the disciples of ʿAqiba, who themselves probably favored the war of Bar Kokhba and therefore insisted their master, ʿAqiba, was among his supporters (see Appendix I), and retroactively turned into militarists not only Eliezer, but also Yoḥanan himself, indeed along with the whole of the Yavnean consistory assembled, according to their claim, *on that day*. Then only Gamaliel is left out of the war-party. It would have been difficult to claim otherwise, with Gamaliel's son Simeon in charge of the Ushan authority and his grandson Judah in closest ties with the Roman regime itself. The revision of the historical Eliezer into an xenophobic militarist therefore does not stand alone in the treatment of the Yavnean materials. The disciples of ʿAqiba did far more to revolutionize the former picture of Yoḥanan (*Development of a Legend*, pp. 16-17, 27-29). Eliezer cannot be seen as a particularly important figure. What appears likely is that wherever they could invent stories to show Yavneans favored war against Rome, they did so. When it was possible to turn an uncompromising statement in favor of pacifism into an ambiguous statement that study of Torah would guarantee success, they also did so. These larger tendencies touched—if lightly—upon the traditions about Eliezer and produced allegations strikingly at variance with the first, and more accurate picture. But this revision was not everywhere effected in the formulation of traditions about Eliezer and did not evidently produce the systematic effort to falsify existing allegations to the contrary.

The Eliezer of tradition therefore is represented in a way we could not have anticipated on the basis of the materials behind the Eliezer of history. The changes, though few, are discrete and unrelated and do not look as though they are the product of a single hand or a single circle. They therefore should be seen as representative of a larger tendency on the part of a considerable part of a generation of authorities to justify war and foster militarism and xenophobia. But the historical Eliezer ought to have had no part in such an approach to the Jews' relationships to other peoples in general and to Rome in particular. He had lived through the disastrous war and witnessed the destruction of the Temple. How he proposed to secure the right to rebuild the Temple and reconstitute its cult we do not know. He might, to be sure, have expected that war would serve to accomplish these messianic purposes. But having seen the inability of the Jews to unite in one war and their proved tendency to alienate the neighboring peoples, he ought to have sought another, more promising way toward the same end. That way can only have been collaboration with Rome, not sedition or rebellion.

Since Gamaliel, alleged to have been Eliezer's brother-in-law, almost certainly advanced exactly that policy, it is not far-fetched to claim that Eliezer did likewise. Among the masters of the Yavnean period, he ought to have taken the part of the patriarch. Among the opposition should have been both ʿAqiba and his close associate, Joshua. Since both the deposition of Gamaliel and the excommunication of Eliezer are represented as the result of encounters with Joshua—in the one case because of the patriarch's "high-handedness" and in the other because of Eliezer's failure to accede to the opinion of the "majority"—it would appear that the war party was led by, or at least claimed to rely upon the authority of, Joshua and ʿAqiba. Now that claim in regard to ʿAqiba stands against the internal evidences already surveyed, which have ʿAqiba as a major authority for Eliezer's traditions overall and for the ones friendly to Samaritans and others in particular. If we rely upon the materials attested by ʿAqiba and Ilai, we have to reject those evidently produced by the Ushan successors of ʿAqiba. But then ʿAqiba's testimony with respect to Eliezer contradicts the later view of ʿAqiba himself. Similarly, the sayings attributed to Yoḥanan in favor of peace are contradicted by those appearing in documents attributed to ʿAqiba's disciples. So it is the disciples—or authorities claiming to be disciples—who have revised the pictures not only of Eliezer and Yoḥanan, but possibly of ʿAqiba himself. Of this, obviously we cannot be certain.

v. Eliezer and the Houses

Eliezer's relationship to the Houses of Shammai and Hillel is no more important a subject and no more consistently treated here than in the historically most useful traditions. The pertinent materials are as follows:

1. M. Nid. 1 : 3—Eliezer rules on the same issue as Shammai and Hillel, but differs from both.
2. M. Kil. 5 : 8—One's actions fully reveal intent. Therefore keeping thorns in the vineyard indicates they are of value. This is consistent with the view of the House of Shammai.
3. M. Shev. 9 : 9—One may eat the produce of the Seventh Year by favor, the opinion of the House of Shammai.
4. M. Ter. 5 : 4—Eliezer is represented as parallel to the House of Shammai, but in point of fact the result of his ruling is consistent with the opinion of the House of Hillel (= "The Houses agreed with the Hillelite opinion, and Eliezer afterward made *his* rule.").
5. M. Shab. 1 : 10—Eliezer is in accord with the lenient tendency of the House of Hillel.
6. M. Shab. 2 : 3—*If* the issue is intention, Eliezer is consistent with the House of Shammai, ʿAqiba, of Hillel.
7. M. Pes. 6 : 1—Eliezer is in the position of Hillel, ʿAqiba of "them" (= Bené Bathyra).
8. M. Ned. 10 : 5-6—Eliezer is consistent with the House of Shammai's view that the word (M'MR) effects acquisition, so b. Ket. 74a.

At Usha the Houses constituted a far less important element in the formation of traditions than they had earlier. The allegation that they had really loved one another or that the Shammaites had not carried out the law in accord with their own opinions was important, as we have seen (*Phar.* II, pp. 190-193), in connection with the Bar Kokhba war. It follows that the assignment of an authority to a given House should have been less important than earlier, when, with the Houses present in the Yavnean gathering, the issues dividing them still were vital. And it should have been less important than later on, in Rabbi's time and afterward, when it became convenient to settle most points in Mishnaic law by a systematic decision in favor of one party and against another. Eliezer then was placed in the House of Shammai by those Palestinians, following Judah the Patriarch himself, who were engaged in a larger effort at systematization of the decision-making process, with formulae and patterns imposed upon what earlier were random and episodic differences. Consequently, we find Eliezer's relationship to the House of Shammai is of no great consequence in the formulation of the traditions, which themselves rely upon historically viable but highly contradictory materials assigning Eliezer to the House of Shammai, or the House of Hillel, or neither House.

vi. Eliezer and the Old Law

It is difficult to assess in detail the relationship between Eliezer's legal sayings and the antecedent law. At some points it seems Eliezer with his contemporaries attempted to make sense of obscure traditions. So, first, there was an old tradition in the hands of the Yavneans. But this tradition was not clear and cannot have come down in a single, fixed, final, "oral" formulation. At other points, second, Eliezer and others seem to have applied established principles—e.g., on the Seventh Year—to new, or formerly unconsidered details, or Eliezer differed from the old law. At still others, third, Eliezer and his contemporaries seem to have worked out laws for situations formerly not dealt with at all or not subjected to precise definition.

In the first category are X.i.1 and X.ii.7, 11, 13, 14, 27, 29, 44 [60], 66, 98-99.

In the second category are X.ii.5, 6, 8, 9, 10, 12, 16, 17-19, 20, 22, 26, 26A, 28, 30, 31, 32, 33, 35, 37, 41, 45, 46, 55, 56, 57, 58, 59, 62, 83-90, 100-110, 118-120.

In the third are X.ii.1-2, 3, 4, 23, 24, 25, 26B, 34, 38, 39, 40, 42, 43, 43A, 47, 48, 49, 51, 52, 53, 54, 61, 63, 64, 65, 66 (all), 67, 68, 69-78, 91-97, 111-111A, 112-115, 116-117, 124, 125.

X.i.1. M. Nid. 1 : 3—Eliezer, Joshua, Shammai, and Hillel all differ on when a woman is deemed unclean. Joshua refers to having "heard 'only a virgin.'" Perhaps some antecedent tradition on the subject existed, but we do not know what it was.

X.ii.1-2. M. Ber. 1 : 1-2—No rule on exactly when the *Shemaʿ* is to be said could have come before Eliezer's time.

X.ii.3. M. Ber. 4 : 3-4—Eliezer favored the earlier situation, in which there evidently was no fixed text for the Prayer.

X.ii.4. M. Ber. 5 : 2—Eliezer and ʿAqiba had no firm tradition on where to insert *havdalah.*

X.ii.5. M. Pe'ah 3 : 6—Eliezer, Joshua, Ṭarfon, Judah b. Batyra, and ʿAqiba cannot have had any tradition at all on the size of a field liable to *Pe'ah.*

X.ii.6. M. Pe'ah 7 : 7—A field composed wholly of defective clusters presents a new problem. Eliezer's and ʿAqiba's difference suggests there was no earlier rule.

X.ii.7. M. Kil. 5 : 8—Thorns in a vineyard—Eliezer is consistent with the principle of intention as formulated by the House of Shammai.

X.ii.8. M. Shev. 5 : 3—The poor may enjoy arum in the Seventh Year. Joshua differs, so there probably was no antecedent rule.

X.ii.10. M. Shev. 9 : 5—Pickled vegetables are prohibited at the Seventh Year according to the earliest date. The rule that the prohibition applies to stored food when it applies to the same part in the field is taken for granted.

X.ii.11. M. Shev. 9 : 9—The Seventh Year produce is free to all, an old rule.

X.ii.12. M. Ter. 4 : 5—How large a portion of the crop may be given as Heave-offering does not appear to have been decided before Eliezer's time.

X.ii.13. M. Ter. 5 : 2, 4, 5, 6—The Houses debated the same sort of problem. Eliezer's fundamental principle, that what has fallen in may be lifted out, does not suggest what the old law might have decreed.

X.ii.14. M. Ter. 6 : 6—The old law should be opposite Eliezer's, as in M. Ter. 2 : 1. ʿAqiba should represent the old law, if it ruled on the question.

X.ii.16. M. Ma. 4 : 3—The old law held that when the processing is completed, produce is liable for the tithes. Eliezer and the sages apply that rule.

X.ii.17-19. M. Ma. 4 : 5, 6, Tos. Ma. 3 : 7—The law of tithing is applied to unimportant herbs and fruits.

X.ii.21. Tos. M.S. 3 : 16—The old law cannot have been clear on this point.

X.ii.22. Tos. M.S. 4 : 5—If a person has set aside the value of the Second Tithe but not the added fifth, he may eat the produce, so Eliezer. The earlier law would not seem to have settled the question.

X.ii.23. M. Hal. 2 : 1—The liability of Palestinian produce taken abroad does not appear to have been decided before Eliezer and ʿAqiba.

X.ii.24. M. Hal. 2 : 4—The law before Eliezer does not seem to have settled the question.

X.ii.25. M. Hal. 4 : 7—The earlier law cannot have determined the status of Syria. The issue is political, not legal.

X.ii.26. M. Orl. 1 : 7—The earlier law is clear. Eliezer applies it to a trivial detail.

X.ii.26A. M. Orl. 2 : 11—The earlier rule ought to be represented by the sages: Only a quantity sufficient by itself to do the leavening will prohibit the dough.

X.ii.26B. M. Orl. 2 : 13—Here it is difficult to see that the law before Eliezer dealt with the problem.

X.ii.27. M. Shab. 1 : 10—The old law is made by the Houses, and Eliezer stands close to the House of Hillel.

X.ii.28. M. Shab. 6 : 4—The principle is old. Its application is moot.

X.ii.29. M. Shab. 2 : 3—The issue is signifying intention.

X.ii.30. Tos. Shab. 4 : 6—Application of established principle.

X.ii.31. M. Shab. 12 : 4—Scratching on flesh is prohibited as writing—perhaps Eliezer's contribution.

X.ii.32. M. Shab. 13 : 1—Definition of an established prohibition.
X.ii.33. M. Shab. 17 : 7—Definition of an established prohibition.
X.ii.34. M. Shab. 19 : 1—Sabbath-sanctity is no greater than that of other commandments—Eliezer's own innovation (in context).
X.ii.35. M. Shab. 20 : 1—Application to a new case of an established principle.
X.ii.37. M. Eruv. 1 : 2—New definition for an established custom.
X.ii.38. M. Pes. 6 : 1—Same as No. 34.
X.ii.39. M. Pes. 9 : 2—Eliezer's definition of "a distant journey" in effect abrogates the old law.
X.ii.40. Tos. Kip. 3 : 14—We do not know the established rule.
X.ii.41. Tos. Suk. 1 : 9—New application of an established law.
X.ii.42. Tos. Y.T. 3 : 2—No earlier ruling seems evident.
X.ii.43. M. Ta. 1 : 1—No antecedent tradition is likely.
X.ii.43A. M. Ta. 3 : 9—No antecedent tradition is likely.
X.ii.44. M. Yev. 8 : 4—The old traditions were contradictory. ʿAqiba and Eliezer interpret them.
X.ii.45-46. M. Yev. 12 : 2-3—Eliezer's opinions do not reflect the earlier state of the law. The exegetical dispute with ʿAqiba suggests there was no established law.
X.ii.47. M. Yev. 13 : 6-7—No antecedent traditions seem evident.
X.ii.48. M. Yev. 16 : 2—No antecedent tradition seems evident.
X.ii.49. M. Yev. 16 : 7—Eliezer and Joshua repeat Gamaliel's rule, for which antiquity is not claimed. So the whole is new.
X.ii.51-54. M. Ket. 1 : 6-9—No antecedent tradition is indicated.
XII.ii.55-56. M. Ned. 10 : 5-6—The earlier law should have held the opposite of Eliezer's view.
XII.ii.57. M. Ned. 10 : 7—The earlier law should have held the opposite of Eliezer's view.
X.ii.58-59. M. Naz. 6 : 11, 7 : 1—Eliezer's rule seems new, since the precedent looks like a good one. So the earlier law held as do the sages.
X.ii.60. M. Naz. 7 : 4—Not relevant. Eliezer does not contribute to the illumination of the earlier tradition.
X.ii.61. M. Sot. 3 : 4D—Eliezer's opinion does not suggest the earlier rule.
X.ii.62. M. Sot. 6 : 1—The application of the established law seems new in theory.
X.ii.63-5. M. Sot. 9 : 2-4—The issues look new.
X.ii.66. M. Qid. 3 : 13—Ṭarfon's theory looks like his own invention, in which case Eliezer would stand for the *status quo.*
X.ii.66A-E. M. B.Q. 6 : 4—The issue is new.
M. B.B. 9 : 7—*If* the issue is how to acquire real estate and movables, then the antecedent law should be given in the precedent.
M. Sanh. 1 : 4—The issue must be new.
X.ii.67-68. M. Zev. 1 : 1, 7 : 4—Eliezer's theory is his own.
X.ii.69. M. Hul. 2 : 6—The old law cannot be before us.
X.ii.70. M. Hul. 12 : 2—The old law cannot be before us.

X.ii.71. M. Bekh. 1 : 5—The old law cannot be before us.
X.ii.73. M. Bekh. 5 : 3—The old law cannot be before us.
X.ii.74. M. Ar. 6 : 3—The old law cannot be before us.
X.ii.75-6. M. Tem. 3 : 3, 6 : 5—The old law cannot be before us.
X.ii.78. M. Ker. 6 : 1, 3—The old law cannot be before us. But the allegation is that Baba b. Buṭi did as Eliezer said.
X.ii.83-90. M. Kel. 2 : 8, 3 : 2, 5 : 10, 14 : 1, 15 : 2, 17 : 1, 27 : 12, 28 : 2—In these instances it looks as if Eliezer and the sages differ on applying established principles.
X.ii.91-97. M. Oh. 2 : 2, 2 : 4, 9 : 15, 12 : 3, 14 : 4-5, 17 : 2—It is difficult to see what, if any, traditions might have come before Eliezer's rulings on what seem to be problems introduced by him or first raised in his time. 14 : 4-5 seems a new problem spun out of an established law.
X.ii.98-99. M. Neg. 9 : 3, 11 : 7—In both cases the old tradition was unclear.
X.ii.100-110. M. Par. 1 : 1, 2 : 1, 3 : 5; 4 : 1, 3; 5 : 4, 10 : 1, 10 : 3, Tos. Par. 10 : 4, M. Par. 11 : 2, 7—We may assume, from the observation that in *Parah*-law, Eliezer introduced a lenient viewpoint, that the earlier law in all instances was strict and imposed the normal sanctuary law on the *Parah*-rite, even though it was done outside the Temple. But in matters of purity, it is alleged that the Pharisees in general agreed with him.
X.ii.111-111A. M. Toh. 2 : 2, 8 : 7—The earlier law cannot have settled either problem.
X.ii.112-115. M. Miq. 2 : 4, 2 : 7, 2 : 8, 2 : 10—Eliezer's several distinctions look new, but we cannot be sure Joshua represents the old law.
X.ii.116-117. M. Nid. 4 : 2, 4—Eliezer's and Joshua's problem seems to be new.
X.ii.118-120. M. Maksh. 6 : 6, Zab. 5 : 3, 7—Eliezer says the *Zab's* semen is not a liquid; that he who carries carrion or a *Zab's* semen is unclean—his own glosses of existing law, so it would seem.
X.ii.124. Tos. Sanh. 11 : 5—We do not know the earlier rule, if any, regarding sorcery. Eliezer's distinction looks original.
X.ii.126. M. Yad. 4 : 3—There was no earlier law.

The old law, attested by Eliezer's sayings either in agreement or disagreement, therefore laid down general rules about the agricultural tithes and offerings; Eliezer and his colleagues applied them. Or, as in the cases of the *Shemaʿ* and of the liability to *Peʾah*, among many other matters, Eliezer and his colleagues gave precise definition to what formerly seems not to have been defined at all. Established prohibitions furthermore were defined and applied to new cases. Sometimes such definitions actually abrogated existing rules. But the claim is not made that a new rule has been laid down. Certainly in respect to *Kelim*, the established principles ought to have come long before Eliezer's time; the issues all are trivial and do not pertain to fundamental definitions of law, rather to applications of existing rules. The several pericopae in *Ohalot*, by contrast, contain problems probably invented by Eliezer, along with Joshua, for the application of existing rules; the basic principles cannot have been set down by the early Yavneans, and the pericopae make no such claim.

By contrast, Eliezer's tendency in *Parah*-law is noteworthy for its leniency. But the principle that the *Parah*-ceremony is subject to less severe rules than those applying to the Temple is introduced into pericopae involving Yoḥanan b. Zakkai and the Sadducees. So the issue should have been current in Yavnean times and certainly was resolved in favor of the position attributed here uniquely to Eliezer and elsewhere to the Pharisees as a whole.

In all, the work of Yavneh as revealed by Eliezer's legal pericopae consisted, as stated, of three separate but closely related tasks: first, the clarification of obscure traditions; second, and far more important, the application of established laws to new cases and the invention of new problems for solution according to existing norms; third, the development of some new legal interests and the consequent generation of new rules. If our rough estimate of the pericopae before us is sound, then the second and third tasks should have been of approximately equal importance. Eliezer on the whole appears more often as an innovator than as a conservative.

vii. Eliezer's Own Contribution

We shall now review the legal materials produced by the evolving traditions about Eliezer, in order to isolate elements possibly originated by Eliezer himself.

X.i.1. M. Nid. 1 : 3—We do not know whether Eliezer's opinion begins with him. The issue probably does not.

X.ii.1-2. M. Ber. 1 : 1, 2—Eliezer said the *Shemaʿ* had to be read early in the evening and late(r) in the morning.

X.ii.3. M. Ber. 4 : 3-4—There should be no fixed text for the Prayer. This is certainly original to Eliezer but is in the setting of current issues.

X.ii.4. M. Ber. 5 : 3—The insertion of *Havdalah* is a current issue, part of the formulation of the liturgy.

X.ii.5. M. Peʾah 3 : 6—The size of a field liable to *Peʾah* was a current issue, on which all opinions are new. Eliezer's is that the field is defined by the seed one may plant in it. Others do not differ in principle.

X.ii.6. M. Pe'ah 7 : 7—A field made up of defective clusters belongs to the owner, not to the poor.

X.ii.7. M. Kil. 5 : 8—Eliezer has applied the attested principle, regarding intention, of the House of Shammai.

X.ii.8. M. Shev. 5 : 3—The poor may use Seventh Year fruit, a very lenient law, but not necessarily laid down by Eliezer.

X.ii.10. M. Shev. 9 : 5—Eliezer's principle that the pickled vegetables follow the earliest prohibition at the advent of the Seventh Year is his own.

X.ii.11. M. Shev. 9 : 9—One may give Seventh Year produce to those who do not observe the taboo—a rule originated by Eliezer, but consistent with the House of Shammai.

X.ii.12. M. Ter. 4 : 5—One may give Heave-offering to the extent of a tenth of the crop, a new rule. Heave-offering may not exceed Heave-offering of Tithe, to which it is comparable.

X.ii.13. M. Ter. 5 : 2, 4, 5, 6—"What has fallen in may be lifted out"—Eliezer's principle is new. It is known in cases attested before M.-Tos.

X.ii.14. M. Ter. 6 : 6—Eliezer's rule that one may pay back from one kind for another is new to him and consistent with his principle that one may give Heave-offering for unclean produce from the clean.

X.ii.16. M. Ma. 4 : 3—Eliezer applies the old rule by making a new distinction between clean and unclean.

X.ii.17-19. M. Ma. 4 : 5, 6; Tos. Ma. 3 : 7—Eliezer holds the established laws of tithing impose the tax on dill, caperbush, and mustard.

X.ii.21. Tos. M.S. 3 : 16—One who is known to have given Second Tithe is assumed to have given the First. The sages give the contrary rule.

X.ii.22. Tos. M.S. 4 : 5-6—Eliezer's opinion that the added fifth presents no obstacle to eating Second Tithe produce which has been redeemed must be original with him.

X.ii.23. M. Hal. 2 : 1—Eliezer probably originated the rule that Palestinian produce taken abroad is liable to Dough-offering.

X.ii.24. M. Hal. 2 : 4—One should not prepare dough in uncleanness, but should make it in quantities smaller than those liable for Dough-offering. ʿAqiba says the opposite. Eliezer then introduces the principle, in general consistent with ʿAqiba's view-point, that if one does prepare the dough in small quantities, it will readily be combined to form the liable amounts.

X.ii.25. M. Hal. 4 : 7—Syria belongs rightfully to the Jews. Gamaliel opposes this claim.

X.ii.26. M. Orl. 1 : 7—The sap of *ʿorlah* is prohibited, an application of an old prohibition to a new detail.

X.ii.26A. M. Orl. 2 : 11—If a prohibited substance completes the quantity needed to leaven, the whole is prohibited—Eliezer's own view, far stricter than the earlier rule.

X.ii.26B. M. Orl. 2 : 13—One should wash his dishes with unclean, then clean oil.

X.ii.27. M. Shab. 1 : 10—Eliezer's rule is not new.

X.ii.28. M. Shab. 6 : 4—Eliezer's opinion on war is his own, but not unique.

X.ii.29. M. Shab. 2 : 3—Eliezer applies the established principle of the House of Shammai.

X.ii.30. Tos. Shab. 4 : 6—Not a new principle.

X.ii.31. M. Shab. 12 : 4—Possibly a new application of the rule against writing.

X.ii.32. M. Shab. 13 : 1—New to Eliezer is only the application of the rule.

X.ii.33. M. Shab. 17 : 7—Eliezer applies a rule against adding to a Tent.

X.ii.34. M. Shab. 19 : 1—Eliezer's view of the Sabbath is a major innovation (in context).

X.ii.35. M. Shab. 20 : 1—Eliezer applies an old rule to a new case.

X.ii.37. M. Eruv. 1 : 2—Eliezer defines in his own way the appropriate *ʿeruv*.

X.ii.38. M. Pes. 6 : 1—Same as No. 34.

X.ii.39. M. Pes. 9 : 2—Eliezer says anyone not in the Temple keeps the second Passover—a radical revision of the old law. In his day it would include everyone!

X.ii.40. Tos. Kip. 3 : 14—Eliezer's philosophy should be his own.

X.ii.41. Tos. Suk. 1 : 9—The rule is old, its application new.

X.ii.42. Tos. Y.T. 3 : 2—Eliezer and Joshua apply festival law to a complex case.

X.ii.43. M. Ta. 1 : 1—No antecedent rule, so both opinions probably are innovations.

X.ii.43A. M. Ta. 3 : 9—The rule is Eliezer's, and Ṭarfon applies it.

X.ii.44. M. Yev. 8 : 4—Eliezer's interpretation is his own.

X.ii.45-46. M. Yev. 12 : 2-3—Eliezer's view is his own.

X.ii.47. M. Yev. 13 : 6-7—Eliezer's view is his own.

X.ii.48. M. Yev. 16 : 2—Eliezer's view is his own.

X.ii.49. M. Yev. 16 : 7—Eliezer's and Joshua's view certainly is new to them.

X.ii.51-54. M. Ket. 1 : 6-9—The problem looks new, so too the opinions.

X.ii.55-6. M. Ned. 10 : 5-6—Eliezer's effort to ease the annulling of vows is his own.

X.ii.57. M. Ned. 10 : 7—Eliezer's effort to ease the annulling of vows is his own.

X.ii.58-59. M. Naz. 6 : 11, 7 : 1—Eliezer's opinion seems to be his own contribution. The three offerings must be brought together.

X.ii.60. M. Naz. 7 : 4—Eliezer says no logical argument is acceptable here.

X.ii.61. M. Sot. 3 : 4D—Eliezer's view about not teaching Torah to women certainly is his own—but others reached the same conclusion.

X.ii.62. M. Sot. 6 : 1—Eliezer's opinion is new, but the difference with Joshua is trivial.

X.ii.63-5. M. Sot. 9 : 2-4—Eliezer's opinions are new, but the differences with Joshua and ʿAqiba are trivial.

X.ii.66. M. Qid. 3 : 13—Eliezer probably enunciates the old law.

X.ii.66A-E. M. B.Q. 6 : 4, B.B. 9 : 7, Sanh. 1 : 4—In all instances, Eliezer's opinion is likely to be new, and so are the problems.

X.ii.67-68. M. Zev. 1 : 1, 7 : 4—Eliezer's theory certainly is his own.

X.ii.69. M. Hul. 2 : 6—Eliezer's rule is new.

X.ii.70. M. Hul. 12 : 2—Eliezer's rule is new.

X.ii.71. M. Bekh. 1 : 5—Eliezer's rule is new.

X.ii.73. M. Bekh. 5 : 3—Eliezer's rule is new.

X.ii.74. M. Ar. 6 : 3—Eliezer's rule is new.

X.ii.75-76. M. Tem. 3 : 3, 6 : 5—Eliezer's rule is new.

X.ii.78. M. Ker. 6 : 1, 3—We cannot be certain that Eliezer cites an established law.

X.ii.84-90. M. Kel. 2 : 8, etc.—In general it is difficult to locate new principles introduced by Eliezer. The issues appear to be the application of established laws to new, trivial objects.

X.ii.91-97. M. Oh. 2 : 2, etc.—The cases look new, but the fundamental principles are well-established.

X.ii.98-99. M. Neg. 9 : 3, 11 : 7—The interpretation of unclear traditions is not Eliezer's.

X.ii.100-110. M. Par. 1 : 1, etc.—Eliezer certainly introduced the distinction between the Temple's requirements and the *Parah's* less strict ones. This is made explicit.

X.ii.111-111A. M. Toh. 2 : 2, 8 : 7—Eliezer's opinions are his own.

X.ii.112-115. M. Neg. 2 : 4, 7, 8, 10—Eliezer certainly introduced distinctions, tending toward stringency, where no distinctions earlier existed.

X.ii.116-117. M. Nid. 4 : 4, 6—Eliezer's and Joshua's problem may be new, but their principles cannot be their own contribution.

X.ii.118-120. M. Maksh. 6 : 6, M. Zab. 5 : 3, 7—Eliezer's rulings seem to be his own. Semen of a *Zab* is not a liquid. Carrying is like moving in respect to uncleanness—the latter a move toward greater consistency in purity laws.

X.ii.124. Tos. Sanh. 11 : 5—The distinction between sorcery and illusion in context looks like Eliezer's.

X.ii.126. M. Yad. 4 : 3—The law is not attributed to Eliezer.

While, as in section vi, it is difficult to distinguish Eliezer's own innovations from his application to new problems or cases of established principles, it seems probable that a number of principles do originate with him, and he also participated with his colleagues in the solution of problems heretofore not resolved or even considered.

The liturgical issues probably begin with the early Yavneans. In this regard Eliezer's position is his own and contrary to that attributed to everyone else. He did not wish to standardize the supplicatory part of the Eighteen Benedictions and insisted that the former situation prevail. That is, he wished prayer to remain primarily an expression of the private person and not subject to the discipline of law. Still, he accepted the need to define when the *Shema*ʿ was to be said morning and night, so he evidently acceded to the tendency to standardize important elements of liturgy, preserving the individual's initiatives in those matters particularly pertinent to his own situation, particularly the supplications in the Prayer.

His view that the poor may use Seventh Year fruit is consistent with the principle of the House of Shammai. In several other cases involving Seventh Year fruit, he was consistently lenient. And this is an established trait of his laws.

His principle on the neutralization of mixtures of sacred substances, e.g., in the cult, or Heave-offering, surely begins with him. Likewise, the tradition has developed the view about giving Heave-offering from clean produce to its logical next step: One may pay back from one *kind* for another.

As observed, many laws constitute nothing more than the application to new, trivial matters of established rules, e.g., tithing was everywhere required, but Eliezer said dill, caperbush, and mustard had also to be tithed.

If Eliezer actually is responsible for the sayings about the liability of Syria and other neighboring countries to Palestinian agricultural taxes, then of course these sayings are originated by him. Likewise, his approval of war begins with him—in context. But it was a commonplace opinion.

The view, already known, that the Sabbath is subordinate to other commandments—circumcision, the Passover—is new to Eliezer and a major innovation, extending the principle that the cult is carried on to other matters.

He likewise would evidently require everyone not in the Temple to keep the second, not the first, Passover. This means that after 70 everyone will have to keep Passover at the same time, and the (alleged) earlier practice will have been abrogated.

Most of the opinions on the problem of Levirate marriage and on accepting the testimony of a woman in explanation of her sexual status look new. The tradition has developed Eliezer's effort to make it easy to annul vows to some new matters, no more extreme than the original allegation.

It is difficult to claim that with Eliezer begins the view that acquiring real estate is done differently from acquiring movables. The distinction is old. But the pericope, according to our analysis, lays the claim that Eliezer said one requires the one to be done in a more elaborate way than the other. The issues and rules in respect to slaughter and the firstling look new but do not exhibit an important or fundamental attitude. The cases of *Kelim* and *Ohalot*, as stated, reveal nothing more than a tendency to apply old principles to new objects, in the one case, or to invent new problems for consideration according to established laws, in the other.

The distinction between the *Parah*-rite and the normal Temple rite is represented as original to Eliezer, and so it may have been. But the same distinction is present in other materials attributed to early Yavneans. Eliezer's new distinctions in respect to the ritual pool, which tended to make the law more stringent, look like his own.

viii. The Application of Eliezer's Law

We have not a shred of evidence that Eliezer ever was able to enforce the law outside of his own household. Occasionally it is alleged that people did what he said, but it is never claimed that they did so because he had the authority to tell them to or the power to force them. The evidence is as follows:

X.i.1. M. Nid. 1 : 3—b. Nid. 9b has a story of Rabbi's applying Eliezer's rule. It is further alleged that during Eliezer's own lifetime people would behave according to his opinion—or Joshua's—but after he died, they followed Joshua's—or Eliezer's. But we do not have evidence of how (if at all) Eliezer applied the law.

X.ii.1. M. Ber. 1 : 1—Evidence of applying the law pertains only to Gamaliel's own sons.

X.ii.2. M. Ber. 1 : 2—No evidence of law-enforcement.

X.ii.3. M. Ber. 4 : 3—No evidence of law-enforcement. But the stories about praying too long or too briefly show Eliezer with his own disciples, so he presumably could tell them what to do.

X.ii.4. M. Ber. 5 : 2—No evidence of law-enforcement.

X.ii.5. M. Pe'ah 3 : 6—No evidence of law-enforcement.

X.ii.6. M. Pe'ah 7 : 7—No evidence of law-enforcement.

X.ii.7. M. Kil. 5 : 8—No evidence of law-enforcement.

X.ii.8. M. Shev. 5 : 3—No evidence of law-enforcement.

X.ii.10. M. Shev. 9 : 5—No evidence of law-enforcement.

X.ii.11. M. Shev. 9 : 9—No evidence of law-enforcement.

X.ii.12. M. Ter. 4 : 5—No evidence of law-enforcement.

X.ii.13. M. Ter. 5 : 2, 4, 5, 6—No evidence of law-enforcement.
X.ii.14. M. Ter. 6 : 6—No evidence of law-enforcement.
X.ii.16. M. Ma. 4 : 3—No evidence of law-enforcement.
X.ii.17-19. M. Ma. 4 : 5, 6; Tos. Ma. 3 : 7—No evidence of law-enforcement.
X.ii.21. Tos. M.S. 3 : 16—No evidence of law-enforcement.
X.ii.22. Tos. M.S. 4 : 5-6—No evidence of law-enforcement.
X.ii.23. M. Hal. 2 : 1—No evidence of law-enforcement.
X.ii.24. M. Hal. 2 : 4—No evidence of law-enforcement.
X.ii.25. M. Hal. 4 : 7—No evidence of law-enforcement.
X.ii.26. M. Orl. 1 : 7—No evidence of law-enforcement.
X.ii.26A. M. Orl. 2 : 11—No evidence of law-enforcement.
X.ii.26B. M. Orl. 2 : 13—No evidence of law-enforcement.
X.ii.27. M. Shab. 1 : 10—No evidence of law-enforcement.
X.ii.28. M. Shab. 6 : 4—No evidence of law-enforcement.
X.ii.29. M. Shab. 2 : 3—No evidence of law-enforcement.
X.ii.30. Tos. Shab. 4 : 6—Story about Hyrcanus, Eliezer's son.
X.ii.31. M. Shab. 12 : 4—No evidence of law-enforcement. Eliezer cites a precedent to demonstrate scratching is writing, but Ben Saṭra(?) is not claimed to have been subject to Eliezer's authority.
X.ii.32. M. Shab. 13 : 1—No evidence of law-enforcement.
X.ii.33. M. Shab. 17 : 7—No evidence of law-enforcement.
X.ii.34. M. Shab. 19 : 1—A. Eliezer's village followed his rule *re* circumcision on the Sabbath.
B. Rabbi ruled in accord with Eliezer.
X.ii.35. M. Shab. 20 : 1—No evidence of law-enforcement.
X.ii.37. M. Eruv. 1 : 2—Eliezer applied the law to his disciple.
X.ii.38. M. Pes. 6 : 1—Temple law, purely theoretical.
X.ii.39. M. Pes. 9 : 2—Temple law, purely theoretical.
X.ii.40. Tos. Kip. 3 : 14—Temple law, purely theoretical.
X.ii.41. Tos. Suk. 1 : 9—Eliezer applied the law to his own situation.
X.ii.42. Tos. Y.T. 3 : 2—No evidence of enforcement.
X.ii.43. M. Ta. 1 : 1—No evidence of enforcement.
X.ii.43A. M. Ta. 3 : 9—Ṭarfon enforced Eliezer's fasting-rule in Lydda. Eliezer and Joshua did the same, Tos. Ta. 2 : 5.
X.ii.43B. Tos. Suk. 2 : 1—Eliezer tells Ilai not to leave home on the festival.
X.ii.44. M. Yev. 8 : 4—A case is cited to establish a medical fact. No evidence of law enforcement.
X.ii.45-46. M. Yev. 12 : 2-3—No evidence of enforcement or application of the law. But Judah's saying on the wooden sandal suggests that it was routine to carry out the rite of *ḥaliṣah.* We have no stories of how Eliezer's opinion was applied.
X.ii.47. M. Yev. 13 : 6-7—No evidence of enforcement.
X.ii.48. M. Yev. 16 : 2—No evidence of enforcement.
X.ii.49. M. Yev. 16 : 7—The case does not pertain to Eliezer's opinion.
X.ii.51-54. M. Ket. 1 : 6-9—No evidence of enforcement.
X.ii.55-56. M. Ned. 10 : 5-6—No evidence of enforcement.

X.ii.57. M. Ned. 10 : 7—No evidence of enforcement.
X.ii.58-59. M. Naz. 6 : 11, 7 : 1—The precedent, opposing Eliezer's opinion, pertains to pre-70 times. For 7 : 1: No evidence of enforcement.
X.ii.60. M. Naz. 7 : 4—No evidence of enforcement.
X.ii.61. M. Sot. 3 : 4D—No evidence of enforcement, but Eliezer's *wife* did know Torah.
X.ii.62. M. Sot. 6 : 1—No evidence of enforcement.
X.ii.63-5. M. Sot. 9 : 2-4—No evidence of enforcement.
X.ii.66. M. Qid. 3 : 13—No evidence of enforcement.
X.ii.66A-E. M. B.Q. 6 : 4—No evidence of enforcement.
M. B.B. 9 : 7—The precedent does not indicate Eliezer's rule was enforced.
M. Sanh. 1 : 4—No evidence of enforcement.
X.ii.67-68. M. Zev. 1 : 1, 7 : 4—Temple law, purely theoretical.
X.ii.69. M. Hul. 2 : 6—No evidence of enforcement.
X.ii.70. M. Hul. 12 : 2—No evidence of enforcement.
X.ii.71. M. Bekh. 1 : 5—No evidence of enforcement.
X.ii.73. M. Bekh. 5 : 3—No evidence of enforcement.
X.ii.74. M. Ar. 6 : 3—No evidence of enforcement.
X.ii.75-76. M. Tem. 3 : 3, 6 : 5—Temple law, purely theoretical.
X.ii.78. M. Ker. 6 : 1, 3—Temple law, purely theoretical.
X.ii.83-90. M. Kel. 2 : 8, etc.—No evidence of enforcement.
X.ii.91-97. M. Oh. 2 : 2, etc.—No evidence of enforcement.
X.ii.98-99. M. Neg. 9 : 3, 11 : 7—No evidence of enforcement.
X.ii.100-110. M. Par. 1 : 1, etc.—Temple law, purely theoretical.
X.ii.111-111A. M. Toh. 2 : 2, 8 : 7—No evidence of enforcement.
X.ii.112-115. M. Miq. 2 : 4, 7, 8, 10—No evidence of enforcement.
X.ii.116-117. M. Nid. 4 : 4, 6—No evidence of enforcement.
X.ii.118-120. M. Maksh. 6 : 6, M. Zab. 5 : 3, 7—No evidence of enforcement.
X.ii.124. Tos. Sanh. 11 : 5—No evidence of enforcement.
X.ii.126. M. Yad. 4 : 3—No evidence of enforcement.

Stories about Eliezer's enforcement of the law are strikingly limited to household matters, involving his own practice and his disciples', on the one side, and that of his own village, on the other. Presumably Eliezer's disciples accepted his view that sometimes a long prayer is called for, other times a short one. His own son did as he said. His village is alleged to have followed his rule about circumcizing on the Sabbath. Eliezer told his disciple Ilai not to leave home on the festival. Ṭarfon in Lydda enforced Eliezer's rule on fasting for rain.

Other precedents or cases, when cited, do not allege Eliezer's view was enforced either by his own efforts or by those of others. They claim only that others earlier had done what Eliezer claims is supposed to be done. We therefore cannot demonstrate that Eliezer enforced the laws he taught, as either a village-authority, or an officer of a larger rabbinical government, or a Roman official. In fact the only laws, except ones on fasting and circumcision on the Sabbath, which do indicate practical enforcement pertain to the private affairs of Eliezer's family and immediate circle of disciples. At most it may be claimed that Eliezer exercised severely limited religious authority in his own town. Since the larger number of the laws which might have produced stories about enforcement pertains to agricultural, family, and cleanness law, it is striking that no evidence suggests either how such laws might have been enforced or that they actually were carried out, on Eliezer's instructions or otherwise, by ordinary folk.

That fact, however, does not suggest that the bulk of Eliezer's laws consisted of purely theoretical rulings. Apart from the Temple laws of various kinds, it seems likely that Eliezer's laws were made because people were expected to keep them. But those who would keep them would do so because they acknowledged Eliezer's authority as a learned man, not because he could either coerce or frighten people to do what he said as a government official or holy man. Who would have been expected to keep the agricultural and cleanness laws, if not loyal Pharisees, by whom Eliezer, among others, presumably was regarded as a great master of the old tradition and its disciplines and a reliable authority on new issues, practical or otherwise? The absence of precedents and case-reports therefore should suggest that the *nature* of the application of sectarian law was different from that of common law—civil, criminal, and the like, or of religious law pertinent to people not part of the sect—Sabbath, festival, and holy day rules, slaughtering and other laws, and the laws of menstrual purity. The Pharisees after 70 would have been instructed in the law as they were before then, by men whose qualification consisted not of 'official' recognition but of the consensus of the sect itself. The status of authority was conferred, therefore, within the group, by processes we cannot now describe, and not achieved by some objectively demonstrated accomplishments or imposed by institutionalized, governmental recognition or by rabbinical support.

The later rabbinical government, which formally authorized its members to effect the law in courts or local authorities, and which enjoyed official status within the Roman and Iranian regimes, seems to have had no counterpart in Eliezer's time, at least so far as he was concerned. Such authority as Eliezer may have exercised outside of his limited circle depended upon nothing more than respect for his opinions on the part of other Pharisees. We have, however, slight knowledge, if any, about where such Pharisees might have been located, how they knew about Eliezer's opinions, or why they accepted them.

ix. Eliezer's Program for Yavneh

Eliezer's program for Yavneh conforms to that already revealed in the historically reliable pericopae. In general he seems to have taken a moderate and often lenient position on the application of the Pharisaic discipline. Along with others of his time he evidently added to the former concerns the effort to define in a fairly precise way the procedures for keeping laws formerly not so carefully applied in detail. Such exact rules include the size of a field liable for *Pe'ah*, what to do with a field wholly consisting of defective clusters (an unlikely phenomenon), how much Heave-offering beyond the minimum requirement may be given, and similar matters. Eliezer opposed the imposition of fixed rules on the supplicatory part of the Eighteen Benedictions, which he hoped to preserve as a spontaneous expression. In Sabbath laws we find a tendency to a somewhat strict application of established rules. Some distinctions introduced by Eliezer, in regard to the ritual pool for instance, seem to have produced strict aspects for what were formerly lenient rules. Of this we can be less certain. The only important innovation in the historical picture introduced by the traditions concerns the central issue of Yavneh: relationships to the Romans and the possibilities of a new war (pp. 347-350).

x. Eliezer and the Christians

The traditions introduce one further, curious point of contact with the Synoptics' picture of Jesus:

11. He said to [the Pharisees]: Which of you, having an ass or an ox that has fallen into a well, will not immediately pull him out on a Sabbath day?" And they could not reply to this—Lk. 14 : 5-6 (Matt. 12 : 9-14: sheep; Mk. 3 : 1-6; Lk. 6 : -11; 13 : 10-17)

11. Tos. Y.T. 3 : 2: Eliezer says that if an animal and its offspring fall into the pit on the festival, one raises the first on condition of slaughtering it and does slaughter it, and feeds the second in its place, so that it will not die.
Joshua says one does not actually slaughter the first, and then raises the second to slaughter that one. So he is able to remove both from the pit.

In point of fact, neither Eliezer nor Joshua would approve immediately removing the animal from the pit on the festival except for the sake of slaughter, all the more so on the Sabbath, when slaughtering is not done. One maintains it there until it is permissible to remove it. Here Jesus's saying takes for granted a law quite the opposite of that attributed to the early Yavneans. I do not know what to make of the Gospels' certainty that the law does not prohibit doing what the early Yavneans take for granted is not allowed.

A second, and far more important pericope first occurs in Tos. Hul. 2 : 24. Eliezer was arrested because of *minut.* The story is in two parts. In the first, it is alleged that Eliezer was arrested because of *minut* but managed to hoodwink the judge by saying he will rely upon the judge. That ends the matter. The judge frees him. Nothing more is said about *minut.*

The point of the story is strikingly similar to that of the trial of Shila (b. Ber. 58a), in which Shila persuades the Iranian judge that he accepts his authority: "Blessed is the All-merciful who has made earthly royalty on the model of heavenly royalty and has invested you with dominion and made you lovers of justice." Forthwith the *parastak* frees Shila and sets him up as a judge. The stories do not use the same language and deal with quite different problems. They have in common the allegation that the rabbi is able to elude gentile justice by making the judge think the opposite of what is really the case; the rabbi speaks of heaven—so both Tos. Hul. and b. Ber. explicitly allege—but the judge supposes the rabbi means the gentile judge himself. The primary element of the story therefore contains a commonplace motif.

The second episode, tacked on to the first, is connected to the foregoing by the allegation that Eliezer was embarrassed at his arrest. Then ʿAqiba proposes that Eliezer has enjoyed something he learned from a *min.* Eliezer admits that was the case, and explicitly admits what is in ʿAqiba's question—therefore is made to accept the ʿAqiban viewpoint that one should have no intercourse whatever with *minim.* Later versions of the story explain what Eliezer had approved in Jesus's sayings: money which may not be used for the Temple may be used for a privy for the high priest. This is consistent, in a general way, with Eliezer's opinions on the purchase of a *Parah*, which is not sacrificed in the Temple, by money of the same origin.

Certainly, Tos. is told in a Roman setting. Lieberman has established that fact. But despite the superficial marks of authenticity, we are unable to assess the beginnings of the account or of the allegation that Eliezer was arrested on suspicion of *minut*. We do not know when he died, and, unless we follow Graetz in finding in the story evidence that Domitian persecuted Christians, we cannot be sure that the story pertains to a persecution during Eliezer's own lifetime. We do not know why Eliezer should have been linked to *minim*. To make the point that clever rabbis can outwit stupid Roman judges, one need not have introduced the question of *minut* at all. So that detail should be integral to the tradition. But then the tradition itself ignores the occasion for the trial—it is excluded from the account of the proceedings—and stresses simply the rabbi's cleverness. Then ʿAqiba's insinuation is made the moral of the narrative. Eliezer merely accepts it and admits he was guilty of violating it. So part B is a story in which ʿAqiba is the master, Eliezer the disciple—thus an ʿAqiban story alleging that the Torah requires the Jews to separate themselves from the *minim*. Clearly, such a story conforms to the viewpoint of the Bar Kokhban supporters. It is commonly supposed, in Bar Kokhba's times, the *minim* seen as Jewish-Christians made their final break with the Jews. Whether this is so cannot be said with certainty.

The tradition thus alleges Eliezer held one should have nothing whatever to do with *minim*. Such an allegation is entirely consistent with the view that Eliezer favored the xenophobic militarists, said gentiles cannot enter the world to come, favored war against peace, and otherwise supported the policies behind the Bar Kokhba War. ʿAqibans seem to stand behind this view of Eliezer. But one cannot show it was ʿAqiba himself who so stated with reference to Eliezer. Nor do we know that the allegations with regard to Eliezer were true. He certainly cannot have been a *min*. But it seems difficult to say whether the account before us reports something which actually happened. It is the first narrative about something Eliezer has done, not merely a chriic setting for an important saying of his.

xi. Forms and the Formation of Traditions about Eliezer

Our form-historical inquiry (pp. 18-62) showed that the dispute-form, developed for use with materials attributed to the Houses of Shammai and Hillel, underwent some interesting, but not very fundamental, structural developments in its application to Eliezer-materials. It furthermore was used for a wider range of types of traditions.

We found it, however, impossible to show that pericopae involving

Eliezer with a given contemporary were set in one form in preference to some other. We cannot, therefore, claim that tradents of, e.g., the ʿAqiba + Eliezer-group made use of a particular form, so that other pericopae in that same form may be supposed to originate in that same circle or to have been generated by it. This negative result is not unimportant, for it removes from consideration the possibility that an element in the history of the formation of Eliezer's traditions is the use of forms peculiar to, or preponderant in, those traditions alone. Form-history is not central in the present consideration of traditions-history, though it did become crucial in connection with the history of the traditions attributed to the Houses of Shammai and Hillel.

Eliezer therefore appears as only one among a number of early Yavneans—and later masters as well—whose sayings were set into fixed forms as part of some larger (as yet unexplored) literary scheme. Since one cannot isolate the forms of Eliezer's materials from those of other masters, his materials obviously were included among those of others of his generation and not preserved apart from the rest. So the history of Eliezer's traditions as we have them has a pre-history, no longer easily recoverable, during which time his opinions ought to have been handed on and organized without reference to the opinions of other masters or "the sages." When we encounter Eliezer's materials, it almost invariably is after they have been put together with those of other masters, rarely, if ever, in their prior state. That does not mean we cannot postulate the state of the traditions before their amalgamation with those of other Yavnean authorities. But it does mean that virtually nothing can still be in its original condition, that is, in the exact language and form given by Eliezer himself.

xii. The Formation of the *Eliezer + Sages*-Type of Tradition

Of the approximately 183 pericopae of all sorts and all strata in which Eliezer's opinion differs from either an anonymous one or a saying attributed to "sages," roughly 115 will come under consideration within the best, better, and fair traditions. Approximately 26 of these derive from Ilai or his son, Judah, or later members of the family. We have no idea of the source(s) of the other exempla.

Ilai and his son Judah are the sole authorities who supply authentic chains, involving themselves, for traditions going back to Eliezer. Ilai's and Judah b. Ilai's chains rarely contain the names of masters other than Eliezer. (The sole exception is Tos. R.H. 2 : 10: Judah says Eliezer says *vs.* ʿAqiba says *to him*, meaning Eliezer, not Judah). In addition, pericopae attested by Ilai never involve named masters, but always present as Eliezer's opposition *the sages*. That obviously cannot mean all pericopae involving Eliezer and sages derive from Ilai's and Judah's stemma of the tradition. This is probably not the case, for some "sages" of M. turn out in Tos. to be ʿAqiba or Joshua. But clearly, the materials preserved in the chains of Ilai and Judah b. Ilai not only have undergone a different formative process, but also appear to go back to sources other than those which contain the names of ʿAqiba or Joshua. The materials, distributed according to tractates and orders, are as follows:

1. *Ilai's Chains*

1. Tos. Ter. 3 : 18/M. Ter. 2 : 1.
2. Tos. Hal. 1 : 10/M. Hal. 2 : 8.
3. Tos. Hal. 1 : 6—Ilai asked Joshua, then Eliezer. M. Hal. 1 : 6 gives Eliezer's opinion, omits both his name and Joshua's opinion.

[4. M. Eruv. 2 : 5-6—No contrary opinions are included in Ilai's list. But Eliezer differs from Judah b. Bava + ʿAqiba. So Ilai's tradition omitted the opposed opinions *and* the authorities behind them. This is probably the earliest formulation of Eliezer's materials —according to lists of Eliezer's opinions without the intrusion of different viewpoints.]

5. Tos. Dem. 1 : 3.
6. ARN Chap. 15: Repent.

2. *Judah's Chains*

1. Sifré Num. 110/M. Hal. 2 : 1: Fruit from abroad.
2-5. Tos. Kip. 2 : 10 etc.: Atonement rites.
6. Tos. Y.T. 1 : 3: Houses.
7. Tos. R.H. 2 : 10: Lev. 23 : 24.
8. Tos. Ket. 11 : 4/M. Ket. 11 : 6: Orphan has right to usufruct.
9-10. Tos. Nez. 2 : 12-13/M. Naz. 3 : 3-5: Nazir-penalties.
11. Tos. Sanh. 9 : 61, M. Sanh. 6 : 4: Hanging woman.
12. Tos. Ah. 7 : 3/M. Oh. 6 : 2.
13. Tos. Par. 5 : 9/M. Par. 5 : 7: *Parah*-water.
14. Tos. Par. 7 : 7/M. Par. 7 : 10: *Parah*-water.

Judah along with other Ushans also attests numerous disputes between Eliezer and named masters, e.g.:

1. Tos. Ter. 9 : 9C/M. Ter. 11 : 2: Eliezer + Joshua.
2. Tos. Men. 2 : 16M. Men. 3 : 1: Eliezer + Joshua.

3. Tos. Ah. 9 : 7/M. Oh. 5 : 6: Eliezer + Joshua.
4. M. Ter. 4 : 7-11/Tos. Ter. 5 : 10-11: Eliezer + Joshua.
5. Tos. Zev. 8 : 20/M. Zev. 8 : 8: Eliezer + Joshua.
6. Tos. M.S. 2 : 16/M. M.S. 3 : 13: Eliezer + ʿAqiba.

3. *Other Chains*

1. Tos. Orl. 1 : 8: Yoḥanan b. Nuri—No *ʿorlah* abroad. No other authority included with Eliezer.

As alleged earlier, Eliezer's traditions certainly began without the inclusion of contrary opinions. That is, he probably said, "One does such and so." He probably did not then add, "But R. ʿAqiba says ["said to me"], 'One does not do such and so.'" That addition will have had to be added later on or in other circles, formed by masters possessing different opinions on the same list of problems deriving from separate masters. They would have had reason to include both the names of authorities as well as their respective opinions. The traditions of Eliezer—as those of all other masters who had their own circles of disciples—could not to begin with have been presented in the dispute-form. In that case, Ilai's list in M. Eruv. 2 : 5-6 supplies the best model, if, alas, the sole significant example, of the original condition of Eliezer's traditions. The dispute involving Eliezer and sages then will have evolved out of such an original tradition; at that point the responsible disciple or tradent (Ilai, Judah) would have registered Eliezer's opinion along with the fact that a contrary view was held by someone else ("sages").

It is all the more striking, therefore, that no pericope involving a chain of either Ilai or Judah also contains the name of another master. This would seem to mean that Ilai's and Judah's chains produced disputes other than through agreement on a common agendum with other circles of named masters. Such disputes would have been developed simply to register a view contrary to Eliezer's, and to assign that view to the majority. Presumably it was on such condition that it was possible to introduce Eliezer's teachings into whatever corpus lies behind the Mishnah, for, as we have observed, the great majority of the chains are in Tos. And when a tradition with a chain behind it is introduced into Mishnah, it may occur as often not with Eliezer's name attached to it at all as in the *Eliezer vs. sages*-form.

By contrast, *Eliezer + Joshua* and *Eliezer + ʿAqiba*-materials probably come from the amalgamation of traditions originally held separately and independently in their respective circles. The materials were brought together when these circles collected their traditions on common agenda and formulated them as a single corpus of law. Since Eliezer normally comes first, his group (or he himself, though this seems less likely) must have had a predominant position. But the preservation and transmission of the joint traditions were the work of Joshuans and ʿAqibans, or, more likely, ʿAqiban continuators of the work of Joshua + ʿAqiba. The agreed-upon materials—centered, as we shall see, in a few particular chapters of a limited number of tractates—were carefully preserved by later ʿAqiban tradents, and the predominant position accorded Eliezer was preserved.

Most Eliezer-materials, however, contain opposed opinions; all come at a second or later stage in the development of Eliezer's tradition; and all take for granted the importance of his opinions on given, fixed agenda. Why his opinions on other matters were not handed on in the preserved materials we cannot now say. Since, as we have seen, Eliezer certainly was a Pharisee and seems to have been an important one, perhaps his opinions on particularly *Pharisaic* aspects of the law evolving at Yavneh were given priority, and others were set aside or ignored or to begin with never formulated for transmission in the normative tradition. The opinions of others, better informed about, or regarded as more authoritative on, other aspects of the law, were elsewhere given priority. But this is a circular argument, for it is by the substance of the laws that we have established Eliezer as a Pharisee; we cannot now claim the preserved substance was what it was *because* he was a Pharisee.

We have already observed that substantive differences in the perspective on Eliezer in the *Ilai + Judah—Eliezer + sages*-type of pericopae and in the *Eliezer + Joshua/ʿAqiba*-type of pericopae are difficult to perceive. I do not find any tendencies at variance or other grounds to suppose that one group deliberately formulated a picture of Eliezer different from that of the other. Overall, one repeatedly comes to the conclusion that materials, once formulated, were not greatly revised, except in the Ushan manner.

xiii. The Formation of the *Eliezer + Named Master*-Type of Tradition

Pericopae which present the opinions of Eliezer with those of some other, named master are assumed to derive chiefly from the circles of Joshua and ʿAqiba, often in tandem.

1. *Eliezer and Joshua*

1. M. Ber. 1 : 2: Reading *Shema'*.
2. M. Shev. 5 : 3: Poor peoples' rights to arum in Seventh Year.
3-7. M. Ter. 4 : 7: Rules on Heave-offering neutralization.
8-10. M. Ter. 8 : 1-3: Deed begun licitly and completed illicitly.
11. M. Ter. 11 : 2: Date-honey, etc., as liquids.
12. Tos. Hal. 1 : 6 = M. Hal. 1 : 6: Cakes of Thank-offering and wafers of Nazirite *re* Dough-offering. Joshua rejects Eliezer's distinction and rules strictly.
13. M. Orl. 1 : 7: Sap of *'orlah*.
14. M. Shab. 12 : 4: Scratching on skin on Sabbath—Tos.: *sages*.
15. M. Shab. 19 : 4: Circumcision on Sabbath.
16. Tos. Shab. 1 : 17: On that day.
17. M. Eruv. 7 : 10: Food for *'eruv*.
18. M. Pes. 1 : 7: Burning Heave-offering of *ḥameṣ*.
19. M. Pes. 6 : 5: Passover slaughtered not for its own sake on Sabbath.
20. M. Sheq. 4 : 7: Cattle sanctified to Temple (= intention).
21. Tos. Y.T. 3 : 2: Raising animal and offspring from pit.
22. M. Ta. 1 : 1: When say rain-prayer.
23. Tos. Ta. 2 : 5: Story—both agree *re* not fasting on *Ḥanukkah*.
24. Tos. Yev. 13 : 3-5 (M. 13 : 2 lacks Joshua): Minor *re ḥaliṣah*, etc. Ishmael praises Eliezer's consistency.
25. M. Sot. 1 : 1: Warning wife.
(26. M. Sot. 3 : 4: Not teach Torah to daughter. Not a dispute.)
27. M. Sot. 6 : 1: Testimony for *Soṭah*.
28. M. B.B. 9 : 7: The oral-will version has Eliezer and Joshua in opposition on the Sabbath/weekday distinction. N.B.: M. Tem. 3 : 3: *Eleazar* instead of Joshua.
29. Tos. Zev. 1 : 1 (M. Zev. 1 : 1): Sin-offering = Guilt-offering.
30. Tos. Pis. 4 : 5-6: Other sacrifice for its own name as a Passover on 14th Nisan.
31. Tos. Zev. 2 : 16 (M. Zev. 3 : 3 omits J): Intention in the cult.
32. M. Zev. 7 : 4: Whole-offering of bird offered like Sin-offering of bird (= No. 29 expanded.)
33. M. Zev. 8 : 10: Take action *vs.* do nothing *re* mixture of bowls of sacrificial blood.
34 = 31. Tos. Men. 2 : 16: Eleazar introduces Joshua. M. Men. 3 : 1 omits him.
35. M. Men. 3 : 4: Residue of Meal-offering may affect Meal-offering.
36. Tos. Men. 8 : 19: Tos. introduces Joshua as opponent of Eliezer. M. Men. 7 : 3 has "sages." Issue: If slaughter is invalid, is bread sanctified? Eliezer says it is. Sages/Joshua say it is not.
37. M. Ar. 6 : 1: Dedicate goods and owe *Ketuvah*.
38-39. M. Ker. 4 : 2-3: Offering where unsure of what sin has been done, or whether one has sinned. Tos. Ker. 1 : 14—*sages*. M. Ker. 6 : 1A—sages.
40. Tos. Zev. 4 : 1-2: Flesh +/− blood.

41. M. Kel. 14 : 7: Metal vessels purified when broken.
42. M. Kel. 17 : 1: Joshua extends rule opposed by Eliezer.
43. M. Oh. 2 : 4: Sealing-stone of grave unclean by carrying. But Tos. Ah. 3 : 7 has Eliezer *vs.* ʿAqiba, and introduces Joshua on ʿAqiba's side.
44. Tos. Ah. 9 : 7: = Eliezer *vs.* Joshua on two jars in two rooms, etc. M. Oh. 8 : 6 ignores dispute, gives Eliezer's view as law.
45. M. Oh. 9 : 15: Tomb.
46. M. Oh. 12 : 3: Window-sill.
47. M. Oh. 12 : 8: Door-jamb.
48-9. M. Oh. 14 : 4-5: Wall-projection.
50. M. Oh. 17 : 2: Grave-area.
51. M. Par. 5 : 4: Reed pipe for *Parah*-rite.
52. M. Par. 9 : 4: Intention for *Parah*-rite.
53. M. Par. 10 : 1: Uncleanness for *Parah*-rite. Sages make a compromise between the two positions.
51. Tos. Ah. 7 : 11: Jar of ashes on window-sill (*Parah*-law + Tent-law).
55. M. Toh. 2 : 2: Food-uncleanness in various degrees.
56. M. Toh. 8 : 7: Outer parts of vessels + Simeon brother of ʿAzaryah differing from both.
57. M. Miq. 2 : 7: Wine jars collect rain.
58. M. Miq. 2 : 8: Lime pot.
59. M. Miq. 2 : 10: Mud in ritual-pool.
60. M. Nid. 1 : 3: Differing traditions *re Niddah.*
61. Tos. Nid. 2 : 3: Wean child after two years *vs.* five years.
62-63. M. Nid. 4 : 4, 6: Woman in labor.
64. Tos. Ed. 1 : 10: Creeping thing in mouth of weasel.
[65. Tos. Ed. 3 : 1: Joshua and Pappyas testify against Eliezer's view in M. Kel. 15 : 2.]
66. M. Ned. 6 : 2: Joshua and Neḥunya b. Elinatan testify against Eliezer's opinion on limb from corpse of a living being.
67. M. Ed. 6 : 3: Joshua *vs.* Eliezer *vs.* Neḥunya *re* flesh from limb of living being.
68. M. Ed. 8 : 6: Eliezer + Joshua *re* Temple—no apparent contradiction.
69. Tos. Sanh. 13 : 2: Gentiles in world to come.

2. *Eliezer + ʿAqiba*

1. M. Ber. 5 : 2: *Havdalah* in 'Thanksgiving.'
2. M. Pe'ah 7 : 7: Vineyard wholly defective clusters.
3. M. Ter. 6 : 6: Pay back from one kind instead of another. ʿAqiba is consistent in a general way with the sages of M. Ter. 2 : 1.
4. M. Ma. 4 : 6: Tithing caperbush.
5. Sifré Deut. 303= M. M.S. 5 : 12: Use of Second Tithe for shroud.
6. M. Hal. 2 : 1: Produce from abroad.
7. M. Shab. 2 : 3: Cloth as wick.
8. M. Shab. 19 : 1: Circumcision on Sabbath.

9. M. Pes. 9 : 2: Distant journey *re* second Passover.
10. M. Sheq. 8 : 7: Unclean things—where burned?
11. M. Yoma 7 : 3: Order of sacrifices on Day of Atonement.
12. Tos. R.H. 2 : 10: Lev. 23 : 24 *re* Additional Service on New Year.
13. M. Yev. 8 : 4: ʿAqiba and Eliezer explain Joshua's tradition about a eunuch and *ḥaliṣah.*
14. M. Yev. 12 : 3: *Ḥaliṣah* without spitting + exegeses.
15. M. Naz. 7 : 4: ʿAqiba relates Eliezer told him one does not reason *re* Nazir. Joshua told him the same thing.
16-17. M. Sot. 9 : 3-4: Neglected corpse.
18. M. Sanh. 1 : 4: Trial for wild beast.
19. M. Ker. 3 : 10: How many offerings for repeated sin? Compare M. Shev. 2 : 5.
20. M. Me. 1 : 2-3: Blood +/− flesh. Compare M. Men. 3 : 4 + Tos. Zev. 4 : 5, 8. Tos. Zev. 4 : 1-2: Eliezer *vs.* Joshua + Tos. Zev. 4 : 1-2: Eliezer *vs.* Joshua.
[21. Sifra Shemini 10 : 5-6/M. Kel. 5 : 1: Heating oven to complete its processing.]
[22. M. Kel. 14 : 1: ʿAqiba's comment is irrelevant to Eliezer's.]
[23. Tos. Sanh. 11 : 5: ʿAqiba cites Eliezer *re* magic.]
[24. Tos. Hul. 2 : 24: ʿAqiba involved with Eliezer *re minut.*]
25. M. Sanh. 10 : 3: Generation of wilderness.

3. *Eliezer, Joshua, ʿAqiba*

1. M. Pes. 6 : 1-2: Sabbath + Passover. Eliezer holds the latter overrides the former. Joshua opposes this view (= *the sages* of 6 : 1), then ʿAqiba does so (= *the sages* of 6 : 1). ʿAqiba's intrusion is unexplained. Joshua could as well have been given the entire contrary argument.
2. M. Yev. 16 : 7 (Eliezer + Joshua *vs.* ʿAqiba): Woman remarries on evidence of a single witness.
3. M. Ned. 10 : 6 (Eliezer *vs.* Joshua; ʿAqiba *vs.* Joshua [+ Eliezer]): Annulling vow of her who awaits Levirate marriage.
[4. M. Naz. 7 : 4: ʿAqiba, first person, *re* Eliezer, Joshua.]
5. M. Kel. 28 : 2: Uncleanness of rag—Eliezer *vs.* Joshua, with ʿAqiba compromising between their positions.
6. M. Nid. 10 : 3: *Zab* inspected on first day only—Eliezer *vs.* Joshua, with ʿAqiba compromising between their positions.

4. *Eliezer + Gamaliel*

1. M. Ber. 1 : 1: Reading *Shemaʿ.*
2. M. Hal. 4 : 7: Status of Syria.
3. M. Bik. 2 : 6: Status of *etrog.*
4. M. M.Q. 3 : 6: Juxtaposed opinions *re* festivals after 70.
[5. M. Git. 1 : 1: Certification of foreign *Geṭ*—not a dispute. Both gloss the same rule.]
6. M. Hul. 2 : 6: Slaughtering dying animal—signs of life.

5. *Eliezer, Joshua, Gamaliel*

1. M. Shev. 9 : 5: Three vegetables in a jar—Gamaliel takes the middle position.
2. M. Ter. 8 : 8: Protecting cleanness of Heave-offering—Gamaliel takes the middle position.
3. M. Yev. 13 : 7 (Eliezer, Gamaliel, Joshua): Deaf-mutes *re* Levirate marriage.

4-7. M. Ket. 1 : 6-9 (Gamaliel + Eliezer *vs.* Joshua): Testimony of woman in her own behalf.

6. *Eliezer vs. Gamaliel, Joshua, ʿAqiba*

1. M. Ber. 4 : 3: Fixed text for Eighteen Benedictions.

7. *Eliezer, Joshua, Ṭarfon, Judah b. Batyra, ʿAqiba*

1. M. Peʾah 3 : 6: Ground liable to *peʾah.*

8. *Eliezer, Ishmael, Ṭarfon + ʿAqiba*

1. M. Ter. 4 : 5: Excess Heave-offering.

9. *Eliezer, Judah b. Batyra vs. Joshua*

1. M. Pes. 3 : 3: Separating Dough-offering in uncleanness on 15 Nisan.

10. *Ṭarfon + Eliezer*

1. M. Qid. 3 : 13: Eliezer rejects Ṭarfon's rule *re mamzer.*

11. *Eleazar b. ʿAzariah, Eliezer, ʿAqiba (+ Simeon)*

1. M. B.Q. 6 : 4: Fine.

12. *Eliezer, ʿAqiba, Ishmael*

1. M. Shav. 2 : 5: How many offerings for how many sins?
2. M. Ker. 3 : 10: How many offerings for how many sins? But now, ʿAqiba agrees with Ishmael's position of M. Shev. 2 : 5 (!).

13. *Eliezer + Judah b. Batyra*

1. M. Neg. 9 : 3.
2. M. Neg. 11 : 7: Judah explains a law Eliezer is unable to rationalize, and Eliezer approves his explanation.

14. *ʿAqiba +Eliezer vs. Judah b. Batyra*

1. M. Par. 2 : 5: Black hairs on Red Heifer.

15. *Yoḥanan b. Zakkai + Eliezer (etc.)*

1. M. Avot 2 : 8-10

Clearly, *Eliezer + Joshua*-pericopae constitute the largest single corpus of the *Eliezer + Named Master*-type of traditions. The second considerable collection is Eliezer + ʿAqiba. Only a few exempla have

Eliezer with a single other master, chiefly with Gamaliel. Gamaliel further occurs in Eliezer + Joshua pericopae, supplying a compromise position between the opinions taken by the chief authorities. Additionally, Eliezer, Joshua, and ʿAqiba appear together. Sometimes it is difficult to see why the pericopae have joined Joshua + ʿAqiba as separate authorities, since they appear with the same opinion, or opinions so close as to be materially undistinguishable. Occasionally, to be sure, ʿAqiba will compromise between Eliezer and Joshua. All other combinations of Eliezer with another named master are episodic; no pattern emerges. Others included, once or at most twice, with Eliezer are as follows: Ṭarfon, Judah b. Batyra, Ishmael, Eleazar b. ʿAzariah, and, in M. Avot 2 : 8-10 only, Yoḥanan b. Zakkai.

It further appears that a single issue will produce several distinct pericopae. But these normally are generated by Joshua's and ʿAqiba's tradents. The more important examples give Joshua and ʿAqiba the same opinion or base their discrete ruling on a single principle. Issues common to a number of circles are as follows:

1. M. Ber. 1 : 1: Eliezer + Gamaliel + M. Ber. 1 : 2: Eliezer + Joshua *re Shemaʿ*.
2. M. Ter. 8 : 1-3: Eliezer + Joshua *re* deed begun licitly and completed illicitly is debated by the Houses.
3. M. Shab. 19 : 1, 4: Circumcision on Sabbath. 19 : 1: Eliezer lenient, ʿAqiba strict. 19 : 4: Eliezer strict, Joshua lenient.
4. M. Pes. 3 : 3, Eliezer, Judah b. Batyra, Joshua = M. Ter. 8 : 11, Eliezer + Joshua *re* taking action to prevent a transgression (Eliezer) *vs.* doing nothing (Joshua). M. Zev. 8 : 10, same issue, same authorities.
5. M. Pes. 6 : 1-2, Eliezer + Joshua, then ʿAqiba is inserted, *re* Sabbath and Passover. This is explicitly made parallel to M. Shab. 19 : 1.
6. M. Shab. 2 : 5: Eliezer, ʿAqiba + Ishmael—Eliezer + ʿAqiba: No separate offering for each sin; Ishmael: Separate liability for each sin. M. Ker. 3 : 10: Eliezer *vs.* ʿAqiba.
7. Tos. Zev. 2 : 16: Eliezer *vs.* Joshua *re* intention in the cult. Sifra Ṣav: Eliezer *vs.* ʿAqiba.
8. M. Men. 3 : 4, Tos. Zev. 4 : 1-2: Joshua *vs.* Eliezer *re* effect of impairment of residue of Meal-offering on Meal-offering. M. Me. 1 : 2, 3: Parallel issue: Flesh +/− blood—ʿAqiba *vs.* Eliezer, with ʿAqiba parallel to Joshua. Tos. Men. 4 : 10—Eliezer *vs.* ʿAqiba *re* issue of Eliezer + Joshua in M. Men. 3 : 4. Tos. Zev. 4 : 5: Eliezer *vs.* ʿAqiba *re* flesh +/− blood. Tos. Zev. 4 : 1-2—Eliezer *vs.* Joshua *re* flesh +/− blood.
9. M. Sanh. 10 : 3: ʿAqiba *vs.* Eliezer + Tos. Sanh. 13 : 2: Eliezer *vs.* Joshua *re* world to come. Positions reversed.

The *Eliezer + Named-Master*-type derives, therefore, primarily from the circles of ʿAqiba and Joshua, normally by themselves, but sometimes in tandem, occasionally including the opinions of other masters as well. The *Eliezer + ʿAqiba* and *Eliezer + Joshua*-materials presumably originate in the first instance, as stated, from the joint efforts of Eliezer and ʿAqiba or the disciples of the respective masters, we cannot be sure which. What has happened, however is that the transmission of Eliezer's traditions has been taken over by Joshua with his associate—perhaps disciple?—ʿAqiba. Gamaliel bears a markedly smaller part of the responsibility for Eliezer's tradition.

xiv. The Distribution of Traditions from Identifiable Sources

The pericopae involving Eliezer and a named master are not evenly distributed according to the several masters among the various tractates and orders.

1. *Zeraʿim*

Eliezer + ʿAqiba

1. M. Ber. 5 : 2.
2. M. Pe'ah 7 : 7.
3. M. Shev. 8 : 9.
4. M. Shev. 8 : 10—ʿAqiba declines to report Eliezer's opinion.
5. M. Ter. 6 : 6: + Eliezer.
6. M. Ma. 4 : 6.
7. Sifré Deut. 303 = M. M.S. 5 : 12.
8. M. Hal. 2 : 1.

Eliezer + Joshua

1. M. Ber. 1 : 2.
2. M. Shev. 5 : 3.
3. M. Ter. 4 : 7.
4. M. Ter. 4 : 8.
5. M. Ter. 4 : 9.
6. M. Ter. 4 : 10.
7. M. Ter. 4 : 11.
8. M. Ter. 8 : 1.
9. M. Ter. 8 : 2.
10. M. Ter. 8 : 3.
11. M. Ter. 11 : 2.
12. Tos. Hal. 1 : 6.
13. M. Orl. 1 : 7.

Eliezer + Gamaliel

1. M. Ber. 1 : 1: + sages.
2. M. Hal. 4 : 7.
3. M. Bik. 2 : 6.

Eliezer + Joshua, ʿAqiba, Gamaliel

1. M. Ber. 4 : 3-4.

Eliezer, Joshua, Ṭarfon, Judah b. Batyra, ʿAqiba

1. M. Peʾah 3 : 6.

Eliezer, Ishmael, Ṭarfon, ʿAqiba

1. M. Ter. 4 : 5.

Eliezer, Joshua, Gamaliel

1. M. Shev. 9 : 5: (Gamaliel settles the issue with a compromise).
2. M. Ter. 8 : 8: (Gamaliel compromises) 8 : 9, 10, 11: Spelling out the principles of the original dispute.

Ishmael

1. Tos. Hal. 1 : 10: Ishmael accepts Eliezer's opinion that Dough-offering is taken from clean for unclean dough—thus opposed to ʿAqiba on a parallel issue, M. Ter. 6 : 6.

2. *Moʿed*

Eliezer + ʿAqiba

1. M. Shab. 2 : 3.
2. M. Shab. 19 : 1.
3. M. Pes. 9 : 2.
4. M. Sheq. 8 : 7.
5. M. Yoma 7 : 3.
6. Tos. R.H. 2 : 10.

Eliezer + Joshua

1. M. Shab. 12 : 4.
2. M. Shab. 19 : 4.
3. Tos. Shab. 1 : 17.
4. M. Eruv. 7 : 10.
5. M. Pes. 1 : 7.
6. M. Pes. 6 : 5.
7. M. Sheq. 4 : 7 (+ ʿAqiba's rule in favor of Joshua).
8. Tos Y.T. 3 : 2.
9. M. Ta. 1 : 1.
10. Tos. Ta. 2 : 5: Story.

Eliezer, Joshua, ʿAqiba

1. M. Pes. 6 : 1-2.

Eliezer, Judah b. Batyra, Joshua

1. M. Pes. 3 : 3.

Eliezer + Gamaliel

1. M. M.Q. 3 : 6.

3. *Nashim*

Eliezer + ʿAqiba

1. M. Yev. 12 : 3.
2. M. Naz. 7 : 4. (A reports E instructed A; then A reports J agreed with E.)
3. M. Sot. 9 : 3.
4. M. Sot. 9 : 4.

Eliezer + Joshua

1. Tos. Yev. 13 : 3-5.
2. M. Sot. 1 : 1.

(3. M. Sot. 3 : 4 [individual sayings].)

4. M. Sot. 6 : 1.

N.B. The *sages* of M. Git. 9 : 1 must include Ṭarfon, Yosi the Galilean, Eleazar b. ʿAzariah, and ʿAqiba, possibly also Joshua. Yosi otherwise never occurs with Eliezer.

Joshua, ʿAqiba + Eliezer

1. M. Yev. 8 : 4: A + E explain J's tradition.
2. M. Yev. 16 : 7: E + J *vs.* A.
3. M. Ned. 10 : 6: E *vs.* Joshua, ʿAqiba *vs.* Eliezer + *vs.* Joshua.

(4. M. Naz. 7 : 4: ʿAqiba *re* Eliezer, *re* Joshua.)

Eliezer + Gamaliel vs. Joshua

1. M. Yev. 13 : 7.

2-5. M. Ket. 1 : 6-9: Gamaliel + Eliezer *vs.* Joshua.

Eliezer, Joshua, Ben ʿAzzai, ʿAqiba, Judah b. Batyra, Eleazar b. ʿAzariah

1. Tos. Sot. 1 : 2. (How much time in intercourse?)

Eliezer + Gamaliel

1. M. Git. 1 : 1: Not a dispute.

Ṭarfon + Eliezer

1. M. Qid. 3 : 13.

4. *Neziqin*

Eliezer + ʿAqiba

1. M. Sanh. 1 : 4.

Eliezer + Joshua

1. M. B.B. 9 : 7.

Eliezer, Eleazar b. ʿAzariah, ʿAqiba

1. M. B.Q. 6 : 4.

Eliezer, ʿAqiba, Ishmael

1. M. Shav. 2 : 5.

5. *Qodashim*

Eliezer + ʿAqiba

1. M. Ker. 3 : 10.
2-3. M. Me. 1 : 2-3.

Eliezer + Joshua

1. Tos. Zev. 1 : 1 (M. Zev. 1 : 1 omits Joshua).
2. Tos. Pisḥa 4 : 5-6.
3. Tos. Zev. 2 : 16 (M. Zev. 3 : 3 and M. Men. 3 : 1 omit Joshua).
4. M. Zev. 7 : 4 (No. 1 expanded).
5. M. Zev. 8 : 10.
6. Tos. Men. 2 : 16: Eleazar introduces Joshua's name, omitted in M. Men. 3 : 1. Tos. Men. 4 : 5: Yosi parallel to Eleazar. Tos. Men. 4 : 6: Eliezer *vs.* Joshua.
7. Tos. Men. 8 : 19: Meir + Judah introduce Joshua's name, left out in M. Men. 7 : 3, which has Eliezer *vs.* sages. b. Men. 47a-b: ʿAqiba instead of Joshua. Tos. Men. 4 : 10: ʿAqiba instead of Joshua.
[8. M. Bekh. 1 : 6: Joshua and Ṣaddoq testify contrary to Eliezer's position. But it is not a formal dispute. Eliezer's opposition is *sages.*]
9. M. Ar. 6 : 1.
[10. M. Tem. 3 : 1: Joshua and Pappyas give testimony in support of *the sages* but are not the same as *the sages.*]
[11. M. Tem. 3 : 3: Eleazar instead of Joshua for issue of No. 1.]
12-13. M. Ker. 4 : 2-3.

Eliezer vs. Gamaliel

1. M. Hul. 2 : 6.

Eliezer + Eleazar b. ʿAzariah

[1. M. Ar. 8 : 4: Eleazar b. ʿAzariah approves Eliezer's law]

6. *Ṭoharot*

Eliezer + ʿAqiba

[1. Sifra Shemini 10 : 5-6/M. Kel. 5 : 1.]
[2. M. Kel. 14 : 1.]

Eliezer + Joshua

1. M. Kel. 14 : 7.
2. M. Kel. 17 : 1.
3. M. Oh. 2 : 4.
4. Tos. Ah. 9 : 7.

5. M. Oh. 9 : 15.
6. M. Oh. 12 : 3.
7. M. Oh. 12 : 8.
8-9. M. Oh. 14 : 4-5.
10. M. Oh. 17 : 2.
11. M. Par. 5 : 4.
12. M. Par. 9 : 4.
13. M. Par. 10 : 1.
14. Tos. Ah. 7 : 11.
15. M. Toh. 2 : 2.
16. M. Toh. 8 : 7.
17. M. Miq. 2 : 7.
18. M. Miq. 2 : 8.
19. M. Miq. 2 : 10.
20. M. Miq. 1 : 3.
21. Tos. Nid. 2 : 3.
22. M. Nid. 4 : 4. Tos. Ah. 3 : 7 has Eliezer *vs.* ʿAqiba.
23. M. Nid. 4 : 6.
[24. M. Yad. 4 : 3: Joshua supports Ṭarfon; Eliezer + Yoḥanan b. Zakkai agree.]
25. Tos. Ed. 1 : 10 = Eliezer in M. Toh. 4 : 2.

Eliezer, Joshua, ʿAqiba

1. M. Kel. 28 : 2: Eliezer *vs.* Joshua, compromised by ʿAqiba.
2. M. Nid. 10 : 3: Eliezer *vs.* Joshua, compromised by ʿAqiba.

Eliezer + Judah b. Batyra

1. M. Neg. 9 : 3.
2. M. Neg. 11 : 7.

ʿAqiba, Eliezer vs. Judah b. Batyra

1. M. Par. 2 : 5.

Eliezer + Joshua + Neḥunya b. Elinatan

1-2. M. Ed. 6 : 2-3.

7. *Historical and Exegetical Pericopae*

Yoḥanan b. Zakkai + Eliezer, etc.

1. M. Avot 2 : 8-9.

Eliezer vs. Joshua

1. M. Ed. 8 : 6.
2. Tos. Sanh. 13 : 2.

ʿAqiba re Eliezer

1. Tos. Sanh. 11 : 5.
2. Tos. Hul. 2 : 24.
3. M. Sanh. 10 : 3.

8. *Summary*

	Eliezer + ʿAqiba	Eliezer + Joshua	Eliezer + Gamaliel	Other
Zeraʿim	8	13 (+2)	3 (+2)	3
Sheviʿit	2	1		
Terumot	1	9 (+1)	—(+1)	
Rest scattered				
Moʿed	6 (+1)	10 (+1)	1	1
Shabbat	3	3		
Rest scattered				
Nashim	4 (+4)	4 (+4)	1	8
Scattered	1 (+2)	1	—	2
Neziqin	1 (+2)	1	—	2
Scattered				
Qodashim	3	13	1	1
[N.B.: M. gives *sages* in place of Tos.'s Joshua.)				
Zevaḥim-Menaḥot	—	6		
Rest scattered				
Ṭoharot	(2) (+2)	25 (+2)	—	5
Kelim	— (+1)	2 + 1		
Ohalot	—	8		
Parah	—	2		
Miqva'ot	—	3		

The important tractates therefore are *Terumot, Zevaḥim-Menaḥot*, and *Ohalot.* In all three, considerable numbers of Eliezer + Joshua pericopae are collected. These not infrequently are located in the same chapter; they center upon a narrow problem or principle of law. Indeed, where several pericopae occur in a single tractate or chapter, the several exempla frequently turn upon the repetition of a single principle in a number of discrete examples.

One cannot suppose that the only traditions handed on by Eliezer dealt with the matters now before us. Nor is it possible to claim that we have a complete repertoire of Eliezer's rulings. The contrary seems more likely to be the case, with him as with all other masters. What we do have are materials *preserved* in a number of different ways. One way was through the immediate disciple, Ilai, and Judah. Another clearly was through the amalgamation of Eliezer's traditions with Joshua's, following a pre-arranged agendum, and, to a less extent, ʿAqiba's.

The masters before us taught many more laws than are preserved according to the very limited agendum, and that agendum cannot be regarded as random. Those of Eliezer's materials which were handed on in the dispute-form with Joshua's and ʿAqiba's were not episodically or accidentally preserved but reveal some sort of plan or an agreement on the part of Eliezer's and Joshua's or ʿAqiba's disciples—if not of the masters themselves—to work out a fixed, limited agendum and to supply a full repertoire of the masters' principles and opinions appropriate *only* to that agendum.

It is, moreover, entirely likely that the plan or agreement involved many other subjects and themes. The elements which actually did survive should be seen not solely as those preserved by the masters or disciples, but as those *selected* from the preserved pericopae by later tradents and redactors, perhaps in later Yavneh, certainly at Usha and afterward. The elements which survived were presumably chosen in preference to other traditions available from other circles, for we cannot suppose that only Eliezer and Joshua specialized on *Ohalot* or *Terumot* (at the specific points at which they predominate); or that only they had opinions on the issues they are represented as discussing.

Evidence that a process of selection was underway derives from the survival of many singletons—traditions of Eliezer + Joshua or Eliezer + ʿAqiba which stand by themselves and do not relate either to other items in the composite traditions of the combined masters or to the context in which they are cited. These singletons suggest a much more substantial corpus of agreed-upon traditions was produced than now is preserved in the specified tractates. And other materials attributed to Eliezer, produced not by the Eliezer + Joshua or Eliezer + ʿAqiba or Ilai/Judah-chains, certainly were taken over in the normative tradition. Those of Eliezer's teachings which had their beginning not in dispute-form and not in chains have not been entirely lost. But their small proportion in the whole suggests that the preservation of Eliezer's traditions depended upon enlisting the efforts of others—first disciples, then contemporaries—in their formulation and transmission. But still others, outside of the circle of disciples and close contemporaries, must bear the major responsibility for making selections of what was to survive and what to be dropped or ignored.

We discern a three-stage redactional process. First comes Eliezer's formulation of his own ideas, whether according to a set of contemporary issues, as with the *Shemaʿ*, or through the application to general rules of a set of precise definitions. Second was the amalgamation of Eliezer's formulations with those of others. These must have required an agreement to disagree on a group of fixed problems and principles, e.g., intention, the process of neutralization, and the like. Finally, later authorities, presently assumed to be chiefly the Ushan ʿAqibans, used some of the materials produced by Eliezer and others in his time in the making of a composite, eventually comprising Mishnah-Tosefta. That third stage cannot be analyzed just yet, for further critical study of the sources of the Mishnah-Tosefta is not to be undertaken on so narrow a base as the very small sample of evidence before us.

xv. Eliezer and the Tannaim (1): Yavneh

We have now proved that Eliezer's circle—Ilai is the only member of whom we are certain, though some disciples mentioned only once or in passing may have been part of it—intersected with the circles of Joshua and ʿAqiba, and to a considerably smaller degree, Gamaliel. Other Yavneans, who bulk large in the total corpus of preserved sayings attributed to masters of that period, occur not at all or only in passing: Ishmael, Eleazar b. ʿAzariah, and Ṭarfon. Eleazar b. ʿArakh, supposed to have been a fellow-disciple, along with Joshua and Eliezer, of Yoḥanan b. Zakkai, Simeon b. Natanel, not only a disciple of Yoḥanan, but also married to Gamaliel's daughter and therefore related by marriage to Eliezer, and Yosi the Priest—all are striking omissions. But not much can be made of them, for the total number of sayings attributed to the three is inconsequential. More striking still, as already observed, is Yoḥanan's own absence. Among the earliest group of Yavneans, on the other hand, a fair representation—both in pericopae just now reviewed as well as elsewhere—may be found: Ṣaddoq and his son Eleazar, the Batyrans (Judah, Joshua, and others), Gamaliel—and even Agrippas!—all are present. If one reviews the names of Yavnean masters, apart from the disciples, associated with Yoḥanan b. Zakkai, only the following are missing: Ben Bukhri, Admon and Ḥanan, Ḥanina b. Dosa, Dosa b. Harkinas, and "the Sadducees." Of these, only Dosa is of any significance at all; his absence is noteworthy as already observed (Vol. I, p. 335).

On the other hand, we may compile an impressive list of Yavneans who appear seldom, if at all, in traditions about Eliezer, while predominating in other materials. They are, for the period toward 70: Dositheus of Kefar Yatma, Abba Eleazar b. Dolai, Ḥananiah b.

Ḥezeqiah b. Garon, Ḥanina Prefect of the Priests, Yoḥanan b. Gudgada, Yoḥanan haḤorani, Yoʿezer of the Birah, Naḥum the Mede, Naḥum the Scribe, Simeon b. Gamaliel, Simeon of Miṣpah, Zekhariah b. HaQaṣṣav; for the period toward 90: Eleazar b. Diglai, Eliezer b. Jacob, Ḥalafta, Ḥanina b. Gamaliel, Yeshebav, Joshua b. Hyrcanus, Neḥuniah b. HaQanneh, Samuel the Small, Abba Saul, Simeon b. Batyra, Simeon son of the Prefect; and for the period toward 110: Eleazar b. Ḥisma, Eleazar b. Judah, Eleazar b. Perata, Eleazar the Modite (interpolated), Elisha b. Abbuyah, Ḥananiah b. Ḥakinai, Ḥananiah b. Teradion, Yoḥanan b. Beroqa, Yoḥanan b. Nuri (seldom), Yosi the Galilean (very seldom), Judah b. Baba, Judah the Priest, Simeon b. ʿAzzai (once), Simeon b. Nanos, and Simeon b. Zoma. Among these, the most remarkable absences or instances of substantial underrepresentation, given their place in the Yavnean corpus, are Ṭarfon, Ishmael, Yosi the Galilean, Eleazar b. ʿAzariah, Simeon of Teman, and Simeon of Shezur.

xvi. Eliezer and the Tannaim (2): Usha

The Ushans involved in the study and revision of Eliezer's traditions are as follows: Joshua b. Qorḥa, Judah b. Ilai, Meir, Nathan, Jacob, Simeon b. Yoḥai, Simeon b. Eleazar (later), Yosi b. Ḥalafta, Simeon b. Gamaliel (seldom). Strikingly, while the Ushans may revise the protasis, or occasionally the apodosis, of a tradition about Eliezer, they never correct the names of the authorities mentioned in Eliezer's traditions. It is taken for granted that Eliezer will be in dispute with ʿAqiba or Joshua or some other, earlier master. No effort is made to change the names of the masters represented along with Eliezer. Normally the Ushan contribution is to refine the law under dispute, claiming that the Yavneans disputed a much finer point than now is represented in Mishnah.

Tannas of the generation of Yavneh occasionally express an opinion about Eliezer and his rules, e.g., Ishmael praises his consistency, so too does ʿAqiba. It is very rare for an Ushan to do so. They and the following generation (excluding Judah the Patriarch) never are made to pass an opinion about the man or about the quality of his traditions. He is not seen as a controversial person. His opinions are taken to be important and sometimes authoritative. It would be difficult to claim that the Ushans deliberately distorted Eliezer's materials. Concomitantly, no Tanna—Yavnean or Ushan—states that the law follows Eliezer or that the law follows Eliezer's opponent. This must mean that the motive to exchange Eliezer's opinion for that of his opposition so as to secure its acceptance did not affect the formation of the materials in Ushan times. The evidence deriving from chains, attestations, and citations is overwhelmingly favorable toward Eliezer as a person and toward the excellence of his legal opinions and traditions.

xvii. Conclusion

The Eliezer of tradition is therefore portrayed by the most important authorities of the second century. Every effort seems to have been made to hand on generally consistent traditions, normally —though not always—developed out of, or closely related to the antecedent materials. No effort, systematic or otherwise, evidently was made either to suppress Eliezer's materials, to distort or falsify them, or to assign to them a negative value, as deriving from the House of Shammai or from a master who had been excommunicated. Neither theme so important in the period of the formation of the legends about Eliezer makes an appearance. To be sure, other important themes and subjects of the Eliezer-legend, beginning with his origins and ending with his death, likewise do not appear.

CHAPTER SIXTEEN

ELIEZER'S EXEGESES

i. Introduction

Exegetical pericopae involve not merely an allusion to or a citation of a verse as illustration or embellishment but sustained interest in the legal implications or theological or historical content of a given Scriptural verse. Our present interest is to see whether any patterns emerge among the various exegetical pericopae to reveal the approaches or methods in the interpretation of Scripture characteristic of Eliezer. A fair criterion for the establishment of such a particular approach or method will be the recurrence of a fixed technique or a consistent attitude in many unrelated pericopae involving separate masters and distinct questions. If we observe consistencies and have no reason to suppose they are wholly fabricated or anachronistic, we may suppose they may reflect Eliezer's own exegetical techniques.

ii. Legal Exegeses

The first and most important question is, Did Eliezer derive law from exegesis, or did the legal interpretations of specific Scriptures follow after, and provide pretexts for, laws which had already been formulated on entirely other grounds. To answer this question, we shall rapidly review the pertinent legal exegeses.

Eliezer and ʿAqiba have an exegetical dispute in M. Peʾah 7 : 7 (Sifra Qedoshim 3 : 1, Sifré Deut. 285). Eliezer interprets Deut. 24 : 21 to mean that the application of the law of defective clusters depends upon a grape-harvest. If there is no harvest, the law does not apply. ʿAqiba stresses Lev. 19 : 10, which says that one should not take defective clusters from the vineyard—even if the whole vineyard consists of them. ʿAqiba further deals with Deut. 24 : 21; it assigns a time for the poor to collect their clusters—after the vintage, not before. Sifré Deut. 230 provides an exegetical dispute between Eliezer and the sages to account for their disagreement in M. Kil. 5 : 8 *re* thorns in a vineyard. M. Ter. 6 : 6, on paying back from one kind for another in the case of misappropriated Heave-offering, includes a dispute between Eliezer and ʿAqiba on the meaning of Lev. 22 : 14.

Eliezer says the Scripture states one gives to the priest what is holy, meaning, what is appropriate to be holy. ʿAqiba says "what is holy" means what the man has actually consumed. Sifra Emor 6 : 6 has ʿAqiba's exegesis, not Eliezer's. b. Yev. 70a contains a dispute on whether an exegesis is needed to prove that an uncircumcized priest may not eat Heave-offering. Eliezer says Ex. 12 : 45 and Lev. 22 : 10 are linked by a *heqqesh*, based on the common occurrence of *sojourner* and *hired servant.* In both cases an circumcized person may not participate. ʿAqiba says Lev. 22 : 4, *Whosoever*, alludes to the uncircumcized. Sifré Deut. 303 has Eliezer's interpretation of Deut. 26 : 14. He says the requirement not to give from tithe to the dead means one does not buy with it a coffin and shrouds for the dead. ʿAqiba says that rule would apply also to a shroud or coffin for a living person. It means, "I have not exchanged it even for something clean." M. M.S. 5 : 12 preserves Eliezer's exegesis without his name.

M. Pes. 3 : 3—the dispute between Eliezer and Joshua about separating Dough-offering in uncleanness on 15 Nisan—is given an exegetical basis in Tos. Pis. 3 : 7. Eliezer points out Scripture says (Ex. 12 : 9) that one must not have leaven. Joshua says this is limited by Ex. 12 : 16, *Only what is eaten by every soul*—and this is not eaten by *every* soul. In M. Pes. 9 : 2, ʿAqiba interprets the plain sense of Num. 9 : 9, while Eliezer gives it a most limited and fanciful meaning, in connection with the distant journey. Sifré Num. 69 develops the dispute by giving Eliezer a *heqqesh*, tying tithes to Passover. Eliezer proves one must not bring the Passover from tithes (Mekhilta deR. Simeon, p. 39, ls. 7-14). In Egypt were no tithes, so the Passover of that time was not brought with tithe-money, and likewise afterward it should not be brought from tithe-money. ʿAqiba says it was impossible to do so there, but that does not tell us the law applying when it *is* possible to do so. But, ʿAqiba adds, just as in Egypt the Passover had to come from unconsecrated beasts, so in the future it has to come from unconsecrated beasts. In Sifré Deut. 133 Eliezer and ʿAqiba dispute the meaning of the commandment to sacrifice in the evening (Deut. 16 : 6). Eliezer says one sacrifices the Passover in the evening, eats it at sunset, and burns it at midnight. ʿAqiba says one sacrifices in the evening, eats at sunset and until midnight. b. Ber. 9a has Joshua. Sifré Deut. 140 provides an exegesis for Eliezer's rule that one must make use of his own *lulav* and his own *Sukkah*: You will make *for yourself.* The sages distinguish between the *lulav* and the *Sukkah.* The latter may be shared or borrowed. Tos. R.H. 2 : 10 has Judah +

Eliezer say that Lev. 23 : 24 refers to the sanctification of the day, the Memorial verses, and the Shofar verses. ʿAqiba says the reference is to the Memorial verses, the Shofar-verses, and the Sanctification of the Day. b. R.H. 32a omits Judah. Mekh. Vayassa 5 : 41ff. = b. Bes. 15b give Eliezer a proof for *ʿeruvé tavshilin* (M. Bes. 2 : 1). M.-Tos. know nothing of the exegesis. The same is so for the release of vows, b. Hag. 3a. Here Joshua likewise participates.

M. Yev. 12 : 3 has an exegetical dispute between Eliezer and ʿAqiba, following upon their disagreement on omitting the spitting in the *ḥaliṣah* rite. Eliezer says, *Thus will be done* (Deut. 25 : 9) means that all things must be done as stated. ʿAqiba says *To the man* means that the man must do his part, but the failure of an element in the ceremony pertaining solely to the woman will not disqualify the rite. This exegesis follows closely from, or may in fact yield, the legal dispute; it does not look as though it were attached after the fact. Sifré Deut. 212 presents the dispute of Eliezer and ʿAqiba on Deut. 21 : 12. Eliezer says the captive maid should cut her nails. ʿAqiba says she should let them grow. Eliezer presents a *heqqesh.* ʿAqiba accepts the principle of the *heqqesh* but supplies a different interpretation. Sifré Deut. 213 has a dispute between the same masters on Deut. 21 : 12. Eliezer says the verse refers literally to her father and mother, for whom the captive maid should weep. ʿAqiba says the reference is to idolatry. In b. Sanh. 58a Eliezer says Gen. 2 : 24 refers to the father's sister, and the mother's sister; ʿAqiba says it means the father's wife and the mother is meant literally.

In b. Hag. 10a Eliezer and Joshua supply proofs for the dissolution of vows. Eliezer says Lev. 27 : 2 and Num. 6 : 2 contain two references to *clearly uttering* a vow. One refers to binding, the other to dissolving. Joshua points to Ps. 95 : 11 as an example of God's releasing himself from a vow. Sifré Num. has an exegesis for Eliezer for Num. 30 : 2: "To make the utterance like an oath." ʿAqiba denies such an exegesis is required. Likewise, Sifré Deut. 61 has Eliezer prove from Deut. 12 : 3 that one must uproot an *asherah.* ʿAqiba says a proof-text is unnecessary for that purpose. The text means one has to change the name of the place where the *asherah* has been cut down. Sifré Num. 24 provides an exegesis of Num. 6 : 4 in support of Eliezer's position in M. Naz. 6 : 11: All the required deeds must be completed before the end of the Naziriteship. Sifré Deut. 205 adds ʿAqiba's disagreement to Eliezer's law in M. Sot. 9 : 2: if a neglected corpse is found between two cities, both have to bring a heifer. M. knows nothing of ʿAqiba's position. No exegesis seems to be involved. Sifré Deut. 206 has the *sages* as the opposition. Tos. Qid. 1 : 4 has Eliezer on harlotry (Lev. 19 : 29). b. Sanh. 76a has Eliezer and ʿAqiba, with entirely different opinions from Tos. Here Eliezer says harlotry is marrying a young girl to an old man. ʿAqiba says it means delaying in marrying off a mature daughter. In b. Yev. 61b, Eliezer says a whore (Lev. 21 : 7) is a faithless wife, and ʿAqiba says it is a prostitute—the plain sense of the word.

Tos. Sanh. 3 : 1 provides Eliezer with an exegetical basis for his opinion that an ox which has killed a man is tried by a court of twenty-three, but other animals which have killed are not. The exegesis is based on Lev. 20 : 16. Similarly, b. Sanh. 45b gives Eliezer an exegesis for Deut. 21 : 22 to prove that all who are stoned are hanged. Sifré Deut. 221 ignores that issue and focuses upon whether a woman is hung. Eliezer has no Scriptural proof for that opinion. M. Shav. 2 : 5 has exegeses for Eliezer and ʿAqiba to prove that a person is liable for being unaware of a creeping thing in the Temple but not for being unaware of the Temple itself. Ishmael has an exegesis for his contrary opinion, based on a *heqqesh, And it is forgotten*, said two times, one for each sort of sin. Lev. 5 : 2 is the verse for all parties' exegeses. The only difference between Eliezer and ʿAqiba is in the exegesis of the Scriptures; they agree on the practical consequence.

Eliezer compares Lev. 5 : 9 and 5 : 19, references to the Sin- and Guilt-offering, to show the two are treated the same way. Joshua is given a contrary proof. Tos. Zev. 1 : 1, which contains these proofs, is not cited in M. Zev. 1 : 1, where the law is presented without Scriptural support. The argument between Eliezer and Joshua about whether one must take action to prevent a transgression from taking place is given an exegetical formulation in M. Zev. 8 : 10. Both parties explain the meaning of Deut. 12 : 32. But other applications of the same principle are not associated with Scriptural proofs. Sifra Ṣav 8 : 1 (b. Zev. 29a) has Eliezer prove from Lev. 7 : 18 that one who slaughters his offering with the wrong intention—in order to eat it on the third day—has rendered it invalid. ʿAqiba differs. The legal issue is whether one retrospectively renders an offering unfit. Eliezer says one can do so. Tos. Zev. 4 : 1-2 gives Joshua and Eliezer proof-texts for their opinions on whether, if there is no blood, there is no flesh, and *vice versa.* Joshua says Deut. 12 : 27 proves if there is no blood, there is no flesh, and *vice versa.* Eliezer says Deut. 12 : 27 shows that even if though there is no flesh, there may be blood; he then explains the meaning of the verse adduced in evidence by Joshua. Sifré Deut. 75 has the same repertoire of proofs. Tos. Ar. 4 : 24 provides an exegetical basis for Eliezer's law in M. Ar. 8 : 4. Tos. Ker. 2 : 12 provides an exegesis for Eliezer's opinion in M. Ker. 4 : 2-3. Lev. 4 : 23 refers to a sin of any kind. Joshua says the same verse means one must know just what sin he has done. Sifra Vayiqra 7 : 26-31 gives an exegesis to Joshua alone. Eliezer's view that the *Parah*-sacrifice is not subject to normal Temple requirements is supported by an exegesis of Deut. 23 : 19 (M. Par. 2 : 3), though the exegesis relates to one matter only, using the hire of a harlot to purchase the heifer.

b. Nid. 68b provides an exegetical dispute for Eliezer's and Joshua's difference in M. Nid. 10 : 3 that the first and seventh days are counted and cover the intervening ones—so Eliezer. Eliezer says Lev. 15 : 28 proves that after all of the days are done—counted without interruptions—the *Zab* or *Zabah* is clean. Joshua draws his proof from Num. 6 : 12. Lev. 13 : 45 is interpreted by Eliezer to mean that the leper should let his hair grow loose. ʿAqiba interprets the verse through a *heqqesh* based on *shall be*—things external to his body are at issue. The leper should not wear *tefillin*—so Sifra Tazriʿa 12 : 6. b. M.Q. 15a has the same argument.

The legal exegeses thus are scattered among the various orders of the Mishnah. They are not concentrated on any legal theme or problem. A great many laws—the vast majority—are not related to a Scriptural proof-text, and at least some of the legal exegeses seem to come after the fact. M. Ter. 6 : 6 and the related rules about giving clean Heave-offering for unclean cannot have depended upon the exegesis of Lev. 22 : 14. The dispute connected to M. Pes. 3 : 3 seems important only for Joshua's position; one does not have to present an ingenious interpretation of the verse to prove Eliezer's point about not having leaven on Passover. Often, moreover, disputes between ʿAqiba and Eliezer will turn on whether a Scriptural exegesis is required to produce a law; Eliezer will prove what to ʿAqiba is already clear. Some interpretations of Scripture clearly are intended to support established practice, for instance, the proof for the release of vows and that for the acceptability of *ʿeruvé tavshilin.* In addition, some laws in legal-exegetical compilations are not represented as based on exegeses at all, for instance, M. Sot. 9 : 2 in Sifré Deut. 205. And other exegeses will produce related, but distinct laws, as in b. Sanh. 45b/Sifré Deut. 221. Still other exegeses deal with only a detail of a much larger issue, as M. Zev. 8 : 10, which relates only to the cult, but *not* to the cases cited in M. Ter., and M. Par. 2 : 3, which is not alleged to cover all the applications of the same principle in the very same pericope. In all, therefore, it seems highly unlikely that Eliezer normally produced laws on the basis of antecedent interpretations of Scripture. Sometimes this may have been the case; in others it is not entirely clear. But in the main the exegesis of Scriptures follows after the formulation of the law. And in most cases the law is generated entirely independent of exegesis, frequently by logical extension of established principles.

iii. Plain vs. Fanciful Interpretation

It cannot be shown that Eliezer exhibited a preference for a simple and obvious of Scripture over a fanciful or imaginative one. Indeed, we have about as many of the one sort of interpretation as of the other.

1. *Pericopae in which Eliezer prefers the simple meaning over the fanciful one*:

1. Tos. Pis. 3 : 7: Ex. 12 : 19 means one cannot separate Dough-offering on the festival.
2. Sifré Deut. 140: One must own his own *lulav, Sukkah.* Sages: All Israel may dwell in a single *Sukkah.*
3. Sifra Tazriʿa 12 : 6: Eliezer parses Lev. 13 : 45. ʿAqiba supplies a *heqqesh*: Shall be.
4. M. Yev. 12 : 3: Eliezer interprets Deut. 25 : 9 verse in the plain sense. ʿAqiba treats *to the man* as an exclusionary clause.
5. Sifré Deut. 213: Eliezer says Deut. 21 : 12 is meant literally. ʿAqiba says it refers to idolatry.
6. Sifré Num. 24: *Re* Num. 6 : 20.
7. Sifré Zuṭṭa 24: The *Soṭah* is forced to drink against her wishes, as Scripture says.
8. Sifra Ṣav 8 : 1: Lev. 7 : 18 means intention alone may render the slaughter invalid.
9. M. Zev. 7 : 7: Lev. 7 : 7 means the Sin- and Guilt-Offerings are subject to the same law.
10. b. Men. 65b: Deut. 16 : 9 says you should count *for yourself*—meaning the date of Pentecost is set by the court. Joshua proves the same proposition in a somewhat more complex manner. Judah b. Batyra uses a *heqqesh*.
11. Tos. Ker. 2 : 12: Lev. 4 : 23 means any kind of sin is covered by a Sin-offering. Joshua: *In which he sinned* means the man must know what sin he has done.
12. b. Nid. 68b: Lev. 15 : 28—*After that* meaning without intervening uncleanness.
13. Mekh. deR. Simeon, p. 106: Ex. 16 : 4 means one should not be anxious about food for the morrow.

14. Gen. R. 70 : 5: Deut. 10 : 18 is literally interpreted. Joshua says it refers to Torah.
15. Sifra Emor 17 : 11 = Mekh. Pisḥa 14 : 11ff.: *Sukkot* (Ex. 12 : 37) means *Sukkot* literally. ʿAqiba: Clouds of glory. b. Suk. 11b reverses.
16-17. b. Bekh. 5b, b. Sanh. 106a: *Rephidim* and *Shiṭṭim* were place-names.
18. Mekhilta deR. Simeon p. 38: Ex. 13 : 5 is interpreted in a plain sense by both Eliezer and ʿAqiba.
19. Sifra Beḥuqotai 5 : 1: God warns Israel before punishment.
20. Sifré Deut. 29: Deut. 3 : 26.
21. Sifré Deut. 32: Deut. 4 : 6 applies to property and body.
22. Sifré Zuṭṭa 13 : 24: Jer. 36 : 27-8 proves a man's agent is like himself. [N.B.: ʿAqiba and Joshua also give plain-sense of the Scriptures.]
24. y. Ta. 1 : 1: Is. 30 : 15 means one must repent to be saved.
25. Gen. R. 61 : 3: Qoh. 11 : 6 means one should sow early and late in life.
26. Gen. R. 98 : 4: Gen. 49 : 3—Eliezer + Joshua.

2. *Pericopae in which Eliezer prefers the fanciful meaning over the simple one*:

1. M. Pes. 9 : 2: *Distant journey* (Num. 9 : 9) means outside of the Temple itself. Tos. Pis. 8 : 2 makes this a *heqqesh.*
2. b. Yev. 48a-b: ʿAqiba says Deut. 21 : 12 means the nails are not to be cut. Eliezer proves from a *heqqesh*-(disfigurement)—that they are to be disfigured.
3. b. Sanh. 58a: Eliezer says Gen. 2 : 24 refers to aunts. ʿAqiba holds it means his father's wife; his mother is taken literally.
4. b. Hag. 10a: Eliezer uses the principle that a repetition of words produces two separate laws. Joshua proves the point on the basis of a simple Scriptural reference.
5. M. Ned. 10 : 7: Eliezer rejects the sages' interpretation of the simple sense of Num. 30 : 14.
6. b. Qid. 18b: BGD means cloak, so ʿAqiba. Eliezer: it means deceit.
7. b. Sanh. 76a: Eliezer says harlotry is marrying a girl to an old man. But ʿAqiba's explanation is equally fanciful.
8. b. Yev. 61b: Lev. 21 : 7—harlot—Eliezer says it is a faithless wife. ʿAqiba says it is a prostitute.
9-10. M. Sanh. 10 : 3: ʿAqiba says Num. 14 : 35 proves the generation of the wilderness perished. Eliezer says Ps. 50 : 5 refers to that generation. Similarly: the sons of Qoraḥ—Num. 16 : 33 *vs.* I Sam. 2 : 6.
11. y. Suk. 4 : 3: II Sam. 7 : 23 shows the Israelites brought idols out of Egypt.
12. Mekh. Pisḥa 14 : 113ff.: Ps. 81 : 45 means redemption will take place in Tishri. N.B.: Mekh. deR. Simeon, p. 135, uses Ps. 121 : 30 + Ex. 12 : 42 to make a completely different point.

14. b. R.H. 10b: I Kings 8 : 2 proves Patriarchs were born in Tishri.
15. Mekh. Beshallaḥ 7 : 109ff.: Ex. 14 : 31 proves there were 200 plagues at the sea. [All exegeses fanciful.]
16. b. Sanh. 95b: Ex. 14 : 31 applies Sennacherib.
17. Mekh. Vayassa 1 : 1-12: Ex. 15 : 22 proclaims the excellence of Israel.
18. Mekh. Amalek 2 : 186: Ex. 17 : 16 interpreted in a fanciful way by all parties.
19. Mekh. Amalek 1 : 173-5: Ex. 17 : 13 shows the war was at the divine command.
20. Mekh. Amalek 1 : 131: Ex. 17 : 11 shows when Israel is loyal to Torah, it prevails.
21. Sifra Mekhilta deMilu'im 2 : 35: Eliezer says the sons of Aaron died outside. ʿAqiba: *Before the Lord* means inside the tent.
22. Sifré Num. 136: Deut. 34 : 1 means God strengthened Moses' eyes.
23. y. Shab. 9 : 3: ŠNYM means years.

iv. Techniques of Exegesis

Three techniques of exegesis, all of them commonplace, recur in Eliezer's exegetical materials: the *heqqesh*, often applied to legal problems, the exclusion or limitation, and the parsing of a Scripture, in which individual clauses are explained according to a single scheme, extant mostly for non-legal verses. None of these techniques is claimed to begin with Eliezer, and all of them frequently occur in the sayings of his contemporaries.

The sole significant discovery is that we do not find among Eliezer's exegetical materials a single instance of the use of a device or technique generally assigned to the authority of Naḥum of Gimzu + ʿAqiba. This would be a decisive mark of the general reliability of the exegetical materials, if the validity of the ʿAqiban devices were ever an explicit issue, and if Eliezer were represented as opposing their use. But ʿAqiba, who occurs with great frequency in the exegetical traditions assigned to Eliezer, himself never employs any of the ʿAqiban principles.

1. *The Heqqesh*

The *Heqqesh* links one legal Scripture to another by reference to a word common to two or more such legal verses or other analogical links. It is attributed first to Hillel. While it appears with some frequency in Eliezer's traditions, it is never alleged that Eliezer was the first to introduce it, nor does its use appear controversial, nor is Eliezer's introduction of the device countered by rejection of the device itself. ʿAqiba and Joshua differ not on the validity of the hermeneutical device but on its implication in a particular setting.

1. b. Shab. 131a: *Bringing* in Lev. 23 : 10, 17 links two showbreads, *ʿomer.*
2. M. Pes. 6 : 2: *Appointed time* means one may slaughter the Pass-over on the Sabbath and do *all* other required actions. ʿAqiba: *Appointed time* applies only to the actual slaughter. The two are not exactly comparable, and Eliezer does not apply the *heqqesh* to other necessities of the slaughter. The *heqqesh* is developed in the Hillel-stories and more appropriately spelled out in Sifré Zuṭṭa 9 : 2.
3. Tos. Pis. 8 : 2/M. Pes. 9 : 2.
4. Sifré Deut. 212: Eliezer and ʿAqiba both use the *heqqesh re* Deut. 21 : 12.
5. Mekh. Neziqin 9 : 29-30: *Sending out* means with a writ.
6. Tos. Sanh. 3 : 1: Ox tried by a court.
7. Tos. Zev. 1 : 1: Lev. 5 : 9, 19 link Sin- and Guilt-offering.
8. Sifra Vayiqra 13 : 4: *Aviv* links the *ʿomer* to barley.
9. b. R.H. 10b: Gen. 30 : 22 + Lev. 23 : 24 + I Sam. 2 : 21 = *remembering.*

2. *Exclusion or Limitation*

The principle of exclusion (*Miʿuṭ*) occurs, though never so designated. It is a logical principle that if Scripture specifically prohibits one among several possible items, then by implication it permits the others. Or if it particularly alludes to one part of a proposition, it then means to lay stress on that single item and to exclude the others from consideration.

1. Mid. Tan. to Deut. 4 : 6, b. Ber. 13a: *These words* limits the requirement of intention to the opening sentence of the *Shemaʿ.* ʿAqiba: It is not necessary—the whole passage requires *intention.*
2. M. Peʾah 7 : 7: *When* you gather grapes—but if you do not gather grapes, the law does not apply. ʿAqiba: You will not take defective clusters *under any circumstances.*
3. b. Sanh. 45b: Deut. 21 : 22—Hang only blasphemer.
4. M. Shav. 2 : 15: Lev. 5 : 2 excludes unawareness of Temple.
5. b. Zev. 76b: Lev. 2 : 12 excludes the altar but permits the fire.
6. Tos. Ar. 4 : 24: Lev. 27 : 28 proves one may sanctify part of a field but not a whole field.
7. Sifré Deut. 75 = Tos. Zev. 4 : 1: Deut. 12 : 27—The blood of your sacrifices will be poured out *even* if the sacrifice is impaired.
8. M. Par. 2 : 3: Deut. 23 : 19 says a harlot's hire may not be brought to the Temple, but it may be used for the purchase of a *Parah.*

3. *Parsing*

Parsing a Scripture involves assigning a particular meaning to the principle elements of a single verse or of consecutive verses. This may require the interpretation of the simple meaning of the verse, or it may demand the explanation of one verse in terms of another or in the light of a different set of interpretive ideas.

1. Sifré Deut. 133: Deut. 16 : 6—*re* Passover.
2. Tos. R.H. 2 : 10: Lev. 23 : 24—*re* New Year Prayers.
3. Sifra Tazriʿa 12 : 9: Eliezer parses Lev. 13 : 45. ʿAqiba interprets the verse through a *heqqesh*: *Shall be*. In this case, Eliezer prefers the simple meaning.
4. Mekh. deR. Simeon p. 143: Song 2 : 14 + Ex. 14 : 13-14.
5. Gen. R. 42 : 1: Gen. 14 : 15 + Ps. 37 : 14.
6. ARN Chap. 36: Gen. 13 : 13.
7. Mekh. Beshallaḥ 1 : 57-69: Ex. 13 : 18 (+ Joshua—both fanciful).
8. b. Shab. 55b: Gen. 49 : 4.
9. b. Eruv. 40b: Qoh. 11 : 2.
10. b. Hul. 92a: Gen. 40 : 10.
11. b. B.B. 10b: Prov. 14 : 34.

v. Redactional Devices

Two redactional devices recur. First is the redactional structure built out of the names of Eliezer, Joshua, Gamaliel; then Gamaliel will say: "We still need the Modite," finally Eleazar the Modite, is introduced, as in b. Shab. 55b. The same redactional formula—Eliezer, Joshua, then Gamaliel, "We still need the Modite"—occurs in b. Hul. 92a. The *We still need the Modite*-structure is in b. B.B. 10b, this time amalgamated with Yoḥanan + disciples (Eliezer, Joshua, then, *The answer of... is best, for he says...*). Pesiqta deR. Kahana (Mandelbaum, p. 20, ls. 6-11ff.) repairs the construction: Liezer, Joshua, and the rabbis, but then yields Liezer, Joshua, Gamaliel, then (!) Leazar b. ʿArakh, and the formula, "I prefer the opinion of Leazar b. ʿArakh."

Second, ʿAqiba's comment on an interpretation or a proposition of Eliezer will occasionally begin with the assertion that what Eliezer has claimed requires Scriptural proof is so obvious that no such proof is needed; or the Scripture's plain meaning has already made Eliezer's point clear, and a more subtle meaning will be involved; or what Eliezer says Scripture proves in fact lies beyond the possibility of proof altogether. These several assertions serve primarily to introduce ʿAqiba's alternative interpretation and to link his saying to what has come before. They therefore seem to function chiefly as redactional devices, not entirely integral to ʿAqiba's own statement. Perhaps what is alleged is that Eliezer's statement was before ʿAqiba when the latter's comment was introduced. We have seven instances, six involving exegetical problems:

1. Mekh. deR. Simeon, p. 39: Passover does not come from tithes. ʿAqiba: You cannot prove what is possible from what is impossible.
2. b. Yev. 70a: Eliezer says one may prove an uncircumcized priest may not eat Heave-offering. ʿAqiba: Unnecessary proof.
3. y. B.Q. 4 : 5: Eliezer says Ex. 21 : 28 proves what ʿAqiba says is obvious.
4. Sifré Num. 153: Eliezer says Num. 30 : 2 proves an utterance is like an oath. ʿAqiba says this is obvious.
5. Sifré Deut. 61: One must uproot an *asherah*—proved by Deut. 12 : 3. ʿAqiba: No proof is needed.

[6. Sifra Shemini 10 : 5-6: ʿAqiba tells Eliezer one cannot decide what is impossible from what is possible. But no exegesis is involved.]

7. Mekh. Baḥodesh 4 : 36ff.: Ex. 19 : 19 proves Israel accepted Torah before it heard God's voice. ʿAqiba: This is obvious.

vi. Conclusion

Our survey of Eliezer's exegeses produces inconsequential results for the study of Eliezer's own contribution. It cannot be shown that Eliezer's legal opinions normally depended upon the exegesis of legal parts of Scripture. Occasionally that appears to have been the case. But for the most part the exegesis seems to be a post-facto addition to an already formulated legal opinion, a Scriptural pretext for a position taken on entirely logical grounds. Logic, not Scriptural exegesis, predominates in the formulation of Eliezer's laws. We moreover cannot show that any exegetical techniques assigned to him either certainly were originated by Eliezer or certainly cannot have been used by him at all. The *heqqesh* is commonplace among exegeses of his contemporaries; the exclusionary principle and the parsing of Scripture are found routinely not only in rabbinic exegesis but elsewhere. We cannot demonstrate that Eliezer preferred either a simple meaning of Scripture or an imaginative and fanciful one. The tradition gives no evidence of the predominance of the one or the other. To be sure, b. Bekh. 34a assigns to Eliezer what is probably an anachronistic issue. He is supposed to prefer the traditional vowels rather than the received text of Scripture. But this saying is attributed to Rav Judah + Samuel; the issue is important in the early Amoraic stratum; and there is no reason to believe that the problem figured in the debates between Eliezer and Joshua. For the rest, we cannot claim that Eliezer is made to use techniques which he could not have used. The absence of the ʿAqiban interpretation of particles is noteworthy but is not probative of Eliezer's rejection of such alleged innovations. So we cannot claim that any specific approaches to, or methods in, the interpretation of Scripture were particularly characteristic of Eliezer and therefore illuminate his hermeneutical philosophy. The contrary seems the firm result of our survey: by themselves the exegetical pericopae supply no important information about Eliezer, other than what they allege in respect to episodic opinions or interpretations of individual verses. But these are best considered in the context of non-exegetical pericopae.

CHAPTER SEVENTEEN

THE ELIEZER OF LEGEND

i. Introduction. Eliezer and the Amoraim

Legendary stories about Eliezer's life and times generally are unrelated to legal sayings. They tend to appear in the later strata of the *Gemarot* and in the late compilations of *midrashim.* Their formal and literary traits exhibit little in common with pericopae in the legal tradition. The disciplined articulation of Eliezer's legal principles and discrete opinions, in close association with Joshua's and ʿAqiba's, on the one side, and Ilai's and Judah's, on the other, has no counterpart in the legendary materials. The legends introduce personal and professional relationships which bear slight, if any, parallels, either external or internal, to the evidences of the legal traditions. For example, while in the legal materials ʿAqiba, Joshua and Eliezer are regarded as equals, in the legendary ones ʿAqiba is made into the disciple of Eliezer, sometimes also of Joshua, and not infrequently Joshua and Eliezer will be represented as co-disciples of Yoḥanan. And the relationship to Yoḥanan b. Zakkai figures prominently in the legendary sort of stories, even though it is virtually unknown to the legal stratum. Clearly the use of the poor traditions for biographical and historical purposes will not be easy. Yet one cannot evade the task, for the purpose of the presentation and analysis of the traditions is not entirely carried out without posing historical questions to, not only *about*, those traditions.

It remains to ask, Was any particular Amora, individually or as part of a circle, especially involved in the formation and development of materials about Eliezer? The following tables suggest that only Rav Judah, through both Samuel and Rav, made a disproportionate number of references to the Eliezer-tradition. But what he contributed was the allegation that the law will be in accord with Eliezer's opinion. Otherwise only in specific and isolated pericopae do we find special interests introduced into the formulation of Eliezer-stories, i.e., Joshua b. Levi (important also in the Yoḥanan-tradition, at exactly the same points). Ba and Ḥiyya b. Ba seem to have had a good opinion of Eliezer. For the rest, the Amoraic allusions are episodic, and reveal no pronounced tendency either to favor him or to denigrate him or to treat him other than routinely, as part of the larger group of early masters.

I. *The Palestinian Talmud*

1. y. Ber. 5 : 2: Isaac Rabban + Rabbi—The law follows Eliezer *re* M. Ber. 5 : 2.
2. y. Shev. 8 : 8: Yosi curses Eliezer's opinion *re* the hide anointed with Seventh Year oil. Hezeqiah + Aḥa—the hide is permitted. Then Yosi says Eliezer permits marrying the daughter of an *ʿam haʾareṣ*. Hezeqiah + Aḥa—Eliezer permits Samaritan leavened products after Passover.
3. y. Ter. 2 : 1: Ṭabi + Josiah b. R. Yannai—The law follows Eliezer. Yiṣḥaq b. R. Naḥman + Hoshaia—The law follows Eliezer. Huna, Ḥananiah, Yosi b. R. Bun, Judah + Samuel—The law does not follow Eliezer.
4. y. Ter. 4 : 4: Jeremiah + Jacob b. R. Aḥa + Simeon b. Laqish—Eliezer follows the House of Shammai.
5. y. M.S. 4 : 5: Bar Qappara—the House of Shammai is in accord with Eliezer *re* Tos. M.S. 3 : 15-16.
6. y. Hal. 4 : 4: Abbahu explains Eliezer's rule in M. Hal. 4 : 7.
7. y. Pes. 5 : 1: Jeremiah says what Eliezer says in b. Ber. 9a.
8. y. Yoma 7 : 2: Huna + Joseph—Eliezer agrees with the House of Shammai *re* M. Yoma 7 : 3.
9. y. Ber. 3 : 1: Zeʿira, Jeremiah + Rav—The law follows Eliezer in the mourner's putting on *tefillin*, and Joshua in taking them off.
10. y. Yev. 13 : 2: Abbahu tells story of Eliezer's marriage to his niece.
11. y. Yev. 13 : 7: *Haggai* before Zera, Menaḥem + Yoḥanan—The law follows Eliezer in M. Yev. 13 : 7.
12. y. Ned. 9 : 2: Simeon + Joshua b. Levi—Eliezer's opinion on releasing vows derives from Moses. [N.B.: b. Ned. 64b—*Ḥisda*].
13. y. Naz. 7 : 1: Abin—The sages and Eliezer agree in certain respects.
14. y. Naz. 7 : 1: Huna + Joseph—Eliezer agrees with the House of Shammai.
15. y. Sot. 1 : 1: Leazar b. R. Yosi before Yasa—Eliezer agrees with House of Shammai.
16. y. Sot. 9 : 16 = y. A.Z. 3 : 1: Jacob b. Idi + Joshua b. Levi—Eliezer's death-scene linked to Yoḥanan b. Zakkai's.
17. y. M.Q. 3 : 1: Ḥanina comments on the excommunication-story but is not central to it. Jeremiah adds the story of Eliezer's evil eye.
18. y. M.Q. 3 : 1: Qerispai, Yoḥanan + Rabbi—I should accept Eliezer's opinions, but the Tannas mix them up.
19. y. Meg. 1 : 9: Jeremiah + Ḥiyya b. Ba: Eliezer and Joshua approved ʿAqiba's translation. [N.B.: b. Meg. 3a—They dictated it.]
20. y. Sanh. 1 : 2: Ba—Yoḥanan b. Zakkai ordained Eliezer and Joshua.

II. *The Babylonian Talmud*

1. b. Ber. 33b: Zera + Ḥiyya b. Abin + Yoḥanan—The law follows Eliezer *re* M. Ber. 5 : 2.
2. b. Nid. 8a: Eleazar—The law follows Eliezer *re* M. Ber. 5 : 2.

[3. b. Ber. 62a: Rabbah b. b. Ḥana has the opinion of Eliezer in b. Ber. 62a, *re* wiping with left hand.]

4. b. Nid. 8a: Eleazar—Eliezer stands behind M. Shev. 7 : 6.
5. b. Bekh. 34a: Judah + Samuel, Resh Laqish, Naḥman + Rabbah bar Abbuha—Eliezer follows the traditional views, plus an exegesis for his rule in M. Ter. 8 : 11.
6. b. Pes. 48b = b. Nid. 8a: Judah + Samuel—The law (M. Hal. 2 : 4) follows Eliezer.
7. b. Shab. 130a: Isaac—A town which followed Eliezer's rule in M. Shab. 19 : 1 was safe from evil decrees.
8. b. Shab. 130b: Zera + Assi—Simeon b. Laqish + Judah the Patriarch: "They followed Eliezer's opinion. How could they accept the opinion of a Shammaite?"
9. b. Eruv. 63a: Rabbah b. b. Ḥana + Yoḥanan—The disciple who taught law in Eliezer's presence was Judah b. Guria.
10. b. Pes. 48a: Rabbi says the law follows Eliezer *re* M. Pes. 3 : 3. Isaac says the law follows ben Batyra.
11. b. Pes. 69b: Judah + Rav—In M. Pes. 6 : 2 + M. Shab. 19 : 1 the law follows ʿAqiba.
12. b. Yev. 108a: Judah + Samuel explains Eliezer's opinion in M. Yev. 13 : 6.
13. b. Yev. 110a = b. Nid. 8a: Judah + Samuel—The law follows Eliezer in M. Yev. 13 : 7.
14. b. Ket. 12b: Judah + Samuel—The law follows Gamaliel + Eliezer in M. Ket. 1 : 6-9.
15. b. Ket. 73b: Rabbah—Eliezer and the First Mishnah are in agreement *re* M. Ned. 10 : 7.
16. b. Giṭ. 83b: Rava—*Re* disproofs of Eliezer in M. Giṭ. 9 : 1.
17. b. Shav. 19a: Sheshet would confuse Eliezer's and ʿAqiba's sayings in M. Shav. 2 : 5, because they were identical in principle.
18. b. Men. 17a-b: Yoḥanan explains Eliezer's opinion in M. Men. 3 : 1.
19. b. Men. 47a-b: Father of Jeremiah b. Abba has a version of a dispute between Eliezer and ʿAqiba.
20. b. Nid. 7b: Judah + Samuel—The law follows Eliezer in M. Nid. 1 : 3, 4 : 4, 10 : 3, and M. Toh. 8 : 7.
21. b. Nid. 9b: Rabbi ruled in agreement with Eliezer and explained that it is all right to do so in an emergency.
22. b. Sanh. 101b: Rabbah b. b. Ḥana—When Eliezer fell ill, disciples comforted him. ʿAqiba said suffering now insures future bliss.
23. b. Sanh. 17b: Judah + Rav: Eliezer knew seventy languages.

Palestinian Amoraim

1. Isaac Rabbah: I, 1; II, 7, 10.
2. Rabbi: I, 1.

3. Yosi: I, 2 (2).
4. Hezeqiah + Aḥa: I, 2 (2).
5. Ṭabi + Joshua b. R. Yannai: I, 3.
6. Huna, Ḥananiah, Yosi b. R. Bun: I, 3.
7. Jeremiah + Jacob b. R. Aḥa + Simeon b. Laqish: I, 4.
8. Bar Qappara: I, 5.
9. Abbahu, I, 6, 10.
10. Jeremiah: I, 7.
11. Zera, Jeremiah + Rav: I, 9.
12. Ḥaggai before Zera: I, 11.
13. Menaḥem + Yoḥanan: I, 11.
14. Simeon + Joshua b. Levi: I, 12.
15. Abin: I, 13.
16. Jacob b. Idi + Joshua b. Levi: I, 16.
17. Ḥanina: I, 17.
18. Jeremiah: I, 17.
19. Qerispai, Yoḥanan + Rabbi: I, 18.
20. Jeremiah + Ḥiyya b. Ba: I, 19.
21. Ba: I, 20.
22. Zera + Ḥiyya b. Abin + Yoḥanan: I, 1.
23. Eleazar [b. Pedat]: I, 2, 4.
24. Resh Laqish: I, 5.
25. Zera + Assi—Simeon b. Laqish: I, 8.
25. Rabbah b. b. Ḥana + Yoḥanan: I, 9.
26. Yoḥanan: II, 18.
27. Father of Jeremiah b. Abba: II, 19.
28. Rabbah b. b. Ḥana: II, 22.

Thus: Isaac 3
Simeon b. Laqish 2
Jeremiah 6
Abbahu 2
Yoḥanan 5
Joshua b. Levi 2
Ba 1
Eleazar b. Pedat 2
Rabbah b. b. Ḥana 2
Rest scattered

Babylonian Amoraim

1. Yiṣḥaq b. R. Naḥman + Hoshaia: I, 3.
2. Judah + Samuel: I, 3; II, 5, 6, 12, 13, 14, 20.
3. Huna + Joseph: I, 8, 14.
4. Naḥman + Rabbah b. Abbuha: II, 5.
5. Judah + Rav: II, 23.
6. Rabbah: II, 15.
7. Rava: II, 16.
8. Sheshet: II, 17.

Thus: Rav 3
Samuel 7
Joseph 2
Rest scattered

III. *Tanḥuma*

1. Ḥuqat 24: Aḥa + Yosi b. R. Ḥanina—Eliezer descends from Moses.

IV. *Gen. R.*

1. Gen. R. 5 : 3: Levi, Abba b. Kahana, Huna, Joshua + Eliezer.
2. Gen. R. 25 : 2: Yoḥanan, Jonathan = Eliezer, Joshua.

ii. Origins, Early Life, Education

The legends do not provide Eliezer with much of a biography. They add three important stories, the origins, excommunication, and the (closely-related) death scenes. Otherwise, Eliezer tends to appear not as an individual but as part of a redactional formula, along with Joshua, or with Joshua and ʿAqiba.

It is difficult to show that any details in the stories of Eliezer's origins (above, Vol. I, pp. 394-452) actually derive from his life. Eliezer and Joshua are routinely alluded to in y. Meg. 1 : 9 as the wonder-children who explain the mysterious meanings of the final letters. y. knows nothing about the story of Eliezer's beginning his studies as a mature man. It takes for granted that he spent his childhood with Joshua. It is difficult to see how the legends of Eliezer's origins could have been known to the authority behind the interpolation of Eliezer's and Joshua's names into a story about the wonder-children. So on the face of it the stories about Eliezer's origins ought to come after the interpolation of Eliezer's and Joshua's names in y. Meg.—that is, late in Amoraic times, not much before the beginning of the fourth century at the earliest.

ARN, the first in the several versions, takes for granted the relationship to Yoḥanan, which it (obviously) has learned from M. Avot itself. But where did it get the notion that Eliezer came only after the others in the circle—Joshua, Yosi the Priest—had already assembled as Yoḥanan's disciples? Only the story-line requires it. ARN also omits reference to the name of the father-in-law, Gamaliel's father, Simeon. This is not a noteworthy omission; it is not central to ARN's account. But the chria about bad breath is important, the second major theme in the account, after the story about leaving the plough to study Torah. Then the third theme, about the disinheritance which produced the contrary action, completes the account. This is surely homiletical. Gen. R. has all three elements, but adds the subject of the homily: Gen. 14 : 15. Tanḥuma contributes to the repertoire a substantial elaboration of the disinheritance motif. Eliezer is made the bad son, who leaves his father in time of troubles. Then comes the bad-breath chria. Then a colloquy further develops the story about the disinheritance. Finally Hyrcanus gives the son more than his brothers. Of these three stories, the first, about leaving the family to study Torah, seems to allege the most as biography. It claims factual knowledge of a specific person and is not merely a setting for a striking saying. The "bad breath" element is a chria in which the result of studies in poverty is represented as eventual fame. The disinheritance-motif, however fully developed, is nothing more than a homily in the guise of a biographical narrative; Torah not only is worth more than material wealth, but also produces great wealth from penitent parents. If the first element is historically sound, then Eliezer ought to have come from a wealthy family but to have displeased his family by adhering to Yoḥanan. We have very little evidence about Eliezer's own material situation; he may have had some orchards, but that does not make him a wealthy man. If he came from Lydda, on the plain, then he should not have been given a field in the mountains to plough, so that detail is probably imaginary. It is not easy to suggest what details might not be equally imaginary.

An interesting set of materials links Eliezer to Yoḥanan and omits reference to all the other disciples. These materials in part are merely redactional but in some cases represent Eliezer as the sole disciple and an exceptionally loyal one. Eliezer is tied to Yoḥanan in Sifré Deut. 144, expanded by b. Sanh. 32b to include many other masters, down to Rabbi. What is taken for granted in Sifré is that Yoḥanan and Eliezer are alike, and both conducted good courts. y. Ber. 2 : 3 joins Eliezer to Yoḥanan. Yoḥanan wore his *tefillin* all the time "and so did his disciple Eliezer." y. Sanh. 1 : 2 presents the saying of Ba, that Yoḥanan ordained Eliezer and Joshua; Joshua ordained ʿAqiba; and Eliezer is dropped. That Yoḥanan was the master of the two is taken for granted. None of these pericopae knows anything about the other disciples of Yoḥanan. Sifré Deut. may have been formulated before M. Avot. But Ba stands behind y. Sanh.; he may have drawn the correct conclusion from the absence of materials about the other disciples: they were not very important.

The stories that make Eliezer into *the* disciple of Yoḥanan then stand quite separately. They make the point that Eliezer was the loyal disciple and did everything his master did. This allegation would later be developed into the claim that he also never said anything his master had not said. Since the link between Eliezer and Yoḥanan is unattested before M.-Tos., it would seem to be of particular importance in the third century, at which time the contrary allegation that Eliezer was a Shammaite also was repeatedly made. This is furthermore when the Mishnah's promulgation produced the necessity to systematize the rules of deciding the law in moot cases. One rule clearly was that the law follows the House of Hillel. Another was that Eliezer was a Shammaite; therefore the law will not follow him. That point, to be sure, cannot have registered with the Rav Judah-Samuel circle, to which are attributed several rulings in favor of Eliezer's law. The contrary polemic was that Eliezer either was not a Shammaite; or that, whatever he was, he did just what his master did, and his master was Yoḥanan—therefore his laws should be regarded as normative because he was a Hillelite like his master. It therefore seems likely that the allegations about Eliezer's disciplehood to Yoḥanan were important in post-Mishnaic times. That he actually was Yoḥanan's disciple is unlikely. We do not know with whom he studied, and the legends do not supply much credible evidence on that subject.

Separate from the allegation that Yoḥanan was Eliezer's master is the repeated claim that Eliezer always copies his master(s)—who are not named. That claim should be prior to the one linking Eliezer to Yoḥanan and perhaps generated the further necessity to specify the master's name. Tos. Yev. 3 contains the earliest allegation that Eliezer's enigmatic replies were on account of his lacking traditions from his masters. It looks like an interpolated gloss, for other Tos. versions know nothing of this reason for his peculiar replies to questions. Tos. Suk. 1 : 9 has a story in which Eliezer gave enigmatic answers to his disciple's questions. At the end, b. Suk. 27b's *baraita*-version glosses: "Not in order to evade, but because he never said anything he had not heard from his master." The story in Tos. Kip. 3 : 14 about the rites of the penitential goat represents Eliezer as giving enigmatic answers to the several questions. b. Yoma 66b likewise glosses the story, not only adding new questions, but also alleging that he did not wish to put the disciples off, but he would not repeat a law he had not heard from his master. Consequently he would not answer their questions. The interpolation takes for granted the allegation that Eliezer never said anything other than traditions of his master(s). But it does not allude to Yoḥanan, as does b. Suk. 27b-28a. In b. Suk. 27b-28a,

Eliezer's stay with Yoḥanan b. R. Ilaʿi at Caesarea is narrated, with the moral that Eliezer did not evade the question but had never said anything he did not hear from his master. To this is adjoined a summary, with an interpolation of Yosi b. Judah. Then Eliezer is asked, "Are all your words only reproductions of what you have heard?" He replies that he never says anything he has not heard: "During all my life no man was earlier than myself in the school house. I never slept or dozed, nor did I leave anyone behind me when I left, nor did I ever utter profane speech, nor did I ever say a thing I did not hear from my teachers." Then comes Yoḥanan b. Zakkai, of whom it is alleged that he never uttered profane talk, never came after anyone else to the school house, never slept or dozed in the school house, never left anyone when he went out, and never said anything he had not heard from his teacher. Finally Hillel, with the eighty disciples, of whom Yoḥanan was least, is attached. Eliezer is dropped. And finally comes Jonathan b. ʿUzziel. The complex pericope stresses, therefore, that Eliezer copied Yoḥanan, Yoḥanan copied Hillel. Thus Eliezer is the true heir of Hillel. But the *redactor* has made that point, which is absent in the prior materials.

Of Eliezer's personal life, the legendary stratum says little. Eliezer was firm that one does not mourn the death of a servant (y. Ber. 2 : 8). Gamaliel did so. Thus Eliezer was supposed to have been part of the slave holding-class, as were (other) third- and fourth-century masters. Abbahu (y. Yev. 13 : 2) tells the story of Eliezer's marrying the daughter of his sister at his mother's request, despite his view that such a marriage to a minor is not legal. ARN drops the attribution to Abbahu and also the reference to Eliezer's mother. The niece is given the chief part.

Two other allegations about Eliezer's education are made. First, he and Joshua showed an interest in cosmological questions. Second, they traded information on how to produce children or male children. Eliezer and Joshua debate the source of rain-water. Eliezer says it comes from the ocean, Joshua, from the waters of the firmament (b. Ta. 9b). Their dispute extended to other cosmological questions: whether the world is completely enclosed by the firmament or not (b. B.B. 25a-b); whether the world was created from the center or from the sides; and whether the world was created from separate materials —heaven and earth—or from the same materials (b. Yoma 54b). I see no connection to *Maʿaseh-Bereshit*-mysticism. Eliezer and Joshua discussed (b. B.B. 10b) what to do in order to produce sons. Eliezer says one should give generously to the poor. Joshua says one should be considerate of the wife's sexual desires. Later versions will have Eliezer give that advice and greatly elaborate it.

Rav Judah-Rav (b. Sanh. 17b) say Eliezer, Joshua, ʿAqiba, and Simeon the Temanite all could speak seventy languages. So it is alleged that his education included the study of languages. y. Meg. 1 : 9 has Jeremiah in Ḥiyya b. Ba's name say ʿAqilas translated the Torah [= presented his translation] before Eliezer and Joshua. They approved it. b. Meg. 3a turns this into the allegation that they dictated the translation to him. On this basis S. Lieberman alleges Eliezer (and Joshua) knew Greek, for the translation was into that language, so *Greek in Jewish Palestine* (N.Y., 1942), pp. 16-19: "In the court of Jabneh . . . there were four members who spoke them [many languages] . . . It is possible that he [Eliezer] acquired his secular learning in his youth, while still at home . . . Here [with reference to ʿAqilas] there can be no doubt whatever that TP speaks of the Greek translation of the Bible by Aquila, who read it before R. Eliezer and R. Joshua, and was highly praised for it. This commendation can be appreciated only if the men who uttered it were qualified to pass judgment on the style and exactness of the translation. And it is obvious that the source in TP regarded them as able critics of Greek style." While it is clear that Ḥiyya b. Ba took for granted Eliezer knew Greek, it is difficult to find much evidence of that fact in the more reliable materials. The sayings based on Aristotelian science and cosmology do not much change the picture.

One cannot positively demonstrate that any of these folkloristic materials contains historically reliable information on Eliezer's origins, early life, and education.

iii. Eliezer's Active Career. Eliezer and Hillel

Eliezer certainly taught law to disciples. Just as it is alleged that he never taught what he had not heard, so it is claimed that disciples were prohibited from passing their opinion in his presence. This allegation is contradicted by the stories about ʿAqiba's numerous disputes with Eliezer, accompanied by the allegation that ʿAqiba was Eliezer's disciple. Sifra Shemini Mekhilta deMiluʾim 2 : 32-3 presents Eliezer's rule that a disciple must not teach the law in his master's presence. A story is also told to illustrate the same point. Eliezer further explains the death of Nadab and Abihu on account of their having taught in Moses's presence. This view does not depend upon a close exegesis of a verse. Sifra Mekhilta deMilu'im = b. Sanh. 52a presents a dispute between Eliezer and ʿAqiba about where the sons of Aaron died. Eliezer says it was outside, ʿAqiba says it was within the sanctuary. This dispute does not seem closely connected to Eliezer's view of the cause of their deaths.

ʿAqiba reports (y. Naz. 7 : 1) that he studied with Eliezer and Joshua. The two masters are represented as conducting a single academy. ʿAqiba's studies with Eliezer and Joshua, furthermore, are routinely alluded to in b. Ned. 50a, the "rich wife, poor scholarly husband"-version of ʿAqiba's beginnings. y. B.Q. 4 : 5 has ʿAqiba address Eliezer as "rabbi" and say that Eliezer's Scriptural exegesis is unnecessary, for its point is obvious. b. B.Q. 41b-42a has the same story, but greatly expands it. M. B.Q. 4 : 5 lacks Eliezer's exegesis and attributes the law to an anonymous, general rule. b. Pes. 69a and y. Pes. 6 : 3 take for granted that ʿAqiba was Eliezer's disciple. y. Pes. says the argument in M. Pes. 6 : 2 took place thirteen years after ʿAqiba began his studies. Joshua claims Eliezer had formerly despised ʿAqiba and now, after thirteen years, had to take him seriously. This element must be intended to account for the several composite pericopae, in which Eliezer opposes Joshua, then ʿAqiba, in that order.

The two are contrasted, with Eliezer at a disadvantage; for example, Eliezer prayed for rain without success. Then ʿAqiba's prayer was answered. ʿAqiba was forebearing, and Eliezer was not, so b. Ta. 25b. We find no story of how ʿAqiba obeyed Eliezer's rule against teaching law in the master's presence, but a great many which implicitly, and some which explicitly, state the opposite. The illness of Eliezer (Mekh. Baḥodesh 10 : 58-86) is a story about ʿAqiba's excellent instruction. All that is important for Eliezer is that he was ill. Ṭarfon, Joshua, Eleazar b. ʿAzariah, and ʿAqiba then supply the important characters, the first three setting the stage for the last and best. It is a story about ʿAqiba, and its point is a commonplace in the ʿAqiban corpus, that suffering is a good thing. Eliezer is not even given a chance to praise ʿAqiba's saying. The structure knows nothing about Eliezer and Joshua as disciples of Yoḥanan. Joshua is no different from Ṭarfon, ʿAqiba, and Eleazar; he calls Eliezer "my master," not "my brother." This genre of chriic settings was popular among those responsible for the midrashic compilations. The Avot-list of Yoḥanan's disciples, for example, generates ARN Chap. Fourteen, the story of the death of Yoḥanan's son, with Eliezer, Joshua, Yosi, Simeon, and Eleazar coming to pay respects. Eleazar comes at the end and is given the best saying. The same genre, not so well developed through narrative, occurs with reference to Ps. 14 : 34, the kindness of the peoples. But we should have further examples of the same "standard list" of disciples of Eliezer: Ṭarfon, Joshua, Eleazar b. ʿAzariah, and ʿAqiba. This is the only such "list"—a strange anomaly.

A second important associate was Joshua. While the interpolation of their names, as wonder-working children, suggests they were together from their earliest years, other stories treat them as associates only in their active careers. Eliezer and Joshua are joined in a number of stories. In b. B.B. 74b they are on a ship. Joshua sees a light, and Eliezer says it is the eye of Leviathan. The story about Eliezer, Joshua, and the insolent widow's son (b. Qid. 31a) has Eliezer as the reasonable party, Joshua as the irritable one. In Gen. R. 70 : 5 Eliezer treats the proselyte, ʿAqilas, in a short-tempered way, and Joshua is patient, parallel to Shammai and Hillel in b. Shab. 30b-31a. Qoh. R. 1 : 8.4 has the same pattern. Eliezer and Joshua are introduced into the story (y. Hag. 2 : 1) of the circumcision of Elisha b. Abbuyah. They were in Jerusalem and invited to the celebration. While others caroused, they studied Torah. But their studies produced supernatural effects—the effects like those described in the *Merkavah*-stories—and so Elisha's father decided he wanted his son to have the same power. This spoiled the effect of the pious deed, and Elisha eventually went bad. So study of Torah should not be undertaken in order to attain supernatural or magical power—a standard rabbinical piety.

Eliezer, Joshua, and ʿAqiba are routinely joined in connection with the Abba Judah-story (y. Hor. 3 : 4). They are not differentiated and play no important role in the story; they represent "the sages," nothing more. The story (Sifré Deut. 38) of Eliezer, Joshua, and Ṣaddoq at Gamaliel's banquet has nothing to do with Eliezer. He serves merely to raise question to be answered by the others—Joshua and Ṣaddoq.

Three legal issues are well-attested for the Yavnean period, the initiation of proselytes, the date of Pentecost, and the rules on saying the *Shemaʿ* and the Prayer. The first clearly was debated among Jewish- and gentile-Christians; the second was a matter of sectarian debate, distinguishing Pharisees from Sadducees, and the third certainly goes back to the redactional agendum of Eliezer, Joshua, and Gamaliel. b. Yev. 46a/y. Qid. 3 : 12 has the dispute between Eliezer and Joshua on the initiation of proselytes. Eliezer says it is all right if the proselyte is circumcized but not baptized. Joshua says it is all right if he is baptized and not circumcized. The sages say both are required. b. Men. 65b gives Eliezer and Joshua differing proofs for the proposition that Pentecost does not have to fall on the day after the Sabbath. Eliezer's depends upon the words, *For yourself* (Deut. 16 : 9)—just as with reference to the *Sukkah* and *lulav* Joshua says there has to be something distinctive at the commencement of the counting. Ishmael offers a different proof entirely, and Judah b. Batyra gives a *heqqesh.* In Sifra Vayiqra 13 : 4 = b. Men. 68a, Eliezer proves from a *heqqesh* that the *ʿomer* must be barley. ʿAqiba provides a proof from logic.

Eliezer proves that the whole *Shemaʿ* does not require the heart's intention. Only the first line does. Scripture says *These words*—so the foregoing will require intention ("Be upon thy heart") but not the rest. ʿAqiba says that the continuation, *Which I command you this day on your heart* means the whole passage requires intention (Midrash Tannaim to Deut. 6 : 6, Hoffmann, p. 26 = b. Ber. 13a). An *ʿam haʾareṣ* is one who does not read the *Shemaʿ* morning and evening, so Eliezer. Joshua says it is a person who does not put on *tefillin*, Ben ʿAzzai says it is a person who does not have *ṣiṣit* on his garment (b. Ber. 47b). One should wipe with the left hand, not the right, because he eats with it. Joshua says it is because one writes with it. ʿAqiba says because one points with it to the accents in the Scroll (b. Ber. 62a). Such ritualization of everyday routine is a mark of rabbinism, but that does not mean the sayings cannot be authentic. Eliezer says (b. A.Z. 7b) that one asks for his own needs and then recites the Prayer. Joshua says the opposite. These opinions are tied to proof-texts (Ps. 102 : 1, Gen. 24 : 63 *vs.* Ps. 142 : 3, respectively), but the proof-texts are not integral to the argument.

The most important event in Eliezer's active career was the excommunication. y. M.Q.'s story about Eliezer's excommunication is attested by Ḥanina and Jeremiah. b. B.M. 59a-b reorganizes and develops y.'s primitive version. The issue is the same; the authority of Heaven in deciding the law. Eliezer is on the side of the House of Hillel, which believed in heavenly echoes, against the Shammaites, represented by Joshua, who do not. The intrusion of Nathan is curious. ʿAqiba occurs in both versions as the leading disciple. He is the suitable person—and Joshua is not mentioned. Gamaliel's absence is explained: he is on a voyage. But he is subject to the supernatural wrath attendant upon the rejection of the heavenly opinion, so should have been involved. Then Imma Shalom is introduced. Her story stresses Eliezer's supernatural power. y. knows nothing about either Gamaliel or Imma Shalom. y. limits supernatural elements to the claim that the echo may decide the law. Eliezer's ability to curse and Gamaliel's tidal wave are unknown. In general, therefore, b. tends to introduce supernatural and magical elements unknown to y. and to give them an important place in the narrative. Jeremiah in y. knows only of his being able to cast an evil eye; that element does recur in b. (I), without attribution to Jeremiah. It is exceeded by the stories that accompany it. The "oven of ʿAkhnai" plays no role in the narratives. Once it is mentioned it is forgotten—so it looks like an interpolation, for it is superfluous to the account. I cannot imagine why it has been introduced.

We have four last-illness-and-death stories. First, y. Shab.'s version of Eliezer's death-scene has only Hyrcanus, his son, and "the disciples"—Joshua is the only one named. Joshua again appears as the sole disciple. Later on, his saying will be given to ʿAqiba and expanded into a chria, with ʿAqiba witnessing the funeral cortege on its journey from Caesarea (not mentioned in y. Shab.) to Lydda. It is taken for granted that the disciples will come to the death-scene, but they are not given individual parts to say. They simply affirm that he is "clean." This must mean that the excommunication is in the background, and F makes it explicit: Joshua says the "vow" has been released. b. Sanh. 68b changes everything. It first accounts for the transfer of the cucumbers/magic saying from Joshua to Eliezer. Eliezer is sick, but, clearly, a death-scene is in hand, so the parallel to Mekh./Sifré is clear. ʿAqiba is now the chief mourner and disciple. Joshua is subordinated but is still made to announce "the vow" is released. Once it is shown that Eliezer is lucid, it is possible to raise legal questions. These are introduced first of all to show that Eliezer had been excommunicated. So that theme, subordinated in y., becomes important in b. ʿAqiba is rebuked for not coming sooner. His death as a martyr is alluded to—thus the ʿAqiban martyrdom stories are in hand as well. The 'decline of the generations' is now given explicit details. Eliezer learned a great deal but not all of what his masters knew, and he taught a great deal but not all of what he knew. Then comes a separate story about Eliezer's mastery of magic—a unique pericope. The five cleanness-rules are then reaffirmed. At the end ʿAqiba is given the honor of delivering a eulogy.

Second, Rabbah b. b. Ḥana's story about Eliezer's (last) illness is strikingly different from Mekhilta's. Rabbah knows nothing of the "four disciples." All he knows is that ʿAqiba will say the opposite of the others. They weep. He rejoices. Eliezer is now certified as a candidate for entry into the world to come. So he is happy. But Eliezer is then told by ʿAqiba that he is not perfect. Rabbah's story is remarkably ignorant of the other death-scenes. We have no hint as to the excommunication, let alone the colloquies and events surrounding the death. The Babylonian last-illness-story cannot be composed by people aware of the Palestinian one(s).

b. Ber. 28b presents a third sort of death scene, following, but not closely modeled on, that of Yoḥanan, and redacted along with it. Eliezer gives three sayings. The scene supplies background for the sayings. Nothing happens. No illusion is made to the excommunication; no disciples are mentioned. ʿAqiba's priority is not alluded to.

ARN Chap. 20 comes last of all. First, b. Ber. is summarized, though the difficult saying about keeping children back from 'reasoning' is dropped. This leaves two sayings, to be careful for one another's honor and to pray with diligence. Eleazar b. ʿAzariah is now credited with the uncleanness-teachings—a role he does not have in b. Sanh.

ARN Chap. 25 then repeats b. Sanh. The cucumbers/magic problem is omitted. It is central to b. Sanh. but irrelevant to the story, therefore represents a Babylonian embellishment generated by the problem of the confused traditions on cucumbers/magic. ARN's new version further expands the story in various details, for instance, "three hundred laws about the bright spot," and the litany about how much Eliezer had learned and how little he taught. Eleazar b. ʿAzariah is introduced as the first mourner.

A fourth sort of death-scene (y. Sot. 9 : 16) is produced by Jacob b. R. Idi-Joshua b. Levi. Now two scenes are explicitly modeled on one another—Eliezer's on Yoḥanan's. Yoḥanan says Hezekiah is coming; Eliezer says Yoḥanan is coming. Both take account of the cleanness-considerations attendant upon the momentary presence of a corpse (their own) in the courtyard. This composite is joined to still another. First, it is announced that "the elders" are told Hillel is worthy of the holy spirit, and Samuel is also worthy. Then the story is expanded to include Eliezer. So Eliezer is represented by Jacob-Joshua as the third in line from Hillel, the worthy disciple. y. A.Z. rearranges the pericopae but does not change the picture. Clearly, Joshua b. Levi is responsible for the stories linking Eliezer to Hillel. Yoḥanan is not mentioned, but Joshua has other stories about him.

And Yoḥanan's death-scene is attached, so he cannot be out of mind in the second story. There can be no doubt that, so far as Joshua b. Levi is concerned, Eliezer is a Hillelite—and one of the most important of them. He knows nothing of Eliezer's having been excommunicated. That element, central to b. Sanh. and alluded to in y. Shab., plays no role at all.

Of the legendary allegations concerning Eliezer's active career, most may be taken as fact. He certainly taught disciples. Ilai is the only one clearly a disciple in the earliest strata of the tradition. ʿAqiba probably was not a disciple; the predominance of his redactors in the formation of composite pericopae seems ample evidence that he was an equal, not a subordinated, master. I see no reason to suppose Ṭarfon, Eleazar b. ʿAzariah, and Joshua were Eliezer's students. Ṭarfon may have had some sort of close association. Eleazar and Joshua were independent masters. Gamaliel is underrepresented in the legends. He should have a more important role, considering his position at Yavneh. He is left out where he clearly belongs, in the excommunication story, only in the later developments being introduced chiefly on account of supernatural considerations, and then because of his sister. The legal issues connected with Eliezer's active career all look genuine, though we cannot take for granted Eliezer's particular part in settling them. The date of Pentecost required numerous masters' proofs, Eliezer among them. The *Shemaʿ* certainly was an important Yavnean problem; Eliezer's opinion may be genuine. The discussion on when to say a prayer for one's own needs contradicts Eliezer's better-attested opinion that one should not have a fixed text for the Prayer to begin with, therefore is spurious.

The stories about Eliezer's excommunication and death are closely linked. One death-scene takes for granted the excommunication story and should be regarded as part of the same picture. It then is to be linked to the masters who give evidence of knowing it—but not of having told it: Jeremiah, Ḥanina. So it was a Palestinian story, known in, and developed by, Babylonian circles. What lies behind it is difficult to say. It was in the third century that the acceptability of Eliezer's legal rulings was much discussed; then he was called a Shammaite; it was alleged that the Tannas do not carefully transmit his teachings; and in other ways it was made clear that one does not rely upon laws in his name. Then how to account for the inclusion of his many pericopae? The reason is that at the end he was released from the ban.

But what to begin with produced a story of a debate on heavenly intervention and the rule of the majority, ending in Eliezer's excommunication? Here only the most tentative speculation seems possible. First, in the background of every debate on heavenly intervention must lie the allegation that Hillel would have received the holy spirit had the generation been worthy of it, so anyone in the rabbinical movement who enjoys heavenly support should be represented as a follower of Hillel. This, indeed, is made clear by the Shammaite rejection of the heavenly testimony.

Now, that Eliezer is linked to Hillel is one of the fundamental implicit assertions of the legendary materials. This point has already been made clear in both legal traditions and *aggadic* sayings. For example, Eliezer's saying that one should not worry about the morrow (b. Sot. 48b) makes him a disciple of Hillel, who said the same thing. Shammai said something different. Mekhilta deR. Simeon b. Yohai then develops the idea into a dispute with Joshua, who agrees with the Shammaites. The *heqqesh*-argument (*bringing* is said with reference to the *ʿomer* [Lev. 23 : 10] and to the showbreads [Lev. 23 : 17]) is attributed to Eliezer in b. Shab. 131a. Hillel's argument based on the *heqqesh* drawn from *In its season* is attributed to Eliezer in M. Pes. 6 : 2-3. But the relation to Hillel is explicit as well, for Eliezer's master now is Yoḥanan. He always did as his master did, said only what his master said. One set of death-stories stresses this very point. Eliezer's death was modeled after Yoḥanan's. And in that same pericope is the story of Hillel's being worthy of the holy spirit, and of Eliezer's like merit. So *every* important exemplum of the Eliezer- Yoḥanan connection will contain allegations about the further connection to Hillel. Palestinian masters, Jacob b. R. Idi-Joshua b. Levi stand behind these allegations.

Receiving the holy spirit, moreover, now is set against the will of the majority of the sages. So one must ask, Of whom is it alleged both that he had supernatural power and that he also had the power to subvert the will of the majority? One obvious candidate is Judah the Patriarch—of his heirs we can presently say nothing—who both was regarded as of the Messianic seed and claimed descent from the Messiah through Hillel. Elijah used to come to his academy (b. B.M. 85b); when Rabbi lay dying, he had knowledge of what was happening in distant places (b. Qid. 72a); he was called the Messiah (y. Shab. 16 : 1, b. Sanh. 98b); he had the power to cause a tooth-ache for Ḥiyya (b. B.M. 85b); he was as great as Moses (b. Git. 59a, b. Sanh. 36a).

Clearly, Rabbi was portrayed as a supernatural figure, not exactly as was Hillel and Eliezer in respect to the Holy Spirit, but in other important ways as having been more than an ordinary sage.

One way of opposing the patriarchal preeminence was to assert that supernatural authority carries no weight against the consensus of the sages. The story about Eliezer stresses that very point. To be sure, Gamaliel is inserted into the story of Eliezer's excommunication. But he is not integral to the story; his name is introduced only later on in its development; and he plays no important role. The story represents Joshua as the leader of those who deny supernatural authority in the formation of the law; Joshua likewise is represented as the leader of those who threw out Gamaliel for his high-handedness. In all, the patriarchal authority, which rests upon the claim of descent from Hillel and thence to the Messiah, stands over against the right of the majority of the sages, led by Joshua, to make decisions. In that context the story of Eliezer's excommunication ought to have been generated. And it strikingly accords with sayings attributed to Rabbi about Eliezer's authority—"I would decide the law in accordance with his opinion, but the Tannas do not accurately portray his opinion."

While the excommunication is important to the death-scene involving the declaration that the ban has been lifted, it plays no role in the others, which know nothing about a ban or the need to release it. Rabbah b. b. Ḥana's story is simply a chria for two sayings of ʿAqiba, first, that Eliezer is suffering now but will enjoy the next world, second that Eliezer was not perfect—both routine sentiments. b. Ber.'s version of Eliezer's death ties Eliezer to Yoḥanan, but the death-scene provides merely a dramatic setting for some wise sayings on Eliezer's part. Joshua b. Levi's scene also links Eliezer to Yoḥanan, but the relationship now is integral, and produces not only the same last words—not *clean* (as with ʿAqiba the martyr) but *prepare a throne*, but also a further allegation about Eliezer as the continuator of Yoḥanan-Hillel. Whether Joshua b. Levi's stories form a part of a larger case in behalf of a patriarchate, which alleged itself to enjoy access to supernatural counsel, we cannot yet determine. The story of the excommunication plays no part in Joshua b. Levi's sayings, so the stemma may be entirely separate from the excommunication + death sequence involving ʿAqiba, Joshua, and Eleazar b. ʿAzariah.

That any of these materials goes back to events in Eliezer's own life seems to me unlikely. They all form part of the third-century rabbis' effort to supply the first and early second century authorities with biographies. But the biographies manifestly ignore the personal traits of the individuals under discussion and focus upon either homiletical or political themes pertinent to the third-century rabbinical estate, on the one side, or to the patriarchal-rabbinical institution, on the other.

iv. Eliezer's Historical Situation

The destruction of the Temple figures more prominently in the legends than in the historical and traditional materials. To be sure, Eliezer's egress from Jerusalem—if he was there before 70—is not the subject of an individual story. Eliezer's and Joshua's part in Yoḥanan's escape consists in serving as names for the disciples who carried the bier, so b. Git. 56a and all other, and later versions. The two disciples play no important part in the story, which simply takes for granted that they were the chief assistants and ignores the other members of Yoḥanan's Avot-circle.

The saying of Eliezer *the Great* (M. Sot. 9 : 15) relates the decline of the generations to the destruction of the Temple. The redactional framework involves nearly the whole of the Tannaitic movement, but omits Eliezer; the close relationship to the saying of Pinḥas b. Yaʾir has already been noted (Vol. I, p. 394). The saying produces a commonplace sentiment about the destruction of the Temple. Eliezer regretted it, along with everyone else. But it is not for that reason to be regarded as not genuine. Eliezer is given a number of similar sayings in quite unrelated materials; he stresses the inevitable loss of learning, though this is not tied to the destruction of the Temple. In all, he may well have regarded the decline of the generations as a trait of the times. If he did, he was wrong, for Yavnean times were marked by noteworthy creative achievements, in which Eliezer himself took an active part.

Eliezer occurs in the colloquy of Yoḥanan and the disciples on the meaning of Prov. 14 : 34 (b. B.B. 10b). All agree that the peoples are incapable of doing real kindness (*ḥesed*). Such a sentiment is congruent to the xenophobic stratum of Eliezer's materials, but not to the historically more reliable assertions about relationships to gentiles, Samaritans, and non-Pharisees.

Mid. Tan. to Deut. 14 : 22, Hoffmann ed. pp. 77-8, gives Eliezer and Ishmael the "rabbinical" sentiment that the Temple was a place where Torah was studied and service to the Temple led to the study of

Torah—so was subordinate to it. This is the most important rabbinical sentiment attributed to Eliezer and is very likely to be spurious. Nothing in Eliezer's salvific message (below) stresses *study* of Torah and practicing the commandments exactly as rabbis do; only the reference in Mekh. to Moses's hands at the battle with Amalek comes close to such a rabbinical notion. One does not have to be a rabbi to say Israel will prosper by loyalty to Torah; this was the message of Deuteronomy. But one had to be a rabbi to say that the Temple was important because Torah was studied there. I doubt Eliezer, whose piety was shaped by the cultic purity laws and by the priestly claims on the produce of the holy land, said any such thing.

The major theological issues of Yavnean times—the nature, meaning, and permanence of the covenant, the means of atonement and the scheme of redemption—all figure prominently in the legendary materials. These issues were made urgent by the destruction. Did the end of the cult signify the dissolution of the ancient covenant between God and Israel? Others asserted just that. What was to be the sign of the covenant in the period in which the Temple lay in ruins? Eliezer is made to say that *tefillin*, or the Sabbath, or circumcision will now represent the covenant. Eliezer the Great (b. Ber. 6a) says that the *tefillin* represent the sign of God's preference for Israel. The covenant referred to in Ex. 19 : 5 is variously interpreted by Eliezer. Mekh. Baḥodesh 2 : 43-5 says Eliezer holds the reference is to the Sabbath; ʿAqiba, to [not practicing] idolatry. Mekh. deR. Simeon, p. 41, has Eliezer refer to Passover, ʿAqiba to *tefillin*; Pesiqta Rabbati says Eliezer told ʿAqilas that the covenant is the Sabbath and circumcision; Mekhilta deR. Simeon, p. 139, has Eliezer say the covenant is circumcision; ʿAqiba refers to the Sabbath, and sages now say it is not to practice idolatry. The value of circumcision and the Sabbath is further stressed by Eliezer in his interpretation of Qoh. 11 : 2 (b. Eruv. 40b). Joshua says the reference is to Passover and Sukkot.

Deut. 4 : 6 is interpreted by Eliezer to mean that a person who loves his body more than his money and one who loves his money more than his body both must love God with all they have (Sifré Deut. 32, b. Ber. 61b). ʿAqiba says the Scripture refers to love, even to the sacrifice of one's life, or martyrdom. Martyrdom plays no role in any saying attributed to Eliezer.

The nature of atonement and the course of the redemptive process constitute important parts in the response to the destruction. Eliezer's position emerges from a number of discrete sayings, none of which on the face of it is irrelevant to his situation. First, Eliezer says that God testifies against or warns Israel and then punishes them. Joshua says that the possibilities of further disaster are endless (Sifra Beḥuqotai Pereq 5 : 1). God's justice could destroy even the best men: Abraham, Isaac, and Jacob could not stand in judgment (b. Ar. 17a).

Eliezer and Joshua further discuss the forgiveness of sins, for example, y. Shab. 9 : 3, on the meaning of Is. 1 : 18. Both say that however long-standing are the sins, they can be whitened. y. Ta. 1 : 1 presents the dispute on the precondition of redemption. Eliezer says if the Israelites do not repent, they will not be redeemed. Joshua challenges this opinion. Then Eliezer says God will raise up a harsh king who will move the people to penitence, so it is inevitable that they will repent. b. Sanh. 97bff. changes this picture. Now *Joshua* says the harsh king will move the people to penitence—so he is made to agree with Eliezer that penitence is the precondition of redemption. But the process of redemption will begin with God's moving the people to penitence. The best rendition of the dispute is Tanḥuma Beḥuqotai 5, which has Eliezer say simply that if the Israelites repent they will be redeemed. Joshua says whether or not they repent, they will be redeemed at the inevitable end.

Eliezer, third, praises the faith of Israel at the sea, as do Shemaʿiah and Abṭalion (*Phar.* I, p. 142), so Mekhilta deR. Simeon. Mekh. Baḥodesh 4 : 36ff. has Eliezer emphasize the submission of Israel to the divine will. God spoke to them only after they had accepted what he would say. ʿAqiba takes for granted that this was so and interprets Ex. 19 : 19 to mean that God served to strengthen Moses's voice so that everyone heard just what Moses heard. Joshua says Israel in the wilderness made one journey at Moses's command, the rest at God's. Eliezer says *all* journeys were at God's command (Mekh. Vayassa 1 : 1ff.). At the redemption from Egypt God tried to tire the people out in order to test and refine them. Joshua says he showered beneficence upon them, giving them the Torah, *manna*, and doing miracles (Mekh. Beshallaḥ 1 : 57ff.). Eliezer, however, also says the Israelites brought an idol with them when they passed through the sea (y. Suk. 4 : 3). ʿAqiba says the verse to which Eliezer refers (II Sam. 7 : 23) means the Israelites redeemed themselves. Eliezer says the reason the people believed in God was that he met their needs. Joshua says it was God's omnipotence which persuaded the people (Mekh. Vayassa 7 : 68ff.). This saying is congruent to Eliezer's contempt for those who are anxious about their material needs.

Fourth, Eliezer and Joshua argue about how the angel smote the Egyptians (b. Sanh. 95b). Eliezer says it was with his hand, Joshua says with his finger. Joshua corresponds to Yosi in Mekhilta, and Eliezer corresponds to ʿAqiba. The Eliezer in Mekhilta has no counterpart. But Mid. Ps. 78 : 15 has Eliezer as b. Sanh.'s Joshua; God smote the Egyptians with his finger. Mekh. Beshallaḥ 7 : 109ff. presents the opinions of Yosi, Eliezer, and ʿAqiba on how many times the Egyptians were smitten in Egypt and at the sea.

Moses's war against Amalek is the theme of a set of Scriptural comments. Joshua says that Moses treated the Amalekites with a measure of mercy. Eliezer says the war against Amalek was at the divine command (Mekh. Amalek 1 : 173ff.). Presumably any new war must await a divine command. God took an oath that nothing would remain of the people of Amalek (Midrash on Psalms 9 : 10). Lam. R. gives this opinion to Joshua and has Eliezer explain that the destruction of Amalek will result in the coming of the Messiah and the final victory of monotheism (Lam. R. 3 : 66 : 9). Amalek came with defiance and not secretly (Mekh. Amalek 1 : 9ff.). The gesture of Moses in the battle meant that when Israel is strong in the words of Torah, to be given through Moses's hands, it would prevail, and otherwise it would not (Mekh. Amalek 1 : 131ff., Mekh. deR. Simeon b. Yoḥai, p. 121, ls. 15-17). Rephidim was a real place. So too was Shiṭṭim (Num. 25 : 1). The former concerns the story of Amalek, the latter, of the Moabites (b. Bekh. 5b, b. Sanh. 106a).

Fifth, the preconditions for redemption figure in Mekh. deR. Simeon, p. 1. Eliezer says that when Israel is at its lowest point, God will descend and redeem them. Joshua interprets the descent to the bush differently, but his point is not greatly at variance. The inevitability of redemption is stressed by Eliezer with reference to Ps. 139 : 16. No foreordained event has failed to take place on its appropriate day. Joshua agrees (Tanḥuma Bereshit 28, Pesiqta Rabbati 23 : 1). Both therefore hold redemption is inevitable, but, as noted, depends upon Israel's repentence. Joshua says that the redemption took place in Nisan and in the future will take place in Nisan. Eliezer says the future redemption will take place in Tishri (Mekh. Pisḥa 14 : 113-117; b. R.H. 10b and *seq.*). Creation took place in Tishri, according to Eliezer, and in Nisan, according to Joshua. The issue then extends to when the natural cycle of nature begins. Eliezer says it is in Tishri, Joshua, in Nisan. The same issue pertains to the birth of the patriarchs—therefore the beginning of the people of Israel.

If we may now compose a picture of Eliezer's message in the aftermath of the destruction, it will appear something like this:

"Israel prospers when it does the will of God and suffers when it does not. Punishment is preceded by appropriate warnings. But God cannot deal with Israel solely according to the requirements of justice. Even the patriarchs could not have emerged guiltless. God has to forgive sins, and his mercy is without limit. There is, therefore, hope for the generation that has undergone punishment.

"But the generation must, nonetheless, do appropriate penance. (Joshua, who claims that grace does not depend upon atonement, is made to agree, for part of divine grace is the imposition of suffering which leads to penitence.) Another element in the penitential process is faith, which marked the redemption from Egypt and will therefore be required once more. Israel's atonement will include replication of the faith of the people at the sea and in their journeys through the wilderness.

"Just as at that time God tried the people in order to refine them, so now there will be trials and troubles. Just as now there are those who lack faith, so then there were Israelites who brought idolatry out of Egypt with them and whose faith depended upon material considerations.

"God punishes the oppressors of Israel. The Egyptians were smitten in times of old. The war against Amalek provides a model of divine support for Israel's cause. Just as nothing will remain of the memory of Amalek, so nothing will remain of the new oppressor. (The Amalek-story is given a rabbinical twist: Israel's victory depends upon Torah. But that theme is not central to the exegetical treatment of the Amalek-story.)

"When will the redemption come? It will be when Israel is at its lowest point. But it is inevitable. Just as every foreordained event in Israel's history took place at its appointed time, so will the last and greatest triumph surely come. One may even posit the date of redemption. It will be in Tishri and so, corresponding to the natural order, will conclude the story of creation and the history of the children of the patriarchs, rather than (as Joshua claims) in Nisan, as a counterpart to the Exodus."

Eliezer's message therefore stresses four main themes: punishment and suffering, sin and atonement, the ultimate bad end for the oppressors, and the inevitability of redemption. One important theme is remarkable for its absence, and that is the Messianic expectation.

Eliezer has no messianic sayings. The composite of his sayings about the age and its destiny leaves no room for a Messiah, a Messianic war, or a Messianic general. The generalized expectation of inevitable redemption does not produce a particular allegation that redemption is near at hand or that what is needed is merely a little patience. On the contrary, central to Eliezer's salvific story is Israel's own repentence. Upon repentence all things depend. So Israel can do something to extricate itself from its present state. But what it can do is not to make war, but rather, to repent and return to God. This viewpoint is very reliably attributed to Yoḥanan b. Zakkai. The Eliezer who stressed irenic relationships to the gentiles and had nothing to say about making war against Rome or laying claim to vast lands outside of Jewish Palestine also ought to be the Eliezer who stressed that the true struggle for redemption lay within the soul of Israel itself. The theological sayings pertinent to the aftermath of the destruction are not only in theme appropriate, but also in substance precisely what should have accompanied the best attested legal sayings of Eliezer about the dominant question of the day: the disaster and Israel's place in the world-empire of Rome.

We find ourselves, therefore, in the position of Judah b. Batyra (M. Neg. 9 : 3, 11 : 7). Our conclusion is that Eliezer really did carry on the tradition of his master. And in substance, if not in fact, his master really was Yoḥanan b. Zakkai. What Yoḥanan said about the situation of 70 is what Eliezer is likely to have said in later years. The message of both was that all depends not upon a Messianic war but upon Israel's own repentence and fulfillment of the requirements of the Torah. Nothing in Eliezer's message goes beyond what had already been stated by Yoḥanan. Nothing in Yoḥanan's message has been omitted. And behind Eliezer and Yoḥanan stands Hillel, whose affect upon Pharisaism was to turn a political party capable of partisan hatred into an irenic table-fellowship sect, with the Temple and the priesthood as the model of its piety. The path from Hillel through Yoḥanan to Eliezer may, therefore, have been discovered only in much later times. But the late-second-century and third-century masters who posited such a single, straight line from Eliezer to Yoḥanan to Hillel—for reasons pertinent to their own politics, to be sure, for it was in the patriarch's interest to avoid talk of Messianic wars and a fast-approaching end of time—from our perspective were absolutely right.

APPENDIX I

THE ROLE OF ʿAQIBA IN THE BAR KOKHBA REBELLION

G. S. Aleksandrov

Translated by

Sam Driver

Brown University

[The following article, translated from Russian, was originally published in *Kratkie soobshcheniia Instituta Narodov Azii*, No. 86, pp. 79-89. Professor E. J. Bickerman kindly called it to my attention. Because of the curious fact that ʿAqiba represents Eliezer as a pacifist in the historically more reliable materials, while Eliezer is portrayed as a militarist in the traditional stratum, it seemed necessary to reconsider the axiom that ʿAqiba himself favored the messianic war of Bar Kokhba. Aleksandrov here raises still more important questions than are presented above, pp. 346-350. For this reason I have included his article.—J.N.]

The question of the role of ʿAqiba ben Joseph in the Bar-Kokhba[1] rebellion (132-135 A.D.)[2] has been and continues to be considered both in Hebrew and in general historiography. The assertion that ʿAqiba ben Joseph was the ideologist of the Bar-Kokhba rebellion is almost universally accepted. It occurs in all the basic works on the history of the Hebrew people (Grätz, Dubnov), on the history of Palestine (Derenbourg), on the history of the so-called "oral Torah" (Frankel, Weiss), and on the philosophy of the history of the Hebrew people (Krochmal).[3] It also occurs in general encyclopedias

[1] Documents of the Bar-Kokhba archive discovered in Wadi-Muraba'at, permit the establishment of the precise name of the leader of the rebellion: Simon Bar-Koziba. Under this name, he figures on the Talmudic and Midrashic sources, and in the Christian ones as Bar-Kokhba. The author of the present article keeps to the name Bar-Kokhba, already established in historical study.

[2] In publishing the documents of the Bar-Kokhba archive (P. Benoit, J. T. Milik, R. de Vaux, *Les grottes de Murabbaʾat. Discoveries in the Judean Desert* II, I-II (Oxford, 1961), Milik comes to the conclusion that the rebellion began on I Tishri, 131 A.D. See also I. D. Amusin, "Dokumenty uz Badi-Murabba'ata," II, *V.D. I,* 1961, No. 4, pp. 136-147.

[3] H. Grätz, *Geschichte der Juden*, Vol. IV (Berlin, 1853) (Hebrew Translation: S. P. Rabinovich [Warsaw, 1893], Vol. II); S. Dubnov, *Vseobshchaia istoria evreev*, Vol. II (St. Petersburg, 1905) (Hebrew Translation: Tel Aviv, 1958, Vol. III); J. Derenbourg, *Essai*

in various languages. It has gone into all the school text-books on the history of the Jews. Since this assertion has become a kind of commonplace, it has penetrated even the works of some Soviet historians[4] and is accepted almost uncritically; it has also penetrated belles-lettres. Sometimes, it is true, individual scholars, such as L. Ginzberg,[5] and Isaac Halevy,[6] came out against certain details of this assertion, but their voices have been drowned in the general chorus. ʿAqiba is unanimously acclaimed as the inspirer of the Bar-Kokhba rebellion. This idea occurs in its shortest and most condensed formulation in S. M. Dubnov: "Bar-Kokhba was the strong right arm of the nation, whose head was Rabbi ʿAqiba. People like ʿAqiba inspired others, and Bar-Kokhba with his 'epic heroes' fearlessly went into battle."[7] S. W. Baron, author of one of the newest histories of the Jews, voices an analogous idea: "ʿAqiba was an intellectual, and Bar-Kokhba a military and political leader."[8]

The point of departure for the creation of such a wide-spread claim concerning ʿAqiba as the ideologist for the Bar-Kokhba rebellion is the following (y. Ta. IV, 68a): Says Simeon ben Yoḥai: "My teacher interpreted the verse, *The star comes up from Jacob* thus—'Koziba comes up from Jacob.' When ʿAqiba met Bar-Koziba, he said: 'Here is the king-messiah.'" Yoḥanan ben Torata said to him, "ʿAqiba, sooner will grass grow out of your cheeks than the Son of David come."[9]

This is the only place in all the Talmudic and Midrashic literature in which there is a reference to ʿAqiba as related to the Bar-Kokhba

sur l'histoire et la géographie de la Palestine (Paris, 1867) (Hebrew Translation: M. Bronstein, Petersburg, 1897); Z. Frankel, *Darkhé haMishnah* (Leipzig, 1859); I. Weiss, *Dor dor-we-Dorschaw*, Vol. II (Vienna, 1876); N. Krochmal, *Moreh Nebukhé Hazeman* (Lemberg, 1863). Henceforth, only the names of the authors will be cited.

4 G. M. Livshits, *Klassovaia bor'ba v Iudee u vosstania protiv Rima* (Minsk, 1957), Ch. X.

5 *Jewish Encyclopedia*, Vol. I, pp. 304-308.

6 I. Y. Halevy, *Doroth ha-Rischonim* (Frankfurt, 1897).

7 S. Dubnov, pp. 44, 45; Hebrew Translation, pp. 26, 27.

8 S. W. Baron, *A Social and Religious History of the Jews* (N.Y., 1952) Vol. II, p. 98.

9 y. Ta., IV, 68a; Eikha Rabba, II. The matter concerns the interpretation of Numbers 24 : 17-18: "... there shall come a star out of Jacob, and a sceptre shall rise out of Israel, and shall smite the corners of Moab, and destroy all the children of Sheth. And Edom shall be a possession." [Translator's Note: The Russian says: "A star shall come up from Jacob, and a rod (as in Aaron's rod) shall rise up from Israel, and will cut down the princes of Moab, and will destroy the sons of Sheth. And Edom will be its inheritance."] The interpretation is built on the consonance of the words "Kokheba" (star) and "Koziba."

rebellion. It has been broadly interpreted. Legendary and half-legendary material about ʿAqiba was introduced; this material existed in abundance in the works of the Talmudic tradition—especially the notes on his travels and his numerous disciples—in order to prove that ʿAqiba himself was not only an ideologist, but also an organizer of the rebellion. As a result, a whole conception was created which, in broad outlines, amounts to the following:

The greatest of the *Tannas* of the first half of the second century A.D., ʿAqiba, a contemporary of Bar-Kokhba, made numerous trips with the purpose of preparing the Jews of the diaspora for the rebellion. His numerous disciples made up the basic nucleus of the rebels under the leadership of Bar-Kokhba. This ʿAqiba, who enjoyed exclusive authority among the Jewish masses of Palestine and the diaspora proclaimed Bar-Kokhba to be the messiah. As a result, the whole movement under Bar-Kokhba's leadership bore a messianic character. This movement, directed against the rule of Rome, was supported by the majority of *Tannas* of the time. ʿAqiba was thrown into prison by the Roman authorities and died a martyr's death.

It is interesting to note that a number of medieval Jewish chronographers who deal with the Bar-Kokhba rebellion do not mention a word about ʿAqiba as an ideologist for the rebellion or about any part he may have played in it.[10] Doubts concerning the ideological and organizing role of ʿAqiba in the rebellion were later voiced by Rabbi Yeḥiel Heilprin (1666-1746) in his famous work *Seder ha-Doroth.* He writes, "Maimonides says at the end of the section *Mishpatim* of Ben Koziba, that ʿAqiba was his arms-bearer. But nowhere in the Midrashim have we discovered that he was indeed his arms-bearer; he [ʿAqiba] only supposed that Ben Koziba was the Messiah on the basis of his successes and his heroic conduct in war. When he saw that he (Bar Kokhba) did not have the gift of judging by intuition (that is, to determine by intuition who is guiltless and who is guilty—which was required of the messiah), he rejected him; Sanhedrin 93b discusses this. When they (the learned men) saw that he could not judge by intuition, they killed him."[11] This extremely important reference is not cited by Grätz. He merely indicates in

[10] Neither Abraham ibn David, *Sefar haQabbalah*, nor Gedalia ibn Yaḥia mentions anything at all about ʿAqiba as a participant in the rebellion. (*Sefer haQabbalah* and *Shalshelet haQabbalah*, 1588, respectively). Nor do Christian sources mention ʿAqiba's name.

[11] Yeḥiel Heilprin, *Seder haDoroth* I (Warsaw, 1878), p. 159.

general terms that corresponding notes on Bar-Kokhba introduced into the Talmud were composed by his enemies. But he does not introduce any arguments to discredit these statements.

As has been noted above, the references to ʿAqiba's travels have been used as an argument in favor of the assertion concerning the ideological and organizational role of ʿAqiba in the Bar-Kokhba rebellion. According to allusions in various tracts of the Talmud,[12] ʿAqiba visited Babylonia, Media, Arabia, Italy (Brindisi and Rome), Gallia, and Africa. What was the purpose of these journeys?

In the beginning of the chapter on the Bar-Kokhba rebellion, Grätz recounts the countries visited by ʿAqiba and indicates that ʿAqiba was preparing the people for rebellion, that he moved carefully and energetically, and that the purpose of these travels, "as has been properly pointed out," was to incite the Jews of the diaspora to rebellion against Rome and to create a Judaic state.[13] However, Grätz does not cite any sources, nor any names of those who support the opinion with which he agrees. The point is that in the Talmudic tracts concerning the countries visited by ʿAqiba, there is not the least reference to suggest that their purpose was to prepare the Jewish population for rebellion.

In this regard, the statement of Naḥman Krochmal is typical: "ʿAqiba's numerous travels to Arabia, the regions beyond the Euphrates and to Ginzak (Media) had for their purpose to enlist the aid of the diaspora in preparing the rebellion, *although there is no corresponding information in the Talmud.*"[14] L. Ginzburg came to the proper conclusion from the absence of any information: "The many journeys which, according to Talmudic sources, were undertaken by ʿAqiba, can scarcely be brought into connection with political agitation."[15] And another scholar, Isaac Halevy, proved convincingly in his own time that these journeys were made in the reign of Trajan or even earlier and could not have any connection at all with the rebellion in Judea during the reign of Hadrian.[16] Nevertheless, many historians continued to speak of the political purpose of ʿAqiba's journeys, even after these works were published, and, moreover, the

[12] b. Yev. 121b; b. A.Z. 34a; b. R.H. 26a; b. Shab. 96b, 97a; b. B.Q. 113b; and elsewhere.

[13] Grätz, p. 158; Hebrew Translation II, p. 235.

[14] N. Krochmal, p. 78.

[15] L. G. Ginzberg, "ʿAqiba," *Jewish Encyclopedia*, I, p. 621.

[16] Y. I. Halevy, *Doroth haRischonim*, part I, Vol. V, pp. 620ff.

historians did not consider it necessary even to enter into polemics with them.

What can be the cause of the many journeys undertaken by ʿAqiba? In the Talmud, there is concrete information which permits a definition of their real character. A number of indications show that ʿAqiba was one of the most authoritative persons in questions concerning the determination of the new moon and leap year. This so-called "secret of leap year" was one of the most important prerogatives of the patriarch of Palestine, since it helped the Jews of Palestine and the diaspora observe religious holidays at the same time. It also permitted the Palestinian patriarch to extend his authority to Jews of the whole diaspora. Special persons were authorized to announce the leap year and the dates of holidays to the European population of the diaspora; some of these persons, the most authoritative ones, had the right to establish the dates by themselves. ʿAqiba was one of these. In one Talmudic tract, it is stated clearly that ʿAqiba came to Nehardea to determine leap year.[17] It also tells that patriarch Gamaliel II reproached ʿAqiba because he prevented witnesses from appearing to give depositions about the new moon, in order not to break the Sabbath rest.[18] Even during ʿAqiba's time in prison, people turned to him concerning leap year.[19] As to ʿAqiba's authority in this matter, there is the well-known episode of the attempt by the Jews in Babylonia to emancipate themselves from the Patriarch of Palestine. Ḥananiah, nephew of Joshua ben Ḥananiah, who lived in Babylonia, instituted a special *Synedrion* and published the calendar dispositions necessary for the Jews of Babylonia. To the charges of the Palestinian learned men who were representatives of the Patriarch that Ḥananiah had no right to establish the leap year and the holidays independently, without first asking Palestine, he answered by saying that even ʿAqiba in his time had fixed the leap year in countries of the diaspora. To this, the patriarch's representatives said that Ḥananiah did not have the right to compare himself with ʿAqiba, whose authority in this regard was unimpeachable.[20] All this factual information gives reason to suppose that ʿAqiba's travels could be

[17] b. Yev. 122a; it is supposed that the trip to Nehardea to determine leap year (or announce it) took place in 110. See L. Ginzberg, "ʿAqiba" in *Jewish Encyclopedia*, Vol. I, p. 621.

[18] b. R.H. 25a.

[19] b. Sanh. 12a.

[20] b. Ber. 63a; y. Ned. VI, 8.

connected with the fixing of the calendar and determining leap year.

The Talmud also shows other reasons why the *Tannas* of the second century A.D., among them ʿAqiba, had to travel to other lands. They concern the Jewish missionaries who went to pagan countries to propagate Judaism; their activity was intensified during the era of the rise of Christianity. To this, in part, is related the statement: "Woe unto you, scribes and Pharisees! Hypocrites! You go over land and sea to make one proselyte."[21] The sources say of ʿAqiba that he successfully attracted proselytes.[22]

The historians thus ignored factual material in the sources and preferred to build hypotheses, for which, by their own admission, there is no basis in the sources. This conception, a basically theological one, runs like a thread through the major work of I. H. Weiss on the history of "Oral Torah." In the beginning of Volume II, he praises ʿAqiba "famous for his travels in the near and far countries of the diaspora, and who aroused nationalistic feelings in the scattered people in order to prepare them for the general rebellion against Rome."[23] Without citing any proof, Weiss does not limit himself to the statement but tries to prove that not only ʿAqiba, but other *Tannas* of the first half of the second century secretly prepared for the rebellion. Here is a sample of his proofs: Eliezer ben Hyrcanus was in his time excommunicated for not submitting to the *Synedrion* in matters of ritual purity, and it was ʿAqiba who informed him of this excommunication. When Eliezer fell fatally ill, the *Tannas* who had participated in his excommunication decided to lift the excommunication from him, and thus came to see him. Eliezer asked them why they had not come to see him before, and they replied that they had not had the time. Then Eliezer prophesied to them that they would not die a natural death, and he said that ʿAqiba would be the most tormented. Weiss comments on this information in the following way: Eliezer understood that the *Tannas* who had come to him had no free

[21] Matthew 23 : 15.

[22] Legend has it that while he was in Rome, ʿAqiba became a close aquaintance of an influential Roman by the name of Cetius bar-Shalom, who later converted to Judaism (some scholars identify him as Flavius Clement, nephew of the Roman Emperor Domitian, who was punished for his conversion to Judaism). Cetius, according to legend, gave all his possessions to ʿAqiba before his execution. Another legend says that under the influence of conversations with ʿAqiba, the wife of Tinnaeus Rufus was converted; Rufus was the governor of Judea during the Bar-Kokhba rebellion. She also gave all her possessions to ʿAqiba. Midrash Tanḥuma, Terumot 3; b. Ned. 50a.

[23] Weiss, p. 3.

time because they were preparing the rebellion, and he was opposed to it. Foreseeing grave consequences for the fomenters of the rebellion, Eliezer warned his visitors of what awaited them. For ʿAqiba, who took the most active part in the affair, he predicted the most painful death.[24] The naiveté and lack of proof in this "commentary" need no further comment.

Nevertheless, despite the total absence of support, the contemporary Israeli historian Gedalia Alon tries to convince us in every way possible in his works that the *Tannas* who were contemporaries of Bar-Kokhba were active supporters of the rebellion. Proceeding from the premise that "as is well known, from the time of the Hasmonaeans and earlier, the Pharisees made up the majority of the population," Alon says that "the most reliable support of this premise is the Bar-Kokhba rebellion, in which one of the chief leaders was ʿAqiba. There is practically no doubt that the majority of the Pharisees were in agreement with ʿAqiba and Bar-Kokhba, since in the opposite case, this rebellion, which lasted three and a half years and in which many tens of thousands of Jews participated, could not have been developed from the very beginning." Further, Alon says that precisely this situation contributed to the great successes of Bar-Kokhba in the initial period of the rebellion, in comparison with the Judaic War of 66-73 A.D.[25] The proofs one should expect are not brought by Alon. S. Yeivin also basically agrees with Alon's conception, differing with him only in certain details.[26]

It must be said that Alon proceeds from two premises which are equally incorrect and unfounded. Is the assertion correct that "from the time of the Hasmonaeans and earlier, the Pharisees made up the majority of the population"? Nothing of the sort. Josephus Flavius, to whom Alon refers in support of his assertion,[27] speaks only of the *influence* the Pharisees had among the people in the times of the Hasmonaeans and the dynasty of Herod, but this by no means signifies that they made up the majority of the population. The majority of the Hebrew people in Palestine, as of any other people, was made up (the slaves apart) of small farmers, trades-people, and small

[24] *Ibid.*, pp. 128-130. Weiss supposes that "many of the leaders of the people" (not naming them) secretly fomented the rebellion over the course of several years.

[25] G. Alon, *Meḥqarim betoledot Yisra'el* (Tel Aviv, 1955) Vol. I, pp. 29ff.

[26] Shemuel Yeivin, *Milḥemet Bar-Kokhba* (Jerusalem, 1952).

[27] I. Flavii [Josephus Flavius], *Iudeiskie drevnosti* [*Jewish Antiquities*] XVIII 1, 3; cf. XIII 15, 5.

merchants. The authority of the *Tannas* in the period under discussion was not only *not* generally recognized, but quite the contrary, there was extreme enmity between the basic mass of the population, which the learned men derogatorily called *ʿam haʾareṣ* (people of the soil, and in the extended sense, clods) and the learned men themselves. Testifying to this fact are numerous statements touching on the relations between the learned men and the *ʿam haʾareṣ*, the "simple folk."[28] With such inimical relations, one can hardly speak of the authoritativeness of the *Tannas* among the Hebrew masses of Palestine in the period of the Bar-Kokhba rebellion.

Being unable to support his conception, Alon is forced to take another tack. He introduces statements made by those opposed to the rebellion and adds that "such people were very few," evidently supposing that this does not need to be proven. He cites, for example, a contemporary of ʿAqiba, Yosi ben Kisma. On meeting Ḥaninah ben Teradion, who taught the Torah to the people despite the decree of Hadrian, he reproached him in these words: "This people [that is, the Romans] is set up by God. It annihilated his house. It burned his palace. And still it continues to exist until now." Further, Yosi ben Kisma threatened Ḥaninah ben Teradion that he would perish together with the roll of the Torah he was teaching, because he was breaking an imperial decree. The sources also say that when Yosi ben Kisma died, there walked behind his bier "the great leaders of Rome," that is, the outstanding representatives of Roman power in Palestine.[29] And Yosi ben Kisma was not the only one. The Roman rulership had begun to be looked upon as something fated, established by God himself against which it was impossible to rise. The rulers of Rome were regarded as instruments in the hand of God, with whose help He chastises the people of Israel for its sins. In this regard, such a conception was a continuation of the teachings of the prophets Isaiah and Jeremiah, who looked upon Assyria and Babylonia in their time

[28] b. Pes. 49b; b. B.B. 8a; Bereshit Rabbah. Cf. A. Ranovich, *Ocherk istorii drevneevreiskoi religii* (Moscow, 1937), pp. 342, 343; M. I. Shakhnovich, *Reaktsionnaia sushchnostʾ iudaisma* (Moscow-Leningrad, 1960) pp. 95, 96 [*The Reactionary Essence of Judaism*]. Many scholars (A. Büchler. *Der galiläische ʿam-haʾares* [Vienna, 1907], L. I. Katsnelson in several articles in *Voskhod* for 1897-1898 and in *Evreiskoi entsyklopediia*) correctly suppose that the sharply critical statements of the *Tannas* concerning the ʿam-haʾareṣ "relate for the most part to the period after the destruction of Jerusalem and after the persecutions of Hadrian." The following statement, surely made during the period in question, is especially characteristic in this regard: "Not a single misfortune has ever been visited upon Israel without the *ʿam-haʾareṣ* being guilty for it."

[29] G. Alon, Vol. I, pp. 29ff.; b. A.Z. 18a; cf. Grätz, Hebrew translation, p. 257.

as knouts of God to lash His disobedient people. An analogous idea was developed by another contemporary of ʿAqiba—Joshua ben Ḥananiah, "God will raise up a king like Haman with cruel laws, and the Israelites will repent."[30] N. Krochmal is thus correct in his assertion that all the learned men were of like mind in convincing the people that this nation (the Romans) was established by God.[31] This pro-Roman orientation of the majority of the *Tannas* had its beginning in the "peace-lovers" of the period of the Jewish War. This orientation not only did not grow weaker with time, but on the contrary grew stronger in certain circles. This is illustrated by an editor of the Mishnah, Patriarch Judah I, who tried "to eradicate the fast of the *9th of Av*" in memory of the destruction of both Temples. But even the obedient Synedrion could not make up its mind to take such a step, which meant the destruction among the people of the very memory of its former independence.[32] To this same Patriarch is attributed the interpretation of Bar-Kokhba's name in the pejorative sense, that is, "son of a lie."[33]

The hypothesis regarding the majority of *Tannas* of the second century and contemporaries of Bar-Kokhba as almost the initiators and ideologists of the rebellion is just as unfounded as the hypothesis concerning the revolutionary nature of ʿAqiba's travels. Neither is supported by any facts at all. Among other things, Alon claims in one place that the majority of the *Tannas* supported the rebellion at its very beginning when Bar-Kokhba was winning. But later, when the rebels began to sustain significant losses, the *Tannas* began to desert him. Being unable to prove his claim with facts, Alon refers to the "fact" that so it was under the reigns of Vespasian and Titus.[34]

The only place in the Talmudic and Midrashic sources where there is information on the relation of ʿAqiba to Bar-Kokhba is the y. Ta. IV, 68a, in which ʿAqiba proclaims Bar-Kokhba the Messiah. Grätz insists upon this point especially.[35] ʿAqiba himself, naturally, is raised

[30] b. Sanh. 97b.

[31] N. Krochmal, p. 76.

[32] b. Meg. 5b; y. Meg. 70b. There are many legends about the friendship between Rabbi (Patriarch Judah I) and Antonius scattered through various tractates in the Talmud. It is not yet known which Emperor is meant here: Marcus Aurelius, Septimus Severus, or Caracalla. Although lacking historical basis, these legends nevertheless characterize the extremely Romanophile orientation of the Patriarch.

[33] Eikha Rabba, Ch. II.

[34] G. Alon, *Toledot HaYehudim be'Ereṣ Yisra'el*, Vol. II (Tel Aviv, 1955) Vol. II, pp. 42-43.

[35] Grätz, p. 160; Hebrew translation, p. 237.

on the highest pedestal.[36] However, Derenbourg categorically rejects Grätz's assertion: "I cannot believe that one could find a single place in the Talmud which would support Grätz's opinion that ʿAqiba was a leader and head of the Jews."[37]

On the question of ʿAqiba's authority in connection with the Bar-Kokhba rebellion, Z. Frankel has taken an original position. Differing with Grätz, who supposed that ʿAqiba was arrested after the rebellion was crushed, Frankel says that ʿAqiba was arrested *before* the rebellion, explaining: "In y. Ta. we find no indication that ʿAqiba was in Betar, or that he aroused the people to rebel, or that he helped Bar-Kokhba with advice. And in b. Ber. we similarly find no indication that ʿAqiba was arrested for cooperating with Bar-Kokhba. From this, one may conclude that ʿAqiba was arrested before the rebellion." But why was ʿAqiba arrested? If one considers the only real proof of ʿAqiba's participation in the rebellion to be his journeys "during which he incited the Jews of near and distant lands to rebellion against Rome" (for which, as we already know, there is no proof whatever), Frankel theorizes that these journeys connected with secret councils created suspicion on the part of the Roman authorities, who arrested ʿAqiba before the rebellion. They did not kill him, however, since the Roman legion in Palestine was then insignificant, and they were afraid that the murder of the outstanding man of the time would lead to rebellion. When ʿAqiba was in prison and the rebellion broke out, they put him to torture.[38] Thus, in Frankel, one unknown is solved by another unknown.

The contemporary Israeli historian Shemuel Yeivin also dealt with the question of ʿAqiba's leadership role: "It is possible to establish with almost complete certainty that there was at this time a High Synedrion of wise men, although we have no data at all on its composition or on who was at its head." On the following page, Yeivin "having no data at all," says that the president of this Synedrion was ʿAqiba, "known as one of the most active leaders of the rebellion."[39] If a rebellious Synedrion of wise men did indeed exist, this would mean that precisely they, the "wise men," with ʿAqiba at their head, led the rebellion, if only in the early period. There is thus every reason to suppose that the hypothesis of ʿAqiba's

36 Grätz, p. 158; Hebrew translation, p. 236.
37 J. Derenbourg, p. 220.
38 Z. Frankel, pp. 121, 122.
39 Yeivin, p. 79.

exclusive role in the Bar-Kokhba rebellion and his authority at the time is entirely baseless.

Did the Bar-Kokhba rebellion have a messianic character? Comparing the information of Josephus on the "false prophets" of the first century B.C. and the first century A.D. with the figure of Bar-Kokhba in the Talmudic and Midrashic legends, we note an essential difference between them. In the *Antiquities* and the *Jewish War*,[40] Josephus speaks of false prophets who promised miracles, the working of which, according to Biblical legends was ascribed to the outstanding heroes—to Moses, to Joshua and others. The actions of all these false messiahs were transistory and had only a local character, attracting only individual groups of fanatics who followed after them like madmen, thinking that the Lord would repay their perception with some foresign of freedom.[41] Bar-Kokhba is described in the Talmudic and Midrashic sources in quite a different light. He has the exclusive strength of the epic hero; with his knees he throws back at the Romans the stones hurled at him by Roman slings.[42] The sources also say that Bar-Kokhba, in order to test the strength and endurance of his soldiers, ordered each of them to cut off a finger. The "wise men" railed against him for this and advised him instead to order that each horseman, galloping at full speed, tear out a Lebanese cedar by the roots. As a result of both tests, an army of 400,000 men was formed under Bar-Kokhba.[43] Hieronymus says that Bar-Kokhba, according to certain tales, vomited forth burning tow.[44] All these legendary tales show that the people saw in Bar-Kokhba an epic hero, an organizer of an army, but scarcely a messiah.

Did Bar-Kokhba consider himself to be the messiah? There is not the least doubt that those Jewish and Christian sources (especially Eusebius)[45] which say that Bar-Kokhba proclaimed himself Messiah were products of groups or individuals inimical to the rebellion. On this point, the Christian sources leave no doubt at all.[46] As to the

[40] I. Flavii [J. Flavius], *Iudeiskie drevinosti* [*Jewish Antiquities*] XX, 8, 6; and *Iudeiskaia voina* [*The Jewish War*], II, 13, 4.

[41] I. Flavii, *Drevnosti*, XX, 5, 1.

[42] Eikha Rabba, II, 2.

[43] y. Ta. *loc. cit.*

[44] Hieronymus, *Annal.* II, *Adv. Rufini.*

[45] Eusebius, *Hist. Eccl.* IV, 6.

[46] On the inimical relations of Christian circles toward the Bar-Kokhba rebellion see E. Schürer, *Geschichte des jüdischen Volkes im Zeitalter Jesu Christi* (Leipzig, 1890) Vol. I, pp. 571, 572.

Hebrew sources, the latter give reason to state that Bar-Kokhba made no attempts to proclaim himself Messiah. Bar-Kokhba, under the influence of his first victory, shouted: "God, you don't have to help us. Just don't help our enemies!"[47] Grätz is inclined to think that this haughty phrase, unsuitable for a man who had proclaimed himself Messiah, was incidentally pronounced by Bar-Kokhba when he was convinced of the strength of his army. In fact this is not so at all.

In y. Ta. we read: "When he (Bar-Kokhba) would go into battle, he would say: 'God, do not help us and do not interfere, for you, God, have denied us, and you do not come out with our soldiers.'" The last part of this exclamation corresponds to Psalm 60 : 10. Here, therefore it is a matter not of a single instance, but a motto or device coined by Bar-Kokhba; in any case it has to do with an often-repeated action. It is known also that two rebel brothers who were hidden in Kefar-Ḥananiah after the rebellion was put down, greeted those passing through with a similar statement-device.[48] The same words are ascribed also to Bar-Derom, an active participant in the rebellion and hero of the battle near Tur-Malka. All this information, whether legendary or not, shows clearly that Bar-Kokhba had not the slightest intention of proclaiming himself Messiah. It is therefore impossible to agree with Soviet historian, G. M. Livshitz, who claims that it is "quite difficult to imagine that Bar-Kokhba actually pronounced these words which are ascribed to him by legend.[49] The logical question obtrudes as to whether all legend is merely a fiction from beginning to end."[50]

What role could ʿAqiba's proclamation of Bar-Kokhba as Messiah have played, given this situation? As is obvious from the sources, there were no generally held ideas about the messiah among the *Tannas* of the period or among the later *Amoras.* In contradistinction to eschatological ideas of the messianic epoch, such as the millenium, ʿAqiba limited it to forty years, so that the epoch, like the reigns of David and Solomon, included only the lifespan of one man.[51] Detailed discussions of this matter are included in b. Sanh. 93a-97b. R. Nathan says that one should not listen to the opinions of those "of our

[47] S. Dubnov, p. 44; Grätz, p. 162; Hebrew translation, pp. 238, 239.
[48] Yalqut Deut. 946.
[49] b. Git. 56a-47a.
[50] G. M. Livshits, *Klassovaia bor'ba v Iudes...*, p. 319.
[51] Midrash Tehillim 90 : 15.

teachers" who proclaimed the future in the form of visions and apocalyptic writings based on calculation of the time of prophecies not yet fulfilled. ʿAqiba is mentioned among these teachers; he based his visions on the interpretation of the lines of the prophet Haggai (2 : 6 and 2 : 2): "Once again, and this will be soon, I shall cause to tremble heaven and earth, the sea and the land, and shall cause all peoples to tremble. And I shall bring low the thrones of kingdoms and destroy the power of the gentile kingdoms; I shall overturn the chariots and those upon them." Such people came to be called "calculators of the end of days." ʿAqiba engaged in such "calculations." S. L. Rapoport gives information on this, referring to the appropriate place in the *Bereshit Rabbah.*[52] It is quite possible that after the first victories of Bar-Kokhba over the Roman army, the army of "the gentile kingdom," ʿAqiba pronounced the victor a king-messiah. There were many such "calculators" at the time, and their actions were sharply criticized later. The following sentence is ascribed to the disciple of ʿAqiba, Yosi bar Ḥalafta: "Whoever shall await impatiently the appearance of the Messiah, that person has no portion in the future world."[53] It is not by accident that following information about teachers one should not listen to, and among them ʿAqiba, there is the statement of *Amora* Samuel bar Naḥmani, in which he calls down destruction on those who engage in "calculating the end," since they claimed that if the Messiah did not appear after the time period set by them, he would never appear.[54]

Such "calculators of the end" were, of course, not alone, but their influence usually spread only to individual groups of fanatics, their "disciples." One should understand precisely in this sense those "disciples of ʿAqiba" referred to in b. A.Z. 25b:[55] It is said of the disciples of ʿAqiba who set out for Kezib that they were met by bandits. They [the bandits] said to them, "Where are you going?" They answered, "To Akko." When they came to Kezib, they went away.

[52] S. L. Rapoport, *Erech Milin* (Prague, 1852) Vol. I, p. 7.

[53] Derekh Ereṣ Rabbah, I.

[54] b. Sanh. 97b.

[55] There is no doubt that the contradictory figures for the numbers of followers of ʿAqiba in the Talmud and Midrash (12,000—Bereshit Rabbah 61 : 3; 24,000—b. Yev. 62b; 48,000—b. Ned. 50a) are the usual *aggadic* hyperbole, as L. Ginzberg noted in the above-mentioned article. Moreover given the context, there is no reference at all to any participation of these "disciples" in the Bar-Kokhba rebellion. As to the note in b. Yev. 62a, on the perishing of a group of ʿAqiba's disciples as a result of *shamda*, one may give here the explanation that they died of diphtheria.

They were asked, "Whose disciples are you?" They answered, "The disciples of Rabbi ʿAqiba." They were told, "Fortunate are Rabbi ʿAqiba and his disciples, whom bad people never meet." From this rather obscure information one may conclude that on the eve of the Bar-Kokhba rebellion or at its very beginning the rebels kept watch on travellers going to Akko and Kezib.[56]

Keeping in mind the ideological situation of Jewish society in Palestine in the second century A.D., one may say that such "calculators of the end" and those around them gave moral support to the rebels. They could carry on corresponding agitation at least in the milieu of those who believed in these "calculations" or who would yield to them. In a like manner, one should understand the reply of Yoḥanan ben Torata cited earlier: "ʿAqiba, sooner will grass grow out of your cheeks, than the son of David come." This reply becomes especially understandable if one considers that ʿAqiba had defined the time span of the messianic epoch as the span of one man's life—forty years.

In summation, one can come to the following conclusions on the basis of the analysis of Talmudic and Midrashic sources at hand:

1. The sources at hand give no indication that ʿAqiba was the ideologist and organizer of the Bar-Kokhba rebellion.
2. The sources give no indication that allow us to connect the numerous travels of ʿAqiba with the preparation of the Bar-Kokhba rebellion.
3. The conception of Weiss, Frankel and others concerning the exclusive role of the clergy in preparing the Bar-Kokhba rebellion, now resurrected in new variants by Israeli scholars (Alon, Yeivin), has no factual basis at all. On the contrary, there are numerous indications that the majority of the *Tannas* contemporary to the Bar-Kokhba rebellion looked upon the power of Rome as a fated phenomenon against which it was impossible to rise, continuing the line of pro-Roman orientation inherited from Yoḥanan ben Zakkai.
4. Between the basic mass of participants in the Bar-Kokhba rebellion and the majority of *Tannas* at the time, relations were distinctly inimical, demonstrated by the many statements of the *Tannas* concerning the *ʿam haʾareṣ*.

[56] b. A.Z. 25b. It is supposed that Kezib is the same as the Biblical Akhzib (Joshua 15 : 44, 19 : 29; Micah 1 : 14).

5. There is no reason to suppose that Bar-Kokhba ever called himself the Messiah. Related information originating in the Jewish and Christian sources inimical to Bar-Kokhba cannot be trusted.
6. Our sources give reason to suppose that ʿAqiba was one of the so-called "calculators of the end," whose influence at the time was quite limited. Nevertheless, given the ideological situation of Jewish society at the time, ʿAqiba could have given moral support to the rebels.

APPENDIX II

DEVELOPMENT OF A LEGEND: STUDIES ON THE TRADITIONS CONCERNING YOḤANAN BEN ZAKKAI:

CORRECTIONS AND RECONSIDERATIONS

The study of the history of the rabbinic tradition in antiquity is at its beginnings. No results may be regarded as final. Everything is to be subjected to further consideration and revision in the light of new findings. Here I therefore continue the work begun in *Development of a Legend.*

i. Corrections

A fair number of errors, both in minor details and in analysis of pericopae, construction of synoptic tables, and other substantive matters, occurred in *Development.* These are deplorable and much regretted. My teacher Morton Smith has kindly supplied lists of various sorts of corrections of detail, for which I am very grateful.

1. *Erroneous Cross-References*

P. 112, Table, Pal. Tal. column, line 3. for II.i.3 read III.i.3.
P. 17 comment, paragraph 2, line 2, for I.i.1 read I.i.2.
P. 19, first comment, line 1, for II.iii.8 read II.iii.7.
P. 19, first comment, line 10, for IV.i.11 read IV.i.9.
P. 19, first comment, line 10, for III.ii.1a read III.ii.1b-c.
P. 55, line 4 for (b) read (b, part 2).
P. 61, General Comments , line 3, for III.i.3 read II.i.3.
P. 65, first comment, line 5, for I.i.8 read I.ii.8.
P. 84, second comment, line 7, for II.ii.6 read I.ii.6.
P. 86, item 6, end, for 3.2 read 3.3.
P. 92, first comment, line 2, for 2.31 read 3.31.
P. 101, line 8 from bottom, for III.ii.19 read I.i.5(a).
P. 101, line 5 from bottom, for II.iii.19b read III.ii.19b.
P. 110, second paragraph, line 2, for 24 read 24b.
P. 110, second paragraph, line 4, for II.i.6 read III.i.6? (But both i.5 and the following i.15 seem wrong.)
P. 111, Table 1, Bab. Tal. column, line 3 for III.ii.8 read III.ii.9.
P. 112, Table, Pal. Tal. column, line 3. for II.i.3 read III.i.3.
P. 118, note 1, line 6, for II.iii.8e and f, read II.iii.8f and g.
P. 132, Table 1, Mishnah col., line 7 for II.i.18 read II.i.18a; line 8, add II.i.18b-d; line 9 add II.i.18d.

P. 135, item 8, for 8 : 4 read 8 : 6.
P. 137, line 5, for 9 : 16 read 9 : 17.
P. 144, item 7, line 1, for III.ii.6 read III.ii.5.
P. 145, item 10, b. Suk. 31b is wrong.
P. 150, line 9 f.b. delete (a).
P. 154, line 11 for 38 : 26 read 38 : 27.
P. 157, Table 1, Bab. Tal. column, line 1, add V.ii.6.
P. 157, Table 1, Bab. Tal. column, item 7, for V.ii.10 read V.ii.21.
P. 157, Table 1, Bab. Tal. column, item 11, to V.ii.7 add III.ii.24.
P. 157, Table 1, Bab. Tal. column, item 15, add V.ii.20.
P. 157, Table 1, ARN column, item 11 add IV.i.5.
P. 157, Table 2, Bab. column, item 4, for III.ii read III.ii.12.
P. 180, Comment, for III.iii.15 read II.iii.15.
P. 192, line 3, for II.i.22 read II.i.21.
P. 203, Disputes, line 2, for II.i.1 read II.i.3.
P. 206, line 11 f.b., for II.i.5, 6, 7a, 7b, 20 read II.i.7.
P. 206, line 4 f.b., for Men. 68b read R.H. 30b (III.ii.9).
P. 207, line 4, (III.ii.9) belongs in the following line after R.H. 30b.
P. 208, item 6, line 1 (V.ii.10) is wrong.
P. 208, line 8 from bottom, for 8.4. read 8.6.
P. 216, line 3, for III.ii.24 read III.ii.23.
P. 221, for y. Sot. 9.16 read y. Sot. 9.17.
P. 225, line 2, for III.i.24 read III.ii.24.
P. 232, line 2 of comment, for VI read VII.
P. 234, headings of outlines, for VI.v.3 read VI.i-i.4; for VI.iii.14 read VI.ii.1.
P. 236, center, for (III.ii.6) read (III.ii.16).
P. 251, line 5 from bottom, for (II.ii.12) read (III.ii.12); the missing ref. for b. Pes. 94a-b is (V.ii.4).
P. 255 refs. for outlines, for (VI.ii.12) read (VI.vii.2); for (VI.ii.13) read (VI.iii.3); for Pesiq. Rab. 14 supply (VI.iv.1).
P. 256, line 11 f.b. for 17 : 19 and 19 : 7 read 17 : 4 and 19 : 6.
P. 256, line 8 f.b. for 44 : 18 read 44 : 21.

Errors of this sort seem considerably more frequent than misprints, and therefore not wholly due to the printer. The misprints are mostly trivial, but note:

P. xv, paragraph 2, line 3 from end, read, "all along";
P. 146, line 9, for "leather," read "litter";
P. 167, text, line 4 f.b., "Sias," read "sins."

2. *Mistranslations*

The following passages have been mistranslated.

P. 26, item 4, last line, for "will be" read "shall render."
P. 139, item 15, last two lines, read "an object already holy cannot be used as a substitute for the redemption of another holy object."
P. 172, item 2. The spirit is not "wandering" but "of madness"; the twigs

are not "smoked," but the doctors "fumigate" the man; the water is not "placed on the fire" but "sprinkled on the man."

P. 174, item 1. Paragraph 3 is Yoḥanan's reply; it should begin with "He said (to him)." The two following sentences are not statements, but questions.

3. *Significant Criticisms and Improvements*

The following substantive comments have been contributed by Professor Smith:

Pp. 15-6: It is not noticed that the story is an insertion, breaking the sequence of the exegesis.

P. 16, item 2(a). This is not part of the Yoḥanan material.

P. 19, comment. The passage does not recur as a *ḥomer* exegesis. The homily in the death-bed scene is not identical.

P. 38, comment, paragraph 2. The conclusions are too strongly stated. MT might show either a correction of SD or an invention to fill out what its sources lacked.

P. 61. In the "General Comments" on Ch. I items 6, 7, 8 and 23 are overlooked.

P. 65, item 1. In the parallel, p. 83, the speaker is definitely Joshua and he would normally be understood to be the speaker here. This therefore probably does not belong in the Yoḥanan material.

P. 68, paragraph 2. The miracle does not begin before the sermon, but interrupts it—a clear sign of insertion.

P. 70. It is not reported in the passages cited that Yoḥanan abrogated the rite of breaking the heifer's neck, he merely stated that it had been abrogated. The exegesis referred to concerns a different rite.

P. 78. In the General Comments on Ch. II, item 10 is overlooked.

P. 82, line 5. The Mishnah's statement refers to a different decree.

P. 83, comment. R. Joshua does not tell the story; it is told about him.

P. 85, line 12 f.b. Not an "exposition attributed to two disciples," but *a story about* an exposition by two disciples.

P. 91, comment, lines 6-5 from end. The complex does not appear in III.ii.23; V.ii.7 is presented as if identical with III.ii.5 (though by error in cross ref. the text has 6 for 5).

P. 116, comment. Part (d) is clearly an addition tacked on to the original story which reached its climax and logical conclusion with the last sentence of (c). Moreover, it is the only element in the story that could have been produced by imitation of Josephus.

P. 126, lines 15-14 f.b. Not "after the master's death" but after the consolation scene. The suggestion is that he did not go to Yavneh. Curiously, this detail of ARN matches the b. Git. escape story, which supposes Yavneh was a center of study before Yoḥanan went there; whereas the ARN 4 escape story supposes Yoḥanan established the school there.

P. 131, comment, line 6. We can suppose that someone later on wanted to attribute eschatological expectations to Yoḥanan.

P. 142, item 1. Yoḥanan's saying is connected with Abbaye's by the fact that they have the same final phrase, "even a gentile in the market place."

P. 147. A new section begins with the second sentence of (c); this is overlooked again on p. 162, item 2.b.

P. 151, line 7. For "there are only a few connections with" read "the basic outline is the same as that of."

P. 157, table 1, items 3-5. The content of these *for the Yoḥanan tradition* is not, "Did Yoḥanan contradict the Torah?" (secondary discussion) but solely the reports of Yoḥanan's three decrees.

P. 161, item 5. There are five elements in the item, not four.

P. 162, item 1. It is unlikely that the last sentence belongs to the Yoḥanan material.

P. 166, paragraph 3: Yoḥanan is accorded the hearing before he predicts that Vespasian will become emperor.

P. 167, line 7. Yoḥanan's ability to tell time in the dark was not magical.

P. 167, item 1. The saying of R. Gamaliel is, as it stands, a *non sequitur*, therefore it must be supposed an abbreviation of the form of the saying found in b. B.B. 10b, where, however, it is attributed to R. Joshua. The additional elements (of this saying) from B.B. should have been given here in parentheses, since knowledge of them is unquestionably presupposed.

P. 175, item 3. Qohelet Rabbah has the traditional three rich men, whereas Lam. R. 1.5.31 has made two persons of Naqdimon ben Gorion; consequently Q.R. does not "clearly depend" on L.R.

P. 179, comment. Yoḥanan followers are probably fruits at the entrance of the orchard.

P. 187, last paragraph. The units of the Yoḥanan tradition have in many cases not been readily discerned, and when discerned are often not "original," and even when essentially original are usually not in their original forms. Like the stories in the Gospels, they must be peeled.

P. 194, paragraphs 2-4. The contexts are not "completely different"; all deal with devices of cheats. The point of law raised by the saying is in all cases the same: Should legal teaching include material which may instruct the students in criminal practices? Yoḥanan's saying on this point has been attached to various cases which raise the issue.

Pp. 195-197. This is the reverse of the preceding case. Here the sayings quoted in various contexts have no specific legal reference of their own, but indicate only approval ("Ḥanan spoke well") or disapproval ("I fear he may be liable for a sin offering") of a preceding opinion or action. Therefore they can never have existed by themselves (*versus* p. 197, line 15); their uniformity suggests that there were once collections of opinions Yoḥanan approved, or disapproved, or both, with this approval or disapproval expressed in stereotyped forms.

P. 199, sec. v., item 1. An independent story, not part of the Yoḥanan-material; that it follows immediately in all versions is evidence of some earlier collection.

Pp. 200-201. Omission of the T. Oholot parallel is unfortunate; its close agreement with the T. Parah text against Sifré shows the consistency of the editor of T. The break between 6a and 6b should come after "forgotten"; the present arrangement produced the false impression (lines 5-6 f.b.) that there was no equivalent to 6b in T. Parah 7b of Sifré combines two elements, first the equivalent of T.P. 7a, then the exact mate of T.P. 7b. Hillel is not "intruded, then excluded," and T.P. 7a-b is not "a garbling of Sifré 8 : 11," but part of the original report which runs almost identically in both versions through 8. The differing comments appended to the reference to Hillel are secondary in both versions.

P. 202. The outline conceals the fact that both Sifra and Mishnah add a final proof text not in the Tosefta. T. does not lack "Scripture," but only the following phrases.

P. 203, line 8 f.b. Yoḥanan is not "introduced as a self-described Sadducee," but merely speaks as would a Sadducee, presumably in *reductio ad absurdum*, i.e. he cites a Pharisaic ruling with which the Sadducees would agree and uses their argument to refute their other objection.

P. 207, item 3. This is really two items. II.i.8a has a parallel; 8b does not. Ergo, they probably circulated separately. From here on one begins to find in the discussion references to traditions of or about Yoḥanan which were not presented in the section on sources; such are passages from b. R.H. 31a (p. 207), 31b (pp. 208, 213), b. Beṣ. 5b (p. 208); b. San. 41b (p. 213); ARNb 28 (p. 216); b. B.B. 134a-b and b. Suk. 28a (p. 219); ARNb 6 (p. 228); ARNb 31, b. Shab. 153a and Qoh. R. 9.8.1 (p. 257).

P. 208, last paragraph. "Precisely" is false. b. R.H. 31b has "who converted," and "Ben Eleazar," lacking in b. Ker. 9a. In the section on sources (III.ii.30 and V.i.8) the texts given for b. Ker. 9a and Y. Sheq. 8.4 (read, 6) are identical, and do not exactly agree with the Hebrew of either passage.

P. 213. This table is full of minor inaccuracies in its reports of wording; worse, it combines three different units of tradition, which should have been treated separately.

P. 216, Table 1. The last two lines of all three columns are not part of the pericope. The most important variant (ARNa 14: "worthy to intercalate the year") is not presented.

Pp. 221-2. This table again combines three different units of tradition; the story of R. Eliezer's death is not lacking from y. Sotah 9.17 (vs. p. 222, line 4 f.b.; p. 224, line 4f.). The table does not show that ARNa 25 has the saying about the chair for Hezekiah.

P. 223, lines 9-8 f.b. The homilies are declared "practically identical" because the table does not accurately represent their differences (nor their similarities). "Whose death penalty is of this world" is not in ARN; "whom I cannot persuade . . . or bribe" is in b. Ber. 28b; etc. Neither story is dependent on the other; they are diverse developments of a common source.

P. 225, line 3 f.b. For "is cited without any change" read "appears with slight differences." One of these differences is the omission of Yoḥanan's title by b. Yev. 105a. Since the context shows this cannot be contemptuous, the passage casts some doubt on the interpretation of other such omissions as evidence of contempt, cp. pp. 32, 52.

P. 226, paragraph 4. The death scene does not show much development from simple to complex, but three completely different pericopae of which all appear in b. Ber. 28b, only two in the other texts.

P. 232, lines 5-4 f.b. That the guards wanted to stab the corpse does not appear in ARN but is in b. Git. and Lam R.

P. 233, lines 9-8 f.b. The ARN escape story is surely more primitive than the b. Git. and Lam. R. parallels. In particular, it has the prophecy of Vespasian's kingship (probably inspired by Josephus) tacked on at the end as a separate element, whereas the parallels have built it into the heart of their stories.

P. 234, Table. One version of the story (VI.v.3) is not noticed. Pesiqta has the element, "This is the school house."

P. 235. y. Meg. lacks the question, but the elements it does have are fuller, not briefer: name of reporter, detailed exegesis of Scripture, lacking in all three later (?) versions.

P. 238. Of the five elements listed as common to Sifré D., b. Ket. and ARNa, two and two-thirds are not so. The author himself brackets the fourth; the last appears in S.D. and b. Ket. only; of the third, "what happened to your father's wealth" appears only in b. Ket. and ARN; the carpets only in SD and ARN.

Pp. 244-5. The list of six elements common to all the Eliezer stories omits two (he went hungry till his breath stank, thus Yoḥanan discovered he was starving) and includes two which are not common. ("Between us he would have perished" is not in Gen. R.; that Eliezer refused to be sole heir is not in ARN.)

Pp. 248-9. The synoptic tables generally are very negligent about getting like elements side by side and showing unique elements without parallels. These errors would take too long to describe, so I have not specified them, but this table deserves notice as a really outstanding muddle that conceals more than half of the essential divisions of the material. (There are also omissions—from the y. Hag. column the descent of the fire and the dancing angels.) Consequently the relationship of the stories is misstated (p. 249). In the Tosefta version some sayings have been expanded and some others added at the end of the story, but in the story itself the only major element not in the Mekhilta is the statement that Y. got off his ass, wrapped himself in his cloak, and sat down. This at least might be true, whereas Mekh. has the appearance of the fire, not in T. and presumably mythological.

P. 250, paragraph 2, lines 4ff. For "the blessing is greatly expanded" read, "a new blessing is added." Doubling of the blessing does not prove dependence—if a dependent account could be expanded, so could an independent one. The Tosefta version contains nothing to indicate that the Joshua tradition was superior to that of Eleazar; this inference is peculiar to b. Hag.

P. 255, lines 3-4. For "there is no close relationship between the two accounts," read, "the two accounts are expansions of an identical core—the question about Moses, based on Ex. 38.26f. and the answer." The following table omits one of the four versions of the story (VI.5.2).

P. 256. The notion that such stories did not circulate widely runs counter to their preservation in many versions.

P. 257, paragraph 3. The saying of b. Hag. 5a does not recur in Tanḥuma Shofeṭim 7; the sayings in these two passages are essentially different.

P. 258. More muddled tables. Of the first, the last two sections were not given in the sources and do not belong here, they are not Yoḥanan-material but secondary exegesis. The second omits the question in Mekh. (making it parallel to all the other versions) and obscures the parallelism of the y. Qid. version to those of Tosefta and b. B.Q. It also fails to show that the *kemin ḥomer* comment appears in different places in the different versions (and is therefore probably secondary—*versus* p. 259).

P. 261. The table omits the statement of the law peculiar to Mekh. and the differences from T. of Mekh. (in point 3) and b. B.Q. (in point 4); the following statement that "there are no variations whatever" is false. It is not noticed that the "related, though different" exegesis in Mekh. is paralleled with only minor differences in b. B.Q. 79b.

P. 289, paragraph 3, line 6. There is no omission.

Smith also observes in connection with Antoninus, Antonius, Agentos, etc. (*Development*, p. 156) that it is likely the several names are corruptions of Antoninus. They presumably come afrom a single series. Antoninus was the traditional interlocutor of Rabbi Judah the Patriarch and the common imperial name from 137 to c. 285. So here we have another example of the Yoḥanan b. Zakkai = Rabbi theme, shaped in this century and a half, probably rather late in it.

4. *Further Comments*

Professor Smith further states:

> The potential value of the synoptic and form-critical methods should not be concealed by the faults in this first application of them. Even in this application it appears, in spite of the faults, in the important results that have been achieved. To estimate these one must remember that ninety percent of the book consists of texts, references, and statements of fact; therefore, the listed errors—and even the doubled or trebled list that might be produced by an exact check against the original texts—affect only a small part of the data presented, and in many instances, the effects are of little or no importance to the arguments. My impression is,

therefore, that most of the arguments are sound, and a number of major points are established. These I now list:

1. The material reported in the earlier rabbinic collections is *on the whole* much more reliable, historically, than that in the later collections (pp. 212, 227, 265-6). The latter often clearly represents inference, fanciful elaboration, and the like. The author recognizes that abbreviation also occurs and more elaborate accounts may *sometimes* be primary (p. 227). I think he is sometimes too hasty (e.g. pp. 265-6) in denying credibility to items that appear for the first time only in late collections. It must also be remembered that the collections are collections, their formation went on through centuries, most were, for one or another period contemporary, the dates given them are only *closing* dates, and even these are extremely uncertain. Given these facts, how much importance is to be attached to these dates? Apart from the question of oral tradition, we must suppose that there was a lot of written material now lost (students, note books, teachers' and preachers' notes and collections of exempla, sayings, etc.) from which the later collections may have drawn. A distinction must therefore be made between the *essential* elements of items that first appear in late collections, and the later elaborations of stories known from early collections. The latter have now been shown to be usually products of invention; the reliability of the former is therefore brought into serious question, but not wholly disproved.

2. Yoḥanan is often cited, but never cites his own teachers (pp. 3, 59). He evidently stood at the beginning of a radically new phase of the tradition.

3. We have relatively little material from Yoḥanan and that little is spottily distributed and often not of much importance. There is nothing amounting to a major revision of the Law. Why, then, does a radically new phase of the tradition begin here, and what has happened to those teachings that must have been necessary to begin it? Evidently the development from Yoḥanan to Usha was complex and in the process much of what Yoḥanan must have taught was superceded if not suppressed (p. 6).

4. Most of the Mishnaic material about Yoḥanan is preserved in forms other than those Rabbi usually used for legal data (pp. 62, 193), and Yoḥanan's exegeses rarely appear in the most common exegetic forms (p. 262). In general the importance of fixed verbal forms in the Yoḥanan material is very small (p. 262; p. 211 goes too far; notice the use of similar forms for stories in Tanḥuma's similar legal points, pp. 204ff. and 193ff. on which see above.) These observations go to confirm the suggestion above, that Yoḥanan stands at the beginning of a new phase of the legal and exegetical traditions, and that the forms later fixed for those traditions became fixed only after his time.

In this event, by the way, it is a striking testimony to the overall accuracy of the tradition that the later conventional forms were not generally imposed on his sayings. Another testimony to the same effect is the remarkable verbal similarity between most versions of most traditions, in their parallel elements. This resembles some of the Q. material in the Gospels; contrast the bulk of the Gospel material in which the wording of the parallel stories differs widely. All this goes to confirm my strictures on Gerhardsson's ignorant *Memory and Manuscript.* Rabbinic literature is the product of a sort of mnemonic tradition quite different from that which lies behind the bulk of the Gospels.

5. There are very few parallels between the Yoḥanan material in the Tannaitic midrashim and that in the Mishnah, and whereas the Yerushalmi mostly repeats both Mishnaic and midrashic material, the Bavli brings a lot of new material with new characteristics, much of it close to ARN (pp. 63, 226, 267-275). The author is inclined to explain these differences as the results of invention, and therefore wants to reconsider the date of ARN (pp. 226, 274). He may be right, but I should like, before deciding, to see more investigation of the possibility that different rabbinic circles might have perpetuated different bodies of tradition. The prosopographic approach to rabbinic history through the study of chains of tradition may have much to contribute here. But the observation of the differences and distribution of the material is of primary importance.

6. Finally, the concluding account of the development of the legend (pp. 276-end) is extremely persuasive. Particularly good is the explanation of the peculiarity of the material from the circle of Rabbi (p. 291); but even better that of the use of the Yoḥanan tradition in Pumbedita and its consequent development there (pp. 295-97). The evidence and arguments here seem conclusive. The estimate of "the historical Yoḥanan" on p. 298 seems to me just about right.

5. *Omitted Parallels*

Professor Jakob J. Petuchowski kindly calls to my attention that Tos. B.Q. 7 : 4, cited on p. 257 as having no parallels, in fact recurs as follows: 1. Tanḥuma Tisa Chap. 30, without Yoḥanan's name; 2. Deut. R. ʿEqev Chap. 17, ed. Lieberman, p. 91; 3. Yalqut Shimeʿoni Tisa No. 397. Petuchowski further comments, "I have a hunch that Yoḥanan's 'original' statement may not have been quite so elaborate as the version in Deut. R., but I also cannot believe that it was quite so laconic as the text preserved in Tos. B.Q. 7 : 4."

6. *Other Observations*

Professor Joseph Heinemann comments as follows:

P. 23, to Sifré Deut. No. 357: The second version (8b) does not allude to the one hundred twenty years and their division into forty-year segments.

P. 35: Beside the stated alternatives, there may not have been *occasion* to mention the escape.

Ben Zion Wacholder (*Journal of Biblical Literature*, Vol. 91, No. 1, 1972, pp. 123-124), corrects the translation, *Development*, pp. 26-27, of "the second loaf" and "the third loaf." The phrases mean a "loaf that is in the second or third degree of uncleanness in relation to its source." This the context makes clear, but it was not made explicit. His correction of *and they tell* to *but some say it* on p. 142 seems to me not much of an improvement. Wacholder does not say what he understands by TQLH (p. 154); he is sure that it does not mean "disorder." Wacholder's corrections are of interest.

His "review" otherwise does not materially advance the study of the problems considered in *Development.* It is difficult, first, to know exactly how he has grasped the main outlines of the argument, since he does not bother to report them. The problems of the book and the way these are solved are not described. Wacholder alleges that "Missing in Neusner's discussions is the bulk of the secondary literature . . ." But that literature is extensively cited in *Life*, both in the text, and in the notes, not to mention in the bibliography. Since the work is offered as a companion to *Life*, there seemed to be no reason to repeat what was already available. He says it is erroneous to say that Hoffmann "provides no introduction to his edition of Midrash Tannaim." My copy of MT contains no introduction. Wacholder states that the writer erred in saying J. N. Epstein "rather than Hoffmann, was *the first* to assign many of its citations to Ishmael's school." What is stated is that J. N. Epstein "attributes it to the school of R. Ishmael." It may be picayune, but not having said Epstein was the first to suggest so, I wonder how carefully Wacholder examined the sentence before he took umbrage at it.

Wacholder is far more interested in the dates assigned to various compilations of Talmudic materials than he is in *Development.* He uses the occasion of his "review" to repeat his already published theory that Mekhilta is post-Talmudic (a theory not fully worked out in his suggestive but inconclusive article in *HUCA* 1968 and criticized in *Development*, pp. xiii-xiv, n. 2). He further announces his opinion that ARN is later than b. He adds, "It is also true that the Tosefta contains a large number of passages that merely reproduce chunks of the Palestinian and (sometimes) Babylonian Talmuds." I am not clear as to Wacholder's theory, but it seems to be that Tos. is post-Talmudic. It is odd that he announces so grand a theory in a little book review and then criticizes the book under review for ignoring it, as though the theory were generally known and widely held.

No one can differ from the first part of Wacholder's conclusion: "There is an urgent need for basic chronological, historical, and literary studies of early rabbinic literature." He adds, "Before ambitious monographs such as Neusner's could be productive." But not having analyzed the various theses of the work, Wacholder has not spelled out exactly why it is not "productive." The editors assigned the book for review to a scholar whose theory is explicitly rejected in the book. The result is a review which berates the author for not accepting the date for Mekhilta proposed by the reviewer—though *not* dealing with the detailed criticism of that theory. And then Wacholder announces, as noted, several new and equally "revolutionary" theories, likewise ignored by the hapless author, who, alas, is insufficiently prescient to know what is still germinating in the reviewer's mind but as yet unavailable for the study and consideration, not to mention criticism, of colleagues.

ii. Reconsiderations

1. *Introduction*

Development of a Legend was based on a sample body of traditions far too small to make possible substantial form-critical, form-historical, and literary- and historical-critical inquiries. In retrospect Yoḥanan b. Zakkai hardly appears as the ideal choice for the first such experiments. The traditions are severely limited in number and exhibit in common remarkably few traits, either formal or substantive. In all, I had in hand approximately 90 items, by contrast to approximately 350 items on the pre-70 masters, 225 items on the pre-70 Houses, and 320 items on Eliezer b. Hyrcanus—most of these in numerous versions. In the latter works it was possible to make observations on the recurrence of a few fixed forms, on mnemonic patterns or their absence, and, especially, on the stages in the development of the several traditions. With the Houses and Eliezer, as noted, we have materials of a quality and quantity unavailable for Yoḥanan. I was unaware, in beginning on Yoḥanan, of just how poor a corpus I had chosen for my methodological inquiries.

Furthermore, at the outset I had to solve elementary problems, such as how to deal with details of a story which first appear in what seem later collections, how to cope with the changes in wording in various versions of a single story, and similar matters. Even the simplest tasks of presentation posed major difficulties; I did not—as Smith's list makes clear—develop a satisfactory system of numbering pericopae.

Much more seriously, I had not fully mastered the construction of synoptic tables. The analyses of individual pericopae produced experience valuable in later inquiries but were in themselves of limited value. I moreover took greater interest in the Amoraic treatments of Yoḥanan than in the ones found in earlier strata—partly, to be sure, because the paucity of Tannaitic participation in the formation of Yoḥanan's materials. The very limited number of attestations made it difficult to say much about the Tannaim and Yoḥanan. Still, what I set out to accomplish, as specified in the preface, was to show precisely the points listed by Smith (above, pp. 443-445).

Since the two subsequent efforts have shown the availability of critical methods not applied in *Development*, it is necessary to criticize and to bring up to date the results of the earliest work.

2. *Attestations*

Work on the Houses and especially on Eliezer has shown the importance of working by stages demarcated by the attestation of knowledge of pericopae on the part of masters of Yoḥanan's own time and thereafter. In *Development* I ignored this side of things, for I did not notice any important attestations and did not distinguish among types of possible attestations. I therefore relied, far too heavily, on the order in which various compilations are presently believed to have been completed.

Attestations of Yoḥanan's materials are as follows:

1. *Yavnean Attestations*

[1-2. M. Ket. 13 : 1-2, *Development*, pp. 47-8; Yoḥanan and Dosa not only disagree about, but seem to attest the little list of rulings. But Yoḥanan's saying, attached to the list, is itself unattested.]

3. M. Avot 2 : 8-9, *Development*, pp. 54-55; Yoḥanan praised Eliezer. Abba Saul says he really praised Eleazar b. ʿArakh. This seems to be a late-Yavnean or early Ushan attestation.

2. *Ushan Attestations*

[1. Mekh. Ishmael, Lauterbach Vol. III, p. 99, *Development*, p. 18: Meir says the rule in Ex. 22 : 1 shows labor is highly regarded. Yoḥanan says dignity is highly regarded. The two sayings are closely related in exegetical principle and ideas. Meir knows nothing of Yoḥanan's exegesis and does not explicitly differ. The two are simply juxtaposed. This is the opposite of an attestation.]

2. M. R.H. 4 : 1, 3-4, *Development*, pp. 43-7: Decrees of Yavneh are attested by Eleazar b. Shammuʿa, Joshua b. Qorḥa. Eleazar: *Shofar*; Joshua: Witnesses *re* New Moon. Tos. R.H. 2 : 9: Joshua b. Qorḥa: witnesses.

3-4. M. Ed. 8 : 3, 7, *Development*, pp. 53-54; Joshua and Judah b. Batyra testify a priest may marry the widow of an *isah*-husband. Simeon b. Gamaliel: We should accept your testimony, but Yoḥanan said we cannot set up a court for this purpose, for the priests will not obey. 8 : 7: Joshua has a similar tradition.
5. M. Men. 10 : 5, *Development*, p. 55: Judah comments on the Day of Waving decree.
6. Tos. Hag. 2 : 1-2, *Development*, pp. 66-68: *Merkavah.*
[7. b. Ker. 9a/y. Sheq. 8 : 4, *Development*, p. 135: Simeon *re* bird-offering of proselyte—*if* it is Simeon b. Yoḥai.]

3. *Attestations in the Circle of Judah the Patriarch*

[1. Mekh. Ishmael, Lauterbach II, p. 290, *Development*, pp. 16-18: Simeon b. Eleazar: No sword on altar because altar prolongs life, sword shortens it. Yoḥanan: Altar makes peace. Yoḥanan's saying begins with *whole stones/peace.* Simeon does not attest Yoḥanan's saying; he does not allude to it and therefore—given the similarity of structure and ideas—probably did not know it. This again is the opposite of an attestation.]

4. *Pericopae First Attested by Appearance in Mishnah-Tosefta*

1-2. M. Shab. 16 : 7, 22 : 3: *Development*, p. 41: Not cover scorpion, not pierce cask. In 16 : 7 Judah reports a case came to Yoḥanan in ʿArav, in 22 : 3 he cites Yoḥanan's precedent in support of his own opinion. Judah does not attest the two stories—he tells them. The principles in both cases are absent in Eliezer's Sabbath-laws.
2. M. Sheq. 1 : 4, *Development*, pp. 42-3; Judah *re* Yoḥanan *re* Ben Bukhri on priests' paying *sheqel.*
3. M. Suk. 2 : 5, *Development*, p. 43: Story *re* Yoḥanan and Gamaliel, showing random-meals must be eaten in the *Sukkah.*
4. M. Suk. 3 : 12/Tos. Men. 10 : 26, *Development*, p. 43: *Lulav* [+ Day of Waving].
5. See List 1, No. 1.
6-7. M. Sot. 5 : 2, 2/Tos. Sot. 5 : 13, *Development*, pp. 48-50: Joshua cites Yoḥanan's opinion on issues discussed by ʿAqiba and Joshua b. Hyrcanus.
8-9. M. Sot. 9 : 9, 15/Tos. Sot. 14 : 1, *Development*, pp. 50-51: Yoḥanan abrogated *Soṭah*-rite. When he died, the splendor of wisdom ended.
10. M. Sanh. 5 : 2, *Development*, pp. 51-52: Ben Zakkai tested evidence.
11. M. Kel. 2 : 2, *Development*, pp. 56-57: Capacity of fragments of large stone-jars, etc.
12. M. Kel. 17 : 16/Tos. Kel. B.M. 7 : 9, *Development*, p. 58: "Woe if I speak of them."
13. M. Yad. 4 : 3/Tos. Yad. 2 : 16, *Development*, pp. 58-60: Ammon and Moab.

14. M. Yad. 4 : 6/Tos. Yad. 1 : 19, 2 : 9, *Development*, pp. 60-61: Holy Scriptures unclean *vs.* Sadducees.
[15. Tos. Ma. 2 : 1, *Development*, p. 65: Tithing dates (Joshua, not Yoḥanan)].
[16. Tos. Hag. 2 : 1, *Development*, pp. 66-68: *Merkavah.*]
[17. Tos. Hag. 2 : 1, *Development*, p. 67: Yosi b. Judah *re* Joshua taught *Merkavah* before Yoḥanan.]
18. Tos. Hag. 3 : 33, *Development*, pp. 68-69: Ṭarfon says Yoḥanan taught him *re* Heave-offering.
19. Tos. B.Q. 7 : 1, *Development*, p. 70: Thief/robber.
20. Tos. B.Q. 7 : 3-7, *Development*, pp. 71-73: *Kemin ḥomer.*
21. Tos. Ah. 16 : 8, *Development*, pp. 74-75: One who searches.
22. Tos. Par. 3 : 8, *Development*, pp. 75-76: Sadducee *re parah*-sacrifice + uncleanness-status.
23. Tos. Par. 4 : 7, *Development*, pp. 76-77: Garments for *parah*-rite.

5. *Pericopae First Attested by Appearance in Tannaitic Midrashim, ARN, and the Beraita-Stratum of the Gemarot*

1. Mekh. Ishmael, Lauterbach Vol. II, pp. 193-5, *Development*, pp. 15-16: Because you did not serve = Sifré Deut. 305: Daughter of Naqdimon (+ b. Ket. 66b).
2. See above, List 3, No. 1.
3. Mekh. Ishmael, Lauterbach Vol. III, p. 16, *Development*, p. 18: Pierce ear.
4. See above, List 2, No. 1 = Sifra Qedoshim 10 : 4.
[5. Mekh. Ishmael, Lauterbach Vol. III, p. 115, *Development*,pp. 18-19: Ex. 22 : 7 shows the robber feared God more than man, the thief *vice versa.* See List 4, No. 19.]
[6. Sifré Num. 123, *Development*, pp. 19-20: White garments for Red-Heifer-sacrifice. The same story is told of Hillel-Eliezer. See List 4, No. 23.]
7. Sifré Deut. 357, *Development*, p. 23: Yoḥanan lived 120 years. Yoḥanan is linked to ʿAqiba.
8. Mekhilta Simeon p. 157, *Development*, p. 24 = Stones that make peace, No. 4—Now: Sons of Torah are atonement for the world.
[9. Mekh. Simeon, p. 158, *Development*, pp. 25-26: Eleazar b. ʿArakh + *Merkavah* + Eleazar outweighs all disciples. See List 1, No. 1, and List 4, No. 16.]
10. Sifra Vayiqra 5 : 1, *Development*, p. 26: *Nasi* brings Sin-offering.
11. Sifra Shemini 7 : 12, *Development*, pp. 27-28: ʿAqiba says the loaf unclean in the second degree renders the third unclean. Joshua: Yoḥanan predicted such a teaching would one day be given. Joshua does not attest the pericope; he is intrinsic to it. Yoḥanan's original saying is not preserved.
12. Sifra Emor 10 : 10, *Development*, p. 29: Day of Waving.
13. Sifra Emor 16 : 9, *Development*, p. 29; *Lulav* + Day of Waving.
14. Sifré Deut. 144, *Development*, p. 30: Good court.
15. Sifré Deut. 192, *Development*, p. 31: draft-exemptions.

16. Midrash Tannaim, p. 58 = ARNb., Chap. 31, *Development*, p. 58: Do not destroy pagan altars.
17. Midrash Tannaim, pp. 175-6, *Development*, p. 37: Joshua reports letters of Simeon and Yoḥanan regarding the *Removal.*
18. Midrash Tannaim, p. 215, *Development*, p. 37: Agrippas is told there are two Torahs.
19. b. Ber. 28b, *Development*, pp. 87-8: Death-scene + Eliezer. [Not marked as Tannaitic in y. Sot. 9 : 16, which has Jacob b. Idi + Joshua b. Levi.]
20. b. Ber. 34b, *Development*, pp. 88-89: Ḥanina b. Dosa.
21. b. Yoma 39b, *Development*, p. 89: Forty years before destruction.
22. b. Suk. 28a, *Development*, p. 90: Hillel + Yoḥanan.
23. b. R.H. 18a, *Development*, pp. 91-92: Family whose sons died at eighteen.
24. b. R.H. 29b, *Development*, pp. 93-94: Yoḥanan + Bené Batyra *re shofar.*
25. b. Hag. 13a, *Development*, pp. 95-96: *Shiʿur Qomah.*
26. b. B.B. 10b, *Development*, pp. 102-104: Righteousness exalteth a nation.
27. b. B.B. 115b-116a, *Development*, pp. 105-106: Sadducees *re* inheritance.
28. b. Ker. 9a, *Development*, p. 109: Proselyte's bird-offering after 70.
29. ARN Chap. 4, *Development*, pp. 113-114: Atonement.
30. ARN Chap. 4, *Development*, pp. 114-119: Escape.
31. ARN Chap. 6, *Development*, pp. 119-121: Eliezer comes to Yoḥanan.
32. ARN Chap. 14, *Development*, pp. 124-125: Death of son.

6. *Pericopae without Attestations before Occurrence in the Gemarot and Some Later Compilations of Midrashim*

1. y. ber. 2 : 3, *Development*, p. 113: Tefillin—Yoḥanan + Eliezer.
2. y. Shab. 16 : 8, *Development*, pp. 133-4: ʿUlla *re* ʿArav.
3. y. Sheq. 2 : 3, *Development*, p. 135: Ten words.
4. y. Ta. 3 : 11, *Development*, p. 136: Hair cut.
5. y. Sanh. 1 : 2, *Development*, p. 138: Ba *re* ordination.
6. y. Sanh. 1 : 2, *Development*, pp. 138-9. Ox put to death.
7. y. Sanh. 1 : 4, *Development*, pp. 139-141: Census, *sheqel.*
8. y. A.Z. 3 : 11, *Development*, pp. 141-142: Temple-shadow.
9. b. Ber. 17a, *Development*, p. 142: Said hello.
10. b. Pes. 3b, *Development*, pp. 142-3: Students before Hillel/Yoḥanan
11. b. Suk. 28a, *Development*, p. 144: Good traits + Eliezer.
12. b. Suk. 32b, *Development*, pp. 144-145: Thorn-palms.
13. b. Suk. 31b, b. Bes. 5a, *Development*, p. 145: Fourth-year fruit.
14. b. Hag. 5a, *Development*, p. 145: Mal. 3 : 5.
15. b. Git. 55b-56b, *Development*, pp. 146-151: Escape.
16. b. B.B. 10a, *Development*, pp. 151-152: Give to charity.
17. b. Men. 65a-b, *Development*, p. 153: Date of Pentecost.

18. Gen. R. 17 : 4, *Development*, p. 159: Gen. 2 : 19 *vs.* Gen. 1 : 24.
19. Gen. R. 19 : 6, *Development*, pp. 159-160: Gen. 3 : 7.
20. Gen. R. 44 : 21, *Development*, p. 161: Gen. 15 : 18.
21. Pesiqta deR. Kahana, p. 74, *Development*, pp. 168-169: Corpse-uncleanness.

We observe that of approximately 90 items in the Yoḥanan-tradition, pre-Mishnaic attestations are available for no more than six, an exceedingly small proportion. The most important of these are the Ushan attestations of several of the *taqqanot*, List 2, Nos. 2, 4, possibly 7. These are, moreover, excellent attestations, for they involve not a single master and one *taqqanah* but a number of important Ushans dealing with several different *taqqanot*. Probably the firmest fact in the Yoḥanan-tradition therefore is that he issued *taqqanot* at Yavneh. These certainly pertained to the Temple rites on festivals after the destruction. The *Merkavah* transmission seems attested by Yosi b. R. Judah [b. Ilai], who says Joshua spoke on the *Merkavah* before Yoḥanan, ʿAqiba before Joshua, Ḥananiah b. Ḥakhinai before ʿAqiba, a late Ushan attestation for the *Merkavah*-theme, but not for its details (!). (I perceive no connection between Ḥakhinai and ʿAkhnai/Ḥakhnai of the famous oven.) It seems that Yoḥanan himself should attest M. Ket. 13 : 1-2; I am inclined to regard that as a good tradition. But the state of the Yoḥanan-corpus overall is so poor that one cannot come to a firm opinion without a better attestation than we have for Yoḥanan's own saying.

That leaves Abba Saul in M. Avot 2 : 8-9. His attestation for Yoḥanan's saying about Eliezer b. Hyrcanus seems as good as any. That should mean the good-way-evil-way-pericope ought to come by late Yavneh or early Usha. Either the original structure begins with Yoḥanan and was changed by Abba Saul. Or Abba Saul presents the original structure, which has been revised by Eliezer's disciples, who did not accept his excommunication and so gave anonymously the version they preferred and as the opinion of a single master the Eleazar b. ʿArakh-construction. In either case it would seem to be a very early pericope. Two problems present difficulties.

First, as we have observed, the whole of the Eliezer-tradition, up to M. Avot, is silent on the Yoḥanan-relation. Eliezer neither cites Yoḥanan nor is linked to him, except here and in M. Yad. 4 : 3.

Second, the redactional tendency to link Yoḥanan and Eliezer b. Hyrcanus occurs throughout the Amoraic strata—Yoḥanan did so-and-so and thus also did Eliezer his disciple. The "correction" attributed to Abba Saul therefore has not registered among important Amoraic circles.

Moreover, and equally striking, the preserved Eleazar b. ʿArakh-corpus is similarly reticent about linking Yoḥanan to Eleazar, except here and in the *Merkavah*-materials. That fact by itself is unimportant, for Eleazar's extant traditions are inconsequential. But of far greater significance, the Amoraim *never* produce redactional or substantive links between Eleazar and Yoḥanan (unless we suppose that every reference to Eliezer/Yoḥanan is really to Eleazar). So we cannot show they even knew it! I am therefore perplexed about interpreting Abba Saul's saying.

On the other hand, we have already observed (*Phar.* I, pp. 1-16) that M. Avot 1 : 1-18 seems to be the work of Ushans and Abba Saul's attestation would thus accord with our findings about the redactional structure of M. Avot. 1-2.

In the balance, I propose the following: Abba Saul does supply a valid attestation for the Yoḥanan-Eliezer connection. What he actually attests is that in late Yavnean or early Ushan times, an antecedent—therefore fairly early and certainly authentic—tendency to link Eliezer to Yoḥanan did exist and was expressed in the pericope's basic structure: Yoḥanan at the head, with Eliezer as the leading disciple. But by the end of Yavnean or the beginning of Ushan times, the tradents represented by Abba Saul's saying severed the link between Yoḥanan and Eliezer. The later masters, perhaps beginning in the circle of Rabbi himself, then ignored Abba Saul's revision, and the Amoraim reversed it entirely, for reasons I cannot now suggest.

As to the absence of connections between Yoḥanan's laws and Eliezer's, the most probable explanation is that the sum of Yoḥanan's legal traditions down to Usha consisted of the *taqqanot* and possibly the comments on M. Ket. 13 : 1-2. The *taqqanot* of early Yavneh simply do not register in Eliezer's legal corpus. M. Ket. 13 : 1-2 deals with matters similarly external to Eliezer's preserved traditions. And Eliezer has no links to the *Merkavah*. I do not know why not. What is alleged, at best, is that Yoḥanan stands at the beginning of the Yavnean enterprise, with Eliezer alleged to have been his foremost "disciple."

Or, to put it otherwise, Yavneh stands at the head, with Lydda second, and Emmaus (Eleazar b. ʿArakh) last. Of the other places (if that is the issue) on the list, we can say nothing.

Another fairly firm tradition about Yoḥanan has to do with his strained relations with the priesthood. Simeon b. Gamaliel in M. Ed. 8 : 3 seems to me to provide a good, if not ideal, attestation for that theme, and M. Sheq. 1 : 4 provides another. Perhaps M. Yad. 4 : 6 and Tos. Par. 3 : 8 and similar materials in List No. 4 serve the same purpose.

One cannot reject the exegetical traditions labelled *Kemin Ḥomer*. They are secondary in importance, but Tosefta's testimony has to be taken seriously.

I am inclined to regard the rest of the exegetical, theological, and biographical-historical tradition as of severely limited historical reliability. But the escape- and related stories do develop the sole solid fact: Yoḥanan issued *taqqanot* after the destruction. Therefore he presumably came at the beginning of Yavneh, and some story about the founding of the "academy" and how the Romans permitted it—therefore how Yoḥanan parted company with the rebels—will have to have been generated. This major motif will have further been expressed by the sermons about Israel's failures to serve God before 70 and how they produced the disasters thereafter; the importance of fear of heaven more than of man; "stones that make peace"—which may be genuine; draft-exemptions; not destroying pagan altars; and the many related items in the peace/destruction/study of Torah-repertoire. In all, therefore, the later traditions exhibit close thematic, if not traditional, links to the sole historical fact about Yoḥanan.

3. *Form-History*

A history of the forms used for the redaction of the Yoḥanan-corpus is not possible, for the Yoḥanan-corpus, unlike those of the Houses and Eliezer, wholly lacks a discipled redactional-formal structure. It is, from a form-critical viewpoint, random and episodic. In retrospect I am surprised at such progress as was possible in the study of forms through the examination of the Yoḥanan-corpus. When we compare the use of a single form—the dispute—for the vast Houses' corpus and the repetition of that single form, with some minor, if interesting, developments for Eliezer's, we perceive a remarkable parallel between the results of the search for attestations and the consideration of the form-critical situation. In both instances we find Yoḥanan's preserved corpus different from (and I think probably later than) those of the Houses and Eliezer. A more apt comparison is to the materials on the pre-70 named masters, who, except for Hillel, likewise exhibit no important traits for form-critical inquiry.

A fruitful working hypothesis emerges: much of the biographical-historical, exegetical and theological materials probably follow the establishment of legal traditions—forms *and* content—for the several early masters. Disciplined forms for the preservation of traditions were used primarily for the legal legacies, which are apt to be prior in time and historically far more reliable than the bulk of the exegetical and historical materials. These lack both a clear formal structure and exhibit stylistic and narrative traits wholly at variance with the legal materials and Tannaitic attestations of any value whatsoever. An alternative hypothesis is that separate circles of contemporaneous redactors stand behind the non-legal materials. I cannot demonstrate the greater probability of the former hypothesis.

4. *The Interpretation of Pericopae*

The most important difficulty in *Development* is the tendency to take at face value far too much of what is alleged by the various sayings and stories. It is normally assumed that an attribution to ʿAqiba means either ʿAqiba really said such a thing, or, far more commonly, the circle of ʿAqiba attributed such a saying to him. The attribution of Tannaitic *midrashim* to the "schools" of ʿAqiba and Ishmael is taken at face value. The beginning of all interpretations is that ʿAqiba favored the war of 66 and sponsored that of 132. On this basis a history of the substance of traditions is attempted, and, within the presuppositions of the established interpretative framework, is on the whole successful.

But what if the materials in the post-Mishnaic compilations do not come from ʿAqiba at all? What if, as observed in our present inquiry, his disciples—or masters fraudulently claiming to have been his disciples—stand behind the several documents attributed to ʿAqiba? Then the historical ʿAqiba will not be accurately represented, and Yoḥanan b. Zakkai-materials will derive not necessarily from Yoḥanan, but from the interests of later authorities with no firm traditions at all about the historical Yoḥanan. Our picture of the historical Yoḥanan would be substantially smaller than we had supposed and would have to be divorced from a great part of the traditions which include his name.

To be sure, the central facts change very little. These are, as stated earlier, (1) Yoḥanan's *taqqanot* and (2) his presence in the earliest stages of the Yavnean enterprise. And these facts will produce an argument from history. First, someone who did what I am fairly sure

Yoḥanan did will have elicited a hostile reception from the priesthood. Gamaliel is the obvious candidate but is ignored—because Yoḥanan did found Yavneh. Second, he surely will have opposed the war—at least in its later stages—and will have suffered the consequent hatred of those who favored and fought in it and survived. Around these two facts is centered the bulk of the stories and sayings. But we are hardly justified on that account in the detailed analyses of individual pericopae, in the assumption that, because their substance is thematically congruent to the established facts, their details therefore may be critically investigated as though they contain stories produced in response to the period of which they speak.

Two examples will suffice. First, my analysis of Sifré Num. 123 (*Development*, pp. 19-21) takes for granted that underneath the complex materials is a Sadducean story of a forgetful teacher of the law. This story was used against Yoḥanan and Hillel. It was then corrected by Eliezer or Joshua. It was then glossed by someone who knew a similar story about Hillel, and so forth. All this is plausible, but no more than that.

Second, the whole range of ʿAqiba/Yoḥanan/war-interpretations, represented by the discussion of Sifra Shemini 7 : 12 (*Development*, pp. 26-27) seems to me somewhat rigid and mechanically reproduced. As stated, the introduction into virtually every ʿAqiba/Yoḥanan-pericope of the problem of war seems dubious. Admittedly, what is conjecture is honestly labelled as such. But the supposed facts upon which conjectures are based have been too readily taken for granted.

I am inclined, however, to stand by the single most striking incidence of the war-issue: the change from *the man who brings peace* to the *students of Torah* in Sifra Qedoshim 10 : 4 (*Development*, pp. 27-28), Mekhilta deR. Ishmael, Lauterbach II, p. 290 (*Development*, pp. 16-17), and Mekhilta deR. Simeon, p. 157 (*Development*, p. 24). The change here is so exact and striking that it cannot be interpreted other than as an effort to change a condemnation of war into something else. But we do not have for one instant to suppose ʿAqiba or ʿAqibans are responsible. Considering the importance of the issue of war later on—certainly on the times of Judah the Patriarch, but also in third and fourth-century Palestine, fourth- and fifth-century Babylonia, and elsewhere—we can hardly take for granted that the deliberate change was made by people who fought in the Bar Kokhba War or who survived it and came to Yavneh.

In all, one has to show that a pericope existed in a given place and time before one can undertake the interpretation of its contents in terms of the issues of that place and time. Such a demonstration is not always possible, and, even when possible, not necessarily conclusive. But it must be attempted. That does not mean a change from *peace-makers* to *students of Torah*, is not noteworthy and important. But accounting for the change is more difficult than has been supposed. In *Development* I relied far too heavily on the supposition that the disciples of ʿAqiba stand behind certain Tannaitic compilations, those of Ishmael behind others. That supposition made it all too easy to suppose Yoḥanan's own situation and consequently his actual teachings lay not far in the background. But if ʿAqibans—even excluding ʿAqiba himself—did not change in the supposedly ʿAqiba compilations the tradition in the supposedly Ishmaelean compilations, then we cannot claim to have Yoḥanan's own words in the latter. All we may say is that someone has taken a pro-peace saying attributed to Yoḥanan and rendered it neutral in regard to the issue of peace. But who has done so, when, where, and in response to what contemporary issues—these questions are not easy to answer.

5. *Conclusion*

Development produced the six results listed by Smith, and these have not been called into question by subsequent research. On the contrary, *Pharisees* and the present work have confirmed every one of them, either by the contrasts between the new materials and those considered in *Development*, or by substantive demonstration of the correctness of the original surmises. The further interpretation of the Yoḥanan-pericopae clearly will produce fewer, rather than more, solid historical-biographical results. It is difficult to see how the picture will be greatly changed, though as Smith makes clear, further analysis will improve both the interpretation of individual pericopae and the synoptic comparisons.

As stated, the choice of Yoḥanan b. Zakkai was hardly auspicious. We now see that his traditions, if more abundant, are much like those of the pre-70 masters, rather than like the Houses' and Eliezer's, in their formal, literary, and redactional traits. That means the historical Yoḥanan b. Zakkai is not likely to develop through the results of work on Joshua, ʿAqiba, Eleazar b. ʿAzarian, Yosi, Gamaliel, and the other Yavneans. By contrast, I am certain further studies will enrich our appreciation of the traditions about Eliezer and the Houses. The difference, as perceived in the present work, is that for Eliezer and the Houses we have more than traditions and legends, but also pericopae of considerable historical interest, that is, fairly good historical sources. For Yoḥanan, as for the pre-70 masters, we do not.

That does not mean *Development* is without interest, or that *A Life of Yoḥanan b. Zakkai* tells us nothing of historical value. The former does do what it set out to accomplish, which is to trace the development of the traditions and legends told about Yoḥanan. The latter provides an account of a hero portrayed by the rabbinical traditions and therefore helps in the description and understanding of rabbinic Judaism in late antiquity.

I therefore affirm my conclusion in *Development* (pp. 300-301). Three sorts of 'lives' of Yoḥanan b. Zakkai are possible. The first is the account of the actual man. The answer is meager. Second is the story of the life of the man after his death. The answer consists of a considerable corpus of facts, for the sources accurately testify to the mind of the schools of the second, third, and fourth centuries that originated them. The evidence in *Development* on these questions is not inconsequential. The third is the composite portrait of the first two, done for the purposes of characterizing the phenomenon that produced the portrait: the rabbinic movement of late antiquity. Who was a typical hero? What religious values are revealed in him? The third kind of 'biography' depends upon the results of the first two, but constitutes a quite different historical statement, one meaningful in the context of the history of religions. Whether or not things really happened is not the only important question. Indeed, for the study of the history of rabbinic Judaism in antiquity, it is not even a very important one. What is important is, What view of reality shaped the minds of the men very told these stories, lived by these laws, believed these myths? That question is accurately answered in, among other works, *Life* and *Development*.

INDICES [1]

I. BIBLE

Acts

5:34 II 304

Amos

3:2 I 334

II Chronicles

33:1-2 I 404
33:10 I 406
33:10-13 I 404
33:12 I 406
36:10 I 366

Daniel

4:11 I 456
4:12 I 456
4:24 I 491
4:27 I 490
7:12 I 479
12:7 I 478-79

Deuteronomy

3:26 I 474; II 14, 23, 72, 393
4:6 I 475; II 29, 72, 393, 417
4:11 I 430
5:30 I 463
6:5 I 475
6:6 I 22
8:15 I 463
8:16 I 463
9:18 I 26
9:25 I 27-28
10:10 I 427
10:12 I 478
10:18 I 428, 448-49 II 392
11:11 I 482-84
12:3 I 221; II 230, 389, 397
12:16 I 260
12:23 I 260
12:27 I 274; II 390, 395
12:32 I 235, 237, 395
14:4 I 249
14:21 I 379
15:23 I 260
16:6 I 135; II 388, 396
16:9 I 245; II 238, 392, 410
16:14 I 147
16:16 II 54
16:20 I 408
19:14 I 409; II 87
21:1 I 202, 302
21:3 I 302
21:12 I 180; II 22, 71, 227, 389, 392-93, 395
21:15 I 181
21:22 I 218-19; II 390, 395
21:23 I 218
22:6-7 I 12, 247; II 24
22:14 I 181
23:1-3 I 375
23:19 I 303-304; 401-402; II 391, 395
24:1 I 207-208
24:8 I 298
24:21 I 35; II 387
25:9 I 166; II 389, 392
25:19 I 468
26:14 I 73-74; II 22, 206, 388
28:10 I 479; II 14, 27, 72, 235
28:64 I 469
29:28 I 453
30:12 I 422
32:49 I 476; II 23, 72
33:21 I 420
34:1 I 475; II 23, 72, 394
34:5 I 117

Exodus

2:14-15 I 470
2:23 I 420
3:8 I 473

[1] The index was prepared by Mr. Arthur Woodman, Canaan, New Hampshire, on a grant from Brown University.

4:11 I 471
4:31 I 421
6:6 I 462
8:14 I 466
8:15 I 464-65
11:7 I 365
12:1 I 458; II 13, 23, 71, 228
12:6 I 364, 476
12:8 I 22
12:9 II 388
12:11 I 364
12:16 I 121; II 388
12:19 I 120-21; II 392
12:24 I 365
12:27 I 223-24
12:37 I 458; II 23, 71, 228, 393
12:42 I 459-60; II 23m 71, 393
12:45 I 179; II 71, 234, 388
12:47 I 462
12:48 I 179
13:5 II 72, 229, 391
13:7 I 121
13:10 I 471
13:18 I 463; II 13, 23, 71, 396
14:2 I 464 II 13, 23, 71
14:13 I 421; II 230, 396
14:14 I 421; II 230, 396
14:15 I 26-28; II 22
14:31 I 464-66; II 23, 71, 394
15:2 I 466; II 23
15:22 I 467; II 23, 71, 229, 394
15:25 I 26-27
16:3 I 466; II 23, 71
16:4 I 421; II 230, 392
17:7 I 421
17:11 I 469; II 23, 394
17:13 I 22; II 23, 71, 394
17:14 I 468
17:16 I 22; II 23, 71, 394
18:4 I 303, 470; II 23
19:1-5 I 472
19:4 I 471
19:5 I 471-72; II 13, 23, 64, 229, 417
19:8 I 458
19:19 I 472; II 13, 23, 72, 397, 418
21:8 I 208; II 22, 71, 234
21:1i I 371
21:24 I 213
21:28 I 212; II 397
21:29 I 377
22:1 II 438
22:5 I 211
22:7 II 450
22:17 I 399, 419; II 27
22:20 I 424
22:24 I 424
22:31 I 379
23:2 I 423
23:9 I 424, 427
27:18 I 103
32:27 I 494
34:34 I 458
35:25 I 141, 450; II 237

Ezekiel
1:1 I 466
16:1 I 10, 369

Ezra
6:10 I 489

Genesis
1:2 I 460
1:11 I 460
1:24 II 452
2:4 I 486
2:6 I 460, 482, 484
2:19 II 452
2:24 I 281; II 389, 393
3:7 II 458
4:3 I 463
4:25 I 446
7:11 I 462
8:22 I 493
13:13 I 455; II 23, 396
14:1 I 438, 442
14:15 II 241, 396, 404
15:18 II 452
18:8 I 408
21:1 I 461
24:63 I 29; II 410
28:20 I 448-49
30:14 I 494
30:22 I 461, 495; II 395
33:17 I 458
37:29 I 495; II 15
40:10 I 488; II 14, 30, 72, 235, 396
46:4 I 473
47:3 I 470
49:3 I 493; II 14, 242, 393
49:4 I 479, II 14, 23, 72, 235, 396

Hosea
12:11 I 466

Isaiah
1:18 I 477; II 14, 29, 72, 418
1:21 I 494
2:4 I 87-88
3:8 II 72
4:5-6 I 458
4:15 I 227
7:14 II 28, 71, 78
12:18 II 72
22:25 II 72
23:23 II 72
27:13 I 462
30:15 I 477-78; II 393
35:10 I 458
49:7 I 478
52:3 I 477-78
52:12 I 365
55:10 I 487
58:5 I 496
60:22 I 477, 479

Jeremiah
1:27 I 180-81
3:14 I 478
3:22 I 478
4:1 I 477
30:7 I 477
36:27-28 I 477; II 393
39:3 I 494
40:3 I 490
47:3 I 470

Job
1:21 I 447
3:10 I 495
9:24 I 487; II, 23, 72
19:21 I 465
35:28 I 484
36:27 I 482-84
37:6 486-87
37:9 I 485
37:10 I 485
38:6 I 485
38:8 I 495; II 15
38:16 I 492
38:38 I 485
41:10 I 428

Judges
5:31 I 140-41, 427
17:1 I 459
17:2 I 491
17:18 I 491; II 242
17:50 I 491
18:31 I 491
20:18-28 I 491; II 22, 242
20:28 I 492

I Kings
6:1 I 461
8:2 I 461; II 394
8:8 I 366
18:44 I 481
21:10, 13 I 491; II 22, 242

II Kings
2:12 I 410, 412, 416
20:17 I 366
21:1 I 405

Leviticus
1:2 I 275
2:12 I 233-34; II 395
2:14 I 30; II 71
3:2, 8, 13 I 382
3:17 I 260
4:2 I 494; II 242
4:23 I 260, 262, 382; II 391-92
4:24 I 223-24
5:2 I 220; II 390, 395
5:2-3 I 220
5:6, 7, 11 I 382
5:9 I 223; II 390, 395
5:15 I 228, 268
5:17-18 I 262
5:19 I 223; II 390, 395
5:21 I 268
7:7 I 240; II 392
7:13 I 243
7:18 I 227, 272; II 390, 392
7:26 I 260
10:1-5 I 473
10:3 I 447
10:14 I 260
11:1 I 114
11:4 I 379
11:33 II 263
16:34 II 262
11:42 I 379
12:2 I 327, 495; II 15, 242

12:3 I 96
13:2-3 I 389
13:14-15 I 389
13:23 I 300
13:43 II 22
13:45 I 162; II 391-92, 396
13:55 I 301
14:2 I 268
14:4 I 390
15 I 392
15:2 I 311
15:25 I 311, 326-27; II 392
15:28 I 330; II 391
16:1 I 473; II 23
16:18 I 139
17:10 I 260
17:10 I 260
17:16 I 384-85
19:10 I 35; II 387
19:15 I 36
19:18 I 397
19:19 I 209
19:20 I 268
19:26 I 260
19:29 I 210-11; II 390
19:33 I 424
20:7 I 117
20:16 I 218; II 390
21:1 I 197
21:7 I 211; II 390, 393
21:11 I 197
22:4 I 279; II 388
22:10 I 179; II 234, 388
22:14 I 58; II 387, 391
23:8 I 476
23:10 I 95; II 395, 414
23:11 I 245
23:14 I 209
23:16 I 245
23:17 I 95; II 395, 414
23:24 I 254-55, 461; II 29, 65, 125, 132, 136, 369, 389, 395-96
23:43 I 458
25:17 I 424
26:18 I 474; II 23, 72
27:2 I 186, 189; II 389
27:28 I 252; II 395
27:31 I 74

Luke

5:17 II 304
5:33-39 II 330
6:1-5 II 330
6:11 II 365
6:40 II 331
7:30 II 304
10:29-37 II 105
10:35 II 304
10:51 II 102
11:37-41 II 331
11:39 II 331
11:42 II 331
11:45, 52 II 304
12:22-23 II 331
13:10-17 II 365
14:3 II 304
14:5-6 II 365
18:12 II 332

Malachi

3:7 I 478
3:8 I 333
3:19 I 456

Mark

2:16 II 304
2:18-22 II 330
2:23-28 II 330
3:1-6 II 365
7:1, 5 II 304
7:3-4 II 331
7:9-13 II 331
7:14 II 331
8:31 II 304
10:33 II 304
11:18 II 304
14:1, 43, 53 II 304
15:1, 31 II 304
27:14 II 304

Matthew

2:4 II 304
5:20 II 304
5:33-37 II 330
6:25-33 II 331
7 II 333
9:14-17 II 330
10:5 II 103
10:24-25 II 331
12:1-8 330
12:9-14 II 365
12:38 II 304
15:1 II 304
15:1-6 II 331
15:10-12 II 331

16:21 II 304
20:18 II 304
21:15 II 304
21:27 II 304
23:23 II 331
22:35 II 331
23 II 333
23:2, 13 II 304
27:41 II 304

Micah

1:7 I 403
6:2 I 461

Nehemiah

8:10 I 148

Numbers

5:2 I 364
5:13 I 201
5:14 I 200, 204
5:18 I 199
5:27 II 241
5:28 I 496; II 15
6:2 I 186, 189; II 389
6:4 I 197; II 22, 389
6:7 I 197
6:9-12 I 192
6:12 I 192, 268; II 391
6:13 I 195-96
6:18 I 196
6:20 I 197; II 392
8:9 I 449
9:2 I 126
9:3 I 123, 125
9:9 II 181, 388, 393
9:10 I 133
9:23 I 467
12:7 I 420
12:13 I 26-28
14:35 I 453-55, 357; II 22, 393
15:19 I 76
15:20 I 357
16:33 I 453, 456; II 393
18:8 I 66
19:1 II 127, 368
19:9 I 312; II 195
19:12 I 125
19:15 I 386
19:16 I 288
23:5 I 497
23:24 I 463
24:21 I 461
25:1 I 470; II 23, 419
25:2 I 470
28:2 I 126
28:23 I 143
29:8 I 143
29:11 I 143
30:2 I 221; II 230, 389, 397
30:14 I 187; II 393
33:7 I 458

Proverbs

2:19 I 450
5:8 I 400-403
6:23 I 463
7:20 I 477
7:26 I 400-403
8:15 I 449
8:34 I 437
9:5 I 448-49
14:34 I 489, 491; II 14, 241-42, 396, 416
18:16 I 432
20:11 I 420
21:24 I 490
25:1 I 404

Psalms

1:5 I 455
9:7 I 468
9:17 I 454, 465
9:18 I 386
14:34 II 409
18:12 I 484
24:1 I 445
24:6 I 488
25:14 I 333-34
37:14 I 438
45:2 I 429
49 I 465
50:1 I 485-86
50:2 I 486
50:5 I 453-55, 457; II 393
65:14 I 461
72:5 I 467
78:47 I 465
78:49 I 465
81:4 I 462
81:4-5 I 460
81:4-6 I 462
81:7 I 462
81:45 II 393

82:6 I 494
90:4 I 497; II 243
90:15 I 497; II 15
93:3 I 492; II 14
95:10 I 455
95:11 I 186, 454, 457; II 389
102:1 I 29; II 410
102:24 I 463
104:35 I 456
106:7 I 463
106:22 I 464
112:9 I 435
113:7 I 425
118:25 I 367
119:89 I 463
119:128 I 445
121:30 I 460; II 393
139:16 I 495-96; II 15, 243, 417
142:3 I 29; II 410
148:1 I 486-87
148:7 I 486
154:17 I 420

Ruth
4:1 I 497; II 15, 243

I Samuel
1:19 I 461
2:6 I 453, 456, 485; II 14, 72, 393
2:21 I 461; II 395
4:19 I 495
7:12 I 488
30:30 I 488
20:33 I 488

II Samuel
7:23 I 459, 489; II 393, 418
12:24 I 447
22:12 I 482-83

Song of Songs
2:8 I 461
2:14 I 421; II 396
5:11 II 15, 243
6:10 I 497; II 15
7:14 I 451

Zechariah
4:10 I 421
10:11 I 459
19:9 I 469

Zephaniah
1:15 I 490

II. MISHNAH

ʿArakhin
3:1 I 384
3:2 I 384
4:1 I 251
5:6 I 251
6:1 I 5, 250-51; II 8, 66, 79, 84, 117, 153, 166, 215, 315, 321, 324, 372, 380
6:3 I 12, 251; II 8, 24, 51, 69, 189, 356, 359, 363
7:2 I 385
8:4 I 252; II 8, 26, 64, 79, 112, 311, 319, 322, 380, 391

ʿAvodah Zarah
1:8 I 12, 380
2:6 I 42
2:7 I 12
3:9 12, 381

Avot
1:1-18 II 38, 4593
2:8-10 I 396; II 344, 375, 382, 448, 452
2:9 II 344
2:10 II 397, 413; II 12, 27, 64, 74, 123, 198, 202

Bava Batra
3:8 I 378
4:4 I 378
4:5 I 379
9:7 I 214, 216; II 9, 21, 66, 69, 125, 187, 312, 320, 359, 363, 372, 379
9:8-9 II 33, 55

Bava Meṣiʿaʾ
3:12 II 33, 55
6:8 I 378
7:8 I 378

Bava Qamma
1:4 I 377
2:5 I 328
4:5 I 213; II 79, 84, 214, 228
4:9 I 377
6:4 I 211-12; II 8, 26, 69, 79, 187, 354, 359, 363, 375, 380

Bekhorot
1:4 I 248
1:5 I 12; II 8, 25, 51, 69, 79, 356, 359, 363
1:506 I 247; II 59, 69
1:6 I 12, 112, 248-49, 145; II 8, 20, 64, 79, 112, 189, 309, 217, 320, 378
4:7 I 12, 383
5:2 II 33
5:3 I 12, 249, 299; II 8, 20, 69, 79, 356, 363
7:1 I 384
7:6 I 12, 384
7:7 I 304

Berakhot
1:1 I 3, 18-22, 30; II 26, 67, 76, 172, 227, 356, 361, 374, 376, 378
1:1-2 I 31; II 68, 172, 352, 356, 372
1:2 I 4, 18-20, 30; II 3, 26, 361, 377
1:3 I 19, 30; II 33-34
1:4 I 19
1:5 I 19, 30
1:11 II 3
3:1 II 84, 212
4:1, 2 I 23
4:3 I 6, 24-25; II 28, 67, 76, 352, 356, 361, 375, 379
4:4 I 23, 26; II 28, 67, 78, 352, 356, 378
4:5 II 3
5:1 I 30
5:2 I 6, 29-30; II 3, 23, 42, 67, 78, 172, 352, 361, 373, 378, 401
5:3 I 30; II 356
6:1 I 31
6:5 II 53, 48
6:6 I 31
8:1 I 8, 31, 346-48; II 37
8:1-8 II 54
8:6 I 31

Beṣah
1:1 I 150; II 65, 74, 83, 210
1:3 I 152
1:1-3, 509 II 55
1:7 I 4
1:8 II 33
2:1 I 151; II 83, 211, 227, 389
2:1-2 II 41, 47
2:1-7 II 55
2:4 II 33
3:4 I 154; II 84, 182, 211
4:6 I 110, 151, 153; II 6, 28, 58, 65, 75, 78, 151, 164
4:7 I 10, 152; II 6, 28, 58, 65, 75, 78, 151, 164
5:2 I 92, 125; II 83

Bikkurim
2:6 I 3, 84; II 4, 28, 63, 78, 98, 310, 374, 378

Dema'i
4:1 I 355
4:3 I 8, 350
5:9 I 8, 37, 42
6:3 I 8, 351
6:6 II 34

ʿEduyyot
1:1-3 II 34
1:3 I 321; II 196
1:5-7 I 345
1:6 I 337; II 88
1:7 II 33-34
1:7-14 II 58
1:14 II 33
2:7 I 87-88, 338; II 11, 27, 64, 73, 81, 83-82, 114, 121, 123, 208, 217, 309, 317, 320
4:1-12 II 56
5:1 I 39
5:1-5 II 56
5:2 II 42
5:4 I 393
5:4-5 I 4
5:5 I 393
6:2 I 6, 340, 342; II 81, 373
6:2-3 I 6, 344; II 12, 26, 52, 68, 157, 165, 217, 379

6:3 I 342, 344; II 81, 373
7:1 I 12, 13, 345; II 8
7:5 I 311, 345; II 10, 21, 80
7:6 I 12, 345; II 78
7:7 I 12-13, 282, 345; II 9, 80, 191
8:3, 7 II 149; II 349, 464
8:4 I 345; II 59, 124, 310, 317, 323
8:6 I 345, 399; II 12, 30, 70, 81, 190, 373, 381

ʿEruvin
1:1 I 101
1:2 I 3, 100; II 5, 21, 33, 68, 117, 128, 354, 358, 362
2:3 I 103, 105
2:5 I 104-108; II 68, 74, 86, 123
2:5-6 I 8; II 99, 308, 316, 322, 369-70
2:6 I 7, 103, 105-108; II 5, 58, 86, 220
3:1 I 112, II 65, 88, 209
3:3 I 10, 360; II 85
3:6 I 10, 109; II 5, 28, 58, 78, 148, 314, 321
3:7 I 110; II 248, 312, 319
4:5 I 361-62
4:11 I 361-62
6:3 I 106; II 99, 101
7:10 I 4, 112-13; II 5, 28, 58, 77, 209, 372
7:11 I 10, 112-13; II 5, 28, 58, 65, 74, 128, 148, 209, 313, 323
8:4 I 318
9:2 I 113; II 5, 19, 65, 77
9:4 II 67, 156
10:10 I 362
10:13 I 127

Giṭṭin
1:1 I 3, 205; II 7, 24, 51, 65, 79, 152, 166, 324, 346, 374, 379
1:2 I 205; II 65, 152, 166, 314, 321, 324
6:3 I 11, 374
6:4 I 11, 374
8:5 I 375
8:8 I 11, 375
8:8-9 II 55
9:1 I 12, 205; II 7, 20, 64, 76, 110-12, 114, 159, 311, 319, 322, 401
9:10 I 201; II 33

Ḥagigah
1:1 I 186; II 41, 47, 78, 234
1:1-3 II 54
2:2 I 313; II 33
1:3-4 II 55
2:7 I 312
2:8 I 445
3:8 I 11, 369

Ḥallah
1:3 I 9, 357
1:6 I 82; II 4, 63, 83, 97-98, 130, 207, 310, 317, 322, 369, 372
1:7 II 178
1:8 II 322
1:9 I 48, 78-79
1:10 I 79; II 310
2:1 I 6, 76; II 4, 19, 68, 74, 124m, 312, 319, 323, 353, 357, 362, 369, 373, 377
2:3 I 76, 79
2:4 I 9, 77; II 4, 24, 50, 68, 77, 176, 353, 357, 362, 401
2:7 I 78-79
2:8 I 9, 45-46, 78-79; II 4, 24, 50, 63, 74, 86, 95, 122, 369
2:10 I 78-79
2:18 II 317
4:1 I 77
4:7 I 3, 80; II 4, 19, 58, 68, 77, 353, 357, 362, 374, 378, 400
4:8 I 81

Horayot
2:7 I 382

Ḥullin
1:2 II 41, 47
2:6 I 246-47; II 8, 20, 69, 76, 79, 158, 188, 354, 359, 363, 374, 380
2:7 I 12, 383
6:1 I 248
12:2 I 12, 247; II 8, 24, 51, 69, 354, 359, 363

Kelim
1:1 I 289
1:2 I 331; II 198
2:2 II 141, 349

2:8 I 12, 276, 339; II 9, 21, 69, 79, 190, 356, 359, 363
3:2 I 12, 277, 281; II 9, 25, 51, 69, 80, 356
5:1 I 277-78; II 230, 342, 274, 380
5:4 I 47
5:8 I 278
5:10 I 12, 278, 339, 345, 426; II 9, 21, 69, 80, 356
8:1 I 13, 279-80; II 9, 25, 51, 64, 66, 76, 112, 311, 319
9:2 II 33
10:1 I 13, 386
10:6 I 278
11:2 I 282; II 191
11:5 I 13, 386
11:8 I 13, 387-88
11:9 I 387
14:1 I 13, 277, 280-81; II 9, 25, 51, 69, 80, 190, 356, 374, 380
14:2 II 42, 47
14:7 I 5, 281-82; II 9, 29, 66, 76, 156, 165, 320, 373, 380
15:1 II 44, 380
15:1-18 II 48
15:2 I 13, 282, 339-40, 345; II 9, 21, 69, 80, 191, 356, 373
17:1 I 5, 283; II 9, 25, 51, 69, 80, 191, 356, 373, 380
17:7 I 306
17:16 II 43, 48, 140
18:1 II 44, 322
18:9 I 13, 283-84; II 68, 76, 158, 165, 171, 315, 322, 324
20:2 II 33
20:4 I 282
20:6 II 42, 47
22:4 II 56
23:1 I 284; II 84, 215-16
24 I 312
25:6 I 318
26:2 I 13, 284-85; II 9, 21, 66, 76, 155, 159, 165, 315, 319
26:4 I 13, 285, 339, 413; II 9, 21, 64, 76, 113, 159, 311, 319, 322
26:5 I 13, 387
27:2 II 9, 51, 382
27:5 I 13, 388
27:6 I 388
27:12 I 13, 286; II 25, 69, 80, 191, 356
28:2 I 5, 286; II 9, 29, 69, 80, 191, 356, 374, 381
28:4 I 33
29:8 I 56

Keritot

1:2 I 268
3:7 I 257, II 121-22
3:8 I 257; II 122
3:9 I 257; II 122
3:10 I 256-57; II 8, 30, 69, 74, 121-23, 191, 312, 319, 323, 374-76, 380
4:2 I 259, 261, 266-67; II 59-60
4:2-3 I 268; II 8, 20, 76, 153, 160, 162, 184, 189-90, 213, 315, 321, 324, 372, 380, 391
4:3 I 5m, 6, 260-61
4:23 II 66
5:5 I 266
5:6 I 266
5:7 I 267
5:8 I 267
6:1 I 12, 267-68; II 8, 20, 69, 79, 154, 189, 356, 359, 363, 372
6:3 I 267-68; II 8, 20, 69, 79, 118, 154, 189, 312, 319, 323, 355, 359, 363

Ketuvot

1:6 I 7, 181
1:6-9 I 7; II 7, 19, 58, 69, 78, 184, 354, 358, 360, 375, 379, 401
1:7 I 182
1:8 I 182
1:9 I 182-83
4:5 I 188
4:8 I 184
5:2 I 188
5:5 I 371
5:6 II 41, 116, 371
8:6 II 41, 116
9:4 I 372
11:4 II 113
11:6 I 11; II 65, 74, 125, 152, 214, 312, 323, 369
13:1-2 II 43, 48-49, 57, 140, 304, 448, 452-53
16:6 II 84

Kila᾽im

2:10 I 9, 352
3:4 I 9, 352
3:5 I 353
3:6 II 173
4:1 II 54
5:3 I 9, 353-54
5:8 I 9, 38; II 3, 18, 67, 77, 173, 351-52, 357, 361, 387
6:2 I 354
9:2 II 128
9:3 I 9, 39; II 3, 23, 50, 64, 75, 128, 144, 313, 320, 323

Maᶜaserot

2:1-2 I 356
2:4 I 9, 355-56
3:5 I 62
4:1 I 70
4:2 I 62
4:3 I 9, 70, 72; II 4, 23, 50, 68, 77, 85, 353, 357, 362
4:5 I 9, 71; II 4, 24, 50, 68, 77, 175, 353, 357, 362
4:6 I 6, 71-72; II 4, 28, 68, 77, 175, 353, 357, 362, 373, 377
5:5 I 80

Maᶜ aser Sheni

2:3-4 II 54
2:7 II 33-34
2:9 II 33
3:6-7, 9 II 54
3:9 II 41, 117
3:12 II 40, 47
3:13 II 106, 308, 322, 370
5:2 I 75; II 83, 207
5:12 I 74; II 206, 373, 377, 388
5:15 I 350

Makkot

3:5 I 12, 379

Makshirin

1:1 I 330
1:2-4 II 33, 56
1:4 II 164
4:4-5 II 56
5:9 II 43, 48
6:4 I 69, 71; II 83, 206
6:6 I 8, 330, 332; II 11, 25, 52, 70, 81, 198, 356, 359, 363

Megillah

3:6 I 11
4:10 I 10, 369

Meᶜilah

1:2 I 228, 269, 272-73; II 21, 79, 171, 215
1:2-3 I 6; II 8, 66, 152, 162, 314, 374, 380
1:3 I 269, 271, 273; II 21, 79
2:2 I 229

Menaḥot

2:3 I 243
3:1 I 12, 240; II 8, 24, 51, 75, 128, 313, 323, 369, 372, 380, 401
3:4 I 5, 241; II 8, 20, 66, 79, 372, 374, 376
7:3 I 12, 243; II 8, 20, 66, 128, 380
8:1 II 66
10:1 II 34

Miqva᾽ot

1:5 II 42, 47
2:4 I 14, 320-21; II 11, 29, 70, 80, 197, 356, 363
2:7 I 5, 321; II 70, 80, 197, 356, 373, 381
2:8 I 5, 372; II 11, 22, 70, 80, 197, 356, 363, 373, 381
2:10, I 5; II 11, 22, 80, 197, 356, 363, 373, 381
3:4 I 391
4:1 II 44, 48
5:6 II 42, 47
7:1 I 323
8:1 I 14, 391
9:3 I 14, 392
9:7 I 392

Moᶜed Qaṭan

1:9 I 163; II 74, 84, 125, 127, 312
3:4 I 158-59; II 65, 84, 125, 132, 212
3:5 I 158
3:6 I 158; II 6, 27, 78, 374, 379

Nazir

1:1-2 II 55
1:3 I 193
3:1 I 11, 192-95; II 27

3:3-5 II 7, 58, 65-66, 74, 125, 185, 312, 320, 323, 369
3:4 I 11, 192-93; II 24
3:5 I 11, 192; II 24
5:1-3, 5 II 33, 55
6:1-5 II 106, 311
6:6 I 193
6:7 I 193
6:11 I 11, 195; II 7, 20, 78, 185, 354, 358, 363, 389
7:1 I 11, 197; II 7, 20, 69, 78, 185, 354, 358, 363
7:2 I 198-99; II 185
7:4 I 6, 199; II 30, 69, 78, 354, 358, 363, 374, 379
8:1 I 196; II 185
12 I 188

Nedarim
3:1 I 191
3:2-4 II 55
3:4 II 41, 47
4:1 I 373
4:3 I 11, 373
4:21 I 372
6:5 II 7
9:1 I 11, 186; II 7, 29, 58, 64, 78, 110, 311, 319, 322
9:2 I 11, 185-86; II 7, 29, 58, 64, 78, 110, 311, 319, 322
10:5 I 187; II 7, 20, 58, 69, 78, 184, 351, 354, 358, 362
10:6 I 7, 187-88, 191; II 5, 20, 58, 69, 78, 184, 351, 354, 358, 362, 374, 379
10:7 I 188, 191; II 5, 20, 58, 69, 78, 185, 354, 358, 363, 393, 401

Nega'im
1:4 II 34
2:4-7, 8, 10 II 359
6:7 II 13, 389
7:4 I 299; II 26
7:4-5 I 13, 300; II, 10, 52, 59, 66, 75, 128, 189, 313
7:5 I 299; II 21, 128
8:3 I 299
9:1 I 301
9:2 I 301
9:3 I 13, 300-301; II 10, 26, 70, 80, 86, 193, 221, 347, 355, 359, 363, 375, 381, 421
11:7 I 301; II 10, 26, 52, 70, 80, 86, 193, 221, 347, 355, 359, 363, 375, 382, 421
13:1 II 85
14:1 I 390-91
14:9 I 389

Nezirot
11:7 I 13
14:9 I 13

Niddah
1:1 I 323; II 34, 171
1:3 I 5, 323-25; II 11, 25 , 67, 80 86, 171, 351-52, 356, 361, 373, 401
1:4 II 257
1:5 I 14, 323-24; II 11, 25, 52, 67, 80, 86
2:1 II 43-44, 47-49
2:4 II 33, 43, 47, 49
2:6 II 43, 48
4:3 II 33, 56, 117, 393
4:4 I 6, 325-28; II 11, 22, 70, 80, 117, 197, 356, 359, 373, 387, 401
4:4-6 II 59, 359, 363
4:6 I 14, 326; II 11, 25, 52, 70, 80, 197, 373, 382
5:1 I 163
5:9 I 4, 329; II 33, 81, 117
10:1 II 56
10:3 I 6, 325, 329; II 11, 22, 67, 81, 156, 165, 171, 374, 381, 396, 401

Ohalot
1:7 I 340; II 26
2:1 I 387
2:2 I 13, 287; II 9, 21, 159, 356, 359, 363
2:3 II 42, 44, 47-48
2:4 I 5, 288; II 9, 25, 56, 69, 80, 192, 355, 373, 380
2:6 I 344; II 85, 217
3:7 I 280, 296
5:1-4 II 33, 56
5:4 II 33
5:6 II 370
6:1 I 13, 289; II 10, 25, 51, 66, 75, 80

6:2 I 13; II 66, 75, 84, 126, 155, 216, 312, 320, 323, 369
7:3 II 42, 47, 56
8:6 I 5, 291; II 66, 75, 84, 128, 155, 216, 313, 373
9:3 I 279
9:15 I 5, 292, 294; II 10, 21, 69, 88, 192, 356, 373, 381
11:1 II 44, 48, 56
11:3-6, II 56
12:3 I 5, 293; II 10, 21, 70, 80, 192, 356, 373, 381
12:8 I 5, 294-95; II 10, 21, 59, 66, 76, 84, 155, 159, 214, 373, 381
13:1, 4 II 56
14:2 I 296
14:4 I 295-96; II 80, 193, 356
14:4-5 I 5; II 10, 21, 59, 70, 192, 356, 373, 381
14:5 I 295-96; II 80
15:4 I 279
16:1 I 290
17:1 I 297
17:2 I 5, 297; II 10, 29, 70, 80, 193, 356, 373, 381
17:5 I 12, 297-98; II 29, 66, 75, 128, 155, 313
17:8 II 165
18:1, 4, 8 II 56
18:7 II 85

ʿOrlah

1:7 I 4, 82; II 4, 28, 68, 77, 353, 357, 362, 372, 377
2:1 I 355, 500
2:4 I 48, 55; II 83, 208
2:7 I 9, 84
2:8 I 9, 82; II 208
2:11 I 9, 82-83; II 78, 83, 177, 207-208, 353, 357, 362
2:13 I 83; II 77, 177, 353, 357, 362

Parah

1:1 I 13, 302; II 10, 29, 70, 80, 86, 194, 221, 238, 244, 355, 359, 363
2:1 I 13, 303; II 10, 29, 70, 80, 194, 356
2:3 I 13, 303-304; II 10, 21, 70, 194, 375, 381
2:4 I 304
2:5 I 7, 304; II 10, 21, 70, 194, 375, 381
3:2 I 312
3:7 I 306
3:8 I 305
4:1 II 13, 305; II 10, 25, 51, 70, 80, 194, 355
4:3 I 13, 305, 309; II 10, 25, 51, 70, 80, 194, 355
5:4 I 5, 306; II 10, 21, 70, 80, 194, 355, 373, 381
5:7 I 13, 307; II 75, 84, 126, 216, 218, 312, 320, 323, 369
7:1 II 1
7:10 I 13, 307-308; II 25, 51, 66, 75, 126, 156, 313, 323, 369
8:2-7 I 319
9:1 I 13, 308-10; II 21, 59, 62, 80, 156
9:3 I 13, 308; II 10, 25, 51, 80, 156, 216
9:4 I 5, 309-10; II 10, 21, 67, 80, 156, 165, 315, 322, 324, 373, 381
9:7 I 13, 309; II 10, 25, 51, 67, 80, 156
10:1 I 5, 311; II 10, 21, 70, 80, 186, 355, 373, 381
10:3 I 13, 311-14, 345; II 10, 21, 70, 80, 195, 355
11:1 I 308-309; II 51, 84, 216
11:2 I 14, 314; II 10, 25, 52, 70, 80, 355
11:7 I 14, 315; II 10, 25, 52, 70, 80, 355

Pe'ah

3:6 I 7, 34; II 3, 28, 67, 77, 172, 352, 356, 361, 375, 378
4:9 I 8, 348-49
5:2 I 8, 348-49
5:4 I 8, 350
6:1 II 42
6:1-3, 5 II 54
6:2 II 33, 144, 313, 320, 323
7:4 I 35; II 172
7:6 I 35; II 54, 173
7:7 I 6, 35; II 3, 18, 67, 77, 172, 352, 357, 361, 373, 377, 387
7:8 I 36
8:6 I 350

Pesaḥim

1:1 II 40, 44, 47
1:6 I 117-18; II 38, 107, 149
1:7 I 117, 119; II 5, 27, 65, 75, 83, 149, 158, 163, 209-10, 314, 321, 324, 372, 378
3:1 I 10, 363
3:3 I 8, 119, 120-21; II 5, 26, 63, 78, 103, 157, 310, 318, 322, 375-76, 379, 388, 391, 401
3:8 II 5
4:5 II 41, 47
5:1 I 135
5:5-8 I 363
5:9 I 10, 363
6:1 I 10, 122-23, 127; II 351, 354, 358, 362, 374, 376, 378
6:1-2 I 61; II 24, 50, 68, 78, 150, 179-80, 244
6:2 I 6, 123-24, 126; II 150, 374, 376, 378, 395, 401, 408, 414
6:2-3 I 363
6:5 I 4, 130, 132; II 5, 19, 65, 75, 158, 161, 314, 321, 324, 372, 378
9:2 I 6, 132; II 5, 26, 68, 78, 181, 354, 358, 362, 374, 378, 388, 393, 395
9:4 I 10, 364
10:6 II 33
10:8 II 44, 48
13:1 I 119

Qiddushin

1:1 II 41, 44, 47
1:9 I 12, 209; II 7, 24, 51, 64, 76, 84, 98, 130
3:12 I 210
3:13 I 8; II 7, 29, 69, 79, 186, 354, 359, 363, 375, 379
4:1 I 376
4:3 I 12, 210, 475
4:13 I 12, 376

Rosh Hashanah

1:1 I 85; II 33
1:2 I 156
1:8 II 84, 217
4:1 I 10, 368
4:1-4 II 57, 141, 448

Sanhedrin

1:4 I 6, 217, 379; II 9, 25, 51, 69, 79, 187, 354, 359, 363, 379
3:3 I 14, 338; II 11, 84, 114, 217
4:1 I 166
5:2 II 141, 449
6:1 I 12
6:4 I 218; II 9, 29, 58, 66, 75, 118, 125, 187, 311-12, 319, 323, 369
7:4 I 370
7:11 I 400; II 27, 70, 85, 199, 217
10:1 II 59
10:3 I 454; II 13, 22, 67, 70, 81, 157, 199, 374, 376, 381, 393

Shabbat

1:3 I 85; II 233
1:4 I 100
1:4-8 I 85, 359; II 146
1:4-9 II 54
1:10 I 9, 85; II 5, 24, 50, 68, 77, 177, 233, 351, 353, 358, 362
2:3 I 6, 86; II 5, 19, 68, 78, 351, 353, 358, 362, 373, 378
2:5 II 376
2:13 II 178
3:1 II 55
6:1 I 14, 88, 338; II 11, 81, 83, 114, 208
6:3 I 9, 89; II 208
6:4 I 9, 87; II 5, 24, 50, 68, 77, 358, 362
6:5 I 88; II 83, 208
7:2 I 99
10:6 I 10, 90, 357
12:4 I 4, 89; II 5, 19, 68, 77, 178, 353, 358, 362, 372, 378
13:1 I 10, 91; II 5, 28, 68, 77, 178, 354, 358, 362
16:7 II 449
16:17 II 240
17:7 I 10, 92; II 5, 68, 77, 179, 354, 358, 362
19:1 I 6, 93, 97, 123; II 5, 68, 75, 148, 158, 179-80, 354m, 358, 362, 373, 376, 378, 401
19:1-2 I 123-24
19:2 I 93-94

19:4 I 4, 96-98; II 5, 19, 64, 75, 147, 158, 163, 179, 314, 320, 372, 376, 378
20:1 I 10, 92, 99; II 5, 28, 68, 77, 179, 354, 358
22:1 I 10, 359
22:3 II 140, 449

Shavuᶜot

2:3 I 220
2:5 I 7, 220; II 9, 29, 69, 79, 121, 190, 213, 312, 319, 323, 375, 380, 390, 395, 401
5:3 I 380
8:3 I 380

Sheqalim

1:4 II 140, 449, 454
2:3 II 55
4:7 I 6, 136-37; II 6, 19, 63, 65, 74, 86, 105, 121, 123 150, 221, 311, 318, 322, 372
4:8 I 136-37; II75, 158
6:1 I 365
7:3 I 233
8:6 II 33, 106, 117, 318, 322
8:7 I 6, 137; II 6, 28, 63, 106-108, 317-18, 374

Sheviᶜit

1:1 II 38
2:5 II 372
2:6 II 254
3:10 II 75, 128, 313, 320, 323
4:2 II 62, 123
4:4 II 33, 54
4:28 II 122
5:3 I 4, 39-40; II 3, 18, 67, 77, 173, 353, 357, 361, 372, 377
5:4 I 40
5:5 I 40
5:8 II 34
7:6 I 40; II 83, 206, 401
8:1 I 41-42
8:2 I 42
8:3 II 43, 48
8:8 I 41-43
8:9 I 42; II 4, 18, 377
8:9-10 I 9, 37; II 59, 68, 73, 86, 100, 121, 123, 310, 318, 322, 377
8:10 I 41-42; II 27

9:4 I 44
9:5 I 7, 44; II 4, 18, 68, 77, 173, 353, 357, 361, 375
9:8 I 40: II 173
9:9 II 4, 17, 68, 351, 357, 361
10:7 I 9, 336; II 11, 22

Soṭah

1:1 I 5, 199; II 7, 20, 67, 76, 111, 159-60, 166, 170, 237, 315, 322, 324, 372, 379
1:2 I 200
3:4 I 201; II 7, 27, 69, 78, 111, 186, 354, 358, 363, 372, 379
4:3 I 11, 373
5:2 II 57, 449
6:1 I 5, 202; II 7, 20, 69, 79, 111, 186, 354, 359, 363, 372, 379
9:2 I 11, 202-203; II 20, 79, 214, 389, 391
9:2-4 II 7, 57, 69, 186, 354, 359, 363
9:3 I 6, 203; II 20, 79, 379
9:3-4 I 6; II 374, 379
9:4 I 203; II 20, 79
9:15 I 395-96; II 12, 27, 70, 81, 198, 304, 416

Sukkah

1:1 II 6, 58, 65, 151, 159, 164, 314, 321, 324
1:4 I 145
1:11 I 10, 145-46; II 19
2:5 II 140, 367, 449
2:6 I 367
3:12 II 65, 449
4:6 I 10, 368

Taᶜanit

1:1 I 5, 156-57; II 6, 26, 65, 68, 78, 151, 164, 314, 321, 324, 354, 358, 362, 372, 378
2:10 I 157; II 84, 211
3:9 I 10, 156; II 6, 24, 50, 354, 358, 362

Temurah

1:1 I 253
2:2 I 254
3:1 I 12, 253, 345, 385; II 8, 20, 66, 79, 153, 162, 382

3:3 I 8, 254, 256, 385; II 8, 20, 59, 69, 79, 189, 355, 359, 363, 380
6:1 I 255
6:3 II 8
6:5 I 12, 255; II 20, 69, 79, 189, 355, 359, 363
7:1 I 136

Terumot
1:3 I 57
1:4 I 46; II 95-96, 115-16
1:5 I 46
1:7 I 46
1:8 I 46
1:9-10 II 115
2:1 I 9, 45-46, 48, 57; II 4, 23, 50, 63, 74, 95, 310, 317, 322, 369, 373
2:2 I 45
2:5 I 47
3:6-7 I 356
4:3 I 48
4:5 I 9, 48; II 4, 18, 68, 77, 174, 353, 357, 361, 375, 378
4:7 I 49-50, 501; II 4, 28, 370, 372, 377
4:7-11 I 4; II 58, 75, 128, 377
4:7-12 I 58
4:8 I 49-50, 52-54, 500-501; II 4, 28, 64, 128, 145, 314, 320, 323
4:9 I 29-50, 52-53; II 4, 28, 64, 145, 314, 320, 323
4:10 I 49-50, 53-54; II 4, 18, 64, 145, 320, 323
4:11 I 50-51, 53, 500-501; II 4, 18, 64, 145, 314, 320, 323
5:1 I 55, 61, 64
5:1-7 I 57
5:2 I 55, 61, 236; II 4, 18, 58, 68, 77, 128, 174, 353, 357, 362
5:3 I 55
5:4 I 56-55; II 18, 33, 58, 68, 77 115, 174, 351, 353, 357, 362
5:5 I 55-58; II 18, 58, 68, 77, 174, 353, 357, 362
5:6 I 55-57, 83; II 18, 58, 68, 77, 174, 353, 357, 362
6:5 I 60
6:6 I 6, 59; II 4, 28, 68, 77, 174, 353, 357, 361, 373, 377, 387, 391
8:1 I 61-62; II 18, 64, 77
8:1-3 I 4, 64, 68, 86; II 4, 18, 58, 177, 372, 376-77
8:2 I 61; II 18, 64, 77
8:3 I 60-62; II 18, 64, 76, 146, 159, 314, 320
8:8 I 63-64, 119, 314; II 18, 27, 65, 77, 83, 146, 375, 378
8:8-11 I 118; II 4, 18, 58. 68, 149, 157, 210, 310, 318, 322
8:9 I 63-66; II 18, 77
8:10 I 63, 65-66; II 18, 77
8:11 I 4, 64-66, 120, 238; II 18, 63, 77, 104, 401
11:2 I 4, 66, 68, 70; II 4, 18, 58, 64, 74, 129, 148, 159, 170, 175, 313-14, 323-24, 369, 372, 377
11:3 I 66, 69; II 147

Ṭoharot
2:2 I 5, 316-17; II 11, 29, 70, 80, 196, 355, 359, 363, 373, 381
2:4 I 316
2:5 I 316
2:6 I 316
4:2 I 6, 338; II 85, 217, 381
4:5 I 314
6:4 I 314
6:5 I 14, 317; II 11, 22, 67, 80, 156
6:6 I 14, 31
8:1, 5, 7 II 56
8:7 I 5, 318, 325; II 11, 22, 80, 86, 119, 196, 220, 331, 333, 355, 359, 363, 373, 381, 401
9:1 II 33, 42, 47
9:3 I 14; II 11, 22, 67, 76, 156, 159, 165
9:5, 7 II 33
10:1 I 314

ʿUqṣin
3:8 II 33
3:10 I 9, 336; II 11, 68, 75, 128, 313, 320, 323
3:11 I 336

Yadayim
4:2 I 332, 334; II 7, 81, 345
4:3 I 344, 447; II 12, 31, 70, 81, 86, 119, 140, 178, 199, 202, 221, 345, 355, 359, 363, 381, 449
4:6 II 141, 450, 454

Yevamot

1:4 II 33, 55
2:5 I 178
3:1 I 4, 173, 370; II 4, 40, 50, 117, 183
3:5 I 393
4:1 I 372
4:3 II 33, 116, 452
6:6 I 373
8:4 I 7, 164-65; II 6, 30, 68, 78, 354, 368, 374, 379
8:6 I 370
10:2 I 179; II 84, 213
10:5 I 11
10:6 I 190
10:7 I 11, 190
12:1 I 165
12:2 I 11, 165-66; II 6, 24, 50, 65, 68, 78, 84, 152, 212, 354, 358, 362
12:3 I 6, 166; II 6, 19, 58, 68, 354, 358, 362, 374, 379, 389, 392
12:4 I 170; II 58, 63, 84, 313
13:1 I 167, 173; II 24, 55, 109
13:2 I 11, 168-70, 173; II 6, 24, 26-27, 63, 67, 84, 109, 170, 311, 318, 322
13:6 I 11, 169, 172-73; II 6, 24, 50, 68, 78, 183, 401
13:6-7 I 163; II 6, 352, 356, 360, 373, 401-402
13:7 I 7, 172-74; II 19, 64, 78, 109, 311, 319, 379
13:11 I 11, 167
16:2 I 11, 176; II 6, 24, 50, 68, 78, 183, 354, 358, 362
16:7 I 7, 177; II 6, 24, 50, 69, 78, 84, 183, 354, 358, 362, 374, 379

Yoma

3:4 I 143
4:1 I 10, 138; II 83
5:3 I 10, 138
5:4 I 139
5:5 I 10, 139; II 6, 19, 50, 65, 74, 125
6:3 II 210
7:1 I 142
7:3 I 6, 141, 144; II 6, 28, 65, 74, 83, 85, 210, 374, 400

8:1 I 366
8:2 I 144
8:11 I 10

Zabim

1:1-2 II 56
1:2 II 33
2:2 I 14, 392
4:6 I 340
5:1 I 331
5:3 I 14, 331; II 11, 25, 52, 70, 81, 198, 354, 359, 363
5:6-7 I 14, 331; II 198
5:7 I 14, 331; II 16, 25, 70, 81, 355, 359, 363
5:12 I 316

Zevaḥim

1:1 I 12, 222, 224, 226, 238; II 7, 24, 51, 69, 79, 150, 162, 188-89, 314, 354, 359, 363, 372, 380, 390
1:3 I 222
1:4 I 382
2:2-3 I 383
2:3 I 226, 269, 274
2:4 I 274; II 84, 215
3:1 I 237
3:3 I 12, 226, 228, 241; II 7, 24, 51, 67, 75, 79, 170, 372, 380
7:1 I 228
7:2 I 228
7:3 I 228-30
7:4 I 5, 229; II 7, 20, 69, 79, 188, 354, 359, 363, 372, 380, 392
8:2 I 232
8:3 I 232
8:4 I 233; II 7, 20, 68, 75, 79, 128, 313, 323
8:5 I 12, 234, 236-37; II 8, 20, 68, 79, 104, 128, 316, 318, 322
8:6 I 234; II 104, 310, 318, 322
8:7 I 12, 234, 237-38, 240; II 8, 24, 51, 79, 104, 310, 318, 320
8:7-12 II 8, 58, 104, 310, 318, 322
8:8 I 12, 235, 237, 239; II 20, 75, 79, 104, 128, 310, 313, 323, 370
8:9 I 12, 235, 237-39; II 20, 79, 104, 310

8:10 I 5, 235, 237, 240; II 20, 79, 104, 310, 370, 380, 390-91
8:11 I 6, 236, 238, 240; II 20, 79, 104, 310
8:12 I 136, 238; II 20, 104, 310
8:15 II 128
9:3 I 243; II 66
12:4 II 38
13:5-6 I 240

III. TOSEFTA

Ahilot
2:7 I 344; II 67, 85, 157, 185, 217
3:4 II 33
3:7 I 289; II 9, 69, 373, 381
3:8 I 289; II 69, 192
5:11 II 33
7:1 I 290; II 10
7:3 I 13, 290; II 66, 75, 84, 126, 155, 216, 312, 320, 323, 369
7:11 I 13, 314; II 10, 80, 195, 373, 381
9:7 I 5, 291; II 66, 75, 84, 128, 155, 165, 216, 313, 370, 373
10:8 I 292-93; II 69
13:3 I 293; II 40, 63
13:10 I 294; II 10, 66, 76, 84, 155, 159, 165, 216
13:12 I 196; II 10, 70, 193
16:8 II 119, 450
17:6 I 298; II 66, 75, 128, 155, 313

ʿArakhin
2:1 I 304
4:5 I 5, 251; II 33, 84, 117, 309
4:6 I 252; II 8
4:24 I 252; II 8, 391, 395

ʿAvodah Zarah
6:4 I 222

Bava Batra
1:9 I 213
2:6 I 284
2:11 II 8, 69, 187
3:1 I 379
4:3 I 285
4:7 I 285
6:8 I 286
10:12 I 215, 217; II 9, 66

Bava Meṣiʿaʾ
1:19 I 12
4:2 I 13
4:14 I 282
6:4 I 280
7:1 I 297
8:8 I 284

Bava Qamma
2:8 I 276
2:11 I 213
5:7 I 377
6:22 I 212; II 8
7:1 II 450
7:3-7 II 57; II 450
7:4 II 446
8:17 I 213; II 27, 187

Bekhorot
3:15-16 II 33, 56

Berakhot
1:1 I 21
2:1 II 77
3:7 I 24-25; II 76, 233
3:10 I 32; II 3
3:11 I 8, 32; II 3
3:13 II 54
4:3 I 8, 347-48

Beṣah
2:15 I 134

Bikkurim
1:6 I 78

Demaʾi
1:3 I 9, 37; II 3, 23, 50, 64, 74, 122-23, 308, 312, 319, 323, 369
5:22 I 8, 37, 43

ʿEduyyot
1:3 II 34
1:4 I 337; II 81, 86, 220

1:10 I 6, 338; II 11, 85, 114, 117, 373, 381
2:1 I 276, 285, 339-40; II 9, 59, 81, 113
2:2 I 339
2:7 I 14
2:8 I 339; II 81
2:10 I 344; II 67, 217
3:1 I 13, 339; II 373

ʿEruvin

1:2 I 102; II 5
2:7 I 107; II 5
2:8 I 107-108; II 5
2(3):15 I 360
4(5):1 I 111; II 5, 57, 148, 314, 321, 324
4(5):2 I 111; II 5, 57, 148, 314, 321, 324
5:5 I 112

Giṭṭin

9:1-5 I 207; II 7, 68, 110

Ḥagigah

2:1 II 450
2:10 II 33
3:33 II 450

Ḥallah

1:6 I 7, 82; II 4, 63, 74, 83, 97-98, 123, 207, 310, 317, 322, 369, 372, 377
1:10 I 7, 337; II 24, 63, 74, 86, 95, 122-23, 310, 317, 323, 369, 378
2:24 II 70, 199

Ḥullin

2:24 II 12
2:11 I 247, II 8, 76, 158, 166
2:24 I 401; II 31, 81, 86, 220, 366, 374, 381

9:24 I 402

Kelim

1:6 I 388
1:9 I 13, 387
2:6 I 284; II 216
2:8 I 276; II 9, 69, 190
4:2 I 13, 281; II 9, 182
4:3 I 285; II 9, 66, 76, 155, 159, 165, 315, 321, 324
4:5 II 42, 47
4:7 I 285; II 9, 64, 76, 113, 159
4:14 I 282; II 9, 66, 76, 154, 159, 165, 315, 321, 324
4:16 II 33
5:7-8 II 56
6:4 I 280; II 9, 66, 76, 112
6:8 I 286
7:1 I 297
7:6 I 386
7:9 II 449
8:8 I 284; II 67, 76, 158, 165, 171, 315, 322, 324

Keritot

1:14 I 261; II 372
1:19 I 268
2:12-15 I 263; II 8, 66, 76, 153, 160, 162, 315, 391-92
3:5-8 I 265-66; II 66, 153, 315
4:4 I 267; II 8

Ketuvot

1:4 II 84
1:6 I 183; II 7
5:6 I 371
11:4 I 11, 184; II 7, 27, 65, 74, 125, 152, 312, 323, 369

Kilaʾim

3:10 I 9, 354
4:4 I 9, 354
5:18 I 9, 39; II 3, 64, 75, 128, 145, 163, 313, 320

Kippurim

2:10 I 10, 138; II 24, 50, 65, 74, 125, 210, 319, 323, 369
2:16 I 10, 138; II 6, 19, 74, 125, 210, 319
3:1 I 10, 139; II 65, 74, 125, 319,
3:14 I 10, 140; II 6, 31, 68, 78, 83, 181, 221, 354, 358, 362, 405
3:19 I 143; II 6, 65, 74, 83, 125
4:3 I 10, 145; II 78
5:14 II 210

Maʿaserot

2:1 II 450
2:2 I 9, 356
3:7 I 9, 72; II 4, 68, 175, 362

Maʿaser Sheni

1:4 I 72; II 324
1:14 II 4, 27, 68, 75, 163, 315, 322
2:16 I 73; II 107, 370
2:18 II 47
3:15 I 73; II 176, 400
3:16 I 9, 73; II 4, 28, 58, 77, 175, 353, 357, 362, 400
4:5-6 I 74; II 4, 18, 58, 68, 176, 353, 357, 362
5:15-16 I 75; II 77, 83, 120, 207

Makshirin

1:4 I 330; II 81

Megillah

4:34 I 10, 369

Meʿilah

1:4 I 269; II 8
1:6 I 270; II 8, 66, 152

Menaḥot

2:16 I 12, 241; II 8, 66, 75, 128, 320, 323, 369, 372
2:17 II 313
3:1 II 320
4:2 I 242; II 8
4:2-6 II 8, 66
4:5 I 242; II 8, 66, 380
4:5-6 I 5
4:6 I 242; II 8, 380
4:10 I 270; II 8, 68, 152, 376, 380
4:14-15 I 271; II 8, 152
8:19 I 244; II 8, 68, 75, 128, 372, 380
10:26 II 449
14:15 II 66

Miqvaʾot

3:1 I 321
3:9 I 391

Moʿed Qaṭan

2:9 II 116, 138

Nazir

2:2-13 II 7
4-8 II 7
4:9-10 II 7
5:1 I 199

Nedarim

6:5 I 190

Negaʿim

1:13 I 202
2:12 I 389
3:5 I 300; II 68, 75, 128, 313
4:8 I 261
8:2 I 390
8:12 I 13
9:7 I 262

Nezirot

2:12-13 I 11, 194; II 65, 74, 125, 312, 320, 323, 369
3:19 II 55
4:8 I 194-95, 262
4:9-10 I 196; II 20

Niddah

1:5 I 324; II 67, 171
1:9 II 86, 221
2:3 I 6, 235; II 7, 80, 373, 381
5:5-7 II 33, 119
5:6 I 4, 325; II 80
6:8 I 326; II 80
9:13 I 330; II 11, 77, 156, 165, 171

ʿOrlah

1:8 I 8, 84, 209; II 63, 76, 84, 100, 124, 177, 214, 310, 317, 322, 370

Parah

2:2 I 304; II 194
3:7 I 390
3:8 II 448, 452
4:7 II 119, 450
5:6 II 10, 194
5:7 I 306
5:9 I 13, 307; II 75, 126, 216, 312, 320, 323, 369
7:7 I 308; II 10, 66, 75, 126, 156, 313, 320, 323, 369

9:3 I 310; II 10, 84
9:5 II 10
9:6 I 310; II 10, 67, 156, 165
10:2 I 313
10:4 I 313-14; II 10, 70, 80, 195 356
10:5 I 313; II 10
11:8 I 315; II 195

Pe'ah

3:2 I 36; II 64, 144, 162, 320, 323
3:3 II 313
4:2 I 350

Pisḥa

1:5 I 119; II, 65, 75, 83, 149, 158, 163, 321
1:6 II 33
3:7 I 121; II 5, 388, 392
3:8 I 121-22; II 5, 29, 67, 149, 166
4:5-6 I 128, 225; II 7, 150, 372
4:8 II 69
4:12 I 131
4:13 I 125-26, 128; II 160
5:1 I 6, 123-24, 128; II 68, 180
5:4 I 4, 132; II 5, 65, 75, 150, 158, 162, 314
7:14 II 33
8:2 I 133; II 5, 68, 395
8:18 I 2n
9:18, 20 I 385
10:9 II 33

Qiddushin

1:4 I 210; II 79, 390
5:1 I 376

Rosh Hashanah

2:9 II 448
1:6 I 6, 155; II 29, 65, 74, 125, 151, 312, 319, 323, 369, 374, 388, 396

Sanhedrin

3:1 I 218; II 9, 69, 388, 396
9:6 I 12, 219; II 9, 86, 75, 125, 312, 369
11:4 I 400
11:5 II 12, 27, 70, 81, 85, 199, 217, 355, 359, 363, 374, 381

13:2 I 455; II 13, 67, 70, 157, 166, 199, 373, 376, 381
13:3 II 36
13:10 I 455; II 13, 70

Shabbat

1:16 I 100
1:17 I 4, 99; II 19, 68, 77, 180, 372
4:6 I 9, 87-88, 92; II 5, 27, 68, 73, 83, 208, 353, 358
4:11 I 89; II 5, 24, 50, 208, 362
5:12 I 9, 89
9:12 I 10, 358
9:13 I 10, 359
11:15 I 4, 90; II 5
12:1 I 10, 91; II 5
12:4 II 19
12:14 I 10, 92, 146; II 5
15:10 I 4, 94, 97; II 5, 64, 75, 147, 158, 163, 170, 314, 321, 324
15:16 I 93-95; II 5, 148, 179

Shavu'ot

1:6 I 7, 221; II 9, 69, 121

Sheqalim

2:10 I 6, 137; II 6, 63, 65, 75, 150, 158
2:18 I 365-66
3:16 I 137; II 6, 106, 308

Shevi'it

1:5 I 40
4:2 II 33
4:3 I 4, 40; II 3
4:21 I 3, 85; II 63, 98, 300, 322

Soṭah

1:1 I 5, 200; II 67, 76, 159, 166, 170, 315, 322, 324
1:2 I 201; II 26, 78, 379
5:13 II 449
13:1 I 366
14:1 II 449
14:3 I 396
15:3 I 396; II 12, 86, 222, 223

Sukkah

1:9 I 8, 147; II 6, 31, 68, 78, 181, 354, 358, 362, 405

1:10 I 146; II 6, 65, 78, 151, 159, 314, 321
2:1 I 7, 129; II 74, 123, 181, 362
3:1 I 368

Taᶜanit
2:5 I 4, 157; II 84, 211, 372, 378

Temurah
1:9 I 255

Terumot
3:16 I 47; II 33, 95-97
3:18 I 9, 45-48; II 4, 63, 74, 95, 123, 310, 317, 322, 369
5:10 I 53; II 4, 64, 75, 163, 314, 320, 323
5:10-12 I 4; II 128, 145, 372
5:11 I 54; II 64, 75, 163, 323
5:12 I 355
6:4 I 56; II 4, 33
7:9 I 59-60; II 4
7:9-10 I 6; II 4
7:10 I 60, 62; II 64, 76, 146, 159, 163, 314, 320, 323
7:18 I 119
8:15 I 9, 84; II 177
9:8 I 4, 67-69; II 4, 64, 76, 83, 146, 159, 170, 206
9:9 I 4, 68-69; II 4, 64, 74, 127, 147, 163, 170, 234, 313-14, 323, 369

Ṭevul Yom
1:8 I 319; II 11, 196

Ṭoharot
2:1 I 317; II 11
6:6 I 14
7:7 II 67
7:9 I 318; II 67, 84, 216

ᶜUqṣin
2:15 II 320
3:15 I 336; II 11, 67, 75, 128, 313, 323

Yadayim
1:19 II 450
2:9 II 450
2:16 I 334; II 70, 449

Yevamot
1:4 II 184
1:7-14 II 33
2:4 I 213
3 I 178; II 31, 78, 181, 187, 221, 405
5:1 I 370; II 33
10:2 I 370
11:4 I 11, 179; II 7, 19, 69, 78, 84, 213
12:1 II 212
12:11 I 11, 167; II 6, 65, 84, 168, 314, 324
12:12 I 11, 170; II 6, 63, 78, 213
13:3-5 I 5, 169; II 6, 26-27, 86, 105, 109, 221, 372
13:7 I 175
14:3 I 176; II 6, 24

Yom Ṭov
1:1, 3 I 4, 150, 339; II 19, 65, 74, 83, 210
1:3 I 150; II 74, 125, 306, 369
3:2 I 4, 154; II 6, 19, 68, 78, 84, 182, 211, 354, 358, 360, 365, 372, 378
3:18 I 153; II 6, 65, 151, 164
4:4 I 10, 92; II 83, 178, 208

Zabim
1:4 II 33
4:9 II 55
5:2 I 332; II 11

Zevaḥim
1:1 II 69, 150, 314, 372, 380, 390, 396
1:5 I 382
1:11 I 12, 224
2:16 I 12, 226, 241; II 7, 67, 75, 128, 170, 372, 376, 380
4:1 I 242, 275; II 65, 162, 395
4:1-2 I 241, 274; II 7, 29, 79, 84, 152, 215, 314, 321, 324, 372, 374, 376, 390
4:5 I 271; II 66, 374, 376
4:5-8 II 8, 152
4:8 I 272; II 66, 374
7:16-20 I 231; II 7
8:15 I 233, 239; II 7, 66, 75, 128, 313, 323

8:19 I 238; II 8
8:20 I 239; II 8, 66, 75, 104, 128, 313, 323, 370
8:21 I 239; II 8
8:23 I 240; II 8
8:24 I 240; II 8

IV. SIFRA

Aḥarē Mot

4:10 I 140
6:5 I 143

Behar

1:5 II 122
3:4 I 44; II 4

Beḥuqotai

5:1 I 475; II 14, 23, 72, 82, 229, 393, 418
11:5 I 384

Emor

6:6 I 60; II 4
10:10 II 450
11:1 I 155
16:9 II 140, 450
17:11 I 460; II 13, 228, 393

Mekhilta de Miluʾim

2:35 I 475; II 14, 23, 72, 82, 229, 394

Meṣoraᶜ Zabim

5:4 I 329

Nedavah

4:12 I 275

Qedoshim

3:1 I 36, 393; II 3
10:4 II 450, 454

Ṣav

1:9 II 38
3:2 I 382
4:3 I 382
4:4 I 225
4:6 I 226
8:1 I 227; II 79, 390, 392
8:1 I 227, 236; II 67, 79, 170, 390, 392
8:5 I 382
8:6 II 33
8:7 I 137
14:1 I 364

Shemini Mekhilta de Miluʾim

2:32-33 I 115; II 72, 77, 86, 230, 407

Shemini

7:10 I 2
7:12 II 140, 450, 456
8:5 I 345; II 118, 124, 312, 319, 323
10:5-6 I 134, 278; II 72, 230, 374, 380, 397

Tazriᶜa Negaᶜim

2:1 I 299
6:7 I 300
13:2 I 301

Tazriᶜa

Ch. 2 II 268
Ch. 3 II 267
2:4 I 326
12:6 I 162; II 6, 22, 71, 78, 227, 391-92
12:10 I 301
13 II 267

Vayiqra

1:13 I 258; II 8
5:1 II 450
5:4 I 136
6:5 I 370
7:26-31 I 266; II 391
11:9 I 222
12:7 I 220
12:4 I 266
13:4 I 246; II 22, 71, 228, 395, 410
13:13 II 33
17:11 I 382
21:4 I 267

V. SIFRÉ

Deuteronomy

29 I 475; II 14, 23, 72, 82, 229, 393
32 I 407, 476; II 14, 29, 72, 82, 228-29, 393, 417
38 I 408; II 12, 31, 71, 81, 228, 409
59 I 209
61 I 222; II 72, 79, 230, 389, 397
75 I 275; II 391, 395
133 I 135; II 6, 22, 71, 78; 227, 388, 396
140 I 149; II 72, 230, 388, 392
143 II 54
144 I 409; II 12, 71, 81, 119, 228, 404, 444
188 I 410; II 81, 87, 220
192 II 450
205 I 203; II 389, 391
206 I 203; II 84, 214, 390
212 I 180; II 22, 71, 78, 227, 389, 395
213 I 180-81; II 22, 71, 227, 389, 392
221 I 219; II 9, 118, 311, 319, 323, 390-91
221 I 219; II 9, 118, 311, 319, 323, 390-91
228 I 247
230 I 39; II 3, 387
261 I 303
269 I 207; II 33
285 I 36; II 3, 387
291 I 167; II 6
303 I 74; II 4, 22, 71, 77, 83, 206, 227, 373, 377, 388
305 II 450
338 I 477; II 14, 23, 72, 82, 229
357 II 445, 450

Numbers

7 I 201
24 I 197; II 22, 389, 392
69 I 133; II 5, 386
84 I 460; II 13
105 I 27; II 3, 227
110 I 76; II 4, 74, 125, 312, 319, 323, 369
123 I 302; II 119, 140, 450, 456
135 I 475
136 I 475; II 14, 23, 72, 82, 229, 394
153 I 188, 221; II 72, 79, 230, 397

Zuṭṭa

6:12 I 192
9:2 I 128; II 395
13:34 I 478; II 14, 72, 82, 230, 393
18:19 I 288
19:2 I 304; II 5
24 I 204; II 20, 72, 79, 230, 392
19:16 I 289, 297

VI. MEKHILTA DeR. ISHMAEL

16 II 450
99 II 448
115 II 450
193-95 II 450
290 II 454

Neziqin

18:9-16 I 428

Pisḥa

6:88-91 I 134; II 71
15:25-30 I 2n
17:204-10 I 417

Amalek

1:9-18 I 470; II 419
1:131-37 I 470; II 23, 82, 394, 419
1:173-75 I 469; II 14, 23, 71, 82, 229, 394, 419
2:186-92 I 468; II 14, 23, 71, 82, 229, 394
3:127-40 I 472; II 14, 23, 71, 82, 229

Baḥodesh

2:18-21 I 472
2:43-45 I 472; II 14, 23, 72, 82, 229, 417

4:36-44 I 474; II 14, 23, 72, 82, 229, 397, 418
6:39-44 I 383
10:58-86 I 405; II 12, 31, 71, 81, 228, 408

Beshallaḥ

1:57-69 I 465; II 13, 28, 71, 82, 228, 396, 418
2:8-15 I 465; II 14, 23, 72, 82, 228
4:1-9 I 26; II 77, 227
4:58-60 II 34
7:109-21 I 465; II 14, 23, 71, 82, 228, 394, 419

Kaspa

2:75-79 I 3

Neziqin

9:29-30 I 208; II 71, 79, 228, 395
10:125-30 I 377
14:37-42 I 211
16:13-24 I 134
18:9-16 II 72, 231

Pisḥa

1:114-18 I 459; II 13, 23, 71, 81, 228
5:106-109 I 364
6:40-43 I 22; II 76
6:88-91 II 227
7:5-20 I 365
11:106-108 I 365
14:11-22 I 459; II 13, 23, 71, 81, 228, 393
14:95-7 I 460; II 13, 27, 71, 82, 228
14:113-17 I 461; II 13, 23, 71, 82, 228, 393, 419

Shirata

3:28-39 I 467

Vayassa

1:1-12 I 468; II 14, 23, 71, 82, 229, 394, 418
1:93-105 I 27; II 227
5:41-50 I 151; II 78, 84, 211, 227, 389
6:47-49 I 467; II 14, 23, 71, 82, 229
7:68-74 I 423; II 72, 81, 230, 418

VII. MEKHILTA DeR. SIMEON

Page

1 I 474; II 14, 29, 71, 82, 229, 419
8 I 114
35 I 461; II 228
38 I 474; II 72, 82, 229, 393
39 I 134; II 5, 28, 71, 78, 229, 388, 397
41 I 472; II 229, 417
57 II 227
88 I 408
103 I 27; II 3, 227
106 I 422; II 72, 230, 392
121 I 469; II 419
135 II 393
139 I 473; II 229, 417
143 I 422; II 72, 81, 230, 396
154 I 467
155 I 467
157, 158 II 450, 454
181 I 218

Mekhilta deR. Simeon to Exodus,

12:42, 13:5, 13:10, 19:5 II 13

VIII. OTHER MIDRASHIC COMPILATIONS

Aggadat Bereshit

12:7 I 473
17:2 I 473; II 14

Avot DeR. Natan

Ch. 3 I 438; II 13
Ch. 4 I 435; II 12, 451
Ch. 6 I 398, 439; II 13, 31, 81, 451
Ch. 13 II 451
Ch. 14 I 398, 449; II 13, 81, 241, 441, 451
Ch. 15 I 399; II 12, 64, 74, 1123
Ch. 16 I 171

Ch. 20 I 415; II 412
Ch. 25 I 417; II 412, 441
Ch. 36 I 458; II 23, 71, 396
Ch. 40 I 33
Ch. 63 II 445
Page 196 I 284
Page 226, 267-75 II 445

Derekh Ereṣ Rabbah
7:6 I 33
56b I 419

Midrash Tanḥuma Beḥuqotai
5 I 480; II 418

Midrash Tanḥuma Bereshit
28 I 497; II 15, 243, 419

Midrash Tanḥuma Ḥuqat
24 I 303; II 86, 238

Midrash Mishlé
21:2 I 408

Midrash on Psalms
9:10 I 469; II 14, 419
9:15 I 458; II 13
18:16 I 484
22:11-12 I 498; II 15, 243
78:15 I 467; II 419
90:4 I 499; II 15, 243
90:17 I 398

Midrash Tanḥuma Pinḥas
13 I 367

Midrash Tanḥuma Teṣé
18 I 469

Midrash Tannaim
10 I 442
58 I 451
175-76 II 351
215 II 451

Midrash Tannaim to Deuteronomy
3:26 I 467; II 14
4:6 II 395
6:5 I 475
9:6 I 22; II 3, 68, 72, 76, 230, 410
11:10 I 408
12:1 I 209
12:4 I 222
12:15 I 275
12:26 I 275
13:1 I 235
14:22 I 477; II 14, 23, 72, 229, 416
21:2 I 203
21:22 I 219
22:7 I 247
24:2 I 35; II 3
25:9 I 167
26:3 I 61
32:49 I 477
34:3 I 117

Pesiqta de R. Kahana (page)
20 I 492; II 15, 396
52, 53 I 469
73 I 302
74 II 452
333 I 464
356 I 496; II 15
393 I 116
419 I 482

Pesiqta Rabbati
14 I 302
23 I 473; II 14
23:1 I 497; II 15, 419
23-24 I 452
52:4 I 480

Pirqé de R. Eliezer
Ch. 1, 2 I 446

Midrash Rabbah
Deuteronomy R
2:24 I 452
4:8 I 433

Exodus R.
2:5-15 I 474
21:8 I 28
23:9 I 466

Genesis R.
1:11 I 421
5:3 I 493; II 15, 242, 403

11:1 I 488
12:11 I 487; II 15
13:9 I 484, 488; II 15
13:10 I 484; II 15
15:2 I 488
17:4 II 452
19:6 II 452
22:4 I 464
25:2 I 494; II 15, 242, 403
33:3 I 494
34:11 I 494
41:10 I 213
42:1 I 440; II 13, 241, 396
44:21 II 452
61:3 I 494; II 15, 242, 393
70:5 I 449; II 13, 393, 409
84:19 I 496
98:4 I 495; II 15, 242, 393
98:64 I 481
100:7 I 160

Kallah Rabbati

1:11 I 436
2:1 I 437; II 13
51b I 436
52a I 437; II 13
52b I 436; II 13
53b I 419-20

Lamentations R.

5:31 II 340
3:66.9 I 470; II 14, 419
27 I 475

Leviticus R.

4:1 I 494; II 15, 242
5:4 I 433
14:4 I 496; II 15, 242
19:1 II 15, 243

Numbers R.

1:15 I 452; II 13
8:9 I 450; II 13
9:10 I 201
9:25 I 498; II 15, 243
9:30 I 204
9:48 I 451; II 7
16:26 I 460
19:7 I 303
20:18 I 498; II 15, 243
29:1 I 464

Qoheleth R.

1:1 I 482
1:6.1 I 485
1:8.4 I 404, 451; II 13, 241, 409
3:16 II 15
7:8 I 450
7:8.1 I 431; II 13
7:26 I 453
9:8 I 399
11:2 II 14
11:5.1 I 494
12:11 I 324

Ruth R.

6:4 I 431
7:7 I 498; II 15, 243

Song R.

1:3 I 420
7:14 I 452

IX. PALESTINIAN TALMUD

ʿAvodah Zarah

2:1 I 303
2:3, 7 I 383
3:1 I 419; II 12, 81, 87, 222, 400
3:8 I 222
3:11 II 451
3:12 I 381
3:13 I 381
5:11 I 82

Bava Batra

3:11 I 378
4:4 I 378
4:5 I 379
9:7 I 214-15

Bava Meṣiʿaʾ

6:6 I 378

Bava Qamma
1:5 I 377
4:5 I 212; II 73, 79, 84, 235, 397, 408
4:9 I 377
6:6 I 211-12

Berakhot
1:1 I 22
1:2 I 18
2:3 I 429; II 12, 30, 81, 239, 404, 451
2:4 I 472
2:8 I 161; II 73, 78, 235, 406
3:1 I 159-61; II 78, 212, 400
4:4 I 23, 26
5:2 I 29, 31; II 172, 400
6:1 I 8, 347-48
7:5 I 32, 347

Beṣah
1:1 I 150
1:4 I 151-52
1:12 I 285
2:1 I 151
3:4 I 154
4:6 I 151, 153
4:7 I 152

Bikkurim
2:4 I 85

Demaʾi
1:1 I 37; II 3, 74, 122
4:3 I 350, 355
4:4 I 374
4:35 I 73
6:2 I 350
6:4 I 350

ʿEruvin
1:2 I 100; II 5
2:5 I 103
2:7 I 103, 106
2:8 I 203
3:1-7 I 112
3:3 I 360
3:7 I 109, 111
4:10 I 361
7:10 I 111-12
9:3 I 113
10:4 I 121, 235
10:7 I 120
10:10 I 362
10:14 I 120

Giṭṭin
1:1, 2 I 205
1:2 I 116
4:4 I 208
8:7 I 375
9:1 I 205, 207

Ḥagigah
2:1 I 430; II 12, 36, 81, 239, 409
3:2 I 316
3:8 I 369

Ḥallah
2:1 I 76
2:2 I 77
2:3 I 48, 78
4:4 I 80-81; II 178, 400

Horayot
2:7 I 382
3:4 I 433; II 12, 81, 409
3:5 I 419

Ketuvot
1:6 I 181
1:7 I 182
1:8 I 182
1:9 I 182
5:6 I 185, 325; II 7, 29, 71, 78, 234
5:7 I 371
9:4 I 372

Kilaʾim
1:1, 5-7 I 38; II 3
2:8 I 352
3:4 I 352
5:3 I 353
5:7 I 38; II 3
6:4 I 354
9:6 I 91

Maʿaserot
1:4 I 152
2:3 I 355-56
3:4 I 61

4:2 I 70; II 4
4:4 I 71
4:6 I 72
5:2 I 76, 80

Ma'aser Sheni

3:3 I 73
4:5 I 73; II 400

Makkot

3:5 I 379

Megillah

1:4 I 157
1:8 I 326, 392
1:9 I 421, 430; II 12, 81, 239, 400, 407
4:12 I 369
3:1 I 163; II 170

Mo'ed Qaṭan

3:1 I 410, 426; II 87, 220, 234, 400
3:5 I 5, 59-60; II 6, 26, 29, 78, 84
3:6 I 158

Nazir

3:3 I 192
3:4 I 192
3:51 I 192
6:11 I 195
7:1 I 142, 197-98, 421; II 12, 81, 239, 400, 408
7:4 I 199

Nedarim

4:3 I 373
8:1 I 157
9:1 I 185
9:2 I 185-86; II 400
10:4 I 187
10:5-6 I 187-88
10:6 I 190
10:7 I 188, 190

Niddah

1:2 I 323-24
1:4 I 323-25; II 6
4:4 I 326
4:6 I 326

'Orlah

1:5 I 82
2:1 I 49
2:6 I 82
2:7 I 83

Pe'ah

1:1 I 452
3:6, 7 I 34
5:2 I 34, 349
6:2 I 36
7:6 I 35
8:2 I 73

Pesaḥim

1:8 I 63, 117
2:7 I 70; II 5, 30, 71, 234
3:1 I 363
3:3 I 120 21, 154, 222, 235
3:6 I 120-21
5:1 I 135; II 400
5:4 I 130
5:9 I 363
6:1 I 122, 131
6:2 I 122-3, 125
6:3 I 128:29, 132; II 237, 408
6:5 I 98, 130
7:5 I 241, 364
9:4 I 364
9:12 I 132

Qiddushin

1:3, 5 I 213
1:8 I 209
3:12 I 180; II 409
3:13 I 211
4:3 I 375
4:2 I 179
4:11 I 376

Rosh Hashanah

1:1 I 463
1:2 I 85
1:7 I 338; II 84
2:3 I 93
4:1 I 368

Sanhedrin

1:2 I 217, 432; II 12, 81, 87, 222, 240, 400, 404, 451

1:4 II 451
3:5 I 338
6:6 I 218
7:13 I 400; II 12, 27, 70, 199
10:4 I 455

Shabbat
1:4 I 99
1:10 I 85
2:3 I 86, 286
2:7 I 411; II 12, 31, 71, 87, 234
6:1 I 88; II 208
6:4 I 87
7:1 I 263
9:3 I 478; II 14, 30, 72, 82, 234, 394, 418
10:4 I 260
10:6 I 357
12:4 I 89-90; II 5, 178
13:1 I 91-92; 259
14:3 I 261
16:1 II 414
16:8 II 451
17:7 I 92
18:1 I 55
19:1 I 93, 95, 128; II 5, 179, 203
19:4 I 96-97
20:1 I 10, 92, 98-99; II 5

Shavuᶜot
2:1 I 220
2:5 I 220
7:4 I 338

Sheqalim
2:3 II 451
4:4 I 136
6:1 I 365
8:3 I 137
8:4 II 441

Sheviᶜit
5:2 I 39-40; II 3
6:1 I 116
8:8 I 37, 41, 43; II 4, 86, 400
9:4 I 44; II 4
9:6 I 44-45
10:3 I 336
10:4 I 336
10:6 I 336

Soṭah
1:1 I 199, 201, 204; II 67, 79, 237, 400
1:2 I 201
3:4 I 201
4:3 I 373, 432
6:1 I 202
6:3 I 199
9:2 I 11, 202
9:3 I 203
9:4 I 203
9:16 I 418-19; II 12, 120, 234, 238, 400, 412, 451
9:17 II 440

Sukkah
1:12 I 145-46
2:5 I 147
2:7 I 148-49, 367
2:8 I 55, 61
2:10 I 148
4:3 I 368, 460; II 27, 393, 418

Taᶜanit
1:1 I 156, 479; II 14, 30, 72, 82, 235, 393, 418
2:12 I 157
3:11 I 156; II 451

Terumot
2:1 I 45-48, 78; II 4, 400
4:4 I 48; II 400
4:6 I 49, 53; II 4
4:7 I 9, 53-54
4:8 I 50, 53
5:1 I 55
5:2 I 56-57
6:1, 3 I 59, 248
6:3 I 59
7:2 I 61-62
8:1 I 61-62, 374
8:2 I 61
8:4 I 63, 117
11:2 I 66-67
11:3 I 68

Yevamot
3:1 I 172
5:6 I 323
8:3 I 179
8:4 I 164

8:6 I 370
12:2 I 165-67
12:3 I 166
13:2 I 168-71; II 6, 63, 78, 400, 406
13:6 I 172
13:7 I 172, 174-75; II 400
16:8 I 177

Yoma
5:5 I 139
5:6 I 139
6:3 I 140
6:5 I 478
7:2 I 142-44; II 400
8:1 I 366
8:2 I 145

X. BABYLONIAN TALMUD

ʿArakhin
14a-b I 384
16b I 489; II 15, 90
17a I 489; II 15, 27, 72, 82, 235, 418
18a I 251
23a I 250; II 117
23b I 251
24a I 251
28a I 252

ʿAvodah Zarah
7b I 29, 71; II 72, 235, 410
9a I 317
16b-17a I 402; II 12, 199
19b I 380
23a I 303
24a I 304
25b II 434
35b I 82
45b I 222
46b I 123, 303
49a I 82
49a-b I 381
49b I 82
70a-b I 317
73b I 82

Bava Batra
10a II 13, 451
10b I 436, 491; II 15, 26, 82, 240, 396, 406, 416, 440, 451
15a-b I 486, 488
16a I 488; II 5, 23, 72, 82, 235
25a II 38; II 15, 72, 82, 235, 406
27b I 34, 378
55b I 317
55b-56a I 317
56a I 318
60a I 378
65b I 336, 379
66a I 282
66a-b I 379
67a-b I 378-79
74b I 429; II 12, 30, 71, 81, 234, 409
78b I 379
80a-b I 336
100a I 113, 213; II 78 , 148
115b-116a II 451
121b I 429; II 12, 27, 71, 81, 234
150a I 34
156a-b I 214
156b-157a I 215
157a I 216; II 66, 75, 125, 187, 312, 320, 323

Bava Meṣiʿaʾ
54a I 74
59a-b I 413, 425; II 81, 410
59b I 278-79; II 9, 12, 31, 71, 87, 222, 230, 234
82b I 378
85b I 414-15
96 I 348

Bava Qamma
15b I 377
16b I 377
25a I 332
41b-42a I 213; II 84, 214, 235, 408
45b I 377
46a I 377
55b I 377
61a-b I 211
79b II 443
83a I 213
84a I 213

Bekhorot
2a I 71
5b I 471; II 14, 71, 234, 393, 419

7a I 249
12a-b I 248
12b I 248
13a I 248
18a I 203
22b-23a I 55
23a-b I 299
29b I 383
33b I 63
34a I 66, 208; II 4, 401
34a-b I 249-50
40b I 384
42a-b I 255
42b I 164
45b I 384
47a I 370
65b II 82

Berakhot

2b I 4, 21
3a I 22; II 3, 26, 70, 76, 233
6a I 480; II 14, 27, 72, 82, 235, 417
9a I 22, 135; II 6, 22, 71, 388, 400
13a I 22; II 3, 22, 70, 230, 395, 410
13b I 23
16b I 162
17a II 451
19a I 278, 425
23a I 33
25b I 18
26 II 3
28b I 414; II 81, 120, 332, 412, 442, 451
29a I 29
29b II 3
29b I 23; II 3, 26, 78
33a-b I 29
33b I 31, II 401
34a II 3
34a I 28; II 3
34b II 451
36a I 71
38a I 66-67
43b II 32
47b I 33; II 3, 26, 70, 77, 233, 410
48b I 32
50b I 347-48
51b I 198
52a I 425
57a I 480
58a II 366
61b I 476; II 417
62a I 33; II 3, 26, 70, 77, 233, 401

Beṣah

3b I 54
4a I 49-50; II 125
5a I 75; II 120, 337
15a I 151
15b I 148; II 22, 181, 389
16a II 34
17a I 32
33a-b I 151
33b I 153
34a-b I 152
35a I 60-61, 70
37a I 154
38a-b I 152

ʿEruvin

6a II 33
7a I 85
11b-12a I 100; II 5
13b II 36
23a-b I 10
26b I 103
27a I 72
27a-b I 112
29b I 59
34b, 35a I 360
38a-b I 109, 111
39a I 109
40b I 32, 481; II 15, 23, 241, 396, 417
42b I 363
44a I 92, 361
45a-b I 361
46a I 323, 325-26
52b I 361-62
54b I 114; II 5, 28, 65, 73, 77, 149, 166, 235, 314, 321, 324
63a I 115-16; II 401
67a-b I 112
70b II 82
80a I 112
81a-b I 112
94a I 113, 214; II 187
100a I 235
101b I 362
102b I 93
103a I 122
146 I 100

Giṭṭin

4a I 205
12a I 348

21b I 207
42b I 208; II 71
45b I 383
55b-56b II 451
56a I 434; II 12, 81, 240, 416
59a II 414
65a-b I 374
80a-b I 375
82a-b I 205-206; II 76, 110, 159
83a-b I 207
83b I 206; II 401
84a I 205
86a I 205

Ḥagigah

3b I 334
5a II 443, 451
10a I186; II 72, 78, 234, 389, 393
12a II 29, 36
13a II 451
23a I 306
23b I 313
26b-27a I 369

Horayot

5a I 220
9a-b I 382

Ḥullin

13a I 383
22b-23a I 55
33b I 63, 316
34a I 317
37a I 246
38a I 246
38b-39b I 383
41b I 267
58a I 255
69b I 247
89a I 480
92a I 490; II 15, 30, 72, 82, 235, 396
116a I 96
116b I 383
120b I 66
129b I 342
132a I 247
138b I 147
140b I 247

Keritot

2b I 382

9a II 441, 451
15a I 257
16a-b I 256
17a I 91, 263
17a-b I 256
18a I 167
19a I 265
19a-b I 259
19b I 91, 263
20a I 259
23b I 267
24b I 267
25a-b I 267
25b I 268

Ketuvot

4b I 160
6a I 371
11b I 181
12a I 184
12b I 181-82; II 401
13a I 182
13a-b I 182
13b I 183
16a I 181-82
17a II 36
52a I 5, 184; II 65, 78
57a I 189
57b I 187
59b I 371
60a I 185, 323, 325; II 29
61b I 371
62b I 371
73a-b I 172; II 401
74a I 172, 189; II 351
86b I 372
101a I 184

Makkot

11b I 61
12a I 254
20a-b I 379
20b I 380
21a I 379

Megillah

3a I 430; II 241, 400, 407
10a I 399
10b I 345
16b I 480
25a-b I 369
26a I 163, 369

Meʿilah
3b I 271
4b I 271
6b I 269
7a I 273; II 153

Menaḥot
9a I 241, 274
9a-b I 242
12a I 242
12b I 240
17a-b I 240; II 407
17b I 179, 226-27
18a I 240
26a I 241, 274
28a I 222
35a I 437
35b I 480
36b I 472
47a-b I 244; II 380, 401
47b-48a I 269
48a I 233
48a-b I 63
65a-b II 451
65b I 245; II 8, 29, 79, 238, 392, 410
68a II 410
68b I 246; II 22, 79
78b I 243
78b-79a I 244
79a I 243
82a I 167
82a-b I 134; II 5
82b I 245
95a-b I 122
96a I 93
102b I 267
106b I 233

Moʿed Qaṭan
10a I 11, 163; II 65, 74, 84, 125, 151, 212, 312, 320, 323
15a I 163; II 391
19a I 11, 158-59; II 65, 74, 84, 125, 151, 212, 316, 320, 323
20a I 163; II 6, 29, 65, 116, 158, 170
21a I 5, 161; II 6
24a I 158
27a1 I 159-60

Nazir
6b I 192
14b I 195
16a-b I 192
16b I 195
18b I 194-95
19a-b I 194
20a I 194-95
28a I 196
32b I 185
47a I 195, 197
52a I 199
53a I 199
54a I 194
56b-57a I 199
62a I 189
63a I 195
65a I 326
65b I 392
66a I 331

Nedarim
20a I 436
20b II 89; II 13, 240
33a I 373
33b II 48
38a I 373
40b-41a I 379
50a I 434; II 12, 81, 240, 408
64a-b I 185-86; II 400
70b I 187
72b I 187
73b I 187
74a I 191; II 184
74a-b I 187-88
75a I 190
75a-b I 188
76a I 192
84a-b I 350

Niddah
3a I 323
6a-b I 323
7a-b I 323
7b I 325-26, 329; II 221, 401
8a I 29, 31, 41, 77, 172; II 83, 206, 401
8a-b I 323
8b I 82
9b I 323, 325; II 67, 171, 220, 361, 401
10a I 323

16b II 48
18b-19a I 345
28b I 220, 287
35a I 392
36b I 326
37a I 392
37b I 167, 326
38b I 326
47b I 329
48a I 329
48b I 326
68b I 329-30; II 391-92
69a-b I 330

Pesaḥim

3b II 451
10a I 317
14a I 117
15a I 63, 117, 119
20b I 63, 117
21a I 63, 117
25a I 476
26b-27a I 82
27a I 381
32a I 59
34b I 234
36a I 70; II 5, 71, 233
38b I 79, 81; II 97
39a I 103, 108; II 100
42a-b I 363
43a-b I 363
44a I 363
46a-b I 120
48a I 120, 122; II 401
48b I 77; II 401
52a, 53a I 44
62a I 128
62b I 130
64a-b I 363
65a-b I 363
65b I 122
66a I 122
67b I 364
68b I 122, 129; II 5
69a I 93, 129; II 237, 408
69a-b I 122
69b I 129; II 401
71b I 130
72a I 86, 98
72a-b I 130
72b I 61, 132
73a I 254
73a-b I 130
72a I 134
77a I 241, 274-76; II 65, 152-53, 314
77a-b I 243
78b I 364
81a I 199
92a I 133
93b I 132
94 I 133
95b I 364
117a I 483; II 15, 22, 72, 82, 235

Qiddushin

3a I 84
18a I 208; II 79
18b II 22, 72, 234, 393
24b I 208
26a I 34
31a I 435; II 13, 31, 81, 240, 409
32b I 409
37a I 209
39a I 209; II 64, 78
41a-42a I 364
43a II 38
69a I 210
72a II 414
73a I 209
74a I 182, 375
75a I 375
76a I 375
82a I 376

Rosh Hashanah

10b-12a I 463; II 13, 31, 82, 228, 394, 395, 419
11b I 461
14a I 85
14b I 84
18a II 451
18b I 157
28b I 235
29b II 362, 451
31b I 75; II 120, 337, 441
32a I 155; II 389

Sanhedrin

2a I 217
7a I 476
10a-b II 81
15b I 218
17b I 437; II 13, 240, 401, 407
32a II 12

32b I 410; II 404
36a II 414
45b I 218-19; II 390, 395
46a I 218
51a I 211
52a I 475; II 407
58a I 181; II 389, 393
68a I 411, 413; II 12, 31, 64, 71, 87, 113, 222-23
68b I 284; II 84, 114, 215, 222-23, 234, 411
76a I 211; II 79, 390, 393
87b I 326
88a I 199, 203
92b I 486; II 15, 30, 72, 82, 235
95b I 467; II 82, 394, 419
97b-98a I 480; II 14, 418
98b II 414
101a-b I 407; II 228, 401
105a I 456; II 13
106a I 471; II 14, 23, 234, 393, 419
110b II 13, 67
111b I 456

Shabbat

12a II 4, 27, 71, 77, 233
13b I 391
14a I 316
14b I 285
17a I 99
19b I 359
20a I 85
24a I 32
28b I 86
29a I 286
29a-b I 86
30b-31a I 451; II 241, 409
36b I 380
39a I 286
55b I 481; II 15, 23, 72, 82, 235, 396
59b I 88
62a I 89
63a I 87-88
65a I 89
94b I 10, 357-59
95a I 359
96a I 281
103a-132a I 93, 95-96
104b I 91, 263; II 5, 178
104b-105a I 89-90
105a I 263
107b I 85; II 4, 19, 71, 77, 233
117a I 100
117b I 154
124a I 154
125b I 92, 99
130a II 401
130b II 179, 203, 401
131a II 179, 395
131a-b II 5
136a I 93
137a I 4; II 64, 75, 147
137a-b I 96-98
137b I 92, 99; II 5
138a I 88, 99
141b II 64
142a I 56
147a I 89
153a I 398; II 12, 27, 64
153b I 99

Shavuʿot

12a I 254
14b I 220
16a I 399
18b-19a I 220, 259
19a I 221; II 401
28a I 196
35b I 493; II 15, 22, 82, 242
39b I 196
46a I 196
113b II 79

Soṭah

2a-b I 199
2b I 200
13b I 117
17a I 480
19b I 204
20a I 201
21b I 201
23a I 233-34
24a I 373
26a I 373
30a I 78, 316
31a I 202
42a II 38
44a I 201
45b I 203
48b I 421; II 12, 27, 71, 81, 230, 234, 331, 414
49b I 369

Sukkah

7b I 145
9a I 148
11b I 460; II 393
16a I 145
19b I 145-46; II 65, 78, 151, 159, 164, 314, 321, 324
20a I 145-4
27a-b I 10, 149, 367; II 78
27b I 147-48; II 405-406
28a I 142, 367; II 86, 120, 221, 244, 264, 405, 451
31a I 10, 149
31b II 451
32b II 451
39b I 84
40a I 85
43a I 6, 149
45a I 368
116 I 459

Ta'anit

2a-b I 156
2b I 158; II 65, 151, 314
4a-b I 156
9b I 483, 488; II 15, 30, 72, 82, 235, 406
19a I 156
25b I 157; II 58, 73, 235, 408
31a I 429
96 I 493

Temurah

11a I 255
13a I 55, 82-83
16b I 255
17a I 255
18a-b I 253
18b I 254
19a I 254
20a I 136
20b I 254
30b I 255
31a I 255
126 I 297

Terumot

34a I 61

Yevamot

14a I 96
15a I 85
16a I 334-36; II 12, 86, 199
17a I 180
26a I 370
28a I 172, 370
29b I 187
34a I 179
34b I 184; II 7, 71, 78, 234
36b I 372
41a I 172
46a I 134, 180, 245; II 5, 7, 19, 71, 78, 234, 409
48a-b I 181; II 393
60b II 7
61b I 170, 211; II 79, 390, 393
70a I 179; II 7, 26, 71, 78, 234, 397
78b I 179
79b I 164
80a I 4, 163-65, 329
81a I 370
82b I 370
83b I 370
84a I 255, 370
85b I 210
89b I 4, 168, 171; II 33, 63, 116
104a-b I 165-66
105a I 166; II 442
107b I 168
108a I 168-69; II 67, 170, 401
109a I 172
110a I 172; II 401
120a I 177

Yoma

49a I 138; II 38
39b II 451
47b I 233-34
53a I 116
53b I 365
54b I 487-88; II 5, 30, 72, 82, 406
58b-59a I 139
59a I 140
64a I 234
66b I 141, 178; II 6, 221, 256, 260, 405
70a-b I 142
70b I 143
73b I 366
78b I 366
80a I 145; II 33, 116
82a I 476

Zevaḥim
2a I 222
3a I 279
5a I 222
8b I 224
10a I 222, 226
10a-b I 224
10b I 236
11a I 130
11a-b I 225
13a-15b I 382
28a I 226
29a I 227-28, 272; II 390
29b I 226, 274
31b I 226
35a I 226
40a I 140
47a I 383
52b I 140
66b I 229
67a I 229, 231-32; II 5
73a I 49, 54
74a I 234
76b I 233; II 395
76b-77a I 233
77a I 233
77b I 234
77b-78b I 234
79b-80b I 235
80b I 308
81a I 236, 239
82a1 I 236
83a I 236
85b I 370
89b-90a I 269, 274
103a I 136
104a I 274-75
107b I 399
115a I 222

XI. GENERAL INDEX

Aaron
Death of sons, I 473-74; II 14, 72, 229, 394, 408
Learning Mishnah, I 113-14
Abba Eleazer b. Dolai, I 322; II 384
Abba Ḥanin, I 36, 365; II 254, 260
Abbahu, R., II 177
Marriage, I 170- 71
Prayer, new daily, I 25-26
Rain, power of, I 156
Abba b. Kahana, R., I 492
Abba Judah, I 431-32
Abba Saul
Disciple and Yoḥanan ben Zakkai, I 396; II 228, 238, 241, 384
Early views, II 251, 281, 344
Forms II 32
Abba Siqra, I 433-34
Abba Yosah b. Dostai, R., I 349
Abba Yudan, II 2
Abihu, I 114-16; II 64, 230, 407
Abin, R., I 198
Abraham, I 438-39
Abṭalion, I 115; II 42
Forms, II 42
Ritual pool, I 321; II 197
Academies
Scholars following, I 408-409
Torah transmitted, I 419-20
Accident, Goat sent away, I 10, 140; II 5
Admon, II 390
Agricultural rules, II 287-88
Agricultural taboos abroad, I 209; II 7, 162-63, 168, 214
Agrippas, I 472
Agrippas II, II 253, 282, 384
Aḥa, R.
Heifer rite, I 302-303
Hides, I 43
Repentence, I 478
Shemaʿ, time of reading, I 21
Aḥai, R.
Shemaʿ, I 4, 21
ʿAkhnai
Excommunication, I 422-27
Oven of, I 12, 131, 278, 339, 422-27; II 9, 12, 21, 25, 31, 69, 71, 190, 206, 234, 260, 263, 275, 284, 344, 411
Akko, II 439
Albeq [Albeck], Ḥanokh, I 14, 16
Animals for altar, I 136, 232
Courtyard validity of, I 106
Dough offering, I 78
Grapecluster, place of eating, I 62
Heave offering, I 64-65, 67, 314, 316, 356, 500
Heifer rite, I 302, 304-305, 307

Ketuvah and dedicated goods, I 250
Liability for damages, I 212
Metal vessels, cleaning, I 281-83
Nazir and vows, I 193
Objects, clean and unclean, I 276
Sabbath and festival, I 99, 109, 112
Sacrilege, I 273
Tithes, I 152, 352
Tomb unclean, I 292, 301
Vows, releasing, I 186
Aleksandrov, G.S., "The Role of ʿAqiba in the Bar Kokhba Rebellion," II 422-436
Alexander Jannaeus, I 90
Alon, Gedaliah, II 428-30, 435
Altar
Immersion not needed, I 11, 369-70
Sayings when leaving, I 10, 368
Sprinkling, I 10, 139; II 5
Wood for, I 428
Amalekites, I 467-71; II 14, 232, 245, 417, 419-20
ʿ*Am Haʾareṣ*, I 32-33; II 1, 3, 26, 70, 164, 233, 252, 400, 410
Bar Kokhba rebellion, II 429, 435
Daughter of, I 43
Ammon and Moab, Tithes, I 332-35; II 12, 31, 70, 141, 199, 342, 345, 347
Amraphel, I 438-39, 441
Animals
Cattle for altar, I 135-37; II 63, 74, 105-106, 150-51
Offspring in pit, I 4, 154; II 6, 19, 68, 182, 211, 338, 363-64, 372
For Sacrifice, I 135-37; II 5, 75, 311
Slaughter for Passover on Sabbath, I 4, 130, 132, 363-64; II 5, 8, 19, 65, 372
Slaughter of dying animal, I 246-47; II 8, 20, 69, 188, 374
Sin offering, I 232-34
Anointing
Hide, seventh year oil, I 9, 41; II 3, 86
Vessels, I 83
Anonymous law, I 13
ʿAqavyah b. Mehallel, II 32-34
ʿAqiba, R., I 2, 6, 8, 346; II 89-91, 120, 228-32, 234, 236
Aaron, death of sons, I 474; II 229
Academies, I 410
Acts in a single category, I 6
Ammon and Moab tithes, I 334
Animals altar, I 135-37; II 19, 63, 74, 105
Asherah, cutting, I 221-22; II 230, 389
Atonement, II 127, 210
Attending scholars, I 437
Bar Kokhba rebellion, II 422-36
Barleycorn, bulk of bones, I 198-99
Blood blemished, I 236, 238; II 21, 152
Blood of corpse, Nazir unclean, I 6
Blood sprinkling, I 6, 244; II 104, 292
Circumcision and Sabbath, I 6, 93-94; II 147, 179, 199
Circumcision of proselyte, I 180; II 234
Cleanliness, Temple court, I 220-21
Clusters, field defective, I 6; II 18
Continual sacrifice, I 142-43
Corpse between two cities, I 202-203
Corpse, neglected, I 430; II 20, 186
Corpse unclean, I 287-89
Court of twenty-three judges, I 6
Courtyard, validity of, I 100-102, 104-105
Covenants, I 471-72
Cucumbers and sorcery, I 399
Deathbed, I 410-16
Decline of generations, I 394-95
Despised by Eliezer, II 237, 408
Disciples and Yoḥanan ben Zakkai, I 397, 431
Discipleship, II 254, 258, 260-63, 269
Disfigurement, I 180-81
Distant journey, I 6, 132-34; II 26, 388
Divorce, I 103, 206-207, II 64, 110-11
Dough offering, I 76-77, 79; II 337
Dough, unfit, I 70; II 228, 233
Early life of Eliezer, II 296-98, 307-308
Eliezer ill, I 403-406, II 31
Emancipation, I 208
Etrog, I 84-85; II 63, 98-99
Eunuch, I 7; II 182
Eunuch and *ḥaliṣah*, I 164-65
Excommunication, I 423-26; II 221, 346, 366
Exodus, I 459, 464-65; II 27
Faith, I 421; II 230
Father-mother relationship, I 181
Fish, II 137

Fleece offering, II 135
Forms, II 33-38, 47-49, 51-52, 58-59, 62
Fourth year fruit, II 135
Generation of the wilderness, I 453-54; II 22, 157, 294
Grace after meals, I 31
Grain, liability of tithes, I 71
Grape clusters and poor, I 34-36
Grave area, II 137
Grave stone unclean, I 287-89; II 24, 192
Guilt offering in own name, I 12
Guilt offering, suspensive, I 264, 266
Ḥaliṣah, I 6, 165-67; II 19, 182, 339, 389
Ḥallah sent abroad, II 176
Hallel, reciting, II 135
Ḥameṣ and heave-offering, I 117-18; II 149
Hands, use of, I 33; II 233
Harlotry, I 211; II 390
Havdalah, II 23
Heave offering, II 135, 171, 174, 336, 387-88
Heave offering and uncircumcized priest, I 179
Heave offering, eating not giving, I 6, 58-60
Heave offering, neutralizing, I 4; II 145
Heave offering, quantity, I 9, 48; II 18
Heave offering, repaying, I 6, 58-60; II 174
Heave offering and *se'ah*, I 499-500; II 336
Heifer rite, I 6, 7; II 21, 194
Heresy, I 401-402; II 199
Hide, seventh year oil, I 41, 43; II 73
Hospitality, I 407
Itch inside itch, II 137
Ketuvah, II 109
Lambs for sacrifice, II 28
Lepers, I 162-63; II 227, 391
Leprosy signs, I 298-99
Levir and vows, I 7; II 19
Liability for damages, I 211-13, 217; II 187
Lost goods, I 431
Lulav, I 6, II 388
Man like agent II 29, 229
Maṣṣah with fruit juices, II 71
Meal offering, I 246
Men of the Great Synagogue, I 451
Milk and honey, I 473
Mishnah, learning, I 114; II 28, 235
Mourning, I 419
Nazir, uncleanness, II 69, 186, 389
New Year, additional service, I 6
Neutralizing mixed produce, I 49-51, 53
Objects, clean and unclean, I 277-78, 280, 286-87; II 25, 29, 191
Ox that gores, I 212; II 235
Palestinian produce taken abroad, I 6; II 18, 26
Passover not from tithes, I 134; II 28, 227, 388
Passover offering, roasting, I 134-35; II 22
Passover and Sabbath, appurtanences, I 6, 10; II 68, 180
Pe'ah, liability for, I 34; II 28, 335
Pigeon racer, testimony of, II 64, 217
Poor and grape clusters, I 34
Power of rain, I 157
Prayer, length of, I 23-24, 26; II 28
Prayer, routine prayer, I 6; II 172
Property given temple, I 6
Proselytes, I 448-49
Relations and influences, II 399-421
Releasing vows, II 184
Remarriage, evidence of witness, I 176-77; II 183
"The Role of ʿAqiba in the Bar Kokhba Rebellion," II 422-36
Sabbath lamp, wick for, I 6, 86-87; II 18, 178
Sabbath observances, II 265
Sabbath and Passover, I 122-29; II 68
Sacrilege, I 268-73
Samaritan, bread of, I 9, 43-43; II 100-102
Sanctities, burning, I 6; II 28, 63, 118-19
Semen, issue of, II 137
Seven lambs sacrificed, I 6
Seventy languages, I 437
Sexual behavior, I 436-37
Shofar verses, I 154-55; II 389
Sin, I 495
Sin and guilt offering, I 6
Sin offering and Passover, I 227-28
Sin offering, individual actions, I 256-58; II 292, 298

Sorcery, I 400, 403; II 27, 199, 204, 217
Soul and might, I 475
Succoth, I 458-59
Study with Eliezer and Joshua, I 432-33
Suppressed traditions, II 205, 218, 220-22
Taboos abroad, I 208-209
Thank offering slaughter, I 243
Tiara on Sabbath, I 88, 337-38; II 64, 73-74, 208
Tithe, I 6, 71; II 25, 106-109, 175, 199, 227
Tithe, dead, given from it, I 73; II 206, 388
Torah and masters, I 403-406; II 31
Torah, power of, I 430
Torah, transmitting, I 420
Traditions, I 6-8; II 96, 99-103, 114-15, 121-22
Trees, New Year date, II 135
Unawareness, creeping things, I 7; II 29, 390
Unclean sacrifices, burning, I 137; I 28, 63
Vows, levirate marriage, I 187-89, 191
Water of bitterness, I 200-201
Wild animals, judged, I 217; II 25
Woman drinking against wishes, II 20
Words on heart, I 22
World to come, I 453-55, 457
Zab, I 329-30
Zab, examination, I 329-30; II 22, 156
ʿAqiba b. Joseph, I 420
ʿAqilas the proselyte, I 428, 471
Aristeus, II 306
Arqablin, I 108
Ark in exile, I 365-66
Arrest, heresy charges, I 400-403; II 12, 31
Arum, I 39-40; II 3, 18, 173, 335, 353, 372
Asherah, cutting, I 221-22, 380-81; II 72, 232, 389, 397
Ashes, corpse cremated, I 13, 287; II 9, 21, 69
Heifer ashes mixed, I 13, 309; II 10, 25
Sin-offering ashes, unclean jar, I 13, 311-14, 345; II 10
Ashqelon, hanging women, I 218-19; II 118, 132
Aspamia, I 67
ʿAṣṣeret, I 158; II 6, 27
Mourning, I 11, 158; II 6
Assi, R., II 179
Attribute of Justice, I 494

Ba, R., I 431; II 404
Baba b. Buṭa, II 118
Baba ben Buṭi, I 267
Bacher, Benjamin Zeʾev (Wilhelm), II 253, 282
Bailment, I 377-78, 380; II 55, 137
Baking, Sabbath and Festival, I 9, 85-86, 150-51; II 5, 16, 22, 24, 41, 55, 68, 71, 178-79, 229
ʿEruv, money for, I 10, 111-13; II 5, 28, 74
Baker's shelf, I 13; II 9, 21, 69, 342
Balsam, I 40; II 4, 206
Bar-Derom, II 433
Bar Kappara, I 73
Bar Kokhba War, II 296, 298, 422-34
Barley, II 71
Tithes, I 71-72; II 4, 22, 71, 228, 410
Barleycorn, bulk of bones, I 198-99, 341-44
Baron, Salo W., II 258, 423
Baroshi, II 254
Bar Qappara, II 258
Baruch ben Neriah, I 478
Baruch the Scribe, II 306
Bassfreund, J., II 252
Bath towels, I 9, 39; II 3, 23, 64, 75, 144, 169
Beam of a balance, II 43, 141
Bed, I 13, 283-84; II 67, 76, 315
Sign of mourning, I 4, 159-60, 163; II 6, 26, 29, 116, 138
Beehive, I 9, 336; II 11, 67, 75, 112-13, 131, 157, 294, 311, 319
Sabbath, extracting on, I 335-37; II 22, 128, 133
Beer, Georg, I 15
Benai Beraq, I 409
Ben ʿAzzai
ʿAmHaʾareṣ, I 33; II 410
Decline of generations, I 394
Reproof, I 488
Torah, taught daughter, I 201-202; II 186
Water of bitterness, I 200-202

Ben Baṭṭiaḥ, I 435
Ben Bukhri, II 384
Ben Dinai, I 278
Benediction, I 493; II 43
  Eighteen benedictions, I 31-32, 155-58; II 3, 343, 360, 365, 375
Ben Kalba Shavuʿa, I 438-39, 444
Ben Megusat, I 164
Ben Pantera, I 403
Ben Satra (Sutra), I 90; II 178
Bet Shearim, II 75, 98
Ben Sira, I 397; II 302, 304
Ben Ṣiṣit Hakkeset, I 438-39, 444
Ben Stada, I 90; II 256
Ben Stara, I 404
Ben Zoma, I 196, 394
Berekhiah, R., I 497
Berekhiah b. Abba b. Kahana, R., I 450
Beror Ḥēl, I 409
Betar, I 436; II 431
Bird, whole offering, I 5, 228-31; II 7, 20, 69, 188, 340
Bitter-herb, I 7, 103, 105-107; II 99, 102, 136, 289, 297
Black, Matthew, II 258
Blood, childbirth and immersion, II 138, 387
  Corpse, Nazir unclean, I 6, 198; II 7
  Gentile woman, II 56
  Mixed, II 58, 290, 313, 328, 372
  Sacrificial blood blemished, I 12, 234-40; II 8, 20, 24, 58, 65, 128, 133, 152-53, 162, 395
  Sprinkling, I 5, 6, 122-28, 138-41; II 5, 19, 21, 65, 74, 104, 161, 168, 200, 289, 291, 314, 323
  Unclean, II 43
Boards, loosely fastened, I 14, 313; II 10, 25, 70, 195, 341
Bokser, Ben Zion, II 259-61, 278, 283
Boundary stone, I 409
Braunschweiger, M., II 250, 280
Breach is neutral, I 10, 113; II 5, 19
Bread
  Sabbath baking, I 9, 85-86, 150-51; II 4, 6, 22, 24, 337
  Of Samaritan, I 9, 41-43; II 73, 86, 102-104, 130, 138
  Sanctified if offering blemished, I 12, 243; II 8, 20, 66
Breast feeding, I 6, 184-85; II 6, 29, 71, 234, 373
Bride, dancing, II 36
Brine, tithe money for, I 72; II 14
Brothers, sisters, levirate marriage, I 172-76, 370
Brüll, J., I 90; II 251, 254, 381

Caperberries, I 6, 71; II 4, 68, 336, 357 360, 373
Captivity, wife and ransom, I 5, 184; II 6
Carob, II 135
Carrion, I 14, 330-31; II 11
Caesarea, I 412, 416
Canaan, I 476
Cattle
  Feed and thorns mixed, I 11, 38; II 3
  Feeding cattle of another, I 372
Chajes, H. P., II 257
Cheese, *ʿOrlah* sap, I 4, 82; II 4, 28, 68, 177
Child
  Shirt of , I 13
  Who is, II 54
Christians, II 330-341, 365-67
  Bar Kokhba rebellion, II 422-36
  Heretical charges, I 400-403; II 249-273
Circumcision, II 144, 247, 249
  Covenants, I 471-73; II 71-72, 229, 253
  Heave offering, I 60, 179; II 1, 71, 234
  Proselyte, I 180; II 6, 19, 234, 236
  Sabbath, instruments, etc., I 4, 6, 93-98, 471-73; II 5, 19, 28, 37, 64, 68, 75, 147-48, 163, 291, 314, 346, 360, 362-64, 372-73
  Slaves, I 2
Cistern, I 5, 322
City of gold, Sabbath, I 9, 14, 88-89, 337-38; II 4
Cloth, used for other purposes, I 5, 286; II 9, 25, 191
Clouds of glory, I 458
Clusters, field defective, I 6, 34-36; II 4, 18, 172-73, 200
Cock-partridge, I 12, 247; II 8, 24, 69, 188, 201, 343
Comb and water-cooler, I 12, 339
Combed wool, I 13
Comfortors of Yoḥanan ben Zakkai, I 446-48; II 13, 241

Commandments
Covenants, I 471-73
Observed abroad, I 12, 209
Continual sacrifice, I 142-44; II 5, 74
Coriander, tithes, I 71-72; II 4
Corpse, I 187-98; II 9, 11, 22, 66, 70, 156, 166, 273
Ashes when cremated, I 13, 287; II 9, 21, 69, 341
Bearers by portico, I 13
Between two cities, I 202-203
Blood of, I 6, 198
At entrance, II 42
Heifer-rite, I 5, 311; II 10
High Priest and neglect, I 11, 197; II 69, 340
Living being, flesh from limb, I 6, 344; II 77
Neglected, I 11, 197-98, 430-31; II 7, 20, 58, 69, 186, 201, 214, 239, 374, 389
Olive and Bulk of, I 290-91, 293-95, 340-44; II 10, 12, 66, 155
Tithe, given from, I 73; II 4, 71, 206
Unclaimed, breaking neck of heifer, I 6, 202-203; II 10
Worm from, I 13, 287; II 9, 21, 191-92
Cosmetics, I 10
Sabbath, use on, I 9, 357-59
Court of Twenty-three judges, I 6, 217; II 8, 25, 69
Courtyard
Breach, public domain, I 10, 113; II 5, 19
Sweeping, I 151-54; II 6, 28, 65, 151
Validity of, I 100-108, 378-79; II 5, 19, 68, 99-100, 117, 130, 136, 288-89, 318, 327, 338
Covenants, I 471-73; II 14, 24, 72-73, 229, 254, 417
Creation, shape of world, I 485-88; II 14, 419-20
Cremation, I 13, 287; II 9, 21
Cucumbers and sorcery, I 399-400; II 12, 70, 199, 217, 411-13

Dama b. Nethina of Askelon, I 451
Damage, liability for, I 211-13, 217-18, 376-77; II 26, 187, 201, 214-15
Date-honey, I 4, 66-70; II 4, 18, 64, 76, 146-47, 170, 206, 229, 314, 372
Dathan, I 470
Daughter, and Torah, I 201-202; II 7, 27, 69, 111-12, 186
Davies, W. D., II 333
Day of Atonement, I 495-97; II 243, 299
Drinking, I 10, 144-45; II 116, 131, 136, 308
Leniencies, I 10; II 132, 210, 312
Mourning, I 158
Prohibitions, I 366
Suspensive guilt offering, I 259-60, 262-63, 265, 267
Temple rites, I 138-41, 144; II 5, 134, 139, 289, 274
Dead, given from tithe, I 72-74; II 4, 13
Death
Firstling, I 12, 248-49, 345
Redemption-lamb, I 12, 248-49, 345
Deathbed, I 410-17, 419-20, 409-16, 418-19; II 12
Death scenes, I 409-19; II 31, 71, 120, 234, 236-38, 346, 400, 403, 411-15
Decline in generations, I 394-95; II 11, 27, 70, 198, 201, 222, 342, 416
Decline of sages, II 152
Dedication of goods, II 55, 106, 112, 131, 139, 189, 201, 292, 311, 340
Ketuvah, I 5, 250-52; II 20, 27, 64, 66, 153, 215, 292, 314, 319, 328
Derenbourg, J., II 251, 281, 422, 431
Dill, tithes, I 9, 71-72; II 4, 24, 68, 336, 357, 360
Dirt, grave-area, I 13, 297-98; II 29, 66, 75, 128, 133, 137, 293, 313
Disciples, I 180
Disfigurement, I 180
Distant journey, I 6, 132-33; II 5, 26, 68, 181, 200, 338, 354, 374, 388, 391
Ditch, lattice work, I 9
Divorce, II 55, 138, 166, 192, 237, 319, 339
Advanced notice, I 203-204
Dedicated goods, I 250-51; II 8, 20, 66, 138
Get from abroad, I 204-208, 370, 372-75; II 7, 24, 152, 314
Limitations, I 205-208; II 7, 20, 64, 76, 110-12, 127, 131, 138, 289-90, 311, 329
Mamzerim, I 207-208
Priest son of divorcee, I 60
Remarriage and levir, I 171-76; II 24
Two brothers and two sisters, levirate marriage, I 172-76

Dogs, I 13, 303-304; II 201, 343
Domitian, II 256-57, 367
Dosa b. Harkinas, II 119, 384
Forms, II 34, 48
Tithes, I 334-35; II 199
Dosetai b.R. Yannai, II 254
Dositheus of Kefar Yatmah, II 45, 384
Dough offering
Clean and unclean, I 9, 79-81; II 4, 63, 74, 95, 122, 287, 375, 388, 392
Designated when, I 119-21; II 5, 26, 63, 103-105, 135, 291, 310
Liability to, I 9, 77, 357; II 4, 200, 233
Passover, unclean on, I 8, 119, 120-21; II 5
Measure, I 48, 76-79; II 4, 24, 65, 68, 150, 164, 176
Produce from abroad, I 76-79; II 4 18, 166, 337, 357
Thank offering cakes, I 7, 81; II 4, 83, 97-98, 123, 129, 135-36, 207, 288, 310, 317, 372
Drinking, Day of Atonement, I 10, 144-45; II 116
Driver, Sam, II 422-36
Dubnov, S., II 422-23

Edersheim, A., II 257
Egg, born on festival, I 4, 150, 339; II 19, 65, 74, 125, 132, 136, 155, 210
Egypt, exodus, I 463-67; II 71
Eight, and seven, meaning of, I 480-81
Eighteen benedictions, I 31-32, 155-58; II 3, 343, 360, 365, 375
Eleazar
Guilt-offering, substitute, I 8; II 20, 28
Liquids, re *Zab*, I 8
Meal offering, I 241
Eleazar b. ʿArakh, R., I 1; II 376, 384
Comfortor of Yoḥanan ben Zakkai, I 447
Disciples and Yoḥanan ben Zakkai, I 395-96
Early life, II 298, 302, 344
Early views, II 251
Righteousness, I 491
Torah and masters, I 404
Eleazar b. ʿAzariah, I 1; II 97, 118, 120, 130, 187, 228, 242, 384-85, 412
Ammon and Moab tithes, I 332-35
Circumcision and Sabbath, I 95
Deathbed, I 416; II 413
Decline of generations, I 394
Dedication of property, II 72, 112
Divorce, conditional, I 206-208; II 110-11
Early life of Eliezer, II 298
Forms, II 33
Illness of Eliezer, I 403-406; II 31, 228
Hospitality, I 407
Ketuvah and dedicated goods, I 252
Liability for damages, I 211-12
Liturgy, I 30
Metal vessels, cleaning, I 284
Mourning, I 417-18
Nazir and thank offering, II 207
Rain water, I 484
Rome and Jews, I 451
Shemaʿ, reciting, II 172
Shoe on last, II 64, 113
Suppressed traditions, II 218
Tithes, I 37; II 99, 345
Torah and masters, I 403-405
Water of bitterness, I 200
World to come, I 455
Zab, I 330; II 198, 206
Eleazar b. Dama, heretics, I 452
Eleazar b. Diglai, II 384
Eleazar b. Ḥarsom, II 258
Eleazar b. Ḥisma, II 384
Eleazar b. Perata, II 384
Eleazar b. Judah, II 384
Eleazar b. R. Ṣaddoq, II 384
Forms, II 33, 170
Mourning, I 163
Prayer in danger, I 25
Ritual pool, I 322
Eleazar b. Shammuʿa, II 250
Eleazar b. R. Simeon, R., I 251; II 117, 258
Eleazar the Modite, II 242, 384
Amalekites, I 467
Grapeclusters, I 489
Righteousness, I 490
Sins, I 480
Eliezer b. Jacob, I 1, 2n, 9, 353; II 100, 116, 384
Corpse between two cities, I 203
Arqablin at Passover, I 108
Sins, I 481
Eliezer b. Joshua, I 407
Eliezer b. Shammuʿa, I 1
Eliezer b. R. Yosé, I 209

Elijah, I 423
Elisha, I 452
Elisha b. Abbuyah, II 384, 409
  Heretics, I 452
  Torah, powers of, I 429-30
Eltester, Walter, II 257
Emancipation of slave, I 208-209; II 71
Enelow, H. G., I 428
Ephraim, I 476
Epstein, Y. N., I 3
  Animals for altar, I 136-37
  Arms on Sabbath, I 87, 90
  Barleycorn, bulk of bones, I 199
  Beehive and *prosbul*, I 337
  Blood blemished, I 238
  Bread baking on Sabbath, I 86
  Circumcision and Sabbath, I 96
  Cleanliness and uncleanliness, I 288, 294, 298, 302
  Cleanliness, Temple court, I 220
  Cock-partridge, I 247
  Courtyard, sweeping, I 153
  Courtyard, validity of, I 101
  Decline of generations, I 395
  Distant journey and Passover, I 133
  Dough offering, I 48, 357
  Dough offering, produce from abroad, I 76-77, 79, 81
  Early views, II 249
  Etrog, I 84
  Firstling, I 249-50, 345-46
  Forms, II 43-44, 47, 49
  Geṭ from broad, I 205, 374-75
  Grapecluster, I 62
  Guilt offering, I 261
  Ḥaliṣah at night, I 166
  Ḥameṣ and heave-offering, I 118-19
  Hanging as punishment, I 219
  Heave offering, I 65, 317
  Heifer rite, I 302, 304-305, 308, 346
  Ketuvah and dedicated goods, I 252
  Levirate marriage, I 174-76
  Levirate vows annulled, I 189
  Liability for damages, I 212
  Mamzer, purifying, I 210
  Marriage and minor, I 168
  Meal offering, I 241
  Menstrual period, I 323-24
  Midras and *maddaf*, I 313, 315
  Mishnah, learning, I 114
  Nazir and vows, I 193, 196
  Neutralizing mixed produce, I 53, 58
  Objects, clean and unclean, I 276-77, 279, 281-82, 284-86
  ʿOrlah sap and cheese, I 82
  Passover and sin offering, I 222, 364
  Peace offering, progeny of, I 254
  Power of rain, I 156
  Property, bequeathing, I 214
  Remarriage, evidence of witness, I 177
  Ritual pool, I 322-23
  Sabbath and festival, I 99, 110, 113
  Sabbath and Passover, I 126, 131, 359
  Sabbath, scratching flesh, I 90
  Shemaʿ, time of reading, I 20
  Sin offering and Passover, I 226
  Sin offering, individual actions, I 258, 358
  Slaughter of dying animals, I 247
  Sterility, I 329
  Suspensive guilt offering, I 268
  Taboos abroad, I 209
  Temple rites, I 139
  Sacrifices, I 143
  Sukkah, cone shaped, I 145
  Tithe, dead given from, I 74; II 206
  Tithes, liability for, I 71
  Torah taught daughter, I 202
  Vows, releasing, I 186
  Weaving on Sabbath, I 91
  Wife warned, I 202
  Witness, I 338
  Zab, I 330, 332
Epstein-Melamed, I 473
Escape of Yoḥanan ben Zakkai, I 433-34, 434-35; II 12
Estate, division of, II 55, 138
Esther, I 467
Etrog
  Like tree, I 3, 84-85; II 4, 63, 98-99, 130, 135, 288, 308, 310, 317, 374
  Tithes, I 84-85; II 4, 28
Eunuch
  Age of, I 4, 163-65, 329; II 6
  Ḥaliṣah, I 163-65; II 6, 68, 182, 338, 374
  Joshua and ʿAqiba, I 7, 163-65
Eusebius, II 432
Evidence, I 5, 202; II 20
Excommunication, I 423-28; II 238, 249-77, 342-43, 345-46, 350, 366-67, 400, 403, 410-15

Exodus
Idol crossing sea, I 450
Red Sea crossing, I 463-67
Ezra, II 305

Faith
Israel at the sea, I 421-23; II 72
Portion everyday, I 420-21; II 12, 71-72, 230, 332
Family affairs, II 187-88
Family law, II 166, 168
Farmer, pledge of utensils, I 12, 251-52; II 8, 25
Fasting, II 58
Ḥanukkah, I 4, 157; II 211
Father-mother, honoring, I 181; II 110, 131, 198, 252, 254, 289, 331
Feldblum, M. S., I 15
Fenugreek, II 54
Tithes, liability for, I 71; II 4, 162
Festival, II 163-64, 168
Animal in pit, I 4, 154; II 6
Courtyard, sweeping, I 151-54; II 6, 28, 65
Egg born on, I 4, 150, 339; II 19, 65, 74, 164
Fasting, II 55
Filters, I 98-99; II 28, 68
Following Sabbath, I 31-32
Fringe of blue thread, I 11, 158-59
Immediate Days of, prayers, I 32; II 273, 328
Lulav, appurtenances, I 6, 149
Millstone, I 11, 163; II 65, 74, 127
Observance, I 147-49; II 6, 74, 163-64, 211, 320
Pick pulse, II 136, 164
Sabbath, I 108-11; II 5, 54, 58, 83, 136, 208, 314
Sabbath separate, I 10, 108; II 5
Sacrifices, II 55
Sweeping courtyard, I 151-54; II 5, 28
Tents for, I 92-93, 99, 146-47
Field, corner, I 46, II 3
Inheritance vs purchase, I 12
Figs
First fruits, I 37-38; II 3
Mixed produce, neutralizing, I 49-56; II 3, 18, 75, 132, 135
Filter, festival and Sabbath, I 10, 98-99; II 5, 28, 68
Finger-nails, Sabbath, I 10, 89: II 4, 389
Finkelstein, Louis, II 259-63, 278, 284
Fire, I 225; II 8, 69, 187, 201
First fruits, I 37-38; II 3, 23, 64, 122-23, 132, 135, 299, 312, 319
Leᶜi, I 9, 37; II 3, 74
Firstling, I 345; II 56, 59
Blemished, I 12, 249-50
Died, I 12, 248-49, 345
Redemption, I 12, 248-49; II 7, 20, 24, 69, 188-89, 200, 340, 361
Slitting ear, I 249-50; II 8, 20, 69, 189
Violator of law of, purchase from, I 12
Fish, unclean, II 137
Flask
Mouse drinking from, I 13, 308
Water falling in, I 13, 308-10
Fleece offering, II 135
Flesh and blood in cult, I 273-76; II 29, 128, 215, 390
Flood, II 242
Forgotten sheaf, I 36, 46, 349-50, 357; II 54, 64, 135, 144, 162
Offering eaten not given, I 59-60; II 4, 313
Four brothers married to sisters, I 4, 173; II 6
Fourth year
Etrog, I 84-85; II 4
Fruit, II 135, 162, 207
Grapes, II 54
Vineyard, I 74-75; II 207
Frankel, Zekhariah, II 256-57, 269, 271, 287, 422, 431, 435
Freudenberger, R., II 259
Friday, baking bread, I 9, 85; II 4
Friedlander, Gerald, I 446; II 255
Fringe, blue thread, festival days, I 10, 158-59; II 312
Fruits
Blessing, I 30-31
First fruits and *demai*, I 37-38; II 3, 23
Poor and Sabbatical year, I 4, 39-40; II 3
Seventh-Year, gift or inheritance, I 9, 44-45; II 3, 18, 162, 336, 357

Galilee, Eliezer spent Sabbath, I 141-42
Gamaliel, R., I 2, 362, 366; II 120-21, 235
Academies, I 410
Ammon and Moab, tithes, I 334-35
Decline in the generations, I 394-95

Dough unfit, I 70
Early life of Eliezer, II 295-96, 298-99, 317
Early views, II 250-52, 259, 263-65
Etrog, I 3, 84-85; II 28, 98-99, 288
Excommunication, I 423-24, 427; II 350
Fasting, II 211
Forms, II 33, 47, 51-52, 62
Fourth year vineyard, I 75
Geṭ from abroad, I 3, 204-205; II 24, 152
Grace after meals, I 31
Grain, for tithes, I 71
Grapeclusters, I 389; II 146
Heifer rite, I 308; II 216
Hospitality, I 401-408; II 409
Israelites in Syria and tithes, I 79-80; II 337
Jar of heave offering, unclean, I 63-64; II 18
Leprosy signs, I 298-99
Levirate marriage, I 172, 174-75; II 19
Levirate, status of minor, I 7; II 64, 109, 339
Men of the Great Synagogue, I 451
Mourning, I 158-61; II 338
On that day, II 346, 349
Pickles, I 43-44; II 18
Poor traditions, II 227
Prayer, length of, I 23-24; II 28
Privy, conduct in, I 33-34
Relations and influence, II 399-421
Remarriage, evidence of witness, I 7, 77; II 183, 213
Righteousness, I 490-91
Rome and Jews, I 451
Sexual behavior, I 435
Shemaʿ, time of reading or reciting, I 3, 18-21; II 172
Sins, I 480
Sin offering, individual action, I 257; II 292
Slaughter of dying animals, I 246-47; II 20, 188
Son's wedding, I 407-409; II 12, 31, 71, 228
Study, I 441
Sukkah, I 148, 267
Tithes, I 3; II 19, 28, 176, 345
Vegetables, kinds in jar, I 7, 44; II 18, 173, 236
Virginity claims, I 7, 181-84; II 184
Gamaliel II, II 263
Bar Kokhba rebellion, II 426
Festival, pick pulse, II 136
Gentiles, wine of, II 138
Peʾah, II 135
Scroll wrappers, II 137
Gedya, I 417
Generation of the wilderness, I 453-58; II 13, 22, 67, 70, 72, 157, 166, 168, 199-200, 229, 294, 348, 374, 393
Gentiles
Bread of, I 43
Heifer of, I 13, 303
Hostility towards, II 273
Slaughter for, I 351
Tithes, I 36-37; II 3
Wine, drinking of, II 138
World to come, I 455-58; II 13, 72-73, 199, 201-202, 242, 342, 348, 367, 373
Gilead, circumcision and Sabbath, I 95, 98-99
Geṭ (writ of divorce),
From abroad, I 204-208, 370, 372-75; II 24, 290, 374
Heave offering when effective, I 11
Levirate marriage, I 172, 175
Quittance, I 11
Refusal of marriage, I 168-70
Testimony of messenger, I 3, 204-205; II 24, 65, 166, 168
Gibeah of Benjamin, I 491; II 22, 242
Gift, Seventh-Year fruits, I 9, 44-45; II 3, 18, 68
Gilat, Yitzhak D., II 249-50, 256, 266-78, 281-82, 284-86
Ginsberg, M.,
Neglected corpse, I 431
Privy, conduct in, I 33
Ginzberg, L., II 423, 425
Girl before puberty and marriage, II 56
Gleanings, I 46, 357
Offering eaten not given, I 59-60; II 4
Standing corn mixed, I 8, 349-50, 357
Goat
Falls ill, I 140-41; II 6, 31, 68, 181
Nasi bringing he-goat, I 12
Sent away, accident, I 10, 140; II 5, 338, 405
Goldberg, Abraham, I 287-88, 290, 292-94, 296-98; II 66
Golden calf, I 494-95; II 242

Goldstein, Morris, II 257
Goodblatt, David, I 408
Grace
  Abounding in, II 36
  After meals, I 31-32; II 3
Graetz,Heinrich, II 252, 256, 282
  Bar Kokhba rebellion, I 422, 425, 430-31, 433
Grains
  Liability for tithes, I 71-72
  Vegetables, sown with, I 9, 352-53
Grapeclusters, I 488-89; II 161, 163
  Defective, I 34-36; II 3, 335, 352, 357, 365
  Eating, I 61-62; II 4, 76, 146
Grapes
  Fourth year, II 54
  Heave-offering, wine from, I 4, 68-69; II 4, 74, 95, 115-16, 127, 131, 135, 287, 313
Grave area, I 5, 13, 296; II 10, 29, 56, 66, 70, 75, 128, 133, 137, 193, 341, 371
  Stone sealing, I 5, 288; II 9, 25, 69, 192, 373
  Tomb in rock, I 5, 291-92
Great Hallel, I 156
Green, William Scott, I 499-500
Guilt-offering: see Sin-offering
Guttmann, Alexander, II 263-65, 284

Haberman, A. M., I 15
Hadrian, II 259
  Bar Kokhba rebellion, II 425, 429
  Rain water, I 482, 484, 487-88
Haftarah, I 10
Ḥaggai, R., I 174
Hair, I 12, 379-80
Ḥalafta, II 384
Halevy, Y. I., II 44
  Bar Kokhba rebellion, II 423, 425
  Early views, II 257, 282-83
  Ḥaliṣah, I 175, 370; II 58
  Eunuch,I 163-65; II 6, 67,182-83,338
  Levirate marriage, I 167-70, 172
  Mamzer, I 178
  Minor, I 5, 11, 167-70; II 6, 213, 372
  Night, left foot, I 11, 165-66; II 24, 68, 182-83, 339
  Widow remarrying, I 179
  Without spitting, I 6, 167; II 6, 19, 68, 389
  Woman performing, at night, I 165-66
  Wooden sandal, I 166-67; II 65, 152, 166, 212-13, 362
Hallel, II 136
Ḥaluṣah, I 60
Haman, I 478-480
  World to come, I 469
Hamburger, J., II 251, 281-82
Ḥameṣ, II 40
  Heave-offering, I 4, 117-19, 157; II 5, 65, 149, 168, 209, 314
Ḥanan, II 43, 49, 384
Ḥanan b. Menaḥem, I 200
Ḥanania b. Teradion, I 410; II 384
Ḥananiah
  Bar Kokhba rebellion, II 426
  Heretics I 453
  Vows, releasing, I 186
  World to come, I 456
Ḥananiah b. Ḥakinai, II 384
Ḥananiah b. Ḥezeqiah, II 384
  Se'ah, overfilling, I 100
Handkerchiefs, re *Kila'im*, I 9, 39; II 3, 23, 64, 75, 144, 162, 168, 294, 313
Hands, wiping with, I 33-34; II 3, 70
Hanging, I 2, 18-20
  Man and woman both, I 12, 219; II 8, 75, 125, 132, 137, 369
  Stoning, I 12, 219; II 9, 29, 58, 66, 118, 321, 388, 395
Ḥanina
  Excommunication, I 425-26; II 234, 410, 413
  *Shema*ᶜ, time of reading, I 4, 20-21
Ḥanina b. Antignos, R.,
  Levirate marriage and halisah,I167-68
  Peace offering, progeny of, I 254
Ḥanina b. Dosa, I 395; II 384
Ḥanina b. Gamaliel, II 384
Ḥanina b. Teradion, II 254, 429
Ḥanina the Prefect of Priests, I 365-66; II 384
  Forms, II 34, 38
  Ḥameṣ and heave-offering, I 117-18
  Sanctities, burning unclean, II 106-107
  *Shema*ᶜ, time of reading, I 20
Ḥaninah, II 258
Ḥannah, I 461-62
Ḥanukkah
  Fast on, I 4, 157; II 211
  Prayers, I 31; II 3

Hard labor, II 59
Harlotry, I 210-11, 401-404; II 390, 393
Havdalah, in Thanksgiving, I 29-30; II 3, 23, 164, 172, 343, 352, 373
Heavenly echo, II 36, 161, 410
  Law, teaching of, I 116-17
Heave offering, II 5, 167-77, 174, 200
  From clean for unclean, I 9, 45-58, 66-67, 314-18, 372-73, 381; II 4, 23, 63, 68, 74, 95-97, 122, 126, 129, 135, 174, 317, 321, 327-28, 358, 388, 391
  Demai produce, I 74, 355-57
  Dough offering portions, I 76-79; II 4
  Eating not giving, I 58-61; II 4, 68, 170
  Forms, II 44, 54, 162, 259-60, 287, 310
  Grapes of, wine from, I 4, 68-69; II 115-16, 127
  Ḥameṣ, burning, I 4, 117-19; II 5, 65, 149, 162-63, 209, 287, 307, 372
  Jar unclean, I 62-66; II 4, 18
  Juices unclean, I 66-67; II 4
  Leaven in unconsecrated food, I 9, 82-83; II 4, 207-208
  Neutralizing, I 4, 9, 48-56; II 4, 64, 68, 75, 145, 163, 288, 314, 360, 372
  Olives, I 46-47, 67-70; II 4, 148-49, 162
  Olives unclean, I 319-20
  Portions, I 48; II 4, 68, 336, 353, 357, 365, 375
  Priest uncircumcised, I 60, 179; II 1, 7, 71, 397
  Produce clean or unclean, I 9, 45-58, 314-18; II 3-4, 63, 68
  Produce from abroad, I 76-79; II 4
  Quantity, I 9, 48; II 4, 18, 68
  Restoring, I 6, 58-61; II 4, 68, 174, 336-37, 353, 387-88
  Se'ah, I 499-500; II 18, 207-208, 290, 308, 336
  Slave eating, I 60-62
  Tithes, I 37-38, 355-57, 372-73; II 3
  Tithes separated, I 73; II 4
  Vessels and unclean liquids, I 318-19
  Weasel, I 6, 338
  Woman eating, I 60-62; II 4, 18
Heifer
  Age of, I 13, 302
  Ashes of, I 13, 309; II 11, 70, 195
  Breaking neck for unclaimed corpse, I 6, 202-203
  Corpse unclean, I 5, 311; II 11, 216
  Gentiles, I 13, 303
  Pregnant, I 13, 303
  Price of dog, I 13, 303-304
  Slain man between two cities, I 11, 202-203
Heilprin, Yeḥiel, II 424
Heinemann, Joseph, II 445
Henna, I 40; II 206
Heresy, I 401-404; II 11, 31, 70
Heretics, I 451-53
Herford, R. Travers
  Early views, II 256-57
  Heresy charged, I 404
Herod, II 305, 428
Hezekiah, I 404, 406
  Throne for, I 417; II 412
Hezeqiah, R., I 43
Hides, I 43, 388; II 3
  Anointed, Seventh Year oil, I 9, 41; II 4, 18, 68, 73, 86, 100-101, 135, 288, 297, 310, 327, 400
  Combed wool, I 13; II 3
Hieronymus, II 432
High Priest, neglected corpse, I 11, 197
Hillel, House of, I 3; II 88-89, 115-18, 232-33, 238
  Boundary stone, I 410
  Bread baked on Sabbath, I 85-86
  Cattle for altar, II 106
  Courtyard sweeping, I 152; II 151, 289
  Courtyard, validity of, I 100-101; II 68, 117
  Disciples and Yoḥanan ben Zakkai, I 396
  Divorce, I 204; II 183, 237, 290
  Egg born on festival, I 4, 150, 339; II 65
  Eliezer b. Hyrcanus, II 313-16, 412-21
  Etrog, I 84
  Eunuch, age of, I 4
  Faith, I 422; II 230
  Four brothers married to four sisters, I 4
  Grave area, I 297
  Ḥaliṣah and minor, I 167
  Heave offering, I 9; II 95-96
  Heave offering produce, I 46, 48; II 115-16

History of forms, II 32-49
Influences on Eliezer, II 253, 262-63, 272-73, 280, 282, 286
Ketuvah and dedicated goods, I 250; II 215
Law, teaching of, I 115
Levirate marriage, I 173, 370
Levirate vows annulled, I 190
Liturgy, I 30
Men of the Great Synagogue, I 451
Menstrual period, I 323, 325; II 171, 339
Minor, inheriting wife of, I 4; II 116-17
Minor wife, I 171
Mourning, I 163, 417-18; II 116
Nazir and high priest, II 185
On that day, II 180
Proselytes, I 450
Ritual pool, I 321
Sabbath and Passover, I 124-26, 131, 359; II 180
Sanctities unclean, burning, II 63
Se'ah unclean, I 55; II 131
Seed mixed, I 38
Sterility, I 328-29
Tithes, I 73; II 95-96, 106-108, 122-23
Traditions, II 53-68, 119
Water of bitterness, I 201
Ḥirot, I 465; II 13, 71, 228
Ḥisda, R., I 186
Hive, I 13, 279-80
Ḥiyya b. Abba, I 430
Ḥiyya b. Abin, R., I 31
Ḥiyya b. R. Ba, I 428; 407
Hole
Lamp, measure of, I 12, 277, 281; II 8, 25
Leather bottle, I 13, 281
Metal vessel, I 13, 277, 280-81; II 10, 25
Holidays, prayer, I 31-32; II 3
Honey and milk, I 474; II 76, 116
Honeycomb, I 10, 335-37; II 128, 135, 137, 313
Honor, I 396-97; II 198
Horowitz, H. M., I 192; II 256
Hoshaia, R., I 48
Hospitality, I 407-409
Holiness, I 198
Sacrifices, I 144
Water and flood, I 492
Ḥuna b. Ḥananiah, R., I 48
Hybrid, redeeming firstling, I 12; II 8, 25, 69
Hyman, A. M., I 353; II 254, 282
Hymen, testifying to lack of, I 7, 181
Hyssop, I 13-14, 315; II 11, 25, 70, 195, 341

Idolatry
Covenants, I 471-73
Object redeemed, I 12
Ilai, II 114, 413
Arqablin at Passover, I 108
Courtyard, validity of, I 101, 103, 106-107
Disciples and Yoḥanan ben Zakkai, I 399
Dough-offering, cakes of thank-offering, I 7; II 63, 74, 97
Early life of Eliezer, II 296-97, 308
ʿEruv, rulings on, I 7; II 63, 74
Festival observance, I 147; II 74
First fruits, II 64, 74, 122-24
Forms, II 33, 35, 46, 50, 58-59
Heave offering, I 46-47; II 74, 95-97
Hides, seventh year oil, II 100-101
Kor's space, I 7
Passover bitter-herb, I 7
Samaritans, bread of, II 100, 102
Seventh year produce, II 102-103
Sin offering and Passover, I 227
Stories and sayings, II 250, 254, 260
Sukkot, visit on, I 7
Suppressed traditions, II 220-21
Temple rites, II 74
Thank offering cakes, I 81; II 63, 74
Traditions of Eliezer ben Hyrcannus, I 2; II 99-103, 115, 120
Illness of Eliezer, I 403-406; II 2, 31, 228, 401, 408-409
Imma Shalom, I 114-16, 423, 427; II 240, 257, 410-11
Sexual behavior, I 435-36
Study with Yoḥanan ben Zakkai, I 441
Immersion, I 50, 52; II 71, 138
Childbirth, II 138
Temple altar, I 11, 369-70
Immersion pool, drawn water, I 56-58, 391-92; II 70
Impotency, I 11
Infant, breast feeding, I 184-85; II 6

Inheritance, II 168
Field, redemption, I 12, 384-85
Mamzer, I 178-79
Minor, I 4, 168, 171; II 131, 137
Seventh-Year fruits, I 9, 44-45; II 3, 18
Intention, rendering unfit, I 13, 305; II 127, 133, 135
Isaac, R.,
Day of Atonement, I 496
Grace after meals, I 31
Mourning, I 417
Redemption, date of, I 460
Vows, releasing, I 186
Isaac the Smith, R., I 485
Ishmael, R., II 91, 120-21, 228, 376, 382-83
Ammon and Moab, tithes, I 332
Cleanliness, temple court, I 220-21
Dough offering, II 74, 122
Early life of Eliezer, II 296
Early views, II 269-70, 286
Emancipation, I 208
Forms, II 33-34
Guilt offering, I 266
Ḥaliṣah of minor, II 213
Heave offering, I 9, 48; II 18, 336
Ketuvah and refusal of marriage, I 169; II 105, 109
Law, approval of, I 7
Menstrual period, I 326
Passover and Pentecost, I 245
Passover offering, I 134
Suppressed traditions, II 220-21
Tithes, I 476; II 199, 345
Unawareness, I 7; II 29
Water of bitterness, I 200-201
World to come, I 458
Ishmael b. Phiabi, I 394
Ishmael b. Yoḥanan b. Beroqah, R., I 121
Israel
At the sea, I 421-22
Repentence, I 477-79
Ritual pools of, I 14
Israelstam, J., I 495
Issi of Caesarea, R., I 4
Heretics, I 451-52
Issi the Babylonian, I 226-27

Jacob, R., II 127, 385
Olives, bulk and corpse, I 294-95
Olives for oil, I 67, 69
Tithes, II 64
Jacob bar Aḥa, R., I 48
Jacob b. Idi, R., II 222, 234, 238, 421
Mourning, I 417
Jacob of Kefar, I 400-402, 452
Jacob the Min, II 256
Jars
Heave offering unclean, I 62-66; II 4, 18, 141
In house *re* tent, 1 5, 291
Rain water in wine jars, I 5, 321; II 197
Sin-offering, I 13, 311-14, 345; II 21, 137
Upside-down, I 13
Jawitz, early views, II 250, 253, 282
Jeremiah, R.,
Eliezer follows Yoḥanan ben Zakkai, I 429; II 407
Excommunication, I 422, 425-27; II 234, 410-11, 413
Heave offering portions, I 48
Mourning, I 159, 161
Passover offering, I 135
Targum approved, I 430
Torah, transmitting, I 420
Water of bitterness, I 200
Jeremiah b. Abba, R., I 244
Jesus, I 90; II 103, 178
Comparing, II 302
Christianity and excommunication, II 252, 256-57, 259
Traditions and Eliezer b. Hyrcanus, II 330-34, 365-67
Virgin birth, I 403
Jesus b. Pantiri, I 400-403
Joab, II 306
Job, I 447; II 15, 235
Jonathan, R., I 492
Jonathan b. Uzziel, II 406
Targum approved, I 429
Joseph, R.,
Holiness, I 198
Redemption, date of, I 460, 462
Sacrifices, I 144
Joseph b. Peridah, II 258
Courtyard, validity of, I 102
Josephus, R.
Law, teaching of, I 115
Rain water, I 482
Josephus Flavius, II 428
Life, II 305
War I, II 305-307

Joshua, R., I 2, 6, 8, 12-13; II 228, 232
Academies, I 409
ʿ*Am ha*ʾ*areṣ*, I 32
Ammon and Moab tithes, I 333-35
Animal and offspring in pit, I 4, 154; II 19, 182, 211
Animals for sacrifice, I 135-37; II 19, 63, 65, 105-106
ʿAqiba studies with, I 432-34
Arum, seventh year, I 39-40; II 18, 173, 336
Attending scholars, I 436-37
Baking for Sabbath, I 151; II 22
Barleycorn, bulk of bones, I 198-99
Bird, whole offering, I 228-31; II 20
Blood blemished, I 235; II 29
Blood to be sprinkled, I 5; II 104
Bread of Samaritans, I 42
Breast-feeding, I 5, 184; II 29, 236
Cheese making, ʿ*Orlah* sap, I 82; II 28, 177
Circumcision, I 4, 96-98; II 19, 64, 147, 234, 239
Clean and unclean, I 338-40; II 119, 293
Cloth, used for other purposes, I 5
Comfortor of Yoḥanan ben Zakkai, I 446-47; II 241
Completion of action
Corpse, heifer-rite, unclean, I 5
Corpse, neglected, I 430-31
Corpse and olive bulk, I 340-41; II 66, 155
Corpse unclean, I 288-89; II 155
Covenants, I 473
Date-honey, I 4; II 18, 146
Deathbed, I 410, 412-13
Decline in the generations, I 394-95
Dedicate goods and *Ketuvah*, I 5; II 20, 153, 292
Disciples and Yoḥanan ben Zakkai, I 395-96, 431
Divorce, advance notice, I 203-204; II 20, 237
Divorce, conditional, I 207; II 64, 110-11
Dough offering, I 121; II 97, 388
Dough-offering unclean on Passover, I 8
Dough unfit, I 70; II 233
Early life of Eliezer, II 295-96, 298, 307
Early influences, II 250, 252-54, 259-60, 263-64, 268, 271, 277
Eliezer follows Yoḥanan ben Zakkai, I 428
ʿ*Eruv*, I 4; II 28, 117, 209, 289
Escape of Yoḥanan ben Zakkai, I 433-34; II 240
Eunuch, I 7
Eunuch and *Ḥaliṣah*, I 163-65
Evidence woman gone aside, I 5
Excommunication, I 422, 425-26; II 221
Exodus, I 464-67
Faith, I 421
Fast on *Ḥanukkah*, I 4; II 211
Festival observance, I 148
Firstling, I 248-49, 345; II 112, 292
Flesh and blood in cult, I 272-75; II 29, 65, 215
Forgotten sheaf, I 36
Forms, II 32-33, 38, 45-47, 50-52
Grace after meals, I 31
Grapeclusters, I 61-62, 489; II 416
Grapes of heave-offering, I 4
Grave-area, I 5, 294-97; II 25, 198
Guilt offering, slaughter for, I 231-32
Ḥaliṣah of minor, I 5
Ḥameṣ and heave-offering, I 4, 117-19; II 65, 149, 209-10
Hands, use of, I 33
Ḥanukkah, fasting, I 157
Heave offering, clean and unclean, I 316-17; II 65, 170, 175
Heave-offering, neutralizing, I 4, 49-50, 53-54, 66; II 18
Heave offering, *se*ʾ*ah*, I 499-500
Heave offering and weasel, I 5
Heave-offering, wine from grapes of, I 4
Heave offering, woman eating, I 60-62; II 18
Heifer rite, I 306, 308-10
Heretics, I 452
Hospitality, I 406-408; II 228
Illness of Eliezer, I 403-406; II 31, 228
Jars in tent, I 5
Jar of heave offering, unclean, I 62-66
Juices for heave offering, unclean, I 66
Ketuvah and dedicated goods, I 250-51; II 215

Ketuvah and refusal of marriage, I 168-69
Land of Israel, I 476
Leprosy signs, I 298-99
Levir and vows, I 7; II 19
Levirate marriage, I 172, 174-75
Levirate, status of minor, I 7; II 64, 109, 339
Levirate vows annulled, I 187, 189-91
Lime pot in cistern, I 5
Living being/corpse and flesh from limb, I 6
Lost goods, I 431-32
Maṣṣah from fruit juice, II 71
Meal-offering, I 5, 241-42; II 20
Men of the Great Synagogue, I 451
Menstruation, I 5, 323-28; II 22, 25, 171, 339
Messiah, day of, I 497
Metal vessels, cleaning, I 5, 281-83; II 68, 154
Midras and *Maddaf*, I 310, 312-14
Minor, status of marriage, I 5
Mourning, I 419
Mourner and *tefillin*, I 4; II 29, 212
Mourning, turn over bed, I 4; II 29
Names, sacred and secular, I 491; II 22, 242
Nazir, I 196; II 185-86
Neutralizing offering, I 48-56; II 145
Numbers, meaning of, I 480-81
Objects clean and unclean, I 286; II 29
Olive's, bulk and corpse, I 194; II 21, 66
Olives for oil, I 67-69
"On that day", I 4; II 19, 202
ʿOrlah, sap of, I 4; II 28, 337
Passover and Pentecost, I 245; II 29
Passover offering, I 135, 365; II 22, 388
Passover and Sabbath, I 10; II 68, 180
Peace offering, progeny of, I 253-55; II 153, 292
Peʾah, liability for, I 34; II 28, 172, 336
Pickles in jars, I 43-44; II 18
Poor, fruits of Sabbatical year, I 4
Prayer, Israel distressed, I 26-28
Prayer, length of, I 23-25; II 28
Priest, son of divorce, I 60-62
Privy, conduct in, I 33-34
Property, bequeathing, I 6, 214-16
Proselytes, I 448-50
Proselyte and circumcision, I 180; II 19
Punishment, warning of, I 474-75
Rain, power of, I 155-57
Rain, prayer for, I 4
Rain water, I 482-84, 487-88
Rain water in wine jars, I 5
Ransom of wife, I 184
Redemption, I 459, 463; II 30, 112, 235
Reed-pipe, I 5; II 21, 194
Relations and influences, II 404-406
Relief, how long, I 5
Remarriage, testimony witness, I 7, 177; II 24, 183
Repentence, I 477-79; II 30
Reproof, I 488
Resurrection, I 485
Righteousness, I 489-91
Righteous, prayer of, I 27-29
Ritual pool, I 321-23; II 22
Rome and Jews, I 451
Ruth and Naomi, I 497
Sabbath and festival, I 111-13
Sabbath and Passover, I 122, 124-25, 127, 129-31; II 187
Sabbatical year and fruits for poor, I 4
Sacrifice, bird, whole-offering, I 5
Sacrilege, I 272-73; II 20
Samaritans, bread of, I 42
Scratching on Sabbath, I 4; II 19
Seʾah, overfilling, I 99-100
Seed, age for sowing, I 493
Seventy languages, I 436
Sexual behavior, I 435-36; II 26
Shemaʿ, time of reading, I 417-21; II 172
Sins, I 480, 494-97
Sin offering, I 223-28; II 66, 153
Sin offering, individual action, I 257; II 292, 391
Sin-offering water, I 5; II 156, 291
Slaughter animal for Passover on Sabbath, I 4; II 19, 65, 67, 150
Sorcery, I 399; II 27, 199, 204, 217
Stone sealing grave, I 5
Study with Yoḥanan ben Zakkai, I 438
Suppressed traditions, II 205, 220-23

Suspensive guilt offering, I 259-68
Targum approved, I 430; II 239
Temple walls, I 398-99
Thank offering cakes, I 81
Thank offering slaughter, I 243-44
Threshold, I 5
Tiara on Sabbath, I 88-90, 338
Tithes, I 476-77; II 345
Tomb unclean, I 5, 291-92; II 21
Torah and masters, I 403-405
Torah, powers of, I 429-30
Torah taught daughter, I 201-202
Torah, transmitting, I 420
Traditions, I 4-8; II 57-58, 62, 120-21
Troops with banners, I 497
Two sins, liability for, I 5; II 391
Uncleanness, grades of, I 5; II 29, 196
Vegetables, kinds in jar, I 7; II 18, 173, 336
Vermin killed on Sabbath, I 85-86; II 19
Vessels, unclean, I 5, 318-19; II 22, 29, 196
Virginity claims, I 7, 181-83; II 19
Vision, I 428; II 236
Vows, releasing, I 186-88; II 29, 184, 234
Wall-projection, I 5, 295-96; II 21, 192
Water and flood, I 493; II 242
Water and mud, I 5; II 22
Water of bitterness, I 199-202
Weasel and heave-offering, I 5
Widow's son, I 434
Wife, ransom, I 5; II 65, 152
Wife, warned, I 5, 202; II 20
Window-sills projecting, I 5, 293; II 21, 192
Woman gone aside, I 5
Wooden vessels, hole in, I 5; II 191
World, creation and shape, I 485-86; II 29-30
World to come, I 454-56, 467-68, 470; II 22, 157, 200
Zab and *Zabah*, I 5, 329-30; II 22, 156, 389
Joshua b. Batyra
Eunuch, I 7
Eunuch and *Ḥaliṣah*, I 164-65; II 182
Heifer rite, I 304; II 21, 194
Joshua ben Ḥananiah [see Joshua]
Bar Kokhba rebellion, II 426, 430
Disciples and Yoḥanan ben Zakkai, I 395-96
Dough offering, designated when, I 120; II 63, 103-104
Early life of Eliezer, II 302
Forms, II 33
Neglected corpse, I 431
Produce, removal at Nisan, II 135
Sorcery and cucumbers, I 399
Study with Yoḥanan ben Zakkai, I 443
Tree, shaking of, II 137
Water and flood, I 492
Joshua b. Hyrcanus, II 384
Joshua b. Levi, R., II 412-13, 415
Grapeclusters, I 489; II 222, 234, 238
Mourning, I 417-18
Repentence, I 478
Joshua b. Peraḥiah, I 90; II 178
Joshua b. Qorḥa, R., I 284; II 386
World to come, I 455; II 67
Josiah b. R. Yannai, R., I 48
Journey, distant journey, I 6, 132; II 5
Judah, I 366; II 161-66, 190
Animal and offspring in pit, I 154; II 182, 211
Animals for sacrifice, I 233; II 75
Atonement, II 210
Beehive and *Prosbul*, I 336-37; II 67
Blood blemished, I 234, 236, 239-40
Blood, sprinkling, I 138-40; II 19
Courtyard, validity of, I 101-140, 113
Disciples and Yoḥanan ben Zakkai, I 399
Dough offering, produce from abroad, I 76-77, 80
Egg born on festival, I 150; II 65
ʿEruv, I 361; II 209
Forms, II 42
Geṭ, origin of, II 65, 152, 166
Goat falls ill, II 181
Grave area, I 298; II 66
Guilt offering, I 259-66
Ḥaliṣah, I 11, 166-67; II 65, 152, 166, 182, 212
Ḥallah sent abroad, II 176
Handkerchiefs, II 64, 75, 144
Hanging, I 219-20; II 66
Heave offering, I 318; II 64, 162-63, 170, 288
Heave offering produce, I 47; II 75
Heave offering unclean, I 66

Heifer rite, I 7, 303-305, 307-308; II 66, 216
Ketuvah and refusal of marriage, I 169
Leprosy signs, I 299-300; II 66
Levirate marriage, I 172
Liability for damages, I 212
Meal offering, I 241; II 66
Menstrual period, I 325; II 165
Millstones, I 163; II 65, 212
Mishnah, learning of, I 113; II 65
Mourning, I 158-61
Nazir and vows, 193-95; II 166
Nazir, unclean, I 11; II 65
Neutralizing offering, I 53-54; II 145
Objects clean and unclean, I 277-78, 285-86
Olive bulk and corpse, I 290-91; II 66
Olives for oil, I 68-69
ʿOrlah laws abroad, I 84; II 98
Orphan, *melog* rights, I 184; II 65, 213
Peace offering, progeny of, I 254
Property, bequeathing, I 216-17
Punishment, warning of, I 474
Ritual pool, I 322-23
Sabbath apparel, I 89
Sabbath and Passover, I 129
Sabbath laws, I 337; II 163, 187
Sacrifices, I 143; II 65-66
Sanctities, burning unclean, II 106
Seventy languages, I 436
Sexual behavior, I 435
Shemaʿ, time of reading, I 4, 20
Shofar verses, I 154-55
Sin offering, I 226-27; II 66, 154
Spinning blue wool, II 212
Suspensive guilt offering, I 259-66, 268
Temple rites, II 65, 347
Tent unclean, II 216
Thank offering, II 66
Tithes, II 64, 176
Winepress, I 354
Wooden sandals, I 11, 166-67; II 65, 152, 166
Wrappers, I 39
Judah b. Baba, R., II 161, 384
Remarriage on evidence of witness, I 176-77
Judah b. Bathyra, I 7; II 221, 291, 376, 410, 421
Academies, I 410
Anonymous law, I 13
Dough offering, designated when, I 120; II 63, 103-104
Dough offering, unclean on Passover, I 8; II 26
Early views, II 260
Leprosy signs, I 300-302; II 193-94
Passover and Pentecost, I 145
Peʾah, liability for, I 34; II 28, 172
Rain, power of, I 158
Water of bitterness, I 200-201
Judah b. Bava, I 8; II 99
Courtyard, validity of, I 102-105, 107
Judah b. Gaddish, R., II 254, 260
Tithe money for purchases, I 72
Judah b. Guria, I 116
Judah b. Ilai, R. [see Judah], I 8, 346, 366; II 87, 90, 120, 161, 280, 385
Animals for sacrifice mixed, I 234
Arum, seventh year, I 40
Beehive, II 75
Courtyard, validity of, I 101, 104-105, 107
Dough offering, produce from abroad, I 76
Egg born on festival, II 74
ʿEruv, I 361; II 74, 99-103, 148
Forms, II 45
Grapeclusters, I 35
Heave offering, I 47; II 74, 170-71
Leprosy, signs of, II 75, 293
Liability for damages, I 212; II 189
Millstones on festival, II 74
Mishnah, learning, I 114; II 149
Nazir, losing days, II 74
Orphan and *melog*, II 74
Peace offering, progeny of, I 255
Peʾah, liability, II 172-73
Rain, I 158; II 25, 151
Sabbath apparel, I 89
Sabbath and festival, I 110
Sanctities, burning unclean, II 107-109
Shoe on last, II 113
Sin offering and Passover, I 227
Temple rites, I 138; II 74
Tithe, dead given from, I 74; II 206
Tithes, fruit from abroad, II 74
Traditions of Eliezer ben Hyrcanus, I 2; II 74-75, 124-29
Weaving blue wool, II 74
Judah b. Naqosa, I 453
Judah b. Sepphoraeus, II 305
Judah the Patriarch, II 90, 170-71

Academies, I 410
Bar Kokhba rebellion, II 430
Blood blemished, I 239
Circumcision and Sabbath, I 95 96; II 179
Corpse and olive bulk, I 343
Courtyard, validity of, I 107
Decline in the generations, I 395
Early views, II 258
Excommunication, I 426-27
Heave offering, I 74
Menstruation, II 340
Metal vessels, I 283
Night watches, II 70
Olives for oil, I 69; II 129-30
Prayer, routine, II 172
Sacrifices, I 144
Shemaᶜ, time of reading, I 21-22
Sin offering and Passover, I 227
Suppressed traditions, II 221-22
Temple rites, I 138
Tent, clean and unclean, II 112-13
Tithes, II 64, 176
Justice, I 495

Kalba Shavuᶜa, I 432
Kefar Ludim, I 204
Kefar Pagi, I 273
Kefar Ṭabi, I 74-75
Ketuvah
Dedicate goods, I 5, 250-52; II 27, 153, 166, 215, 372
Orphan and rights, I 184
Ransom of wife, I 184; II 168
Refusal of marriage, I 168-70; II 67, 109
Sterile woman, I 373
Virginity claims, I 181-83
Wife warned, I 202; II 339
Key, lost, I 10, 359-60
Kezib, II 439-40
Klausner,J., II 257
Klein, S., I 409
Konovitz, Yisra'el, II 254, 282
Kor, carrying in *Kor*'s space, I 7, 103, 105-107; II 99
Krochmal, N., II 422, 425, 430

Lamb
Redemption-lamb dies, I 12, 248-49, 345; II 131
Sacrifice of, I 6, 142, 144
Lamp
Hole in, I 12, 277, 281; II 9, 24, 56, 68, 190, 341-42
Sabbath lamp, wick for, I 86-87; II 5, 19, 68, 337
Land
Pe'ah, liability for, I 8, 34; II 3
Land of Israel, I 475-76
Lattice work, I 9
Law
Anonymous law, I 13
Approval of, I 7, 337
Formation, I 1
Teaching in presence of master, I 114-17; II 5, 72, 86, 230, 407-408
Leather bottle, I 13, 281
Leaven
Cosmetics and Passover, I 10
Unconsecrated food mixed, I 9, 82-83
Leazar, R.,
Courtyard, validity of, I 107
Heave offering, eaten not given, I 59
Liability, I 144
Leazer b. ᶜArakh, I 190-91
Leazer b. ᶜAzariah, I 81
Leazer b. R. Yosah, R., I 7, 83-84
Leazer b. R. Yosi
Divorce, advance notice, I 204; II 68, 237
Water of bitterness, I 201
Leᶜi, first fruits, I 8, 37
Leniences, I 10
Leper
Sin offering, I 261-62; II 21
Tefillin, I 162-63; II 6, 71, 391
Leprosy, I 389-90; II 59
Signs of, removal, I 13, 298-302; II 10, 26, 66, 70, 75, 128, 133, 137, 156, 193, 200, 293, 313
Letter writing, I 91-92
Levi, R., I 438, 492, 496
Leviathan, eye of, I 427; II 13, 30, 71, 234, 409
Levir, I 11, 168-69, 172-73; II 24
Annuls vows, I 7, 187-88, 191; II 7, 19, 20, 339
Minor refusing, I 167-70; II 64, 138
Levirate marriage, I 174-76; II 6, 24, 68, 137, 201, 339, 360, 375
Co-wives, surviving brothers, II 55
Divorce conditions, I 206
Eunuch, I 164
Ḥaliṣah, I 167-70; II 6, 24, 152

Minor, status of, I 7, 11, 174-76; II 6, 68, 109-10, 339
Pregnancy, I 372
Remarriage to divorced wife, I 171-76; II 6, 68
Sterile woman, I 328-29
Two brothers, sisters, I 172-76, 370; II 130, 137
Vows, I 187-92; II 19
Liability
Acts in single category, I 6, 256-57, 259-61
Cutting hair, I 12, 379-80
Damages, I 211-13
Dough offering, I 9, 76-77; II 74
Neglected corpse, I 430
Ox that gores, I 212-13, 217-18
Lieberman, Saul, I 2n, 15-16
Animals for altar, I 137
Arum, seventh year, I 40
Barleycorn, bulk of bones, I 199
Blood blemished, I 238
Circumcision and Sabbath, I 97
Cleanness and uncleanness, I 289-91, 293, 296
Courtyard, sweeping, I 153
Courtyard, validity of, I 102, 107-108
Deathbed, I 410
Demai, I 37
Distant journey and Passover, I 132
Dough offering, I 121
Dough offering portions, I 78-79
Early views, II 249, 258
Egg born on festival, I 150; II 210
Etrog, I 76
Fourth year vineyard, I 75
Harlotry, I 210
Heave-offering, I 119, 318, 354-56
Heave offering eaten not given, I 60
Heave offering produce, I 46-47
Heave offering and *se'ah*, I 499
Heifer rite, I 304, 306-307, 310
Heresy charges, I 400, 403
Ketuvah and dedicated goods, I 251-52
Levirate marriage, I 175-76
Levirate vows annulled, I 190-91
Liability, I 145
Mamzer, purifying, I 178
Menstruation, I 324-26
Metal vessels, cleaning, I 284
Midras and *maddaf*, I 313-14
Nazir and vows, I 194, 196
Neutralizing mixed produce, I 53-54
'Orlah laws, I 84
Orphan, *melog* rights, I 184
Power of rain, I 157
Prayer, I 23-26, 32
Remarriage, evidence of witness, I 176
Sabbath and festival, I 111
Sabbath and Passover, I 127-28, 132
Sacrifices, I 143-44, 154
Sacrilege, I 271
Shofar verses, I 155
Sin offering, I 263, 359
Sin offering and Passover, I 225
Sukkah, I 146-47
Temple rites, I 138, 140
Thank offering cakes, I 81
Tiara on Sabbath, I 88-89
Tithes, I 67-68, 72-74, 334
Unclean sacrifices, burning, I 137
Vessels, greasing, I 83
Virginity claims, I 183-84
Weaving on Sabbath, I 91-92, 94-95, 99
Wrappers, I 39
Zab, I 332
Liezer b. Jacob, I 354-55
Mourning, II 116
Liezer the Great, R., I 7, 83-84
Lime pot in cistern, I 5, 322; II 373
Liquids
Defined, I 4, 66-67; II 4, 18, 64, 146-47, 163, 167, 170, 200, 206, 261-63, 264, 287, 293, 312, 319, 324
Zab, I 8, 330, 332; II 11, 25, 118
Liturgy of prayer, I 29-30; II 3, 132, 164, 360
Living being/corpse and flesh from limb, I 6, 340-342
Livshitz, G. M., I 438
Lost goods, I 431-32
Lost key, I 10
Lot, I 438-39
Lotus, I 40; II 3, 206
Lud, I 74-75, 204, 234; II 62
Lulav, I 149; II 140
Appurtenances of, I 6, 149; II 136, 410
Power of rain, I 156; II 6
Privately owned, I 10, 149; II 388, 392
Waving, II 136
Lydda, I 79, 333, 409, 412, 416

Maddaf, I 340; II 10, 21, 70, 341
Uncleanness, I 310-15; II 10, 21, 185
Maimonides, II 424
Make-up on Sabbath, I 10, 357-59
Male offspring, I 434-35; II 13, 25, 239, 400
Mamzer, purification, I 8, 209-10; II 7, 12-13, 29-30, 69, 186, 201
Divorced woman, I 207-208
Manasseh, I 476
Mantel, Hugo, II 258
Marinus, R., I 317
Marriage, II 166, 168
Erroneous, sin-offering, II 6, 69
Four brothers to sisters, I 4, 173, 369
Geṭ and refusal, I 168-70
Girls past puberty, releasing vows, I 11
Ḥaliṣah, performing at night, I 165-66; II 6, 19
Intermarriage, assured stock, I 12, 209-10, 375-76
Levirate marriage: see Levirate marriage
Minor and *ḥaliṣah*, I 167-70; II 6
Minor and priest, I 170; II 141
Minor, rights of, I 167-70; II 6
Minor wife, I 171; II 309
Niece and Liezer, I 170-71; II 400, 406
Priest, I 170; II 141
Property of husband, woman retaining, I 372
Refusal and *Ketuvah*, I 168-70
Remarriage, divorce valid for, I 11, 205; II 191
Remarriage, sin offering each action, I 179; II 6, 69
Remarriage, testimony of single witness, I 7, 11, 176-77; II 6, 12, 20, 24, 84, 200, 213, 339, 374
Seed, age for sowing, I 493; II 393
Sex in doubt, I 370
Status of minor, I 5, 169; II 6, 68
Sterile woman, I 11, 373
Water of bitterness, I 199-202
Woman, work for husband, I 371
Maṣṣah, II 71, 97
Mathia, R., I 410
Mattiah b. Ḥeresh, R., I 420
Meal offering, I 240 42, 245 46; II 8, 20, 133, 135, 291, 313, 320, 372, 376
Eating something not eaten, I 12, 226, 228, 241; II 8, 24
Residue unclean, I 5; II 8, 20
Meals, II 37, 54
In Sukkah, I 10
Measurements, II 267-68
Megillah, I 158-63
Meir, R., II 161-166, 190, 385
ʿAmHaʾareṣ, I 33; II 233
Arum, seventh year, I 40
Circumcision and Sabbath, I 98; II 147
Courtyard, I 113
Decline in the generations, I 394
Dough offering, I 76
Early influences, II 251
Egg born on festival, II 163, 210
Emancipation, I 208
Forms, II 42
Guilt offering, I 267-68
Ḥameṣ and heave-offering, I 117-19; II 65, 209
Handkerchiefs, II 64, 144
Heave offering, II 64, 162-63, 288
Heretics, I 452
Men of the Great Synagogue, I 451
Neutralizing offering, I 53-54; II 145
Objects clean and unclean, I 276, 286-87; II 164-65
Offering eaten not given, I 60
Olives for oil, I 67, 69
Property bequeathing, I 217
Ritual pool, I 323
Sabbath and Passover, I 130-31; II 163, 187
Sanctities burning unclean, II 107-109
Shemaʿ, time of reading, I 4, 20-22
Slaughter, II 65, 161
Suspensive guilt offering, I 267-68
Thank offering, I 243-44; II 66
Tiara on Sabbath, I 88; II 208
Torah, power of, I 430
Winepress, I 354
Melog, minor, rights of, I 11, 184; II 27, 65, 74, 125, 132, 138, 213-14
Memorial verses, I 154-55; II 6, 389
Menaḥem, R., I 174
Mendelsohn, S., II 253, 282
Men of the Great Synagogue, I 452
Menstruation, I 323-52; II 11, 25, 52, 165, 273
Sin offering, I 256-58

Women unclean, I 5, 323-25; II 11, 67, 171, 339
Messiah, II 274
Day of, I 497-98
Metal vessels, cleaning, I 281-82; II 9, 29, 154, 165, 168
Hole in, I 13, 277, 280-81; II 9, 69, 190-91, 294, 373
Purifying, I 5, 281-82; II 9, 66, 76
Meyers, Eric M., I 293
Midras, I 310-15, 388
Micah, I 491; II 242
Might and soul, I 475; II 14
Milk and honey, I 473; II 13
Millstone, I 11, 163; II 65, 74, 125, 132, 136, 212, 289, 312
Minor
Ḥaliṣah, of, I 5, 11, 167-70; II 6
Inheriting, I 4, 168, 171; II 116-17
Levirate marriage, I 174-76; II 6, 26, 109-10, 138
Marriage and divorce, I 171; II 125, 183, 191, 289
Melog, rights to, I 11, 184; II 27, 65, 74, 125, 138
Priest marrying, I 170
Status of, I 7, 11, 163, 175; II 6, 63-64, 183, 289, 318
Status of marriage, I 5, 169; II 6, 27, 130, 311
Woman annulling vows, I 186-88; II 67, 109, 138, 170
Minut, arrest for, I 400-403; II 12, 31, 70, 201, 203
Minyamin
Water of bitterness, I 200; II 203
Miriam the Palmyrean, I 195-96
Mishael, I 455
Mishnah
Before 70, II 44-53
Order of learning, I 113-14; II I, 5, 28, 65, 149, 166, 168, 235, 312, 319
Mixing, sacrifice, I 12, 234, 236-37
Moab and Ammon, tithes of poorman, I 332-35; II 11, 31, 70, 141, 234
Money pouch, I 13, 285; II 9, 21, 68, 78, 155, 165, 168, 294, 315
Moore, George Foot, II 254
Morag, Shelomo, I 15
Mordecai, I 467
Moses
Covenants, I 472
Land of Israel, I 475-76
Law, teaching of, I 116-17
Learning Mishnah, I 113-14
World to come, I 467-71
Mourning, I 158-63, 180-81, 416-19; II 1, 6, 271
Aṣṣeret, I 11, 158; II 6, 338, 346-47
Benediction, I 492
Lepers and *tefillin*, I 162-63; II 6
Slave, I 161-62; II 389
Tefillin, I 5, 158-63; II 6, 29, 400
Turn over bed, I 5, 159-60, 163; II 6, 28, 29, 118, 140, 172
Mouse, drinking from flask, I 13, 308
Mud
Crown holding water in trough, I 13, 307; II 126
Ritual pool, I 5, 307; II 21, 70, 197, 373
Mustard, tithes, I 9, 71-72; II 4, 68, 137, 336, 357, 360

Naboth, I 492; II 15, 22
Nadav, I 114-16; II 72, 407
Naḥman, R., I 66
Naḥman b. Isaac, R.,
Hands, use of, I 33-34
Reproof, I 488
Naḥum the Mede; II 384
Forms, II 37
Naḥum the Scribe, II 384
Nail, unclean, II 42
Nakdimon ben Gorion, I 439-40, 445
Names, sacred and secular, I 491-92; II 15, 22
Naomi and Ruth, I 497
Nasi, I 12
Nathan, R., II 166, 385
ʿAmHaʾareṣ, I 33
Bar Kokhba rebellion, II 433
Date-honey, tithes, I 67; II 64, 146, 163, 206
Deeds found illicit, II 64
Dough offering, I 121; II 65, 164
Early views, II 260
Excommunication, I 423, 426; II 410
Grapeclusters, eating of, II 76, 146
Heretics, I 452
Objects, clean and unclean, I 282, 285; II 66, 76, 154-55, 159, 165
Olives for oil, I 68
Offering eaten not given, I 60, 62
Ransom of wife, I 184; II 65, 152

Sukkah cone shaped, I 145-46; II 65, 76, 159
Tithes, II 76
Nathan b. R. Joseph, R., I 33
Nazir
Barleycorn's bulk of bones, I 198-99; I 185-86
Blood of corpse, unclean, I 6, 198; II 7
High priest, I 197-98; II 19-20, 69, 185
Neglected corpse, I 11, 197-98, 430-31; II 7, 69
Unclean, II 58, 320
Unclean during sacrifices, I 11, 192-97; II 7, 19-20, 69, 185, 389
Unclean, loss of days, I 11, 192-97; II 7, 24, 69, 74, 125, 127, 132, 293, 312, 369
Unclean end of period, I 11, 192-95; II 24, 65, 138
Vows, I 192-97; II 24, 65, 69, 74, 125, 166, 328
Wafers for dough offering, I 81; II 63, 288
Necklace, broken, I 13, 387
Nehardea, I 176
Nehemiah
Punishment, warning of, I 474
Succoth, I 458
World to come, I 456
Nehemiah of Bet Deli, R., I 176
Neḥuniah b. HaQanah, R., I 490; II 242, 384
Prayer, length of, I 23
Neḥunya, I 6
Forms, II 52
Neḥunya b. Elinatan of Kefar HaBavli, R., I 340-44
Nero, II 256
Neutralizing mixed produce, I 48-56, II 4
New Moon, I 32; II 3, 141
New Year
Additional service, I 6, 155; II 312, 319, 372
Mourning, I 158; II 6, 338
Sabbath, I 368-69; II 54, 300
Shofar verses, I 154-55; II 6, 132, 136, 300, 396
Trees, date for, II 135
Niddah, I 435-36
Legal traditions, I 323-30; II 373
Night watches, I 22; II 3, 71, 233
Nose-hooklet, I 13, 387-88
Nursing child, I 5, 184-85; II 7, 29, 71

Olives, II 261-63, 284, 336
Bulk of corpse, I 290-91, 293-95, 340-44; II 9, 12, 21, 66, 157, 168, 217, 293, 341
Clean and unclean, I 287-98; II 10, 135, 137
Dipping in salt, I 9, 70, 72; II 4, 336
Heave-offering, I 46-47, 67-70; II 4, 74, 135
Pe'ah, II 135
Pressing, II 54, 135, 162, 319
Sap from, I 14; II 11, 22, 67, 156, 165, 168, 293
Tithes, I 70-71; II 4, 23, 68
Unclean, II 56
Unclean for heave offering, I 319-20
Onqelos, I 430; II 12
Discipleship, II 254
"On that day", I 4, 99-100; II 19, 68, 180, 201-202, 342, 345, 349, 372
Oppenheim, Hayyim, II 256, 278-79, 282, 284
ʿOrlah
Abroad, I 209; II 27, 76, 131, 214, 288, 310, 317, 319
Cheese-making, I 4, 82; II 4, 28, 68, 177, 337, 357, 372
Fruit, II 40
Laws, application outside Palestine, I 8, 82-84; II 4, 63-64, 98, 135
Legal traditions, I 82-84; II 4, 200, 357
Ornaments, making for fee, I 12, 380-81
Sabbath, wearing on, I 87-89; II 4
Orphan, *melog* rights, I 184; II 7, 125, 369
Oven, II 55, 72, 342
ʿAkhnai, I 12, 131, 278, 339, 423-28; II 9, 12, 21, 25, 31, 64, 69, 190, 206, 234, 263, 275-76, 284
Hive protecting, I 13, 279-80; II 112-13, 131, 230, 346

Pacifism and the Bar Kohkba rebellion, II 428-42
Palestinian produce taken abroad, I 6, 76; II 4, 19
Papa, R., I 318
Papyas, R., I 12, 13; II 153, 221

Animals for altar, I 136; II 105
Clean and unclean, I 339-40
Heifer rite, I 345
Peace offering, progeny of, I 253-54; II 292
Parah rites, I 302-15; II 29, 329, 356, 361, 366, 369, 373, 393, 396
Parents, honoring, I 450-51; II 13, 31
Paschal lamb, I 2n, 364-65
Passover, II 167-68
Arqablin, I 108
Barbecuing offering, I 134-35; II 6, 22, 71
Bitter-herb, I 7; II 99, 1021, 136
Distant journey, I 6, 132-33; II 5
Dough-offering, I 8, 70, 119, 120-21; II 5, 97-98, 103-105, 388
Ḥameṣ, clean or unclean, I 117-18; II 5, 65
Not from tithes, I 133; II 5, 28, 71, 227, 388, 397
Pentecost, I 244-45
Sabbath, I 6, 10, 121-35; II 14, 24, 68, 180-81, 291
Sabbath, appurtenances for, I 6, 10, 122-23, 126; II 5, 19
Sin offering, I 222-28
Slaughter animals, I 4, 129-32, 332, 363-64; II 6, 65, 71, 75, 150, 161, 314, 372
Zab to sanctuary, I 10
Patience, I 396-97
Peace offering, I 222-25; II 55, 105
Progeny of, I 12, 252-55, 298, 346, 385-86; II 8, 20, 66, 153, 162, 168, 292, 340
Pe'ah
Legal traditions, I 8, 34-36, 348-51; II 3, 28, 135, 172-73, 200, 335, 352, 356-57, 375
Olives and carob, II 135
Poor man, I 8, 34-36, 348-51
Pedat, R., I 40; II 206
Pentecost, II 55, 237-38
Passover, I 244-45; II 1, 6, 8, 29, 409-10, 413
Peqiʿin, I 409
Petuchowski, Jacob J., II, 451
Pharisaism and Eliezer b. Hyrcanus, II 294-334, 347-50
Pickles, I 43-44; II 3, 18, 68, 353
Pigeon-racer, I 14, 338; II 11, 27, 64, 74, 114, 131, 217, 284, 311, 319
Pingree, David, I 487
Pinḥas, R.,
Water of bitterness, I 200, 474
Pinḥas b. Ya'ir, I 395; II 416
Lost, I 221
Pompeius Longinus, II 256
Poorman
Arum, seventh year, I 39-40; II 3
Demai as tithe, I 8
Fruits of Sabbitical year, I 4, 37-40
Grapeclusters, I 8, 34-39; II 3
Pe'ah, I 8, 34-36, 348-51
Tithes, I 37-38; II 3, 70, 141, 199
Prayer
Grace after meals, I 31-36; II 3
Holidays, I 31-32; II 3
Israel distressed, I 26-28; II 18
Length of, I 23-27; II 1, 3, 28, 30, 70, 226-27
Liturgy, I 29-30; II 3
Rain, prayer for, I 5, 155-58; II 6, 26, 65, 68
Righteousness, I 26-29; II 3
Text not fixed, I 6, 23-24; II 3, 172, 201, 343, 352, 356, 409, 413
Price, dog and heifer, I 13, 303-304
Priest
Heave offering when uncircumcised, I 60, 179; II 6
Minor and marriage, I 170
Tithes, I 8
Private domain, doubt in, I 13, 318
Produce, for heave-offering, I 45-58; II 3-4
Imported, I 76-79; II 4, 19, 68, 125, 127, 176, 373
Removal at Nisan, II 135
Seventh year, I 41; II 12, 43, 123, 130, 135, 174, 351, 353
Through Jerusalem, II 54, 162
Progeny
Peace-offering, I 12, 252-55, 385-86; II 8, 20, 153, 200
Ṭerefah, I 12, 255; II 20, 69
Property, II 272, 363
Bequeathing and acquiring, I 6, 213-17; II 9, 21, 69, 187, 201, 343, 372
Sale of, I 378
Proselytes, I 449-51; II 71, 163, 409-10
Circumcision, I 180; II 1, 7, 19

Prosbul
Beehive, I 335-37
Pe'ah, liability for, I 34
Psalms, numbers, meaning of, I 481-82
Puberty, I 328-29; II 168
Punishment
Stoning to death, I 218-20
Warning of, I 474-75; II 14, 72, 229, 393, 418
Purim, I 31

Qerispai, R., I 425-26; II 221, 234
Quittance and *Geṭ*, I 11

Rabbah bar Abbuha, I 66
Rabbah b. b. Ḥana, II 228, 411-12, 415
Hands, use of, I 33-34
Law, teaching of, I 116
Torah and masters, I 405-406
Rabbinism and Eliezer b. Hyrcanus, II 298-334, 347-50
Rachel, I 460-61
Rags, I 13, 286; II 9, 25, 29, 69, 191, 374
Rain
Fast Day, early rain, I 10, 155-57; II 6, 24, 65, 151, 164, 338, 363
Prayer for, I 5, 155-58; II 6, 26, 68, 73, 168, 235-36, 289, 314, 372, 406, 408
Water in wine jars, I 5, 321
Rain water, source, I 482-84, 487-88
Ransom of wife, I 5, 184; II 152, 168
Rapoport, S. L., II 434
Rav, II 267, 407
Mourning, I 159, 161
Reproof, I 488
Sabbath and Passover, I 129
Seventy languages, I 436
Rava, I 33, 207-208
Raw flesh, I 13
Redemption
Date of, I 460-64; II 13-14, 71, 228-29, 259, 393
Firstling, I 12, 248-49; II 7, 20, 24, 69, 112, 311
Redemption-lamb, I 12, 248-49, 345; II 112, 292, 319
Repentence, I 477-79; II 30, 72, 115, 235-36, 418-21
Red heifer rite, I 302-10, 345, 391; II 10, 21, 25, 66-67, 70, 140, 161, 194, 200, 261, 273, 312, 340-41, 375
Red Sea crossing, I 464-68; II 27, 71, 228, 230, 232, 394, 418-19
Reed pipe, I 5, 305-310; II 10, 21, 70, 194, 341, 373
Remarriage, I 12, 176; II 6, 19, 24, 138, 183, 201
Repentence, I 397-98, 478-80; II 15, 74, 136
Before death, I 422-27; II 15, 30, 64, 131, 138, 198, 296, 311, 319, 332, 343, 393
Rephidim, I 470; II 14, 71, 234, 393, 419
Reproof, I 488; II 15, 27, 72, 235
Resh Laqish, I 66
Resurrection, I 485
Reuben, story of, I 369; II 6
Righteousness, I 489-91
Ritual pool, I 14, 320-23, 391-92; II 11, 22, 29, 44, 70, 165, 200, 315, 342, 361, 365
Rokeah, David, I 403
Roman lady, I 450; II 241
Rome, I 409
Eliezer b. Hyrcanus, II 299-300
Jews in world of, I 451
Rose, seventh year, I 40; II 3, 83, 206
Rosenthal, Ludwig A., II 256

Sabbath, I 337-46, II 163, 168, 200, 254, 266-67, 284, 332, 365
Alley-way, validity of, I 100-108; II 5, 19
Arms on, I 87-88; II 5, 24, 68, 274, 337
Aṣṣeret like, I 158; II 6, 27
Bread baking, I 9, 85-86, 150-51; II 5, 7, 22, 41, 68, 177-78
Benediction for mourners, I 492
Circumcision, I 4, 93-98, 471-73; II 5, 19, 30, 37, 64, 68, 71-72, 75, 149-50, 181, 202, 330, 333
City of gold, I 14; II 4
Courtyard, validity of, I 100-108; II 5, 19
Covenants, I 471-73; II 72-73
Festival separate, I 10, 31-32, 108-13, 360-62; II 5, 54, 58, 83, 293-94, 319, 328, 332-33
Filtering winc, I 10, 98-99; II 68, 179-80
Finger-nails on, I 10, 89, 357-59; II 5

Honeycomb, extracting, I 10, 335-37; II 128, 133
Instruments for circumcision on, I 6, 93, 96, 123; II 5
Lamp, cloth for wick, I 6, 86-87; II 5, 19, 68, 178, 373
Lamps and *tefillin*, I 409-16
Laws, I 337-46
Letter writing, I 91-92
Lulav and, I 149
Make-up on, I 10, 87-89; II 4
New Moon, sanctification, I 8, 32
New Year, I 368-69; II 54
Ornaments on, I 9, 87-89; II 4
Passover, I 6, 10, 121-35; II 5, 19, 24, 68, 333, 338, 374
Property, bequeathing, I 213-17
Scarf on, I 9, 89; II 4
Scratching flesh on, I 4, 89-90; II 5, 19, 68, 178, 200
Seven and eight, meanings, I 480-81
Shofar, II 140
Slaughter animal for Passover on, I 4, 122-35, 332; II 5, 65
Spice box on, I 9, 89; II 5, 24
Sukkah, I 141-42, 146-47; II 5-6
Sword on, I 9, 87; II 4, 178, 338
Tefillin and Sabbath lamps, I 409-16
Tents, I 146-47; II 6
Tiara on, I 9, 88-89, 337-38; II 5, 27, 64, 68, 74, 178
Vermin killed on, I 85; II 1, 19, 27, 71
Weaving on, I 10, 91-92; II 5, 28, 68, 178, 200
Window-shutter, I 10, 92-93; II 4, 19, 68, 179
Work on, II 54, 138, 352-53
Sabbatical year, poor and fruits of, I 4, 39-40; II 3
Sacred names, I 491-492; II 15, 22
Sacrifice, II 292-93
Acceptable and unacceptable, mixing, I 12, 234, 236-37; II 68, 292
Animal and offspring in pit, I 4, 154; II 6, 19, 68
Animals for altar, I 135-37, 232-34; II 6, 63, 75
Bird, whole-offering, I 5, 228-311
Blood blemished, I 12, 234-40; II 8, 20, 24, 28, 128, 152-53
Continual, I 142-44; II 5, 74
Dying animals, I 246-47; II 7, 20
Festival, II 55
Goat falls ill, I 140-41; II 6, 68
Guilt offering, slaughter for, I 231-32, 255; II 7
Meal offering, I 240-42, 245-46; II 7
Nazir unclean, I 192-97; II 69
Order of, I 142-44
Paschal lamb, I 2n
Priest unfit, I 60-62
Progeny of peace offering, I 252-55
Seven lambs, I 6, 142, 144
Slaughter for other purpose, I 222-28; II 67
Temple rites, I 138-41; II 6, 22, 65
Thank offering, I 243-45
Unclean, burning, I 137; II 6, 63
Sacrilege, I 268-73; II 9, 20, 69
Ṣaddoq, R., I 12
Early life of Eliezer, II 295-96, 298, 384
Escape of Yoḥanan ben Zakkai, I 434
Firstling, redeeming, I 248-49; II 112, 292
Hospitality, I 406-408; II 228
Vows, releasing, I 185-86; II 64, 110, 289
Saffron, tithe money purchasing, I 72; II 4, 27, 68, 75, 163
Salt, olives, dipping in, I 9, 70, 72; II 4
Samaritans, I 351; II 348, 350
Bread of, I 9, 41-43; II 73, 86, 100-102, 130, 138, 297, 310, 316, 328-29
Tithes, I 8, 36-37; II 3
Samuel,
Dough offering, portions, I 77
Heave offering, I 48, 66
Ketuvah and refusal of marriage, I 169
Levirate marriage, I 172
Menstrual period, I 325
Reproof, I 488
Virginity claims, I 184
World to come, I 467-68
Samuel b. R. Isaac, I 420
Samuel the Small, II 384
Sanctities, burning, I 6, 137; II 5, 28, 65, 75, 106-109, 130, 149, 311, 318, 336
Sanhedrin, I 217-22
Sap from olives, I 14; II 11, 22
Scapegoat, I 140-41; II 5
Scarf on Sabbath, I 9, 89; II 4
Schürer, Emil, II 251-52, 282, 304
Schwabe, I 408

Scorpion, I 13, 387; II 140
Scratching flesh on Sabbath, I 4, 89-90; II 5, 19, 68, 338, 353-54, 372
Scribism, ideology of, II 302-304
Scriptures, unclean hands, II 141
Se'ah, I 499-500; II 44
  Heave offering, I 49-52, 54-58, 499-500; II 18, 131, 174, 336
  Overfilling, I 99-100
Second tithes, II 54, 106-107, 135, 288
  First fruits, I 37-38; II 3, 299
  Money exchanged, I 72; II 4
  Reliability for, I 9, 73; II 4, 28, 68, 176
Seed
  Age for sowing, I 493; II 15, 242
  Mixed, I 38; II 3, 75, 98, 130, 135, 214
Sepphoris, I 400-402, 409
Seven, and eight, meaning of, I 480-81
Seventh year, II 316
  Arum, I 39-40; II 3, 18
  Balsam, I 40; II 4
  Designating produce, I 10, 152
  Etrog, I 84-85; II 4
  Fruits, gift or inheritance, I 9, 44-45; II 4, 18, 68
  Henna, I 40; II 3
  Heave offering, I 58-61; II 4
  Hide, anointing, I 9, 41; II 4, 18, 66, 73, 100-101, 135, 288
  Lotus, I 40; II 3
  Produce of, I 41; II 3, 43, 102-103, 123, 130, 297
  Rose, I 40; II 3, 83
  Tithes, eating from, I 152; II 4
  Vegetables, kinds in jar, I 7, 44
  Vineyard, II 54, 206, 357
Seventy languages, I 436; II 13, 240, 401, 407
Sexual behavior, I 371-72, 435-36; II 13, 26, 42, 137, 240, 246, 407
  Sin offering, individual actions, I 256-58
Shammai, House of, I 3; II 88-89, 115-18, 231-33, 238, 307-10
  Boundary stone, I 409
  Cattle for altar, II 106
  Circumcision and Sabbath, I 96
  Courtyard, validity of, I 100; II 68, 117
  Disciples and Yoḥanan ben Zakkai, I 395
  Divorce, advance notice, I 204; II 239
  Egg born on festival, I 4, 150, 339; II 65, 210
  Etrog, I 84
  Eunuch, age of, I 4
  Faith, I 421
  Four brothers married to four sisters, I 4
  Fruits of seventh year, gift or inheritance, I 45
  Ḥaliṣah and Minor, I 167
  Heave-offering, I 9, 46-48; II 95-96, 115-16
  History of forms, II 32-49
  Influences on Eliezer, II 253, 258, 262-63, 268-69, 272, 274-77, 280, 282, 284-86
  Ketuvah and dedicated goods, I 251; II 215
  Levirate marriage, I 173, 370
  Levirate vows annulled, I 188-90
  Liturgy, I 30
  Men of the Great Synagogue, I 451
  Menstrual period, I 323-25; II 171, 339
  Minor, inherit wife of, I 4; II 116-17
  Minor wife, I 171
  Mourning, I 163, 417-18; II 116
  Nazir and high priest, II 185
  Poor, favoring, I 36, 349
  Proselytes, I 414
  Ritual pool, I 321
  Sabbath and Passover, I 131
  Sacrifices, I 144
  Sanctities unclean, burning, II 63
  Se'ah, unclean, I 55; II 131
  Seed, mixed, I 38
  Seventh year produce as gift, II 174
  Sterility, I 328-29
  Suppressed traditions, II 218
  Thorns in vineyard, II 173
  Tithes, I 477; II 95-96, 106-108 122-23
  Tithes, separated, I 73
  Traditions, II 53-60
  Vermin killed on Sabbath, I 85-86
  Water of bitterness, I 201
Shape of world and creation, I 485-88
Sharecropper, I 8, 351-52; II 19, 176, 337
Shema'
  Mourning, I 158-63; II 6

Reciting, I 3, 8, 18-22, 30-33; II 3, 22, 26, 72, 136, 172, 201, 233, 252, 342-43, 352, 355-56, 360, 372, 374, 394, 409-10, 413
Requires attention, I 22; II 3, 70, 410
Sabbath-New Moon, reciting, I 8, 32; II 3
Shemaʿiah
Forms, II 34
Law, teaching of, I 115
Ritual pool, I 321; II 196
Shemaʿiah of Kefar Otnai, I 313
Sheqel, coins for, II 55, 140, 161
Sheshet, R., I 221
Shila, I 372
Shirt of child, I 13, 388-89
Shiṭṭim, I 471; II 14, 71, 236, 393, 419
Shoe on last, I 13, 285, 329; II 9, 21, 64, 76, 113-14, 131, 137, 283-95, 311
Shofar on *Sabbath*, I 368-69; II 140, 300, 388
Siknin, I 409
Simeon, R., I 4, 13, 346; II 158-59, 190
Animal and offspring in pit, I 4; II 211
Animals for altar, I 137; II 63, 65, 150, 188
Bed, purification, II 68, 76
Blood blemished, I 236, 238
Corpse and olive bulk, I 344
Corpse unclean, I 289
Courtyard, sweeping, I 153; II 65, 151
Dying animal, slaughter for sacrifice, I 246
Firstling, I 345
ʿEruv, I 361
Guilt offering, I 259, 262-64, 266
Ḥameṣ and heave-offering, I 119; II 65, 75, 209-10
Heave offering, I 355
Liability for damages, I 211-12
Metal vessels, cleaning, I 283
Nazir and vows, I 194
Objects, clean and unclean, I 276, 286
Olives, bulk and corpse, I 294-95
Passover offering, II 75
Peace offering, progeny of, I 253-54
Ritual pool, I 322
Sabbath and Passover, I 131
Shofar verses, I 155
Tithe, money for purchases, I 72; II 75, 158
Vessels, unclean liquids, I 318-19
Zab, I 329-30
Simeon b. ʿAzzai, II 384
Simeon b. Batyra, II 384
Simeon b. Eleazer, R., II 385
Circumcision and Sabbath, I 98; II 64, 147
Divorce, conditions of, I 206, 208
Forms, II 45
Mourning, I 163; II 116, 170
Passover and Pentecost, I 245
Sin offering, I 263, 358
Simeon b. Gamaliel, R., II 164-66, 349, 384-85
Decline in the generations, I 395
Forms, II 45
Ketuvah and dedicated goods, I 250; II 66
Slaughter of dying animals, I 247
Study with Yoḥanan ben Zakkai, I 441
Tithes from Israelites in Syria, I 80; II 176
Simeon b. Laqish, R.,
Circumcision and Sabbath, I 96; II 179
Heave offering portions, I 48
Simeon b. Leazer, II 45
Simeon b. Nanos, II 384
Simeon b. Natanel, I 396, II 297, 302, 384
Simeon b. Sheṭaḥ, R., I 90
Hanging, I 218-19; II 118, 132, 178
Simeon Shezuri, II 385
Guilt offering, I 266
Objects, clean and unclean, I 285; II 64, 159
Shoe on last, II 113
Sin offering, I 259, 263; II 76, 154
Simeon b. Yoḥai, I 346, 366; II 161-63, 385
Bar Kokhba rebellion, II 423
Circumcision and Sabbath, II 64, 147
Corpse and olive bulk, II 66, 155
Faith, II 72
Grave area, II 69, 192
Peace offering, II 66, 153
Stranger, love for, I 427-28
Simeon b. Zoma, II 384
Simeon of Miṣpah, II 384
Simeon son of the Prefect, II 384
Simeon of Just, II 305
Simeon the Temanite, I 436; II 385

Sin, I 493-97
Individual sins, I 5, 6, 256-57, 259-61; II 6, 8, 132, 184, 292
Tithes for fear of, I 476
Sin offering, I 6; II 58, 167-68, 188, 195, 265-66, 273, 319, 340, 372, 396
Ashes and unclean jar, I 13, 311-14, 345
Bird, whole offering, I 228-31; II 7, 20, 66
Blood blemished, I 234-40
Heifer rite, I 302-305; II 9-10
Individual actions, I 256-58; II 8, 69, 121-29, 189, 200, 213, 292, 312, 374-76
Intention and execution, II 268, 291, 315, 372
Leper, I 261-62
Own name, I 12, 222, 224, 226
Passover, I 222-28
Slaughter for, I 231-32, 332
Substitute, I 8, 255; II 8, 21, 59, 69, 189
Suspensive, I 12, 258-68, 381-82; II 8, 20-21, 66, 69, 76, 118, 153-54, 162, 189-90, 292, 321, 372, 391-92
Water of, I 5, 309-10; II 59, 127, 132, 139, 156, 164, 168, 291, 320
Whole offering confused, I 232-34; II 132-33, 313
Widow remarrying, each action, I 11, 179; II 7, 19
Sisera, I 496
Ṣiṣit, I 32-33, II 3, 136, 410
Sisters and two brothers, levirate marriage, I 172-76, 370; II 6
Slain man, between two cities, I 11, 202-20
Slaughter, II 41, 166, 293
Animal and offspring in pit, I 4, 154; II 6
Dying animals and sacrifice, I 246-47; II 8, 20, 69
Eating something not eaten, I 12, 226, 228, 241
For Gentile, I 12, 351, 382-84
Guilt offering, I 231-32
Passover and Sabbath, I 4, 122, 332, 363-64; II 5, 65, 396
Sacrifice, for other purposes, I 222-28; II 7, 19, 24, 67, 150, 170, 390
Sin offering, I 332
Thank offering, I 243-45
Slaves, II 73, 236
Circumcision, I 2n
Emancipation, I 208-209; II 71
Heave offering, eating, I 60-62; II 4
Mamzer, purifying, I 209-10
Marriage of, I 209-10
Mourning, I 161-62; II 6, 235
Witness, remarriage of woman, I 7, 176-77; II 6
Smith, Morton, II 442, 448-50, 452-53, 462
Solomon, temple walls, I 399
Somogyi, Joseph, II 265
Sorcery, I 400-401, 404; II 12, 27, 70, 199, 201, 203, 359, 374
Christianity and excommunication, II 249-77
Flesh scratching, I 90; II 4
Soṭah
Rites, II 239, 290, 322, 329, 372, 392
Spice box on Sabbath, I 9, 89; II 5, 24
Spinning blue wool, I 158; II 74, 125, 132, 138, 212, 312
Sterility, I 328-29, 373
Stone, sealing grave, I 5, 288; II 69
Stoning to death, I 12, 218-20; II 9, 29 58, 66
Stranger, love for, I 427-28; II 72, 231
Succoth, I 458-59; II 19
Sukkah, II 272, 289
Clean and unclean, I 288-89
Cloth, spreading of, I 146-47; II 6, 31, 68, 76, 181-82, 338, 346
Cone-shaped, I 10, 145-46; II 6, 19, 65, 151, 164, 168, 312, 319
Festival observance, I 147-48; II 6
Legal traditions, I 141-49; II 6, 410
Lulav, I 149; II 6
Meals in, I 10, 367; II 141
Privately owned, I 10, 149; II 72, 230, 388, 392
Rules, II 58, 136, 168
Sabbath, I 141-42; II 6
Visit on, I 7, 128, 147; II 346
Sweeping courtyard, I 151-54; II 6
Sword on Sabbath, I 9, 87; II, 4, 348
Syria
Farmers, II 58
Israelites liable for tithes I 9, 79-81; II 4, 19, 68, 176, 336, 357, 360
ʿOrlah laws, I 84; II 4, 19, 98, 374
Sharecropping, I 80-81

Ṭabi, R.
Heave offering produce, I 48
Mourning, I 162
Taboos, II 287-88
Agricultural taboos abroad, I 209
Ṭarfon, I 7; II 120, 261, 376, 384-85
Ammon and Moab, tithes, I 332-33, 335
Attending scholars, I 437
Cattle for altar, II 101
Divorce, I 206-207; II 110
Early life of Eliezer, II 298
Emancipation, I 208
Forms, II 33, 48-49
Grave area, I 297
Hallel, reciting, II 136
Heave offering, I 9, 48; II 18, 174, 336
Illness of Eliezer, I 404-407; II 31, 228, 413
Mamzer, purification, I 8, 210; II 29, 186
Menstrual period, I 328
Passover offering, I 134
Pe'ah, liability, I 34; II 28, 172
Rain, I 156; II 363
Shema', reciting, II 174
Tithes, II 201, 345
Torah and masters, I 404-405
Teaching
Law in presence of master, I 114-17
Unmarried man, I 12, 376
Tefillin, I 418, 437; II 13, 27, 30, 72, 410, 417
'AmHa'areṣ, I 32-33; II 3
On head, I 479
Mourner, I 5, 158-63; II 6, 29, 212
Privy, II 136
Sabbath lamps, I 409-16; II 13
Temple
Altar not needing immersion, I 11
Cleanness, I 220-21, 389
Cult, II 292-93, 298-334, 376
Property given, I 6, 136-37; II 309
Rites, I 138-41; II 5, 24, 65, 74, 104, 119, 125, 127, 161-62, 187, 273, 289, 294-307, 347, 362-63
Walls, I 399-400; II 12, 170, 198, 201
Ten Commandments and covenants, I 471-73; II 24
Tent
Ashes from corpse, I 13, 287
Clean and unclean, I 279-80, 287-98, 386-87; II 112, 132-33, 137, 168, 216, 294, 312, 358
Corpse, II 55
Festival, I 92-93, 99, 146-47
Men and vessels, uncleanness, I 13, 289, 386-87
Worm from corpse, I 13, 287
Ṭerefah, progeny of, I 12, 255; II 9, 20, 69
Testimony
Get, messenger giving, I 3, 204-205; II 166, 360
Pigeon-flyer, I 14, 88, 338; II 74, 294
Test rags, II 43, 48, 138
Thank offering
Dough-offering from cakes, I 7, 81; II 4, 63, 74, 83, 97-98, 123, 129, 135, 207, 288
Slaughter for, I 243-45
Thanksgiving, sanctification of the day, I 29-31; II 3
Thorns in vineyard, I 9, 38-39; II 3, 18, 173
Tiara on Sabbath, I 9, 88-89, 337-38; II 5, 12, 27, 64, 74, 114, 131, 136, 208, 289, 311
Tiberias, I 362
Tithes, II 162-63, 272-73, 285-86, 331-32, 355
Ammon and Moab, I 332-35; II 12, 31, 70, 141, 197, 201
Caper bush, I 6, 71-72; II 4, 68, 175
Date-honey, I 4, 66-70; II 4, 18, 64, 78, 148
Dead, given from it, I 73-74; II 4, 71, 83, 206, 388
Demai, poor man, I 8, 34-36, 348-51
Dill, I 9, 71-72; II 4, 24, 68, 175
Distant journey and Passover, I 133; II 5
Dough offering portions, I 76-79; II 4
Eating not giving, I 58-61; II 4
Etrog, I 3, 84-85; II 4
Gentiles, I 36-37; II 3
Liability for, I 9, 73-74; II 4, 28, 66, 68, 175-76, 353
Heave offering portions, I 48, 355-57, 372-73; II 4, 327-28
Liquids, I 4, 66-70; II 4, 18, 64, 76, 146-47
Moab and Ammon, I 332-35; II 12, 31, 70, 141, 197, 201

Mustard, I 9, 71-72; II 4, 68, 175
Olives, I 46-47, 67-70; II 4, 23, 68, 146-47, 175
Passover, not from, I 133; II 5, 28, 71, 227
Priest-share-cropper getting, I 8
Principle, not fifth, I 74; II 4, 18, 68
Saffron purchased, I 72; II 4, 27, 68, 75, 288, 315
Samaritan, I 8, 36-37; II 3
Second, II 54, 106-107, 176
Separating, I 73; II 4
Seventh year, I 152
Sins, I 476
Syria, liability in, I 3, 79-81; II 4, 19, 58, 68, 176, 312
Titus, II 430
Toetterman, C. Augustus, II 256-57
Tomb, clean and inclean, I 291-93; II 9, 21, 25, 69, 192, 341
Toothpick, I 10, 151, 153; II 164, 289
Torah
Academies transmitting, I 419-20
Daughter taught, I 201-202, 450; II 7, 27, 111-12, 290, 339, 358, 372
Master of, I 403-406; II 12, 300-301 303, 347
Powers of, I 429-30
Study of, II 294, 416-17
Scroll wrappings, I 9, 39; II 3, 23, 64, 75, 144, 294, 313
Trajan, I 404; II 256, 259-60
Bar Kokhba rebellion, II 430
Troops with banners, I 497
Tsarkes, Eleazer, II 253
Tur-Malka, II 433

Unmarried man, teaching, I 12
Urbach, Ephraim E., II 249, 258
Uriah, I 494
Usha, II 89-90, 167-69
Attestations, II 64-67
Forms, II 40, 42, 46-48, 50, 59, 61
Traditions, II 335-86
Utensils, unclean, I 9, 83

Vegetables
Grain sown with, I 9, 352-53
Kinds in jar, I 7, 43-44; II 4, 18, 68, 173, 336, 357, 375
Vermes, Geza, II 258
Vermin, killed on Sabbath, I 85; II 4, 19, 27, 71, 233
Vespasian, II 430
Escape of Yoḥanan ben Zakkai, I 434
Vessels
Greasing with oil, I 9, 83
Metal vessel, hole in, I 13, 277, 280-81; II 9, 25, 29, 315
Purifying, I 5, 281-82; II 29, 66
Tent unclean, I 13, 289, 386-87
Unclean, I 5, 318; II 11, 22, 119, 196, 220, 294, 331, 333
Unclean liquids, I 318-19
Wooden, hole in, I 5, 283; II 9, 25
Vine and branches, I 488-89
Vineyard
Defective clusters, I 6, 34-36; II 3, 18, 162, 335, 373, 387
Fourth year, I 35, 74-75; II 135
Seed mixed, I 38, 354-55; II 3, 137
Seventh year, II 54
Thorns in, I 9, 38-39; II 3, 18, 173, 200, 335, 351-52, 387
Winepress in, I 9
Virginity, claims of, I 7, 181-83; II 7, 19, 69, 184, 192, 339
Vows, II 41, 55, 58, 185, 289, 358
Girl past puberty, I 11, 186-87; II 6, 339
Levir annuls, I 7, 187-92; II 7, 20, 339
Levirate marriage, I 187-92; II 6, 69, 360, 374
Minor female annulling, I 11, 186-88
Nazir loses days, I 192-97; II 7
Releasing, I II, 185-92; II 7, 29, 64, 69, 112, 130, 138, 184, 200, 234, 311, 319, 328, 388, 391, 411

Wacholder, Ben Zion, II 446-47
Wall-projection, I 5; II 10, 21, 70, 192-93, 373
War, attitudes toward, II 347-50, 394
War of 66, influences of, I 304, 306
Warts, I 12, 384
Water
Crown of mud holding in trough, I 13; II 126
Falling into flask, I 13
Immersion pool and drawn water, I 56-58; II 70, 342
Ritual pool, I 5, 307; II 22, 70
Source of rain, I 482-84, 487-88; II 15, 30, 72, 235
Tree, shaking of, II 137

Unclean guardian, I 13, 307-308; II 75, 126
Water-cooler, comb of, I 12, 339; II 9, 21, 69, 190, 341
Water of bitterness, I 199-202
Weapons, carrying on Sabbath, I 87-88; II 5, 24, 68
Weasel, I 6, 338; II 164, 219
Weaving on Sabbath, I 10, 90-92; II 5, 28, 68, 338
Whole offering, I 142-44; II 7, 66, 125, 133, 290
Bird as sacrifice, I 5, 228-31; II 7, 20, 69, 340, 372
Widow
Remarriage, I 7, 11, 176-77; II 6, 19
Son, I 434; II 240, 409
Wife
Ransom, I 5, 184; II 65, 152, 166, 236
Warning, I 5, 199, 202; II 7, 20, 67, 69, 76, 111, 166, 170, 188, 290, 315, 372
Wild animals judged, I 217-18; II 9, 25, 69, 187, 201, 342, 374
Willow branch, rites of, I 367-68
Window shutter, I 10, 92-93; II 5, 19, 68, 338
Window-sills, I 5, 293; II 9, 21, 70, 192, 373
Wine
Blessing unmixed with water, I 8, 31, 346-48
Heave-offering, I 4, 68-69; II 135, 313
Jars, rain water in, I 5, 321; II 373
Winepress, in vineyard, I 9, 353-55
Wipe with left hand, I 33-34; II 1, 3, 26, 70, 233, 236, 401, 410
Witnesses, I 338; II 11, 64, 141
Remarriage on evidence of, I 7, 176-77; II 6, 12, 20, 24, 138
Water of bitterness, I 199-202
Wife, warning to, I 5, 199, 202; II 7, 20, 67, 76
Woman
Acquiring, II 41
Drinking against wishes, II 20, 72, 230
Finger-nails on Sabbath, I 9, 89; II 4
Girl past puberty, releasing vows, I 11
Gone aside, I 5, 202; II 141
Ḥaliṣah at night, I 165-66; II 6, 19
Hanging, I 218-20; II 8, 75, 125, 292, 311, 390
Hard labor, I 14; II 10-11, 22, 25, 70, 164, 197-98, 339
Heave offering, eating, I 60-62; II 4, 18, 162
Make-up on Sabbath, I 9
Menstruation period, I 5, 323-30; II 10, 25, 352
Minor annulling vows, I 186-88; II 67, 109, 138, 328
Old woman, I 14, 323-24; II 10
Scarf on Sabbath, I 9, 89; II 4
Sterile, I 11, 328-29
Tiara on Sabbath, I 9, 88-89, 337-38; II 4, 12, 27, 64
Torah, teaching daughter, I 202-202; II 329
Virginity, testifying to lack of hymen, I 7, 181; II 6, 69
Water of bitterness, I 199-202
Wood for altar, I 428; II 13, 27, 234
Wood splinter, I 151-54; II 6
Wooden sandal, I 11, 166-67; II 6, 65, 152, 314, 362
Wooden vessels, I 5, 183; II 9, 25, 69
Wool, hide for combed wool, I 13
World, creation and shape, I 485-88; II 15, 29-30, 36, 72, 235, 252, 412
World to come, I 468-71; II 13, 23, 70, 199, 202, 376, 412
Generation of the wilderness, I 453-58; II 13, 22, 67, 70, 157, 168, 199-200, 294, 296, 348
Worm from corpse, I 13, 287; II 9, 21, 69

Yaqqim of Haddar, R., I 345
Yasa, R., I 201; II 237
Yavneh, I 409, 436; II 87-90, 167-69
Attestations, II 63-64, 92-142
Forms, II 32-33, 38-39, 45-47, 49, 52, 61
Mourning, I 417
Pharisaism and Rabbinism, II 287-334
Yeivin, S., II 428, 431, 435
Yeshebav, II 384
Yiṣḥaq b. R. Naḥman, R., I 48
Yoʿezer of the Birah, II 384
Yoḥanan, R.
Grace after meals, I 31
Law, teaching of, I 116

Levirate marriage, I 174
Meal offering, I 241
Reproof, I 488
Taboos abroad, I 209
Water and flood, I 492
Yoḥanan b. Beroqa, II 384
Yoḥanan b. Gudgada, II 384
Yoḥanan b. HaḤorani, II 384
Yoḥanan b. R. Ilai, II 254, 406
Yoḥanan b. Ilai, R., I 7, 146-47; II 31
Yoḥanan b. Nuri, R., I 8, 12, 360-62; II 112-13, 124, 384
Early views, II 260
Forms, II 32, 49
Objects, clean and unclean, I 280, II 64
ʿOrlah laws abroad, I 7, 83-84; II 63-64, 76, 214
Taboos abroad, I 209
Yoḥanan ben Torta, II 423, 435
Yoḥanan ben Zakkai, I 10, 368; II 88, 119-20, 129, 221-23, 228, 231, 234
Ammon and Moab tithes, I 333-35; II 199
Comfortors, I 447-49; II 408
Death scenes, I 414; II 120, 234, 236-37
Decline in the generations, I 395
Disciples, I 396-98, 432
Early life of Eliezer, II 295, 300-304, 307, 326
Early views and influences, II 250-54 256-60, 266, 274-75, 280-81, 286
Eliezer follows, I 428-29; II 339-44
Escape, I 433-34; II 2
Forms, II 39, 43-49, 57
Fourth year vineyard, I 75
Law, teaching of, I 115
Men of the Great Synagogue, I 451
Midras and *maddaf*, I 313
Mourning, I 417-18
Passover and Pentecost, I 245
Relations and influences, II 399-421
Righteousness, I 489-91
Scholars following academies, I 408-409
Study with, I 437-46
Sukkah, I 142, 367
Torah and masters, I 403-405
Yoḥanan the High Priest, I 351
Yoke, pledge of farmer, I 12
Yosah, R.,
Animals for altar, I 137; II 63, 150
Heave offering, I 74
Ḥameṣ and heave-offering, I 119
Tithes, II 176
Yosah b. Durmasqit, R., I 7, 83-84
Yosah b. Ḥalafta, R., I 95; II 434
Yosah, b. R. Judah, R., I 85; II 98-99
Yosi, R., I 12, 362-63; II 99, 162-63, 166
ʿAmHaʾareṣ, I 43
Ammon and Moab, tithes, I 333; II 345
Arum, seventh year, I 40; II 173
Comfortor of Yoḥanan ben Zakkai, I 447; II 241
Covenants, I 473
Courtyard, validity of, I 102, 104-106
Distant journey, I 132; II 181, 200, 238
Divorce, I 204; II 64, 112
Early views, II 260
Excommunication, II 346
Forms, II 33, 42, 47
Fourth year vineyard, I 75; II 207
Grapeclusters, I 35-36
Guilt offering, I 255, 259-63, 265-66
Ḥameṣ and heave-offering, I 117-18; II 209
Heifer rite, I 308, 310
Meal offering, I 242
Menstrual period, I 323-24; II 171, 339
Midras and *maddaf*, I 311, 313
Objects, clean and unclean, I 280, 172
Olives, bulk and corpse, I 294
Oven, cleanness, II 64, 112-13
Passover and Pentecost, I 245
Prayer, I 24-25
Sin offering, II 66, 76, 154
World to come, I 467
Zab, I 329-30
Yosi b. R. Bun, R., I 48
Yosi b. Durmusqit, R., I 334; II 254
Yosi b. Ḥalafta, I 238, 409; II 385
Yosi b. R. Ḥanina, I 302-303; II 238
Disciples and Yoḥanan ben Zakkai, I 399, II 406
Divorce, I 205; II 76, 110, 159
Passover and Pentecost, I 245
Sukkah and Sabbath, I 141
Water of bitterness, I 200-201
Wife, witnesses to warn, I 5; II 76, 170
Yosi Kaṭnuta, I 395

Yosi ben Hisma, II 429
Yosi b. Peridah, I 102; II 118-19
Yosi b. Yoʿezer, II 262
  Clean and unclean, II 137
  Disciples and Yoḥanan ben Zakkai, I 398; II 124, 132
Yosi b. Yosi, I 102
Yosi the Galilean, R., I 7, 83-84, 464; II 120, 228, 384-85
  Blood blemished, I 236
  Divorce, I 206-208
Yosi the Priest
  Disciples and Yoḥanan ben Zakkai, I 396-97, 444
  Early life of Eliezer, II 298, 302, 384

Zab, I 227, 272, 288, 311, 314, 329-30; II 11, 56, 165, 171, 197, 201
  Carrion, I 14, 330-31; II 11, 25, 70, 198, 356
  Examination, I 6, 14, 325, 329-32, 392-93; II 11, 22, 70, 156-57, 168, 293, 341, 359, 374, 391
  Liquids, I 8, 330-332; II 11, 25, 70
  Sanctuary on Passover, I 10
  Zabah, I 323-30; II 11, 201, 341
Zechariah, I 494
Zeʾira, R.,
  Levirate marriage, I 174
  Mourning, I 159, 161
Zeitlin, S., II 257
  Fourth year vineyard, I 75
Zekhariah b. haQaṣṣav, II 384
Zera, R.,
  Circumcision and Sabbath, I 96; II 179
  Grace after meals, I 31